GRAND CANYON
NATIONAL PARK

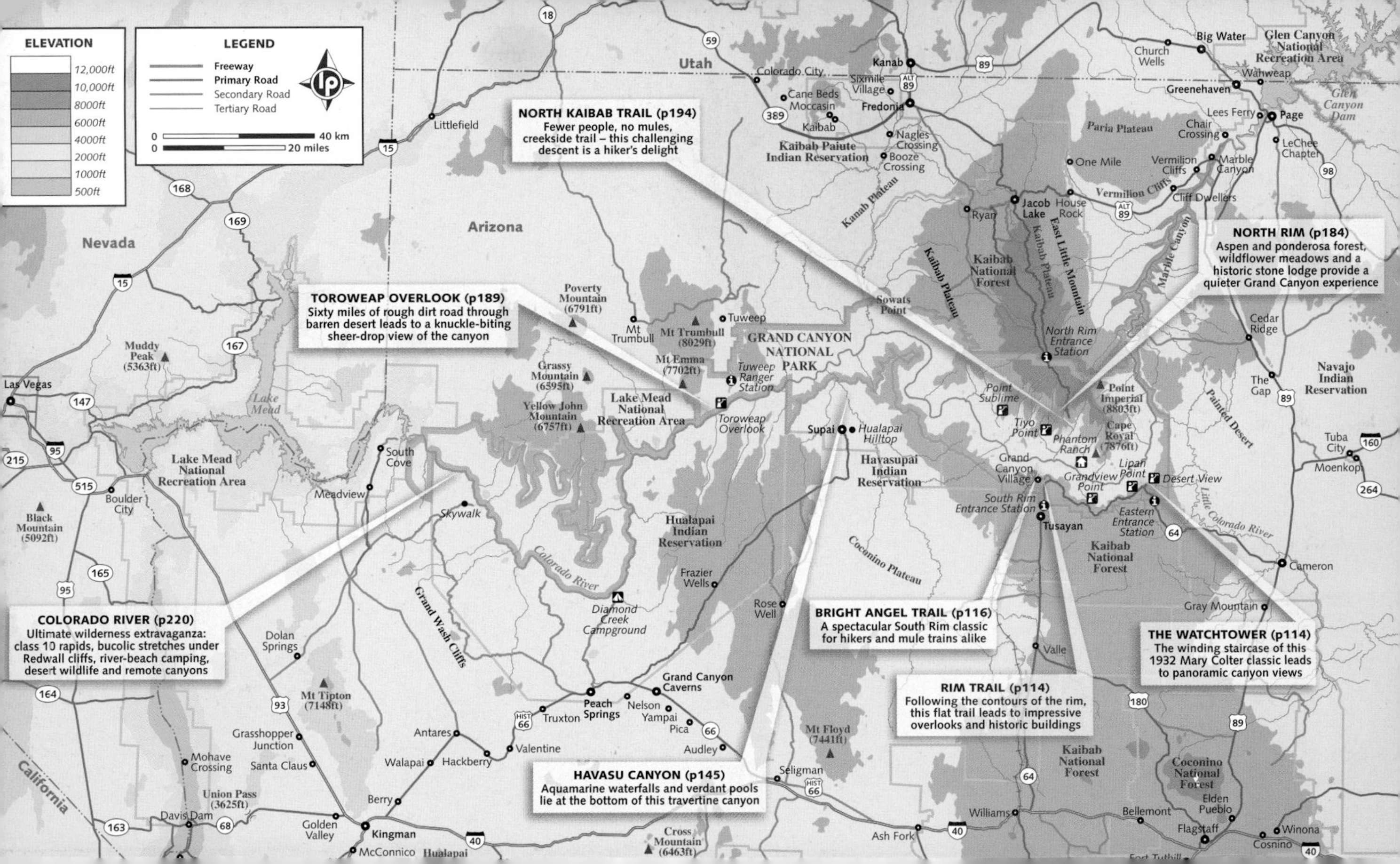

ELEVATION
12,000ft
10,000ft
8000ft
6000ft
4000ft
2000ft
1000ft
500ft
LEGEND
Freeway
Primary Road
Secondary Road
Tertiary Road
0 40 km
0 20 miles
NORTH KAIBAB TRAIL (p194)
Fewer people, no mules, creekside trail – this challenging descent is a hiker's delight
NORTH RIM (p184)
Aspen and ponderosa forest, wildflower meadows and a historic stone lodge provide a quieter Grand Canyon experience
TOROWEAP OVERLOOK (p189)
Sixty miles of rough dirt road through barren desert leads to a knuckle-biting sheer-drop view of the canyon
COLORADO RIVER (p220)
Ultimate wilderness extravaganza: class 10 rapids, bucolic stretches under Redwall cliffs, river-beach camping, desert wildlife and remote canyons
BRIGHT ANGEL TRAIL (p116)
A spectacular South Rim classic for hikers and mule trains alike
THE WATCHTOWER (p114)
The winding staircase of this 1932 Mary Colter classic leads to panoramic canyon views
RIM TRAIL (p114)
Following the contours of the rim, this flat trail leads to impressive overlooks and historic buildings
HAVASU CANYON (p145)
Aquamarine waterfalls and verdant pools lie at the bottom of this travertine canyon
Utah
Arizona
Nevada
California
GRAND CANYON NATIONAL PARK
Lake Mead National Recreation Area
Glen Canyon National Recreation Area
Kaibab Paiute Indian Reservation
Hualapai Indian Reservation
Havasupai Indian Reservation
Navajo Indian Reservation
Kaibab National Forest
Coconino National Forest
Kaibab Plateau
Kanab Plateau
Paria Plateau
Coconino Plateau
Painted Desert
Grand Wash Cliffs
Vermilion Cliffs
East Little Mountain
Marble Canyon
Colorado River
Little Colorado River
Lake Mead
Glen Canyon Dam
Las Vegas
Boulder City
Kingman
Flagstaff
Williams
Page
Kanab
Fredonia
Jacob Lake
Tusayan
Cameron
Grand Canyon Village
Supai
Peach Springs
Seligman
Ash Fork
Littlefield
Colorado City
Big Water
Church Wells
Greenehaven
Wahweap
Lees Ferry
LeChee Chapter
Marble Canyon
Cliff Dwellers
Chair Crossing
One Mile
House Rock
Ryan
Sixmile Village
Cane Beds
Moccasin
Kaibab
Nagles Crossing
Booze Crossing
Sowats Point
Tuweep
Mt Trumbull
Mt Trumbull (8029ft)
Mt Emma (7702ft)
Poverty Mountain (6791ft)
Grassy Mountain (6595ft)
Yellow John Mountain (6757ft)
Muddy Peak (5363ft)
Black Mountain (5092ft)
Mt Tipton (7148ft)
Mt Floyd (7441ft)
Cross Mountain (6463ft)
Union Pass (3625ft)
Tuweep Ranger Station
Toroweap Overlook
Point Sublime
Tiyo Point
Phantom Ranch
Point Imperial (8803ft)
Cape Royal (7876ft)
Lipan Point
Desert View
Grandview Point
North Rim Entrance Station
South Rim Entrance Station
Eastern Entrance Station
Hualapai Hilltop
Skywalk
Diamond Creek Campground
South Cove
Meadview
Dolan Springs
Frazier Wells
Rose Well
Grand Canyon Caverns
Nelson
Yampai
Pica
Audley
Truxton
Valentine
Hackberry
Antares
Walapai
Berry
Golden Valley
McConnico
Hualapai
Grasshopper Junction
Santa Claus
Mohave Crossing
Davis Dam
Valle
Gray Mountain
Cedar Ridge
The Gap
Tuba City
Moenkopi
Bellemont
Elden Pueblo
Winona
Cosnino

GRAND CANYON NATIONAL PARK

One of the natural wonders of the world, the Grand Canyon warrants any hyperbolic language it inspires. Its vastness and staggering beauty are amazing, astounding and awesome – and its many-layered splendor isn't mere metaphor. A short roam along the rim serves up stunning vistas at nearly every turn of the trail, giving glimpses now and then of the Colorado River, which carved the curvaceous gorge. Descend deeper and get intimate with the canyon's rock layers, a beautifully mind-boggling record of geologic time on a nearly incomprehensible scale. Even the existing trails snaking into the canyon follow in the ancient footsteps of the Native Americans who once inhabited this wondrous place. Find a serene spot for solitude, watch the light sculpt the temples of the canyon and let the grandeur reveal itself.

Hiking & Camping

Lying in the stillness of a desert night, counting falling stars, it's hard to remember why you felt so frazzled last week at work or why you tossed the newspaper aside in resigned despair. When you're camping under the aspen and ponderosa, directly on the rim of the canyon, descending its depths in predawn silence or scrambling through the fire-blazed red of its endless expanse, does it really matter?

Author Tip

Read Michael Ghiglieri and Thomas Meyers' *Over the Edge: Death in the Grand Canyon* before any backcountry hike at Grand Canyon National Park – real life stories of average folk drive home the canyon's ferocity. Always check weather forecasts for the entire region. Rain an hour away can create dangerous deluges in canyon country.

❶ Rim to Rim on the Kaibab

Camp under the cottonwood trees, sit with a book in a cold-clear creek, watch the sun scare away the stars in the cool silence of dawn. There's nothing like it (p123) in the world.

❷ Rainbow Rim Trail

An 18.4-mile trail (p201) through ponderosa, aspen and wildflower meadows connects five canyon overlooks. Stretch your bag out on the canyon edge – no fees, no crowds, no noise.

❸ Havasu Canyon

Four gorgeous, spring-fed waterfalls and inviting azure swimming holes sit 10 miles below the rim in the heart of the 83,000-acre Havasupai Reservation (p145).

❹ Buckskin Gulch

Scramble, climb, wade and squeeze your way through this 13-mile slot canyon (p206) with 500ft-tall sandstone walls and miles-long sections no wider than your shoulders.

❺ Colorado River

Slam over white water, float in the stillness, hike to waterfalls, and feast on lavish meals on the beach (p220). No wonder folk wait years to raft through the bottom of time.

❻ Hermit Trail

Follow in the footsteps of the Hermit himself and discover the beauty of this rugged South Rim trail (p125) on your journey to the river and back.

Geologic Wonders

The Grand Canyon's shifting desert light, dazzling colors and multitudes of temples, thrones and arches have inspired centuries of artists. But for geologists, the canyon itself is the canvas, sprawled across half of Earth's lifespan in 6000ft of rock. It's all there, exposed in one awesome expanse of ancient sea floors, lava flows, sand dunes, flood plains, and roots of ancient mountains, each layer marking the slow passing of eons.

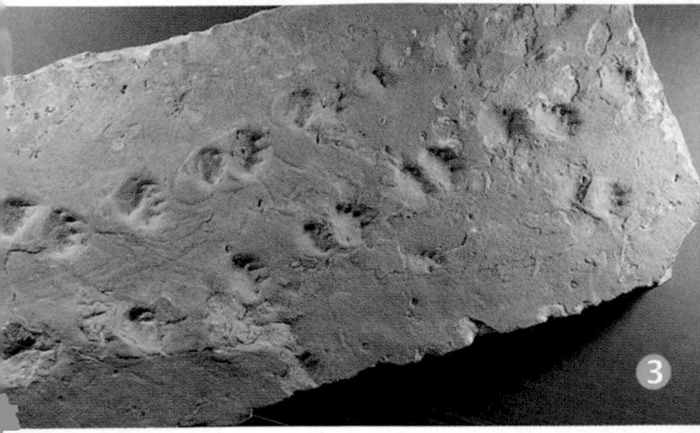

Author Tip

Attend a ranger geology talk early in your trip. Easier to digest than a geology book, talks by rangers transform the abstract into the concrete, with visual aids, stories and handy tricks for grasping the mind-boggling history of the canyon's rocks and formations. For more advanced rock hounds, read the trail with Lon Abbott & Terri Cook's *Hiking the Grand Canyon's Geology*.

1 Vulcans Throne

The park's most impressive cinder cone erupted only 74,000 years ago, leaving behind a massive pile of basalt on the Esplanade Platform – best viewed from Toroweap Overlook (p189).

2 Bright Angel Canyon

An excellent example of how creeks follow fault lines across the landscape – follow Bright Angel Creek through the canyon on the North Kaibab (p194).

3 Coconino Sandstone

Sheer 350ft sandstone cliffs, nothing more than hardened sand dunes, hold millions of fossilized insect and lizard tracks – look for them as you hike through the cliffs on the Bright Angel Trail (p116).

4 Canyon Overlooks

Spread out before your eyes at every overlook (p109 and p187), the Grand Canyon is the ultimate geologic wonder. A single panorama can reinvent itself with every shifting nuance of desert light.

5 Vishnu Temple

This sandstone formation rises from the canyon like a temple in the sky. Amazingly fluid and otherworldly, it seems to change with every few steps along the South Rim's Rim Trail (p114).

6 Redwall Limestone

Perhaps the most prominent feature of the canyon, huge red cliffs (see p69) tower 500ft to 800ft over the Tonto Platform and divide forest habitats above from desert habitats below.

Fall Colors & Sweater Weather

In the fall, that sliver of time when the intensity of summer has passed and the harshness of winter is only a whisper, the Grand Canyon itself seems to pull on an oversized sweater and snuggle down to a quieter, gentler routine. The desert sun doesn't bear down so hotly, the crowds have dispersed, and the cottonwood and aspen yellow to a soft glow.

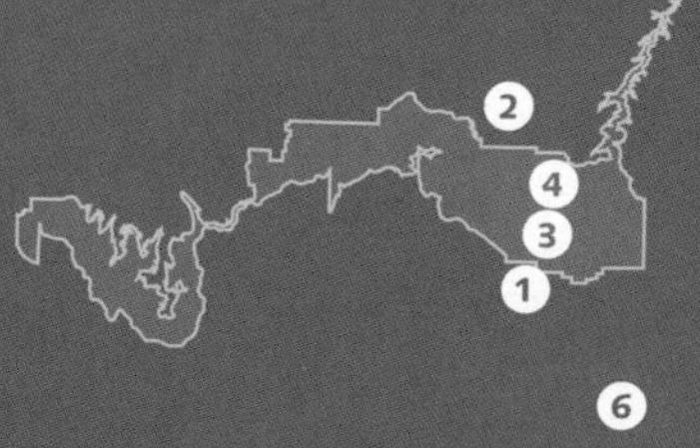

Author Tip

Head to the North Rim in late October, after the lodge and facilities close midmonth and before the first snow makes the road there impassable. You can still hike all the trails, and camp at the campground or spend the night at a rustic cabin at Jacob Lake Lodge, 45 minutes from the canyon rim. Just you, the deer, the falling leaves and the canyon.

❶ South Rim

Avoid summer's mayhem and heat by visiting the canyon's most popular destination in the off-season (p24).

❷ North Kaibab National Forest

High mountain meadows and golden aspen with miles of idyllic dirt roads and hiking trails. Picnic among the leaves at remote canyon overlooks in the national forest (p199).

❸ Phantom Ranch

Strip off your sweater as you descend into the canyon, soak up the warmth at canyon-bottom Phantom Ranch (p132), then hike back out into the fall.

❹ Grand Canyon Lodge

Crunch over fallen leaves and snuggle down with a hot cider by the massive stone fireplace on the back verandah of this historic timber lodge (p197) on the canyon's edge.

❺ Sedona

New-age hot spot with alternative medicine (think crystal healing and past-life regression, tai chi and acupressure), Sedona's wonderland of red rock (p162) becomes even more alluring when fall settles on the desert.

❻ Flagstaff

Coffee shops and bookstores bristle with new-year energy at this college town (p151). Fuel up with breakfast at Macy's (p159) before a hike in the Coconino National Forest.

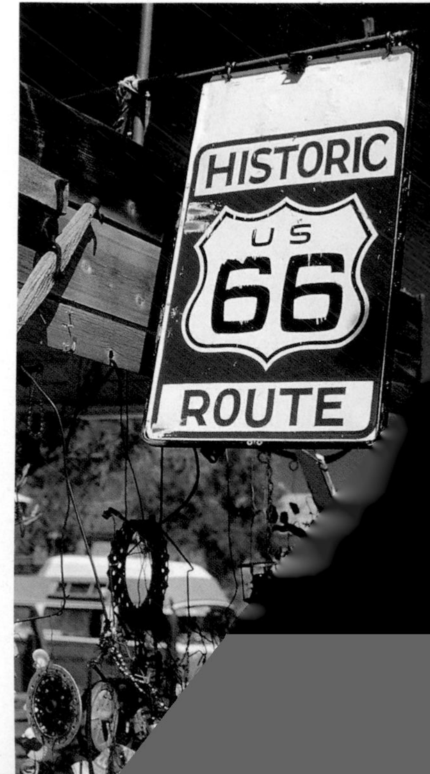

Colorado River

Spotting the Colorado River from the rim, as it winds around buttes and plateaus, elicits awe at what one river can do. But actually rafting the river and experiencing the essential nature of its rapids and rocks takes the wonder to a whole new level. Add to that the geologic record you'll observe along the way and the river ecosystem so different from that on the rim, and you'll have a much deeper understanding of the canyon.

Author Tip

Even if you haven't booked a commercial trip a year in advance, your dreams of rafting the Colorado may not be a wash. People's plans change over the course of a year. If you're really raring to go, get wait-listed, be persistent and patient, and keep your schedule as flexible as you can (easier done as a solo traveler, of course). Cancellations happen – you may luck out.

❶ Redwall Cavern

Poke around the beach at this concert hall of a cavern (p225) and look for animal footprints to identify in the sand.

❷ Little Colorado River

Incongruous not only for its South Pacific tendencies but also because it's a natural amusement-park ride, the Little Colorado (p226) is a big must-do.

❸ Elves Chasm

Like something out of an elysian fairytale, this lush, green grotto (p226) shelters a waterfall to climb up and a pool to dive into at its base.

❹ Tapeats Creek to Deer Creek

Take a day to trek what is universally acknowledged as one of the most beautiful hikes (p226) on the Colorado, with its narrows, waterfalls, Native American pictographs and stellar scenery.

❺ Havasu Canyon

Hike into Havasu Canyon to experience its blue-green waters, from the riverside to the waterfall and pools (p227) that remain largely the domain of rafters.

❻ Lava Falls Rapid

Get your game face on for Lava Falls (p226), the gnarliest rapid on the river with a 37ft drop over fewer than 500yd.

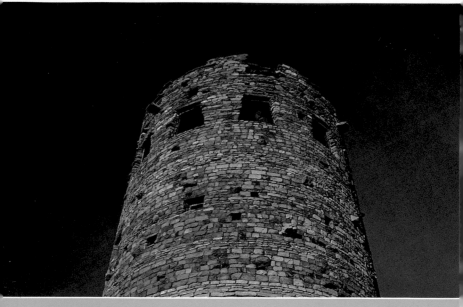

Historic Architecture

Many of the notable structures on the South Rim were envisioned by Mary Colter, who contributed richly to the culture and landscape of the Grand Canyon. But some of her buildings have a history preceding her arrival, as with 'The Hermit' of Hermits Rest and the Hopi of Hopi House. And notable architecture unrelated to Mary Colter tells its own story elsewhere in the Grand Canyon.

Author Tip

Though Mary Colter's influence is inescapable when surveying the structures on the South Rim, the strength of her designs is rooted in how complementary to the canyon landscape they are. Unless you know and care that she designed them, her structures blend so harmoniously into their environment that you might simply take their presence for granted. Could you say that about your own neighborhood?

1 Hermits Rest

This resthouse (p112) at the end of the line on Hermit Rd still makes a welcome stop for a snack after strolling the Rim Trail or ascending the Hermit Trail.

2 El Tovar

El Tovar (p106), the exemplar of national-park-lodge style, is an unmissable landmark with its distinctive silhouette, dark wood and decorative trim.

3 Hopi House

Built to resemble a Hopi dwelling and used as a residence by Hopi artisans in the early 1900s, Hopi House (p108) is now a shop selling high-quality Native American handicrafts.

4 Grand Canyon Lodge

Originally designed by Gilbert Sanley Underwood, the stone verandahs of the low-key, rough-hewn Grand Canyon Lodge (p197) are an architectural reflection of all that's good about the North Rim.

5 The Watchtower

Both this round stone tower (p114) and the spectacular views from the top floor are well worth the climb up the narrow spiral staircase.

6 Lees Ferry

The fort is now open air, but the thick brick walls attest to the culture clash between Mormon John D Lee and the Native Americans of the area (see p215).

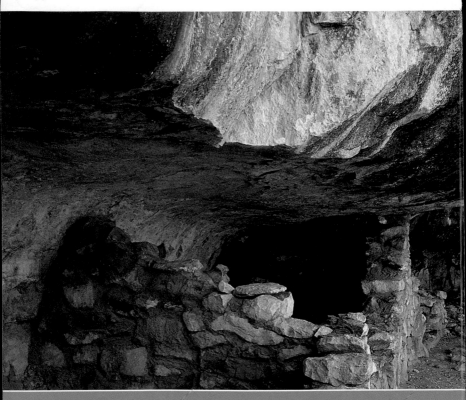

Native Americans

Ancient Native Americans predating the Puebloan cultures that followed have left few clues as to how they lived around the canyon. Modern-day Native American tribes of the region, on the other hand, rely on Grand Canyon tourism to make a living off the land. ou can find everything from skillfully woven ajo rugs to one-day river tours run by pai guides, and can explore the ruins of that lived here before them.

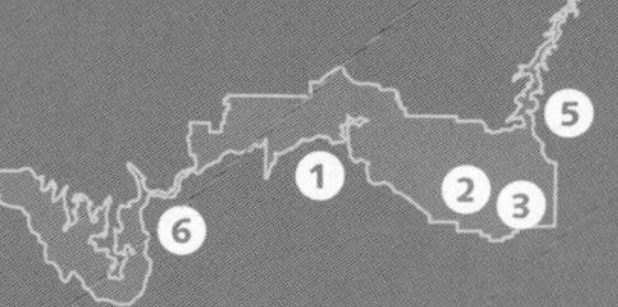

Author Tip

If you're looking for Native American jewelry but aren't a collector, it's easy to find at reputable shops on the South Rim and in the towns around the Grand Canyon. But you'll also see stalls set up on the sides of Hwys 64 or 89 on the Navajo Reservation, where you can shop around and get to know your local dealer.

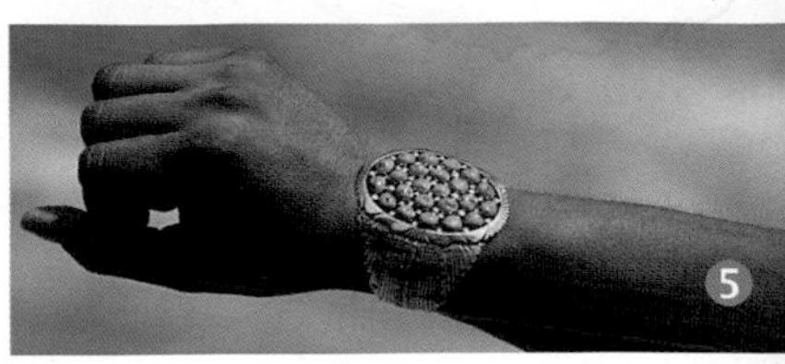

❶ Havasu Canyon

Hike down into the only reservation (p145) inside the canyon, and view the blue-green waters from which the Havasupai take their tribal name.

❷ Indian Garden

Indian Garden (p117) is the very reason the Bright Angel Trail is where it is; the Havasupai blazed the original trail to access this precious water source.

❸ Tusayan Ruins & Museum

As elsewhere in the region, walking through the remains of this ancient Puebloan village (p113) elicits more questions about its inhabitants and the culture that largely disappeared with them.

❹ Walnut Canyon National Monument

Another abandoned settlement of the Sinagua people, the cliff dwellings at Walnut Canyon (p155) perch around a butte in the gorgeous setting of this forested canyon.

❺ Navajo People

The enormous Navajo Reservation (p147) lies to the east of the national park, but you'll find Navajo jewelry and handmade rugs for sale all over the region.

❻ Hualapai Reservation

The Hualapai Nation, whose reservation (p149) borders the quiet southwestern rim of the canyon, runs the only one-day river trips on the Colorado and recently opened the glass-bottomed Skywalk.

Suspended above the abyss at the Skywalk (p149)

Contents

Grand Canyon National Park	**3**
The Authors	**19**
Destination Grand Canyon National Park	**21**
Planning Your Trip	**23**
Itineraries	**30**
Activities	**41**
Kids & Pets	**57**
Environment	**65**
History	**84**
South Rim	**100**
SIGHTS	**106**
El Tovar	106
Bright Angel Lodge	107
Yavapai Observation Station	107
Grand Canyon Depot	107
Hopi House	108
Verkamp's Curios	108
Lookout Studio	108
Kolb Studio	108
Grand Canyon Cemetery	109
OVERLOOKS	**109**
DRIVING	**110**
HIKING	**114**
Easy Hikes	114
Day Hikes	115
Backcountry Hikes	122
BIKING	**126**
OTHER ACTIVITIES	**127**
Mule Rides	127
Flyovers	128
Fishing	128
Ranger Programs	129
Cross-Country Skiing	129
SLEEPING	**130**
Camping	130
Lodges	131
EATING	**133**
Budget	133
Midrange	134
Top End	134
DRINKING	**135**
BEYOND THE SOUTH RIM	**135**
Kaibab National Forest (South Rim)	137
Tusayan	137
Valle	139
Williams	140
Havasupai Reservation	144
Hualapai Reservation & Skywalk	149
Flagstaff & Around	151
Sedona	162
Cameron	170
Lake Mead & Hoover Dam	171
Las Vegas	175
North Rim	**184**
OVERLOOKS	**187**
DRIVING	**187**
HIKING	**190**
Easy Hikes	190
Day Hikes	192
Backcountry Hikes	194
BIKING	**196**
OTHER ACTIVITIES	**196**
Mule Rides	196
Ranger Programs	197
Cross-Country Skiing	197
SLEEPING	**197**
EATING & DRINKING	**198**
BEYOND THE NORTH RIM	**199**
Kaibab National Forest (North Rim)	199
Along Highways 89 & Alt 89	204
Fredonia	207
Kanab	207
Page & Glen Canyon National Recreation Area	213
Colorado River	**220**
PLANNING	**222**
Orientation	222
Permits & Costs	223
Boat Options	223

When to Go 223
Rafting Companies 224
UPPER SECTION: LEES FERRY TO PHANTOM RANCH 225
MIDDLE SECTION: PHANTOM RANCH TO WHITMORE WASH 226
LOWER SECTION: WHITMORE WASH TO SOUTH COVE 228

Directory 229

Accommodations 229
Activities 230
Business Hours 231
Children 231
Climate Charts 231
Courses 232
Discount Cards 233
Festivals & Events 233
Food & Drink 233
Holidays 234
Insurance 234
International Visitors 234
Internet Access 235
Money 235
Post 235
Showers & Laundry 235
Telephone 235
Time 236
Tourist Information 236
Tours 236
Travelers with Disabilities 237
Volunteering 238
Women Travelers 238
Work 239

Transportation 240

GETTING THERE & AWAY 240
Air 240
Bus 241
Car & Motorcycle 242
Train 244
GETTING AROUND 245
Bicycle 245
Shuttle 245
Car & Motorcycle 245

Health & Safety 247

BEFORE YOU GO 247
Insurance 247
Medical Checklist 247
Internet Resources 247
Further Reading 248
IN THE PARK 248
Medical Assistance 248
Common Ailments 248
Environmental Hazards 249
Safe Hiking 251
Safe Biking 254

Clothing & Equipment 256

Clothing 256
Equipment 258
Buying & Renting Locally 261

Glossary 262

Behind the Scenes 264

Index 270

World Time Zones 278

Map Legend 280

Regional Map Contents

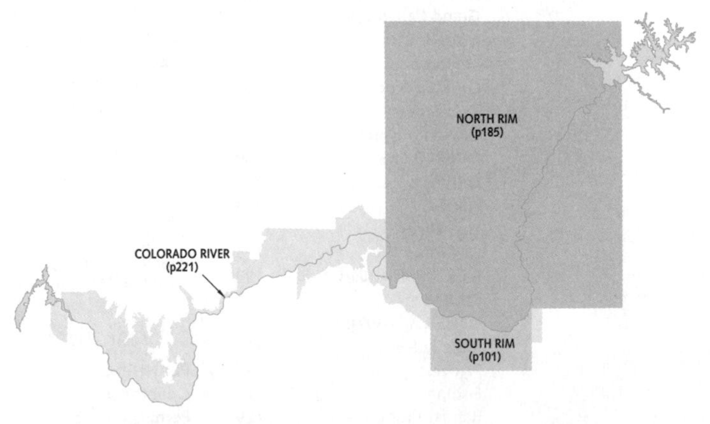

The Authors

WENDY YANAGIHARA

On her first visit to the Grand Canyon on a family road trip at age 13, Wendy discovered RC Gorman and the colors of the Southwestern desert. Upon the family's return to coastal California, she was allowed to paint a mock-up (in ugly primary colors, still on the garage wall) of the sunset-silhouetted cactus mural she envisioned in her bedroom. The mural didn't get approved, but the memory of desert colors never faded.

On this last visit to the Grand Canyon, Wendy spent weeks soaking up the local color – from enigmatic black Vishnu schist to white Moenkopi sandstone, the coolness of the Colorado River to the searing heat of the canyon's trails. Though she has covered national parks in other Lonely Planet guides – including *Indonesia, Mexico* and *Vietnam* – she was thrilled to reacquaint herself, in greater depth, with the grandest canyon of all for her first domestic assignment.

My Grand Canyon National Park

An early morning at Moran Point (p113), drinking in the canyon colors and desert air, is better than coffee. But so is stretching my legs on the 7am ranger hike down the South Kaibab (p117). It's hard to say that one Grand Canyon experience is better than another, but waking to sunrises and falling asleep beneath moonlit clouds and stars on various beaches along the Colorado River (p220) rate up there with memories of first kisses. It's possible that I spent my entire canyon travels with a gleeful smile on my face – how could I not, when pausing 10ft from an unperturbed grazing bighorn on the long haul up the Bright Angel (p117), or watching condors circle on thermals below Yaki Point (p112)? Roaming from river to rim, as I hope to do again and again, I was continually humbled and rejuvenated by the canyon's boundless beauty.

LONELY PLANET AUTHORS

Why is our travel information the best in the world? It's simple: our authors are independent, dedicated travelers. They don't research using just the internet or phone, and they don't take freebies in exchange for positive coverage. They travel widely, to all the popular spots and off the beaten track. They personally visit thousands of hotels, restaurants, cafés, bars, galleries, palaces, museums and more – and they take pride in getting all the details right, and telling it how it is. For more, see the authors section on www.lonelyplanet.com.

JENNIFER DENNISTON

A 10-week trip through Europe with her family hooked nine-year-old Jennifer to travel; by 21, she had traveled independently to five continents. Jennifer discovered America's Southwest during a postcollege stint teaching writing in New Mexico – after years exploring the quirky nooks, crannies and deceptively empty roads of the Southwest, the desert landscape became as much a part of her as the cornfields and dairy farms of her childhood's Midwest America. She earned a masters degree in American Studies, focusing on the American West, taught writing at the University of Iowa, and contributed to Lonely Planet's *Southwest USA, USA, Arizona* and *Grand Canyon* books. Mother to Anna (7) and Harper (4), Jennifer makes travel a cornerstone of her children's lives and education. She and her husband, a geology professor in Iowa, have taken the girls to Singapore, New Zealand and Australia, and the family (including the golden retriever!) spends summers road-tripping through the United States.

CONTRIBUTING AUTHOR

David Lukas is a professional naturalist whose travels and writing take him around the world, but he always returns to his home landscape of the American West. He has contributed environment and wildlife chapters to about 15 Lonely Planet guides. On his last trip to the Grand Canyon he spent all of his time mesmerized by the stunning California condors that circle the South Rim.

Destination Grand Canyon National Park

More than the sum of its archetypal overlooks, iconic Grand Canyon National Park can be an utterly transcendent experience even for those who never delve beyond the scenic viewpoints. The immensity of the canyon's scale and the intensity of its colors and shadows at sunrise or sunset scream for superlatives. Yet the canyon's many facets go beyond the essential beauty of its temples and buttes, with their infinite rock faces.

The very age of the canyon is nearly incomprehensible. At about two billion years old – half of Earth's total life span – the exposed layer of Vishnu schist at the bottom of the canyon is some of the oldest exposed rock on the planet. And the means by which it was exposed is of course the living, mighty Colorado River, which continues to carve its way 277 miles through the canyon as it has for the past six million years. Within the inner gorge of the mile-deep canyon, the riparian ecosystem on the canyon floor is a world away from the high country on the North Rim. Aside from the wildlife and amazing landscapes of the river gorge and its side canyons, evidence of the canyon's rich human history remains in the pictographs on its walls and ancient granaries within its caves. Even as recently as the late 1920s, the Havasupai were cultivating crops at Indian Garden on the Bright Angel Trail, and they are currently the canyon's only inhabitants, with a domain that includes beautiful Havasu Canyon. But backcountry hikers, river runners, scientists and artists continue to visit the inner gorge as did the explorers who came before them – the lore of John Wesley Powell and Glen and Bessie Hyde adding to the formidable allure of the river itself.

'the canyon's scale and the intensity of its colors and shadows at sunrise or sunset scream for superlatives'

Most of the canyon's five million annual visitors stream through during the busy summer season, and 90% visit only the developed South Rim. Situated only about 60 miles north of Interstate 40, the South Rim remains a quintessential stop on cross-country road trips, popular not only for the accessibility of its awe-inspiring viewpoints but also for its historic buildings, Native American ruins and tiny museums. But even here on the fast-view, drive-through rim of the park, you can take it as slow as you like. Escaping the crowds can be as easy as taking a day hike below the rim or merely tramping a hundred yards away from the parking lot of a scenic overlook.

If you seek solitude, however, a simple solution is to bypass the South Rim in favor of the quieter, more remote North Rim. Since it lies more than 200 miles by road from the South Rim, few visit both rims on the same trip. Though its scenic viewpoints are fewer in number and not as dramatically sublime, the North Rim has its own abundant charms: at an elevation of 8200ft (1000ft higher than the South Rim), its cooler temperatures support wildflower meadows and tall, thick stands of aspen and spruce.

Amid these forested roads and trails, what you'll find is peace, room to breathe and a less fettered national park experience.

Hikers could spend years exploring the trails that unfurl down both rims, from the well-trodden Bright Angel Trail on the South Rim to the rugged threshold trails on the North Rim. Though summer is the most popular season for day hikes (despite oppressively hot temperatures of more than 100°F below the rim), experienced canyon hikers know that it's much more pleasant to hike in the spring and fall, when there are also significantly fewer visitors. Exploring the backcountry inside the Big Ditch is also better left for these cooler seasons, as midsummer temperatures can skyrocket to heights of 120°F at Phantom Ranch, down on the banks of the Colorado. And while independent rafters formerly had to wait for a decade or two for their chance to run the Colorado, the park service's switch in 2006 to a lottery system increased everyone's odds of taking their trip of a lifetime.

'the vertiginous experience of walking on a cantilevered glass floor above the canyon is inarguably unique'

Mitigating the impact of tourist traffic to protect the canyon and to ensure visitor enjoyment has been an ongoing concern for the park service. Shuttles serving three routes on the South Rim encourage visitors to get out of their cars and reduce traffic. Additionally, the Greenway Plan that has been put into (slow) motion will eventually manifest itself in multiple-use, accessible paths that lead between key points on the South Rim and even into Tusayan, outside the park's South Entrance. As for noise pollution at the canyon, scenic flyovers have been restricted to specific corridors and are limited to certain hours of the day; none is allowed below the rim (except at Grand Canyon West).

Grand Canyon West, more than 240 miles and four hours west of the South Rim, is its own modern conundrum. Run by the Hualapai Nation, this scenic section of the Grand Canyon has recently been bedecked with the controversial Skywalk, a glass platform allowing visitors to walk beyond the canyon rim to view the maw below them. Some see the Skywalk as a sacrilege and a harbinger of unwise development on the fragile West Rim, but most agree that its construction was a revenue-generating strategy for the struggling Hualapai Nation to keep their tribe afloat. Though the vertiginous experience of walking on a cantilevered glass floor above the canyon is inarguably unique, what it means for the future of the West Rim and the Hualapai remains uncertain.

Despite the amusement-park atmosphere that can tinge both Grand Canyon West and Grand Canyon Village, all it takes to restore one's sense of place is a pause along the Rim Trail to refocus on the canyon's jagged features. The more time you spend at the canyon, the more it will reveal to you its subtle beauty and grandeur.

Planning Your Trip

It's easy enough to do a spur-of-the-moment road trip to the Grand Canyon, crash at a roadside motel, and take a spin around the South Rim. You can have a great time visiting the canyon this way if you're flexible – if you don't mind staying outside the park, or you can forego a mule ride into the canyon. But if you're reading this, it's probably not because the pull of the open road suddenly seized you (or maybe it did, and you stopped into the nearest bookstore before hitting the highway).

Advance planning affords not only peace of mind but also a wider range of options. At some destinations in the summer season you'll find that suites and two-room cabins (which are ideal if you're traveling with

GRAND DECISIONS

North or South?

Each rim offers a different experience of the canyon, and your choice of which to visit will depend on the time you have, the activities you'd like to pursue and what kind of experience you're looking for.

The majority of canyon visitors head for the easily accessed South Rim, whose visitor centers, lodges, eateries, gift shops, sights and services are open year-round. Most of the action centers on Grand Canyon Village, where the bustling atmosphere is particularly circuslike in the summer. Shuttles make regular loops from scenic points to lodges to trailheads, and it's easy to get around on well-marked paths along the rim. The elevation here is about 7000ft, and piñon-juniper forest surrounds the village. Offering panoramic views, the Rim Trail curves along the rim for 13 miles, 5.5 of which are paved. Drivers can choose from among 13 overlooks along two roads, and several spectacular trails descend into the canyon from the South Rim.

Though only 10 miles from the South Rim as the raven flies, the North Rim is a 215-mile, five-hour drive on winding desert roads from Grand Canyon Village. Because it's so remote, only about 10% of park visitors get to the North Rim; thus, it offers a very different experience. At 8000ft to 8800ft, this rim supports wildflower meadows and tall, thick stands of aspen and spruce, and the air is often crisp. Services are limited, and a lone historic lodge overlooks the canyon. You can hike, attend ranger programs and join a mule trip on the North Rim, but overlooks are scarce on this heavily forested rim.

The Kaibab National Forest stretches more than 50 miles north, and except for a few scattered lodges and campgrounds, the nearest facilities are in Kanab, Utah (80 miles north), and Page, Arizona (124 miles northeast). This is a quieter, gentler side of the Grand Canyon, and its remote beauty is well worth an extended trip.

Gateway Towns

These towns make great stops on your way to or from the park, and can also provide overflow accommodations if the park is booked.

If you visit the North Rim, you could stay a few days in Kanab and visit some of the Southwest's most picturesque terrain; many travelers visit the North Rim as one corner of a grand Zion–Bryce–Grand Canyon National Parks triangle, flying in and out of Salt Lake City, Utah or Albuquerque, New Mexico. These parks, as well as Grand Staircase-Escalante National Monument and Glen Canyon National Recreation Area, all lie within two hours of Kanab.

From the South Rim, Flagstaff lies 78 miles south of Grand Canyon Village and is a destination in its own right. Flagstaff makes an excellent base from which to explore several Native American sites, Sedona's red-rock country, and the Prescott, Kaibab and Coconino National Forests. You'll also find great museums and restaurants in town, and the surrounding area offers plenty of outdoor recreation, including downhill skiing, hiking and mountain biking.

children) are often reserved months ahead of time. And if you're looking to get a backcountry permit, ride a mule into the canyon, hike into Havasu Canyon or raft the rapids on the Colorado River, the earlier you make reservations for these popular activities, the better your chances.

The greatest benefit of planning ahead is that you'll have a better understanding of the canyon when you visit. Reading up on the Grand Canyon before you go will enrich your experience tremendously: as you hike down a trail, you'll be able to identify plants and birds you see; as you gaze from the rim, you'll understand how the canyon was formed.

The park distributes a useful free trip planner; call ☎ 928-638-7888 or visit the park's website at www.nps.gov/grca. See Tourist Information (p236) for more planning resources.

WHEN TO GO

All services and facilities on the North Rim are closed from mid-October through mid-May, though you can still drive into the park and stay at the campground until the first snowfall closes the road from Jacob Lake. Snow falls as early as late October and as late as January, and annual snowfall can be more than 200in. Rangers stay at the North Rim year-round, and you can cross-country ski or snowshoe into the park after the road closes.

See Climate Charts (p231) for more information.

The South Rim is open year-round, though ice and snow may temporarily close roads. Some facilities have limited hours during the winter, and Yavapai Lodge closes for several months. From March through November, private cars are not allowed on Hermit Rd.

Seasonal Highs & Lows

Weather is a primary consideration in deciding when to visit the park. June is the driest month, while summer thunderstorms roar through in July and August. These heavy rains can make hiking in the canyon not just unpleasant, but deadly, as flash floods can rip through side canyons with no warning. Temperatures average 85°F on the South Rim in July, the hottest month, and are generally 10° cooler on the North Rim. Expect sweater weather in the evenings on the North Rim. Temperatures on the rim average 20° cooler than at the bottom of the canyon. You could wake up to frost on the rim in April and be basking in 85°F by the time you get down to the river. Summers in the gorge are mercilessly hot, averaging 101°F in June, 106°F in July and 103°F in August. Despite the extreme heat, the summer also draws the biggest crowds; if you'd rather avoid them, visit in the spring or fall instead.

Surprisingly, for all its namesake grandeur, the Grand Canyon is not the biggest, nor the widest, nor even the longest canyon – it's simply unsurpassingly awesome.

Weather is cooler and changeable in the fall. By October, highs on the South Rim average 65°F. Snow and freezing overnight temperatures are likely by mid- to late September on the North Rim and by late October on the South Rim. While fall foliage is not particularly striking on the South Rim, colors on the North Rim peak from the last week of September through mid-October. That's just before the North Rim closes for the season and is an ideal time to visit this rim. There are still warm days breaking up the crisp autumn weather, and it's a spectacular time to hike and bike in the Kaibab National Forest. Both rims see a drop in tourists, and it's the best time to hike the inner canyon. Temperatures in the canyon average 84°F in October and 68°F in November.

The quietest season is winter. Temperatures in January and February average 42°F on the rim and 56°F on the canyon floor. While snow adds to the dramatic beauty of the canyon, snowstorms do occasionally wreak havoc. Trails remain open, though they can be icy and dangerous near the rim.

Rates at the lodges in the park remain the same year-round, but rooms in gateway towns like Flagstaff, Kanab and Williams drop significantly during the winter.

Coping with the Crowds

Everyone has heard horror stories about the crowds at the Grand Canyon, from bumper-to-bumper traffic and long lines to fully booked hotels, campgrounds and activities. But armed with a few simple strategies, you can escape the throngs.

The first trick is to avoid the South Rim in the summer. Peak season at the Grand Canyon ranges from April to September, and the park is busiest from Memorial Day to Labor Day (see p234 for dates). Visiting at other times of the year means you'll have to share the park with far fewer people.

Summer visitors may want to consider visiting the North Rim instead, as its limited services and remote location keep day-trippers to a minimum. You'll encounter few fellow hikers on its many trails. To really escape the crowds, plan to camp at the North Rim after the lodge closes but before the first snowfall shuts down the road to the park. You won't find any water or facilities, but you'll have the whole place pretty much to yourself.

If you do brave the South Rim, don't be discouraged by the half-hour line at the entrance station and your first encounter with the teeming village. Take a few minutes to get your bearings, then take a short stroll or hike – you'll be surprised at how easily you can leave the chaos of the village behind.

Accessing the South Rim via the East Entrance rather than the more popular South Entrance is another simple way to avoid the masses. There is usually no line here (even though it's only 10 miles further from

FESTIVALS & EVENTS

See p151 and p210 for more festivals and events throughout the region.

North Rim

For a couple of weeks in June the Phoenix Amateur Astronomy Society sets up powerful telescopes for a **Star Party** on the Grand Canyon Lodge verandah – guests can see Saturn's rings and the moons around Jupiter. Park rangers on the North Rim orchestrate an informal **Fourth of July** celebration for children, featuring a fire-engine parade and water guns for the kids. Held annually in August, **Heritage Days** celebrates the region's Native American culture. Members of nearby tribes, including the Havasupai, Paiute, Hopi and Navajo (tribal participation varies from year to year), conduct this three-day program. Activities include kachina doll carving classes, musical performances and talks about the history and culture of their tribes. Call the **North Rim Visitor Center** (☎ 928-638-7864) for more information.

South Rim

During the week following summer solstice, the Tucson Amateur Astronomy Association (see Courses, p232) offers a **Star Party** nightly at Yavapai Point, featuring a slide presentation followed by telescope viewing of the June sky.

During the first three weeks of September, the park hosts the **Grand Canyon Music Fest** featuring chamber music at Shrine of the Ages auditorium. Tickets can be purchased in ad online or by contacting the **festival office** (☎ 928-638-9215, 800-997-8285; www.grandcanyon .org; PO Box 1332, Grand Canyon, AZ 86023; adult/child $15/8). Tickets are sometimes available at but don't count on it.

In December the park observes the holidays with a 20ft Christmas tree in the lob and Christmas Eve and Christmas night celebrations at Phantom Ranch.

Flagstaff) and your first experiences in the park won't be marred by the hurly-burly of the village. Stop by the Watchtower at Desert View with its spectacular canyon overlook, then drive the 25 miles to the village along Desert View Dr. If you plan on camping along the South Rim, and are willing to chance the first-come, first-served policy, consider staying at peaceful Desert View Campground beside the East Entrance.

Because so many people stay in Flagstaff, Williams and Sedona and travel into the park just for the day, the South Rim quiets down considerably every evening. This is the time to relax on the porch of El Tovar or take a leisurely stroll along the rim.

Lastly, don't let the crowds scare you off. If you're flexible, you may still be able to find rooms, raft the river or book a mule trip, even if you left planning until the last minute. In fact, same-day mule trips on the North Rim are routinely available. Cancellation rates at some rafting companies are as high as 15%, so if you call a few weeks before your trip, there's a decent chance you can float the Colorado. If you can't book an overnight trip, consider a day rafting trip on the Hualapai Reservation (see p150).

Lodge vacancies are less predictable. You could call the park in mid-May and find vacancies on both rims for June, call a week later and find everything booked, then call two weeks later and find a room at El Tovar. See p230 for tips on finding last-minute accommodations.

COSTS & MONEY

Your biggest expenses will be food and accommodations. If you camp, take day hikes and cook your own meals, you can enjoy the park for about $30 a day. If you stay at a rim-view suite at El Tovar and eat all your meals at this historic lodge, you'll spend upward of $400 a day. Add a rafting excursion, and you're talking an expensive trip. Most visitors spend somewhere between these two extremes.

The $25-per-vehicle (or $12-per-pedestrian) park entrance fee covers shuttles, museums, ranger programs and some classes (for example, the photography and astronomy classes offered in the summer; see p232). Hiking is free, unless you spend the night in the canyon (see p44). See www.nps.gov/grca/planyourvisit/fees-reservations.htm for current information on fees and permits.

For those on a moderate budget, particularly those with children in tow, it's often worth going for higher-quality cabins over motel rooms on the North Rim as the price difference between them is minimal. On the South Rim, rim-view cabins at the Bright Angel Lodge cost a bit more,

BEST FAMILY ACCOMMODATIONS OUTSIDE THE PARK

- Best Western Grand Canyon Squire Inn (Tusayan, p138)
- Canyon Motel & RV Park (Williams, p142)
- Comfi Cottages (Flagstaff, p158)
- Grand Motel (Williams, p142)
- ...nipine Resort (Sedona, p167)
- ...ab Lodge (North Rim, p204)
- ...merica Motel (Flagstaff, p159)
- ...ge (Kanab, p211)
- ...use Inn (Williams, p142)

but they're bright and sunny and have more character than doubles at the other lodges. The least expensive rooms on the South Rim are the basic ones at Yavapai West, which don't have rim views but sit amid ponderosa trees and are among the most peaceful in the park.

Packing your own picnic lunches and snacks will save you quite a bit on pricey meals, especially if you stock up on groceries in one of the gateway towns before arriving at the park. You'll also have the freedom to choose your own picnic spot with a view. Inside the park, Canyon Village Marketplace (p133) on the South Rim carries most everything you may have forgotten, and the lodge cafeterias on both rims offer lower-priced kids' menus, making them good places to fill up on the cheap if you don't feel like cooking.

Most gateway towns offer accommodations to suit every budget, but your expenses will skyrocket if you stay in Sedona, one of Arizona's costliest destinations. Except for the campgrounds, it's difficult to find any lodgings for less than $90 a night.

Expenses	Cost
park admission (per vehicle)	$25
campsite at Mather Campground	$18
double room at Maswik Lodge	$78-139
dinner for 2 at El Tovar	$70
cocktail at Grand Canyon Lodge	$6
souvenir Grand Canyon poster	$10
full-day mule trip	$125-149
train ride from Williams (coach class)	$65
7-day rafting trip	$2400
shuttle ride in park	free!

BOOKS

The Grand Canyon Association publishes an excellent trilogy on the prehistory, geology and ecology of the canyon. No more than 60 pages each, these thorough, well-written illustrated books are geared toward general audiences and ideal for anyone seeking an introduction to the region. You can buy *An Introduction to Grand Canyon Ecology* by Rose Houk (1980), *An Introduction to Grand Canyon Geology* by Greer Price (1999), and *An Introduction to Grand Canyon Prehistory* by Christopher M Coder (2000) individually ($7 to $10) or together at a discount.

Over the Edge: Death in the Grand Canyon by Michael P Ghiglieri and Thomas M Myers (Puma Press, 2001) is an informative and fascinating, if slightly repetitive, survey of death in the canyon. Morbid as the topic might be, the book can be surprisingly entertaining.

Below the rim, hikers will find *Hiking Grand Canyon National Park* (Falcon, 2006) by Ron Adkison to be an indispensable hiking guide. It covers everything from easy day hikes to backcountry treks, as well as providing useful information on hiking in this unique environment.

Meanwhile, down on the river, whitewater guide Brad Dimock investigates the story of missing honeymooners Glen and Bessie Hyde, who disappeared in 1928 on a tragic journey down the Colorado, in his book *Sunk Without a Sound: The Tragic Colorado River Honeymoon of Glen & Bessie Hyde* (Fretwater Press, 2001).

Michael Reisner tells the dramatic story of the damming of the West in *Cadillac Desert* (Pimlico, 2001). This thoroughly researched, interesting read gives a very different account than that told in the visitors center at Glen Canyon and Hoover Dams.

If you're doing a private trip down the Colorado, check out *Day Hikes from the River: A Guide to 100 Hikes from Camps on the Colorado River in Grand Canyon National Park* by Tom Martin.

A solid, interesting overview of the geology, botany and wildlife of the canyon is what Jeremy Schmidt offers up in his *Grand Canyon National Park: A Natural History Guide* (Houghton Mifflin, 1993). The readable descriptions are accompanied by loads of photos.

For more background and further exploration of the region, pick up Lonely Planet's *Southwest USA*.

MAPS

Trails Illustrated/National Geographic publishes a comprehensive waterproof and tearproof topographic map of Grand Canyon National Park that encompasses both rims, the backcountry and all trails.

Sky Terrain's topographic 1:40,000 *Grand Canyon Trail Map* (2007) by Kent Schulte details the most popular areas and trails in the Grand Canyon, making it an excellent planning tool for backcountry adventures in the canyon.

Two United States Forest Service (USFS) maps show sights, viewpoints, primitive campsites, forest service roads and other useful locations in the surrounding Kaibab National Forest. The *North Kaibab Ranger District* map covers the forest north of the canyon, while the *Tusayan, Williams & Chalender Ranger Districts* map covers forest south of the park. They are available at the visitors centers in Flagstaff and Williams, the Tusayan and Williams Ranger Stations, and the Kaibab Plateau Visitor Center in Jacob Lake.

You can also find gems of individual trail maps, like *Hikernut's Grand Canyon Companion – A Guide to Hiking and Backpacking the Most Popular Trails Into the Canyon: Bright Angel, South Kaibab & North Kaibab Trails* by Brian J Lane.

The best road map of the region is AAA's *Indian Country Guide Map*, which, in addition to highlighting the local Native American reservations, shows many dirt roads not included on other maps.

Check camping stores in Flagstaff and Kanab to find detailed topographic United States Geological Survey (USGS) maps, essential for anyone planning backcountry hiking; order in advance by calling ☎ 888-275-8747 or accessing the USGS website at www.us gs.gov.

All but the USGS maps are available at Books & More Store (p104) on the South Rim and can be ordered in advance by calling the Grand Canyon Association at ☎ 800-858-2808. For outdoor activity maps of the entire West, peruse the map center at the Public Land Information Center website (http://plicma pcenter.org/).

Adult males make up the largest demographic of those who fall to their deaths at the canyon. (Hint: peeing over the rim is not as funny as you think it is. Use common sense.)

INTERNET RESOURCES

More resources for planning your Grand Canyon trip are available online.

Arizona Office of Tourism (www.arizonaguide.com) The state of Arizona's tourism website, with links to hundreds of resources, from road conditions and airport information to festivals and events statewide.

Grand Canyon Association (www.grandcanyon.org) Best online bookstore for the park, with links to the Grand Canyon Field Institute, the Grand Canyon Music Festival and other useful sites.

Great Outdoor Recreation Pages (www.gorp.com/gorp/location/az/az.htm) Dude ranches, hiking sites, rafting outfitters and other outdoor activities in Arizona.

Lonely Planet (www.lonelyplanet.com) Home to the Thorn Tree bulletin board, where you can ask fellow travelers for their tips and share your own when you return home.

National Park Service (www.nps.gov/grca) Updated information on the park, including current trail talks and a calendar of events, with a link to the Grand Canyon Association bookstore.

ublic Lands Information Center (www.publiclands.org) Consolidated information on all public lands in the United States, with links to educational programs and online shopping for recreation passes and permits etc.

Xanterra Parks & Resorts (www.xanterra.com, www.grandcanyonnorthrim.com for North Rim, www.grandcanyonlodges.com for South Rim) Primary in-park concessionaire, with information on special promotions, mule trips and accommodations.

USEFUL ORGANIZATIONS

Contact these organizations for more information on projects relating to the park. Also see Tourist Information, p236.

Grand Canyon Association (☎ 928-638-2481, 800-858-2828; www.grandcanyon.org; PO Box 399, Grand Canyon, AZ 86023) Founded in 1932, this nonprofit association runs educational, historical and scientific programs in the park. In 1993 the association established the Grand Canyon Field Institute (p232), which offers educational courses for all ages. Visit the association website to buy books and videos on the park and peruse the various classes it sponsors.

Grand Canyon Chamber of Commerce (☎ 928-638-2901, 888-472-2696; www.grandcanyonchamber.org; PO Box 3007, Grand Canyon, AZ 86023) This chamber of commerce website lists a calendar of events and links to local businesses and area maps.

Grand Canyon National Park Foundation (☎ 928-774-1760; www.grandcanyonfoundation.org; 625 N Beaver St, Flagstaff, AZ 86001) Incorporated in 1995, this nonprofit foundation works to preserve, protect and enhance the park. Through private, corporate and philanthropic donations, it funds wildlife restoration projects, exhibits and interpretive programs.

Grand Canyon Trust (☎ 928-774-7488; www.grandcanyontrust.org; 2601 N Fort Valley Rd, Flagstaff, AZ 86001) The trust supports environmental projects geared toward preserving and protecting the natural resources of the Colorado Plateau. It has worked to control noise pollution by minimizing air tours over the canyon and helped engineer the 1996 flood-flow plan to restore beaches in the canyon, among other projects. The trust also offers many volunteer opportunities through its Grand Canyon Volunteers program (see p54).

National Park Service (NPS; ☎ 928-638-7888; www.nps.gov/grca; PO Box 129, Grand Canyon, AZ 86023) Responsible for overall management of the Grand Canyon, the NPS cooperates with Xanterra, the Grand Canyon Association and other park agencies. Along with updated information on the park, its website can also point you toward an advance trip planner and a backcountry planner. NPS environmental programs instruct teachers, individuals, school and community groups about the park and the need to protect its natural resources. The environmental education office (☎ 928-638-7662; www.nps.gov/grca/forteachers/index.htm) provides materials for teachers and international visitors and offers teacher-training workshops and field trips at the canyon.

Sierra Club, Grand Canyon Chapter (☎ 602-253-8633; http://arizona.sierraclub.org; Ste 277, 202 E McDowell Rd, Phoenix, AZ 85004) This chapter works in its traditional activist capacity with other groups in the area on issues as diverse as monitoring endangered condors and lobbying for limitations on canyon flyovers.

Itineraries

SOUTH RIM IN AN AFTERNOON

One Day

Make the most of your afternoon at the canyon by starting with sights at the rim and a short foray down the Bright Angel before hopping on the Hermit Rd shuttle; the afternoon covers around 20 miles.

- Admire the classic park architecture over lunch at **El Tovar** (p135).
- Shop **Hopi House** (p108) and **Verkamp's Curios** (p108) for Native American jewelry and canyon postcards.
- Roam the **Rim Trail** (p114) and keep an eye out for cruising California condors.
- Shore up your geology knowledge and get the view explained at **Yavapai Observation Station** (p104).
- Hike down to Mile-and-a-Half Resthouse on the **Bright Angel Trail** (p116).
- Hop on a Hermit Rd shuttle to pay respects and snap some photos at **Powell Memorial** (p111).
- Watch a striking canyon sunset at **Pima Point** (p111) or **Hopi Point** (p111).
- Ruminate over the afternoon with dinner at the festive **Arizona Room** (p134).

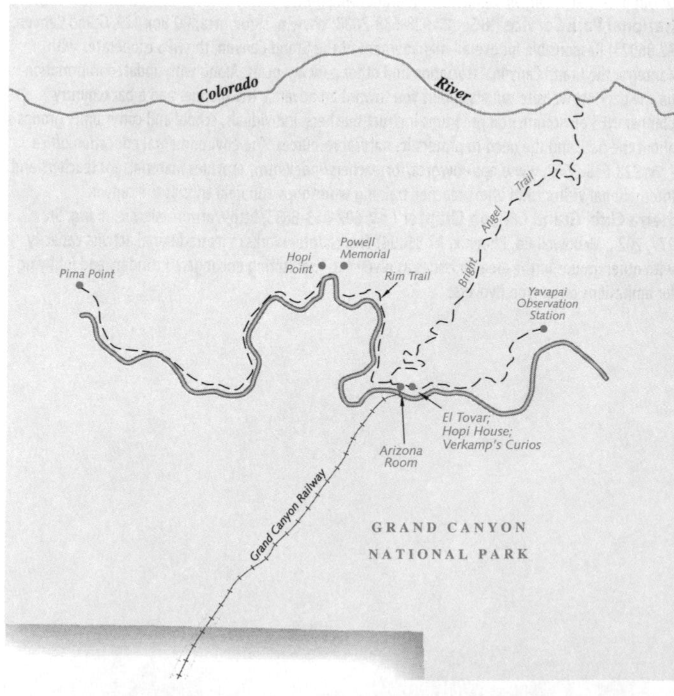

ONE DAY ON THE SOUTH RIM

One Day

- Ride a shuttle to catch the sunrise at **Yaki Point** (p112).
- Show up at South Kaibab Trailhead for the 7am ranger-led **Cedar Ridge Hike** (p129).
- Address more quotidian needs with coffee and a pastry at **Deli at Marketplace** (p134).
- Stroll the Greenway Trail to **Canyon View Information Plaza** (p104) for books, postcards and, oh, information.
- Gape at the view and get a grip on geology at **Yavapai Observation Station** (p104).
- Lunch on the early side to avoid the crowds at elegant **El Tovar** (p135).
- Head to **Hermits Rest** (p112) for a brief detour down the trail (or to the gift shop).
- Get into the car and get started on the **Desert View Drive** (p112).
- Hike out to peaceful **Shoshone Point** (p115) along the way, if the parking lot's empty.
- Wave from the **Watchtower** (p114) at the rafters you might see on the rapids below.
- End with a decadent dinner at **Brix** (p161) in Flagstaff – but book ahead!

Start with sunrise and work your hiking legs; after a relaxed lunch you can do the leisurely 25-mile Desert View Dr before fine-dining 80 miles away in Flagstaff.

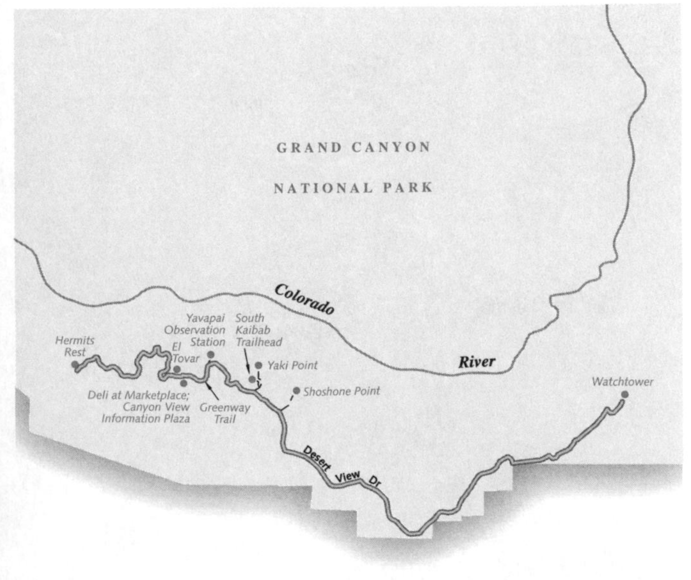

TWO DAYS ON THE SOUTH RIM

Two Days

Travel the 65 miles from Williams on the Grand Canyon Railway and spend a night at the South Rim before catching the next day's train back.

- Board the **Grand Canyon Railway train** (p244) in Williams after the Wild West shoot-out.
- Stretch your legs and check out the rim from the **Lookout Studio terrace** (p108).
- Get inspired at **Kolb Studio** (p108) and shoot the canyon from your own angle.
- Do the **Hermit Road** (p110) drive by shuttle, and hike some of the Rim Trail.
- Take in the sunset at **Hopi Point** (p111) as you circle back in.
- Enjoy a cocktail as you wait for a table at the **Arizona Room** (p134).
- Bring a flashlight and attend an evening **ranger talk** (p129) at Mather Amphitheater.
- Spend the night in a cozy **Bright Angel cabin** (p132).
- Get up early to do the ranger-led **Cedar Ridge Hike** (p129) from South Kaibab Trailhead.
- Hop off at **Canyon View Information Plaza** (p104) for books and postcards.
- Savor a last lunch at **El Tovar** (p135) before catching the train back to Williams.

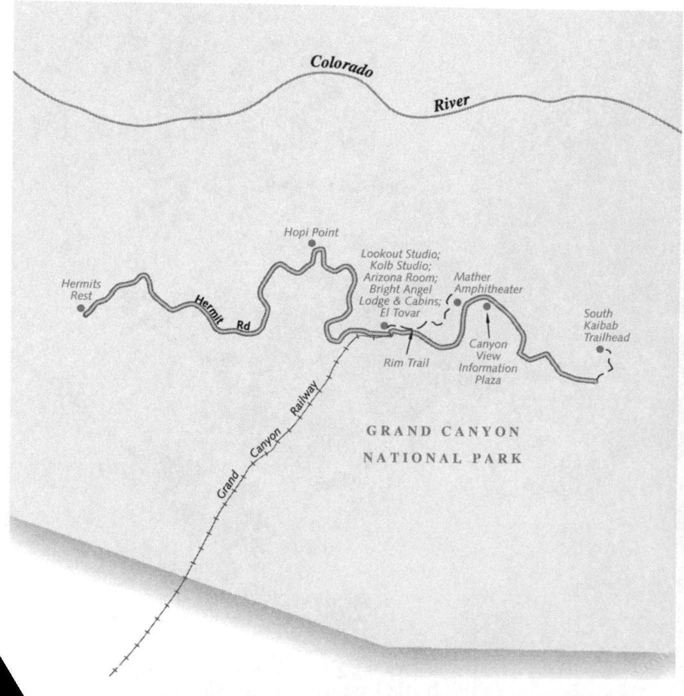

ONE WEEK ON THE SOUTH RIM

One Week

- Take it slow on the **Desert View Drive** (p112).
- Amble out to **Shoshone Point** (p115) for a peaceful picnic lunch.
- See the sights around the village with a stroll along the **Rim Trail** (p114).
- Do dinner and an **IMAX movie** (p139) in Tusayan.
- Get away from it all on the **Dripping Springs Trail** (p121).
- Watch from **Hopi Point** (p111) as the sun paints the canyon at sunset.
- Sip the requisite rimside cocktail at the **Arizona Room** (p134).
- Spend a night by the river – hike down **South Kaibab**, up **Bright Angel** (p124).
- Take on the rugged day hike down the **Grandview Trail** (p119).
- Attend a **ranger walk or evening talk** (p129).
- Put it all into the regional context at the excellent **Museum of Northern Arizona** (p153).

A week allows plenty of time for long day hikes or a backcountry overnight hike, leisurely drives, a movie and an evening ranger talk, all at a sane pace, covering around 150 miles.

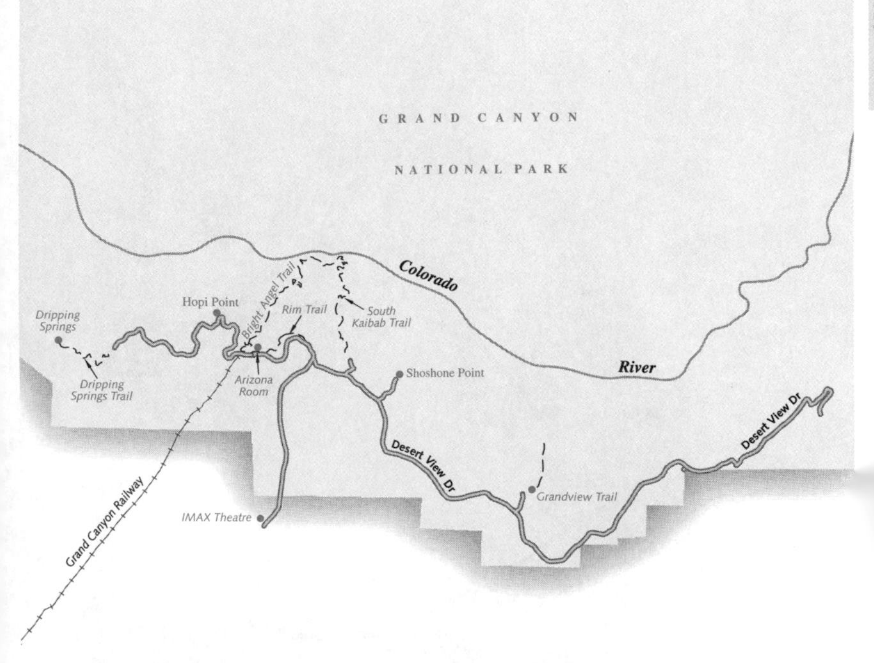

TWO WEEKS ON THE SOUTH RIM

Two Weeks

Start planning for this full two weeks: for a spot at Havasu Campground and a place on a rafting trip, you'll want to book six months to a year ahead. This itinerary covers around 300 miles.

- Leap in at Lees Ferry for a six-day rafting trip on the **Upper Colorado** (p225).
- Hike up to the South Rim on **Bright Angel Trail** (p122).
- See how far you've traveled from **Lookout Studio** (p108).
- Have lunch or a cocktail on the back porch at **El Tovar** (p135).
- Book a course – well in advance – with **Grand Canyon Field Institute** (p232).
- Sit quietly and watch the colors change at sunrise from **Yaki Point** (p112).
- Take in a sunset from **Hermit Road** (p110).
- Have a last look at the river rapids from **Lipan Point** (p113) on Desert View Dr.
- Spend a night in **Williams** (p140), taking in the cool, forested air and small-town feel.
- Drive up historic Route 66 and spend the night in a **Seligman motel** (p144, p150).
- Hike overnight into **Havasu Canyon** (p144) to cool off in the beautiful blue-green waters.

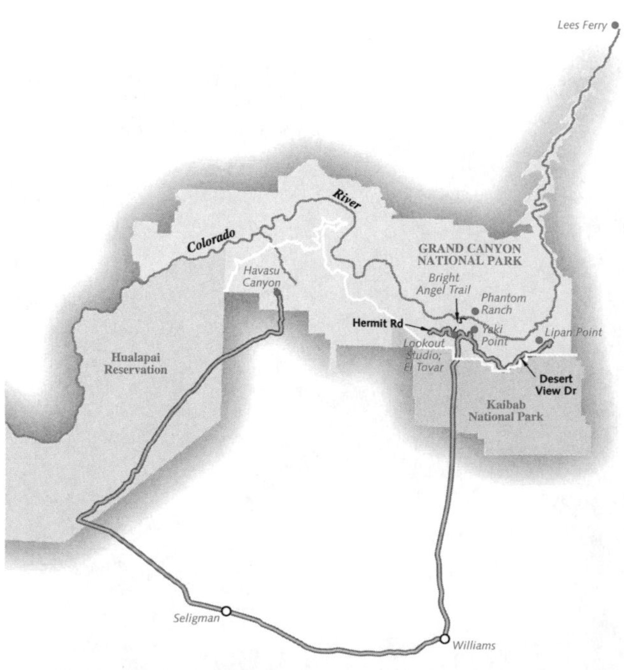

A DAY ON THE NORTH RIM

One Day

- Grab a brew and pastry from the **Roughrider Saloon** (p199) in Grand Canyon Lodge.
- Relax in a rough-hewn rocker on the back verandah of **Grand Canyon Lodge** (p197).
- Stroll along a precarious rocky finger out to **Bright Angel Point** (p190).
- Wind your way to overlooks along **Cape Royal Road** (p188).
- Drive to Point Imperial on **Point Imperial Road** (p189).
- Soak in a fireside **ranger program** (p197) on the lodge's verandah.
- Hike through meadows and aspen on the **Widforss Trail** (p192).
- Grab a bottle of wine and some cheese for an evening picnic at **Marble View** (p201).
- Watch the deer graze in the meadow over dinner at **Kaibab Lodge** (p204).

Wake up with the roosters for the drive from Kanab, 83 miles from the North Rim, and plan on returning to Kanab in time for bed!

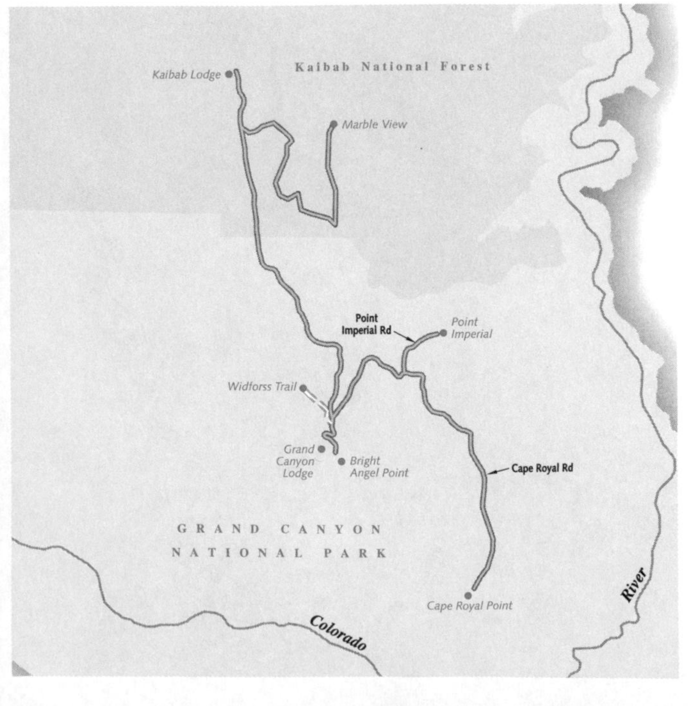

FOUR DAYS ON THE NORTH RIM

Four Days

Fall into the North Rim groove – high mountainmeadows, quiet overlooks, rustic cabins and dinners with panoramic canyon views. Get an early start out of Kanab, 83 miles north, on day one.

- Squeeze through a slot canyon on the **Wire Pass to Buckskin Gulch** (p206) hike.
- Walk along a precarious rocky finger on your way to **Bright Angel Point** (p190).
- Stargaze over the canyon expanse from the back verandah of **Grand Canyon Lodge** (p197).
- Descend into the canyon for sunrise at the **Coconino Overlook** (p194).
- Hike the **Widforss Trail** (p192) for a quiet picnic on the rim.
- Wind along **Cape Royal Road** (p188) and out to **Point Imperial** (p189).
- Sidle into a side canyon on the **Cliff Springs** (p191).
- Stand on **Cape Final** (p191), listen to the silence, breathe deep.
- Take in a **ranger talk** (p197) on ancient Puebloans at Walhalla Overlook.
- Meander through meadows and aspen along the **Arizona Trail: Park Boundary Trailhead to Crystal Spring** (p203).
- Picnic in the meadow at **Marble View** (p201) – read a book, throw a Frisbee, kick back.

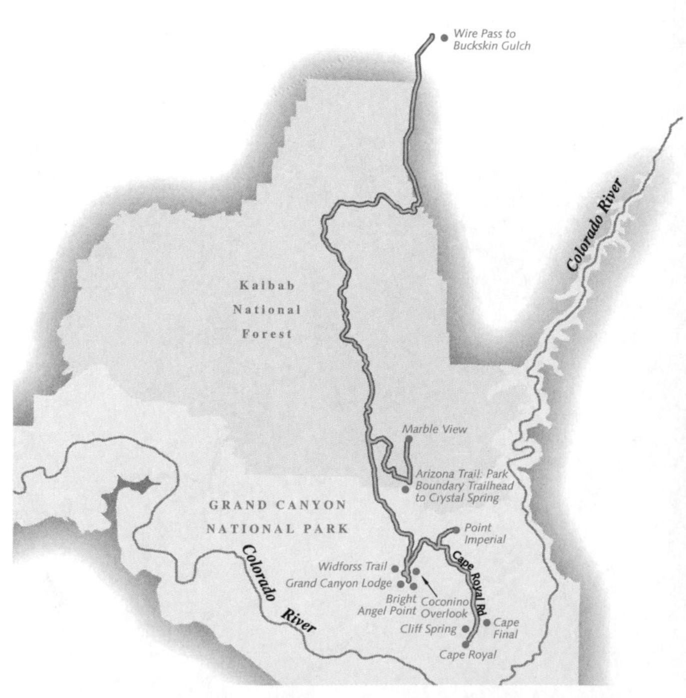

ONE WEEK ON THE NORTH RIM

One Week

- Relax in a rough-hewn rocker and enjoy the spectacular view from the back verandah of **Grand Canyon Lodge** (p197).
- Walk along a precarious finger on your way to **Bright Angel Point** (p190).
- Wind along **Cape Royal Road** (p188) and out to **Point Imperial** (p189).
- Picnic on the canyon edge at **Widforss Point** (p192).
- Bump your way to **Point Sublime** (p189) and simply relax.
- Hike along an old fire road to the rarely visited **Tiyo Point** (p189).
- Stars? Geology? Ancient Puebloans? Take your pick of **ranger programs** (p197).
- Descend into the canyon on the **North Kaibab** (p194) for a night at **Phantom Ranch** (p132).
- Meander through meadows and aspen along the **Arizona Trail: Park Boundary Trailhead to Crystal Spring** (p203).
- Hike from overlook to overlook along **Rainbow Rim Trail** (p201).
- Gaze into nothingness over an evening picnic of wine and cheese at **Marble View** (p201). Perfection.

Enjoy a night in the desert depths of the canyon and several days exploring the cool woods and meadows of the North Rim. From here it's 210 miles to Flagstaff, 280 miles to Las Vegas, 350 miles to Phoenix, and 395 miles to Salt Lake City, Utah.

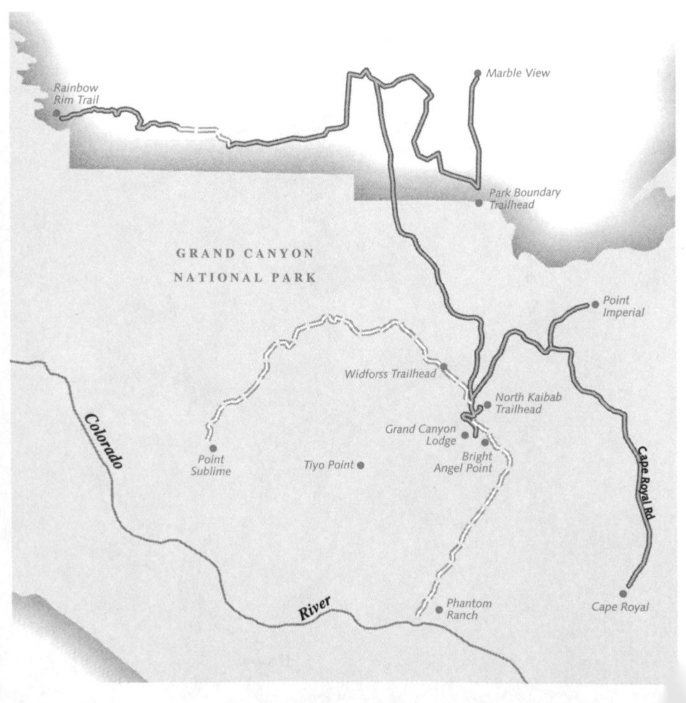

SOUTH RIM WITH CHILDREN

Two Days

This trip loops from Flagstaff up to Desert View (90 miles), includes a night at Grand Canyon Village and exits the park's South Entrance for the 79-mile return drive to Flagstaff.

- Hike 1000-year-old lava flows and explore ancient Puebloan dwellings at **Sunset Crater Volcano National Monument & Wupatki National Monument** (p155).
- Climb the winding staircase of the **Watchtower** (p114) – what stories do the walls tell?
- Stop at canyon overlooks and **Tusayan Ruins & Museum** (p113) along **Desert View Drive** (p112).
- Stroll out to **Shoshone Point** (p115).
- In the village, enjoy drinks and downtime on the lawn off the back porch of **El Tovar** (p106).
- Taste the Wild West under antler chandeliers at the **Arizona Room** (p134).
- Stargaze along the **Rim Trail** (p114).
- Earn **Junior Ranger** (p60) or **Discovery Pack** (p60) badges.
- Hike or ride a mule into the canyon on the **Bright Angel Trail** (p117).
- Exit the park from the South Entrance and catch the Grand Canyon film at the **IMAX** (p139) in Tusayan.
- Kick around **Flagstaff** (p151) and play at **Thorpe Park** (p153).

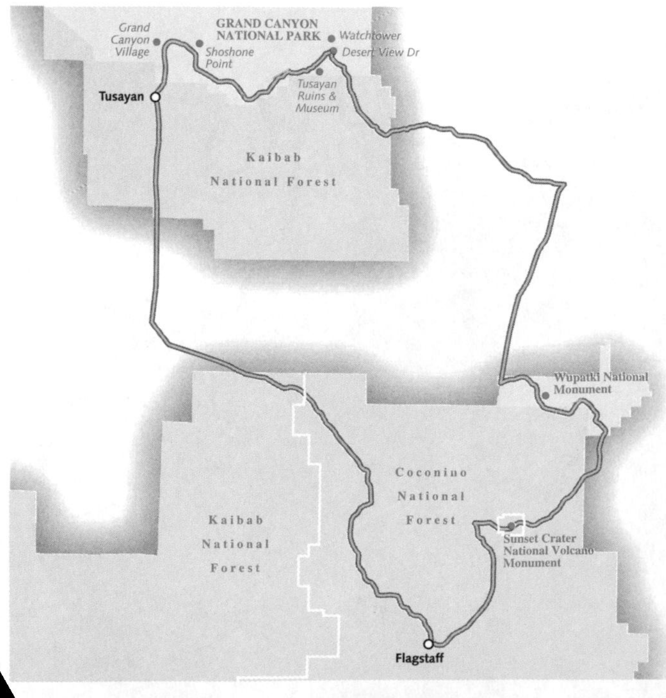

NORTH RIM WITH CHILDREN

Four Days

- Stargaze from the back verandah of **Grand Canyon Lodge** (p197) and overnight in a rustic cabin.
- Hike as much (or as little!) of the **Widforss Trail** (p192) as energy allows.
- Bump on a **mule** (p196) along the rim (two hours) or into the canyon (half-day).
- Relax over a leisurely afternoon earning **Junior Ranger** (p60) or **Discovery Pack** (p60) badges.
- Take a pizza from **Deli in the Pines** (p198) to the **Moon Room** (p198) or drive to **Harvey Meadow** (p194).
- Drive along **Cape Royal Road** (p188), stopping for a picnic at **Greenland Lake** (p188).
- Wander through the woods along the **Transept Trail** (p191) for an ice cream at the **general store** (p198).
- Hunt for fossils and play in the meadow along the **Arizona Trail: Park Boundary Trailhead to Crystal Spring** (p203).
- Kick back with a glass of wine and snacks while the kids play at **Marble View** (p201).
- Splash in the Colorado River at **Paria Beach** (p216) at **Lees Ferry** (p215).
- Picnic by the apricot orchard at **Lonely Dell Ranch** (p215) and continue 45 minutes to **Page** (p213) or two hours to **Flagstaff** (p151).

Arrive at Grand Canyon Lodge from Kanab (83 miles), Page (124 miles), Flagstaff (210 miles), Las Vegas (284 miles) or Salt Lake City (394 miles) in the early evening and spend four nights there. It's 84 miles from the North Rim to Lees Ferry.

TWO WEEKS ON BOTH RIMS

Two Weeks

This itinerary loops 201 miles from Las Vegas to Kanab, the North Rim (83 miles), Lees Ferry (84 miles), the South Rim's Desert View (109 miles), Flagstaff (79 miles), and back to Las Vegas (279 miles). Whew!

- Eat at Kanab's **Laid Back Larry's** (p212) and squeeze through the **Wire Pass to Buckskin Gulch** (p206) hike.
- Drive along **Johnson Canyon Road** (p210) and take in a Western movie at the **Barn** (p212).
- Stock the car with water and food and head out to knuckle-biting **Toroweap** (p189) overlook.
- Stargaze from **Grand Canyon Lodge** (p197) on the North Rim and take in a ranger talk (p197).
- Hike the **Widforss Trail** (p192), drive **Cape Royal Road** (p188), and scramble to **Cliff Spring** (p191).
- Descend predawn into the canyon to tackle the overnight **rim-to-rim hike** (p123) – catch the **Trans-Canyon Shuttle** (p245) on your way back to the North Rim.
- Meander along the **Arizona Trail: Park Boundary Trailhead to Crystal Springs** (p203) and picnic at **Marble View** (p201).
- Wade in the Colorado River and explore historic buildings in **Lees Ferry** (p215).
- Drive along the South Rim's **Desert View Drive** (p112) – don't miss the **Watchtower** (p114) and **Shoshone Point** (p115).
- Compare overlooks on a walk along the **Rim Trail** (p114).
- Gawk at **Hoover Dam** (p171) on the way back to Vegas.

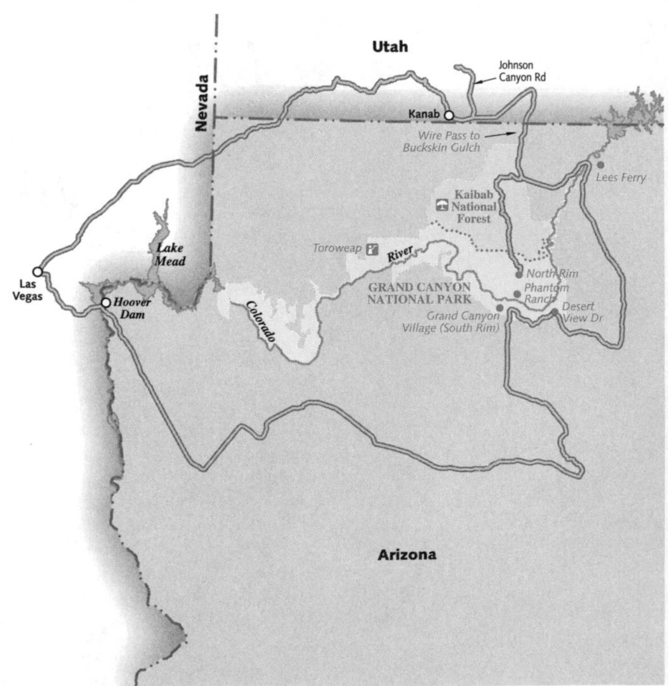

Activities

Encompassing more than 1.2 million acres, the Grand Canyon contains a world to explore beyond the so-enormous-as-to-be-nearly-unreal canyon vistas. To truly arrive at a deeper comprehension of the canyon, you need to get down and dirty on the dusty trails or above it all in a canyon flyover. Conveniently, there are many ways to experience the canyon, catering to all sorts of interests and skill levels. Whether it's by boot or hoof, paddle or motor, delving into the gorge will enormously enhance your intimacy with the canyon.

Hiking is perhaps the finest way to take in the scenery, as you follow the footfalls of ancient people along trails they've traced into the canyon. You'll gaze up at rocky spires, look for condors wheeling above and bighorn sheep foraging below, all the while listening to the crunch of canyon dust beneath your feet and smelling wild sage on the breeze. Hikes can be as gentle as half-hour rim walks or as arduous as multiday backcountry treks, but a popular alternative to descending under your own power is to let a sure-footed mule do the walking. Along the rim, it's also possible to ride a bike or a horse; both activities are better on the North Rim, where winter creates a silent wonderland for cross-country skiers and snowshoers. And on the canyon floor lies the biggest thrill of all: rafting the rapids on the Colorado.

Time of year, advance planning and your individual interests will determine, in part, what activities are available to you. We've listed popular activities here, with information to help you plan your pleasure.

Gourmands who don't mind carrying a little extra weight if it means eating well on the trail will find tasty backcountry recipe ideas and photos of plated results at www.onepanwonders.com.

HIKING

It goes without saying that the best way to see the staggeringly magnificent landscapes within the canyon is to hike right into them. Hiking is the most popular and accessible activity within the park, the beauty of it being that the options make it open to everyone. Hikes range from paved trails that the mobility-challenged and children can tackle to primitive, unmaintained treks that backcountry experts will love.

You can hike the canyon year-round. Though the best seasons are spring and fall, most hikers hit the trail in summer, when hot temperatures exact a toll and require special caution. Promising snow-dusted buttes and crisp blue days, winter hiking is spectacular, though only the South Rim remains open. You can still hike into the canyon from the North Rim after the first major snowfall, but you'll have to purchase a backcountry permit and then ski or snowshoe 44 miles to the rim. Trails are often icy in the early morning; to safeguard against glissading into the canyon, outfit yourself with a pair of crampons, which cost about $10 and are available at **Canyon Village Marketplace** (☎ 928-631-2262; 🕒 7am-9pm), on the east side of Grand Canyon Village.

Hiking here is markedly different from hiking elsewhere. The sheer terrain is uniquely challenging, made even more so by the environment and climate. Many trails begin with sharp descents, which translate into equally steep ascents at the end of the hike, when you're most exhausted. Add the effects of altitude, hefty elevation changes and the desert environment, and you've got a set of circumstances that require heightened awareness and preparation. The key to enjoying the Grand Canyon on foot is to take proper precautions, honestly assess and respect your limitations and select hikes that best match your ability. Please refer to our comprehensive hiking chart (p48) and detailed trail descriptions for suggestions.

AL ASTORGA, VIP

Not only is he a very important person, he's a Volunteer-in-the-Park. Known by many as 'the mountain goat', Al Astorga has been hiking throughout the Grand Canyon for the past decade and has participated as a search-and-rescue volunteer in both the national park and in Coconino County, Arizona, since 1996. As a VIP, he works Preventative Search and Rescue (PSAR) patrol on the main corridor trails like the Bright Angel.

So what's your role as a PSAR volunteer? I basically patrol the trail I'm assigned to, assessing hikers' condition and water supplies. With experience, you develop a way of recognizing people who are in trouble or are getting into trouble. If you just ask them, people will *absolutely* lie about how much water they have with them. **What problems do people most commonly run into?** Heat-related problems: people collapsing on the trail, vomiting, becoming disoriented. Then there's what I call 'canyon anxiety,' when people start heading back up and realize how far up they have to go. Anxiety sweats will flush out electrolytes even more quickly. **Advice you'd give to first-time canyon hikers?** If you're hiking in the daytime, soak your clothes every chance you get. Bring a spray bottle to spray yourself with water, and even stick an umbrella in your pack for shade. Embrace information! The more you know about hiking in the canyon, the better off you'll be. You know, it costs $14,000 to get helicoptered out of the canyon, and there are only two helicopters carrying out multiple missions for both rims, and not just for search and rescue – they also have to fly water in and deal with pipeline breaks. I hate seeing people suffer below the rim; as soon as that happens, all their fun tickets are gone.

For great hiking beyond the park, head north to the Kaibab National Forest (North Rim; p199), where you'll find cooler summer temperatures, fewer people and a robust network of trails. Try Snake Gulch (which connects to Kanab Creek), regarded as one of the best places along the Colorado Plateau to see petroglyphs. The trailhead is at the end of Forest Rd 642, about a half-hour drive from the Kaibab National Forest visitor center on AZ 67 (south of Fredonia). Stop by the **Kaibab Plateau Visitor Center** (☎ 928-643-7298; 🕒 8am-5pm) in Jacob Lake for trail information. Michael Kelsey's *Canyon Hiking Guide to the Colorado Plateau* offers detailed descriptions for dozens of hikes, many of which dip in and out of the park.

Difficulty Level

From first-timers to veteran hikers, everyone will find suitable trails within the park. Most hikes involve some elevation change, from as little as 100ft to as much as 7000ft. But most trails are also out-and-backs that cover the same stretch in both directions, making it easy to cater a hike to your abilities. On trails headed down to the Colorado River, switchbacks are standard, though width and terrain vary. Trails like Grandview and Hermit, for example, are narrow and bumpy, while Bright Angel and South Kaibab are wide and rock-free.

Generally speaking, the only truly easy hikes in the Grand Canyon are those that stay above or close to the rims, along with a handful of fairly flat trails like Uncle Jim (p193) or short jaunts such as Cliff Springs (p191). Another accessible option is to hike short segments of more challenging trails. Rangers cite the average hiking speed as 2mph going down and 1mph climbing up, an important consideration when selecting a trail and distance. On your first hike or two, gauge your speed to learn how long each mile might take.

The hikes in this book are organized into four difficulty levels. Remember that a single trail can have several difficulty ratings, depending on which segment you plan to hike.

Easy An easy hike is less than 2 miles long over fairly even, possibly paved terrain and has no significant elevation gain or loss.
Moderate These hikes involve some elevation change (usually 500ft to 1000ft) and are longer or more exposed than those rated 'easy.' Generally fine for all ability levels.
Difficult Hikes with significant elevation change and longer mileage. Require a bit more hiking experience.
Very Difficult Tough hikes, involving the greatest exposure and mileage, as well as substantial elevation change (2500ft to 4000ft). Better left to the fittest, most experienced hikers.

HIKE CLASSIFICATIONS

The park service classifies canyon terrain into four specific zones, based on maintenance levels and the availability of water and facilities. These, in turn, loosely correlate to different hiking skill levels.
Corridor zone This heavily trafficked zone includes well-maintained trails, sometimes with a water source. The South Kaibab, North Kaibab and Bright Angel Trails lie within this zone. Wide and well-marked, these trails are regularly patrolled by National Park Service (NPS) personnel and provide both hiking and mule access to the inner canyon.
Threshold zone This zone embraces less-traveled trails, such as the Hermit, that are rugged, with little or no water.
Primitive zone Encompasses little-used paths that are not maintained. Best suited to experienced canyon hikers who are comfortable with route finding.
Wild zone Is just that – don't expect to find marked trails, or any trails for that matter.

All hikes listed in this book, both day excursions and backcountry forays, follow established and well-marked trails. The majority lie within the corridor and threshold zones, generally regarded as the safest areas to hike within the canyon; a section or two of the overnight treks may pass through a primitive zone.

Hydration systems like Camelbaks are particularly great for longer day hikes or backpacking trips. You can carry more water without a bottle swinging from your pack, and you'll be more inclined to sip regularly.

Day Hikes

Anyone venturing into the inner canyon (technically, anything below the rim) should know it's a place of extremes. Even on short hikes, preparation is key, especially in this desert climate. Whether you're hiking a short section of the Rim Trail or 6 miles on the Bright Angel, always carry plenty of water. Also bring a wide-brimmed hat, sunglasses and sunscreen.

Perennial favorites include the well-maintained corridor trails – Bright Angel (p116), South Kaibab (p117) and North Kaibab (p194) – which

COOL TRAILS FOR A HOT DAY

Looking for a reprieve from the scorching sun? Take on one of the following trails (see the Hiking Chart, p48–51, for full hike descriptions). Tip: the less-exposed, higher-altitude North Rim is the better choice when trees and shade are priorities.

- **Cliff Springs** (p191) Short and sweet, this trail starts out as a sunny downhill, then cools with each step as it dips beneath overhangs, hugs a sandstone wall and ends at a misty, fern-fringed oasis.
- **Shoshone Point** (p115) An almost entirely shaded ramble through a patch of South Rir forest, this trail ends at a gorgeous, secluded overlook.
- **Transept Trail** (p191) Wending along the rim of its namesake canyon, this trail offe mix of sun and shade, open and hidden overlooks and refreshing breezes from be
- **Widforss Trail** (p192) If you're after a longer cool hike, this is the star. The trail through aspen groves, swings by several views and offers a soothing mix of s with a nice picnic spot at the turnaround.

spiral from rim to river, crisscross the canyon and provide the most direct backcountry access. Though they may feel like superhighways in summer, plan on hiking at least one of these magnificent trails, if only for a short distance. One lovely, rewarding, less-trafficked day hike on the South Rim is the Dripping Springs Trail (p121), while almost any trail on the North Rim will yield solitude on a day hike.

Many day hikes can be extended into the backcountry or combined into overnight excursions. See the Backcountry Hikes sections of the North Rim (p194) and South Rim (p122) chapters for full descriptions.

Backcountry Hikes

If you like challenging terrain, gape-worthy scenery and absolute serenity, plan an overnight hike into the canyon. There's simply no substitute for experiencing the Grand Canyon in the heart of its vast backcountry. While the elevation change can be daunting and the distances long, backcountry hiking is far more accessible than people tend to think. Join the hundreds who trek down the Bright Angel Trail (p122) each year, or head to the Hermit Trail (p125) for a sublime backcountry escape. Or try the legendary Kaibab rim-to-rim hike (p123), a 21-mile classic journey across the canyon. Provided you prepare, plan an appropriate route and itinerary, and take your time, virtually anyone with basic camping and hiking skills and a thirst for adventure can experience the wonders of being on the canyon floor.

Learn more about low-impact camping and the seven principles of the Leave No Trace ethic at www.lnt.org/programs/lnt7/index.html.

You'll need a backcountry permit (below) to stay overnight anywhere within the canyon. Any foray into the canyon also requires decent equipment. If you're at all nervous about tackling the backcountry alone, or feel you might need some guidance, there are plenty of group outings available, offering camaraderie and helpful instruction. For a list of outfitters, see p47.

Before embarking on your backcountry hike, make sure to check with a ranger on the current availability of water; pipelines sometimes break and you can't always assume you'll be able to refill your reserves at established water sources. On long out-and-back hikes along unmaintained trails, you might consider stashing water along the route to ensure you won't run dry.

Minor challenges or injuries can quickly become dangerous in the harsh canyon conditions. Hiking in the backcountry requires keen preparation and caution, even if you're a veteran who's logged thousands of hiking miles. Each year numerous canyon rescues involve both inexperienced hikers and strong backpackers. For more information on key safety issues, see p251.

Generally speaking, you shouldn't put together a hiking itinerary that is beyond the capabilities of any one member of your group. If you'd like to hike the backcountry but don't want to go solo (which increases your risks anyway), there are lots of group hike offerings (see p47). Before setting out on any backcountry excursion, check trail conditions at one of the backcountry offices or call park headquarters at ☎ 928-638-7888.

PERMIT INFORMATION

Overnight backpacking at Grand Canyon National Park requires a backcountry permit, as does camping in undeveloped areas on the rim, such as along the Ken Patrick Trail. The only exceptions are hikers or mule riders with reservations at Phantom Ranch, and those hiking into Havasu Canyon.

Control of camper numbers is very tight, and demand for permits often far exceeds available slots. Due to overcrowding and environmental

THE ARIZONA TRAIL

Established in 1988, the Arizona Trail (Map p185) started out as the vision of Flagstaff schoolteacher Dale Shewalter as he was hiking in the Santa Rita Mountains. Stretching the length of Arizona from Mexico to Utah, the completed trail will cover 800 continuous miles over Arizona's diverse landscapes, even passing through Grand Canyon National Park on its way. Connecting many preexisting trail systems, the AZ Trail was already 93% complete at the time of writing.

Many sections of the AZ Trail make excellent day hikes. On the North Rim, a lovely section of the trail (p203) runs through Kaibab National Forest (North Rim). The trail roughly parallels the highway leading into the North Entrance of Grand Canyon National Park, where, about 10 miles in, it then connects with the North Kaibab Trail.

Beyond the South Rim, the AZ Trail meanders through the Flagstaff area, with a forested section alongside beautiful Walnut Canyon (p156).

Find more information and current news on the Arizona Trail at www.aztrail.org.

concerns, rangers limit the number of people per night at each of the park's backcountry campgrounds. If you're caught camping in the backcountry without a permit, expect a hefty fine and possible court appearance.

Permits cost $10, plus an additional $5 per person per night; the nonrefundable fee is payable by check or credit card. If you plan on backcountry camping in the canyon at least three separate times in a given year, the $25 Frequent Hiker Membership waives the $10 permit fee for all trips following the first one. On your backcountry permit application, simply check the box for membership and include the payment when sending your application.

To get inspired or plan a hike on either rim, poke around www.bobspixels.com/kaibab.org, a terrific online Grand Canyon guide maintained by a photographer with more than 20 years' experience hiking the canyon.

Applications are accepted in person or by mail or fax beginning the first day of the month, four months prior to the planned trip; for instance, if you'd like to hike the Bright Angel in June, you'll want to apply on or after February 1. The Backcountry Permit Request Form and detailed instructions for applying are available online at www.nps.gov/grca/planyourvisit/backcountry-permit.htm, as well as in the Backcountry Trip Planner, available throughout the park. Submit your request to the **Backcountry Information Center** (☎ 928-638-7875; fax 928-638-2125; Backcountry Information Center, GCNP, PO Box 129, Grand Canyon, AZ 86023). Allow three weeks for the permit to be mailed to you. Once a permit is granted, itinerary changes are not allowed, except for emergencies. You can list three alternative dates and routes, which can markedly increase your chances of securing a permit.

If you're denied a permit, there's still hope! Provided you're willing to be flexible about where and when you hike, you can show up in person at the Backcountry Information Center on either rim. Add your name to a waiting list by submitting a request in writing for a permit for the following day. The wait can take anywhere from a day to a week (the wait tends to be longer on the South Rim), and you must show up in person by 8am every morning to maintain your position on the waiting list. Though requests are accepted in person only, you can get an idea of how long the wait is by calling the Backcountry Information Center.

RESPONSIBLE BACKCOUNTRY USE

To help preserve the ecology and beauty of Grand Canyon National Park, strive to make as minimal a footprint as possible when enjoying the backcountry. For more information on low-impact backpacking, learn the seven principles of the Leave No Trace ethic (www.lnt.org; click the Programs link) and live them.

RIM TO RIVER IN ONE DAY

Experienced hikers and fit newcomers alike are often tempted to hike from the rim to the river and back in a single day, an outing that involves close to 9000ft of elevation change. But no matter how early you start, how many previous miles you've logged or how many energy bars you eat, it's simply a bad idea – and rangers, numerous signs and this book will discourage you from attempting this risky stunt. In fact, rangers post themselves at key spots along the corridor trails, gently inquiring how far hikers plan to go, eyeing water supplies and climbing legs. Posted at the visitors centers and key trailheads, one particular warning poster cuts to the chase – it depicts a young, fit hiker on his hands and knees, vomiting on the trail.

While it's certainly possible for strong hikers to accomplish this haul from the South Rim in the cool air of spring and fall, attempting to do so in the summer heat is downright foolish. It makes no difference if you're a fit 25-year-old or a 65-year-old trail veteran. Still not convinced? Read the gripping *Over the Edge: Death in Grand Canyon,* by Michael Ghiglieri and Thomas Myers, or ask a ranger how many costly rescues (at the hiker's expense) occur per day during the summer, many involving heat-exhausted males in their 20s.

Trash

Pack out all waste, including biodegradable items like orange peels. Don't bury trash; not only will it take years to decompose, but it's detrimental to the health of the animals that will likely dig it up.

Human Waste

Where there are no toilets, bury solid human waste in a cathole (about 6in deep and at least 100ft from any water source). Cover the waste with soil and a rock. In snow, dig down to the soil. To further minimize your impact, consider bringing along a 'poop tube' (see www.fastq.com/~jrschroeder/poop.htm for a great DIY version) and dispose of your waste at a local sewage treatment plant or RV dump station after your trek.

If you're camping along the Colorado River, the sheer volume of water makes washing up and peeing in the river an acceptable option. However, this only applies to the Colorado and not to the creeks and rivers flowing into it. In other areas, urinate 100ft from water, preferably on sand or rock, but not in catholes or waste you are packing out.

Washing

For personal washing, use biodegradable soap and toothpaste with a water container; disperse waste water at least 100ft away from any water source, scattering it widely to allow the soil to filter it fully. When washing dishes and utensils, use sand or snow rather than detergent.

Erosion

Hillsides and mountain slopes, especially at high altitudes, are prone to erosion. Stick to existing trails and avoid short cuts.

If a well-used trail passes through a mud patch, walk through the mud so as not to widen the trail. Avoid removing or trampling the plant life that keeps topsoils in place.

Fires & Low-Impact Cooking

Open fires are prohibited in Grand Canyon National Park except at established campgrounds on the rim. Cook on a lightweight kerosene, alcohol or white gas stove and avoid those powered by disposable butane gas canisters. Consider bringing food that doesn't require cooking, and reduce the weight in your pack by not bringing a stove at all.

Wildlife Conservation

Discourage the presence of wildlife by wrapping up and packing out all food scraps (and watch those ravens – they're brave, clever and opportunistic!). Place gear out of reach and tie packs to trees. It is illegal to feed wildlife, as this can lead to animals becoming dependent on hand-outs, to unbalanced populations and to diseases.

Hiking Outfitters & Groups

Group outings are a terrific way for first-time hikers to enjoy safe and social hiking. Even if you're an experienced hiker, group hikes offer opportunities to learn about the canyon in the company of likeminded adventurers. The highly respected Grand Canyon Field Institute (p232) offers many naturalist-led hikes and backpacking trips for all skill levels. These fairly priced, expertly guided expeditions generally last three to nine days.

For short guided hikes, you can't beat the free and justly popular ranger-led hikes, offered year-round on the South Rim and from June to October on the North Rim. Check *The Guide* for listings. The guided Cedar Ridge Hike (p129), departing daily at 7am from the South Kaibab Trailhead, is a fantastic way to assuage nerves and experience this phenomenal walk in the company of a local expert. Don't forget water, snacks and appropriate clothing.

Stash a copy of *Belknap's Waterproof Grand Canyon River Guide*, by Buzz Belknap and Loie Belknap Evans, in your daypack for interesting mile-by-mile facts about the river, canyon geology, history, wildlife and botany.

Lots of local outfitters offer guided hiking excursions in the park. There's a wide range of trips, prices and dates, not to mention styles, so definitely peruse a few before making your choice. Whatever your decision, you're best off reserving a spot at least five months in advance. Pick up a full list of accredited backcountry guide services at the park's visitors centers or through the **Grand Canyon Chamber of Commerce** (☎ 928-638-2901, 888-472-2696; www.grandcanyonchamber.org; PO Box 3007, Grand Canyon, AZ 86023).

Canyon Rim Adventures (☎ 800-897-9633; www.canyonrimadventures.com) Based in Kanab, this outfit offers camping adventures that combine hiking and biking.

Discovery Treks (☎ 888-256-8731; www.discoverytreks.com) This outfit offers a wide selection of guided trips, from one-day hikes on the Grandview or Marble Canyon Trails to five-day backpacking excursions on the North Rim.

Four Season Guides (☎ 928-525-1552, 877-272-5032; www.fsguides.com) Straight outta Flagstaff, this company offers guided multiday backcountry trips, including a rim-to-rim and a Havasu Canyon jaunt.

Just Roughin' It Adventure Co (☎ 480-857-2477, 877-399-2477; www.justroughinit.com) Arizona adventures start here, catering to hikers of all levels who want to challenge themselves and leave a minimal impact.

Pygmy Guides (☎ 928-707-0215, 877-279-4697; www.pygmyguides.com) From day hikes to rim-to-rim, this excellent outfit does it all and attempts to accommodate special-needs travelers as much as possible.

Rubicon Outdoors (☎ 800-903-6987; www.rubiconoutdoors.com) Consummate professionals and minimal-impact wilderness adventurers run the show, which features everything from day hikes to its popular five-day Hermit Trail to Bright Angel trip.

Sky Island Treks (☎ 520-622-6966; www.skyislandtreks.com) Catering to first-time hikers, families and expert backpackers alike, its 'extreme itineraries' feature expedition-level treks to little-visited corners of the Grand Canyon.

Wild Horizons Expeditions (☎ 888-734-4453; www.wildhorizonsexpd.com) If the inn-based hiking trips and intensive backcountry treks are not quite to your liking, this Jackson, WY–based outfit also designs custom tours.

Wildland Trekking (☎ 970-903-3719, 800-715-4453; www.wildlandtrekking.com) Guided by experts, you can choose one of the regularly offered hiking or backpacking tours, or design your own adventure.

HIKING IN THE GRAND CANYON NATIONAL PARK: SOUTH RIM

Name	Hike type	Start location	Round-trip distance	Round-trip duration	Difficulty
Cedar Ridge	day hike/ mule	South Kaibab Trailhead	3 miles	1-2hr	moderate
Phantom Ranch	overnight/ mule	South Kaibab Trailhead	14.4 miles	2 days	difficult
Rim Trail	easy hike	Hermits Rest/ Pipe Creek Vista	13 miles (one way)	varies	easy-moderate
Skeleton Point	day hike/ mule	South Kaibab Trailhead	6 miles	3-5hr	moderate-difficult
South Kaibab to North Kaibab	overnight/ mule	South Kaibab Trailhead	20.9 miles	3 days	difficult
Bright Angel					
Indian Garden	day hike/ mule	Bright Angel Trailhead	9.2 miles	5-7hr	moderate-difficult
Mile-and-a-Half Resthouse	day hike/ mule	Bright Angel Trailhead	3 miles	2-3hr	moderate
Plateau Point	day hike/ mule	Bright Angel Trailhead	12.2 miles	8-10hr	difficult
Three Mile Resthouse	day hike/ mule	Bright Angel Trailhead	6 miles	4-5hr	moderate-difficult
Hermit					
Dripping Springs	day hike	Hermits Rest	7 miles	3-5hr	moderate-difficult
Hermit Creek	overnight	Hermits Rest	15.6 miles	2 days	difficult
Santa Maria Spring	day hike	Hermits Rest	5 miles	2-4hr	moderate-difficult
Grandview					
Coconino Saddle	day hike	Grandview Trailhead	1.5 miles	1-2hr	moderate-difficult
Horseshoe Mesa	day hike	Grandview Trailhead	6 miles	4-6hr	difficult
Other hikes					
Shoshone Point	easy hike	Shoshone Point Trailhead	2 miles	40min	easy
Tonto Trail	day hike	South Kaibab Trailhead	13.1 miles (one way)	5-7hr (one way)	very difficult

 Wildlife Watching  Great for Families 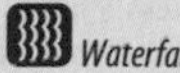 Waterfall  Restrooms  Drinking Water  Ranger Station

ACTIVITIES

Elevation change	Features	Facilities	Description	Page
1140ft			Short, steep and very scenic hike on the only corridor trail that descends along a ridge crest; gorgeous at sunrise	117
4714ft			Tough but rewarding hike to this cool oasis (or to Bright Angel Campground, 13.6 miles) on the Colorado River	122
200ft			Popular paved and dirt point-to-point trail that winds along the South Rim, connecting the stunning South Rim overlooks	117
2040ft			Panoramic views down the ridgeline and a challenging day-hike destination (best not attempted in summer)	122
5770ft			The park's only rim-to-rim hike is a revered classic; can also be started from the North Rim	123
3060ft			The gruelling switchbacks of Jacob's Ladder lead to the leafy bliss of Indian Garden	117
1131ft			Short rewarding hike that passes through two tunnels along the Grand Canyon's most popular trail	116
3120ft			Not recommended for summer day hikes, this sun-baked trail winds out to the edge of the Tonto Plateau for a beautiful glimpse of the inner gorge	117
2112ft			Following the Bright Angel Fault, this trail zigzags down to a shaded resthouse with inner canyon views	116
1700ft			Peaceful and challenging hike to Louis 'The Hermit' Boucher's favorite hangout inner-canyon trek	121
3660ft			Hard but beautiful hike to a sublime camping spot fringed with cliffs, near a creek; can be linked with Bright Angel Trail for a spectacular inner-canyon trek	120
1680ft			Beautiful and serene day hike along a steep wilderness trail to a small but lovely cliffside spring	120
1600ft			This steep rocky challenge winds up at a shady spot with with phenomenal views	119
2699ft			Stay on the steep and narrow on this, one of the park's most popular and exposed day hikes.	119
50ft			Cool, shady walk to one of the South Rim's most sublime views	115
3260ft			Long tough day hike offering a splendid look at the inner canyon along the South Kaibab, Bright Angel and Tonto Trails	121

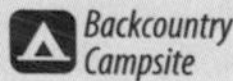

HIKING IN GRAND CANYON NATIONAL PARK: NORTH RIM

Name	Hike type	Start location	Round-trip distance	Round-trip duration	Difficulty
Bright Angel Point	easy hike	Grand Canyon Lodge	1 mile	30min	easy
Cape Final	easy hike	Cape Royal Rd	4 miles	3hr	easy
Cliff Springs	easy hike	Cape Royal Rd	1 mile	45min	easy-moderate
Ken Patrick	day hike	North Kaibab Trailhead parking lot	10 miles (one way)	6-7hr	moderate-difficult
Point Imperial	easy hike	Point Imperial	4 miles	2hr	easy
Transept	easy hike	Grand Canyon Lodge/Campground	3 miles	1½hr	easy-moderate
Uncle Jim	day hike/mule	near North Kaibab Trailhead parking lot	5 miles	3hr	moderate
Widforss	day hike/mule	signed turn-off 2.7 miles north of Grand Canyon Lodge	10 miles	4-6hr	moderate
North Kaibab					
Clear Creek	day hike	North Kaibab 3 miles north of Phantom Ranch	17.4 miles	10hr	difficult
Coconino Overlook	day hike	North Kaibab Trailhead	1.5 miles	1hr	easy-moderate
Cottonwood Campground	overnight	North Kaibab Trailhead	6.8 miles (one-way)	4hr (one-way)	difficult
Redwall Bridge	day hike/mule	North Kaibab Trailhead	5.2 miles	4-5hr	difficult
Roaring Springs	day hike/mule	North Kaibab Trailhead	9.4 miles	7-8hr	difficult
Supai Tunnel	day hike/mule	North Kaibab Trailhead	4 miles	3-4hr	moderate-difficult

Wildlife Watching *Great for Families* *Waterfall* *Restrooms* *Drinking Water* *Ranger Station* *Backcountry Campsite*

ACTIVITIES

RIVER RAFTING

Rafting the Colorado ranks among the top outdoor adventures for many, not only for its thrill factor but also for its romance. It's a geological journey through time, an adrenaline rush, secluded backcountry getaway and riparian paradise all rolled into one phenomenal ride.

Rafting season begins in mid-April and runs into September for motorized boats, November for oared vessels. Though the park carefully regulates the number of rafts on the Colorado, visitors have several options. For those short on time, there are half- and full-day rafting trips (p222), though not necessarily on sections within the Grand

Elevation change	Features	Facilities	Description	Page
150ft			Short, easy paved hike to a narrow peninsula with canyon views on three sides	190
150ft			Flat, easy tramp along the Kaibab Plateau to a nice overlook	191
600ft			Perfect for kids, this short, scenic trail passes ancient ruins, tunnels along a carved rock wall and ends at a verdant spring with views	191
800ft			Point-to-point wooded trail opening up to spectacular views at Point Imperial	193
100ft			Short rim trail with views of the eastern canyon	192
200ft			Enjoyable amble along a narrow dirt path rimming the canyon and connecting Grand Canyon Lodge with the campground	191
600ft			A loop atop the Kaibab Plateau, with views of Roaring Springs Canyon	193
350ft			Lovely forested walk with some of the finest canyon views on the North Rim	192

Elevation change	Features	Facilities	Description	Page
1500ft			Branching off the North Kaibab, this is the most popular inner canyon hike on the north side of the Colorado, rife with views and pretty falls	195
800ft			The flat ledge at the end of this short hike offers clear views of Roaring Springs and Bright Angel Canyons	194
4170ft			Last 2 miles of this trail traces Bright Angel Creek to the campground, where tall cottonwoods provide shade after a long, hot descent	194
2150ft			Challenging descent along switchbacks leads to Redwall Bridge, which crosses Roaring Springs Canyon	194
3050ft			North Kaibab favorite for strong hikers, this features pools in green oasis on the otherwise hot corridor trail	194
1410ft			Steep, spectacular hike to a red sandstone tunnel with sweeping views of the inner canyon chutes	194

Canyon. Most rafters join a commercial outing (p224) with one of many accredited outfitters for trips lasting from three to 21 days. Each year a few hundred private rafting excursions (p222) are allowed on the river as well.

ROAD & MOUNTAIN BIKING

Not exactly known as a cyclist's park, the Grand Canyon nonetheless has some very nice stretches for two-wheeling. Hiking trails (except the Greenway Trail) within the park are closed to bicycles, but they are welcome on all roads open to automobile traffic. The best riding on the South Rim is along Desert View Dr, with successive scenic overlooks from Yaki Point to Desert View. But the biking is much better on the North Rim, where you'll find both long hauls and short spins.

On the North Rim, you can fashion a terrific extended ride out to Point Imperial and on to Cape Royal, about 45 miles each way from Grand Canyon Lodge. The park's 35mph speed limit ensures slow traffic, and the pine-fringed road offers a good riding surface. For a short, sweet ride that's well suited to families, take the Bridle Trail, which leads from the North Kaibab Trailhead to the campground (0.5 miles) and lodge (1.5 miles). Mountain bikes are allowed on blacktop roads only, except for the 17-mile dirt road to Point Sublime, and the Bridle Trail from the campground to the lodge.

Tales told on the river are best when they come with crinkly smiles from your tanned boatman (or woman), but almost as good is *There's This River… Grand Canyon Boatman Stories*, edited by Christa Sadler.

Outside the park, there's plenty of gnarly single-track for mountain bikers in Kaibab National Forest (p199), which teems with old-growth ponderosa pines, steep-sided canyons, aspen groves and velvety meadows. Stop at the **Tusayan Ranger Station** (☎ 928-638-2443, ⌚ 8am-5pm) for trail maps and directions. There are also some fabulous rides around Flagstaff and Sedona (see p156); for trails and route suggestions, look locally for Cosmic Ray guidebooks.

Rental bicycles are not available in the park, but you can rent in Las Vegas (p179), Flagstaff (p157) or St George (p187). For more information on self-guided biking in the Grand Canyon, pick up copies of Sarah Alley's detailed books *Bicycling America's National Parks – Arizona & New Mexico: The Best Road & Trail Rides from the Grand Canyon to Carlsbad Caverns* and *The Mountain Biker's Guide to Arizona.*

Several outfitters offer guided biking trips that include forays into the park.

Backroads (☎ 800-462-2843; www.backroads.com) Offers a nine-day biking/inn adventure to Bryce, Zion and Grand Canyon National Parks for around $3000 per person.

Canyon Rim Adventures, Inc (☎ 800-897-9633; www.canyonrimadventures.com) Offers four-day mountain-biking/camping trips on the Kaibab Plateau for $845 per person, including all equipment and meals.

High Sonoran Adventures (☎ 480-614-3331; www.hikethecanyon.com) Grand Canyon mountain biking and hiking tours include singletracking around the San Francisco Peaks and Arizona Trail before hiking on the South Rim (about $225 per person per day, all-inclusive).

BEST BIKE RIDES IN THE PARK

Though not the park for hard-core bikers, the Grand Canyon nonetheless offers up some great rides. If you aren't traveling with your own wheels, pick up a rental in St George (North Rim; p187) or Flagstaff (South Rim; p157). Stretch out your trail-tested or mule-sore legs on one of these scenic routes. Distances listed are for one-way travel.

- Desert Rim Dr (22 miles) You'll have to concentrate to keep your eyes from wandering off the road to the stunning canyon views. This hot ride is best tackled at sunrise or in the late afternoon.
- Grand Canyon Lodge to Point Imperial (8 miles) A winding, shady ride through pine forests and thickets of aspen and bright-orange Indian paintbrush. Ends at a picnic spot on the rim with a spectacular view.
- Hermit Rd/West Rim Dr (10 miles) Better for mountain bikes, but doable on a sturdy roadie or one with slicks, this relatively traffic-free ride offers a series of breathtaking overlooks. Cold drinks and ice cream await at Hermits Rest.
- Point Imperial to Cape Royal (15 miles) Long and winding with lots of small rolling hills, this delightful pedal along a forest-fringed road eventually opens up to sage-dusted terrain and views. Don't veer off the road when you first glimpse magical Angels Window.

HORSEBACK RIDING

Horseback riding is offered outside the park, mostly in the lovely and cool Kaibab National Forest, on the North Rim; contact Allen's Guided Tours (p203). On the South Rim, near Tusayan, Apache Stables (p137) offers trail rides along the piney trails of the Kaibab and campfire rides (you supply the hot dogs and s'mores). On the Havasupai Reservation (p144), you can travel by horseback from Hualapai Hilltop to the campground at Supai ($150/75 round-trip/one way), or take a tour from the lodge to the waterfalls ($60).

HELICOPTER RIDES & AIRPLANE TOURS

While less of a hands-on activity than hiking, seeing the Grand Canyon from the air does offer an incredible perspective, and the tours are understandably popular. Close to 100,000 flights take almost a million passengers above the canyon each year. Tours operate out of Grand Canyon National Park Airport, just south of Tusayan, as well as the airports in Las Vegas (see p180), Phoenix and the Hualapai Reservation (see p150). You can pick up a partial list of outfitters at the visitors centers.

'Close to 100,000 flights take almost a million passengers above the canyon each year'

The advantages of opting for an airplane tour over a helicopter excursion are lower prices and the ability to cover a lot more distance: in addition to the Grand Canyon, you'll fly over Marble Canyon and Lake Powell. Unlike airplanes, however, helicopters are permitted to dip beneath 1000ft above the rim, offering closer views of the canyon.

The flights are controversial, as flying anything over the canyon can be tricky, involving high-altitude takeoffs (the airport is at 7000ft), sudden wind shifts, unpredictable air currents and few level landing areas should an emergency arise. There have been some 60 crashes over the past half century. Stiff regulations now govern all flights crossing the canyon, to both limit noise and promote safety. More than 75% of the park airspace is off-limits to planes, and flying beneath the rim is prohibited in all but the West Rim area.

RANGER PROGRAMS

The NPS hosts a wealth of free ranger programs in the park, ranging from a half-hour talk on the endangered California condor to a daily three-hour guided hike down the South Kaibab Trail to Cedar Ridge. Particularly enjoyable are the evening programs, which vary in subject but often showcase the stunning night sky. If you're traveling with kids, the Junior Ranger programs (p60) get kids engaged with hands-on projects before they're sworn in as junior rangers.

Ranger programs are offered year-round on the South Rim and between May and October on the North Rim (when the park is open). For a detailed listing of programs, refer to the park newspaper, *The Guide;* you can also check schedules online at www.nps.gov/grca. There's also a daily ranger program at Phantom Ranch (p132), accessed by foot or mule train only (check the bulletin board at Bright Angel Campground or the Phantom Ranch Canteen for that day's topic). Occasionally, the rangers host special events, so be sure to check the park bulletin boards or inquire at the visitors centers.

Beyond the park, the **Kaibab Plateau Visitor Center** (☎ 928-643-7298; 🕑 8am-5pm, closed Oct-May), north of the North Rim in Jacob Lake, presents several ranger programs. Topics include the plateau's geology, the night sky and life on the Kaibab at the turn of the 20th century. Even if you can't attend one of the programs, stop by to peruse the excellent selection of books. Unlike the park visitors centers, this one is rarely crowded, and rangers will happily field your questions about the Grand Canyon and Kaibab Plateau.

VOLUNTEERING

Volunteer opportunities in the park have largely to do with revegetation of native species and the removal of invasive ones, but they aren't limited to botanical projects. If you're more interested in working with people, you can volunteer as an interpretive naturalist or as a trip assistant on youth programs.

AmeriCorps (☎ 202-606-5000; www.americorps.org; 1201 New York Ave NW, Washington, DC 20525) Serving the needs of communities and local environments through a network of local, state and national programs, AmeriCorps offers volunteer opportunities in both the Grand Canyon and the surrounding communities.

Grand Canyon Trust (☎ 928-774-7488; www.grandcanyontrust.org) The volunteer arm of this nonprofit conservation organization offers opportunities to participate in its Grand Canyon Volunteers projects. These range from assisting graduate students with research at Northern Arizona University in Flagstaff to week-long tamarisk removal trips in the backcountry.

'shoot the natural water chute at Slide Rock State Park in Sedona'

Grand Canyon Volunteers (www.gcvolunteers.org) Volunteer through this branch of the Grand Canyon Trust, which offers opportunities from Flagstaff to the inner gorge.

Grand Canyon Youth (☎ 928-773-7921; www.gcyouth.org/pages/volunteer.htm; PO Box 23376, Flagstaff, AZ 86002) Takes young people on river trips to foster teamwork, leadership, personal growth and a relationship with wilderness. The nonprofit organization has openings for longer-term volunteer commitments in Flagstaff and on the river as trip coordinators.

National Park Service (www.nps.gov/grca) The NPS website lists available positions in its Volunteers in the Parks (VIP) program, including year-round openings for revegetation volunteers. You can volunteer for a day or a month, and duties include seed collection, plant propagation and non-native plant removal. Limited free camping may be available. Find job details and apply in advance on the website by clicking on the Support Your Park link.

Sierra Club, Grand Canyon Chapter (☎ 602-253-8633; http://arizona.sierraclub.org; Ste 277, 202 E McDowell Rd, Phoenix, AZ 85004) The Grand Canyon chapter publishes the local newsletter *Canyon Echo* and offers occasional opportunities to volunteer in the area.

Student Conservation Association (SCA; ☎ 603-543-1700; www.thesca.org; 689 River Rd, PO Box 550, Charlestown, NH 03603) This nonprofit organization offers three- to 12-month paid conservation internships that also earn academic credit, as well as summer trail-crew work at locations all over the country.

SWIMMING

Enduring the summertime heat at the canyon makes it easy to understand why hikers are so intensely drawn to the river. Swimming in the swift, hypothermic current of the Colorado is a quick road to bad news (like death, for example), but you can find safe places out of the current where it's possible to dunk yourself in the frigid water. You'll have to do an overnight hike or be on a rafting trip to do so, however.

Since there are no swimming pools on either rim, you'll have to head instead to hotels in Tusayan (p138), on the South Rim, or Kanab (p211), on the North Rim.

Outside the North Rim, there are plenty of spots to swim or wade, including Lake Powell and the start of the Colorado at Lees Ferry (see p216).

The waterfalls and pools of Havasu Canyon (see p145) are probably the most alluring places in the region for swimming, if you can reserve far enough in advance to stay at Supai. But you don't need to plan ahead to shoot the natural water chute at Slide Rock State Park (p163) in Sedona.

If you're passing through Lake Mead National Recreation Area (see p173), be sure to ask at the visitors centers about pollution and water levels before venturing into the lake. Of course, if you're in that area, you can always fall back on the wave pools and decadent artificial beaches of Vegas' casinos (p177).

MOSEYING BY MULE

Riding a mule down into the canyon is a time-honored park tradition. Mule trains have been making their way down the Bright Angel and other trails into the canyon for over a century, taking delighted tourists below the rim and ferrying supplies in and out of the canyon. Traveling the trails on the backs of these mellow, sure-footed creatures is the classic way to get below the rim and makes for a memorable trip.

Mule trains – up to 30 animals per group – are only permitted on the corridor trails, the Uncle Jim Trail and the first mile of the Ken Patrick Trail. Just because you're not doing the walking doesn't mean it's effortless. If you don't ride regularly, you should expect to be rather saddle sore once you dismount – you probably shouldn't plan any ambitious hikes for the day after. Those scared of heights or big animals – gentle and cute though they may be – are best off exploring the canyon by other means.

Rides are offered year-round from the South Rim along the Bright Angel and South Kaibab Trails, though summer treks on the latter are limited to descents only, given the heat and exposure of the ridge. On the South Rim, it's possible to do overnight mule trips with one or two nights spent at Phantom Ranch, giving you the chance to explore the inner canyon before trekking back up to the rim. Overnight trips are not offered from the North Rim, due to the lengthy distance to Phantom Ranch.

For booking details for mule trips on the South Rim, see p127; for the North Rim, see p196.

FISHING

The Colorado is fairly well laden with trout and catfish, as are its permanent tributaries. Fishing is best during the winter months, when spawning trout make their way from the Colorado up Bright Angel Creek. To fish, you'll need an Arizona state fishing license, which you can pick up at **Canyon Village Marketplace** (☎ 928-631-2262; 🕑 7am-9pm), on the east side of Grand Canyon Village on the South Rim, or north of the park in Lees Ferry. For nonresidents, a license costs $17.25 for one day, $32 for five days or $128 for the year (with the trout stamp); the Colorado River–only license (good for a year) is a bargain at $48.75. Arizona residents pay $16.25 for one day or $23.50 for the year. You'll also need to pony up an additional $3 for the Colorado River/Lake Powell fishing stamp.

To fish along the Colorado in the park, you'll also need an overnight backcountry permit (p44). North of the park, there's excellent angling near Lees Ferry, especially along the 16-mile stretch from the outflow of Lake Powell at Glen Canyon Dam. These waters house a treasure trove of fat and feisty rainbow trout, and you're allowed to catch two per person per day. Several outfitters and local lodges offer guided fishing expeditions (see p217). You can also fish for striped and largemouth bass on Lake Mead (see p173); however, if you fish from a boat on the lake or from the Nevada shoreline, you must also have a Nevada use stamp ($3).

CROSS-COUNTRY SKIING & SNOWSHOEING

In winter the North Rim and environs get an average of 150in of snow annually, offering miles of snow-covered forest roads and a patchwork of wide meadows for those willing to make the trek. The park road officially closes from mid-October to mid-May, and visitors must ski or snowshoe the 44 miles to the rim. There are no designated trails, so you can ski or snowshoe virtually anywhere, opening up limitless options for backcountry exploration.

The South Rim boasts a few cross-country loops within the Kaibab National Forest, 0.3 miles north of Grandview Lookout. You can rent skis in Flagstaff, where you'll find several more cross-country circuits, as

RETREAT, REFRESH

After several strenuous days trekking through the backcountry, a shower will feel like a revelation and a spa: nirvana. Head to Sedona and you'll find yoga retreats and lovely spas for all inclinations. But the most luxurious spa in the land, nestled in the red-rock embrace of beautiful Boynton Canyon, skillfully integrates the spiritual with the physical. Features like the kiva-inspired meditation room (whose earth floor encourages a direct connection with the planet) are telltale signs that Miiamo Spa (p168) is distinctly Sedona. If you can absorb the sticker shock with aplomb, this sublime spa experience will unkink all your canyon-weary aches.

well as downhill facilities. The popular Flagstaff Nordic Center (p156) has lovely groomed trails for cross-country skiing, unless you want to explore the surrounding national forest trails for free.

ROCK CLIMBING

Rock climbing is allowed anywhere in the Grand Canyon, except above established trails (for obvious reasons). While Arizona is rife with climbing areas, climbing in the canyon is not extremely popular, nor very visible. Most people tend to hike down from the South Rim to summit one of the various temples within the canyon; if you plan to stay overnight, you'll have to pick up a backcountry permit (p44). Stop by Vertical Relief Climbing Center (p157) in Flagstaff to hit up the employees there for info on climbing throughout the region. It also sells guidebooks, rents equipment and runs climbing classes and workshops.

Stewart M Green's *Rock Climbing Arizona* (Falcon, 1999) is a comprehensive guide to prime Arizona climbing areas and includes topo maps and detailed route information. An updated 2nd edition should be published by the time you read this. If you can find it anywhere, the currently out-of-print *Grand Canyon's Summit Select* by Aaron Tomasi features about 50 climbs to summits in the canyon.

Kids & Pets

Parents, many remembering their own childhood vacation to the desert Southwest, pack the sunscreen and camera, hiking boots and sun hats, and drag their children to the Grand Canyon. Perhaps the kids were pushing for Disneyland, or maybe they argued for staying home and hanging out with friends. It is, after all, nothing more than a big hole. But there's a reason why generation after generation of families flock to this quintessential national park. Here, everything from lazy days along dusty trails, searching for fossils and picnicking on the rim to white-water adventures down the Colorado and the classic canyon mule ride make for memories that imprint not only into photos but into the spirit. Maybe it's the air and the silence, maybe it's the history and the wildlife, maybe it's the geology. Or perhaps it's nothing more than the canyon's grandeur, nothing more than a child's simple recognition that the world is so much more than each individual life. Whatever it is, children don't easily forget their family trip to the Grand Canyon. It remains *the* iconic American destination, amplified in the imagination by cowboy movies and advertisements, and powerfully symbolic of American ideals of freedom, self-reliance and the transformative power of the Western landscape. With a little planning and a lot of patience and flexibility, a trip to this region could go down as one of your best family vacations.

THE ZINKULA FAMILY

In 2006 the Zinkula family – mom, dad and four kids ages four, six, nine and 11 – loaded tents, a cooler, duffel bags and pillows into the car and drove about 1500 miles to the North Rim from Iowa.

Sarah (11) We keep journals from everywhere we go. My favorite part of the Grand Canyon is when we took this little hike to a dead end and there was a railing with telescopes (Bright Angel Point, p190). I felt carsick on the long and bumpy road to Point Sublime (p189). Mom kept saying 'Look out the front window and you'll be OK'. It was worth it though. We sat on the blanket, eating pretzels. There was a group of men camping and we got our journals out and drew pictures and stuff, and it was beautiful. Kyle and Tyler loved climbing around the rocks without getting in trouble. We went to a ranger talk (p60). They made a bonfire while we waited for the ranger to come. He came in costume as a mountain man and brought a mountain-lion skull and a few other skulls. We had to identify the skulls. He told us lots of stories about the stars and the history of the canyon. He said if a mountain lion comes you should stand on a tree stump and try to make yourself look bigger.

Erin Sarah and I volunteered. We had to stand up on a bench and wave our hands in the air and yell 'Ahhhhhhh' pretending we were chasing a mountain lion. It was fun. Afterwards, we got back in our tent and went to sleep.

Sarah I loved the Hopi dance at the Hopi Reservation (p216). We stumbled on it. They were dancing a rain dance so that the rain would come and help their crops. We don't know if the rain ever came.

Mark (Dad) It was called the Katsina dance. It wasn't advertised. The guy we bought a neckl[illegible] from invited us, and there was only one other non-Native there. We weren't sure we should [illegible] be there. The dance, Canyon de Chelly (p216) and Point Sublime were my favorite parts.

And if your family includes Fluffy or Spike, well then, if you know where to go, what to do and what to bring (detailed later), they can have a great time too.

BRINGING THE KIDS

Long drives, precarious canyon overlooks, crowded shuttles and stifling summer heat can be a challenge for parents. The rewards, however, can be found in the most mundane of activities – a sunset picnic at Cape Royal (p188), playing in the grassy area behind El Tovar (p106), watching the condors over the canyon. And the canyon's geology, human history and wildlife, accessible in concrete ways at every turn, makes the park the world's largest classroom – kids learn without even trying.

While any trip should allow plenty of time for serendipitous discoveries, some things require advanced planning. These activities include rafting trips through the canyon (p220), family trips with the Grand Canyon Field Institute (p232), overnight stays at Phantom Ranch (p132), a ride on the Grand Canyon Railway (p244) and mule trips down the South Kaibab from the South Rim (p127). Mule trips from the North Rim can also be booked in advance (p196), but they don't go to the canyon bottom and are often available at short notice. Outside the canyon, the Museum of Northern Arizona (p153) offers fantastic discovery programs (www.musnaz.org/education/discovery.html) for children ages three to 18. Topics include an afternoon field trip to a prairie-dog town and a four-day hiking trip to the North Rim.

www.nationalgeographic.com/grandcanyon/kids.html has printable Grand Canyon – themed coloring pages, games and educational activities that can prepare children for the park and fuel their excitement.

Most tours to the Grand Canyon offer children's discounts. Children 15 or younger arriving on bike, motorcycle or foot, or as part of a noncommercial group (scouts, school etc) do not have to pay the $12 individual entrance fee. Note that there is no place to rent strollers or other such gear at the park. See p38 and p39 for suggested family itineraries to each rim.

Are We There Yet?

You can't avoid long stretches in the car, particularly if you go to the North Rim, but the right frame of mind and some smart packing can minimize backseat whining.

TIP

Crayons melt! Do not bring them on summer road trips.

Try not to squeeze too much in. Endless hours in the car rushing from overlook to overlook, sight to sight, can result in grumpy, tired kids and frustrated parents. After a while, canyon views start to look alike, and the trip becomes a blur. Stop often and stay flexible. Sometimes the best times on road trips are those moments when you're not doing much of anything but pulling to the side of the road and poking around (see the boxed text, p62, for ideas). Bring sunshades for the window, snacks, water, and a football, soccer ball or Frisbee – any grassy area or meadow is a potential playing field.

When restlessness sets in, surprise the kids with a Grand Canyon trip bag filled with canyon books, a special treat, a car-friendly toy and a game. Bring a journal, an enlarged Xeroxed map and colored pencils for each child. Kids can follow along on their map as you drive, drawing pictures on it of what they see and do, and record the trip in their journal. Remember to bring favorite CDs, or more conveniently an iPod and an iTrip (car speaker connector). Books on CD (most rental cars do not have tape players) from your local library can help pass the hours as well.

Arizona law requires that children five years old and younger sit in a car seat except on public transportation. Most car-rental agencies rent rear-facing car seats (for infants under one year old), forward-facing

GAMES FOR THE CAR

- *52 Fun Things to Do in a Car*, by Lynn Gordon – a deck of cards, each card with a game or activity
- *Best Travel Activity Book Ever*, published by Rand McNally
- *Kids Travel: A Backseat Survival Kit*, published by Klutz
- *Mad Libs* – fill-in-the-blank word game
- *Miles of Smiles: 101 Great Car Games & Activities*, by Carole Terwilliger Meyers
- *Regal Travel Auto Bingo Game Card – Car Bingo*
- *Travel Scavenger Hunt*, by Pazow
- *TravelMates: Fun Games Kids Can Play in the Car or on the Go – No Materials Needed*, by Story Evans and Lise O'Haire

seats and boosters for about $10 per day, but you must reserve these in advance. Clarify the correct type of seat when you make the reservation, as each is suitable only for specified ages and weight.

Sleeping & Eating

If you travel with lots of gear, you might prefer to stay at the Yavapai Lodge (p133) or Maswik Lodge (p132) on the South Rim, as you can park right outside your door. Bright Angel Lodge (p132) offers two-room cabins, and El Tovar (p133) has several suites. On the North Rim, Grand Canyon Lodge's Pioneer Cabins (p197) sport two tiny rooms and sleep six. Children under 16 stay free at all Grand Canyon lodgings, but there is a $10-per-day charge for cribs and cots. Most accommodations outside the park do not charge extra for children under 12, and many have suites and pools.

You can spend the night with a borrowed dog, cat or pot-bellied pig at Best Friends Animal Sanctuary (p211) in Kanab, outside the North Rim.

While 'family-friendly restaurant' evokes images of pizza buffets and play areas at McDonald's, even the fanciest restaurants in and around the park welcome families and most provide children's menus. Both rims offer cafeterias and plenty of picnic spots (see boxed text, p134). There's a full grocery store on the South Rim (Canyon Village Marketplace, p133), but because there is only a limited general store on the North Rim consider bringing a cooler and stocking it in Page or Kanab. Only western cabins at Grand Canyon Lodge have refrigerators, but there is free ice behind the visitors center.

When Grand Canyon Lodge first opened in 1928, staff lined up at the door to sing a welcome song to arriving guests. When guests left, they sang a farewell song.

The child-friendly icon (icon) in this book indicates sights, restaurants and hotels that are particularly accommodating to children, such as hotels with kiddie pools or playgrounds.

Health & Safety

Kids pick up bacteria like fly paper picks up flies, and when you're traveling, they're particularly susceptible to whatever bug is floating around. The only place that sells children's medicine is the Canyon Village Marketplace (p133) on the South Rim, so don't forget to pack children's Tylenol and children's Motrin. You'll be glad you did when your child wakes up with a fever of 102°F at 3am. Note that the North Rim is isolated and the closest medical facilities are 1½ hours away in Kanab (see p207), Utah.

It's easy to forget, as you're waiting in line for a shuttle or walking a rim trail with hundreds of other folk, that this is a wilderness. In most areas, there are no guardrails along the rim, and even where there are there is room for a small child to slide through. Children and adults alik have plummeted to their deaths engaging in the most mundane activities in the most populated parts of the park. Secure toddlers in backpacks, always hold young children's hands (some people resort to leashes), and absolutely do not allow anyone to run and scramble along the rim. Hikes into the canyon can be treacherous – consider carefully before bringing children under nine years old.

See the Health & Safety chapter (p247) for other safety issues, including dehydration, altitude sickness, snakes and scorpions.

Fun Stuff for Families

The park offers lots of cool kids' activities beyond mule riding (p196 and p127) and rafting (p220), the quintessential canyon favorites. While the South Rim has more sights, museums and a broader variety of ranger-led interpretive programs designed for children, the chaos and crowds can be intimidating and exhausting. The intimacy of the North Rim attracts families looking for a quieter vacation.

TIP

You can avoid endless digging through bags if you organize with Eagle Creek Pack-It Cubes (www.eaglecreek.com).

Try to factor in a couple of lazy days, and never underestimate the value of simply hanging out. An afternoon at the hotel pool or a playground can recharge the energy and spirits of kids and parents alike. In Kanab, Utah, City Park (Map p209) has an excellent playground. Nestled under the spectacular red rock of the Vermilion Cliffs, it offers a modern play structure, picnic tables, a big grassy area and, best of all, a fountain designed for children to play in (the button to turn it on is an unmarked red circle on the ground). Thorpe Park Playground (off Map p154) in Flagstaff is another favorite. In Page, the playground (Map p214) at the elementary school is open to the public during the summer.

RANGER PROGRAMS

In the Junior Ranger program, geared towards children ages four to 14, children pick up an activity book from the visitors center on either rim, complete three pages and attend a ranger program. Upon completion, a ranger solemnly swears them in as junior rangers and the child receives a junior ranger certificate and a badge ($1.50). While the whole thing sounds rather hokey, we spent a leisurely afternoon on the North Rim completing the project and it was the highlight of our six-year-old's visit. The Discovery Pack Program (ages nine to 14) begins with a 90-minute ranger talk, after which children check out binoculars, a magnifying lens, field guides and other naturalist tools. Children must complete parts of the activity book and return the material by 4pm to become junior rangers.

TIP

Kids love climbing the spiral staircase at the Watchtower (p114). Don't miss it!

Rangers use hands-on activities to teach children about the park's ecology and wildlife at Way Cool Stuff for Kids and Kids Rock. For example, the ranger builds a forest with the children, who pretend to be trees, grasses, bees and other plants and animals. The Junior Ranger Adventure Hike examines the park's rocks, fossils, plants and animals on a one-mile hike. For younger children (ages two to six), the South Rim offers Story Time Adventure on the rimside porch of El Tovar (p106).

'n Play fits into most hotel bathrooms or in the small nooks most rooms seem to have. nts, bring some duct tape and a dark, lightweight sheet or blanket you can hang over This way, the child can sleep in darkness without being disturbed by parents reading TV.

TOP FIVE GRAND CANYON CHILDREN'S BOOKS

Books on the Grand Canyon can be bought in advance from the **Grand Canyon Association** (☎ 800-858-2808; www.grandcanyon.org).

- *101 Questions About Desert Life*, by Alice Jablonsky. Question and answer format and colorful illustrations explore desert life.
- *Brighty of the Grand Canyon*, by Marguerite Henry. True stories about a burro in the late 19th century written through the eyes of Brighty the mule.
- *Exploring the Grand Canyon*, by Lynne Foster. Introduction to the region's geology, history, plants and animals, and canyon-related activities for car and park.
- *I See Something Grand*, by Mitzi Chandler. Ecology, history and wildlife of the canyon through a discussion between a child and her grandfather.
- *Puzzler's Guide to the Grand Canyon*, by Kristy McGowan and Karen Richards. Hidden pictures, word searches, logic puzzles and other activities.

Adults must accompany all children. Except for the Junior Ranger and Discovery Pack programs, specific options vary by year and season. Check *The Guide* (a National Park Service newspaper available on both rims) for current programs, times and locations. You can download a seasonal schedule of ranger programs from the For Kids link on the park's website (www.nps.gov/). National monuments surrounding the park offer Junior Ranger and kid-friendly ranger programs as well.

HIKING

Both rims offer opportunities for kids to get dirty and dusty on the trails, but the North Rim and the bordering Kaibab National Forest (p199) are particularly popular with families who enjoy the outdoors. Their shaded trails and higher altitude entice travelers intent on escaping the desert heat; there are plenty of meadows where children can run around away from the danger of the rim; and it's almost guaranteed that you'll see mule-deer or wild turkeys. The paved Rim Trail (p114) on the South Rim is suitable for strollers, but if you plan on more extensive hiking, consider a front carrier for infants or a backpack carrier for toddlers (available at outdoor supply stores in Kanab, see p212, and Flagstaff, see p162). Recommended family trails include the Rim Trail, Shoshone Point (p115) and a day hike into the canyon on the Bright Angel (p116) on the South Rim; the Widforss (p192) and Cape Final (p191) on the North Rim; and the Sourdough Wells stretch of the Arizona Trail (p203) in the Kaibab National Forest.

BEYOND THE PARK

Families could spend several days, even weeks, exploring the mountains and desert surrounding the park. Flagstaff (p151), with excellent parks, a pedestrian-friendly downtown, and plenty to do in the area, is an exceptionally kid-friendly town and well worth a few days' visit. Explore ancient Puebloan cliff dwellings at Walnut Canyon National Monument (p155), splash around in Oak Creek's Slide Rock State Park in nearby Sedona (p163) and catch an outdoor movie in the town square (p161). See the boxed text (p156) for more ideas.

Outside the North Rim, small and friendly Kanab (p207) offers kitschy Western fun and makes an excellent base for families. Costumed volunteers demonstrate cooking, weaving and other pioneer chores at Pipe

PARK & POKE

Sometimes the best times are had by simply parking the car and poking around – no charge, no destination, no agenda. Here are some of our favorite park and poke stops:

- **Harvey Meadow** (North Rim, Map p185) Explore Uncle Jim's Cave in the sandstone walls.
- **Paria Beach** (p216, in Lees Ferry, Map p200) Splash in a calm, shallow stretch of the Colorado River. Afterwards, enjoy a picnic in the apricot orchard a minute down the road at **Lonely Dell Ranch** (p215, in Lees Ferry, Map p200).
- **Balanced Rocks** (Lees Ferry, Map p200) Scramble and hide among giant boulders.
- **Angel's Landing** (Kanab Canyon Rd, p210) Kick back with a book and sketch pad at this grassy oasis outside Kanab.
- **Greenland Lake** (North Rim, Map p188) Stretch your legs in the meadow and woods and play in the restored salt house.
- **Cameron Trading Post** (Cameron, p170) Escape the heat in the shady green gardens of this bustling roadside stop.
- **Little Colorado River Gorge** (Hwy 64, 11 miles west of Cameron, p170) Peruse Navajo crafts and trinkets and take in the view (a small fee may apply).

Spring National Monument (p209) and kids love sliding down soft pink sand at Coral Sand Dunes State Park (p209). After a day of kicking around the dusty Utah desert, you can sit outside with a cold beer and watch the kids play in an old movie set at Frontier Movie Town (p210). In the evening, catch a free Western movie at the Old Barn Playhouse behind Parry Lodge (p212).

BRINGING THE PETS

While it's certainly possible to enjoy a trip to the Grand Canyon with your pet, there are several restrictions on pets at the park. Dogs and cats are allowed at rim campgrounds and throughout the park's developed areas, but cannot ride the shuttles or enter any lodges, stores or restaurants, and they must be leashed at all times. On the South Rim they can tag along on paved rim trails, but on the North Rim they're allowed only on the Bridle Trail (p192). You cannot take pets below the rim. It is illegal to leave a dog tied up alone at a campground, and you must clean up after your dog. Failure to follow these rules may lead to a $500 citation. Official service animals are welcome throughout the park, but you must register at the backcountry office before taking them below the rim.

The environment can be harsh on pets, and mountain lions, rattlesnakes, scorpions and other critters are prevalent in the region. Prepare your pets for weather extremes. In the summer, do not leave them in the car or RV unattended at any time. Think twice before taking pets on desert hikes in the summer – as it's excruciatingly hot and the sand burns tender paws – and always bring a portable water bowl. In the scorching desert north of the North Rim, dogs can cool off in Kanab Creek in Angel Canyon (p211) and the Paria River at the Pahreah River Town Site (p205), but are not allowed in the Colorado River between Glen Canyon Dam and Lees Ferry. If you're camping, you'll need extra blankets even in the summer as desert nights can be cold even if days are scorching. Babbits in Flagstaff (see p162) and Willow Canyon in Kanab (see p212) sell outdoor gear for dogs, but the only complete pet-supply shop in the region is the **Petsmart** (Map p152; ☎ 928-213-1737; 1121 S Plaza Way; 🕑 9am-9pm Mon-Fri, to 7pm Sat) in Flagstaff.

Horses and pack animals are allowed in the park, and there are corrals on both rims. Contact the backcountry center (p45) for the required overnight stock permit ($10 per person plus $5 per animal). You can ride below the rim on the Bright Angel (p117), North and South Kaibab (p117), the River Trail (p124) and the Tonto Trail (p121), but descents are steep, rocky and treacherous. On the North Rim, horses are allowed on the Arizona Trail (p45), Uncle Jim (p193) and Tiyo Point (p189), as well as on fire roads off Cape Royal Rd (Map p188). There are a few rim trails at Toroweap (p189) open to horses as well, but no rim trails on the South Rim. Access www.nps.gov/grca/planyourvisit/backcountry.htm for updated regulations on private stock at the park.

Dog-Friendly Areas

The Kaibab National Forest (p199) that surrounds the North Rim is dog heaven. You can take them on all trails and dirt roads, there are plenty of big meadows, they are allowed off-leash and even in summer the high elevation and thick shade keep them cool.

Leashed dogs are welcome on the trails to the waterfalls in Havasu Canyon (p144) in the Havasupai Reservation, as well as at the picnic areas at Sunset Crater Volcano National Monument (p155), Walnut Canyon National Monument (p155) and Wupatki National Monument (p155). You can take your dog on the five-day wilderness hike through Paria Canyon (p207), but you must pay $5 per day and pick up special dog-doo bags at the Paria Contact Station (p205).

Several motels in the Grand Canyon region, including the historic Hotel Monte Vista (p158) in Flagstaff, the Grand Hotel (p138) in Tusayan, the Kaibab Lodge (p204) just outside the entrance to the North Rim, and all the hotels in Kanab accept dogs and cats. You may be restricted to a smoking room or have to pay a small fee or deposit. Both Kanab and Flagstaff are particularly dog-friendly towns. In Flagstaff, dog owners head to Buffalo Park (Map p152), an open mesa with a lovely 2-mile gravel loop trail (suitable for sturdy strollers) and views of Mt Elden. Bushmaster Park (Map p152) and Bark Park in Thorpe Park (Map p152) offer off-leash dog areas.

See Renee Guillory's recommended *Best Hikes with Dogs: Arizona* and go to http://phoenix.about.com/od/anim/a/hikingdogs.htm for her tips on hiking in Arizona with your dog. Remember that dogs, like humans, need to be in good shape before taking off on extended hikes, and are susceptible to altitude sickness and dehydration.

Find up-to-date listings of dog-friendly hotels, campgrounds and attractions at www.dogfriendly.com.

Veterinarians

The closest vets to the South Rim are **Canyon Pet Hospital** (Map p152; ☎ 928-774-5197; www.canyonpet.com; 12 S Mikes Pike; 🕑 8am-8pm Mon-Fri, 8am-noon Sat, noon-4pm Sun) or **Aspen Veterinary Clinic** (Map p152; ☎ 928 526 2423; 7861 N US Hwy 89; 🕑 8:15am-5:30pm Mon-Fri, 8am-noon Sat) in Flagstaff; messages direct you to emergency contacts after hours. From the North Rim, you need to drive 1½ hours to **Kanab Veterinary Hospital** (Map p209; ☎ 435-644-2400; 484 S 100 East) or two hours to **Page Animal Hospital** (Map p214; ☎ 928-645-2816; www.pageanimalhospital.com; 87 S 7th Ave).

Kennels

Kennel (Map p103; ☎ 928-638-0534; 🕑 7:30am-5pm) facilities on the South Rim take pets with advance reservations. While convenient, and perfectly fine for one or two days, it's not recommended for extended stays. Twenty concrete-floored, 4ft-by-6ft kennels expand by day to include an added 6ft of outdoor space. There are no large play areas for the dogs, and individual walks are limited to one five-minute walk per day. Eight cages house cats. Costs are $8/11 for a cat/dog for day only and $12/17 for a cat/dog per night. There is no kennel on the North Rim. Kathleen at **Creature Comforts** (☎ 435-899-9245) in Kanab provides personalized cage-free petsitting services in her home ($20 to $25 per night) and **Doggy Dude Ranch** (off Map p209; ☎ 435-772-105; www.doggyduderanch.com; Hwy 9 btwn Rockville & Springdale), 5 miles outside of Zion National Park and about a 50-minute drive (approx 46 miles) from Kanab, offers quality day care and overnight accommodation.

You'll find several kennels, including Canyon Pet Hospital, in Flagstaff. The recommended **Canyon Pet Resort** (Map p152; ☎ 928-214-9324; www.canyonpetresort.com; Suite 300, 1802 W Kristy Lane; 🕑 7:30am-6pm Mon-Fri, 8am-6pm Sat, 4-6pm Sun) offers a cat room ($10), kennel boarding ($16), luxury suites (cageless rooms with a half-door for $27) and doggie day camp ($15). Camp counselors play with the dogs, and there are kiddy pools and shade and dog-runs for like-sized dogs. For extra attention, enroll your pet in the Tender Loving Care Program, which includes private 20-minute walks in a residential neighborhood for dogs and a strategically placed bird feeder for cats!

If you're uncomfortable leaving your dog in a kennel, **Sleepover Rover** (☎ 866-817-0500; www.sleepoverrover.com) offers host families in Phoenix, Flagstaff and Las Vegas who will keep your dog cage-free in their home ($32 to $47 per night). All hosts have dog-safe yards, are home full time, and have been personally approved by the company's founder and owner. There is one host family in Grand Canyon Village (small dogs only).

www.fs.fed.us/r2/coconino/recreation/ has a complete listing of equestrian trails in the Peaks District and Mormon Lake District of the Coconino National Forest that surrounds Flagstaff and Sedona.

Horse Trails & Equestrian Facilities

The Kaibab National Forest that borders the North Rim offers excellent riding opportunities with all trails open to horses and miles of dirt roads. Ranchers who run cattle in the Kaibab have a permit to use corrals within the forest, and while they welcome riders passing through you need to call or stop by the Kaibab Plateau Visitor Center (p199) for locations and current information. Only certified hay is allowed within the forest.

In the Coconino National Forest just outside Flagstaff Little Elden Springs Horse Camp (off Map p152) offers 15 horse-friendly campsites with hitching posts but no corrals. From here, riders can access more than 100 miles of equestrian trails, ranging from easy to the challenging Heart Trail. To get to Little Elden, head 5 miles northeast of Flagstaff Hwy 89. Turn west on FR 556 and drive 2 miles to FR 556A. Turn right to the campground.

Horse boarding facilities in the Grand Canyon region:

Flagstaff Hay & Grain (off Map p152; ☎ 928-526-3556; www.flagstaffhayandgrain.com; 11705 N US Hwy 89, Flagstaff)

MCS Stables (off Map p152; ☎ 928-774-5835; www.mcsstables.com; 5835 S Hwy Alt 89, Flagstaff)

Paria River Adventure Ranch (Map p200; ☎ 928-660-2674; www.pariacampground.com; Hwy 89, 30miles west of Page)

Environment

While neither the longest nor the deepest canyon in the world, the Grand Canyon is certainly one of the most awe inspiring. Hollowed out like a massive inverted mountain range, the Grand Canyon wields a profound influence across hundreds of miles of northern Arizona, dramatically altering the local environment and the lives of the region's plants and animals.

Sprawling across 1.2 million acres, Grand Canyon National Park protects a sizable portion of the vast Colorado Plateau, an elevated tableland that spans the Four Corners states – Arizona, Utah, Colorado and New Mexico. The park also protects 227 free-flowing miles of the Colorado River, among the greatest of all North American rivers.

Want to know how things are looking in the canyon today? Try the webcam at Yavapai Point, www.explorethecanyon.com/WebCam/.

For geologists the canyon showcases a remarkably well-preserved, two-billion-year-old slice of geologic history. In these exposed layers, half of the Earth's life span is revealed, serving as a window into our planet's past. For biologists the region encompasses a rich mix of species and ecosystems, where Rocky Mountain forests and meadows mingle with three great American deserts – the Mojave, Sonoran and Great Basin. All told, the park is home to 1500 plant species, 305 bird species, 76 mammal species, 41 reptile and amphibian species and 26 fish species.

THE LAND

The Story in the Rocks

VISHNU SCHIST & ZOROASTER GRANITE

The story begins in the canyon's innermost recesses, where the Colorado River continues to carve a deep channel into progressively older rock. The bottommost layer, Vishnu schist, is dark and fine-grained, with vertical or diagonal bands that contrast with the canyon's horizontal upper layers. Look carefully to spot intruding bands of pinkish Zoroaster granite. Together, these are among the oldest exposed rocks on Earth's surface.

The schist offers evidence that two billion years ago the canyon region lay beneath an ancient sea. For tens of millions of years, silt and clay eroded into the water from adjacent landmasses, settling to the seafloor. These sediments, along with occasional dustings of lava and ash, accumulated to a thickness of 5 miles and were later buried beneath another 10 miles of additional sediment. By 1.7 billion years ago these layers had buckled and uplifted into a mighty mountain range that rose above the water. In the process, intense heat and pressure transformed the sedimentary layers into metamorphic schist and gneiss.

STROMATOLITES

At the time, the region lay near the equator, but the uplifted landmass soon began a northward migration while undergoing a long spell of erosion. So much of the uplifted material eroded away that it left a significant gap (or unconformity) in the geologic record – from 1.7 billion to 1.2 billion years ago. Lost with hardly a trace was the mountain range itself, which finally wore down into a low coastal plain. Gradually the landmass sank back into the sea, providing a platform for marine algae, which secreted the Bass limestone that now sits atop the Vishnu schist. Marine fossils in the Bass limestone include such primitive life forms as cabbagelike stromatolites.

DR VICTOR POLYAK

It's odd to think that the ancestral Colorado River once flowed through only a small valley in what is today Grand Canyon National Park. Some researchers argue that the canyon dug its way down to its present level in the last six million years, while others think its incision took much longer. Dr Victor Polyak, a geologist at University of New Mexico, has been funded by the National Science Foundation to construct a precise history of incision. He and colleagues Carol Hill and Dr Yemane Asmerom examine mammillary calcite (milky mineral crusts called 'cave clouds') in caves along the canyon walls. Because these deposits form at the water table, they indicate the height of the river at various times in the geologic past. By uranium-lead dating the calcite, he can precisely determine the depth of the canyon at different points in time. Polyak has made about 25 research trips to more than 30 caves.

'There are a lot of caves at the park, including some well-known caves not open to the public. We get permits from the park, as well as the Hopi and Navajo governments, to collect samples. Most of the caves are in the Redwall limestone, usually halfway down from the top, and off-trail. We typically backpack in, but we also had two river trips. Many of the caves required that we rig ropes to rock climb to the entrance – the highest involved 400ft of technical climbing. Strangely, rain was one of our biggest hazards. A storm came on us suddenly one time and we could barely walk down the slopes toward the river. At 3am I was awakened to the sound of running water and clunking noises. A raging stream filled with boulders ran a few feet from my tent, and my buddy narrowly escaped being washed into the river in his tent. We desperately pulled gear to higher ground and were lucky to lose only some chairs and kitchen supplies. Another time storms created hundreds of waterfalls. It made the Grand Canyon look like it was in tropical South America.'

Polyak and his colleagues believe that the mammillary speleothems they have collected are absolute indicators of the canyon's complete history and that analyses of these cave formations will tell the story of the canyon's formation that is different from all previous studies. As this book goes to press, Polyak is writing up conclusions of his work in anticipation of publication.

THE PRECAMBRIAN ERA & THE GREAT UNCONFORMITY

In the late Precambrian era (1.2 billion to 570 million years ago) the region alternated between marine and coastal environments as the ocean repeatedly advanced and retreated, each time leaving distinctive layers of sediment and structural features. Pockmarks from raindrops, cracks in drying mud and ripple marks in sand have all been preserved in one form or another, alongside countless other clues. Much of this evidence was lost as erosional forces scraped the land back down to Vishnu schist. The resulting gap in the geologic record is called the Great Unconformity, where older rocks abut against much newer rocks with no intervening layers. Fortunately, pockets of ancient rock that once perched atop the Vishnu schist still remain and lie exposed along the North and South Kaibab Trails, among other places.

THE PALEOZOIC ERA

The Precambrian era came to an end about 570 million years ago. The subsequent Paleozoic era (570 to 245 million years ago) spawned nearly all of the rock formations visitors see today. The Paleozoic also ushered in the dramatic transition from primitive organisms to an explosion of complex life forms that spread into every available aquatic and terrestrial niche – the beginning of life as we know it. The canyon walls contain an abundant fossil record of these ancient animals, including shells like cephalopods and brachiopods, trilobites, and the tracks of reptiles and amphibians.

The Paleozoic record is particularly well preserved in the layers cut by the Colorado, as the region has been little altered by geologic events such as earthquakes, faulting or volcanic activity. Every advance and retreat of the ancient ocean laid down a characteristic layer that documents whether it was a time of deep oceans, shallow bays, active coastline, mudflats or elevated landscape. Geologists have learned to read these strata and to estimate climatic conditions during each episode. In fact, the science of stratigraphy, the reading of rock layers, stemmed from work at the canyon, at a time when American geology was in its infancy and considered vastly inferior by European geologists.

THE MESOZOIC PERIOD & THE KAIBAB UPLIFT

Considering the detailed Paleozoic record, it's puzzling that evidence of the following Mesozoic period (245 to 70 million years ago) is entirely absent at the canyon, even though its elaborate layers are well represented just miles away on the Colorado Plateau and in nearby Zion, Bryce and Arches National Parks. Towering over the landscape just south of the South Rim, Red Butte is a dramatic reminder of how many thousands of feet of Mesozoic sediments once covered the canyon 70 million years ago. So what happened to all of this rock, which vanished before the river even started shaping the canyon? About 70 million years ago the same events that gave rise to the Rocky Mountains created a buckle in the earth known as the Kaibab Uplift, a broad dome that rose several thousand feet above the surrounding region. Higher and more exposed, the upper layers of this dome eroded quickly and completely.

Evidence from the past 70 million years is equally scarce at the canyon, as the movement of materials has been away from the canyon rather than into it. Volcanism has added a few layers of rock in parts of the west canyon, where lava flows created temporary dams across the canyon or simply flowed over the rim in spectacular lava waterfalls, the latter now frozen in time as at Lava Falls. The stretching of Earth's crust also tilted the region to the southwest, shifting drainage patterns accordingly.

'lava flows created temporary dams across the canyon or simply flowed over the rim in spectacular lava waterfalls'

But the story that interests visitors most, namely how the canyon has changed in the past five million years, is perhaps the most ambiguous chapter of all. Geologists have several competing theories but few clues. One intriguing characteristic is that the canyon's east end is much older than the western portion, suggesting that two separate rivers carved the canyon. This fits into the oft-repeated 'stream piracy' theory that the Kaibab Uplift initially served as a barrier between two major river drainage systems. The theory assumes that the western drainage system eroded quickly into the soft sediments and carved eastward into the uplift, eventually breaking through the barrier and 'capturing' the flow of the ancient Colorado River, which then shifted course down this newly opened route.

Alternate theories assume other river routes or different timing of the erosion, placing it either before or after the uplift. Until more evidence is uncovered, visitors will have to simply marvel at the canyon and formulate their own theories about how this mighty river cut through a giant bulge in Earth's crust millions of years ago.

Reading the Formations

After their initial awe has worn off, many visitors are eager to learn how to identify the formations that so neatly layer the canyon. The distinctive sequence of color and texture is worth learning, as it repeats itself over and over again on each rim, from each viewpoint and along each

A ROCK PRIMER

Rocks are divided into three large classes – sedimentary, igneous and metamorphic – each well represented in the Grand Canyon.

Sedimentary

Sedimentary rock originates as accumulations of sediments and particles that cement together over time. Borne by water or the wind, the sediments generally settle in horizontal layers that preserve many features, suggesting how they formed. Three types of sedimentary rock are present in the canyon:

Limestone Comprises little more than calcium carbonate, a strong cement that softens and easily erodes when wet.

Sandstone Consists of sand particles that stack poorly, leaving lots of room for the calcium carbonate cement to penetrate, making this a very hard and durable rock.

Mudstone (including shale) At the opposite end of the spectrum from limestone, mudstone consists of flaky particles that stack so closely together, there's little room for the binding cement. Thus mudstone is often very soft and breakable.

Igneous

Igneous rock originates as molten magma, which cools either deep underground or after erupting to the surface as lava or volcanic ash. Volcanic rocks are common west of Toroweap Valley, where they form such prominent features as Vulcans Throne and Lava Falls. Granite that cooled deep inside the earth lies exposed along the inner gorge – in fact, canyon explorer John Wesley Powell originally named the river corridor Granite Gorge.

Metamorphic

Metamorphic rock starts out as either sedimentary or igneous, then transforms into other kinds of rock following exposure to intense heat or pressure, especially where the Earth's crust buckles and folds into mountain ranges. Metamorphic rock usually remains hidden deep underground. Two types of metamorphic rock are common in the canyon:

Schist Deriving from shale, sandstone or volcanic rock, schist lines the inner gorge and is distinguished by narrow, wavy bands of shiny mica flakes.

Gneiss Forming light-colored intrusions within the schist, gneiss is characterized by its coarse texture and the presence of quartz and feldspar.

trail. Simply memorize the catchphrase, 'Know The Canyon's History, See Rocks Made By Time,' in which the capital letters represent the formations from rim to canyon floor. The formations are listed in that order here.

KAIBAB LIMESTONE

Starting at the top, a layer of creamy white Kaibab limestone caps the rim on both sides of the canyon. This formation is about 300ft thick and erodes to form blocky cliffs. Limestone surfaces are pitted and pockmarked, and rainwater quickly seeps into the rock to form sinkholes and underground passages. Fossils include brachiopods, sponges and corals.

TOROWEAP FORMATION

The Toroweap Formation is the vegetated slope between the cliffs of Kaibab limestone above and massive Coconino cliffs below. Similar in composition to the Kaibab, the Toroweap is a pale yellow to gray crumbly limestone that also contains marine fossils.

COCONINO SANDSTONE

It's quickly evident how sandstone erodes differently from limestone when you descend past Coconino sandstone along the Bright Angel Trail (p116), one of the few places a trail can negotiate these sheer 350ft cliffs. Inspect the rock face closely to spot fine crosshatches, evidence of windblown ripples that once crisscrossed huge sand dunes. Even more fascinating is the wealth of fossilized millipede, spider, scorpion and lizard tracks found in this formation.

HERMIT SHALE

Below these mighty cliffs lies a slope of crumbly red Hermit shale. This fine-grained shale formed under shallow tidal conditions and contains fossilized mud cracks, ripple marks and the footprints of reptiles and amphibians. Today it supports a distinctive band of shrubs and trees including oak, hop tree and serviceberry. Hermit shale is so soft that in the western canyon it has eroded completely, leaving a broad terrace of Esplanade sandstone.

SUPAI GROUP

Just below the Hermit shale are the red cliffs and ledges of the Supai Group, similar in composition and color but differing in hardness. This is a set of shale, limestone and sandstone layers, and each dominates different portions of the canyon. All formed under similar swampy coastal conditions, where shallow waters mingled with sand dunes. Deposited some 300 million years ago when amphibians first evolved, these formations preserve early footprints of these new animals. Supai cliffs can be stained red by iron oxides or black from iron or manganese.

REDWALL LIMESTONE

Next is the famous Redwall limestone, one of the canyon's most prominent features. Viewed from the rim, the Redwall is a huge red cliff that towers 500ft to 800ft over the broad Tonto Platform. The Redwall also forms a dividing line between forest habitats above and desert habitats below. The rock is actually light gray limestone that has been stained red by iron oxides washed down from layers above. This formation is pitted with many caves and alcoves and contains abundant marine fossils, including trilobites, snails, clams and fish.

'Tonto Platform is the only break in a long jumble of cliffs and ledges'

MUAV LIMESTONE

Muav limestone is a small slope of varying thickness that marks the junction of Redwall sandstone and the Tonto Platform. This marine formation contains few fossils but features many eroded cavities and passages.

BRIGHT ANGEL SHALE

Perched just above the dark inner gorge, the broad, gently sloping Tonto Platform is the only break in a long jumble of cliffs and ledges. The platform is not a formation at all but rather the absence of one, where soft greenish Bright Angel shale has been largely stripped away to reveal the hard Tapeats sandstone beneath.

TAPEATS SANDSTONE

The last and oldest Paleozoic sedimentary layer is the Tapeats sandstone, below which lies the huge gap (the Great Unconformity) that separates the sedimentary layers of the canyon from the ancient Vishnu schist of the inner gorge. Collectively referred to as the Tonto Group, Tapeats, Bright Angel and Muav all formed along the same ocean shoreline. Tapeats originated with coarse cobbles along an ancient beach, Bright Angel shale comprises fine mud deposits that collected just offshore from the beach, and Muav limestone consists of calcium carbonate that fused in deep water.

Forces at Work

What's truly remarkable about the Grand Canyon is not how big it is, but how small it is. In terms of sheer volume, much more material has been removed from the Grand Wash Trough just below the canyon or other stretches where the river meanders across vast floodplains. But the canyon's narrow scale continues to concentrate erosive forces in dramatic fashion. As the canyon widens with age, it may no longer be as impressive a sight.

Interested in geology? Consider the informative but rather technical *Grand Canyon Geology*, edited by Stanley Beus and Michael Morales.

Obviously foremost among the erosive forces is water, which chisels virtually every inch of the landscape. From the smallest raindrop to the mightiest flash flood, water is an immensely powerful erosive force. Its differing effect on various rock types is readily apparent in the canyon's stair-step profile – the softer rock formations crumbling into gentle slopes at the foot of sheer hard cliffs.

On a subtle level, water may simply seep deeply into the rock, dissolving some minerals and converting others to slippery clay. The water gradually weakens the rock matrix, causing large or small bits of rock to break free. In Surprise Canyon a massive landslide totaling 1 cubic mile slid 1500ft, though most landslides are much smaller.

A weathering effect known as frost riving occurs when water works down into cracks and freezes. Freezing water exerts a tremendous outward force (20,000lb per square inch), which wedges into these crevices, prying loose blocks of rock from the canyon cliffs.

Streams have gradually eroded defined side canyons on both rims, cutting back ever deeper into their headwalls. This effect is especially pronounced on the higher-altitude North Rim, as it catches more runoff from passing storm systems. This rim also angles to the south, pouring its runoff into the canyon. While the South Rim likewise slopes to the south, that means its waters flow away from the canyon, slowing the pace of erosion.

As parallel side canyons cut back toward their headwalls, they create the canyon's distinctive temples and amphitheaters. Neighboring streams erode either side of a long promontory or finger of rock, then carve the base of the promontory, leaving the tip stranded in open space. Over time these isolated islands of elevated rock weather into rugged spires called temples, while the headwalls of the side canyons become amphitheaters.

Water is not always as patient and imperceptible. Late-summer thunderstorms cause flash floods that sculpt the landscape over the course of minutes. A tiny trickling brook carrying grains of sand can quickly explode into a torrent that tosses house-sized boulders with ease.

Although the Colorado cut through the soft sedimentary layers at lightning speed, the river has now reached extremely hard Vishnu schist, and erosion has slowed dramatically. As the river approaches sea level, downward erosion will cease altogether, even as the canyon continues to widen. This lateral (sideways) erosion proceeds 10 times faster than downward cutting. Thus, far in the future, the Grand Canyon may be referred to as the Grand Valley.

GEOLOGIC WONDERS

- **Vulcans Throne** (see Toroweap drive, p189) The park's most impressive cinder cone
- **Bright Angel Canyon** (p190) An excellent example of how creeks follow fault lines across the landscape
- **Havasu Creek** (p227) Stupendous travertine formations and beautiful waterfalls
- **Toroweap Overlook** (p189) The canyon's most dramatic viewpoint
- **Vishnu Temple** (see Cape Final hike, p191) One of the canyon's most prominent temples

WILDLIFE

Wildlife in the park ranges from secretive bighorn sheep and prehistoric condors to scampering lizards and nosy ringtail cats, all scattered across a vast region. For some species the Grand Canyon presents an insurmountable obstacle, while for others it's a life-sustaining corridor through a forbidding desert. Only in a few places do animals congregate in conspicuous numbers. If you remain patient and alert, you'll take home lifelong memories, but it also helps to learn some of the park's different habitats.

Life Zones

BOREAL FOREST

On the highest peaks of the North Rim perches boreal forest, an offshoot of the Rocky Mountains and home to many of the same plants and animals. Unlike other canyon habitats, this is a land of cool, moist forests and lush meadows. Snowfall may exceed 150in and persist for six to seven months of the year, conditions that favor trees like the Engelmann spruce, Douglas fir and quaking aspen and animals like red squirrels, blue grouse and broad-tailed hummingbirds.

PONDEROSA PINE FOREST

Broad, flat plateaus on both rims are dominated by ponderosa pine forest. This species forms nearly pure stands of stately, fragrant trees at around 7000ft. Temperatures are moderate, and rainfall averages about 20in a year. Characteristic species include the unique Abert's and Kaibab squirrels, as well as a variety of bird species, ranging from American robins to northern flickers.

PIÑON-JUNIPER WOODLANDS

Sharing the rim with ponderosa pines and cloaking the canyon walls down to about 4000ft are piñon-juniper woodlands. These forests of piñon pines and Utah junipers signal desertlike conditions, where snow scarcely ever falls and annual rainfall hardly exceeds 10in. Shrubs such as cliff rose, sagebrush and Mormon tea thrive here. Animals include rock squirrels, cliff chipmunks, and scrub and piñon jays.

DESERT SCRUB COMMUNITY

Between the canyon's inner gorge and the great cliffs above there is a broad apron known as the Tonto Platform. Here at 3000ft to 4000ft clings the desert scrub community, a zone of blazing summer heat and little rain. Dominating the platform is low-growing blackbrush, along with a handful of other hardy species such as prickly pear cacti. Visitors will spot few birds and only the occasional black-tailed jackrabbit or white-tailed antelope squirrel.

RIPARIAN ZONE

Lining every waterway in the area is a separate and distinct habitat known as the riparian zone. The presence of precious water draws many plants and animals to this zone. Crimson monkeyflowers and maidenhair ferns mark the scattered seeps and springs, while stream banks near the river are choked by tamarisk, an aggressive introduced plant. Red-spotted toads and beavers share these waters with ducks, herons and other birds that come to drink.

Life Through the Seasons

Amateur naturalists should track down *A Field Guide to the Grand Canyon,* by Stephen Whitney, or *A Naturalist's Guide to Canyon Country,* by David Williams, both of which cover the region's common plants and animals.

The canyon encompasses such a wide variety of climatic extremes that the seasons are as complex as the landscape. While one rim celebrates spring, the other rim may still languish in the grip of winter, and in the depths of winter the canyon floor can experience hotter temperatures than in summer elsewhere in the country.

April ushers in the first long spells of fair weather, interrupted by lingering wet winter storms. Even as golden eagles and peregrine falcons nest along the river, the North Rim may remain under many feet of snow. Migrant birds arrive in numbers through May. Along the South Rim and within the canyon itself, wrens, phoebes and warblers fill the air with song and activity. Mammals likewise take advantage of the short season between winter cold and summer heat. Chipmunks and squirrels lead the charge, bounding energetically amid the rocks and trees.

By June, however, temperatures begin to soar, and animal activity slows to a trickle. Daytime temperatures in excess of 100°F are the norm through August. Torrential afternoon thunderstorms alleviate the agony for a few hours each day. June through August is usually the best time to observe wildflowers along the North Rim, while the best time on the South Rim is from August into October.

Clear, cool days make autumn the ideal time for visits to the park, though wildflowers have gone to seed and many birds have already made the journey south. Remaining behind are the resident animals – mammals fattening up for hibernation and a handful of birds that feast on the plentiful seeds. Other animals remain active through winter, especially on the canyon floor, where temperatures remain moderate and snow rarely falls.

Animals

LARGE MAMMALS

Although bighorn sheep stand guard on high cliff faces, while elk and deer wander through mountain meadows and mountain lions lurk in forest nooks, your chances of finding many large mammals are relatively slim. They'll likely show up when you least expect them, so keep your eyes open.

Mountain Lions

Even veteran biologists rarely see the mountain lion. But a large population does live here, and the canyon rates among the best places in North America to spot this elusive cat. While mountain lions roam throughout the park, they gravitate to forests along the North Rim in pursuit of their favorite food, mule deer. Reaching up to 8ft in length and weighing as much as 160lb, this solitary animal is a formidable predator that rarely bothers humans.

Mule Deer

Rim forests and meadows are the favored haunts of mule deer, which commonly graze at dusk in groups of a dozen or more. After their predators were systematically hunted out of the park in the early 1900s (even Teddy Roosevelt came to the canyon to hunt mountain lions), the deer experienced a massive population explosion. Less common on the South Rim and within the canyon, deer move seasonally to find water and avoid deep snows.

Bighorn Sheep

Like solemn statues, bighorn sheep often stand motionless on inaccessible cliff faces or ridgelines and are readily identified by their distinctive curled horns. During breeding season, males charge each other at 20mph and ram horns so loudly the sound travels for miles. Look for bighorns in side canyons along the Tonto Platform (p117) beneath the South Rim. Bring binoculars, as hikers seldom encounter this animal at close range, and never for more than a moment.

Coyotes & Foxes

Wild members of the dog family include the ubiquitous coyote and its much smaller cousin, the gray fox. Both share the same grayish brown coat, and each has adapted to human activity, growing increasingly comfortable around roads, buildings and (of course) any unattended food. You stand a good chance of seeing coyotes in the daytime, especially around meadows, where they hunt for rodents. Foxes often emerge at night, when you might spy one crossing a trail or road.

SMALL MAMMALS

Small mammals are much more abundant than their larger cousins, including many types of common squirrels, chipmunks and small carnivores. Look for these around campsites and picnic grounds or near trails and roadside pullouts.

From expertly guided backpacking trips to geology and archeology classes, the Grand Canyon Field Institute (www.grandcanyon.org/fieldinstitute) makes learning in the park an exciting experience.

Chipmunks & Squirrels

While similar in appearance, the region's three chipmunk species do bear subtle differences. The South Rim is the exclusive domain of the gray cliff chipmunk, an extremely vocal species that can bark an estimated 5800 times in a half-hour, twitching its tail with each call. This species shares the North Rim with least chipmunks and Uinta chipmunks, although cliff chipmunks are relegated to rocky ledges and cliffs. Least chipmunks inhabit open areas and carry their tails erect when they run, while Uinta chipmunks live in forests and are abundant around North Rim campgrounds and picnic sites.

The most conspicuous members of the squirrel family are speckled gray rock squirrels, which scoot fearlessly amid visitors' feet along rim trails and viewpoints. Hoping for handouts (strictly forbidden), these large squirrels will boldly explore unattended gear or sidle up to resting hikers. True to its name, this species nearly always inhabits rocky areas.

Living on opposite rims, Abert's and Kaibab squirrels present a classic evolutionary test case, demonstrating how the canyon divides populations into distinct species. These long-eared squirrels were a single population only 20,000 years ago, when forests grew in the canyon. The squirrels split into two populations when the climate warmed and dried and the canyon was transformed into desert habitat. Today the two remain so closely related that scientists can't agree whether to rank them as separate species despite obvious color differences. Both the light-bellied Abert's squirrel of the South Rim and the dark-bellied Kaibab squirrel of the North Rim depend on ponderosa pine forests for their livelihood, rarely wandering more than 20yd from these trees. Each species is common on its respective rim.

Wood Rats

Although they bear a superficial resemblance to city rats, wood rats are extraordinary, gentle creatures with many interesting attributes. The canyon's four species share a maddening propensity for stealing small shiny objects like watches or rings and leaving bones, seeds or other objects in exchange – hence the animal's common nickname, the trade rat. Wood rats are also famous for building massive stick nests that are used by countless generations. Upon dismantling these nests and examining their contents, biologists have been able to document more than 50,000 years of environmental prehistory in the region.

'enjoy the aerial acrobatics of swifts and swallows atop rimside cliffs'

Ringtail

One of the area's most intriguing creatures is the nocturnal ringtail, which looks like a wide-eyed housecat with a raccoon tail. Once common around park campsites, where they would emerge at night to raid campers' food supplies, ringtails have been discouraged by modern food-storage techniques, though they are still observed along the rims and river corridors.

BIRDS

Whether you enjoy the aerial acrobatics of swifts and swallows atop rimside cliffs or the bright songs of warblers among riverside thickets, there's no question that the canyon's 300-plus bird species are among the region's premier highlights.

Small Birds

A harbinger of spring, the broad-tailed hummingbird zips energetically about the park from May through August. Males bear a notch in their wing feathers that creates a distinctive whirring sound in flight, making this diminutive bird sound impressively big, thus attracting mates. They are common in wildflower-filled forest glades on both rims.

Forests and campgrounds on both rims host large numbers of the sparrow-sized dark-eyed junco. Hopping about the forest floor in search of seeds and insects, this bird is conspicuous for its black hood and its habit of nervously flicking its tail outward to flash white outer tail feathers. Similar in appearance but restricted to trees is the mountain chickadee, a perennial favorite with children because its merry song sounds like *cheese-bur-ger*. Both species are hardy and among the handful of birds that remain in the park year-round.

The first birds many visitors encounter are white-throated swifts, which swoop and dive over towering cliff faces at rim viewpoints. Designed like sleek bullets, these sporty 'tuxedoed' birds seem to delight in riding every wind current and chasing each other in playful pursuit. Flying alongside the swifts are slightly less agile violet-green swallows, which are a familiar sight around campgrounds and park buildings.

Only hikers that descend to the sparsely vegetated Tonto Platform (p117) will spot the beautiful black-throated sparrow, one of the few species able to survive in this scorching desert habitat. Sporting a jaunty black bib and crisp white facial stripes, this bird brightens scrubby slopes with its sweet *chit-chit-cheee* song.

The stirring song of the canyon wren is for many people the most evocative sound in the park. So haunting is this song, it hardly seems possible that this tiny reddish rock-dweller could produce such music.

Starting out as a fast series of sweet tinkling notes, the song fades gracefully into a rhythmic cadence that leaves you full of longing.

Underscoring the importance of water in this desert landscape, it comes as a shock to find American dippers (formerly known as water ouzels) beside streams deep within the canyon. These lovable and energetic bundles of gray feathers rarely leave the cascading streams, where they dive beneath the cold water to capture insects and larvae. Look closely to spot the flash of this bird's whitish, translucent eyelids, which allow it to see underwater.

Birds of Prey

Of the six owl species occurring regularly in the park, none is as familiar as the common and highly vocal great horned owl, which regularly fills the echoing canyons with its booming hoots. This is among the largest and most fearsome of all raptors, and when one moves into the neighborhood, other owls and hawks hurry on to more favorable hunting grounds or run the risk of being hunted down as prey themselves. Hikers may be startled to glance up and spot this bird's huge glaring face and prominent 'horns' (actually long erect feathers) as it peers down at them from a crevice along the rim.

Commanding vast hunting territories of some 50 sq miles, powerful golden eagles may be observed as they travel widely in search of jackrabbits and other prey. Boasting 7ft wingspans, they are among the canyon's largest birds, second in size only to recently arrived California condors. Watch for the characteristic golden tint on the eagle's shoulders and neck.

Given their endangered status in recent decades, peregrine falcons are surprisingly common throughout the park. Here they find plenty of secluded, cliffside nesting sites, as well as one of their favorite food items,

CONDORS

When critically endangered California condors were released at the nearby Vermilion Cliffs in 1996, the canyon experience was forever and profoundly altered. As was the case when wolves were reintroduced to Yellowstone National Park, visitors seem utterly fascinated by the condors. With 9ft wingspans and horridly wrinkled featherless heads, these birds are an unforgettable sight.

It's a miracle condors are around at all, seeing as their world population declined to less than two dozen birds in the 1980s. Many assumed these gigantic prehistoric holdovers were on the brink of extinction. Following a concerted captive breeding effort, however, there are now about 60 condors flying around the park and nearby areas.

Fortunately for park visitors, condors have a strong affinity for large crowds of people. This is an evolutionary trait, as condors are carrion feeders, and crowds of large mammals like humans are more likely to produce potential food. As a result, condors often hang around popular rim viewpoints like Grand Canyon Lodge on the North Rim and Grand Canyon Village on the South Rim. Visitors are granted world-class, close-up views – sometimes too close, as condors seem to delight in swooping up from behind obstacles and gliding mere feet over visitors' heads. Makes you wonder if they're trying to startle someone into falling – dropping in for lunch, you might say!

Condor populations are far from secure, however, even in the park, where they seem to have plenty of food and room to roam. The true test will be whether the species can continue t reproduce successfully. Pairs laid their first egg in 2001 and a total of six chicks have be born in the wild since the reintroduction effort began. The canyon birds are all still young inexperienced, so biologists hope that as the birds mature, more pairs will form and try to b Given that condors live about 50 years, there's plenty of time for these birds to settle d their new home.

white-throated swifts, which they seize in midair. Look for the falcon's long, slender wings and dark 'moustache.'

AMPHIBIANS & REPTILES

Amphibians and reptiles seldom garner the attention they deserve, but a surprising range of beautiful and unique species call the canyon home. Lizards and snakes are especially well represented here. Other resident species include geckos and iguanas, the rare (and venomous) Gila monster, blind snakes and pink rattlesnakes, to name just a few.

Frogs & Toads

The bleating choruses of common canyon tree frogs float up from boulder-strewn canyon streams each night. Gray-brown and speckled like stone, these tiny frogs dwell in damp crevices by day, emerging at night beside rocky pools.

Occupying similar habitat (because water occurs in limited patches) is the aptly named red-spotted toad, a small species with (you guessed it) red-tipped warts covering its body. Its nighttime song around breeding pools is a high musical trill.

'easily the strangest reptile in the park is the rarely seen Gila monster'

Lizards

Perhaps the most abundant and widespread reptile in the park is the eastern fence lizard, a 5in- to 6in-long creature you'll likely see perched atop rocks and logs or scampering across the trail. During breeding season, males bob enthusiastically while conspicuously displaying their shiny blue throats and bellies. Females have dark, wavy crossbars on their backs and only a pale bluish wash underneath.

As delicate in appearance as a fragile alabaster vase, the banded gecko has thin, practically translucent velvety skin. Emerging at night to hunt small insects, this lizard is not readily found unless you're hiking the desert slopes at night with a flashlight.

Easily the strangest reptile in the park is the rarely seen Gila monster, which looks like a 2ft-long orange-and-black sequined sausage. Mostly placid, it is capable of quick lunges and powerful bites with its massive black-rimmed jaws. The lizard holds on tenaciously as its venomous saliva enters bite wounds. While no human deaths have been attributed to this species, the venom is a potent neurotoxin, and victims should seek immediate medical care. Though encounters are rare, this lizard is best left alone.

Snakes

Home to some 20 snake species, the park is a great place to learn about these misunderstood animals. Commonly encountered in a range of habitats is the gopher snake, often mistaken for a rattlesnake because it vibrates its tail in dry leaves when cornered or upset. Sporting an attractive tan body with dark brown saddles, this lithe constrictor preys on rodents and small birds.

The snakes that elicit the most interest are four resident species of rattlesnake – speckled, black-tailed, Mojave and western. Nothing quite approaches the jolt of terror and adrenaline prompted by the angry buzz of a rattlesnake. Both humans and wild animals react with instinctive fear, even though rattlesnakes rarely strike unless provoked. In another show of evolutionary adaptation, the pink rattlesnake resides solely within the canyon depths. Tinted to blend in with the canyon walls, this is a subspecies of the common western rattlesnake.

INSECTS

Summer visitors will likely hear desert cicadas, whose ceaseless rasping and clicking is produced by vibrating membranes stretched over resonating sound chambers. Finding one of these inch-long insects is another matter altogether, as they are masters of camouflage – one reason they're able to screech all day and still avoid predators.

Also notable are inch-long, shiny metallic-blue carpenter bees, which tunnel through dead wood in dry forested areas. Unlike colonial hive-making bees, carpenter bees lead solitary lives and spend much of their time chasing away interlopers who might move into their hard-earned tunnels.

The canyon's many butterfly species are highlighted by the distinctive orange-and-black monarch butterfly, which flutters through the park in large numbers in late summer, en route to Mexican wintering grounds. This large, showy butterfly avoids predation because as a larva it feeds on milkweed plants that contain noxious alkaloids – animals that try to eat monarchs suffer a severe reaction to these plant compounds.

Plants

The park supports a fantastic mix of plant communities and is home to more than 1400 species from four of North America's major biological provinces – the Rocky Mountains and the Mojave, Sonoran and Great Basin Deserts. Each province contributes unique species to the mix. Plants of the Rocky Mountain province are found on both rims, especially the North Rim, where Engelmann spruce and quaking aspen form distinctive moist forests. Plants of the desert provinces occupy the inner canyon, where the climate is much hotter and drier. Mojave plants are found from downriver up to Hundred and Fifty Mile Canyon, Sonoran plants (including ocotillo and mesquite) dominate the central canyon, while Great Basin plants (rabbitbrush, sagebrush etc) take over from lower Marble Canyon to Lees Ferry.

TREES

Pine, Spruce & Aspen

Due to their prominence and longevity, trees serve as excellent indicators of different life zones and local environmental conditions. The stately ponderosa pine, for example, defines the distinctive forested belt between 6000ft and 8000ft. In many places along the North Rim and on the highest points of the South Rim this species forms nearly pure stands that cover many acres. To identify this species, look for large spiny cones, long needles in clusters of three and yellowish bark that smells like butterscotch.

HANGING GARDENS

Even though much of the Grand Canyon region appears arid, there is in fact water locked up inside the layers of porous sandstone – the byproduct of countless torrential rainstorms, which pour down onto the surface and percolate deep into the stone. Over time this water flows laterally and emerges from cliff faces as various seeps and springs. Flowing waters erode soft sandstone, causing the rock to collapse and form cool, shady overhangs. The constant water supply then fosters a rich community of algae on vertical surfaces and below that lush gardens of delicate flowering plants and ferns known as hanging gardens. These gardens of maidenhair ferns, columbines, orchids, monkeyflowers and primroses are a welcome sight to parched desert travelers. Botanists also treasure these alcoves, as many of the plants are unique to the Colorado Plateau, occurring nowhere else but in these hanging gardens.

At higher elevations ponderosa pines mingle with two other species that characterize the Rocky Mountain boreal forest. Engelmann spruce has a curious bluish tinge to its needles and inch-long cylindrical cones with paper-thin scales. To confirm its identity, grasp a branch and feel for sharp spiny-tipped needles that prick your hand. Young Engelmann spruce are a favorite choice for Christmas trees because they flaunt such perfect shapes. Quaking aspen is immediately recognizable for its smooth, white bark and circular leaves. Every gust of wind sets these leaves quivering on their flattened stems, an adaptation for shaking off late snowfalls that would otherwise damage fragile leaves. Aspen groves comprise genetically identical trunks sprouting from a common root system that may grow to more than a hundred acres in size. By budding repeatedly from these root systems, aspens have what has been called 'theoretical immortality' – some aspen roots are thought to be more than a million years old.

Piñon-Juniper Woodlands

Habitats at the lower edge of the ponderosa pine belt are increasingly arid, but two trees do particularly well along this desert fringe. Piñon pines are well known for their highly nutritious and flavorful seeds, sold as 'pine nuts' in grocery stores. These same seeds have been a staple for Native Americans wherever the trees grow, and many animals feast on the seeds when they ripen in the fall. Piñons have stout rounded cones and short paired needles. Together with Utah junipers, piñon pines form a distinctive community that covers millions of acres in the Southwest. Such 'PJ woodlands' dominate broad swathes of the South Rim and canyon walls down to 4000ft. Blue, berrylike cones and diminutive scalelike needles distinguish junipers from other trees. Birds feed extensively on juniper 'berries,' prompting the seeds to sprout by removing their fleshy coverings.

Plant-lovers will appreciate *A Field Guide to the Plants of Arizona*, by Anne Epple, while those interested in how plants can be used will enjoy *Wild Plants & Native People of the Four Corners*, by William Dunmire and Gail Tierney.

Oaks

Consorting with piñons, junipers and ponderosas is the beautiful little Gambel oak, whose dark green leaves turn shades of yellow and red in autumn and add a classy palette of color to an already stunning landscape. Often occurring in dense thickets, oaks produce copious quantities of nutritious, tasty acorns long favored by Native Americans and used to make breads, pancakes, soups and ground meal.

Cottonwood

Rivers and watercourses in this harsh desert landscape are lined with thin ribbons of water-loving plants that can't survive elsewhere. Towering prominently above all others is the showy Fremont cottonwood, whose large, vaguely heart-shaped leaves rustle wildly in any wind. Hikers in the canyon's scorching depths find welcome respite in the shade of this tree. In spring, cottonwoods produce vast quantities of cottony seed packets that fill the air and collect in every crack and crevice.

Tamarisk

Since construction of upstream dams, aggressive weedy tamarisk has replaced ancestral communities of willows and other native plants. Though this delicately leaved plant from Eurasia sports a handsome coat of soft pink flowers through summer, its charms end there, for this plant robs water from the soil and completely overwhelms native plant communities. Producing a billion seeds per plant and spreading quickly, this species now dominates virtually every water source in the Southwest deserts.

SHRUBS

Acacia & Mesquite

Despite the prevalence of tamarisk along stream banks, a few native plants manage to hold on. Easily recognized are catclaw acacia and honey mesquite, thorny members of the pea family that produce seeds in elongated, brown peapods. Each species features delicate leaflets arranged in featherlike sprays, though acacia has little rounded leaflets, while mesquite has long narrow leaflets. Acacia seeds are very hard and must be scratched up in tumbling floodwaters before they'll germinate. Mesquite was a staple among Southwest Indians, providing food, fuel, building materials and medicines. Charcoal of this tree is prized today for the unique flavor it lends to barbecues.

Blackbrush & Banana Yucca

Stretching from the base of rim cliffs to the inner gorge, the broad, flat Tonto Platform is almost entirely covered by a single desert shrub known as blackbrush. Presenting a somber face on a barren, uniform habitat, this dark shrub reaches great ages and is only rarely replaced by young seedlings. Life is spare for this plant; its leaves look like little skinny needles and its flowers lack petals. Scattered among the blackbrush are a few other shrubs, including banana yucca, a stout succulent related to agave and century plants. Growing in a dense rosette of thick leaves that reaches 2ft high, this plant sends up a 4ft flowering stalk in the spring followed by fleshy, bananalike fruit. So much energy goes into this reproductive effort that the plant waits years between blooming cycles.

Fendlerbush

Many shrub species cloak the canyon walls above the Tonto Platform. Here the steep slopes offer a variety of shaded niches and seeps or springs where shrubs form thickets. In spring and early summer these sweet-scented thickets fairly hum with bees, butterflies and birds at work among the abundant blossoms. While blooming, the white-flowered fendlerbush is a powerful magnet for such butterflies as admirals and painted ladies. This 9ft-high shrub sports curious flowers with four widely separated, spoon-shaped petals.

Combining powerful advocacy with a passion for the landscape, the Glen Canyon Institute (www.glencanyon.org) is dedicated to restoring a healthy Colorado River system.

Berries

Another shrub with widely spaced petals (though in fives) is the common Utah serviceberry. Well named, this member of the rose family has been used extensively by countless peoples in the Southwest for food, medicine and other utilitarian purposes. Shaped like tiny apples, the bluish purple berries are not terribly tasty but have been a food staple for millennia.

Common throughout forested areas of the park are seven types of currants and gooseberries. All produce varyingly sweet and edible (though mainly spiny) berries that are an important food source for wildlife and occasionally consumed by humans. Some species bear sticky leaves that are pungent when lightly rubbed.

Big Sagebrush

Abundant on both rims is the distinctive big sagebrush, a plant that dominates millions of acres of dry desert habitat from northern Arizona to Canada. Tolerant of cold and rain to a degree not found in other desert species, sagebrush ranges from valley floors to high desert peaks across the West. Three-lobed leaves and an aromatic scent make identification of this species a cinch.

IN SEARCH OF DARKNESS

If you think that bright glow you see on a moonless night from the north rim is the Milky Way, guess again. What you are seeing is the nighttime glow of Las Vegas, 175 miles away! Sadly, the scourge of light pollution does not stop at the limits of cities but spreads far and wide. In fact, the lights of our industrialized world have become so pervasive that many people have never seen the Milky Way or more than a handful of stars. It is estimated that people in large cities see less than 1% of the stars that someone would have seen in the 1600s.

Some of the darkest corners remaining in the continental United States can be found in the Southwest, but even here the night sky is coming under increasing threat from over-illuminated cities. Members of the nonprofit **International Dark-Sky Association** (www.darksky.org) monitor these changes and work tirelessly to help cities revise their nighttime lighting policies. This may seem like a trivial matter but excessive nighttime lighting not only destroys the quality of your evening reverie, but also wastes electricity and disrupts the lives of plants and animals.

WILDFLOWERS

The park's dazzling variety of wildflowers put on an extravagant show – and because habitats range from arid desert to snowy heights there are always flowers blooming somewhere from early spring on. Even in midsummer, pockets of water foster lush wildflower gardens in shaded recesses within the canyon, while sudden thunderstorms trigger brief floral displays.

Raising eyebrows whenever encountered by hikers, the oddly inflated desert trumpet presents its loose arrangement of tiny yellow flowers any time between March and October. Just below the flowers, the stem balloons out like a long slender lozenge. Old stems maintain this shape and are just as curious as the living plant. Sometimes wasps drill into the plant and fill its hollow stems with captured insects as food for developing larvae.

One of the more conspicuous desert flowers, especially along roadsides, is the abundant peachy pink globe mallow. Shooting forth as many as 100 stems from a single root system, they can tint the desert with their distinctive color. At least 10 mallow species live within the park.

Seeps, springs and stream banks are fantastic places to search for some of the most dramatic flower displays (see boxed text, p77). The brilliant flash of crimson monkeyflowers amid lush greenery comes as something of a shock for hikers who've trudged across miles of searing baked rock. Apparently, someone once saw enough of a monkey likeness to name this wildflower, but you're more likely to notice the 'lips' that extend above and below the flower.

Columbines are also common at these seeps and springs, though some species range upward into moist forested areas of the park. The gorgeous golden columbine is most common in wet, shaded recesses of the inner canyon. Red columbine is a rare find in a wide range of forests and shaded canyons, while the blue-and-white Colorado columbine is a resident of Rocky Mountain spruce-fir forests along the North Rim. The long spurs of columbine flowers hold pockets of nectar that attract large numbers of butterflies and hummingbirds.

Though this hardly seems the place to find orchids, the beautiful giant helleborine is in fact common at seeps and springs within the canyon. The distinctly orchidlike flowers are a medley of green and yellow petals with purple veins. Though it goes without saying you should never pick flowers in a national park, it's especially important that these precious orchids be admired and left undisturbed.

Scarcely noticeable among needle-blanketed forest floors, the intricate lousewort is nevertheless a common plant in the ponderosa pine and spruce-fir zones. Finely cut, fernlike leaves hide the plant's red-tipped white flowers, which grow close to the ground.

OTHER PLANTS

Although they could be classified with wildflowers, the park's two dozen cacti are a group of plants unique unto themselves. Foremost among the cacti are the 11 members of the prickly pear group, familiar for their paddle-shaped pads that resemble beaver tails. In fact, one of the most common species is called beavertail cacti, while a rarer species is known as pancake pear. Both the pads and fruit are commonly eaten after proper preparation. Be aware that the spines (glochids) detach easily on contact and are highly irritating.

Often dubbed the classic beautiful cacti, stunning claret cup hedgehog cacti shine like iridescent jewels in the dusty desert landscape, where they are the first to bloom in spring. Their deep scarlet flowers burst forth from as many as 50 stems per clump, blooming simultaneously for a period of several days.

Of the park's 20-plus ferns the maidenhair fern deserves special mention because it forms dense sheets of bright green at countless desert oases. Lacy and delicate, this fern requires a continuous supply of water but otherwise does well in an imposing landscape. You'll recognize it by its fan-shaped leaflets and wiry black stems.

A close examination of the park's juniper trees reveals an extremely abundant but easily overlooked plant – yellow-green juniper mistletoe. Parasitic, but apparently not harming its host trees, mistletoe produces tiny fruits that birds like robins and bluebirds absolutely love. Carried in the birds' digestive tracts, the seeds adhere to new tree branches once excreted.

ENVIRONMENTAL ISSUES

Locked in by dams at both ends of the canyon, the once mighty Colorado River has undergone profound changes, with significant impacts on the many plants and animals that depend on the river and its natural cycles. Few species, either aquatic or terrestrial, escape the effects of these changes, although some species benefit while others are harmed.

Preserving the environmental health of the vast Colorado Plateau is one task of the Grand Canyon Trust (www.grandcanyontrust.org).

No group of animals has suffered more than the handful of native fish that once thrived in the warm, sediment-laden waters of the Rio Colorado (Colored River) – so named because of its murky soup full of rusty brown sediments. Upstream from the canyon, Glen Canyon Dam now captures nearly all of the 380,000 tons of sediment that once flowed annually through the canyon. The dam instead releases clear cold water in a steady year-round flow that scarcely mimics the ancestral seasonal flood cycle. Under this managed regime, unique fish like the Colorado squawfish, razorback sucker and prehistoric-looking humpback chub have been almost entirely displaced by introduced trout, carp and catfish that flourish in the current conditions.

Some changes to the river environment are dramatic, while others are so subtle that scientists are only beginning to understand them. An obvious change has been the gradual loss of riverside beaches, as the river is no longer depositing sediments in backwater stretches. Beaches have also become overgrown, since the river no longer floods and sweeps away seedlings that take root on open sand. Former sandbanks are now densely vegetated, many with impenetrable thickets of highly invasive tamarisk.

More subtle changes include the chain reaction that begins when sunlight penetrates the now clear water and nourishes algal growth (formerly limited in the murky river). The algae support a food chain that ascends to diatoms, then invertebrates and non-native rainbow trout. Algae also soak up phosphorus, a critical nutrient that otherwise fuels aquatic diversity. Efforts to alleviate this damage include a series of experimental releases of water from the Glen Canyon Dam that have helped rebuild beaches and stabilize humpback chub populations.

It's a grim reminder of modern life that the park suffers from a pall of air pollution that frequently hovers over the canyon, both summer and winter. At the very least it might help obscure the daily swarm of helicopters and sightseeing planes that fly in the canyon, but that's little solace and not much can be done until faraway cities clean up their acts.

The park is also threatened by a modern-day gold rush taking place right on its borders. Over 800 uranium mining claims have been staked within 5 miles of the park since 2003 and there is considerable fear that mining activity on this scale could adversely impact the park environment.

SUSTAINABILITY

The fact that nearly 5 million people a year visit this fragile desert landscape means that tourism and development have a lasting impact. Even an action as simple as walking off the trail is detrimental when it becomes multiplied many times over by a steady stream of visitors. Then there are the inevitable impacts of everyone arriving in their private cars and needing fresh drinking water, plus lodging and showers if they are staying overnight.

The park seems acutely aware of these facts and is trying to mitigate impacts wherever possible. Over the last several years the park has been developing an effective public transit system, and a growing network of pedestrian and bicycle trails on both rims (see boxed text, p105), as a way of reducing traffic congestion and air pollution. Eventually the park hopes to have over 70 miles of trails along the rims linked to points for equipment rental and return, so that visitors can custom-tailor their visits by using a combination of rented bicycles and buses.

Water remains a critical issue because it is gathered from wells and seeps on the Coconino Plateau, and nearby developments (see Grand

CRYPTOBIOTIC CRUSTS

One of the Grand Canyon's most fascinating features is also one of its least visible and most fragile. Only in recent years have cryptobiotic crusts begun to attract attention and concern. These living crusts cover and protect desert soils, literally gluing sand particles together so they don't blow away. Cyanobacteria, among Earth's oldest life forms, start the process by extending mucous-covered filaments that wind through the dry soil. Over time these filaments and the sand particles adhering to them form a thin crust that is colonized by microscopic algae, lichens, fungi and mosses. This crust absorbs tremendous amounts of rainwater, reducing runoff and minimizing erosion.

Unfortunately, this thin crust is quickly fragmented under the impact of heavy-soled boots, not to mention bicycle, motorcycle and car tires. Once broken, the crust takes 50 to 250 years to repair itself. In its absence, the wind and rains erode desert soils, and much of the water that would otherwise nourish desert plants is lost.

Visitors to the canyon and other sites in the Southwest bear the responsibility to protect cryptobiotic crusts by staying on established trails. Literally look before you leap – intact crusts form a glaze atop the soil, while fragmented crusts bear sharp edges.

AN UNCERTAIN SKYWALK

Everyone who has seen the new Grand Canyon Skywalk has something to say about this engineering marvel. This horseshoe-shaped glass walkway extends 20m from the canyon wall, giving pedestrians a heart-in-the-throat view of the river 4000ft below. The 4in-thick glass beneath your shoes is safe enough, but try telling that to the fear shivering up your spine. Built to hold 70 tons of weight, and withstand fierce winds or earthquakes, this thing isn't going to fall down any time soon.

Newly built by the cash-poor Hualapai Indian Reservation, the Skywalk is either a brilliant stroke of commercialism or a vile smear on this sacred landscape. Plenty of people have lined up behind both viewpoints and the project has generated considerable controversy from its inception. Not helping matters much, the tribe is hoping that the Skywalk will be the anchor for a 9000-acre development along a 100-mile stretch of the South Rim that would include hotels, restaurants, a golf course, a museum, and a cable car from rim to river, all of which raise concerns about limited water supplies and overdevelopment of this fragile area. If nothing else, the Skywalk brings these kinds of questions to the forefront.

Canyon Skywalk, p150) threaten to strain the limits of the supply. Because water use in the region is expected to double over the next 50 years, there is growing uncertainty about whether the area's natural seeps and springs (see Hanging Gardens, p77) will start drying up as the aquifer is drawn down.

History

Out in the great wide open of the Grand Canyon lies a rich human history dating back more than 10,000 years, when Paleo-Indian hunters first passed through it in search of big game. Fluctuating with cycles of climate change and the ebb and flow of commercial tides, the ongoing dramas of human existence continue to play themselves out against the canyon's vast backdrop. Even today, stewardship of the canyon and its resources meet with contemporary issues of Native American survival, water management and preservation of the park's pristine places.

ANCIENT CULTURES OF THE GRAND CANYON

Stone points and blades found across the uplands of the Grand Canyon suggest that the earliest inhabitants were the nomadic Paleo-Indian people of the Ice Age. Though there is no evidence to suggest that they occupied the canyon, they passed through the region more than 10,000 years ago in their search for Pleistocene megafauna such as mammoths, camels and giant sloths. Most of their few material possessions have been washed away, so the only record of their existence is the stone remains of their weapons.

The Archaic Periods

By 9000 years ago, Archaic cultures entered the Grand Canyon region from the Basin and Range Province to the northwest and replaced paleoculture. The Archaic cultures span the period 7000 BC to 1000 BC.

The Early Archaic period, characterized by seasonal habitation, atlatl weapons, woven sandals and groundstone tools, saw an increase in population on the plateaus despite the drier climate and the loss of large Pleistocene game.

About 6000 years ago, a drought that would last on and off for almost 2000 years defined the Middle Archaic period. Conditions became even tougher, and many peoples migrated to more amenable lands. Those who stayed moved between canyons and plateaus, sometimes camping in the caves and leaving evidence of their culture.

As the drought waned, about 4000 years ago (2000 BC), people returned to the region, and the 1000-year Late Archaic period began. Late Archaic evidence at the Grand Canyon includes dozens of elaborate split-twig animal figurines depicting common prey, like bighorn sheep,

TIMELINE

8000 BC	7000 BC–1000 BC	1000 BC–AD 1300	1150–1300	1250
Paleo-Indian hunters pass through the Grand Canyon hunting as mammoth and ground [illegible] begin to [illegible]pear	Archaic cultures occupy the canyon, leaving behind evidence of their existence in split-twig figurines	Basketmaker and ancient Puebloan cultures develop farming communities in and around the canyon	Puebloan tribes abandon their settlements for unknown reasons that might include severe drought or hostile invasions	The Cerbat/Pai (ancestors of today's Hualapai and Havasupai) and Southern Paiute migrate to the canyon region

pronghorn antelope and deer, found in Stantons Cave, 50ft above the Colorado River in the Redwall limestone of Marble Canyon. Many are pierced by small twig or cactus thorn, thought to represent arrows, and some were found in shrinelike arrangements, with feathers and human hair attached. Radiocarbon dating tells us that these figurines are 3200 to 5000 years old. Archeologists believe that nomadic groups used the caves for religious rituals, perhaps as a place to offer gifts to the gods in hopes of luring prey. Split-twig figurines found in the Grand Canyon are on display at Tusayan Museum (p113).

BASKETMAKERS & ANCESTRAL PUEBLOANS

Corn (maize), squash and beans, cultivated in Mexico for at least 9000 years, arrived at the Grand Canyon at around 500 BC. The Basketmakers, the canyon's earliest corn-growing people, are named after the intricate coiled and watertight baskets that they made. They lived in rock shelters and pithouses, cultivated cotton, hunted game and gathered wild plants.

In many ways, the Basketmakers were a transitional people who combined the hunting-gathering tradition of the Archaic culture with what would become a decidedly farming culture. They adorned themselves with stone, shell, bone, seed and feather jewelry; wore deerskins and square-toed sandals; and domesticated dogs and turkeys. Trade with other groups contributed to their development, and about 1700 years ago (300 AD), they began to make pottery, and the bow and arrow began replacing the atlatl and dart. A complex religious life is evident through petroglyphs and clay figurines; they smoked ceremonial tobacco, played music on six-hole flutes and made prayer sticks. By about 1100 years ago, pithouses had been replaced with stone structures.

Puebloan culture blurs with the Basketmaker culture, and the gradual shift from one period to the other is a result of complicated migrations and developments. (Anasazi, the term traditionally used to describe the early Puebloan culture, translates roughly as 'Enemy Ancestors.' Because Hopi and Zuni find this term offensive, contemporary scholars refer to the Anasazi as 'ancestral Puebloans,' or 'prehistoric Puebloans.') Puebloan culture, as defined and explained by archeologists, includes corn-growing cultures that inhabited the southern Colorado Plateau and the Four Corners Region. The word 'pueblo' means 'town' and refers to the above-ground adobe or stone structures in which these people lived. Religious ceremonies took place in kivas, circular below-ground buildings reminiscent of pithouses. Ancestral Puebloan culture is a general term

The Grand Canyon Historical Society publishes *The Ol' Pioneer,* a quarterly magazine profiling historical characters and events at the canyon, available for downloading at www.grandcanyonhistory.org.

1540 Spanish explorer García López de Cárdenas and his party of 12 arrive at the south side of the Grand Canyon

1776 Missionary Francisco Tomás Gárces encounters the Grand Canyon and is the first to call the river the Colorado

1803 The Louisiana Purchase makes the young United States the north-eastern neighbor of New Spain

1821 The Mexican Revolution secures Mexican independence from Spain

1820s Trappers and traders hunt for beaver and oth furs in the car exploring th Colorado Ri and its trib

that includes several distinct traditions based on pottery style, geographic location, architecture and social structure; among them are the Chacoan, Mesa Verde, Kayenta, Virgin River, Little Colorado River, Cohonina and Sinagua cultures. By about 700 AD, Basketmaker culture had been completely replaced by Puebloan culture.

From 700 AD to 1000 AD, various strains of early Puebloan culture lived in and around the canyon. On the South Rim, the Cohonina inhabited the canyon west of Desert View (including Havasu Canyon and the Coconino Plateau) and mingled with the Kayenta, living seasonally in the uplands and along the river. Pottery shards found in Chuar Canyon and unearthed during a flash flood suggest that, despite difficult conditions, a farming community thrived in the canyon 1200 years ago.

Paleoclimate research indicates that about 1000 years ago, precipitation increased slightly. For the next 150 years, the Grand Canyon experienced a heyday of farming. Various bands of ancestral Puebloans occupied side canyons, developing complex systems of irrigation to grow squash, beans and corn on any arable land they could find. Taking advantage of the subtle shift in climate, they spread out, strengthened and flourished. While the canyon was by no means lush, the high water table, increased precipitation and wide alluvial terraces made it more amenable to agrarian communities than it would be today.

An intricate trail system allowed access all over the canyon and to the river, and spurs in all directions linked canyon communities and facilitated trade with cultures throughout the Southwest. Remnants of these paths can still be seen today; some were modified by prospectors, early tourist entrepreneurs and the National Park Service (NPS) and are still in use. One of the most striking of these ancestral Puebloan trails is a stick footbridge across a gap in the cliffs called the Anasazi Bridge (Map p221), which can be seen on the north side of the river, upstream from President Harding Rapid.

'Then relatively suddenly between 1150 and 1200, Puebloan Indians abandoned the Grand Canyon'

Then relatively suddenly between 1150 and 1200, Puebloan Indians abandoned the Grand Canyon. Other centers of Puebloan culture, like Chaco Canyon in northwest New Mexico and Mesa Verde in Southern Colorado, were also abandoned during this period, and scientists cannot agree on exactly why such elaborate and thriving communities would so suddenly leave their homes. Analyses of tree rings, stalagmites and lake pollen suggest that a severe drought descended upon the region at about 1150. This drought affected precarious canyon conditions, dropping the table, drying up springs, halting sediment-rich flooding that helped minimize erosion, and reducing the number of acres that could be successfully farmed. After just a few years of drought, corn reserves dwindled, and

1848
Treaty of Guada-
·pe Hidalgo
·ds Mexican–
·rican War

1848
The US annexes Mexico's Northern Territory, which includes Arizona

1848
Gold is discovered at Sutter's Mill, prompting the California gold rush

1850
Territory of New Mexico is formed, which includes the Grand Canyon

1851
Military surveyors begin exploring and mapping the country's new territories

canyon people were faced with malnutrition and starvation. Though there was no single mass exodus from the canyon, Puebloan peoples drifted away. Cohonina migrated towards Flagstaff; Sinagua drifted to and blended with Hopi mesas to the east. The Kayenta villagers stayed a bit longer than their contemporaries to construct fortlike buildings along the South Rim. According to archeologists, these defensive structures suggest that hostile invasions from migrating tribes further weakened the already vulnerable Puebloan communities and contributed to their withdrawal from the canyon. The Tusayan Ruin (p113), on the east side of the South Rim, may have been the last Puebloan community in the Grand Canyon region. Archeological records show that it was not built until 1185 and was inhabited by a community of about 30 people for a mere 25 years.

Whatever the reason – drought, invasion or a combination of the two – by 1300 the Grand Canyon became merely an echo of the once-thriving agrarian Pueblo culture. Though the evidence suggests that they would return periodically, Pueblo Indians never returned permanently.

The Hualapai, Havasupai & Paiute

As the farming cultures of the Pueblo people exited the canyon, other cultures moved in. The Cerbat/Pai, ancestors of today's Hualapai and Havasupai, arrived from the Mojave Desert to inhabit the western side of the canyon south of the river. It's not clear when they took up permanent residence – some scholars believe that they came to the region about 100 years after the ancestral Puebloans left, while others believe that it was their arrival that contributed to the Puebloans' departure.

'The Hualapai trace their origins to Kathat Kanave'

The Hualapai trace their origins to Kathat Kanave, an old man who sometimes took the form of a coyote and lived in Mada Widita Canyon (also known as Meriwitica), on the canyon's westernmost edge. He taught the Pai (literally 'The People') how to live in the canyon, explaining what herbs cured which ailments and how and what to plant. From this sacred canyon, the Pai were separated: a frog led the Havasupai east to his lush home in Havasu Canyon, while the Hualapai remained close to Meriwitica.

The Hualapai and Havasupai developed complex systems of irrigation and spent summers farming within the canyon, at places like Havasu Canyon and Indian Garden. During the winter, they hunted on the plateau. They dressed in sewn buckskin and made coiled baskets and brown or red pottery. Their biggest contact was with other Native American tribes, and through trade with the Hopi, the Northeastern Pai acquired peaches, figs, wheat, melons, cattle and horses.

1856–58
Edward Fitzgerald Beale leads a caravan of camels across the desert to establish the road that later became Rte 66 and is now I-40

1858–59
First Lieutenant Joseph Christmas Ives and his expedition become the first European Americans to reach the river within the canyon

1863
President Lincoln creates the Arizona Territory

1865
The Civil War ends

1865
Hundreds of Navajo die on the 'Long Walk' to Fort Sumner after being force from their traditional lanc

On the other side of the canyon, arriving at about the same time as the Pai (but unrelated), the hunter-gatherer Paiute migrated southward from the Great Basin of Nevada and Utah to inhabit the high plateau country once sparsely populated by the Virgin Puebloans. The few remaining Puebloans likely taught them how to squeeze water from the dust and rock to grow corn and squash in the canyon deltas, and they descended into the canyon to collect salt and other natural resources. Paiute rock art, or *tumpituxwinap*, tells us something about their lives and culture. They wore loincloths, lived in branch and brush shelters, made baskets and reddish-brown pottery, used grinding stones for seeds, hunted with bows and arrows, and crossed the river to trade with the Havasupai. Paiute bands who occupied the Grand Canyon about 800 years ago include the Kaibabits, Uinkarets and Shivwits.

REMOVAL OF NATIVE AMERICANS

From the early 19th century, US military forces pushed west across the continent, protecting settlers and wresting land from the Indians, who had little use for European concepts of land ownership. With the 1848 Treaty of Guadalupe and the discovery of gold at Sutter's Mill in California, Americans crossed the continent in unprecedented numbers. It wasn't long before they intruded into and permanently transformed the lives and homes of Native Americans who had lived in and around the Grand Canyon for centuries.

Wade deeper into the background of the Havasupai with the ethnography *I Am the Grand Canyon: The Story of the Havasupai People*, by Stephen Hirst, told largely in their own words.

After the murder of Hualapai Chief Wauba Yuman in 1866, Hualapai chief Sherum engaged American troops in a three-year war. The US Army destroyed their homes, crops and food supplies until the Hualapai surrendered in 1869. They were forced onto a reservation on the lower Colorado, and deprived of rations and unused to the heat of the lower elevations, many died from starvation or illness. The Hualapai escaped the reservation, only to be confined again when President Chester Arthur set aside the current 1,000,000-acre reservation on the south side of the Grand Canyon.

Though the Havasupai escaped the brutality of the Indian Wars, they too were eventually forced to give up their lands and were confined to a reservation as Americans settled in the Grand Canyon region. In 1880 President Rutherford Hayes established an area 5 miles wide and 12 miles long as the Havasupai Reservation, which eventually was expanded to its present-day boundaries. A few years later, the Bureau of Indian Affairs established schools for the Hualapai and Havasupai children to teach them the ways of the white man. Their canyon home was increasingly disturbed by Anglo explorers, prospectors and intrepid tourists as the

1866
Hualapai Chief Wauba Yuman is murdered, precipitating a three-year war against the military

1868
Navajo Reservation is established on 5500 sq miles in the heart of their ancient lands, eventually growing into the largest reservation in the country

1869
Transcontinental railroad completed

1869
Hualapai people surrender to US military and are confined to a reservation

1869
John Wesley Powell becomes the first to successfully run the Colorado

19th century drew to a close and the Grand Canyon became a destination for European Americans.

Native Americans on the North Rim did not fare any better. US westward expansion brought disease to the Paiute, settlers stole the Paiute's best lands, and by the late 1860s conflict with Anglo pioneers had become common. In the early 20th century only about 100 Kaibab Paiute lived north of the canyon in Moccasin Spring. They were moved onto a reservation in 1907. Today the Kaibab Reservation surrounds Pipe Springs National Monument, in the desert about 80 miles north of the North Rim.

Find more cultural information about contemporary Native American tribes in and around the Grand Canyon on p146.

SPANISH EXPLORERS & MISSIONARIES

Europeans saw the canyon for the first time in September of 1540. Spanish explorer Francisco Vásquez de Coronado believed that seven cities of gold lay in the northern interior of New Spain, and though several efforts had proved fruitless (he instead found Native American pueblos of stone and mud), he continued to traverse the region in search of gold. Native Americans told him about a great river that would reach riches at the Gulf of California, so he sent García López de Cárdenas and his party of 12 to investigate.

It is not clear where Cárdenas and his men stood when they first saw the Grand Canyon, but based on his written record, historians believe it was somewhere between Moran Point and Desert View, on the South Rim. Though Hopi guides knew of relatively easy paths into the canyon, they didn't share them, and Cárdenas' men managed to descend only about one-third of the way down before turning back. The canyon was too much of an obstacle, and the rewards were too little.

'Europeans saw the canyon for the first time in September of 1540'

Finding no gold or riches of any sort, Spanish explorers left the canyon country to the Native Americans – who were not, however, left in peace. The Catholic church of Spain, more interested in converting the natives to Christianity than finding gold, spent the next several hundred years building missions in the Southwest and severely punishing resistors.

Despite the unwelcoming conditions, Spanish missionaries traversed the inhospitable terrain of Northern Arizona in search of both converts and routes to Santa Fe. Inevitably, some stumbled upon the canyon. In 1776, about 200 years after Cárdenas tried to reach the river, Francisco Tomás Gárces reached the canyon in an effort to find a path to Santa Fe from what is now Yuma, Arizona. A kind and gentle man who is widely regarded to be the second European visitor to the canyon, Gárces named the river 'Rio

1870–90 Ranchers and settlers arrive in the Grand Canyon region; by 1890, the non-Native American population of the Arizona Territory reaches more than 88,000

1871 John D Lee starts the first commercial ferry service across the Colorado River at today's Lees Ferry

1871 John Wesley Powell returns to the Colorado River on a second expedition, accompanied by photographer EO Beaman and artist Frederick Samuel Dellenbaugh

1880 President Rutherford Hayes establishes the Havasupai Reservation

1883 President Chester A Arthur confirms the Hualapai Reservation

Colorado,' meaning 'Red River.' He spent several days with the hospitable Havasupai. Because they had been sheltered in their canyon home, the Havasupai had not yet developed a fear and hatred of Spanish missionaries, and they showered him with feasts and celebration. He marveled at their intricate system of irrigation and treated them with courtesy and respect. He continued east into Hopi country, but they refused to give him shelter or food. Later that year, Silvestre Vélez de Escalante, Francisco Atanasio Domínguez and Captain Bernardo Miera y Pacheco came upon the canyon while trying to find a route from Monterey, California, to Santa Fe.

Historians believe that no more than a handful of Europeans visited the canyon from 1540 until the early 19th century. Their influence on the people and land of the region was minimal, for the canyon held nothing of interest for them. For Spanish explorers, it was a barrier to be overcome in their search for gold, and because there was nothing but dry, barren country, the indigenous peoples were left in relative peace. They had no way of knowing that what would begin as a trickle of American traders, trappers and government surveyors in the mid-19th century would end in a tumult of pioneers, prospectors and tourists that would transform their lives forever.

TRAPPERS, TRADERS & SURVEYORS

In 1803 the Louisiana Purchase made the young United States the northeastern neighbor of New Spain, and in 1821 the Mexican Revolution secured Mexican independence from Spain. These two events opened up northern Arizona for trappers and traders, who took advantage of Mexico's lax control of the region.

Delve deeper into the canyon's cultural, political and geological history, as well as contemporary issues, at www.desertusa.com.

Hundreds of fur trappers, employed by trading companies like William Henry Ashley's Rocky Mountain Fur Company, explored the rivers and tributaries of what would become Wyoming, Utah, Colorado, Arizona and New Mexico in search of pelts. Though none of them rafted the Colorado River right through the canyon, French trapper Denis Julien scratched his name and the year (1836) along the cliffs as far downstream as Cataract Canyon. Ashley himself etched his name in rocks at Red Canyon in 1825; when John Wesley Powell (p92) came upon it in 1869, he named the rapids Ashley Falls.

In the mid-19th century several events occurred over the course of a few years that would transform the American Southwest within a half-century. With the Treaty of Guadalupe Hidalgo in 1848, the Mexican–American War ended, and the United States acquired Mexico's northern territory, which would eventually become Arizona, California, Nevada, Utah, Colorado and New Mexico. This, along with the territories acquired

1884
JH Farlee builds the South Rim's first wagon trail from Peach Springs to Diamond Creek, 2 miles from the Colorado, and builds the canyon's first hotel

1884
Miner John Hance takes the first tourists into the canyon down his mining trails

1890
William Wallace Bass begins taking tourists into Havasu Canyon, befriending the Havasupai and facilitating cross-cultural exchange with the relatively isolated tribe

1890s
A stagecoach line runs from Flagstaff to the South Rim

1892–93
Prospector Peter Berry builds the 4-mile Grandview Trail from Grandview Point

with the Louisiana Purchase only 40 years earlier, more than doubled the size of the US and forced the federal government to grapple with the problem of running a Jeffersonian system of representative government while also maintaining a national identity despite great geographical and cultural distances. That same year, gold was discovered at Sutter's Mill in California. In 1850 the territory of New Mexico, including Arizona and the Grand Canyon, was created.

Forty-niners rushing toward gold in California, and pioneers hoping to build homes in the new West, needed wagon roads. Moreover, if the US was to retain control over the vast wilderness they had just acquired, it needed to know exactly what it was. And so the government sent military men to identify and map its new territory in the 1850s. Edward Fitzgerald Beale took a caravan of camels across the desert in the late 1850s, creating the road that would eventually become I-40.

In 1858 army First Lieutenant Joseph Christmas Ives was appointed to explore the still-mysterious 'big canyon' region. Directed to find an inland waterway, Ives set off on the steamboat *The Explorer* on December 31, 1858, from the Gulf of Mexico. He traveled upriver for two months but crashed into a boulder in Black Canyon (near today's Hoover Dam) before ever making it into the canyon. He abandoned his river efforts and set off on Beale's road, along with artists Heinrich Baldwin Mollhausen and Baron Friedrich W Von Egloffstein, a geologist, various Indian guides, soldiers, packers, trail builders and about 150 mules. After about a month, they scrambled down a side canyon north of Peach Springs and became what historians believe to be the first European Americans known to reach the river within the canyon. Mollhausen and von Egloffstein are credited with creating the first visual representations of the Grand Canyon.

Frustrated with the difficulty of the terrain and the lack of water, Ives cut south to Beale's road west of Havasu Falls, and eventually returned east to organize the expedition's maps, landscape etchings and lithographs into a cohesive report on the 'big canyon.' While acknowledging its sublime beauty (perhaps the first to do so), Ives concluded that the region was 'altogether valueless… Ours has been the first and will doubtless be the last party of whites to visit this profitless locality… It seems intended by nature that the Colorado River, along with the greater portion of its lonely and majestic way, shall be forever unvisited and undisturbed.'

'Ours has been the first and will doubtless be the last party of whites to visit this profitless locality'

The idea of nature as a destination in itself, as something to be preserved as an American treasure, did not become a popular notion until the late 19th century. Until that point Americans were interested in nature only in as much as it could be exploited for material gain. Within a quarter-century, this would change. But it would take the work of artists,

1893 President Benjamin Harrison proclaims the Grand Canyon a forest preserve

1896 Bright Angel Hotel is established

1897 John Hance becomes the first postmaster on the rim

1897 Peter Berry opens his luxurious Grand View Hotel

1899 Over 900 people visit the Grand Canyon

who would show the public the splendor and grandeur of the canyon, combined with a national need for an American identity and unity in the wake of Civil War, to shift American attitudes.

JOHN WESLEY POWELL

Fascinated by the reports of initial surveys of the Grand Canyon, John Wesley Powell cobbled together a makeshift team of volunteers and private funding to finance an expedition to the Colorado River. The work of this one-armed Civil War veteran and professor of geology would set the stage for the canyon's transformation from a hurdle to a destination.

In May of 1869, Powell and his crew of nine launched four wooden boats, laden with thousands of pounds of scientific equipment and supplies, from Green River, Wyoming. They floated peacefully until one of the boats, the *No Name,* smashed into rocks at rapids that Powell named Disaster Falls. Despite this and the loss of supplies, they continued down the Green River, joined the Colorado River on July 17 and floated through Glen Canyon without further mishap. The waters of the Colorado in the 'big canyon,' however, were not so kind. They portaged their heavy boats around rapids and ran others, baked under the hot sun, repaired leaks and sustained themselves on dwindling rations of flour, coffee and dried apples. Powell took notes on the geology and natural history, and they spent a great deal of time scrambling over cliffs, taking measurements and examining rocks, canyons and streams in what Powell called their 'granite prison.'

Wallace Stegner's engaging *Beyond the Hundredth Meridian: John Wesley Powell & the Second Opening of the West* recalls Powell's historic first river trip down the Colorado within the context of developing the West.

On August 27 they came to a particularly wild rapid that Powell named Separation Rapid. Here, three men – Bill Dunn and brothers Seneca and Oramel Howland, who were exhausted, fed up with their wilderness conditions and convinced that they would never make it through alive – abandoned Powell and hiked north out of the canyon in hopes of finding civilization. Instead, it is believed that they were attacked and killed by Shivwits Paiute men who mistook them for prospectors who had murdered a Paiute woman. The Powell expedition made it through the wild water, as well as through several other rough rapids, and emerged three days later close to what is now Lake Mead. After 14 weeks on the river, Powell and his crew became the first-known people to explore the Colorado River through what Powell named the Grand Canyon.

Powell returned to the Colorado River in 1871 for a second expedition, this time with photographer EO Beaman, who produced about 350 images of the Grand Canyon, and artist Frederick Samuel Dellenbaugh. In 1873 Thomas Moran, the landscape painter who would become the artist most associated with the Grand Canyon, and photographer John Hiller

1901 The Santa Fe Railroad begins running from Williams to the South Rim

1902 Winfield Hogaboom drives the first car to the Grand Canyon

1903 President Teddy Roosevelt visits the Grand Canyon

1903 Kaibab Trail is constructed from the Colorado River up Bright Angel Canyon to the North Rim

1903 Prospector turned tourism-entrepreneur Ralph Cameron imposes a $1 toll on his Bright Angel Trail

RIVER RUNNERS IN THE CANYON

While tourism on the rims and on inner-canyon trails developed feverishly at the beginning of the 20th century, the idea of rafting on the 277 miles of the Colorado River through the canyon attracted only a few intrepid adventurers. One of the earliest of these was Robert Brewster Stanton, who went down the river in 1889 to survey it for a rail line. He lost several men, and the idea of a rail line along the river was wisely abandoned. After 1900, several prospectors survived the trip, and in 1911 the Kolb brothers filmed their river expedition and began screening it to tourists.

Of the many early tourists who tried to raft the river but never finished, honeymooners Glen and Bessie Hyde would become the most famous. They set out in 1928, without lifejackets, to be the first man and woman pair to run the Colorado through the canyon. They ran the 424 miles from Green River, Utah, to Bright Angel Creek (including the rapids at Cataract Canyon) in 26 days and hiked up to Bright Angel Lodge for a rest, publicity photographs and interviews. Though witnesses say Glen seemed excited to continue, and loved the media attention, Bessie hinted at being less than thrilled to return to the river. As Emory Kolb and his daughter Edith walked them to the trailhead, Bessie noticed Edith's shoes and, looking at her own hiking boots, commented rather sadly, 'I wonder if I shall ever wear pretty shoes again.' As fate would have it, she never would. The honeymooners never emerged from the canyon, and their disappearance remains one of the park's greatest mysteries.

In 1938 Norman Nevills started the first commercial river-running business, but by 1949 still only 100 people had run the Colorado through the Grand Canyon.

visited the rim country with Powell. Powell's 1875 report, entitled 'The Exploration of the Colorado River of the West,' as well as newspaper and magazine articles – and in particular Moran's and Hiller's visual representations that accompanied these written accounts – planted the seeds for the canyon as a tourist destination. Moran's painting *Grand Chasm of the Colorado,* purchased by Congress for $10,000, hung in the National Capitol building and would be influential in securing national-park status for the Grand Canyon. For the first time, the general public saw images of the sublime and spectacular Grand Canyon. Within a quarter of a century, through the combined forces of the prospectors-turned-tourist guides, the railroad and the Fred Harvey Company (see p96), the Grand Canyon would become an iconographic American treasure.

TOURISTS ARRIVE

In the years after the Civil War, the United States accelerated efforts to build a transcontinental railroad in an effort to unite the country and promote Western settlement. Surveyors were sent to find the most advantageous route, and in 1869 the line was completed.

1904	1905	1906	1907	1907
Brothers Ellsworth and Emory Kolb set up their photography studio on the South Rim	Fred Harvey Company opens El Tovar	Grand Canyon Game Preserve is set aside on the North Rim	Tourists cross the Colorado River to the north side in a cage strung on a cable	Kaibab Paiute are moved to a reservation

PROSPECTORS TURNED CANYON GUIDES

Though hundreds of mineral claims for copper, asbestos, silver and lead were located in the Grand Canyon after 1880, most did not pan out. Many prospectors discovered that they'd have better luck making money through tourism than mining. Tourism at the turn of the 20th century revolved around prospectors who developed their mining trails, guided travelers into the canyon and built the South Rim's earliest lodges.

Hance Ranch

Prospector John Hance, who lives on in canyon lore as one of its most colorful characters, is credited with guiding the first canyon tourists. In 1884, having given up on striking it rich from asbestos or copper, he began charging guests $1 for dinner and lodging in his tents (3 miles east of Grandview Point) and guided visitors into the canyon on his mining trails. In 1895 he sold Hance Ranch, then became the canyon's first postmaster in 1897. Though he sold his claim in 1901, Hance remained on the canyon rim, working as a canyon raconteur for the Fred Harvey Company (see p96), until illness forced him to move to Flagstaff in 1918. He died in January 1919, a few weeks before the park was granted national park status, and was the first to be buried in Grand Canyon Cemetery.

Bass Camp

William Wallace Bass, a contemporary of Hance, set up a dude ranch 25 miles west of today's Grand Canyon Village in 1890. He drove to Williams to pick up guests, brought them to his camp over a two-day wagon ride and entertained them along the rim and, by 1901, on over 50 miles of inner canyon trails. He continued to run his lodge while tourist facilities developed around him, and it wasn't until 1923 that he finally closed it down.

Grand View Hotel

Prospector Peter Berry mined copper, gold and silver (including a 700lb nugget of over 70% copper, which was displayed at the Chicago World's Columbian Exposition in 1893) at Horseshoe Mesa. Though his mining was relatively successful, Berry decided to turn to the tourist trade and built the Grand View Hotel in 1897. Unlike Hance's rustic tents, Berry's accommodations boasted Hopi crafts, Navajo blankets, beamed ceilings, hardwood floors and comfortable furnishings. The hotel and trail became hugely popular with the mule-trekking set.

After Harry Smith's Canyon Copper Company bought him out, Smith and Berry joined forces to run a bigger Grandview Hotel from 1903 to 1907. The park service gained control of the land and its remnants in 1939 and razed all of the buildings, but today it's still possible to see the remains of Berry's mine along the Grandview Trail.

Ralph Cameron

Ralph Cameron bought out mining claims at Indian Garden and opened the inner-canyon Indian Garden Camp at the turn of the last century. In 1903 he acquired what was originally the Red Horse stage station and opened Cameron's Hotel next to the Bright Angel Hotel. He retained control of Bright Angel Trail Rd, forcing the park service and the Fred Harvey Company to develop services around him (see boxed text, p116).

1908
President Teddy Roosevelt creates Grand Canyon National Monument

1910
Floods sweep away most of the homes in the village of Supai, on the Havasupai Reservation

1912
Arizona Territory becomes a state

1913
The forest service builds the 56-mile Grand Canyon Hwy to the Bright Angel Ranger Station on the North Rim

1917
Tourists begin staying at Wylie's Way Camp, on the North Rim

With the arrival of the Atlantic and Pacific Railroad to Flagstaff and Williams in the early 1880s, tourists trickled to the canyon's South Rim. In 1883 a total of 67 hardy tourists made the 20-mile trek from Peach Springs (the nearest train line to the Grand Canyon) to Diamond Creek. From there, they descended another two miles along Diamond Creek Wash to the Colorado River. In 1884 JH Farlee eked out the Grand Canyon's first wagon trail to Diamond Creek and built a hotel at the end of the line.

Tourism on the North Rim

Because of its isolation, tourism on the North Rim developed more slowly, and even today it only receives 10% of the park's visitors. The Arizona Strip, the remote desert country north of the rim, was originally settled in the mid-19th century by Mormons, who were trying to escape increasingly strict laws against polygamy.

Most visitors to the Kaibab Plateau went for sport hunting. In June 1906 Teddy Roosevelt created Grand Canyon Game Preserve. The United States Forest Service prohibited deer hunting in the preserve and set about eliminating all of the animal's predators. James T 'Uncle Jim' Owens, in his capacity as the reserve's first game warden, guided hunting trips and oversaw the killing of hundreds upon hundreds of badgers, coyotes, wolverines, cougars and grizzly bears.

Following the arrival of the first car to the North Rim in 1909, the forest service began advertising scenic attractions on the Kaibab Plateau. In 1913 the forest service built the 56-mile Grand Canyon Hwy to the Bright Angel Ranger Station, at Harvey Meadow. Aldus Jensen and his wife ran a small tourist service with tent accommodation. They led guests along the Rust Trail to the river, where they would connect with Fred Harvey wranglers. In 1917 Wylie's Way Camp opened near the fire tower at Bright Angel Point, and Jensen closed down his services. A step above tents, but nothing like the elegance of El Tovar, Wylie's Way Camp could accommodate up to 25 guests and offered tent cabins; guided tours to Cape Royal, Point Sublime and other destinations; mule trips; and a central dining room.

Visitors arriving at the North Rim from the north had to take the 135-mile stagecoach from Marysvale, Utah, to Kanab and then travel the 80 miles or so to the rim by whatever means they could find. Alternatively, beginning in 1907, they could hike into the canyon from the South Rim, cross the Colorado River in a cage strung on a cable, and hike up to the North Rim on the North Kaibab Trail (constructed in 1903). On the canyon's bottom, visitors stayed in a tourist camp at the mouth of Bright Angel Creek, the predecessor to Colter's 1922 Phantom Ranch.

The last wild condor to soar over the Grand Canyon was spotted in 1924 – until the US Fish & Wildlife Service released six endangered California condors in northern Arizona in 1996, the happy result of a captive-breeding program.

1919
The Grand Canyon becomes the United States' 15th national park

1919
A dirt road to the North Rim is built from Kanab

1922
Fred Harvey Company builds Phantom Ranch, designed by Mary Colter, along the Colorado River

1926
Automobiles overtake the railroad as the most popular form of transportation to the canyon

1928
Grand Canyon Lodge is built on the North Rim

FERRYMAN OF THE COLORADO

Believing that stories of good homesteading and plenty of water in Arizona were true, Utah Mormons moved south to the desolate desert land north and east of the Grand Canyon. They built Winsor Castle (now in Pipe Springs National Monument), a cattle ranch and a refuge from Indians, in 1870. That same year, Mormon leaders ordered John D Lee, exiled because of his participation in a massacre of non-Mormon emigrants in Mountain Meadow, to run a ferryboat across the Colorado to service the influx of Mormons to the region. His ferry would be the only river crossing on the upper Colorado, and he spent several years preaching his faith while shuttling prospectors and settlers – along with their mules, wagons and whatever else they needed – across the river. A wanted man, he occasionally had to leave his post to hide from the law. In 1874 they found him and tried him, and in 1879 he was executed for murder. The ferry crossing was used until 1929, when a bridge was built a few miles downstream. Today river runners put in at Lees Ferry (p215), and visitors can tour historic buildings at the site of his ferry launch.

Also in 1922, Gronway and Chauncey Parry began automobile tours to the North Rim, and Will S Rust opened a tourist camp north of the park. In 1919 a rough dirt road from Kanab to the North Rim was completed, and by 1925 more than 7000 visitors arrived at Bright Angel Point. In 1928 Union Pacific architect GS Underwood designed the original Grand Canyon Lodge, and a suspension bridge was built across the river to connect the South and North Kaibab Trails. Though a fire on September 1, 1932, destroyed the main lodge on the North Rim, it was rebuilt in 1937, and the guest cabins, still used today, were left unharmed.

The Railroad & Crowds Arrive

With the arrival of the railroad to the South Rim in 1901, tourism at the canyon accelerated. Instead of paying $20 and enduring a teeth-rattling 12-hour stagecoach ride, visitors could pay $3.95 and reach the rim from Williams in three hours.

In 1902 brothers Ellsworth and Emery Kolb arrived, and within a few years they set up a photography studio (p108) on the rim. Tourists could ride a mule into the canyon in the morning and have a photo of their journey by the next day. Fred Harvey, who joined the Santa Fe Railroad in 1876 to provide hotels and services to its passengers, earned a reputation for luxurious trackside accommodation, fine dining and impeccable service. In 1905, only four years after the train's arrival at the rim, his Fred Harvey Company built El Tovar, an elegant hotel, and established Hopi House. Fred Harvey hired Hopi to live there, demonstrate their crafts, wear native costumes and perform dances for the tourists.

1928	1928	1928	1929	1936
Construction of a igid suspension idge to replace old swinging ge completes oss-canyon Trail	US government takes over Bright Angel Trail	Glen & Bessie Hyde attempt to claim the title of the first couple to run the Colorado River but disappear around river mile 237	Marble Canyon Bridge is dedicated near Lees Ferry, replacing the ferry and making rim-to-rim travel possible	Hoover Dam, a feat of engineering, is built on the Colorado River west of the canyon, creating Lake Mead

Now that the Native Americans had been confined to reservations and the wilderness had been tamed, Americans began to see an innocence and authenticity in Native American culture and in the natural landscape that was lacking in industrialized life. No longer a threat, Native Americans and their crafts and lifestyle became a subject for the tourist gaze.

The Grand Canyon, with its proximity to the Native Americans of the Southwest and its spectacular wilderness scenery that could be enjoyed from the comfort of rimside hotels, offered Americans a safe opportunity to return to a romanticized past. Furthermore, the magnificent landscape of the American West, unique in its geologic features, gave a young country looking for a history and a unifying sense of nationality something to claim. The American West gave the country a unique identity, and tourists flocked to the Grand Canyon.

The Fred Harvey Company hired architect Mary Colter (see p98) to build tourist facilities from indigenous materials that would echo the architecture of Pueblo Indians and blend into the natural surroundings.

THE GRAND CANYON TODAY

In 1908 President Theodore Roosevelt created the Grand Canyon National Monument, and in 1919 President Woodrow Wilson made Grand Canyon the 15th national park in the US. Over 44,000 people visited the park that year. By 1956 more than one million people would visit the Grand Canyon annually.

While the North Rim has not developed much beyond what it was in 1930, the Grand Canyon's South Rim has changed dramatically since the park's pioneer period. The NPS centralized tourist facilities at Grand Canyon Village, a decision that, while resulting in an ever more congested 40-mile stretch along the South Rim, has allowed for vast areas of undeveloped wilderness. Ironically, considering the efforts that are made today to minimize automobile travel to the park, superintendents in the canyon's early days as a national park worked to attract visitors traveling by automobile.

The Great Depression slowed the frenzy of park development, and from 1933 to 1942, the Civilian Corps Conservation, the Public Works Administration and the Works Progress Administration did everything from touching up buildings to creating trails and cleaning ditches. Fewer tourists visited during this period, giving rangers breathing room to develop interpretive programs – the predecessors of today's ranger talks.

The dearth of visitors from the Depression through the end of WWII resulted in a quieter, more relaxed Grand Canyon National Park. However, as soon as the war ended, Americans – in love with their cars and

Proposed construction of two gigantic dams on the Colorado in the mid-'60s was famously quashed by public protest after the Sierra Club published full-page ads in major newspapers asking, 'Would you flood the Sistine Chapel so the tourists can see the ceiling?'

1937

Grand Canyon Lodge, on the North Rim, is rebuilt after a fire destroys the main lodge

1956

Two airplanes on eastward flights from Los Angeles collide over the canyon, resulting in the establishment of a national air-traffic control system

1963

Controversial Glen Canyon Dam is built on the Colorado River east of the canyon, creating Lake Powell and destroying Glen Canyon

1964–67

Dams at Marble Gorge and Bridge Canyon are proposed for the Colorado River, but massive public outrage quashes the proposal

1968

Train service the park is discontin

HISTORY

MARY COLTER'S GRAND VISION

Mary Colter's buildings blend so seamlessly into the landscape that, were it not for the tourists strolling around them, you could conceivably not even notice the structures. Indeed, Colter's buildings add to the beauty of Grand Canyon National Park because they succeed so magnificently in adding nothing at all.

In 1883 at the age of 14, Mary Colter (1869–1958) graduated from high school in St Paul, Minnesota. She studied art in San Francisco and spent her entire career designing hotels, shops, restaurants and train stations for the Fred Harvey Company and the Santa Fe Railway. Beginning in the late 1870s, these two companies worked as a team to transform the American West into a tourist destination.

Colter's work follows the sensibility of the Arts and Crafts Movement. In keeping with the nationalist spirit of the late 19th century, and reacting against industrialized society, the Arts and Crafts aesthetic (or Craftsman style) looked toward American models, rather than European traditions, for inspiration. The movement revered handcrafted objects, clean and simple lines and the incorporation of indigenous material. For an excellent example of well-preserved, classic Arts and Crafts design, stop by the Riordan Mansion in Flagstaff (p153).

Colter spent a great deal of time researching all her buildings, exploring ancient Hopi villages, studying Native American culture and taking careful notes. The Colter buildings in Grand Canyon National Park use local material such as Kaibab limestone and pine, and incorporate stone, wood, iron, glass and brick. They embrace Native American crafts like woven textile and geometric design, and echo Indian architecture with kiva fireplaces and vigas (rafters) on the ceiling.

The conundrum of preserving expanses of Western land as sacred American wilderness while at the same time developing them for tourists was solved in part by Colter's brilliant designs. Her buildings, known as 'National Park Service rustic,' stand in harmony with their natural environment and served as models and inspiration for subsequent tourist services in national parks throughout the country.

Arnold Berke's *Mary Colter: Architect of the Southwest* is a beautifully illustrated and well-written examination of the life and work of Mary Colter.

eager to explore and celebrate their country – inundated the national parks. The flood prompted another flurry of construction, and from 1953 to 1968 the park built more trails, enhanced existing trails, improved roads and built Maswik, Kachina and Thunderbird Lodges. Steel and concrete buildings joined the classic rustic style of El Tovar and Mary Colter's architecture.

Despite the problems and political battles that have surfaced as the park becomes more and more popular, including debates over automobile restrictions, regulations for scenic flights and limits on motorized boats on the Colorado River, the NPS's vision of a centralized South Rim

1974

ffic congestion so bad that rk service shuttle

1976

The park sees more than three million visitors

1979

Grand Canyon National Park is designated a Unesco World Heritage site

1987

The Federal Aviation Administration requires sightseeing planes and helicopters to fly higher over the canyon and bans them from certain areas

1989

Grand Canyon Railway offers a historic train ride to the South Rim from Flagstaff

has prevented sprawling development. It is still possible to take a short hike and feel as if the entire park is your own.

In 1979 Grand Canyon National Park was designated a World Heritage site by the members of Unesco. One hundred years after the first train of tourists arrived at the South Rim, the NPS continues to grapple with the dilemma of how to ensure access to one of America's greatest natural treasures while at the same time preserving the wilderness that everyone comes to experience.

1989

More than four million people visit the Grand Canyon

1993

One hundred and thirty years after Ives predicted that the canyon would be 'forever left unvisited and undisturbed,' almost five million people visit Grand Canyon National Park

2006

National Park Service (NPS) begins changing river permit system from a seriously backlogged waitlist to a weighted lottery

2007

Hualapai Nation opens the controversial glass Skywalk at Grand Canyon West

2007

Three five-week-old mountain lion kittens are captu and tagged wit Grand Canyon National Par park resear

South Rim

Step up to a South Rim overlook, and as the maw dramatically opens out before you – the breeze carrying a soaring California condor along with high-desert hints of piñon and sage – expect to feel very, very small. If you can stake out a quiet spot on the rim to watch the sunrise or sunset color the canyon's jagged spires and temples, it may well be a religious experience. As one helicopter pilot said, 'You get all kinds of reactions when people see the canyon for the first time – some cry, some scream, some are speechless.' And the most stunning Grand Canyon vistas reveal themselves at the South Rim, accessible to visitors of all ages and abilities on scenic drives skirting the canyon edge to threshold trails beckoning the experienced canyon hiker.

Taking in the grandeur from the rim is as far as most visitors go. But ranging below the rim brings the sheer immensity and splendor of the gorge into a whole new context; even hiking down one layer into geological history, you'll catch glimpses of fossils embedded in sandstone, and petroglyphs left by ancient Native Americans. Join a mule train and wind your way down a dusty corridor trail, wondering at the intrepid explorers and native people who survived in this extreme terrain. Though the accessibility of the South Rim means sharing your experience with others, there are thousands of ways to commune with the canyon and its wildlife, and enjoy its sublime beauty one on one.

HIGHLIGHTS

- Rewarding yourself après-hike with a prickly pear margarita on the porch swing at the back of **El Tovar** (p106) while canyon colors evolve in dusk light
- Winding your way up stone steps at the historic **Watchtower** (p114) to discover Hopi-inspired murals inside and sweeping, unparalleled views outside
- Taking in the smells of juniper and piñon with quiet moments at spectacular overlooks on an early-morning meander along **Desert View Dr** (p112)
- Living in each beautiful moment of sunrise at **Lipan Point** (p113), one of the most stunning overlooks on the South Rim
- Feeling the burn on the steep **Grandview Trail** (p119) while feeling blessed with rugged olitude and gorgeous canyon scenery at its sage-tufted mesa

- ND CANYON VILLAGE ELEVATION: FT
- AVERAGE HIGH/LOW TEMPERATURE IN JULY: 84/54°F

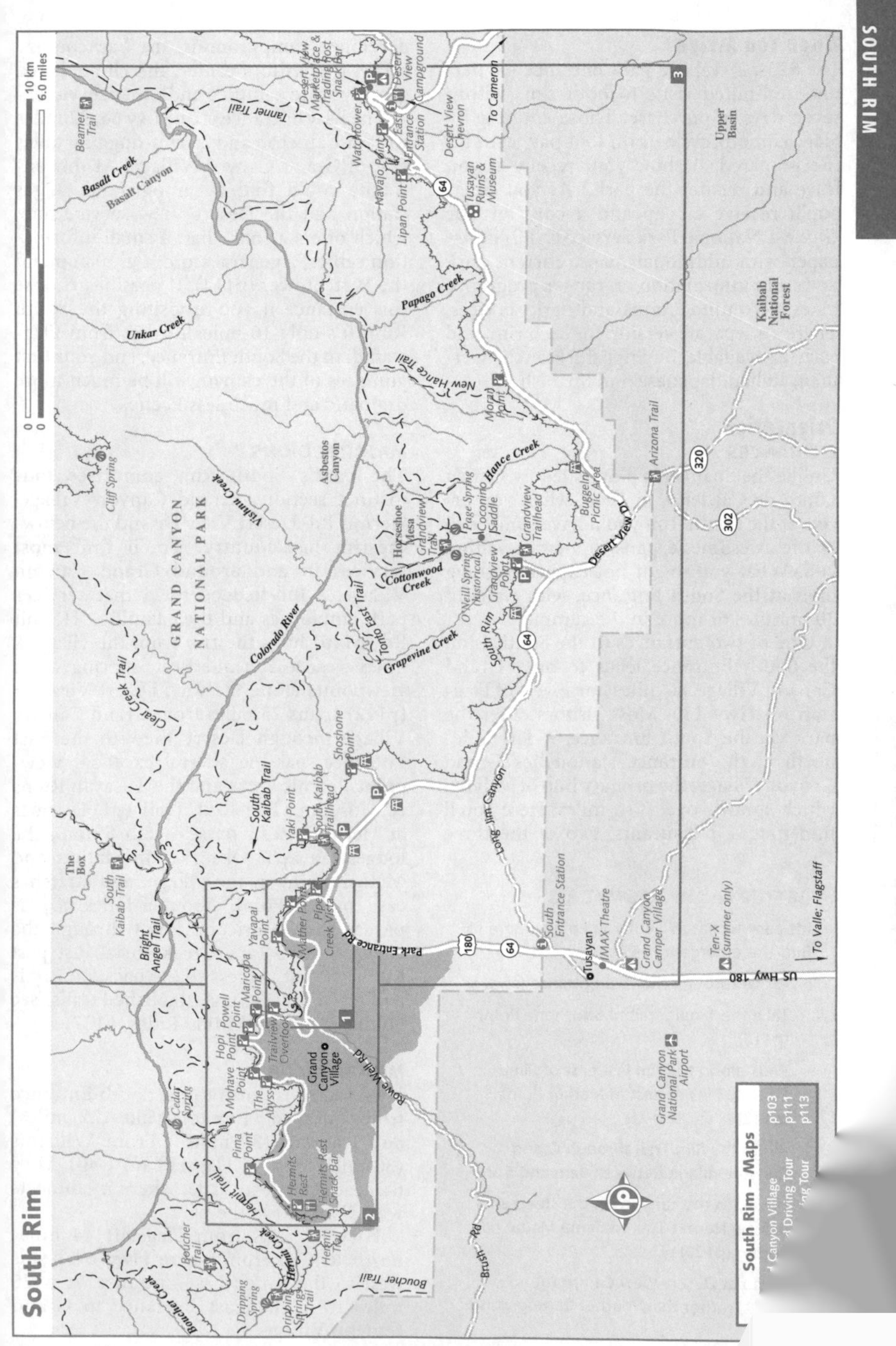
South Rim
0 10 km
0 6.0 miles
GRAND CANYON NATIONAL PARK
Colorado River
Basalt Creek
Basalt Canyon
Beamer Trail
Tanner Trail
Unkar Creek
Papago Creek
New Hance Trail
Vishnu Creek
Asbestos Canyon
Hance Creek
Cliff Spring
Clear Creek Trail
Horseshoe Mesa
Grandview Trail
Page Spring
Coconino Saddle
Cottonwood Creek
Tonto East Trail
Grapevine Creek
O'Neill Spring (historical)
Grandview Point
Grandview Trailhead
Buggeln Picnic Area
Desert View Dr
Arizona Trail
South Rim
Shoshone Point
South Kaibab Trail
Yaki Point
South Kaibab Trailhead
The Box
Long Jim Canyon
Bright Angel Trail
Yavapai Point
Mather Point
Pipe Creek Vista
Park Entrance Rd
Maricopa Point
Powell Point
Hopi Point
Trailview Overlook
Mohave Point
The Abyss
Grand Canyon Village
Rowe Well Rd
Pima Point
Cedar Spring
Hermit Trail
Hermits Rest
Hermits Rest Snack Bar
Hermit Creek
Hermit Trail
Boucher Trail
Boucher Creek
Dripping Spring
Dripping Springs Trail
Brush Rd
Desert View Marketplace & Trading Post Snack Bar
Desert View Campground
Watchtower
Navajo Point
East Entrance Station
Lipan Point
Desert View Chevron
To Cameron
Tusayan Ruins & Museum
Moran Point
Upper Basin
Kaibab National Forest
South Entrance Station
Tusayan
IMAX Theatre
Grand Canyon Camper Village
Ten-X (summer only)
To Valle; Flagstaff
US Hwy 180
Grand Canyon National Park Airport
South Rim – Maps
...d Canyon Village p103
...d Driving Tour p111
...ng Tour p113
1
2
3
64
180
320
302

When You Arrive

The $25-per-vehicle park entrance fee permits unlimited visits to both rims within seven days of purchase. Those entering by bicycle, motorcycle or on foot pay just $12. (Be prepared to show your receipt if you leave and reenter the park.) As you enter, you'll receive a map and a copy of *The Guide,* a National Park Service (NPS) newspaper with additional maps, current park news and information on ranger programs, hikes, accommodations and park services. There's a separate version for each rim, and each is available in English, French, German, Italian, Japanese and Spanish.

Orientation

ENTRANCES

Unlike the Spanish explorers led by García López de Cárdenas in 1540, when you arrive at the South Rim you'll have some idea of the awesome, expansive views awaiting you. What you might not expect are long lines at the South Entrance, with waits of 30 minutes or more in the summer.

One of two entrances to the South Rim, the South Entrance leads to busy Grand Canyon Village, 80 miles northwest of Flagstaff on Hwy 180. Most visitors enter the park via the South Entrance. A few miles north of the entrance station lies Grand Canyon Village, the primary hub of activity, which sprawls over 3 sq miles. Here you'll find lodges, restaurants, two of the three developed campgrounds, the backcountry office, the visitors center, the clinic, bank, grocery store, shuttles and other services.

The East Entrance is on Hwy 64, 32 miles west of Cameron and 25 rim-hugging miles east of Grand Canyon Village. At this entrance you'll find a campground, a gas station and the Desert View service hub, which offers a snack bar, a small information center, a general store, a gift shop and the Watchtower (p114). If possible, choose this entrance if you're visiting the South Rim. It's only 10 miles further from Flagstaff than the South Entrance, and your first glimpses of the canyon will be much more dramatic and much less hectic.

> **GETTING AWAY FROM IT ALL**
>
> It's easy to get away if you know where to find the emergency exits.
>
> - Arrive through the East Entrance (above)
> - Take the 1-mile trail to Shoshone Point (p115)
> - Walk along the rim just east of Pima Point (p111) or east of Mather Point (p112)
> - Avoid the Rim Trail through Grand Canyon Village between 9am and 5pm
> - Hike into the canyon on the steep and narrow Hermit Trail to Santa Maria pring (p120)
> - mp at Desert View Campground 1) rather than Mather Campground

MAJOR REGIONS

The park's South Rim comprises four distinct sections: Grand Canyon Village, Hermit Rd, Desert View Dr and the below-the-rim backcountry. You'll find most services in and around Grand Canyon Village, a full-fledged town that services park employees and their families. Hermit Rd (p110) hugs the rim from the village 8 miles west to Hermits Rest, offering seven viewpoints along the way. Desert View Dr (p112) spans 25 miles from Grand Canyon Village through Desert View to the East Entrance, passing several excellent viewpoints, picnic areas and the Tusayan Ruins & Museum. The Rim Trail (p114) starts at Hermits Rest, passes Kolb Studio, the lodges, Yavapai Observation Station and Mather Point in the village, and stretches east to Yaki Point. About 5 miles of it is paved, from Maricopa Point through the village east to Pipe Creek Vista, just past Mather Point. Access to the backcountry is by foot or mule along established trails (see Hiking, p114, and Mule Rides, p127).

MAJOR ROADS

Hwy 180 runs north to the South Entrance from Tusayan (1 mile), Valle (22 miles) and Flagstaff (80 miles). From Williams (30 miles west of Flagstaff on I-40), Hwy 64 heads north to Valle, where it connects with Hwy 180 to the park.

Hwy 89 runs from Flagstaff 44 miles north to Cameron, where Hwy 64 heads west to the park's East Entrance. It is 25 miles from the East Entrance to Grand Canyon Village.

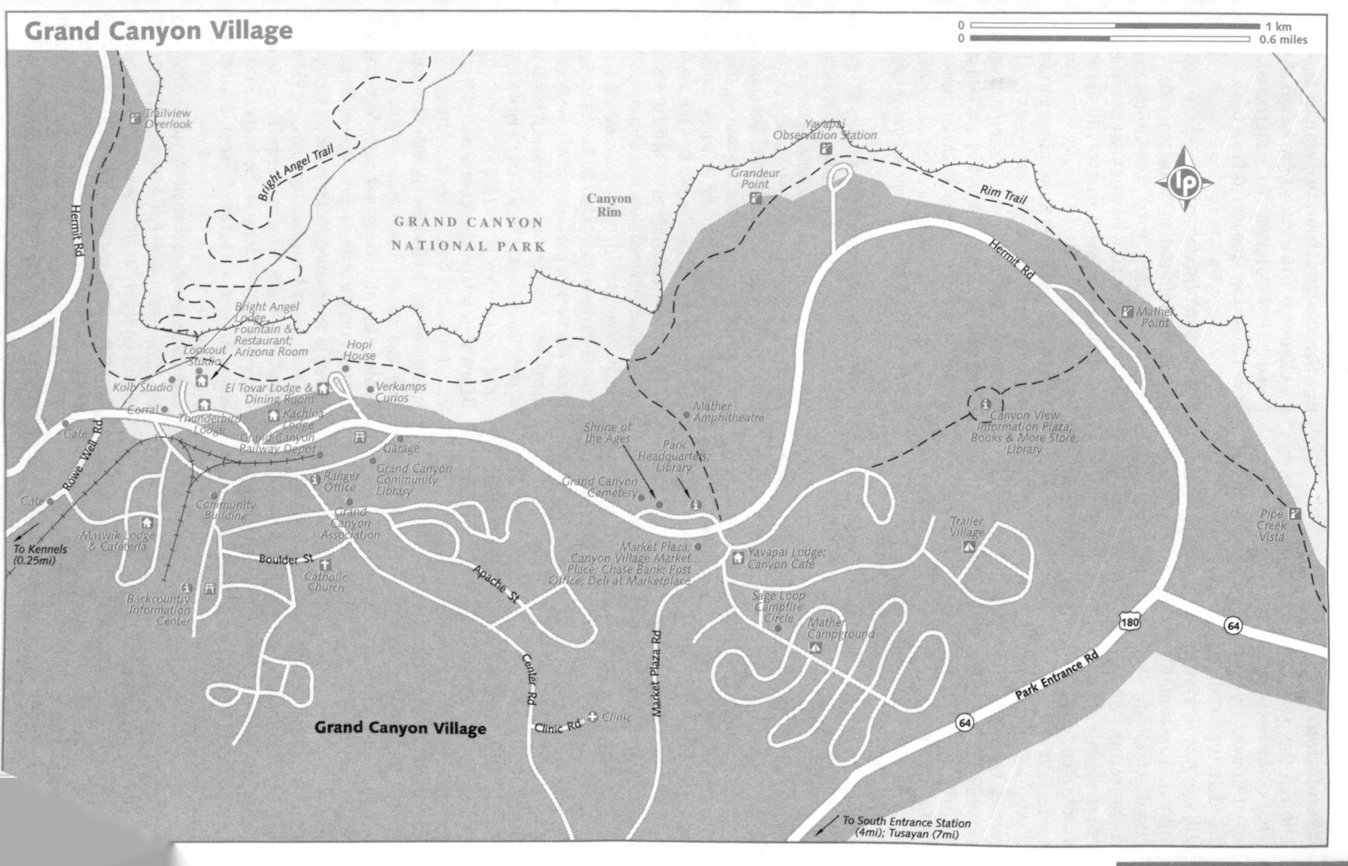
Grand Canyon Village
0
0
1 km
0.6 miles
Trailview Overlook
Bright Angel Trail
Hermit Rd
Kolb Studio
Lookout Studio
Bright Angel Lodge; Fountain & Restaurant; Arizona Room
El Tovar Lodge & Dining Room
Kachina Lodge
Thunderbird Lodge
Grand Canyon Railway Depot
Corral
Gate
Rowe Well Rd
Gate
To Kennels (0.25mi)
Maswik Lodge & Cafeteria
Backcountry Information Center
Community Building
Boulder St
Catholic Church
Grand Canyon Association
Ranger Office
Grand Canyon Community Library
Garage
Hopi House
Verkamps Curios
GRAND CANYON NATIONAL PARK
Canyon Rim
Grand Canyon Village
Apache St
Center Rd
Clinic Rd
Clinic
Grand Canyon Cemetery
Shrine of the Ages
Park Headquarters; Library
Market Plaza: Canyon Village Market Place; Chase Bank; Post Office; Deli at Marketplace
Market Plaza Rd
Mather Amphitheatre
Grandeur Point
Yavapai Observation Station
Yavapai Lodge; Canyon Cafe
Sage Loop Campfire Circle
Mather Campground
Trailer Village
Canyon View Information Plaza; Books & More Store; Library
Hermit Rd
Rim Trail
Mather Point
Park Entrance Rd
180
64
64
Pipe Creek Vista
To South Entrance Station (4mi); Tusayan (7mi)

Information

Though the park can seem overwhelming when you first arrive, it's actually quite easy to navigate, especially when you leave the driving to shuttle drivers. The blue Village Route shuttles stop at all of the following information centers except Hermits Rest, Desert View and Tusayan Ruins & Museum, which are covered by the other shuttle routes. *The Guide* contains a color-coded shuttle-route map in the centerfold.

Almost all services on the South Rim are in Grand Canyon Village, easily accessible via the blue Village Route shuttles. On the east side, Market Plaza (Map p103) includes the grocery/deli/outdoors shop **Canyon Village Marketplace** (☎ 928-631-2262; ⌚ 7am-9pm), **Chase Bank** (☎ 928-638-2437; ⌚ 9am-5pm Mon-Thu, 9am-6pm Fri) with a 24-hour ATM, and a **post office** (☎ 928-638-2512; ⌚ 9am-4:30pm Mon-Fri, 11am-1pm Sat) where stamps are available via a vending machine from 5am to 10pm. The main visitors center is **Canyon View Information Plaza** (Map p103; ☎ 928-638-7644; ⌚ 7:30am-6:30pm), just behind Mather Point.

Limited hours go into effect between October and March. If you have questions, NPS rangers and people who staff the hotels, restaurants and services are typically helpful and friendly.

BOOKSTORES

Books & More Store (Map p103; ☎ 928-638-0199; ⌚ 8am-8pm) Located in the Canyon View Information Plaza, this is the park's most extensive bookstore.

Hermits Rest (Map p101; ☎ 928-638-2351; ⌚ 8am-sunset) At the west end of Hermit Rd, this beautiful stone building houses a small bookstore, gift shop and snack window. For more details, see the Hermit Rd driving tour (p110).

Kolb Studio (Map p103; ☎ 928-638-2771; ⌚ 8am-7pm) Once the home and studio of the Kolb brothers, pioneering photographers of the Grand Canyon, this historic building houses a small but excellent bookstore and an art gallery with changing exhibits (see p108).

NTERNET ACCESS

and Canyon Community Library (Map p103; 928-638-2718; per 50min $3; ⌚ 10:30am-5pm) Just d the garage, this little brown schoolhouse-looking houses the community library and several providing internet access; hours vary seasonally, ad.

Park Headquarters Library (Map p103; ⌚ 8am-noon & 1-4:30pm Mon-Thu & alternate Fri) At the back of the courtyard at Park Headquarters, the small library offers free internet access when someone's staffing it.

TOURIST INFORMATION

Backcountry Information Center (Map p103; ☎/fax 928-638-7875; ⌚ 8am-noon & 1-5pm) Located near Maswik Lodge, this is the place to get waitlisted for a backcountry permit (p44) if you haven't reserved one ahead of time.

Bright Angel, Yavapai & Maswik Transportation Desks (Map p103; ☎ 928-638-2631, ext 6015; ⌚ 8am-5pm) In the lobbies of Bright Angel, Yavapai and Maswik Lodges, these service desks can book bus tours and same- or next-day mule trips. They can also answer questions about horseback rides, scenic flights and smooth-water float trips. Bright Angel can arrange last-minute lodgings at Phantom Ranch (p132), if available.

Canyon View Information Plaza (Map p103; ☎ 928-638-7644; ⌚ 8am-5pm) Three hundred yards behind Mather Point, Canyon View Information Plaza encompasses this visitor center and the Books & More Store. Outside the visitor center, bulletin boards and kiosks display information on ranger programs, the weather, tours etc. One display presents photos from each viewpoint – an excellent orientation to the rim. The center's bright, spacious interior includes a ranger-staffed information desk and a lecture hall, where rangers offer daily talks on a variety of subjects. The store offers a vast selection of books and videos on the park and the region. You can take the blue Village Route shuttle directly to the plaza. Alternatively, simply stroll along the rim to Mather Point, or drive to the small lot by Mather Point and walk to the plaza. If the lot is full, you can park on the side of the road.

Desert View Information Center (Map p101; ☎ 928-638-7893; ⌚ 9am-5pm) Housed in small stone building near the East Entrance, this staffed information center also offers books and maps.

El Tovar (Map p103; ☎ 928-638-2631; ⌚ 8am-5pm) This hotel's helpful concierge can answer questions, arrange same- or next-day bus tours and sell stamps.

Tusayan Ruins & Museum (Map p101; ☎ 928-638-2305; ⌚ 9am-5pm) Three miles west of Desert View, this museum (p113) features exhibits on the park's indigenous people and has an information desk staffed by rangers.

Yavapai Observation Station (Map p103; ☎ 928-638-2631; ⌚ 8am-8pm) Perched on the rim, this observation center features huge windows with expansive views of the canyon, and panels that identify the major geologic features. The station lies 1.75 miles east of El Tovar and 0.6 miles west of Mather Point. As parking can be difficult, you're better off walking along the Rim Trail or hopping on the blue Village Route shuttle.

Park Policies & Regulations

Have a look at p236 for general information on park policies and regulations on both rims.

Getting Around

CAR

Once parked outside your hotel, your car can remain there as long as you're in the village. All services and points of interest are accessible via the free shuttles, a hassle-free alternative to traffic and parking.

If you do drive, consult the Grand Canyon Village map (Map p103) or *The Guide* for parking lot locations. You'll find lots at all the hotels and at Mather Point, though this may change as the Greenway Plan (below) is implemented. Small lots at viewpoints along Hermit Rd and Desert View Dr usually have plenty of open spaces, even during summer peak season. Though Desert View is only 25 miles east, allow at least 45 minutes by car, even if you plan to drive nonstop. While traffic usually moves rather smoothly, the speed limit is 45mph, and cars often turn unexpectedly into the many pullouts. Note that from March through November, cars are not allowed on Hermit Rd, which heads west from the village to Hermits Rest.

The only gas station within the park is the **Desert View Chevron** (Map p101; ☎ 928-638-2365; 🕑 24hr), near the East Entrance. It's open daily from late March through September, though exact dates depend on the weather each year. Gas stations in Tusayan are closer to the village. The village **garage** (Map p103; ☎ 928-638-2631; 🕑 8am-noon & 1-5pm) offers basic auto repair services during business hours as well as 24-hour emergency service. They can also tow you to Williams or Flagstaff if they're unable to repair more complicated problems.

SHUTTLE

Free shuttle buses ply three routes along the South Rim. In the pre-dawn hours, shuttles run every half-hour or so and typically begin running about an hour before sunrise; check *The Guide* for current sunrise and sunset information. From early morning until after sunset, buses run every 15 minutes. *The Guide* features exact seasonal operating hours relevant to your visit, along with a map of shuttle stops. Maps are also posted at all shuttle stops and inside the shuttles themselves.

Hermits Rest Route

The red Hermits Rest Route runs west along Hermit Rd from March through November, during which time the road is closed to private vehicles. You can hop off at any of the viewpoints (it stops seven times on the way from the village to Hermits Rest), enjoy the view and a hike, then catch another shuttle

THE GREENWAY PLAN

The awesome geologic wonder that is the Grand Canyon attracts more than 5 million visitors each year, leading at times to not-so-awesome heavy traffic and crowded parking lots. In an effort to minimize car use and preserve a more peaceful atmosphere along the rim, the National Parks Foundation has been working with the Grand Canyon Association to develop 73 miles of dirt and paved bicycle and pedestrian paths on both rims. As the paths are developed, roads and parking lots may face restrictions.

On the South Rim three accessible trails totaling 11 miles will connect Tusayan, Canyon View Information Plaza, the lodges and the future Heritage Education Campus. A proposed 34-mile trail will link Canyon View Information Plaza with Desert View to the east and Hermits Rest to the west. Greenway projects on the North Rim include a 6-mile trail that will connect Grand Canyon Lodge, the campground and the North Kaibab Trailhead, as well as a 14-mile trail out to Cape Royal (currently accessible only via paved road).

Four miles of Greenway trails are already in use on the South Rim. The first is part of the Rim Trail, stretching east from Yavapai Observation Station past Mather Point to Pipe Creek Vista. Th second trail connects Canyon View Information Plaza with Grand Canyon Village.

The plan is dependent in part on private and corporate donations. For updated informa and details on how to contribute, contact the **Grand Canyon Foundation** (☎ 928-774-1760 .grandcanyonfoundation.org).

further west or back to the village. Or walk part of the way along the Rim Trail (p114) and catch the shuttle. The shuttle stops only at Mohave Point and Hopi Point on its return to the village.

Village Route

The blue Village Route provides year-round transportation between most village facilities, including Canyon View Information Plaza, Yavapai Point, Market Plaza, the backcountry office, hotels, restaurants, campgrounds and parking lots. It does not stop at the clinic.

Kaibab Trail Route

The green Kaibab Trail Route provides service to and from the Canyon View Information Plaza, Pipe Creek Vista, South Kaibab Trailhead and Yaki Point. The trailhead and Yaki Point are on a short road off Desert View Dr that is closed to cars year-round.

Hikers' Express

The early-bird Hikers' Express shuttle leaves from Bright Angel Lodge (with a stop at the Backcountry Information Center) for the South Kaibab Trailhead daily at 4am, 5am and 6am from June to August; 5am, 6am and 7am in May and September; 6am, 7am and 8am in April and October; and 8am, 9am and 10am between November and March.

TAXI

Grand Canyon South Rim Taxi Service (☎ 928-638-2822, 928-638-2631, ext 6563) offers taxi service to and from Tusayan and within the park. Service is available 24 hours, but there are only a couple of taxis, so you may have to wait for one.

TOURS

Narrated bus tours west to Hermits Rest or east to the Watchtower depart twice daily from Maswik, Yavapai and Bright Angel Lodges. These offer a good introduction to the canyon, as drivers stop at [illegible]he best viewpoints, point out the vari[illegible]s buttes, mesas and plateaus, and offer [illegible]orical anecdotes. Tickets are available [illegible]e lodge transportation desks or from [illegible] Tovar concierge, or you can book [illegible]lling ☎ 928-638-2631. Children [illegible]6 ride for free when accompanied [illegible]dult, and wheelchair-accessible vehicles are available with a day's advance notice.

Two-hour tours to Hermits Rest ($18.25) depart daily at 9am and 4pm. A 90-minute sunrise tour or two-hour sunset tour to Hermits Rest ($14.50) departs at various times throughout the year (the sunrise tour can leave as early as 4am in summer).

Four-hour Desert View Dr tours ($31.50) depart daily at 9am and 12:30pm and include an hour at the Watchtower. In summer a sunset tour of Desert View Dr departs at 4pm.

A combination tour ($40) allows you to choose any two of the above options.

SIGHTS

While you'll obviously want to marvel at the main attraction, the South Rim is also the site of notable buildings and museums that offer some fascinating and enriching historical perspective on your canyon experience. Many of the historic buildings on the South Rim were designed by visionary architect Mary Colter (p98), painstakingly researched and designed to complement the landscape and reflect the local culture.

Check out the Desert View driving tour for details about the Watchtower and Tusayan Ruins & Museum, and consider purchasing the self-guided *Walking Tour of Grand Canyon Village Historical District* brochure ($1) at park bookstores. Hours listed here are for the summer season; unless otherwise noted, hours vary seasonally.

EL TOVAR

With its unusual spires and dark-wood beams rising behind the Rim Trail, elegant **El Tovar** (Map p103; ☎ 928-638-2631; ♿) remains a grande dame of national park lodges. El Tovar was built in 1905 for the Atchison, Topeka & Santa Fe Railway and designed by architect Charles Whittlesey as a blend between a Swiss chalet and the more rustic style that would come to define national park lodges in the 1920s. Spacious rooms (many with sleigh beds and rim overlooks), a dining room with panoramic views, and wide, inviting porches with rocking chairs offered visitors a comfortable and elegant place to relax after a long journey to the park.

Today the public spaces look much as they did when the lodge opened, though many of the rooms are smaller, and it remains the most luxurious lodge (p133) on the South Rim. Moose and elk trophy heads, reproduction Remington bronzes and Craftsman-style furniture lend the interior a classic Western feel. A gift shop and restaurant adjoin the lobby, and the helpful concierge can book bus tours and answer questions. The lodge sits about 100 yards from the rim, and though it bustles with throngs of tourists by day, the scene mellows in the evening. The back porch, a sweet spot to relax with a drink, looks out over a small lawn, one of the park's few grassy areas and a great place for small children to play. If the back porch is full, take your drink to the side porch – it's closer to the Rim Trail but has a delightful bench swing that's the perfect perch after a long hike.

BRIGHT ANGEL LODGE

By the 1930s tourism to the park had boomed, and Fred Harvey decided to build a more affordable alternative to the El Tovar. Designed by Mary Colter, the log-and-stone **Bright Angel Lodge** (Map p103; ☎ 928-638-2631; ♿) was completed in 1935. Just off the lobby is the **History Room**, a small museum devoted to Fred Harvey, the English immigrant who, in conjunction with the Atchison, Topeka & Santa Fe Railway, transformed the Grand Canyon into a popular tourist destination. Don't miss the fireplace, built of Kaibab limestone and layered with stones that represent the canyon strata from river to rim.

On the lodge grounds is the **Buckey O'Neill Cabin**, now a guesthouse. Built in the 1890s by William Owen O'Neill, the cabin is the longest continually standing building on the rim. Nicknamed 'Buckey' because he 'bucked the odds' in a card game, O'Neill moved to Arizona in 1879 and worked as an author, journalist, miner, politician and judge. Drawn to a copper deposit near Anita, about 14 miles south of today's Grand Canyon Village, he lived in this cabin and worked on the side as a tour guide. As was the case with so many other prospectors, Buckey found mining to be an unprofitable venture, so he eventually sold his land to the railways and went on to become mayor of Prescott, Arizona. He was one of Teddy Roosevelt's Rough Riders in the Spanish American War and died the day before the assault on San Juan Hill. Today, the lucky few who make reservations well in advance can stay in his cabin (see left).

The first stagecoach to the South Rim left Flagstaff on May 19, 1892. Eventually, stages made the 11-hour ride to the park thrice weekly, and three stations along the way allowed visitors to stretch their legs, dust off and prepare for the next leg of the journey. **Red Horse** (originally called Moqui Station) was built 16 miles south of the village in the 1890s; in 1902 Ralph Cameron, who controlled Bright Angel Trail, moved the building to its present site (on the Bright Angel Lodge grounds) and converted it into the Cameron Hotel. It served as a post office from 1907 to 1935. When Mary Colter designed Bright Angel Lodge in the early '30s, she insisted the station be preserved and incorporated into the lodge.

YAVAPAI OBSERVATION STATION

Panoramic views of the canyon unfold behind the plate-glass windows of **Yavapai Observation Station** (Map p103; ☎ 928-638-2631; 🕐 8am-8pm; ♿) on **Yavapai Point**, one of the South Rim's best viewpoints. Plaques beneath the large windows identify and explain the formation of the landmarks upon which you're gazing. With a topographic relief model of the canyon itself and a model illustrating and explaining the canyon's sedimentary layers, this is an excellent place to bone up on Grand Canyon geology before hiking down. If the exhibits here spark your curiosity, consider attending a ranger talk about canyon geology (check *The Guide* for locations and times).

GRAND CANYON DEPOT

Designed by Francis Wilson for the Atchison, Topeka & Santa Fe Railway, this **train depot** (Map p103; ♿) was completed in 1909, eight years after the first train arrived in the village from Williams. It's one of three remaining log depots in the country and one of only 14 log depots ever constructed in the US. The logs are squared or three sides to create a flat-walled interic The 1st floor was used for passenger se ices, and the 2nd floor was a two-bedr apartment for the ticket agent. Tod Grand Canyon Railway train pulls ir station daily from Williams (see p24

HOPI HOUSE

Another beautiful stone building designed by Mary Colter for Fred Harvey, **Hopi House** (Map p103; 928-638-2631; 8am-8pm May-Aug, 9am-5pm Sep-Apr;) was built largely by Hopi Indians and was finished a few weeks before completion of El Tovar in 1905. It was modeled after the pueblos at Old Oraibi, a Hopi settlement on the Third Mesa in eastern Arizona that vies with Acoma, New Mexico, for the title of longest continually inhabited village in the US. The interior does resemble an ancient pueblo, featuring adobe walls and concrete walls made to look like dirt, corner fireplaces and a timbered ceiling. Exterior ladders and interior staircases connect each story. In the park's early days, Hopi Indians lived here, sold crafts and entertained travelers with nightly dances. Today, it's a wonderful place to shop for high-quality Native American jewelry, basketwork, pottery and other crafts.

VERKAMP'S CURIOS

In 1898 John G Verkamp sold souvenirs from a tent outside Bright Angel Lodge to persevering travelers who arrived at the canyon after long, arduous stagecoach rides. He was a little before his time, however, as there weren't enough customers to make a living, and he closed down his operation after only a few weeks. Arrival of the railroad in 1901 opened up the canyon to more and more tourists, and in 1905 Verkamp returned to build the Craftsman-style **Verkamp's Curios** (Map p103; 928-638-2242; 9am-7pm May-Aug, to 6pm Sep-Apr;) at its present location, beside Hopi House and across the parking lot from El Tovar. He lived on the 2nd floor and sold his wares from the first. Today Verkamp's ancestors run the curio shop.

LOOKOUT STUDIO

Like Mary Colter's other canyon buildings, **Lookout Studio** (c 1914) was modeled after stone dwellings of the Southwest Pueblo Indians. Made of rough-cut Kaibab limestone – e stone that comprises one of the layers the upper canyon walls – with a roof mirrors the lines of the rim, the studio ds into its natural surroundings. The r features an arched stone fireplace, walls and a timber-framed ceiling. Inside, you'll find a small **souvenir shop** (Map p103; 928-638-2631, ext 6087; 8am-sunset) and a tiny back porch that offers spectacular canyon views. There's also stone stairway snaking below Lookout Studio leading to another terrace, which may be closed in bad weather.

KOLB STUDIO

Photographer brothers Ellsworth and Emery Kolb first came to the Grand Canyon from Pennsylvania in 1901 and 1902, respectively. The pioneering brothers built their photography studio in 1904 and made their living photographing parties traveling the Bright Angel Trail. In 1911, after having boats custom-made for the expedition, they filmed their own trip down the Green and Colorado Rivers, and canyon visitors flocked to their small auditorium to see the film, in which both brothers repeatedly tumble into the water. Emery continued to show the film to audiences twice daily until his death at 95 in 1976.

Today, their **studio** (Map p103; 928-638-2771; 8am-7pm), perched on the edge of the canyon, holds a small but well-stocked

PHOTO FINISH

Back in the day, before digital photography or even one-hour processing existed, the Kolb brothers were shooting souvenir photos of mule-riding Grand Canyon visitors as they began their descent down the Bright Angel Trail. In true American entrepreneurial fashion, they'd then sell finished prints to the tourists returning to the rim at the end of the day. Among the adventurous Kolb brothers' many accomplishments, this was one they completed on a regular basis in the early 1900s before there was running water on the South Rim. So how did they process the prints?

After snapping photos from their studio window that strategically overlooked a bend in the trail, one of the brothers would then run 4.6 miles down to the waters of Indian Garden with the negatives, print the photos in their lab there and then run (or perhaps hike briskly) back up the Bright Angel to meet delighted visitors with their mule-straddling mugs in print.

bookstore and an art gallery with changing exhibits. You can still see clips of the original Kolb river picture, though not projected on the big screen nor introduced by the late Emery. Their home, built on two stories and beneath the bookstore, is maintained by the Grand Canyon Association and occasionally opened to the public for tours.

GRAND CANYON CEMETERY

More than 300 people are buried at Grand Canyon Cemetery (Map p103), many whose lives are intricately woven into the history of the canyon, including the Kolb brothers, John Verkamp, Ralph Cameron and John Hance, who ran a hotel a few miles from Grandview Point.

OVERLOOKS

Even if your visit to the canyon is very short, try to carve out some time to simply sit and quietly contemplate this monumental work of nature.

The best times of day to watch the light and shadow bring out the canyon's sculpted features is at sunrise and sunset – of course, these are also prime times for busloads of like-minded visitors to pull up and pile out for photo ops at the most popular overlooks. But you'd be surprised how few of them actually roam beyond the parking lots. Hiking a few minutes along the rim from any overlook is usually all it takes to get you to a secluded spot all your own.

Overlooks are listed here west to east.

Hermits Rest (p112) Stone archway welcomes you to the end of the line.

Pima Point (p111) Good views of Hermit Camp on the Tonto Platform and Hermit Rapids on the Colorado River as well as some sections of the Hermit Trail. A great spot to watch sunrise/sunset.

Abyss (p111) Good place to see very steep walls.

Mohave Point (p111) Great spot to watch sunrise/sunset.

Hopi Point (p111) Great views of various temples and buttes in the canyon.

Powell Point (p111) Standing at this overlook and sharing its name is the Powell Memorial, a monument to none other than John Wesley Powell.

Maricopa Point (p110) Good views of Bright Angel Canyon.

> **TIP**
>
> Check *The Guide* or the kiosk at Desert View Information Plaza for sunrise and sunset times.

Trailview Overlook (p110) Offers an excellent view of most of the Bright Angel Trail and is a very good spot from which to watch hikers and mule trains ascending and descending the trail.

Yavapai Point (p107) A westward alternative to Mather Point, Yavapai gives a good introduction to the lay of the canyon.

Mather Point (p112) With two outcrops, this overlook is the one-stop photo op that's usually crowded with drive-through visitors.

Pipe Creek Vista (p112) A quieter alternative to Mather Point on the same section of the South Rim.

Yaki Point (p112) A superb place to watch the sunrise, with knockout views of several formations.

Shoshone Point (p115) Accessible only by walking, Shoshone Point will reward you with a rocky promontory and some of the canyon's best views.

Grandview Point (p112) Take in expansive views of the canyon from the overlook, or hike down a short way for a bit more solitude.

Moran Point (p113) Excellent view down both directions of the Colorado and of the colorful walls of Red Canyon.

Lipan Point (p113) Magnificent panoramic views taking in the curvy Colorado and the Palisades of the Desert.

Navajo Point (p114) This spot overlooks the river below and vast Navajo Reservation to the east.

Desert View (p114) The South Rim's highest overlook affords views in all directions from the top floor of the Watchtower, as well as from a lower terrace.

> **TOP FIVE OVERLOOKS**
>
> - **Mohave Point** (p111) For a look at the river and three rapids.
> - **Hopi Point** (p111) Catch huge sunset views.
> - **Lipan Point** (p113) Creeks, palisades, rapids and sunrises.
> - **Desert View** (p114) Climb to the top the Watchtower and wave down at river.
> - **Yaki Point** (p112) A favorite poi watch the sunrise warm the ca features.

DRIVING

Two scenic drives hug the rim on either side of the village: Hermit Rd to the west and Desert View Dr to the east. The rim dips in and out of view as the road passes through the piñon-juniper and ponderosa stands of Kaibab National Forest. Pullouts along the way offer spectacular views and interpretive signs that explain the canyon's features and geology.

Millions of visitors simply drive up, jump out of their cars and snap a photo – but photos don't do justice to the enormity of this place.

Take a minute or sixty to walk out, maybe find a quiet place to sit and absorb each view in the present tense. If you're short on time, select a few choice overlooks to enjoy at length. Breathe in the desert air, study the behavior of ravens and the swoop of turkey vultures, peer down at the river and wonder at the forces that carved this canyon.

Though you might expect bumper-to-bumper traffic, this is generally not the case. Yes, there's a constant stream of cars, but you'll rarely come to a standstill and can usually find plenty of parking at the viewpoints. The road to Yaki Point and the South Kaibab Trailhead is closed year-round to all traffic except bicycles and the green Kaibab Trail Route shuttle. From March 1 to November 30, Hermit Rd is closed to all traffic except bicycles and the red Hermits Rest Route shuttle. Both scenic drives may close due to snow or ice buildup from November through March; call ☎ 928-638-7888 for current road and weather conditions.

If you don't have a car or don't want to drive, bus tours (see p106) of both scenic drives leave several times daily year-round. Alternatively, you can hike the Rim Trail ›114) to any of the viewpoints along Her- ‹ Rd. In the heat of summer it's nice to bine shuttle rides with hiking.

the wise: bring water with you on
e – there's no water available until
st.

Books & More Store (p104) sells an audio guide on tape or CD with more information on what you'll see along the rim. Some viewpoints offer good river views, while others are best for sunrises or sunsets. Everyone has a favorite – find your own among the following.

HERMIT ROAD

Duration 2½ hours
Distance 8 miles
Start Grand Canyon Village
Finish Hermits Rest
Nearest Town Grand Canyon Village
Summary Hermit Rd heads out to the western reaches of the Rim Trail all the way to historic Hermits Rest, with exceptional views leading the way.

This popular road offers several exceptional views. It begins at the west end of Grand Canyon Village and ends at Mary Colter's distinctive Hermits Rest, built as a rest stop for early park tourists. Although this drive also makes a great bike ride, the road is very narrow. Because shuttles are not allowed to pass bicycles along Hermit Rd, bicyclists are required to pull off the road to allow vehicles to pass. Hermit Rd is closed to private vehicles from March through November, but the Hermits Rest shuttle route will take you to all the sites detailed here.

Trailview Overlook offers a great view of Bright Angel Trail (p116), the lush vegetation at Indian Garden and Grand Canyon Village on the rim to the east. If you arrive early in the morning, you may see the tiny specks of a faraway mule train descending into the canyon.

In 1890 prospector Daniel Lorain Hogan discovered what he believed to be copper 1100ft below **Maricopa Point**. He filed a mining claim for the area, including 4 acres on the rim, and set about making his fortune. After more than 40 years of minimal success, Hogan realized that the real money at the canyon was in tourism, so in 1936 he built tourist cabins, a trading post and a saloon on the rim. In 1947 he sold the property to Madelaine Jacobs for $25,000.

Ironically, it was Jacobs who would make her fortune off mining interests here. Learning that the gray rock Hogan had ignored in his quest for copper was rich in uranium, she sold out to Western Gold & Uranium. From 1956 through 1969 the Orphan Mine just southwest of this point produced more than a half million tons of uranium ore. Tourists still visited the point during the mining, though the experience must have been somewhat marred by the noise and radioactive dust.

Today, in addition to the wide-angle views of the canyon from Maricopa Point, you can also see the metal remains of the tramway and elevator that moved the ore to the rim. Some areas above the rim are fenced off, in part due to a slight risk from radioactivity.

Perched at Powell Point, the **Powell Memorial** was erected in 1915 in honor of John Wesley Powell, the intrepid one-armed (!) Civil War veteran, ethnologist and geologist who led the first white-water run through the canyon on the Colorado in 1869. It doesn't offer much of a river view, but is a good spot to think about that first brave dive down the unexplored, wild Colorado. The park was officially dedicated at this spot in 1920.

One of the park's best viewpoints, **Hopi Point** juts out further than any other overlook along Hermit Rd and offers huge, spectacular views of plateau upon plateau and the Colorado River a mile below. Notable canyon features here include the Isis and Osiris Temples. Until completion of Hermit Rd in 1912, Hopi Point was the westernmost spot on guided tours. Nowadays, it's a popular place to watch the sunset and is often crowded on summer evenings. If you're here during shuttle season, walking the 0.3-mile segment of the Rim Trail between Powell Point and Hopi Point is a pleasant alternative to getting on the bus.

If you're doing the Grand Canyon speed-demon tour and only have time for a couple stops, make them count at Mohave and Hopi Points. **Mohave Point** serves up a delicious array of cliff views in all directions. It's also a particularly good place to see the Colorado, as three rapids – Salt Creek, Granite and Hermit – are visible below and downstream.

Aptly named, the **Abyss** is a beautiful example of how steep some canyon drop-offs can be. If you're at all acrophobic, consider stopping at a different viewpoint – sheer cliffs drop 2600ft to the Redwall limestone below. If heights don't bother you, walk about a quarter mile westward along the Rim Trail and (carefully) check out the dizzying drop.

The overwhelming maw of the Grand Canyon can truly be appreciated from **Pima Point**, where you can see for miles to the west, north and east. In 1912 the Atchison, Topeka & Santa Fe Railway completed Hermit Camp, a tourist hub with tent cabins, restrooms, showers and a blacksmith forge 3000ft below Pima Point, accessible from a trailhead at Hermits Rest. The camp was a popular mule-train destination, and a tramway was built in 1926 to transport supplies. By 1930, tourists favored Phantom Ranch, the stone lodge and cabins built along the

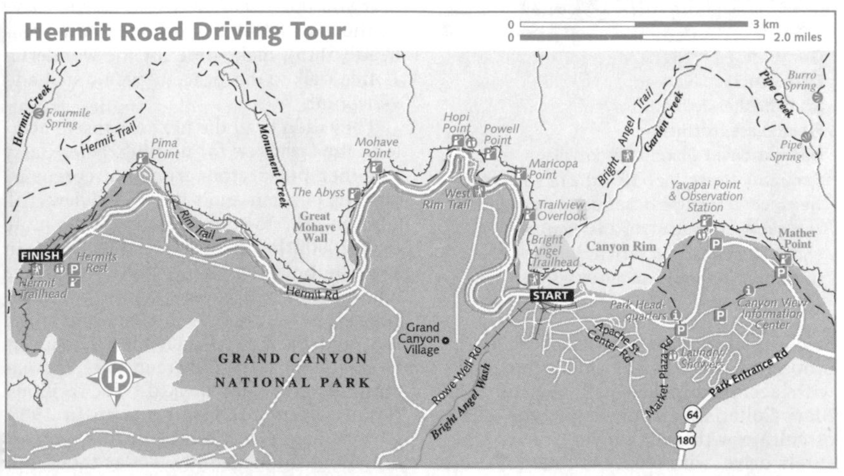

river in 1922, and Hermit Camp was abandoned. In 1936 the railway intentionally torched the camp, the remains of which are still visible from the rim.

Hermits Rest (and Hermit Rd and Hermit Rapid…) is one of the 13 canyon features named after one of the park's most famous residents, Louis Boucher (aka 'The Hermit'). Boucher was a Canadian immigrant who worked as a prospector and tourist guide and lived alone at Dripping Springs in Boucher Canyon, below Hermits Rest, from 1889 to 1912.

Back in the early 1900s, prospector Ralph Cameron held the rights to Bright Angel Trail, prompting the Atchison, Topeka & Santa Fe Railway to develop other trails and services for canyon tourists. In 1909 the railway began work on Hermit Rd. It commissioned none other than Mary Colter to design a resthouse at the end of the road, constructed an 8.5-mile trail from the rim into the canyon and built a camp at the end of the trail. Colter's Hermits Rest, a beautiful stone and wood shelter, offered tourists a place to freshen up before descending into the canyon or after the arduous journey back to the rim.

Today Hermits Rest features a small gift shop and snack bar. You can still take Hermit Trail (p120) into the canyon. If you just want to stretch your legs, hike down about 10 minutes and search the walls for exposed fossil beds.

DESERT VIEW DRIVE

Duration 1–4 hours
Distance 25 miles
Start Mather Point
Finish East Entrance
Nearest Town Grand Canyon Village
Summary Desert View Dr is the red-carpet welcome to the Grand Canyon (sans paparazzi and hype), starting at the East Entrance and including historic architecture, a Native American ruin and inspiring vistas.

Seven well-marked viewpoints (plus an unmarked one), an ancient Puebloan site with accompanying small museum and Mary Colter's Watchtower give you a dash of culture with your canyon views. A leisurely drive, with plenty of time for every stop, takes about four hours. Start early enough and you might be lucky enough to see a loping coyote or grazing mule deer near the road. Desert View Dr could also make an excellent one-way bike ride if you can be dropped off or picked up at one end, or if you don't mind the 50-mile round-trip.

As it sits right beside the parking lot used for Canyon View Information Plaza (300 yards away), **Mather Point** is the most crowded of all the viewpoints. However, its roomy overlooks extend to two promontories that jut out over the canyon, providing views of the Bright Angel and South Kaibab Trails ribboning down into the canyon. Or you can walk 1.3 miles east along the Rim Trail to **Pipe Creek Vista** to escape the crowds. Views from this overlook take in Brahma Temple and O'Neill Butte, as well as Pipe Creek, naturally, and it tends to be less of a traffic circus than Mather Point. From Pipe Creek you can catch the Kaibab Trail Route shuttles (see p106) back to the information plaza.

Closed year-round to private vehicles, **Yaki Point** lies just north of Desert View Dr and is accessed by the green Kaibab Trail Route shuttles. From Yaki Point in 1924 the NPS began the two-year process of blasting rock to create South Kaibab Trail (p117), an effort to bypass Ralph Cameron's Bright Angel Trail. East of the trail, you'll get an excellent look at Zoroaster Temple and Wotan's Throne beyond.

If you don't see many cars as you drive by the unsignposted Shoshone Point Trailhead (p115), make time for the wonderful 1-mile walk to this peaceful picnic spot and viewpoint.

They didn't call the next expansive overlook the **Grandview** for nothing. Peter Berry (another prospector-turned-entrepreneur) and his partners built the Grandview Toll Trail in 1893 to access copper claims more than 2000ft below on Horseshoe Mesa. In 1897 he built the Grand View Hotel here on the rim, and when he wasn't hauling copper, he led tourists into the canyon on foot and by mule. When the railroad arrived 13 miles west of here in 1901, tourists naturally gravitated toward those facilities, forcing Berry to close up shop in 1908. Unfortunately, his mining venture petered out about the same time. Today thousands

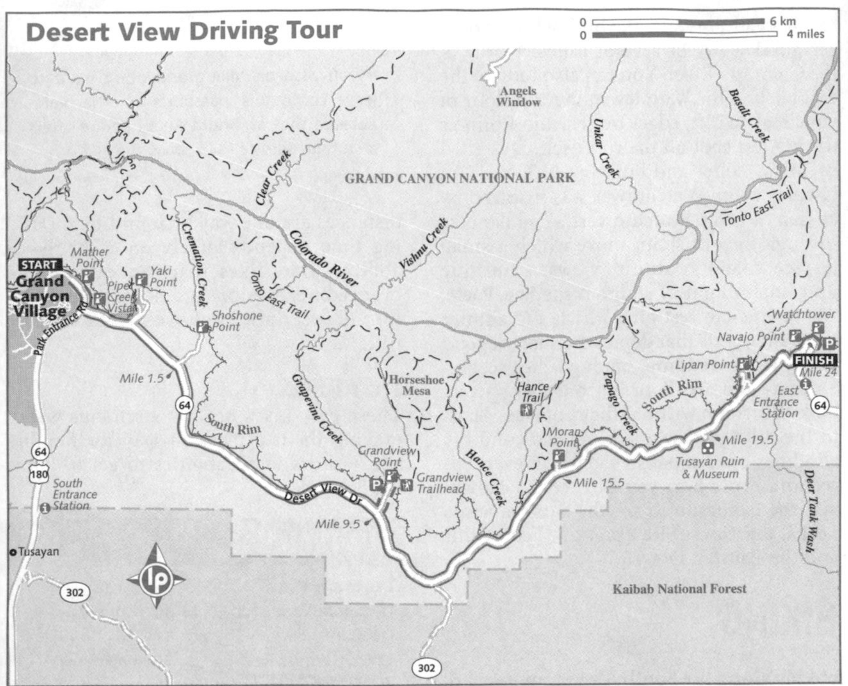

make a steep descent into the canyon via Berry's Grandview Trail (p119), while others enjoy impressive canyon views from the spot where his hotel once thrived.

The oft-visited **Moran Point** is named after Thomas Moran, the landscape painter who spent just about every winter at the canyon from 1899 to 1920 and whose romantically dramatic work was instrumental in securing the canyon's national-park status. From here you can see down the river in both directions, and peer down onto the reddish orange Hakatai shale of Red Canyon below. Particularly in the early morning or evening light, it's easy to see what drew Moran and hundreds of other artists to the canyon.

The tiny **Tusayan Ruins & Museum** (admission free; 9am-5pm) houses only a few displays of pottery and jewelry, but the 4000-year-old twig figures of animals (see p84) on exhibit are worth a stop at this beautiful little stone building. From here you can take a short self-guided walk through the remains of an **ancient Pueblo village** that was excavated in 1930. Tree-ring analyses date the structure to 1185, and archaeologists estimate that about 30 people lived here. Much of the village has been left only partially excavated in order to prevent excessive erosion damage to the unrestored room sections and kiva (ceremonial chamber). Look in *The Guide* for details on ranger-led tours. This is a shaded area with bathrooms, but there are no canyon views.

One of the most spectacular viewpoints on the South Rim, **Lipan Point** gives a panoramic eyeful of the canyon and makes a magnificent spot to watch the sunset. From here, you'll get an unobstructed view of Unkar Rapid just to the west. You can also catch glimpses of both 75-Mile Creek and Unkar Creek, which feed into either side of the Colorado; on the north bank, look for the gentle slopes of Unkar Delta at the sinuous kink in the river. To the northeast, the sheer cliffs called the Palisades of the Desert define the southeastern wall of the Grand Canyon, beyond which the Echo and Vermilion Cliffs lie in the distance.

The Escalante and Cardenas Buttes a the immediate features you'll see fr

Navajo Point (7498ft), beyond which you'll get good views of several miles' worth of the Colorado River. You can also look to the east back at the **Watchtower**, the top floor of which, at 7522ft, edges out Navajo Point as the highest spot on the rim itself. Designed by Mary Colter and built in 1932, the 70ft circular stone Watchtower was inspired by ancient Pueblo watchtowers. You'll enter through the gift shop, above which a small terrace offers beautiful views. Continue up a small flight of stairs to the **Hopi Room**, where you can rest on a bench and admire the wall murals that depict the snake legend and a Hopi wedding, among other scenes. Second- and 3rd-floor balconies also overlook this room. A final flight of steps leads to the 4th floor, where binoculars and big windows offer expansive views in every direction. From here you can see the canyon and the Colorado River, the San Francisco Peaks, the Navajo Reservation, Echo Cliffs and the Painted Desert.

HIKING

Hiking along the South Rim is among park visitors' favorite pastimes, with options for every skill level. The popular river-bound corridor trails (Bright Angel and South Kaibab) span the 7 to 10 miles to the canyon floor, following paths etched thousands of years ago by drainage routes. Several turnaround spots make these trails ideal for day hikes of varying lengths. Both can get packed during summer with foot and mule traffic. For more solitude, opt for a less-trodden trail like Hermit or Grandview.

Most of the trails start with a super-steep series of switchbacks that descend quickly to the dramatic ledge of Coconino sandstone about 2 miles beneath the rim. Hike another 3 miles and you'll hit the sun-baked Tonto Platform, which after another couple miles opens up to inner gorge vistas. From the platform it's a fast and furious pitch to the canyon floor and Colorado River. Most day hikers will want to stay above the Tonto Platform, particularly in summer.

Day hiking requires no permit, just preparation and safety. In the following descriptions, we specify whether the listed distances are one way or round-trip. (Hiking time depends largely on each hiker's ability.) Day hikes that can extend into overnight excursions are noted in the text; for full descriptions of overnight hikes, see p122.

> **TIP**
>
> If you plan on hiking and don't want to leave computers, passports or other valuables in the car, Bright Angel Lodge offers a storage service for a small fee.

EASY HIKES

These easy hikes are not strenuous walks, making them a pleasant way for families and visitors of all abilities to get to know the South Rim.

RIM TRAIL

Duration Varies
Distance Varies (up to 13 miles one way)
Difficulty Easy–moderate
Start Hermits Rest
Finish Pipe Creek Vista
Nearest Town Grand Canyon Village
Transportation Shuttle
Summary The Rim Trail can be walked in its entirety in a day with stops at scenic viewpoints, or explored in short segments by hopping on and off the shuttles.

Stretching from Hermits Rest on the rim's western edge through Grand Canyon Village to Pipe Creek Vista and with an elevation change of a mere 200ft, the Rim Trail connects a series of scenic points and is hands down the easiest long walk in the park. By no means a nature trail, it's paved from Maricopa Point (1.5 miles west of Kolb Studio) to Pipe Creek Vista (1.3 miles), which makes it accessible to wheelchairs and more easily navigable for those with mobility issues.

Still, flexibility is a big draw, with the shuttles making it simple to jump on for a segment and hike for as long as you like. Every viewpoint from Hermits Rest to Yaki Point is accessed by one of three shuttle routes, which means you can walk to a vista and shuttle back, or shuttle to a point, walk to the next and shuttle from there. A helpful map inside *The Guide* shows the shuttle stops and hiking distances along each segment of the trail.

The trail passes many of the park's historical sights, including **El Tovar**, **Hopi House**, **Kolb Studio**, **Lookout Studio** and **Verkamp's Curios**. The 3 miles or so that wind through the village are usually packed with people, but the further west you venture, the more you'll break free from the crowds. Out there the trail runs between Hermit Rd and the rim, and though some segments bump up against the road, elsewhere you can't hear a sound from the shuttle buses.

One very pretty stretch is the mile east of **Pima Point**, where the trail is set far back from the road, offering stunning views and relative solitude. Winding through piñon-juniper woodlands, it passes several viewpoints; see the Hermit Rd drive (p111) for details. **Mohave** and **Hopi Points** offer great views of the Colorado River, with three visible rapids (Salt Creek, Granite and Hermit) below and downstream.

Its accessibility makes the Rim Trail a terrific option for families. It's also a lovely stroll at sunrise, sunset or under a starry sky, times when the crowds really thin out. Runners also favor this trail before the heat hits. When you first arrive in the park, stretch your legs along the trail to take in the canyon air and get the lay of the land.

SHOSHONE POINT

Duration 40 minutes round-trip
Distance 2 miles round-trip
Difficulty Easy
Start/Finish Shoshone Point Trailhead
Nearest Town Grand Canyon Village
Transportation Car
Summary With an elevation change of only 50ft and a sandy trail through ponderosa forest, Shoshone Point puts solitude within easy reach.

The gentle and cool amble out to Shoshone Point, accessible only by foot or bike, can be a welcome pocket of peace during the summer heat and crowds. This little-known hike is also ideal for children. Chances are you won't see another person, which means you can have the spectacular views all to yourself.

The trail starts from a dirt pullout along Desert View Dr, 1.2 miles east of Yaki Point or 6.3 miles west of Grandview Point. There's no official trailhead or signpost, so look for the dirt road barred by a closed and locked gate. The park service deliberately downplays this trail, which they kindly make available from May to October for weddings and other private events. If the parking lot is full of cars, refrain from hiking out, out of respect for any private events taking place. When it hasn't been reserved for a special gathering, and during winter months, hikers are welcome on the trail. Because the trail is sandy, it isn't wheelchair-friendly, and you'll have to saddle up a mountain bike to ride out here.

It's a fast and mostly flat out-and-back walk along the forested trail, which weaves through fragrant ponderosa pines before opening up in a clearing. This is a great spot for a family gathering, as you'll find picnic tables, BBQ grills and portable toilets. Nearby Shoshone Point juts out into the canyon, offering magnificent views of the North Rim's full sweep. Unlike the other scenic points, there are no safety railings here. You can walk to the tip of the slender plateau and its Easter Island moai-like formation, where it feels almost possible to reach out and touch **Zoroaster Temple**.

DAY HIKES

The South Rim offers excellent day hikes for all levels and persuasions. See p251 for safe hiking tips.

Note that some primitive trails not mentioned here are outlined in Scott Thybony's excellent *Official Guide to Hiking Grand Canyon*, available at park bookstores. These trails are better suited to experienced canyon hikers, but for anyone who ventures down them it's important to leave your itinerary with someone, as these trails are not regularly patrolled.

TIP

When hiking out of the canyon, it help gauge your progress by stopping occa ally to look back at how far you've cli instead of only up toward the ri can sometimes feel daunting whelming, especially when yo

BRIGHT ANGEL TRAIL – SHORT DAY HIKE

Duration 2–3 hours round-trip; 4–5 hours round-trip
Distance Mile-and-a-Half Resthouse 3 miles round-trip; Three-Mile Resthouse 6 miles round-trip
Difficulty Moderate–difficult
Start/Finish Bright Angel Trailhead
Nearest Town Grand Canyon Village
Transportation Shuttle
Summary Test out your canyon legs with a hike to either resthouse on the well-traveled Bright Angel Trail; bonuses on the Bright Angel are merciful shade and water.

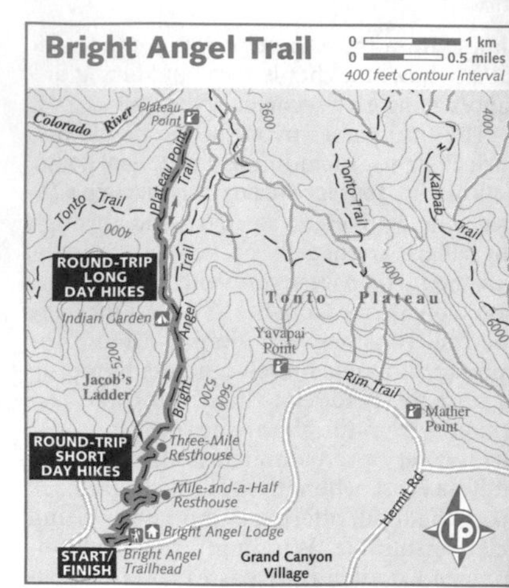

The most popular of the corridor trails, the Bright Angel is wide, well graded and easy to follow. It's equally attractive to first-time canyon hikers and seasoned pros, as well as mule trains, making it a heavily trafficked route. But the din doesn't lessen the sheer beauty. The steep and scenic 7.8-mile descent to the Colorado is punctuated with four logical turnaround spots, including two well-appointed resthouses for opportunities to seek shade and hydrate. Even if you're wary of crowds, you won't regret taking a jaunt of some length on the Bright Angel.

The trail follows a natural route along the Bright Angel Fault and was first used by the Havasupai to reach the glistening water source at Indian Garden and the inner canyon recesses. In the late 19th century, miners improved the trail, enlisted the help of mules and began charging a toll for usage. While numerous individuals and groups, including the Atchison, Topeka & Santa Fe Railway, wrangled for control, the reins eventually went to the NPS in 1928.

There are both shade and seasonal water on the Bright Angel (unlike the South Kaibab). Still, the summer heat can be crippling;
ay hikers should either turn around at one
the two resthouses (a 3- to 6-mile round-
or hit the trail at dawn to safely make
nger hikes to Indian Garden and Plant (see the Long Day Hike, opposite).
the Colorado for the day is not an
ecially during the summer.

head of the oft-crowded Bright
is smack in Grand Canyon
west of Kolb Studio and Bright Angel Lodge. There's ample nearby parking, or you can take the shuttle bus to the Hermits Rest transfer stop and walk from there. The piñon-fringed trail quickly drops into some serious switchbacks as it follows a natural break in the cliffs of Kaibab limestone, the Toroweap formation and Coconino sandstone. The trail soon passes through two tunnels – look for the Indian pictographs on the walls of the first. After passing through the second, **Mile-and-a-Half Resthouse**, 1131ft and

HISTORY OF THE BRIGHT ANGEL

In one form or another, the Bright Angel Trail has been in continuous use for thousands of years. It was originally forged by the Havasupai Indians to access present-day Indian Garden, where they grew crops and farmed until the early 20th century. In the early 1890s prospectors Ralph Cameron and Pete Berry – who built the Grand View Hotel – improved the trail, eventually extending it to the river. Seeing a golden opportunity, in 1903 Cameron imposed a $1 toll on anyone using the trail, a widely criticized decision. In response, the Atchison, Topeka & Santa Fe Railway and others constructed toll-free alternative trails, such as the Hermit, to draw the burgeoning mule tourism trade. In 1928 the park service took the reins of the Bright Angel and lifted the toll, thus ending mule traffic on the Hermit.

nearly an hour's hike from the top, comes into view. It has restrooms, an emergency phone and drinking water from May to September. Turning around here makes for a 2½-hour round-trip.

Continuing downward through different colored rock layers, more switchbacks eventually deposit you 2112ft down at **Three-Mile Resthouse**, which has seasonal water and an emergency phone but no restrooms. Down below, you'll see the iridescent green tufts of Indian Garden tucked into a canyon fold, as well as the broad expanse of Tonto Platform, a nice visual reward before beginning the ascent back to the rim. First-time Grand Canyon hikers should strongly consider making this their turnaround point.

BRIGHT ANGEL TRAIL – LONG DAY HIKE

Duration 5–7 hours round-trip; 8–10 hours round-trip
Distance Indian Garden 9.2 miles round-trip; Plateau Point 12.2 miles round-trip
Difficulty Difficult
Start/Finish Bright Angel Trailhead
Nearest Town Grand Canyon Village
Transportation Shuttle
Summary Continuing down the Bright Angel brings you to the shady oasis of Indian Garden; for a more challenging and very exposed hike, cross Tonto Platform to reach Plateau Point for gorgeous views of the inner gorge. Distances and durations for these hikes reflect round-trips from trailhead to turnaround and back. Follow the Short Day Hike description (opposite) and continue from Three-Mile Resthouse using the following hike description.

If you're continuing down from Three-Mile Resthouse, you'll soon hit a grueling set of switchbacks known as **Jacob's Ladder**, which twist through Redwall limestone cliffs. A bridge ferries you across the transcanyon water pipeline, and soon after you descend into the cool leafiness of **Indian Garden**, where Havasupai still farmed up until a century ago. These days, it's a popular campground, with a ranger station, toilets, year-round drinking water, shaded picnic tables and a mule corral. If this is your day-hike destination, linger in the soothing, albeit crowded, spot: eat lunch under a cottonwood, nap on the grass and splash your feet in the creek. With an elevation gain of 3060ft, it's a hard and hot 4.6-mile climb back up to the rim – particularly the thigh-burning Jacob's Ladder. The round-trip takes about seven hours with a rest here.

From the campground, if you turn left and head west across Garden Creek, you'll soon reach the **Plateau Point Trail** junction, a spur off the Tonto Trail. This ribbon of a trail unfurls north for just under a mile over the flat, barren and yucca-studded **Tonto Plateau**, dead-ending at **Plateau Point** (3120ft below the rim) for a stunning view of the inner gorge. Though it's a popular year-round destination for strong day hikers, rangers nonetheless discourage anyone from making the round-trip trek in summer. The long, exposed stretch can be brutally hot, with the 12-mile round-trip taking up to 10 hours.

From Indian Garden, Bright Angel continues north to the river and is soon intersected by the east–west Tonto Trail. For a description of overnight hikes along the Bright Angel, see p122.

SOUTH KAIBAB

Duration 1–2 hours round-trip; 3–5 hours round-trip
Distance Cedar Ridge 3 miles round-trip; Skeleton Point 6 miles round-trip
Difficulty Moderate; moderate–difficult
Start/Finish South Kaibab Trailhead
Nearest Town Grand Canyon Village
Transportation Shuttle
Summary Day-hike destinations on the South Kaibab give hikers a steep, stark and rewarding challenge on this spectacular South Rim spine; but this party is BYO water, as the trail has no water sources.

One of the park's prettiest trails, the South Kaibab combines stunning scenery and adventurous hiking with every step. The only corridor trail to follow a ridgeline in- stead of a drainage route, the red-dirt pa traverses the spine of a crest, allowing unobstructed 360-degree views. Blaste of the rock by rangers in the mid-192 South Kaibab is steep, rough and wh posed. The dearth of shade and wa bined with the sheer grade, make the South Kaibab particularly d

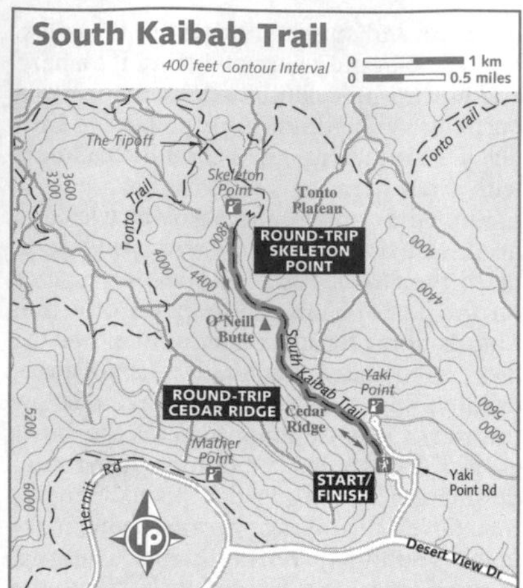

summer, and rangers discourage all but the shortest of day hikes. The main passersby during summer are mule trains taking the shortest route to Phantom Ranch, backpackers planning to ascend Bright Angel and day hikers out for a quick peek. The trail sees a fair number of rescues, with up to a half-dozen on a hot June day. Even if you're just hiking a few miles, plan on bringing a gallon of water.

Summer day hikers should turn around at **Cedar Ridge**, perhaps the park's finest short day hike. Up to a two-hour round-trip with a 1140ft change in elevation, Cedar Ridge is a dazzling spot, particularly at sunrise, when the deep ruddy umbers and reds of each canyon fold seem to glow from within. This hike can also be done with a ranger, see p129. During the rest of the year, the continued trek to Skeleton Point, 1.5 miles beyond Cedar Ridge and 2040ft below the rim, makes for a fine day hike – though the climb back up is a beast in any season.

The trailhead is 4.5 miles east of Grand Canyon Village along Yaki Point Rd, just shy of the point itself. To keep crowds n check during high season, you're only rmitted to park at the trailhead between ember and February; all other times re- a ride aboard either the Kaibab Trail shuttle (p106) or the far more direct Express shuttle (p106). Water and available at the trailhead.

e mule corral the trail starts out gentle, with a long, well-graded switchback that leads to the end of a promontory about 20 minutes from the top. Here the cliff-hugging trail opens up to a shaggy promontory, which juts off the elbow of a switchback and offers a sweeping panorama of the purplish Tonto Platform far below. The ledge, unfortunately dubbed 'Ooh Aah Point,' is a nice spot for rest and refreshment. It's also a good juncture to gauge how you're feeling and consider turning back, ascending the 780ft to the top for a round-trip hike of a little over 1.5 miles.

Soon after, things turn serious, as the trail takes a sharp nosedive and begins to zigzag down a series of steep, tight switchbacks, making its way down the red sandstone. After about 30 minutes, the trail straightens out some when it hits the gorgeous **Cedar Mesa** and its namesake ridge, a striking red-tinged mesa. Stop long enough for a snack and perhaps a visit to the pit toilet. But what you'll linger for are the lovely vast views of Bright Angel Canyon, Devil's Corkscrew and the North Rim. This is considered the last 'safe' turnaround in summer, and the ascent from here takes one to two hours.

The trail then meanders off the mesa toward **O'Neill Butte**, wraps around to the east, then levels out onto another plateau known as **Skeleton Point**, from which you can see the Colorado River. From here settle in for a hefty, scree-covered descent on switchbacks that grind through the Redwall

TOP POSTHIKE TREATS

Recharge and reward yourself with a tasty snack after a long, hot day on the trail:

- **Canyon Crunch Ice Cream** (Bright Angel Fountain; p133) Peanut-butter ice cream swirled with a fudge ribbon, chunks of granola, crispy rice and peanuts.
- **Hiker's Caesar** (Bright Angel Restaurant; p134) Romaine lettuce, grilled chicken breast, tomatoes and crisp veggies dressed in Caesar and Parmesan.
- **Prickly Pear Margarita** (El Tovar; p106) Tequila, prickly pear syrup and lime over ice; for complete electrolyte replenishment (ahem), be sure to order this pink drink with salt.

limestone before fanning out onto the flat skirt of the Tonto Plateau. After traversing the platform, you'll reach its edge and the junction of the Tonto Trail, some two to three hours from the top.

About 19 miles to the east, the Tonto connects with the Grandview Trail (below), while 4.1 miles to the west are Indian Garden and Bright Angel Trail, making for a terrific long day hike (see p121). For a description of backcountry hikes on the South Kaibab, see p122.

GRAND VIEW TRAIL

Duration 1–2 hours round-trip; 4–6 hours round-trip
Distance Coconino Saddle 1.5 miles round-trip; Horseshoe Mesa 6 miles round-trip
Difficulty Moderate–difficult; difficult
Start/Finish Grandview Trailhead
Nearest Town Grand Canyon Village
Transportation Shuttle
Summary The Grandview is the bee's knees for stunning views and solitude – but also a knee-killer; in this case, the pain is your grand gain.

One of the steepest trails in the park – dropping 1200ft in the first three-quarters of a mile – Grandview is also one of the finest and most popular day hikes. The payoff following the stunning (and grueling) descent is an up-close look at one of the inner canyon's sagebrush-tufted mesas and a spectacular sense of solitude. The trail spirals down to a sprawling horseshoe-shaped mesa, where Hopi people once collected minerals.

In 1892 miner Pete Berry improved the former Native American route and constructed the current trail to access his Last Chance Mine at Horseshoe Mesa. For the next 15 years mules carted high-grade copper from there to the rim (see Grand View Hotel, p94).

The trailhead, right beside where the hotel once stood, is at Grandview Point, 12 miles east of the village on Desert View Dr, with year-round parking. While rangers don't recommend the trek to Horseshoe Mesa in summer (there's no water on the very exposed trail, and the climb out is a doozy), it's not overly long and certainly doable for strong hikers strapped with a hydration system and hiking early or late. For a shorter but still rewarding option, you can hike to Coconino Saddle and turn around there. Though it's only a 1.5-mile round-trip, it packs a quick and precipitous punch as you plunge 1600ft over less than a mile. With the exception of a few short level sections, the Grandview is a rugged, narrow and rocky trail and probably not the best choice for those skittish of heights or occasional loose footing. The steep drop-offs can be a bit scary, but although the trail is no longer maintained, Berry's metal-reinforced switchbacks have held up quite nicely.

Steep from the start, the trail first wends down the north end of **Grandview Point** and Kaibab limestone along cobbled and cliff-edged rock stairs fringed with occasional flowers like fiery orange Indian paintbrush, straw-yellow arnica and blue delphinium. The views from the trailhead and just below are extraordinary, so even if you don't plan to hike, do walk down the trail a short way to take in the vistas. After about 30 or so minutes, you'll reach the **Coconino Saddle**, where the trail crosses the slender spur between Hance and Grapevine Canyons.

The saddle is a stunning overlook and a nice leafy spot for a snack and a rest in the shade. From here the trail is more exposed and eventually narrows to a ribbon as it traverses the ruddy Supai sandstone. A little over 2 miles past Coconino you'll hit a second saddle, connecting to **Horseshoe Mesa**, then a short dip later reach pit toilets and remnants of old miners' cabins. There are traces of mining all over the mesa, from the speckled soil to old machinery and mineshafts. Although the many hollowed-out caves may look enticing, it's forbidden, not to mention very dangerous, to enter them.

For backpackers, three different trails descend 1000ft from Horseshoe Mesa to t
Tonto Trail; the easiest to follow is the
that heads west near the pit toilets. Ta
to hike a 7-mile loop around the foot
mesa, following the Tonto and East
shoe Mesa Trails and rejoining G
a little ways up from the mesa, m
16.6-mile round-trip from the
ing overnight on Horseshoe

Tonto requires a backcountry permit (p44). From the Tonto you can also hike 7 miles east to join the primitive New Hance Trail, or 20 miles west to the South Kaibab Trail (p117).

HERMIT TRAIL

Duration 2–4 hours round-trip
Distance Santa Maria Spring 5 miles round-trip
Difficulty Moderate–difficult
Start/Finish Hermits Rest
Nearest Town Grand Canyon Village
Transportation Shuttle
Summary Unmaintained Hermit Trail winds down into the often-shady and usually unpopulated Hermit Canyon, connecting with several other trails to secluded canyon nooks.

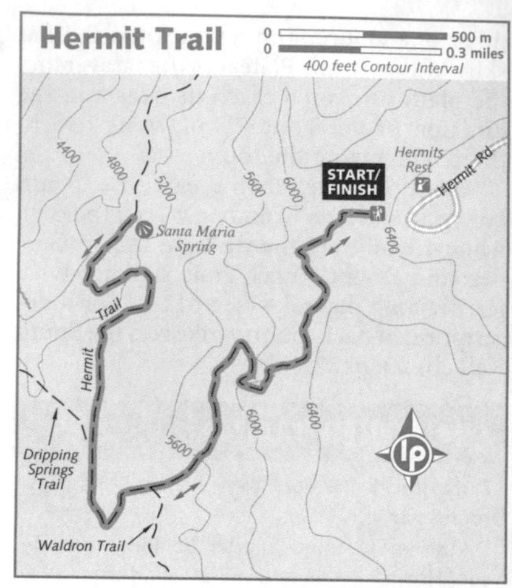

This wilderness trail descends into lovely Hermit Canyon by way of a cool spring. It's a rocky trip down, with some knee-wrenching switchbacks and long traverses that wend through the Supai cliffs. But if you set out early in the morning and take it slow, the Hermit offers a wonderfully serene day hike and glimpses into hidden corners. Offering several good turnaround spots and a clear shot to the Colorado River, the trail is equally appealing to both day hikers and backcountry adventurers.

In 1912 the Atchison, Topeka & Santa Fe Railway developed the trail (originally called El Tovar) for tourists to avoid tolls on the then privately controlled Bright Angel Trail. Mule trains ferried travelers to cushy Hermit Camp, which boasted a fancy stone cabin outfitted with a stove, glass windows, beds, and wood floors adorned with Navajo rugs. Supplies arrived via tram from Pima Point.

The trail was eventually renamed in honor of Louis 'The Hermit' Boucher (see Hermits est, p112). When the NPS gained con- of Bright Angel in 1928, luring away mule tourism business, the Hermit was oned. Though officially untended hen, the trail is in remarkably good n.

t destinations for day hikers are aria Spring (5 miles round-trip, tion change) or to Dripping Springs via a spur trail (6.5 miles round-trip, 1440ft elevation change). For a shorter but still worthwhile hike, turn around at the Waldron Trail junction in Waldron Basin, a round-trip of just under 3 miles with 1240ft of elevation change. The upper section of the Hermit is well shaded in the morning, making it a cool option in summer.

The **Hermit Trailhead** is at the end of its namesake road, 8 miles west of Grand Canyon Village and about 500ft from Hermits Rest. Although the road is only accessible via shuttle bus during the summer peak season, overnight backpackers are permitted to park at the lot near the trailhead throughout the year, and day hikers may do so in winter.

The rocky trail weaves down Hermit Basin toward Hermit Creek along a cobblestone route indented with steps and fraught with washouts. You'll reach the rarely used **Waldron Trail** (jutting off to the south) after about 1.5 miles and 1240ft of descent, followed some 30 minutes later by the spur trail headed for Dripping Springs (opposite). The trail then traces over some flat rocks (a perfect picnic spot) before descending steeply to **Santa Maria Spring**, a cool, shady haven, marked by a pretty stone shelter adorned with green foliage and a welcome wooden bench. The lush scene belies the spring, however, which is actually more of a trickle. You can drink the water provided you treat it.

DRIPPING SPRINGS TRAIL

Duration 3–5 hours round-trip
Distance 7 miles round-trip
Difficulty Moderate–difficult
Start/Finish Hermits Rest
Nearest Town Grand Canyon Village
Transportation Shuttle
Summary An excellent day hike with an elevation change of 1440ft, Dripping Springs is a must-do for South Rim hikers curious to see why Louis Boucher made this secluded spot his home.

What better reason to tackle a hike than to answer the question 'What would the Hermit do?' The trailhead at which you will address this inquiry is at Hermits Rest, and for the first 2 miles you'll be on the Hermit Trail (opposite). At the junction with the Dripping Springs Trail, turn left and head west along the narrow path as it climbs and meanders along the slope's contours. In a mile you'll hit the Boucher Trail and turn left, following the Dripping Springs Trail as it wends up toward the water source, which sprouts from an overhang not far beneath the rim. Droplets shower down from the sandstone ceiling, misting a myriad of maidenhair ferns, and here you will find your answers.

TONTO TRAIL (SOUTH KAIBAB TO BRIGHT ANGEL)

Duration 7–9 hours one way
Distance 13.1 miles one way
Difficulty Very difficult
Start South Kaibab Trailhead
Finish Bright Angel Trailhead
Nearest Town Grand Canyon Village
Transportation Shuttle
Summary A stellar choice for strong hikers seeking solitude, this full-day excursion links two popular corridor trails along a peaceful, winding section of the Tonto Trail – but time it right to avoid charring your epidermis and brain. Distance and duration given for this hike are from start to finish; the hike description, however, details the section linking the South Kaibab and Bright Angel trails.

You want a piece of this? It's a long, difficult hike that's best suited for any season but summer. That said, it is doable in the hot months, provided you're on the trail by 5am and are a truly (be honest!) experienced desert hiker. The Tonto is an unpatrolled wilderness trail with no facilities along its undulating, sun-baked desert terrain – under no circumstances is this route an option for moderate hikers during the summer.

The full Tonto is a 95-mile east–west passage along the entire length of the Tonto Platform, from Red Canyon to Garnet Canyon. Unlike the corridor trails, the Tonto does not extend to the rim, nor does it involve significant elevation change, remaining around 4000ft. But it is by no means easy or level – this 4.1-mile section of the Tonto linking the South Kaibab and Bright Angel trails jumps up and down as it follows the contours and drainage routes while paralleling the river and rim. The Tonto crosses numerous trails, including the Grandview, then 20 miles west the South Kaibab, and another 13 miles west the Hermit. Most hikers hop on the Tonto to connect to other trails. The segment described here – from The Tipoff on South Kaibab to Indian Garden on Bright Angel – is considered the central portion and is officially referred to as the Tonto Trail.

From the South Kaibab Trailhead it's a bone-jarring and hot 4.4-mile descent to the Tonto Trail junction, dropping 3260ft in elevation to the edge of the Tonto Platform. Just past the junction there's an emergency telephone and a toilet, a final reminder you're about to set foot on wilder, unpatrolled terrain.

Heading west on the Tonto, you'll hug the contours as the trail crosses the agave-dotted plateau and darts in and out of gulches. Deep in a canyon fold, the trail skirts through a canopy of cottonwoods near a drainage; just past here on the left is a terrific spot for camping (for backcountry permit information, see p44). The trail remains in shade through midmorning. As the day progresse
however, the Tonto bakes and the surrour
ing landscape is completely parched –
don't want to be caught here midday in
mer, so it's imperative you time you
accordingly. After about two hou
stumble into lush **Indian Garden**, th
shady oasis for cooling off befo
up to the rim. From here it's

and mule-churned 4.6 miles up the Bright Angel – but take heart, the first 1.5 miles are the toughest.

BACKCOUNTRY HIKES

Without venturing below the rim, it's impossible to truly appreciate the grandeur and depth – both literal and figurative – of the Grand Canyon, one of the world's deepest chasms. Hiking down through ancient layers of rock is a singularly surreal journey through geologic time, and the difference in ecology between rim and river is truly unique. Outdoor enthusiasts should plan to spend at least a night or two in the inner gorge to explore side canyons and tributaries of the rich wilderness along the Colorado.

Overnight hikes into the canyon require a backcountry permit, for which applications are taken up to four months in advance. If you didn't secure a backcountry permit in advance, try your luck at the Backcountry Information Center (p104), where walk-ins can fill vacancies or cancellations. Typically, you'll be waitlisted for several days before snagging one; see p44 for more detailed information.

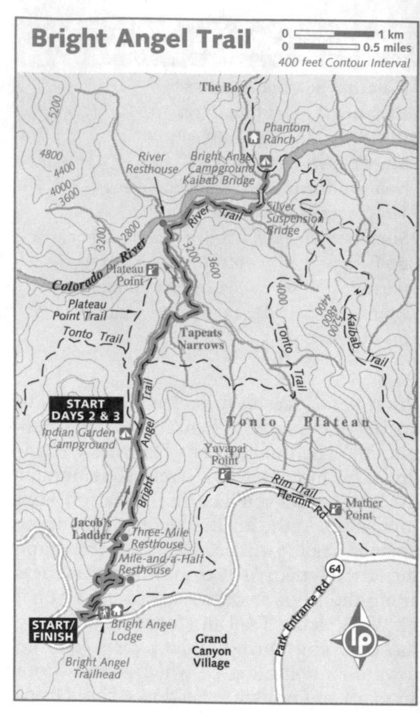

BRIGHT ANGEL TRAIL

Duration 3 days
Distance 18.6 miles round-trip
Difficulty Difficult
Start/Finish Bright Angel Trailhead
Nearest Town Grand Canyon Village
Transportation Shuttle
Summary The most popular path from the rim to the river, the Bright Angel is well maintained and easy-to-follow – fun for first-time canyon hikers and veterans alike.

The Bright Angel, a corridor trail that's wide and well-maintained, opens onto sweeping canyon views that take your mind ff the knee-pounding 7.8-mile, 4380ft de- nt to the Colorado River. Because of its ssibility, it tends to be well traveled at mes of day, but its benefits include spots on the trail and seasonal water

th follows a natural break in the Bright Angel Fault as it winds e productive freshwater spring at Indian Garden and on to the inner canyon. Native Americans were the first to use the route. Arriving in the late 19th century, prospectors improved the trail, introduced mules and began charging a toll. Tourism quickly outpaced mining, and by 1928 the NPS gained control.

Between mid-May and mid-September, extreme heat and sun mandate shorter hiking days. The NPS often restricts summer hiking to mornings and evenings, keeping hikers off the trail between 10am and 4pm. Plan to start hiking at first light – 4:30am in summer and 6:30am in spring and fall. Take advantage of the trail's four day-use resthouses to get out of the sun and hydrate. These open-walled, roofed enclosures offer shade, picnic tables, nearby toilets and an emergency telephone. The two upper resthouses provide drinking water from May to September.

Mules have the right-of-way, so hikers must step aside for mule trains to pass. In winter and early spring the upper reaches can be icy, and you may want to wear crampons.

DAY 1: BRIGHT ANGEL TRAILHEAD TO INDIAN GARDEN CAMPGROUND

2–3 hours; 4.6 miles

The Bright Angel Trailhead (6860ft) is both exhilarating and intimidating. The canyon unfolds before you in all its glory, hikers bustle around making last-minute adjustments to their backpacks, and wranglers acquaint first-time mule riders (is there any other kind?) with the curious beasts. You may even reread the interpretive sign at the trailhead to delay your first steps down a trail that looks like it drops off the edge of the planet.

Start slowly. If you suffer vertigo, look to the left for a while or just stop and close your eyes – the first five minutes are the hardest. Before you know it, you'll grow accustomed and the trail gets interesting.

Quickly pass through **First Tunnel**. Indian pictographs adorn the wall above the piñon- and juniper-lined trail. After passing through **Second Tunnel**, you'll reach **Mile-and-a-Half Resthouse** (5720ft), about 45 minutes from the trailhead. Anyone starting late or hiking for the first time should turn around here, allowing two to three hours round-trip.

About 200 yards before **Two-Mile Corner** look for more pictographs on a boulder. As you approach **Three-Mile Resthouse** (4920ft), about 90 minutes from the trailhead, your views expand over the Redwall limestone cliffs to Indian Garden and Tonto Platform below. Day hikers turning back here should allow four to five hours round-trip.

The switchbacks of **Jacob's Ladder** descend through sheer Redwall cliffs. Beyond, mesquite clumps grow from seasonal streambeds as you cross the transcanyon water pipeline and reach Indian Garden, 45 minutes from Three-Mile Resthouse. Havasupai Indians farmed here until the early 20th century.

The year-round **Indian Garden Campground** (3800ft; 50-camper limit) is an inviting stop, with cottonwoods, a ranger station, a toilet and a resthouse with picnic tables. Year-round drinking water is available just before the Plateau Point Trail junction. Each of the campground's 15 sites offers a picnic table shaded by an open-walled, roofed enclosure. Indian Garden is a day-hike destination only for stronger hikers, who should allow five to seven hours round-trip.

DAY 2: DAY HIKE TO COLORADO RIVER

6–8 hours; 9.4 miles

Passing the Tonto Trail junction after a half-mile, the Bright Angel Trail follows year-round Garden Creek as it cuts through the dramatic sandstone cliffs of **Tapeats Narrows**. Below, you'll cross the creek twice before arriving at a barren saddle.

In front of you is **Devils Corkscrew**, a massive set of switchbacks through the arid Vishnu schist (the oldest exposed rock of the canyon's

RIM TO RIM

The three-day South Kaibab to North Kaibab trek is the classic Grand Canyon rim-to-rim hike and one of the finest trips in the canyon. Backpackers can start on either rim, though the climb up the South Kaibab is the hottest and most exposed in the park. Thus the majority of hikers begin the hike from Yaki Point, descending 6.4 miles to the Colorado River and Bright Angel Campground. From there it's 7 miles to Cottonwood Campground for the second night, and a final 6.8-mile climb up to the North Rim.

You'll need a backcountry permit (p44) to do the hike, and a lift home. Thank goodness for the nifty **Trans-Canyon Shuttle** (☎ 928-638-2820; PO Box 348, Grand Canyon, AZ 86023; one way $70; 🕑 mid-May–mid-Oct). Between mid-May and mid-October, the shuttle departs daily from Grand Canyon Lodge on the North Rim at 7am, arrives at Bright Angel Lodge on the South Rim around 11:30am, and then makes the return trip at 1:30pm, arriving back at the North Rim around 6pm. You must reserve a seat on the shuttle beforehand with a deposit for half the fare (for eac passenger), and credit cards are not accepted. Tip: don't blow all your money on snacks and b at the Phantom Ranch canteen – the shuttle only accepts cash!

Remember that no facilities on the North Rim are open between mid-October and mi and that the weather can be unpredictable – you could leave warm, sunny weather on t Rim and walk into a snowstorm on the North Rim. There is a year-round ranger statio provide shelter if you turn left at the North Kaibab trailhead and walk about a mile turn right at the trailhead, you will encounter a whole lotta nothing for 43 miles.

layers) and the trail's last big descent. At the base of the switchbacks, the trail meets Pipe Creek, whose lush streamside habitat contrasts sharply with the desert. To the west, Garden Creek tumbles over a dramatic waterfall to join Pipe Creek. Ninety minutes from Indian Garden is the **River Resthouse**.

The welcome sight of the Colorado and Pipe Creek Beach below heralds the unsigned junction (2446ft) with the **River Trail**. Follow this undulating trail upstream for 30 minutes, enjoying views of Zoroaster Temple (7123ft), then cross the **Silver Suspension Bridge**. Linking the Bright Angel and South Kaibab Trails, the trail continues a short distance to the black Kaibab Suspension Bridge.

A ranger station, a toilet, drinking water and a telephone are just prior to the Bright Angel Creek footbridge. Cross the bridge, turn left at the junction and follow the creek upstream to Bright Angel Campground, 1.5 miles from the start of the River Trail. **Phantom Ranch** (2546ft) is 0.3 miles further. A right turn at the junction leads to the boat beach, **Anasazi ruins** and **Kaibab Suspension Bridge**. After a picnic, return to Indian Garden to camp. For different campgrounds, hike to Bright Angel Campground the first night, then Indian Garden Campground the second night, breaking the ascent into two days.

DAY 3: INDIAN GARDEN CAMPGROUND TO BRIGHT ANGEL TRAILHEAD

4–5 hours; 4.6 miles

Retrace your steps up to the South Rim.

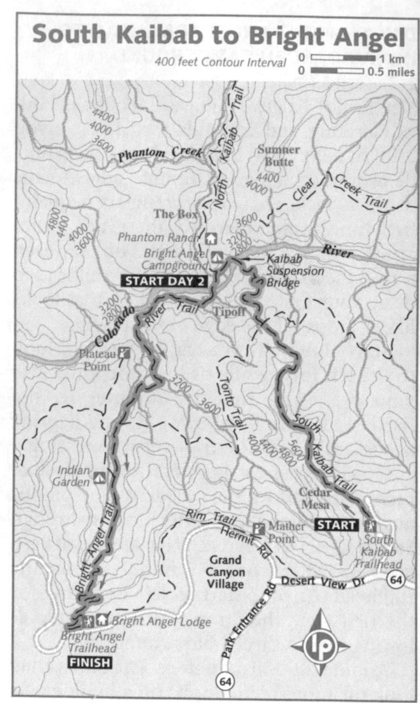

SOUTH KAIBAB TO BRIGHT ANGEL

Duration 2 days one way
Distance 16.1 miles one way
Difficulty Difficult
Start South Kaibab Trailhead
Finish Bright Angel Trailhead
Nearest Town Grand Canyon Village
ransportation Shuttle
mmary This excellent South Rim hike takes down the exposed spine of the South Kaid returns up the more forgiving Bright make it a three-day rim-to-rim hike, the North Kaibab.

ve time to spend one night or you want to start and finish on the South Rim, this hike is a terrific choice.

This hike can also easily be adapted to do the classic rim-to-rim from the South Kaibab to the North Kaibab (p194). More options for rim-to-rim combinations are detailed on p123.

DAY 1: SOUTH KAIBAB TRAILHEAD TO BRIGHT ANGEL CAMPGROUND

4–6 hours; 6.8 miles

From the South Kaibab Trailhead (7260ft) the trail starts out at a gentle decline before spiraling steeply down to **Cedar Mesa** (6320ft), where you'll gain a slight reprieve. Past Skeleton Point the trail continues its precipitous drop over scree and through the Redwall cliffs, eventually opening up onto the Tonto Platform.

Traverse the agave-studded plateau past the Tonto Trail junction, then take a long pause and a deep breath at the **Tipoff** (3870ft), which provides an emergency phone and toilet and marks the beginning of the steep descent into the inner gorge.

After hiking another challenging 1.5 miles and drinking in pretty views of Phantom Ranch, you'll reach the **River Trail**, which skirts the south side of the Colorado River and connects up with the Bright Angel Trail. Soon you'll cross the river via the skinny black **Kaibab Suspension Bridge**; turn left after crossing the bridge and you'll see an ancient **Anasazi dwelling**.

Just shy of a mile from here is the Bright Angel Campground.

As an alternative to camping at Bright Angel Campground, you may prefer spending the night at Phantom Ranch (p132). This picturesque riverside ranch is the only accommodation within the canyon. Dating from 1922, the cluster of buildings – which includes a main lodge and cabins – is fringed with towering cottonwoods and fruit orchards planted more than a century ago.

Used predominantly by people who descend the corridor trails on mules, the ranch is very popular and often fully booked. Spots not taken by mule excursions go to hikers who don't feel like toting camping gear. Reservations must be made far in advance, and you must check in at the Transportation Desk at Bright Angel Lodge by 4pm on the day prior to your hike. You can also see if there are any same-day openings by calling ☎ 928-638-2631, as cancellations for dorm beds do occur and are doled out on a first-come, first-served basis each morning at Bright Angel Lodge.

Family-style breakfasts and dinners are served here, but they must be reserved at the same time as you book your lodgings.

DAY 2: BRIGHT ANGEL CAMPGROUND TO SOUTH RIM

6–9 hours; 9.3 miles

To return to the South Rim, take the River Trail from the campground, pick up the Bright Angel and begin the 9.3-mile ascent, which takes between six and nine hours (see the preceding route description, p122). Provided you have planned ahead, you could also spend a second night on the trail at Indian Garden Campground.

If you're hiking to the North Rim, head up the North Kaibab (p194) to Cottonwood Campground, where you can spend your second night.

HERMIT TRAIL TO HERMIT CREEK

Duration 2 days round-trip
Distance 15.6 miles round-trip
Difficulty Difficult
Start/Finish Hermits Rest
Nearest Town Grand Canyon Village
Transportation Shuttle
Summary Tracing the path of the Hermit, this steep but rewarding out-and-back hike goes down to the river and Vishnu schist, the oldest exposed rock of the canyon's layers.

DAY 1: HERMIT TRAIL TO HERMIT CREEK

4–6 hours; 7.8 miles

From the Hermit Trailhead a steep, rocky path descends 2.5 miles to Santa Maria Spring (for a full description of the day hike, see p120). Backpackers continue past the spring as the trail levels for a mile or so before zigzagging over loose rocks.

Soon after descending the Redwall via a series of extremely steep, compressed switchbacks known as the **Cathedral Stairs**, the

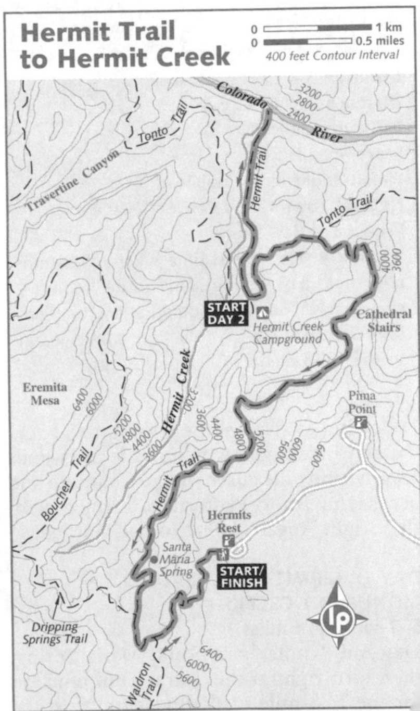

Hermit hits the Tonto (6.6 miles from the trailhead, at 3120ft). One mile west of the junction are stone remnants of the old **Hermit Camp** and near that the cliff-rimmed **Hermit Creek Campground** (3000ft), a glorious place to sleep.

From the campground it's another 1.5 miles to the Colorado, which you can reach by turning down Hermit Creek just before Hermit Camp or following the creek right from the campground. Down at the river, the canyon walls are exquisite black Vishnu schist shot through with veins of pink Zoroaster granite. **Hermit Rapids** mark the confluence of Hermit Creek and the Colorado.

DAY 2: HERMIT CREEK TO HERMIT TRAILHEAD

6–8 hours; 7.8 miles

To return to Hermits Rest, retrace your steps for the arduous but gorgeous climb back to the trailhead. For a longer wilderness excursion, you can pick up the eastbound Tonto and intercept the Bright Angel (see below for a full description).

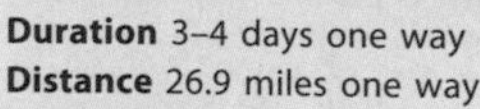

HERMIT TRAIL TO BRIGHT ANGEL TRAILHEAD

Duration 3–4 days one way
Distance 26.9 miles one way
Difficulty Difficult
Start Hermits Rest
Finish Bright Angel Trailhead
Nearest Town Grand Canyon Village
Transportation Shuttle
Summary Not for first-time hikers, this stunning trek may require some route finding – particularly along the undulating and unmaintained Tonto – but you'll find ample water sources and plenty of camping spots.

Following in steps of the hermit, this backcountry hike begins with solitude and wends its way along the curves of the Colorado and across the Tonto Platform to connect with the Bright Angel Trail at Indian Garden.

DAY 1: HERMIT TRAILHEAD TO MONUMENT CREEK

5–7 hours; 11.6 miles

Descend 4 miles past Santa Maria Spring, then turn right at the Tonto Trail junction or the 14.5-mile eastbound passage to the Bright Angel Trail. From the junction it's 3.8 miles to **Monument Creek**, providing water and designated trailside camping sites, after a descent of 3640ft this first day. Alternatively, you can spend the first night at Hermit Campground, then backtrack a mile to embark on the Tonto your second morning.

For a quick side trip, head 2 miles down the drainage to **Granite Rapids**, one of the bigger rapids on the Colorado. If you're lucky, you might catch a raft or kayak running the rapid when you get down to the river; look for the trail sign just south of the monument spire.

DAY 2: MONUMENT CREEK TO INDIAN GARDEN CAMPGROUND

4–6 hours; 10.7 miles

The Tonto snakes along the contour with a mild elevation change of 600ft, reaching Cedar Spring after 1.3 miles and Salt Creek in another 30 minutes; there's seasonal water and camping, as well as a pit toilet just above the campsite at Salt Creek. From there it's just under 5 miles to Horn Creek – don't even think about drinking the water here, as it's been found to have a high radioactive level. In under an hour you'll be at verdant Indian Garden, with treated water available year-round.

DAY 3: INDIAN GARDEN CAMPGROUND TO BRIGHT ANGEL TRAILHEAD

3–5 hours; 4.6 miles

Load up on water at the campground before beginning the hot grind back to the South Rim, the first 2 miles of which are the toughest. It's best to get a very early start so that you're still in the shade for the grueling Jacob's Ladder switchbacks. You'll stay cool and have a spectacular view as the sun inches its way down the red Supai sandstone. (For a full description of the Bright Angel Trail, see p116).

BIKING

Mountain bikers have limited options inside the park, as bicycles are only allowed on roads and the Greenway Trail (this will evolve as the Greenway Plan develops; see p105). Hermit Rd (p110) offers a scenic ride west to Hermits Rest, about 16 miles round-trip from the village. Keep in mind that shuttles ply this road every 10 to 15 minutes between March and November. They are not permitted to pass bicyclists, so you'll have to pull over each time one drives by. The rest of the year, traffic is minimal, making this a very pleasant ride.

Alternatively, you could ride out to the East Entrance along Desert View Dr (p112), a 50-mile round-trip from the village. The route is largely shuttle-free but sees a lot of car traffic in summer. Just off Desert View Dr, the 1-mile dirt road to Shoshone Point (p115) is an easy, nearly level ride that ends at this secluded panoramic vista, one of the few places to escape South Rim crowds.

The Greenway Trail, running between Canyon View Information Plaza and Grand Canyon Village, is open to cyclists but is shared with pedestrians and wheelchairs. Keep your ear open for news on paths to be constructed, which will lead south to Tusayan and east to Desert View.

Options outside the park include Kaibab National Forest (p137), just south, which offers several mountain-biking trails. The closest bike rental is in Flagstaff (p157).

OTHER ACTIVITIES

For information on rafting, see the Colorado River chapter (p220) and p50.

MULE RIDES

Mosey into the canyon the way tourists traveled a century ago, on the back of a sure-footed, velvet-eared mule. One- and two-day mule trips into the canyon depart every day of the year from the corral west of Bright Angel Lodge. The seven-hour day trip ($148) takes riders down the Bright Angel Trail to Indian Garden, then follows the Plateau Point Trail to **Plateau Point**, an overlook of the Colorado River. Here you can hop down and stretch your legs, enjoy the view and prepare for the 6-mile return trip. The mule train will make a stop for lunch at Indian Garden. Overnight trips (one/two people $401/709) and two-night trips (one/two people $566/946) follow the Bright Angel Trail to the river, travel east on the River Trail and cross the river on the Kaibab Suspension Bridge to spend the night at Phantom Ranch. It's a 5½-hour, 10-mile trip to Phantom Ranch, but the return trip up the 8-mile South Kaibab Trail is an hour shorter. Overnight trips include accommodations and all meals.

> **GRAND TEMPLES OF THE CANYON**
>
> In 1880 Clarence Edward Dutton, accompanied by artists Thomas Moran and William Henry Holmes, led an expedition to the canyon under the auspices of the newly formed United States Geological Survey. Dutton likened many of the canyon's elaborate mesas, buttes and pinnacles to temples and towers of ancient cultures of India, Egypt and Scandinavia, among others. So, duly inspired, he dignified these canyons with auspicious monikers like Confucius Temple, Osiris Temple, Krishna Shrine and Freya Castle, still noted as such on the park's maps and interpretive signs.

Don't plan a mule trip assuming it's the easiest way to travel below the rim. It's a bumpy ride on a hard saddle, and unless you're used to riding a horse regularly, you will be saddle-sore afterwards. Riders must be at least 4ft 7in tall, speak fluent English and weigh no more than 200lbs fully clothed. Personal backpacks, fanny packs, purses or bags of any kind are not allowed on the mules. Anything that could possibly fall off and injure someone in the canyon below will be kept for you till your return. Keep in mind that these rules are in place for the safety of the riders, the mules and others on the trails.

When you arrive at the corral, the wranglers will give you a small bag (a 15lb ice bag) that's just big enough for a bathing suit, a change of clothes and a few personal items. These will be put in saddlebags for the trip – your bag will not necessarily be on your mule, so don't put anything in it you may need during the ride. Carry sunscreen and any medications in your pocke You must wear a hat that secures to y head, a long-sleeved shirt and long p (preferably jeans), or you will not lowed on the mule. You should al sunglasses, but they must also your head. The wranglers will rider a water pouch and will ditional water with meals. F something before you leav tiring ride to lunch.

To book a mule trip more than 24 hours and up to 13 months in advance, call **Xanterra** (☎ 303-287-2757, 888-297-2757; www.xanterra.com). If you arrive at the park and want to join a mule trip the following day, ask about availability at the transportation desk at Bright Angel Lodge. If the trips are booked, join a waiting list, then show up at the lodge at 6:15am on the day of the trip and hope there's been a cancellation. But if riding a mule is that important to you, your best bet is to reserve the trip at least six to eight months in advance. Or make tracks to the other side of the canyon: mule rides on the North Rim (p196) are usually available the day before the trip.

If you're not planning a mule trip, just watching the wranglers prepare the mules can be fun, particularly for young children. In summer stop by the mule corral at 8am; in winter they get going about an hour later.

For information on horseback riding in the south side of the Kaibab National Forest, see p137.

FLYOVERS

At press time, flyovers at the Grand Canyon were still departing daily from Tusayan and Las Vegas. However, the NPS and the Federal Aviation Administration are federally mandated to present an environmental impact report in the near future, which may have implications for the number or existence of scenic flyovers at Grand Canyon National Park. Flights have already been restricted in number, altitude and routes due to noise pollution affecting the experience of other visitors and wildlife. If a flyover isn't an option during your visit or isn't the way you want to travel, consider enjoying an aerial view from the safety and comfort of the IMAX Theater (p139).

Standard routes include a 30-minute flight over the western canyon, a 40-minute eastern tour along the rim to the confluence of the Colorado and Little Colorado Rivers, and a 50-minute loop that bridges the two by crossing the North Rim forest. On most flights you'll see Coconino Plateau, Dragon Head (a dramatic ridge jutting from the North Rim) and the Painted Desert. Ask about the Eco-Star helicopters, which provide a quieter experience.

Contact the following companies for specific rates, as each offers several options, but note that their prices are fairly competitive. Ask about trips to Havasu Canyon on the Havasupai Reservation (p144). Flights from Tusayan operate year-round, departing daily at regular intervals between 8am and 5pm.

Air Grand Canyon (☎ 928-638-2686, 800-247-4726; www.airgrandcanyon.com)

Grand Canyon Airlines (☎ 866-235-9422; www.grandcanyonairlines.com)

Grand Canyon Helicopters (☎ 928-638-2764; www.grandcanyonhelicoptersaz.com)

Maverick Helicopters (☎ 888-261-4414; www.airstar.com)

Papillon Grand Canyon Helicopters (☎ 928-638-2419, 800-528-2418; www.papillon.com)

FISHING

You can fish anywhere along the Colorado as long as you have an Arizona fishing license with a trout stamp (see p55 for more details). There are several good fishing

THANEY DA SILVA, LEAD HELICOPTER PILOT

How long have you been doing this? I've been flying helicopters at the Grand Canyon since 2004. Before that, I was flying in California for seven years. **What's your favorite aspect of flying here?** I like the location, the small-town lifestyle – I come from a small town in Brazil. Three million people come through here every year, but it doesn't feel like it. The air is so clean here, and I love the outdoors. **Where do you recommend that people go to get away from crowds during the summer?** Go see the IMAX movie, maybe drive to a quiet point on the rim – Point is my favorite. If you really want to get away, do a Havasu Canyon trip. **Any good s from your experiences flying here?** You get all kinds of reactions when people see the for the first time – some cry, some scream, some are speechless. That's rewarding. Pilots them the highlight of their life. **Do you have a favorite feature in the canyon?** In the d evening the light is so different, like the sunrise at specific angles. I guess monsoon favorite feature, my favorite season. You see these isolated cloud formations and ns, sometimes five to seven all at once.

GETTING HITCHED AT THE GRAND CANYON

To be married in the park, you must first obtain a state marriage license from any Arizona courthouse. The nearest location is the **Clerk of the Superior Court** (☎ 928-779-6353) in Flagstaff. If you want an outdoor wedding, you'll then need to procure a free permit from the park by writing Wedding Permit Information, Grand Canyon National Park, PO Box 129, Grand Canyon, AZ 86023. Include the exact date and time of the event, how many people will be attending, your requested location and who will be performing the ceremony. Several pastors and priests at Grand Canyon Village may be able to officiate. Otherwise, four local justices of the peace or the Flagstaff Municipal Judge can do the honors. For details on locations and other information, call ☎ 928-638-7775.

You can get married at any viewpoint along the South Rim – imagine the spectacular backdrop in your wedding photos! Outdoor weddings of more than 50 people (maximum 85) must be held at Shoshone Point, a beautiful overlook at the end of a 1-mile dirt road. Ceremonies are available by reservation from May 15 to October 15 only; call ☎ 928-638-7777 for details. Remember that summer showers are prevalent from late June to September; consider a morning wedding to minimize the possibility of rain. To make advance reservations for indoor weddings and/or receptions at park lodges, call ☎ 928-638-2525.

It's also possible to get married on the North Rim, though logistics are more complicated, given its remote location. Contact the North Rim District Ranger at the wedding permit address listed earlier. For catering information, call or write the **special events coordinator** (☎ 928-638-2525; c/o Sales, Grand Canyon NP Lodges, PO Box 699, Grand Canyon AZ 86023).

spots near Phantom Ranch, though the most popular area is the 15-mile stretch of water east of Lees Ferry (p215). Several lodges there offer gear and guided trips. Nonresident fishing permits (one/five days $17.25/32) are available at Canyon Village Marketplace (p133).

RANGER PROGRAMS

Free ranger programs are one of the park's greatest treasures. Lasting 30 minutes to four hours, the talks and walks cover subjects ranging from fossils to condors to Native American history. Programs are held throughout the park and often involve a short walk. *The Guide* provides a complete listing of current ranger programs, including a short description and the location, time and duration of each program. A kiosk at Canyon View Information Plaza also clearly explains current programs.

The **Cedar Ridge Hike** is one regular offering. It involves a strenuous 3-mile hike (two to four hours round-trip) 1140ft below the rim on the South Kaibab Trail. While you can take this trail by yourself, the ranger will explain canyon geology and history as you hike. It departs from the South Kaibab Trailhead at 7am. Take the green Kaibab Trail Route shuttle from Canyon View Information Plaza to access the trailhead.

On the one-hour **Geology and Fossil Walks**, both offered daily, you can brush up on your knowledge of brachiopods and learn about the canyon's rich history. The Fossil Walk is an easy half-mile one-way walk to exposed fossil beds along the rim, a particularly nice activity if you plan on hiking into the canyon from Hermits Rest. If you attend the ranger talk, you'll be able to recognize fossils that lie about 10 minutes down the trail.

Each **evening program** at Mather Amphitheater examines a significant aspect of the canyon's natural or cultural history. Subjects change nightly; check the kiosk at the Canyon View Information Plaza or call ☎ 928-638-7610.

For information on ranger programs geared toward kids, check out p60.

CROSS-COUNTRY SKIING

From November through March, depending on snowfall, the surrounding national forest offers several trails for cross-country skiing and snowshoeing. Trails around Grandview Point may be groomed. Contact the **Tusayan Ranger Station** (☎ 928-638-2443) for current information. You can rent skis from several outdoor shops in Flagstaff (p162), where you'll also find plenty of cross-country and downhill trails.

SLEEPING

At the South Rim, you can sleep under the stars in one of the park's three campgrounds or choose a cabin or comfortable lodge room. Mather and Trailer Village campgrounds take reservations and are open year-round, while Desert View is open May through September and does not accept reservations. There's a seven-day limit at all three campgrounds. If you don't find a spot in the park, you can always pitch your tent free of charge in the surrounding Kaibab National Forest (see p137).

Xanterra (☎ 888-297-2757; www.xanterra.com) operates all park lodges, as well as Trailer Village. You can make reservations up to 13 months in advance. Visit Xanterra's South Rim website (www.grandcanyonlodges.com) for more information. For same-day reservations call the **South Rim switchboard** (☎ 928-638-2631).

In summer or during the holidays, you may find that there are no rooms left at the village inns; instead, consider a chain hotel or motel in Tusayan or a roadside joint in Valle. If you want more than just a place to lay your head, however, head to Flagstaff, Williams or Sedona. Several historic hotels and B&Bs in Flagstaff and Williams and gorgeous but expensive inns in Sedona offer far more character than you'll find at most lodgings in or near the park.

CAMPING

The **National Park Service** (☎ 877-444-6777; www.recreation.gov) operates Mather and Desert View Campgrounds. Reservations for Mather are accepted up to six months in advance till the day before your arrival. From mid-November through February, sites at Mather Campground are first come, first served.

Mather Campground (Map p103; sites $; year-round) Though Mather has over 300 campsites, it's actually a pleasant and relatively quiet place to camp. Piñon and juniper trees offer plenty of shade, sites are well dispersed and the flat ground offers a comfy platform for your tent. If you're longing for pristine wilderness, look elsewhere, but if you just want a guaranteed site with ample facilities, this is your best bet. You'll find pay showers, laundry facilities, drinking water, toilets and grills. There are no hookups, though there's a dump station, and the maximum length for trailers and RVs is 30ft. Next door a small general store stocks camping supplies, drinks and basic food items like cereal and canned goods. Pay phones stand just outside, a full grocery store is a short walk away and it even has its own shuttle stop on the Village Route. Mather accepts reservations from March through mid-November – the rest of the year it's first come, first served. Family sites (the official name for standard sites) hold up to six people. Group sites hold up to 40 people, but there is no minimum – if

SOUTH RIM CAMPGROUNDS

Camp name	Location of sites	Number	Elevation (approx)	Open required?	Reservations fee	Daily
Desert View Campground	Desert View	50	7450ft	May–mid-Oct	No	$12
Grand Canyon Camper Village	Tusayan	300	6612ft	Mar-Oct	No	$25-46
Mather Campground	Grand Canyon	317	7000ft	year-round	Yes, up to 6 months in advance	$18
Ten-X Campground	2 miles south of Tusayan	70	6650ft	mid-Apr–Sep	No	$10
Trailer Village	Grand Canyon	84	7000ft	year-round	Yes	$28

you don't mind spending the extra money, you can reserve one all to yourself. Disabled sites are closer to the facilities and on more level ground. If you don't have a car or would just like some distance between you and your fellow campers, ask for a backpacker site. If you think you'll arrive late or need to cancel a reservation, call the NPS reservation line at ☎ 800-388-2733. If you're hoping for same-day reservations, just show up in person and hope for the best (not a smart strategy during the peak summer rush). As crowds diminish in September, some loops are closed. By December only one loop remains open.

Desert View Campground (Map p101; sites $; ⌚ May–mid-Oct) Set back from the road in a quiet piñon-juniper forest near the East Entrance, this first-come, first-served campground is a peaceful alternative to the more crowded and busy Mather Campground. The lovely sites are spread out enough to ensure some privacy. You'll find toilets and drinking water but no showers or hookups. A small cafeteria/snack shop near the campground serves breakfast, lunch and dinner, and there's also a general store that offers basic camping supplies and staples like pasta, canned food, milk, beer and wine. The best time to secure a spot is midmorning, when people are breaking camp. Don't drive in after dark assuming you'll get a site, as it's at least 25 miles to another campground. Before you arrive, call the East Entrance Station (☎ 928-638-0105) to confirm whether any sites are available. Call the Desert View Information Center (☎ 928-638-7893) to confirm the campground's operating dates.

Trailer Village (Map p103; ☎ 888-297-2757, same-day reservations 928-638-2631; sites $; ⌚ year-round) As the name implies, this is basically a trailer park, offering little in the way of natural surroundings. Expect RVs lined up tightly at paved pull-through sites with hookups amid a rather barren, dry patch of ground. Check for spots with trees on the far north side. You'll find picnic tables and BBQ grills, while a coin laundry and showers are a quarter-mile away at Mather Campground.

Along the banks of the Colorado River on the canyon floor, Bright Angel Campground (Map p118) is one of three backcountry campgrounds, along with Indian Garden and Cottonwood, that lie along the main corridor trails between the North and South Rims. You must obtain a backcountry permit (p44) if you intend to stay anywhere below the rim overnight. If you're staying at the campground but don't want to pack down your own stove and food, you can reserve meals at nearby Phantom Ranch (see p135).

LODGES

If you desire or require a room (or bathroom) of your own, the lodges on the South Rim represent a solid range of park accommodations. To reach any lodge, call the central **switchboard** (☎ 928-638-2631).

Facilities	Description	Page
	First-come, first-served campground with well-dispersed sites on the peaceful eastern side of the South Rim	above
	Large campground with showers and playground but little shade; RV sites have full hookups	138
	Park's biggest campground, with wooded, well-dispersed Village sites; no hookups; trailers & RVs limited to 30ft	above
	Spacious campground with picnic tables and fire rings but no showers; pull-through sites have no hookups	138
	Near Mather Campground dump station (closed in winter); hookups and pull-through sites for vehicles up to 50ft	131

Dogs Allowed On Leash 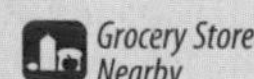 Grocery Store Nearby  Snack Shop

Photographs, including pictures of the rooms, are posted on Xanterra's South Rim website (www.grandcanyonlodges.com).

Phantom Ranch (Map p101; ☎ 888-297-2757; d & dm $-$$) At the bottom of the canyon floor, which means it can only be reached on foot, mule or floating river conveyance. Built along the north bank of the Colorado River, stone cottages offer both private and dormitory-style rooms. Cozy private cabins sleep four to 10 on bunks. There are also dormitory-style bunks in single-sex cabins outfitted for 10 people. Bunk prices include bedding, soap, shampoo and towels; meals are extra. The ranch – a mule, rather – also provides a duffel delivery service for about $60 each way, but these must be soft-sided duffels weighing no more than 30lbs apiece. Reservations for the family-style meals (see p135) must be made at the same time as room reservations. If you'd rather skip the expensive meals, you may bring your own food and stove. After dinner each night, the dining room converts into a canteen that serves beer, wine and hot drinks, as well as a venue to meet fellow riverside ramblers.

Bright Angel Lodge & Cabins (Map p103; d/cabins $/$$; year-round;) Built in 1935 (see p107), this log-and-stone lodge on the ledge offers travelers more historic charm and nicer rooms than you'll find at most other accommodations on the South Rim. Unfortunately, the public spaces have neither the quiet elegance nor rustic Western character found at El Tovar. You will find two restaurants, a snack bar and a small, nondescript bar with a TV. If you want to relax with a drink – tired as you think your legs may be – your cocktail will feel much better if you walk a few doors down to El Tovar. In 2001 all rooms at Bright Angel were refurbished in keeping with architect Mary Colter's original design. The least expensive rooms in the park are the doubles with shared (immaculate) bath, which offer a double bed, a desk and a sink. The bathroom is down the hall, there are no TVs and the pleasant rooms are nothing extraordinary, but this is a great price for a perch right on the rim (no views, however). Powell suites feature two bedrooms and a tub but no shower or TV; each holds up to seven people. Cabins at Bright Angel, many decorated in rustic Western style, offer more character. There are several options, starting with standard cabin and ranging up to the excellent value of rim-view cabins, which are bright and airy, with a queen bed, a full bath, a refrigerator, a partial canyon view and doors that open right out onto the Rim Trail. Four out of the 15 rim-view cabins have a fireplace and are a bit pricier. Because the rim-view cabins face the Rim Trail, there isn't such a feeling of seclusion amid the foot shuffling and tourist musings that last into the evening, especially during summer. One of the more interesting places to stay on either rim, the Buckey O'Neill Cabin ($$$) is a spacious, Western-style cabin with a king bed, separate sitting room, refrigerator, dry bar, two TVs, a full bath and front and back doors. Built in the 1890s, the cabin was home to Buckey O'Neill, a prospector who believed he found copper in Anita, 14 miles south of the canyon. It's the second-oldest building in the park, offering a real sense of history and an escape from the tourist throngs. Canyon breezes more than compensate for the lack of an air conditioner. As with rim-view suites at El Tovar, the cabin is usually booked more than a year in advance through the Bright Angel Lodge.

Kachina & Thunderbird Lodges (Map p103; d $$; year-round) Beside the Rim Trail between El Tovar and Bright Angel, these institutional-looking lodges offer standard motel-style rooms with two queen beds, full bath and TV. Rooms with views of the parking lot are perfectly fine, but it's worth spending up a little for the rimside rooms, some with partial canyon views. The concrete buildings resemble elementary schools complete with green lawns, but they're a short stroll from El Tovar's lovely public spaces. Neither lodge has a lobby or front desk – guests at Kachina check in at El Tovar, while those at Thunderbird check in at Bright Angel, just to keep things interesting.

Maswik Lodge (Map p103; d & cabins $$; year-round) Located a quarter-mile from the rim near the Backcountry Information Office, the Maswik Lodge is named for the Hopi kachina who guards the canyon. The lodge comprises 16 two-story wood-and-stone buildings set in the woods. Rooms at Maswik North feature private patios, high ceilings and forest views, while rooms at the less expensive Maswik South are smaller and don't offer much of a view. Here you'll encounter much less foot traffic and general bustling about than at the rim, but the rooms are standard motel rooms. You'll find a cafeteria and a bar here with a pool table and big-screen TV. Small cabins are available in the summer only.

Yavapai Lodge (Map p103; d $$; ⌚ Apr-Oct) Sure, it's your basic motel, but there are some hidden pluses to the Yavapai Lodge. For one, it lies more than a mile from the traffic and chaos of the central village. Though it may not boast rim views, it's close to Canyon View Information Plaza and within walking distance of the grocery store, post office and bank in Market Plaza. The lodgings are stretched out amid a peaceful piñon and juniper forest, yet you can pull your car right up to your door. Rooms in Yavapai East are in six air-conditioned, two-story buildings, while rooms in Yavapai West are spread out in 10 single-story buildings without air-conditioning. These are basic, clean motel rooms with tubs, showers and TVs. Yavapai closes from November through March, though it does open up briefly for the Thanksgiving and Christmas holidays.

El Tovar (Map p103; d $$-$$$, ste $$$; ⌚ year-round; ♿) Its exposed beams, dark wood interiors, bronzes and stately presence continue to define El Tovar as a quintessential 1905 national park lodge (see p106). It appeals to those visitors seeking more than a roadside motel, and even day-trippers are lured in by the wide, inviting porches that wreathe the rambling wood structure, offering pleasant spots for people-watching and canyon sunsets. Even if you're not a guest, stop by to relax with a book on the porch swing or a drink on the patio. The public spaces hint at the genteel elegance of the park's heyday. The original guestrooms were remodeled to accommodate private baths, thus many of the standard double rooms are incredibly small – ask for the slightly more expensive deluxe room. You can put a cot or a crib in a deluxe double at no extra charge for children (there's an extra charge for adults), but if your party is more than three people, consider getting a suite rather than multiple doubles. The capacity varies by suite: standard suites sleep three, four or seven, while porch suites sleep three, four or five. Those in a mood to splurge can stay in one of three rim-view suites, all with sitting rooms and private porches looking out onto full canyon views. These are the only rooms in the park with a full rim view, and they're often booked more than a year in advance. Themed suites are the next best choice, but standard king rooms (renovated in 2005) also have some atmospheric appeal befitting this elegant institution.

EATING

Grand Canyon Village has all the eating options you need, whether it's picking up picnic parts at Canyon Village Marketplace, an après-hike ice-cream cone at Bright Angel Fountain or a sit-down celebratory dinner at El Tovar. Hours listed here are for the summer and may vary in slower seasons.

BUDGET

Desert View Marketplace (Map p101; ☎ 928-638-2393; Desert View; ⌚ 8:30am-6pm) At the East Entrance, near the Watchtower, Desert View Campground and Desert View Trading Post Snack Bar, this general store sells simple groceries and souvenirs. Expect the same sort of goods you'd find at any convenience store.

Canyon Village Marketplace (Map p103; ☎ 928-631-2262; Market Plaza; ⌚ 7am-9pm) The biggest source for supplies on either rim, this market offers everything you'd expect from your local grocery store. You'll find canned goods, meat, cheese, beer, wine, firewood, diapers and over-the-counter medications, though no pharmacy. You may prefer to stock up on groceries in Williams, Flagstaff or Sedona, as prices and selection are better outside the park.

Bright Angel Fountain (Map p103; ☎ 928-638-2631; Bright Angel Lodge; mains $; ⌚ 8am-8pm) On the rim at Bright Angel Lodge, this cafeteria-style fountain serves burgers, hot dogs, premade sandwiches, yogurt, ice cream, soda and milk. It's cash-only, but you'll only need a few bucks.

Hermits Rest Snack Bar (Map p101; ☎ 928-638-2351; Hermits Rest; mains $; ⌚ 9am-sunset) This walk-up window outside Hermits Rest is basically a human-powered vending machine: you tell the dude what kind of premade sandwich, ice-cream bar or drink you

TEN PRIME PICNIC PICKS

Terrific picnic spots abound in thousands of shady, secluded sites you can find simply by roaming along the rim, away from the shuttle-stop overlooks. Find your own favorite perch and look for circling condors or faraway mule trains, or take a hike to reach these prime picnic spots.

- **Cedar Ridge** (p118) Lunch atop one of the outcrops to stake out photo ops before heading up the South Kaibab
- **Indian Garden** (p117) Heading up or down, this cool oasis on the Bright Angel makes a restful picnic stop
- **Yavapai Point** (p107) Poke around the Observation Station, then picnic at the point
- **Santa Maria Spring** (p120) Spirit yourself away with a sandwich to this secluded spring
- **Widforss Point** (p192) Pad across pine needles to take in peaceful views of five temples
- **Uncle Jim Point** (p193) No need to stray too far for the Uncle Jim Trail to reward you with views
- **Shoshone Point** (p115) Wander under the shade of ponderosa to this atypical South Rim picnic site
- **Point Imperial** (p189) Chow down as you get the lowdown on the layout from the highest point on the North Rim
- **Hermits Rest** (p112) BYO lunch or hit the snack bar before venturing down the trail a little way
- **Cape Royal Wedding Site** (p189) Best bench for a sunrise brunch

want, and then you hand your cash over the counter as he dispenses the goods.

Desert View Trading Post Snack Bar (Map p101; ☎ 928-638-2360; Desert View Trading Post; mains $; 8am-6pm) The only place to eat on the east end of the rim (aside from the general store), this small snack bar serves a limited breakfast, lunch and dinner. Menu items include burgers, corn dogs, mayo-heavy premade sandwiches and soda, and cold cereal, eggs and French toast in the morning.

Deli at Marketplace (Map p103; ☎ 928-631-2262; Market Plaza; $; 7am-8pm) This counter in the village grocery store is the best place to find a fresh-made sandwich for a picnic. If you prefer, you can sit at one of the few indoor tables and enjoy such hot dishes as pizza and fried chicken. In the morning the deli offers doughnuts and coffee.

MIDRANGE

Bright Angel Restaurant (Map p103; ☎ 928-638-2631; Bright Angel Lodge; mains $$; 6:30am-10pm;) With exposed wood beams and an adobe-style interior, this busy family-style restaurant in the back of Bright Angel Lodge is not without its simple charm. The menu offerings include burgers, fajitas, salads, roast turkey and other down-home sorts of dishes. Families with small children gravitate here, so it can get loud, and the harried staff provide the most perfunctory service of the three waitstaffed restaurants on the South Rim. The restaurant serves coffee from 6am and does not take reservations.

Maswik Cafeteria (Map p103; ☎ 928-638-2631; Maswik Lodge; mains $$; 6am-10pm) Based in Maswik Lodge, the term 'cafeteria' should tip you off to the fare, service and seating. Though fairly predictable, the food is pretty good – a nice variety and not too greasy. You'll find pizza, burgers, fried chicken, Mexican fare and other hot dishes, as well as beer, soda and milk.

Canyon Café (Map p103; ☎ 928-638-2631; Yavapai Lodge; mains $$; 6am-10pm) At Yavapai Lodge, this café has the same sort of food and setup as at Maswik Cafeteria, and you can get boxed lunches to go. Hours vary seasonally.

TOP END

Arizona Room (Map p103; ☎ 928-638-2631; Bright Angel Lodge; mains $-$$$; 11:30am-3pm Mar-Oct & 4:30-10pm Mar-Dec) A wonderful balance between casual and upscale, this busy restaurant in Bright Angel Lodge is one of the best options for dinner on the South Rim. Antler chandeliers hang from the ceiling, and picture windows overlook a small lawn, the rim walk and the canyon beyond. Try to get on the waitlist when doors open at 4:30pm, because by 4:40 you may have an hour's wait – reservations are not accepted. There's no indoor bar, but you can sit outside on the small deck, watch passersby on the Rim Trail and enjoy a drink while you wait (but you'd better nurse that costly cocktail!). Mains include steak, chicken and fish dishes, while appetizers include such creative options as toasted cumin onion rings.

El Tovar Dining Room (Map p103; El Tovar; ☎ 928-638-2631; mains $$-$$$; 🕑 6:30-11:00am, 11:30am-2pm & 5-10pm) If at all possible, treat yourself to at least one meal at the historic El Tovar. The memorable surroundings feature dark wood, tables set with china and white linen, and huge picture windows with views of the rim and canyon beyond. The service is excellent, the menu creative, the portions big and the food very good – much better than you might expect at a place with captive customers that knows it's the only gig in town. Breakfast options include fresh-squeezed orange juice, El Tovar's pancake trio (buttermilk, blue cornmeal and buckwheat pancakes with pine-nut butter and prickly pear syrup) and cornmeal-encrusted trout with two eggs. Lunch and dinner menus are equally creative. Though you're welcome to dress up to match the elegant setting, you'll be perfectly comfortable in jeans as well. Reservations are required for dinner. Call Xanterra (☎ 888-297-2757) to make dinner reservations up to six months in advance. El Tovar does not take reservations for breakfast or lunch; to avoid lunchtime crowds, eat before the Grand Canyon Railway train arrives at 12:15pm, as passengers often make lunch at El Tovar their first stop.

Phantom Ranch Canteen (Map p101; ☎ 928-638-2631; mains $$$; 🕑 5am & 6:30am breakfast seatings, 5pm & 6:30pm dinner seatings) On the canyon floor, Phantom Ranch offers family-style meals on a set menu: hearty stew, steaks and vegetarian chili, as well as sack lunches. Seating hours change seasonally. You must make reservations before your trip into the canyon (up to 13 months in advance), ideally when you reserve your cabin, dorm or campsite at Bright Angel Campground. The canteen is open to the public for cold lemonade and packaged snacks between 8am and 4pm, and for beer, wine and hot drinks from 8pm to 10pm.

DRINKING

The park isn't exactly a nightlife hot spot, but for those who still have energy at the end of the day, there are a few places to go.

On the South Rim, the patio off the bar at El Tovar (p106) is a great spot to sit with a prickly pear margarita and watch people strolling along the rim. Inside is a dark and cozy lounge, with big, cushioned chairs and stained glass. Sports fans can catch a game at the sports bar at Maswik Lodge (p132). The dark, windowless bar at Bright Angel (p132) doesn't offer much in the way of character, but it's fun to look at the historic photos on the bar. All bars close at 11pm, and drinks are prohibited along the rim itself.

On Thursday nights park employees head to Tusayan, just outside the park's South Entrance, for dancing at the Grand Hotel (p138). Some opt to catch the latest scores at the popular sports bar in the Best Western Grand Canyon Squire Inn (p138), which also features a video arcade, pool tables and a bowling alley.

BEYOND THE SOUTH RIM

Carved into the stunning landscape of the Southwest, the Grand Canyon has more than its own unique splendor to offer visitors. Stretching both north and south of the canyon is the Kaibab National Forest, the southern ecosystem of which is characterized by piñon and juniper. Grand Canyon National Park itself is bordered on the west by the Hualapai and Havasupai Reservations, where you can hike to turquoise waterfalls in the inner canyon, tiptoe on the glass-floored Skywalk on the West Rim, and raft along the Colorado for a day. Further west, where the Colorado River has been reined in by the massive engineering feat that is Hoover Dam, Lake Mead is a popular recreation area for desert dwellers thirsting for fishing, houseboating and water sports.

The gateway towns leading to the South Rim are destinations in their own right: L Vegas for its slick excess and cardinal si Flagstaff for its cool, outdoorsy feel, Sed for surreal natural beauty and metaph mystique, and Williams for its small- Route 66 atmosphere.

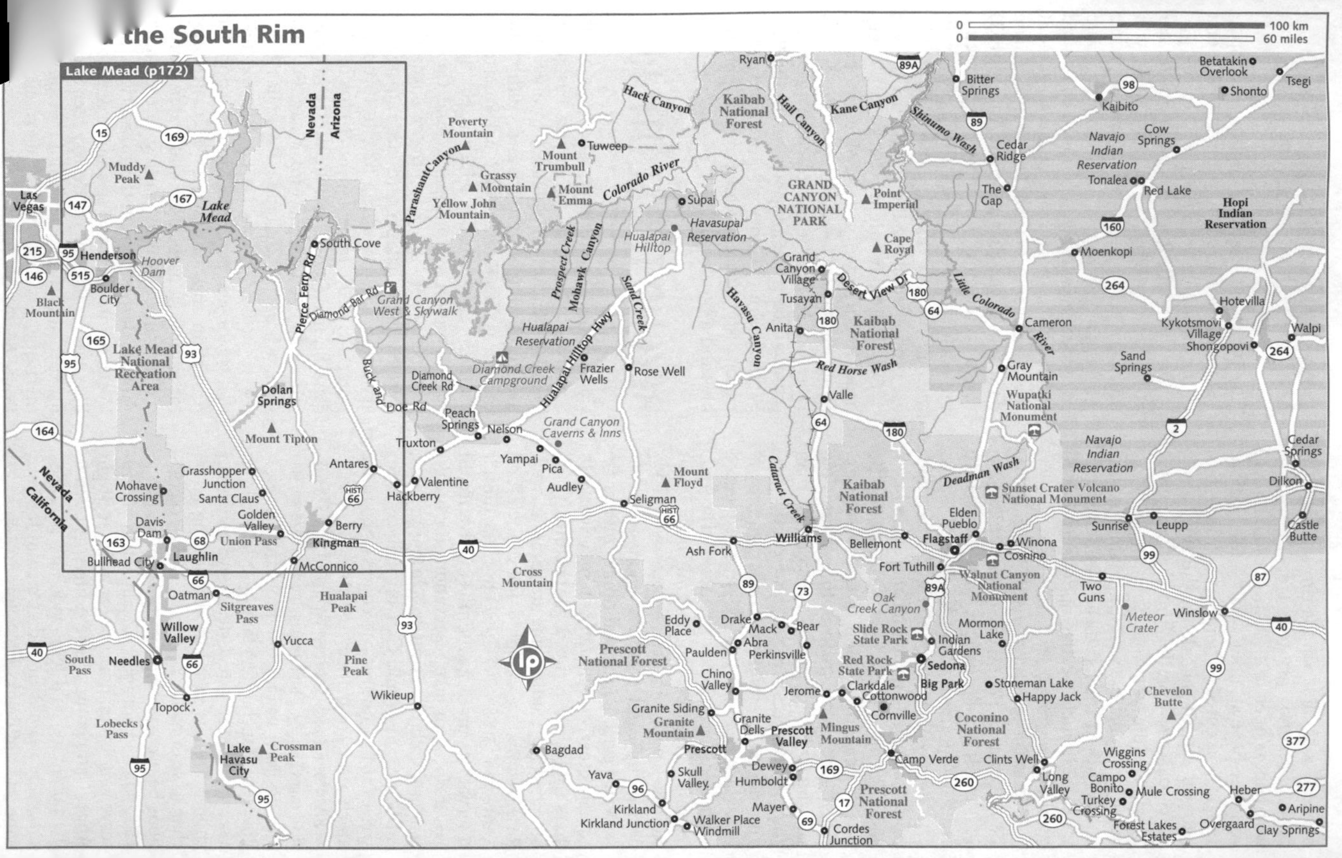

the South Rim
Lake Mead (p172)
0 100 km
0 60 miles
Las Vegas
Henderson
Boulder City
Hoover Dam
Lake Mead
Lake Mead National Recreation Area
Black Mountain
Muddy Peak
Nevada
Arizona
California
South Cove
Pierce Ferry Rd
Diamond Bar Rd
Grand Canyon West & Skywalk
Dolan Springs
Mount Tipton
Kingman
McConnico
Berry
Antares
Hackberry
Valentine
Truxton
Peach Springs
Nelson
Yampai
Pica
Audley
Seligman
Ash Fork
Williams
Bellemont
Flagstaff
Fort Tuthill
Elden Pueblo
Cosnino
Winona
Two Guns
Meteor Crater
Winslow
Leupp
Sunrise
Sedona
Big Park
Oak Creek Canyon
Slide Rock State Park
Red Rock State Park
Cottonwood
Cornville
Clarkdale
Jerome
Camp Verde
Prescott
Prescott Valley
Chino Valley
Paulden
Drake
Mack
Abra
Bear
Perkinsville
Granite Dells
Dewey
Humboldt
Mayer
Cordes Junction
Skull Valley
Walker Place
Windmill
Kirkland
Kirkland Junction
Yava
Bagdad
Wikieup
Yucca
Hualapai Peak
Pine Peak
Crossman Peak
Lake Havasu City
Topock
Needles
Willow Valley
Oatman
Sitgreaves Pass
Laughlin
Bullhead City
Davis Dam
Mohave Crossing
Golden Valley
Union Pass
Santa Claus
Grasshopper Junction
Lobecks Pass
South Pass
Grand Canyon Village
Tusayan
Anita
Valle
Red Horse Wash
Desert View Dr
Cape Royal
Point Imperial
Kaibab National Forest
Grand Canyon National Park
Havasupai Reservation
Supai
Hualapai Hilltop
Hualapai Reservation
Hualapai Hilltop Hwy
Diamond Creek Campground
Diamond Creek Rd
Buck and Doe Rd
Grand Canyon Caverns & Inns
Frazier Wells
Rose Well
Sand Creek
Havasu Canyon
Cataract Creek
Mohawk Canyon
Prospect Creek
Colorado River
Mount Emma
Mount Trumbull
Tuweep
Grassy Mountain
Yellow John Mountain
Poverty Mountain
Parashant Canyon
Hack Canyon
Hall Canyon
Kane Canyon
Ryan
Bitter Springs
Shinumo Wash
Cedar Ridge
The Gap
Cameron
Little Colorado River
Gray Mountain
Wupatki National Monument
Sunset Crater Volcano National Monument
Deadman Wash
Walnut Canyon National Monument
Mormon Lake
Indian Gardens
Stoneman Lake
Happy Jack
Coconino National Forest
Clints Well
Long Valley
Prescott National Forest
Mingus Mountain
Granite Mountain
Granite Siding
Eddy Place
Mount Floyd
Cross Mountain
Moenkopi
Tonalea
Red Lake
Cow Springs
Kaibito
Shonto
Betatakin Overlook
Tsegi
Navajo Indian Reservation
Hopi Indian Reservation
Hotevilla
Kykotsmovi Village
Shongopovi
Walpi
Sand Springs
Cedar Springs
Dilkon
Castle Butte
Chevelon Butte
Heber
Overgaard
Aripine
Clay Springs
Wiggins Crossing
Campo Bonito
Mule Crossing
Turkey Crossing
Forest Lakes Estates

KAIBAB NATIONAL FOREST (SOUTH RIM)

The park's South Rim is bordered by the piñon-juniper and ponderosa-pine woodland of **Kaibab National Forest** (Map p101; ☎ 928-635-8200; www.fs.fed.us/r3/kai/), whose Tusayan Ranger Station sits just outside the park's South Entrance. Offering several great mountain-biking trails, unlimited camping, hiking and cross-country skiing, the forest extends outdoor recreation options beyond the park. You won't find spectacular canyon views, but you won't find the crowds either. Bring plenty of water, as natural water sources are scarce in this arid region. You'll likely spot elks, mule deer, turkeys and coyotes, and on rare occasions you may encounter a mountain lion, black bear or bobcat.

Orientation & Information

The forest's Tusayan Ranger District (327,267 acres) borders Grand Canyon National Park to the north, the Navajo Reservation to the east, private and state-owned lands to the south and the Havasupai Reservation to the west. The main road through the forest is Hwy 64/180, which connects Williams and Flagstaff with the canyon. Hwy 64 accesses the district's northeast corner.

If you plan on hiking or camping in the forest, maps are available at the Williams visitor center and at **Books & More Store** (Map p103; ☎ 928-638-0199; Canyon View Information Plaza, Grand Canyon Village; ⌚ 8am-8pm).

Sights & Activities

Built by the Civilian Conservation Corp in 1936 as a fire tower, the 80ft **Grandview Lookout** offers great views of the region for those willing and able to climb all those stairs. From the park's Desert View Dr (p112), turn at the sign for 'Arizona Trail' between mileposts 252 and 253, about 2 miles east of Grandview Point. You can **hike** or **bike** 1.3 miles on a dirt road to the lookout. Alternatively, take unpaved Forest Rd 302, just past Grand Canyon National Park Airport, in Tusayan.

You can also ride or hike here via the **Tusayan Bike Trail**, a moderate bike trail on an old logging road. The trailhead is 0.3 miles north of Tusayan on the west side of Hwy 64/180. It's 16 miles from the trailhead to the lookout. If you don't want to ride all that way, three interconnected loops offer 3-, 8- and 9-mile round-trips.

From the lookout you can hike or ride part or all of the still-evolving Arizona Trail (p45), a 24-mile one-way ride to the south boundary of the Tusayan Ranger District. This is an excellent and relatively easy ride. Eventually, the Arizona Trail will span the state more than 750 miles from north to south. The northern segment of the trail unfolds beneath ponderosa pines and gambel oaks; further south, the trail passes piñon-juniper stands, sage and grasslands. Bring plenty of water, as there are no dependable sources along the trail. Ask at the ranger station about other hikes.

Apache Stables (☎ 928-638-2891, 928-638-3105; www.apachestables.com) offers one-hour and two-hour horseback rides through the forest. You can also take a one-hour evening saunter to a campfire and return on a wagon. For riders of all ages, the outfitter offers a campfire wagon ride, in which trail riders rendezvous with the wagon for a cookout beneath the stars. For both campfire trips you must bring your own food (think hot dog and s'mores components), drinks and paper plates; if you bring a small cooler, the staff will put it on the wagon.

In the winter the United States Forest Service (USFS) maintains a groomed **cross-country skiing loop** 0.3 miles north of Grandview Lookout.

Sleeping

Free dispersed camping is allowed in the national forest as long as you refrain from camping in meadows, within a quarter-mile of the highway or any surface water, or within a half-mile of any developed campground. Dispersed camping is not allowed inside Grand Canyon National Park.

TUSAYAN

☎ 928 / pop 562 / elev 6612ft

The friendly little town of Tusayan, situated 1 mile south of the park's South Entranc along Hwy 64, is basically a half-mile st of hotels and restaurants catering to Gr Canyon visitors. It makes a good base commodations inside the park are b up, and it does offer convenience general store, gas station, souve and espresso bar with internet a Tusayan Ranger Station sits jus park's South Entrance.

Sleeping

Some of these motels offer a touch more character than you'd find at most other American roadside motels, but don't expect anything particularly memorable.

Ten-X Campground (Map p101; 928-638-7851; sites $; mid-Apr–Sep) Woodsy and peaceful, this first-come, first-served forest-service campground 2 miles south of Tusayan has 70 sites and can fill up early in the summer. You'll find large sites, picnic tables, fire rings and BBQ grills (the campground host sells firewood), water and toilets, but no showers. There are pull-through sites for RVs but they don't have hookups. Pine needles make for soft sleeping grounds. An amphitheater sometimes hosts programs on everything from canyon geology to nature programs for children; check the bulletin board for times.

Seven Mile Lodge (928-638-2291; d $-$$) This simple, friendly motel doesn't take reservations, but you can show up as early as 9am to see if there are any vacancies; rooms are usually filled by early afternoon in the summer.

Grand Canyon Camper Village (Map p101; 928-638-2887, 877-638-2887; tent & RV $$;) A mile south of the park on Hwy 67, this private campground has a ton of sites and a playground on the premises – so if you have kids, it's got that going for it. It's just behind the north end of Tusayan's restaurant strip, making it convenient for walking into town for dinner. Sites are on dirt with no shade or natural surroundings, but there are toilets and pay showers, and if you really do need a place to camp, it's a safe and relatively quiet choice. Full hookups are available.

Rodeway Inn – Red Feather Lodge (928-638-2414, 800-538-2345; www.redfeatherlodge.com; d $$;) This motel offers well-kept rooms in two buildings, as well as an adjacent restaurant, a fitness center and an utdoor pool. Built in 1997, the three-story tel features elevators and interior doors, le the older two-story motor lodge of- utside entrances and stairs.

Western Grand Canyon Squire Inn (928- 800-622-6966; d $$;) Rooms est Western range from standard a two-story 1973 annex, sans spacious interior rooms in the with elevator. With plenty of stuff to keep kids and adults alike busy, this is the only resortlike accommodation in Tusayan. You'll find a restaurant, a coffee shop, a popular sports bar, a bowling alley, pool tables, a beauty salon, an exercise room, a coin laundry, tennis courts and an outdoor pool.

Grand Hotel (928-638-3333, 888-634-7263; www.visitgrandcanyon.com; d $$;) The distinct Western motif in this hotel's open public spaces – including a big fireplace, high ceilings, woven rugs, stone floors and faux pine beams – gives this newish hotel an old look, and it works. And with appropriate Western hospitality, the friendly staff complete the theme. The relatively large, comfortable rooms have been upgraded with pleasing Mission-style furniture, and the ones in back face the woods. Tour buses roll in for the 7pm Native American dance performance at the restaurant, and nightly live country music draws locals and visitors alike from around 10:30pm. The hotel also features an indoor pool and a hot tub.

Canyon Plaza Inn & Suites (928-638-2673, 866-698-2012; www.grandcanyonqualityinn.com; d/ste $$/$$$;) This is one of the better options in Tusayan, featuring spacious rooms and suites, a bright, modern restaurant, an outdoor pool and a hot tub, and an 8ft indoor hot tub set in an atrium. All suites have two rooms, while suites with king beds include pullout couches in the sitting area.

Holiday Inn Express (928-638-3000, 888-465-4329; www.gcanyon.com; d/ste $$/$$$;) Holiday Inn Express offers predictable quality, featuring modern, comfortable interior rooms, an indoor pool and a complimentary continental breakfast. Though attractive, two-room suites cost about as much as you'd pay for a canyon-view suite at El Tovar – not the sweetest of deals. But doubles are more reasonable.

Eating

Considering the number of annual tourists that pass through Tusayan, the village manages to retain a sort of old-fashioned, roadside-hub pace. There's an OK variety of eateries to choose from, but as yet no one has established a notable culinary presence.

Jennifer's Bakery & Internet Café (928-638-3433; mains $; 7am-10pm summer, to 4pm winter;

) In the Grand Canyon Village Shops (opposite the IMAX Theater), this is where USFS rangers come to grab a sandwich and escape the tourists. It's a small place with high tables, highway-robbery internet access ($3 for 15 minutes), coffee, pastries and a limited menu. Breakfast items include yogurt-and-granola parfaits, omelets and Belgian waffles. For lunch it can make sandwiches and panini to order (with a vegetarian option or two). Service tends to be leisurely.

Sophie's Mexican Kitchen (928-638-1105; mains $; 11am-9pm;) Sporting bright turquoise walls and Southwestern chairs, this tiny café in the Grand Canyon Village Shops offers decent Mexican food, including tacos and fajitas. There's a selection of domestic and Mexican beers, but you'll have to sip it out of a foam cup if you don't want to drink it inside. The friendly, low-key spot is a welcome alternative to the bigger, tourist-oriented restaurants in town and on the rim.

We Cook Pizza & Pasta (928-638-2278; mains $$; 11am-10pm;) This cavernous, busy pizza joint beats eating at Pizza Hut (except in price), and is the kind of place where you order, take a number, and unceremoniously chow down at one of the big tables. The pizza isn't particularly compelling, but it's good and no-nonsense like its name, and whaddaya mean you want something fancier than broccoli and Asiago? It also has children's portions and menu items like salads and pastas.

Spaghetti Western (928-638-3230; mains $$; 4-9:30pm;) If you're hankering for Italian of the wine-list and sit-down variety, this is another good choice for lasagna, minestrone and ravioli. It's outfitted with a full bar, checkered tablecloths and candlelit tables, and it offers several vegetarian options as well as a children's menu.

Entertainment

The best show in town is the National Geographic Visitor Center's **IMAX Theater** (Map p101; 928-638-2468; www.explorethecanyon.com; adult/child $13/10; 8:30am-8:30pm Mar-Oct, 10:30am-6:30pm Nov-Feb), screening a terrific 34-minute film called *Grand Canyon – The Hidden Secrets*. With exhilarating river-running scenes and virtual-reality drops off canyon rims, the film plunges you into the history and geology of the canyon through the eyes of ancient Native Americans, John Wesley Powell and a soaring eagle. The IMAX experience affords you a safer, cheaper alternative to a canyon flyover, but if you do have your heart set on a helicopter ride, you'll also find Grand Canyon National Park Airport (Map p101) conveniently located in Tusayan.

Getting Around

You can walk to most places along the highway through Tusayan. **Enterprise** (928-638-2871; 9am-5pm) provides rental cars at Grand Canyon National Park Airport in Tusayan. Pickup service is available.

VALLE

About 25 miles south of the park, Valle marks the intersection of Hwy 64 to Williams and Hwy 180 to Flagstaff. It's not much of a town, just a gas station and a few places to stay and eat if you're really stuck between a rock and a hard place.

Flintstones Bedrock City (928-635-2600; tent & RV $, admission $5; Mar-Oct;) is a little worse for wear, but of course Bedrock City is old! You might not want to stay at the barren, windswept campground, but kids and lovers of camp (the kitsch kind) will love this well-worn roadside attraction. Built in 1972, it features a life-sized Fred and Wilma, a Flintmobile and colorful concrete dinosaurs and houses to clamber around. The campground features coin showers and a laundry, a snack bar (think Bronto Burgers and Dino Dogs) and a recreation area complete with 'concreteosaurs.' It's a must-stop for Flintstones fanatics and connoisseurs of kooky Americana.

At Valle Airport, the small **Planes of Fame Air Museum** (928-635-1000; cnr Hwys 64 & 180; adult/child/under 5 $5.95/1.95/free; 9am-5pm;) has a small collection of immaculately kept vintage airplanes on display. Aviation enthusiasts will find it fascinating; others may not.

Grand Canyon Inn (928-635-9203, 800-635-9203; d $-$$;) is parceled out on either side of Hwy 64, offering standard motel rooms, a restaurant (open 7:30am to 2pm and 6pm t 9pm) and an outdoor pool. All rooms ha TVs and air conditioners, while the lar ones also provide telephones. Next d you'll find a gas station and minimart.

WILLIAMS

928 / pop 2910 / elev 6780ft

A pretty slow spot by day, Williams comes to life in the evening when the Grand Canyon Railway train returns with passengers from the South Rim. Though this small town can't compete with Flagstaff's restaurants, historic downtown or myriad sights, it is a friendly town and caters to canyon tourists. Route 66 passes through the main historic district as a one-way street headed east; Railroad Ave parallels the tracks and Route 66 and heads one-way west.

Lining these two thoroughfares is downtown Williams.

Orientation & Information

Java Cycle Coffee (928-635-1117; 326 W Route 66; 6am-7pm Mon-Wed, 6am-8pm Thu & Fri, 7am-9pm Sat, 7am-6pm Sun) This little café offers internet access.

Library (928-635-2263; 113 S 1st St; 9am-noon, 1-5pm & 6-8pm Tue-Thu, 9am-noon & 1-5:30pm Fri, 9am-1pm Sat)

Police station (928-635-4461; 501 W Route 66; 9am-5pm Mon-Fri)

Post office (928-635-4572; 120 S 1st St; 9am-5pm Mon-Fri, to noon Sat)

Visitors center (928-635-4061, 800-863-0546; www.williamschamber.com; 200 W Railroad Ave; 8am-6:30pm) Inside the historic train depot; offers a small bookstore with titles on the canyon, Kaibab National Forest and other areas of interest.

Williams Health Care Center (928-635-4441; 301 S 7th St; 8am-8pm)

Williams Ranger Station (928-635-5600; 742 S Clover Rd; 8am-4pm Mon-Fri) You'll find USFS rangers at both the visitors center and here.

Sights & Activities

There are plenty of opportunities for **hiking** and **biking** in nearby Kaibab, Coconino and Prescott National Forests. Ask at the visitors center or at the ranger station for maps and information.

GRAND CANYON RAILWAY

Following a 9:30am **Wild West show** by the tracks, the historic Grand Canyon Railway train (see boxed text, p244) departs for its two-hour ride to the South Rim. If you're only visiting the rim for the day, this is a and hassle-free way to travel. You can e the car behind and enjoy the park by shuttle or tour bus.

GRAND CANYON DEER FARM

Children love the **deer farm** (928-635-4073, 800-926-3337; www.deerfarm.com; 6769 E Deerfarm Rd; adult/child/under 3 $7.50/4.50/free; 9am-6pm). Blanketed in wood chips, a trail leads through an open area where the deer roam free. A smaller pen is home to goats (always eager to munch on food, shirts, strollers, whatever). Just $2 buys enough deer food to keep kids busy for a while. Among the more exotic animals in residence (that visitors are asked not to feed) are marmosets, wallabies and 'mini-cattle.' It's 8 miles east of Williams, off I-40's exit 171.

Sleeping

Free dispersed camping is allowed in the national forest provided you refrain from camping in meadows, within a quarter-mile of the highway or any surface water, or within a half-mile of any developed campground.

BUDGET

Railside RV Ranch (928-635-4077, 888-635-4077; www.railsidervranch.com; 877 Rodeo Rd; tent & RV sites $;) The closest campground to downtown Williams. There's no shade, but the campground has coin showers, a pet wash and a small clubhouse. Campsites – 96 RV hookups and an area for about 10 tents – are right beside the tracks for the Grand Canyon Railway train, but it doesn't run at night. To get here turn east from Grand Canyon Blvd onto Edison Ave (three blocks north of the tracks), then left on Airport Rd. After one block, turn right onto Rodeo Rd; the campground is on the left, just before the tracks.

Circle Pines KOA (928-635-2626, 800-562-9379; www.circlepineskoa.com; 1000 Circle Pines Rd; tent & RV sites & cabins $;) Amid 27 acres of ponderosa-pine forest a half-mile north of I-40 (take exit 167), Circle Pines is open year-round and offers plenty of activities for children and adults alike. Options include live music and hayrides on the weekends, miniature golf, an indoor pool, two hot tubs, bike rentals and horse stables. A café with outdoor seating serves breakfast and dinner.

Ponderosa Forest RV Park & Campground (928-635-0456, 888-635-0456; 494 N Parks Rd, Parks; tent & RV sites $;) Offering tranquil wooded sites, this shady and fragrant campground

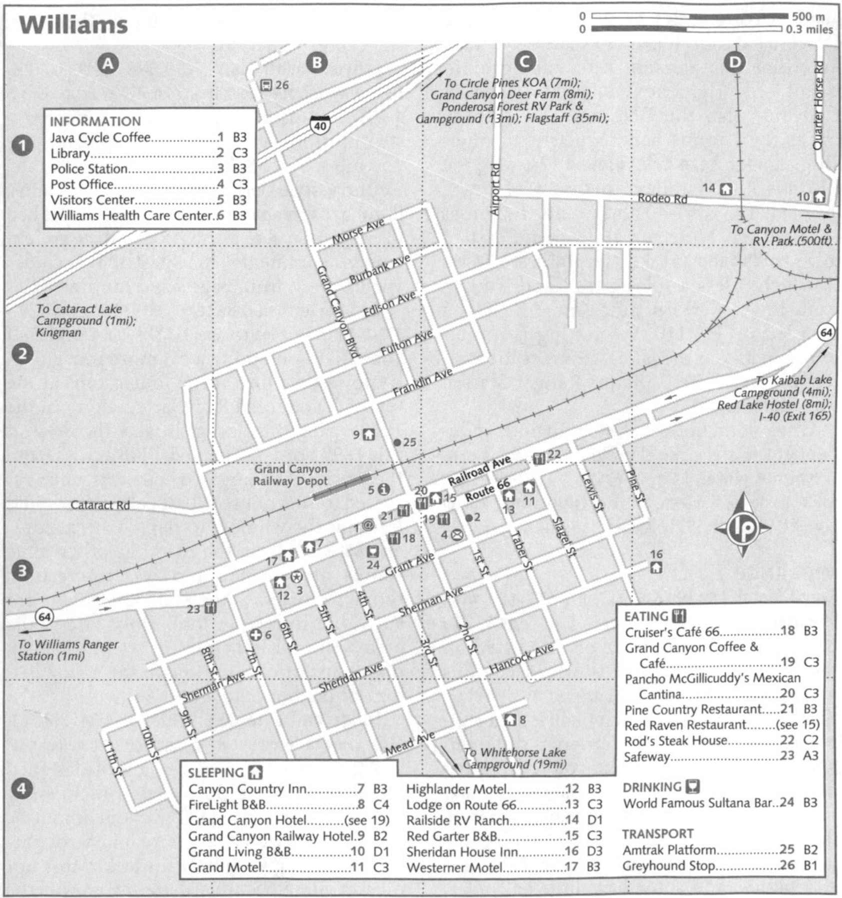

is at exit 178 off I-40, 13 miles east of Williams. Tent sites are at the very back of the property, and there's a camp store out at the entrance to the campground.

Red Lake Hostel (☎ 928-635-4753; 5235 Hwy 64; tent & RV sites, dm & r $) Run in conjunction with a small store alongside Hwy 64, eight miles north of I-40, this place is neither here nor there. It offers some bare-bones budget options: camping in the dirt lot out back, sleeping in a basic dorm room with clean sheets or in a private room with a shared bathroom out back. Though the building is fringed with Indian paintbrush and Native American vendors often set up their wares in front, luxuries like showers are not offered here.

our pick **Grand Canyon Hotel** (☎ 928-635-1419; thegrandcanyonhotel.com; 145 W Route 66; dm & r $) This charming spot is just what this town needed – a European-style hostel in a historic 1889 building right on Route 66. There's air-con in interior rooms, but Williams is nice and cool, and in the exterior rooms you can get a good breeze going with the window open and ceiling fan whirring with white noise. 'Backpacker' rooms, modeled on European hostels are clean and comfortable, and the priva rooms are simply and tastefully decorat Best of all, the charming proprietors go o their way to make you feel at home.

Three pleasant USFS campground Williams offer year-round campin out hookups. Take exit 161 off head north 2 miles to reach **Cataract Lake Campground** (Map p141; tent & RV sites $) but take note that this pleasant little campground is not only right next to pretty Cataract Lake but also the BN-Santa Fe Railway tracks, and trains run regularly all night long. **Kaibab Lake Campground** (Map p141; tent & RV sites $) is 4 miles northeast of town; take exit 165 off I-40 and go north 2 miles on Hwy 64. Nineteen miles southeast of town is **Whitehorse Lake** (Map p141; tent & RV sites $), which offers a hiking trail and fishing; from town, drive 8 miles on 4th St and turn left on FR 110. Swimming is not allowed in any of the lakes. Contact the visitors center or the Williams Ranger Station for information.

Other good budget choices include independent motels like the clean and well-run **Westerner Motel** (928-635-4312, 800-385-8608; 530 W Route 66; s, d & ste $) and **Highlander Motel** (928-635-2541; 533 W Route 66; r $;).

MIDRANGE

Grand Motel (928-635-4601, 877-635-4601; www.thegrandmotel.com; 234 E Route 66; s, d, ste & apt $;) Built in 1936 along Route 66 and listed on the National Register of Historic Places, this vintage roadside motel is capped by a metal-tiled stucco roof made to look like the original faux adobe walls. Each room is different, and all make you feel like you're stepping into a time warp – you can imagine yourself road-tripping to the Grand Canyon before the days of chain motels. All of the rooms include a minifridge, microwave, cable TV and phone, and some have little balconies. In good weather, a good continental breakfast is served outside on the patio.

Canyon Motel & RV Park (928-635-9371, 800-482-3955; www.thecanyonmotel.com; 1900 E Rodeo Rd; RV sites & cottages/train cars $/$$;) Stone cottages and rooms in two railroad cabooses and a former Grand Canyon Railway coach car offer a quirky alternative to a standard motel. Resting on sections of old track, the train cars sport bunk beds and private decks, and even though they're a bit on e cramped side, kids love the experience. e little cottages feature white walls and d floors, with kitchenettes and king or e beds, and there's a heated indoor n the grounds. To get here, turn east rand Canyon Blvd onto Edison Ave ocks north of the tracks), then left on Airport Rd. Drive one block, then turn right onto Rodeo Rd.

Canyon Country Inn (928-635-2349, 877-405-3280; www.thecanyoncountryinn.com; 422 W Route 66; s & d $-$$) Rooms at this family-run inn are a step up from typical motel rooms and give you more of a B&B feel at a reasonable rate. Country-style decor includes frilly curtains, floral bedspreads and a teddy bear on the bed to make you feel at home. It offers an 'extended' continental breakfast that includes yogurt, fresh fruit, bagels and muffins.

Red Garter Bed & Bakery (928-635-1484, 800-328-1484; www.redgarter.com; 137 W Railroad Ave; d $$) If you'd like something a bit more intriguing, try to reserve one of the four rooms at the reputedly haunted Red Garter. Up until the 1940s, gambling and girls were the draw at this 1897 bordello-turned-B&B across from the tracks. The largest room was once reserved for the house's 'best gals,' who would lean out the window to flag down customers. Set back from the road, the other three rooms are smaller and less interesting, though quieter. Some staff are downright surly, but innkeeper John Holst knows the area well and is happy to get out a map, offer suggestions and relate the saucy history of the bordello and the town.

Lodge on Route 66 (928-635-4534, 877-563-4366; www.thelodgeonroute66.com; 200 E Route 66; r/ste $$/$$$;) The Lodge is a well-designed blend of a Route 66 motel with low-key Southwestern style (ie no Kokopelli motif). Sturdy dark-wood furniture and wrought-iron accents give an elegant feel to this upmarket motel. Standard rooms are on the cramped side, with the big beds and little else taking up most of the available space, but roomier suites feature microwaves and minifridges. Continental breakfast is served out on its lovely covered patio.

TOP END

Sheridan House Inn (928-635-9441, 888-635-9345; www.grandcanyonbbinn.com; 460 E Sheridan Ave; d & ste $$-$$$; closed Jan-Feb) KC and Mary Seidner are the gracious hosts at this pine-fringed hilltop inn in the far south end of town. Included in the rates are a full hot breakfast, and you're encouraged to help yourself to a refrigerator full of complimentary soft drinks, and snacks generously left out around the dining area. The inn has a pool table, a sunroom for movie-watching and a video library that includes children's videos. The rooms are nicely appointed in a comfy country style, and some offer CD players, TVs, VCRs and full marble baths. Because it's such a rambling house, there's plenty of room to find a place of your own on a deck, a porch or a cozy chair in a corner.

FireLight B&B (☎ 928-635-0200, 888-838-8218; www.firelightbandb.com; 175 W Meade Ave; r $$$; 💻) Four well-appointed and tastefully decorated rooms in this Tudor-style house all have their own fireplaces. A gourmet breakfast is served every morning by your hosts Debi and Eric, there's a pool table on the premises and this romantic spot is adults only.

Grand Living Bed & Breakfast (☎ 928-635-4171, 800-210-5908; www.grandlivingbnb.com; 701 Quarter Horse Rd; r & ste $$$) Grandly spacious rooms in this B&B boast antique oak and cherry furniture, king- or queen-sized beds, private bathrooms (three with clawfoot tubs), TVs and fireplaces. Terrycloth bathrobes and a basket of toiletries in the bathrooms are a nice extra, and hosts Gloria and Bill will make you feel like a special guest. Old West details include a wraparound porch, hardwood floors and log cabin–style walls, but the rooms are named after flowers and decorated with a softer touch. To get here, turn east from Grand Canyon Blvd onto Edison Ave (three blocks north of the tracks), then left on Airport Rd. Drive one block, then turn right onto Rodeo Rd. Grand Living is just past the tracks, on the corner of Rodeo and Quarter Horse Rds.

Grand Canyon Railway Hotel (☎ 928-635-4010, 800-843-8724; www.thetrain.com; 235 N Grand Canyon Blvd; r $$-$$$; 🚭 ♿) This sprawling hotel caters primarily to passengers heading to the rim on the Grand Canyon Railway train. While the spacious lobby, with a flagstone fireplace and painting of the canyon, hints at the elegance of days past, the Southwestern-style rooms are what you'd expect at any standard hotel. A lounge serves simple meals, and an adjacent restaurant serves breakfast, lunch and dinner. You'll also find a fitness room, pool and hot tub. Ask about room/railway packages (see boxed text, p244).

Eating & Drinking

If all you want is a decent place to grab a bite, several restaurants in Williams feed and entertain the tourist crowd, often featuring live music on summer evenings. One notable new exception is the Red Raven Restaurant, which offers a slightly finer dining experience.

Safeway (☎ 928-635-0500, pharmacy 928-635-5977; 637 W Route 66; 🕒 5am-10pm) You can get groceries here.

Pine Country Restaurant (☎ 928-635-9718; 107 N Grand Canyon Blvd; mains $; 🕒 7am-10pm; ♿) This family restaurant offers reasonably priced American basics and delicious pies. Though the menu offers few surprises, the price is right. Just across the street from the visitors center, it has wide windows and plenty of room to relax in a home-style setting.

Grand Canyon Coffee & Café (☎ 928-635-4907; www.grandcanyoncoffeeandcafe.com; 125 W Route 66; mains $; 🕒 6am-2pm Wed-Sat & Mon, 8am-1pm Sun; ♿) A good choice for a quick meal, this small family-run café serves an eclectic mix of typical diner foods as well as Chinese and Mexican dishes. It also has a limited children's menu.

Pancho McGillicuddy's Mexican Cantina (☎ 928-635-4150; 141 W Railroad Ave; mains $-$$; 🕒 11am-10pm Sun-Thu, 11am-midnight Fri & Sat; ♿) Directly across from the train station, this bustling spot is popular with hungry passengers. It offers passable 'Mexican' food, made for the palate of Midwestern tourists, but it's a lively place to hang out and has a nice bar. The restaurant is housed in an 1893 tavern, and musicians perform on the outdoor patio on summer evenings.

Rod's Steak House (☎ 928-635-2671; 301 E Route 66; mains $-$$; 🕒 11am-9:30pm Mon-Sat; ♿) Locals say the service here depends on owner Stella's mood, so don't rely on service with a smile. The food, however, is consistently good. The cow-shaped sign and menus spell things out – if you want steak and potatoes, this is the place to come. They've been staples since the restaurant opened in 1946, though there are a few non-cow items on the menu. Diners with limited mobility should note that restrooms are down a flight of stairs.

Cruisers Café 66 (☎ 928-635-2445; 233 W Rout[illegible] 66; mains $-$$; 🕒 3-10pm; ♿ 👶) Housed in [illegible] old Route 66 gas station, with photos of [illegible] stations on the walls and meals serve[illegible] a hubcap, this café is a fun place fo[illegible] Expect the usual diner fare, such as [illegible] and grilled cheese, as well as more [illegible] mains, like mesquite-grilled rib[illegible] on the outdoor patio). In summ[illegible] sit outside and enjoy live musi[illegible]

Red Raven Restaurant (928-635-4980; www.redravenrestaurant.com; 135 W Route 66; mains $$; 11am-3pm & 5-9pm Tue-Sun;) Good wine list, creative food, basic menu. Friendly service, family-run restaurant. Wraps, steaks, salads.

World Famous Sultana Bar (928-635-2021; 301 W Old Route 66; 10am-1am) Stop by this quirky bar for a beer and a game of pool. Expect the once-over when you walk in – they don't see many tourists here.

Getting There & Around

Greyhound (928-635-0870, 800-229-9424; www.greyhound.com; 1050 N Grand Canyon Blvd) doesn't have a bus station in town, but it does stop at the Chevron gas station north of downtown. **Amtrak** (800-872-7245; www.amtrak.com; 233 N Grand Canyon Blvd) stops at a platform on the outskirts of town but provides a shuttle connecting to the Grand Canyon Railway Depot. If you'd prefer to arrange private transportation, **Open Road** (928-226-8060, 800-766-7117) offers two shuttles a day to the canyon ($22/17 adult/child) and to Flagstaff ($17/12 adult/child).

HAVASUPAI RESERVATION

One of the Grand Canyon's true treasures is Havasu Canyon, a hidden valley with four stunning, spring-fed waterfalls and inviting azure swimming holes in the heart of the 185,000-acre Havasupai Reservation. Parts of the canyon floor, as well as the rock underneath the waterfalls and pools, are made up of limestone deposited by flowing water. These limestone deposits are known as travertine, which gives the famous blue-green water its otherworldly hue. Because the falls lie 10 miles below the rim, most trips are combined with a stay at either Havasu Lodge in Supai or at the nearby campground. Supai is the only

HISTORIC ROUTE 66

Arizona claims bragging rights for having the longest continuous stretch of Route 66, running east to west from Seligman to Topock. Getting off I-40 for part of a long road trip can be a beautiful alternative to simply blowing through this part of the country, especially on this section of the Mother Road. Driving some parts of this byway can be equal parts eerie, nostalgic and melancholy, while other parts are strongly redolent of scrub and dust, and still others delightfully alive.

Worthy of note west of Williams is Seligman, where Juan Delgadillo once reigned prankishly supreme at his famous **Delgadillo's Sno Cap Drive-In** (928-422-3291; 301 E Route 66;). We won't ruin the fun for you, but his son and family carry on the merry traditions as they serve you frosty (or are they incredibly warm?) shakes and cheeseburgers with cheese. Along both sides of Seligman's stretch of Route 66 are the historic buildings that have survived over the years, as well as good budget motels, restaurants (Roadkill Café, anyone?) and souvenir shops where they lay the kitsch on thick.

Getting back on the westward highway reveals miles upon miles of rolling hills and canyon country, punctuated by the Route 66 attraction of **Grand Canyon Caverns & Inn** (Map p136; 928-422-3223; www.grandcanyoncaverns.com; Mile Marker 115, Route 66; 45-min tour adult/child $13/10; 8am-6pm May-Sep, call for off-season hours;). You'll be greeted by a huge plaster dinosaur and can escape the desert heat in the cool subterranean caverns here, 21 stories below ground via elevator, and see a model of the gigantic Harlan's ground sloth (*Glossotherium harlani*) whose well-preserved skeleton was found inside the cave with a broken hip. The cavern restaurant, about a mile off the highway, is a great little roadside resting spot with a small playground, and you can even stay the night at the inn (rooms $).

Next stop west is Peach Springs, the biggest town on the Hualapai Reservation (p149), with a …otel where you can arrange one-day rafting trips on the Colorado. Moving ever westward, you'll …ss tiny towns like Truxton and Valentine, and teeny Hackberry, whose Old Route 66 Visitor Center … passersby with its eccentrically decorated gas station. Vintage cars in faded disrepair, old … seats and rusted-out ironwork adorn the 1934 general store and dusty parking lot. It's run …ute 66 memorialist and makes a lovely spot to stop for a cold drink and souvenirs.

…ore information on the history of this old highway, check out the **Historic Route 66 …n of Arizona** (928-753-5001; www.azrt66.com).

village within the Grand Canyon, situated 8 miles below the rim. For more on the Havasupai tribe, see the boxed text, p146 and the History chapter, p87.

Orientation & Information

The Havasupai Reservation lies south of the Colorado River and west of the park's South Rim. From Hualapai Hilltop, a three- to four-hour drive from the South Rim, a well-maintained trail leads to Supai, waterfalls and the Colorado River. Information is available from the **Havasupai Tourist Enterprise** (☎ 928-448-2141; tourism@havasupaitribe.com; PO Box 160, Supai, AZ 86435). Visitors pay an entry fee of $35 ($17.50 for children 12 and under) when they arrive in Supai.

The local post office is the only one in the country still delivering its mail by mule, and postcards mailed from here bear a special postmark to prove it. There's also a small emergency clinic in Supai. Liquor, recreational drugs and nude swimming are not allowed, nor are trail bikes allowed below Hualapai Hilltop.

Hiking

Two moderate to difficult trails are on the reservation, leading to waterfalls and a gorgeous swimming hole. Before heading down to Supai, you *must* have reservations to camp or stay in the lodge. Do not try to hike down and back in one day – not only is it dangerous, but it doesn't allow enough time to see the falls, which splash down a few miles further afield in Havasu Canyon.

HUALAPAI HILLTOP TO SUPAI

Duration 3–5 hours one way
Distance 8 miles one way
Difficulty Moderate
Start Hualapai Hilltop
Finish Supai
Nearest Town Supai
Transportation Private
Summary The hike boasts a 2000ft elevation change and starts out steeply but is not terribly strenuous; the travertine walls of the canyon rise on either side as you descend the trail.

The trail from Hualapai Hilltop descends steep switchbacks for 1.5 miles before leveling off in a dry creek bed. In this part of the canyon you'll see beautiful layers of the **Toroweap formation**, **Coconino sandstone**, **Hermit shale**, and **Esplanade sandstone**. The trail then winds through the canyon for the remaining 6.5 miles to Supai. About 1.5 miles before Supai, the trail meets Havasu Creek; follow this trail downstream to the village. Shade trees line the creek, and the sheer walls of the canyon rise dramatically on either side of the trail.

HAVASU CANYON TO WATERFALLS

Duration 2–6 hours round-trip, with stops at pools
Distance 3–6 miles round-trip
Difficulty Moderate–difficult
Start/Finish Supai
Nearest Town Supai
Transportation Hike, mule or helicopter
Summary Heading out of Supai toward the river, this hike reveals the stunning waterfalls and travertine-bottomed pools hidden within Havasu Canyon; be prepared for the 1200ft elevation change.

Just over a mile beyond Supai is 75ft-high **Navajo Falls**, after which you'll cross two bridges to reach beautiful **Havasu Falls**. This waterfall drops 100ft into a sparkling blue pool surrounded by cottonwoods and is a popular swimming hole. Havasu Campground (p148) sits a quarter-mile beyond Havasu Falls. Just past the campground, the trail passes **Mooney Falls**, which tumbles 200ft down into another blue-green swimming hole. To get to the swimming hole, you must climb through two tunnels and descend a very steep trail – chains provide welcome handholds. Carefully pick your way in and out, keeping in mind that these falls were named for prospector DW James Mooney, who fell to his death here. Travertine walls tower over the creek and falls. After a picnic and a swim, continue about 2 miles to **Beaver Falls**. The Colorado Rive[r] is 5 miles beyond.

The trail passes small pools and casca[des] and crosses the creek many times; use e[xtra] caution when the water is high. The [Colo]rado lies 10.5 miles from Supai and 8 beyond the campground. Camping [pro]hibited beyond Mooney Falls, a

NATIVE AMERICANS OF THE GRAND CANYON

Human habitation of the Grand Canyon region dates back at least 4000 years, according to carbon-dating of split-twig animal figurines (see p84), and continues to the present day. Tribes whose reservations now form several of the borders of Grand Canyon National Park and who reside on the land surrounding the park include the Hualapai, Havasupai, Navajo, Hopi and Paiute peoples. To varying degrees, these local tribes rely on the tourism coming through the Grand Canyon region, and visitors may pass through one or two of the reservations on their travels to the national park. Visitors are welcome to visit the reservations as long as they show the proper respect for tribal culture and privacy. You'll be contributing to the tribes' economies if you take tribal-run tours, stay at campsites and lodges on the reservations or purchase handicrafts and art directly from tribal members. Remember that Native American reservations are sovereign nations within the US and that tribal laws may apply (though federal laws supersede them). See p149 for more about etiquette on the reservations.

The Havasupai

Well-known for their beadwork and basketry, the Havasupai (whose name translates as 'people of the blue-green waters') share the Yuman language with the Hualapai (below). Both tribes are together referred to as Northeastern Pai. Their legends tell them that mankind originated on a mountain near the Colorado River. They left their Mojave relatives behind and headed to Meriwitica, near Spencer Canyon (a tributary of Grand Canyon). The Hualapai stayed near Meriwitica, but a frog, enticed by the stream and lush vegetation, led the Havasupai east to Havasu Canyon. Archaeological records indicate that the Northeastern Pai arrived at the Grand Canyon around AD 1150, and the Havasupai have occupied Havasu Canyon since about that time.

Today over 30,000 tourists visit Havasu Canyon (p144) every year, and the Havasupai's lives and economic survival are integrally related to the tourist industry that has developed in and around Grand Canyon National Park. They, along with the Havasupai, do not participate in the gaming industry. In Supai, the village at the bottom of the canyon, the Havasupai run a lodge and campground, as well as a small village store, serving the tourist industry. The village's isolation probably magnifies the tension created by the outside influence of mainstream American culture on the younger generation of Havasupai. The traditional structure of Havasupai society, based on respect for tribal elders and the tribal council, remains in place despite such outside pressures – but as with much of life for many Native Americans, this continues to be a struggle.

The Hualapai

The Hualapai Reservation, bordering a large section of the Grand Canyon's South Rim, stretches as far south as Route 66. The Hualapai (meaning 'people of the pine trees') counts itself among the few tribes in the Southwest that do not generate revenue from gambling; instead, they've tried their hand at tourism, most successfully through motorized rafting tours on this section of the Colorado River, and through tours of one scenic section of the West Rim, known as Grand Canyon West (p150). Package tours are now a requirement for visitors wishing to visit the West Rim, and the tribe hopes that the addition of the Skywalk (p150) will generate much-needed funds to better the fortunes of its people. The infrastructure here is still fairly basic, but the Hualapai have been expanding the West Rim airport and actively hyping their latest attraction. These next few years will be a challenge for the tribe, as they attempt to balance their need to survive with their traditional stewardship of land they consider sacred.

If you plan to travel off Route 66 on the Hualapai Reservation, you must purchase a permit in ny Peach Springs. Peach Springs is also where you'll find the Hualapai Lodge, the hub where e tribe's tourist enterprise meets Route 66. You can base yourself at the lodge if you want to k the only one-day rafting trips (see Hualapai River Runners, p225) on the Colorado River. Peach Springs, you'll be shuttled to the Diamond Creek put-in point, where you'll board a motorized raft. At the end of your river trip, they'll ferry you out via helicopter to the rim at Grand Canyon West.

Like the Havasupai, the Hualapai are renowned for their basketry. You will also find Hualapai dolls at trading posts and in and around the canyon.

The Navajo

The Navajo people comprise one of the largest tribes in North America; about one of every seven Native Americans are Navajo. Bordering the eastern edge of the national park, the 27,000-sq-mile **Navajo Reservation** (☎ 928-871-6436) is the biggest in the US. If you enter the park through the East Entrance, you'll pass through the Navajo Reservation; the tiny outpost of Cameron (p170), also on the reservation, marks the intersection of Hwys 89 and 64, which leads to the East Entrance. Along the way you'll see jewelry stalls along the road, often with hand-painted signs announcing their approach with 'Friendly Indians Ahead!'

The Navajo Nation (also known as the Diné) has historically been adaptable to the ways of other tribes and cultures, which perhaps has contributed to the nation's strength and size. But the Navajo people have certainly not been exempted from the poverty and historical struggle of all Native American tribes.

The Navajo are renowned not only for their jewelry, pottery and sand paintings, but most famously for their weaving. Sought-after Navajo rugs, which can take months to complete, can be found for sale throughout the region, from Sedona to the South Rim. Most of the processes are still done by hand: carding the wool, spinning the thread, dying the threads with natural concoctions, and hand-weaving the designs themselves. You can find some examples at reputable dealers like Hopi House (p108) in Grand Canyon Village or the excellent Garland's Navajo Rugs (p170) in Sedona.

The Hopi

East of the Grand Canyon lies the 2410-sq-mile **Hopi Reservation** (☎ 928-734-3283), which is completely surrounded by the Navajo Reservation. The Hopi are Arizona's oldest tribe and are probably best known for their unusual, often haunting kachina dolls.

According to Hopi religion, kachinas are several hundred sacred spirits that live in the San Francisco Peaks north of Flagstaff. At prescribed intervals during the year, they come to the Hopi Reservation and dance in a precise and ritualized fashion. These dances maintain harmony among all living things and are especially important for rainfall and fertility. Kachina dolls, traditionally carved from the dried root of the cottonwood tree and elaborate in design and color, represent these sacred spirits.

While some kachina dolls are considered too sacred for public display or trade, Hopi artisans carve kachina dolls specifically to be sold to the general public. You can buy these, as well as pottery, basketwork and jewelry at Hopi House (p108) in Grand Canyon Village, at the Watchtower (p114), where Navajo weavers sometimes demonstrate their craft, and at the Cameron Trading Post (p170).

The Paiute

The Southern Paiute people occupy land north of the Colorado River in what is known as the Arizona Strip and have traditionally used the canyon for hundreds of years. After contact and conflict with Navajo and Ute slavers, Spanish explorers, Mormon settlers and the US government, the Southern Paiute now live in scattered settlements and reservations in California, Utah, Nevada and Arizona.

One branch of this tribe, the Kaibab Paiute, occupies a reservation in northern Arizona, just west of Fredonia and south of Kanab, Utah. The tribe is largely involved in both agriculture and tourism and runs a visitors center and campground at Pipe Spring National Monument (p209).

strenuous hike to the river and back. It's generally recommended that you don't attempt to hike to the river; and in fact, the reservation actively discourages this.

Sleeping & Eating

We have to mention again that it's 8 miles to the lodge and more than 10 miles to the campground from Hualapai Hilltop. It is absolutely essential that you make reservations in advance; if you hike in without a reservation, you will not be allowed to stay in Supai and will have to hike all the way back up to your car at the trailhead.

Havasu Campground (☎ 928-448-2121, 928-448-2141; Havasupai Camping Office, PO Box 160, Supai, AZ 86435; sites $; ⏰ check-in 9am-5pm) Two miles past Supai, this campground's 340 sites span three-quarters of a mile along the creek between Havasu and Mooney Falls. You'll find picnic tables, pit toilets and a spring for drinking water (purify it first). While there are no showers, you can swim in the river and pools. Fires are not permitted, but campers can cook on gas stoves. This campground is often packed in summer, so be sure to hike its length before choosing a spot to pitch your tent. Campground rates do not include the entrance fee into the reservation.

Havasupai Lodge (☎ 928-448-2111, 928-448-2201; www.havasupaitribe.com; PO Box 159, Supai, AZ 86435; r $$) In Supai, this lodge offers motel rooms, all with canyon views, two double beds, air-conditioning and private showers. There are no TVs or telephones. Reservations are essential; the lodge is often booked months in advance for the entire summer, and unless you plan to camp, there's nowhere else to stay. A café serves breakfast, lunch and dinner daily, and a general store sells basic but expensive groceries and snacks (supplies are still carried down by mule).

Getting There & Around

Seven miles east of Peach Springs on historic Route 66, a signed turnoff leads to the 62-mile paved road to Havasu Canyon. At Hualapai Hilltop you'll find the parking area, stables and the trailhead into the canyon, but no services. To get to Supai, park your car and then hike, ride or fly the 8 miles down to the village. If you plan on hiking or riding down, you should spend the night either in Peach Springs (ideally), Grand Canyon Caverns or in one of the motels along Route 66. Motels in Seligman are about 90 miles from Hualapai Hilltop.

If you're planning on hiking down after spending the night at the South Rim, be aware that Hualapai Hilltop is a good (ie not so good) three- to four-hour drive from the South Rim.

Don't let place names confuse you: Hualapai Hilltop is on the Havasupai Indian Reservation, not the Hualapai Reservation, as one might think.

A DARK UNDERCURRENT TO THE BLUE-GREEN WATER

Each year about 30,000 visitors are lured into Havasu Canyon by the famed blue-green pools and waterfalls from which the Havasupai take their name. The vast majority of travelers enjoy peaceful stays in Supai, exploring the waters around the village – but in May 2006 one visitor hiked out toward the pools and never returned.

The brutal stabbing murder of 34-year-old Tomomi Hanamure, a solo Japanese woman visiting Havasu Canyon for her birthday, shook the tribe both with its violence and by the mere fact of its occurrence. The mainstream media invaded Supai, reporting on an influx of methamphetamine, the village's deteriorating social structure and its dangerous, disaffected youth. Under the barrage of negative attention, the tribe soon barred journalists from entering the valley and released little information about the developing case. In December 2006 Randy Wescogame, a young Havasupai man, was arrested and charged with Hanamure's murder.

Supai's societal problems are certainly not unique to the Havasupai. A single murder, though tragic, should not deter you from experiencing this magical place, just as Las Vegas' dozens of yearly murders don't deter the millions who visit Sin City.

That said, while most trips to Supai and Havasu Canyon are blissfully uneventful and rewarding, some visitors have reported being harassed by local youth. For the time being, solo travel into Havasu Canyon is not recommended, and female visitors should strongly consider traveling there with male companions.

RESERVATION ETIQUETTE

Visitors are usually welcome on Native American reservations, as long as they behave in an appropriately courteous and respectful manner. Tribal rules are often clearly posted at the entrance to each reservation, but here are some general guidelines.

Alcohol Most reservations ban the sale or use of alcohol.

Ceremonials and powwows These are either open to the public or exclusively for tribal members. Ceremonials are religious events, and applauding, chatting, asking questions or trying to talk to the performers is rude. Photography and other forms of recording are rarely permitted. While powwows also hold spiritual significance, they are usually more informal.

Clothing Modest dress is customary. Especially when watching ceremonials, you should dress conservatively; tank tops and short shorts are inappropriate.

Photography and other recording Many tribes ban all forms of recording, be it photography, videotaping, audiotaping or drawing. Others permit these activities in certain areas only if you pay the appropriate fee (usually $5 to $10). If you wish to photograph a person, do so only after obtaining his or her permission. A posing tip is usually expected. Photographers who disregard these rules can expect tribal police officers to confiscate their cameras and then escort them off the reservation.

Private property Use common sense here – don't walk into private homes unless invited. Don't climb on ruins or remove any kind of artifact from a reservation. Kivas (ceremonial chambers) are always off-limits to visitors. Off-road travel is not allowed without a permit.

Recreation Activities such as backpacking, camping, fishing and hunting require tribal permits. On Native American lands, state fishing or hunting licenses are not valid.

Verbal communication It is considered polite to listen without comment, particularly when an elder is speaking. Be prepared for long silences in the middle of conversations; such silences often indicate that a topic is under serious consideration.

MULE OR HORSE RIDES INTO THE CANYON

If you don't want to hike to Supai, you can arrange for a mule or horse to carry you in and out. It costs $120 round-trip for rides to the lodge, and $150 round-trip for rides to the campground. It's about half that price if you hike in and ride out, or vice versa. Mules depart Hualapai Hilltop at 10am year-round. Call the lodge or campground (wherever you'll be spending the night) in advance to arrange a ride.

HELICOPTER RIDES INTO THE CANYON

On Sundays, Mondays, Thursdays and Fridays from mid-March through mid-October, a helicopter ($85 one way) shuttles between Hualapai Hilltop and Supai from 10am to 1pm. Service is on a first-come, first-served basis and advance reservations are not accepted; you just show up at the parking lot and sign up. There's no hangar or anything – just a helicopter in the dirt. Call **Havasupai Tourist Enterprise** (☎ 928-448-2141) before you arrive to be sure the helicopter is running. From mid-October to mid-March the helicopter operates on Sundays and Fridays only.

Papillon Grand Canyon Helicopters (☎ 800-528-2418; www.papillon.com) offers a daily flight from Grand Canyon Airport, in Tusayan, to Supai for $465 round-trip (with online discount). Flights depart Tusayan at 9:40am; you can spend the day in the canyon and return on the 3:30pm flight, or you can return on a later day. Lodging is not included.

HUALAPAI RESERVATION & SKYWALK

Home to the much-hyped Skywalk, the Hualapai Reservation borders many miles of the Colorado River northeast of Kingman and includes the only road to the river within the Grand Canyon. In 1988 the Hualapai Nation opened Grand Canyon West, a less chaotic alternative to the South Rim. Though the views here are lovely, they're not as sublime as those on the South Rim – but the unveiling of the glass bridge known as Grand Canyon Skywalk in 2007 added a completely novel way to view the canyon. It's a hell of a drive to get here, but that's part of the adventure – you even could consider flying in if you're leery of busting the shocks on your car.

Orientation & Information

The Hualapai Reservation covers the southwest rim of the canyon, bordering Havasupai Reservation to the east and Lake Mead National Recreation Area to the west. **Hualapai Office of Tourism** (☎ 928-769-2219, 888-255-9550; Hualapai Reservation, PO Box 538, Peach Springs, AZ 86434) staffs a desk at Hualapai Lodge (right) in the blink-and-you'll-miss-it town of Peach Springs.

Sights & Activities

GRAND CANYON WEST

Nowadays, the only way to visit **Grand Canyon West** (☎ 877-716-9378; adult/child from $30/23; 🕒 7am-7pm summer, 8am-4:30pm winter), the section of the west rim overseen by the Hualapai Nation, is to purchase a package tour. A hop-on, hop-off shuttle travels the loop road to scenic points along the rim. Tours can include a community picnic-style lunch (vegetarians and picky eaters, bring your own), horse-drawn wagon rides from an ersatz Western town, and informal Native American performances.

All but the cheapest packages include admission to the **Grand Canyon Skywalk** (www.grandcanyonskywalk.com; adult/child $25/18.75; 🕒 8am-6pm summer, 9am-3:30pm winter), the vertigo-inducing, horseshoe-shaped glass bridge cantilevered 4000ft above the canyon floor. Jutting out almost 70ft over the canyon, the Skywalk allows visitors to see the canyon through the glass walkway. Would-be visitors to the Skywalk are required to purchase a package tour, which makes the amazing experience of peering past your feet into the gorge below quite a pricey prospect. *Nota bene:* at press time, no cameras, parachute rigs or other personal belongings were allowed on the Skywalk.

Tours depart several times a day from the Grand Canyon West airport terminal. Allow at least a half-day to get there, have a look around, and drive back out. Day tours from Las Vegas (see p180), including a round-trip flight via helicopter or small plane, can also be arranged.

DIAMOND CREEK ROAD

This 22-mile unpaved scenic road heads north from Peach Springs to the Colorado River. At road's end you'll find picnic tables and a camping area (see right). Don't forget to purchase an entrance permit ($12 plus tax, per person) from the Hualapai Lodge front desk before driving down the road.

RAFTING

Hualapai River Runners (p224) offers one-day rafting trips on the Colorado from Diamond Creek to Pierce Ferry Landing. Its motorized rafts hold up to 10 people, and this is your only opportunity for a one-day white-water rafting trip within the Grand Canyon. River trips include a shuttle to the reservation from Hualapai Lodge (below) in Peach Springs. The Hualapai Lodge can also arrange packages that include accommodations with the river trip.

Sleeping & Eating

Diamond Creek Campground (Map p136; sites incl entrance fee $) On the Colorado, at the end of Diamond Creek Rd, is this small and basic campground, a beach camping spot along the river. The elevation here is 1900ft, so the campground is extremely hot in summer. You'll find toilets and a picnic tables but no drinking water. The campground holds about 10 people and is first-come, first-served; contact the Hualapai Office of Tourism (☎ 928-769-2230) for availability.

Grand Canyon Caverns & Inn (Map p136; ☎ 928-422-3223; www.grandcanyoncaverns.com; MM 115, Route 66; r $; 💻 🏊 ♿) Thirteen miles east of Peach Springs on Route 66 is this inn offering basic motel rooms, a pool and a restaurant (mains $; open 7am to 7pm) serving burgers and fried food. The hotel also operates tours of Grand Canyon Caverns (see p144).

Hualapai Lodge (☎ 928-769-2230; 900 Route 66, Peach Springs; r $$; 🏊 ♿) The only place to stay in Peach Springs is this modern lodge, which has, oddly, a saltwater swimming pool. Connected to the hotel is Diamond Creek Restaurant (mains $; open breakfast, lunch and dinner), serving standard American fare.

Thirty-five miles east of Peach Springs, in Seligman, you'll find several inexpensive, simple motels; the best is **Historic Route 66 Motel** (☎ 928-422-3204; 500 W Route 66; r $).

Getting There & Around

There are no regular shuttles or buses to Peach Springs or the Hualapai Reservation.

At the time of writing, 14 of the 21 miles of Diamond Bar Rd to Grand Canyon West were graded but unpaved. Be prepared for very slow going (as in 20mph slow) on the dusty, bumpy road – while the ride can be fun in a car, it's inadvisable in an RV. You should call the Hualapai Lodge to check road conditions before heading out, especially if it's been raining, as the road may be impassable. If you don't feel up to driving, take advantage of the **park-and-ride service** (☎ 702-260-6506; per person $10); reserve in advance.

To get to Grand Canyon West from Kingman, fill up your gas tank and drive north on Hwy 93 for approximately 26 miles. Then head northeast along the paved Pierce Ferry Rd for about another 30 miles, before turning onto Diamond Bar Rd for the final 21-mile stretch. Directions from other towns are detailed on the **Grand Canyon West website** (www.destinationgrandcanyon.com). At the time of writing, rumor had it that the Hualapai Nation planned to pave Diamond Bar Rd (and save the surrounding Joshua trees from choking to death) by the end of 2008.

Bypass the driving completely by booking a Grand Canyon West tour with a round-trip flight from Las Vegas (see p180).

FLAGSTAFF & AROUND

☎ 928 / pop 58,210 / elev 6910ft

People come to Flagstaff for many reasons: to attend Northern Arizona University (NAU), to break up an interstate jaunt or perhaps to stay while visiting the South Rim. Many end up moving here; that's the kind of place it is. With a pedestrian-friendly historic downtown, lots of great restaurants, fun brewpubs, leisurely coffeehouses, interesting hotels, fantastic scenery and proximity to myriad outdoor activities, Flagstaff is a wonderful city, well worth a few days before or after a trip to the canyon.

Orientation

Approaching Flagstaff from the east, I-40 parallels Old Route 66. Their paths diverge at Enterprise Rd: I-40 veers southwest, while Old Route 66 curls northwest, hugging the railroad tracks, and is the main drag through the historic downtown. NAU sits between downtown and I-40. From downtown, I-17 heads south toward Phoenix, splitting off at Hwy Alt 89 (also known as 89A), a spectacularly scenic winding road through Oak Creek Canyon to Sedona. Hwy 180 is the most direct route northwest to Tusayan and the South Rim (80 miles), while Hwy 89 beelines north to Cameron (59 miles),

FESTIVALS & EVENTS

Flagstaff Winterfest Held throughout February, there's skiing, sled-dog races, skiing, food, skiing and a parade through historic downtown – oh, and skiing.

Sedona International Film Festival (www.sedonafilmfestival.com) A film festival hosted by screen veteran Sedona from late February to early March.

Hopi Festival of Arts & Culture At the Museum of Northern Arizona in Flagstaff, this festival from late June to early July features Hopi art, artisans and traditional dances.

Fabulous Fourth Festivities Celebrating both the 4th of July and the founding of Flagstaff, there's a parade, an arts-and-crafts fair and fireworks.

Navajo Festival of Arts & Culture Another Native American festival at the Museum of Northern Arizona in Flagstaff, this early-August festival features weaving demonstrations, talks on lore, ethnobotany and the Navajo language.

Flagstaff Festival of Science (www.scifest.org) Science presentations, hikes and other excursions bring science to life at this Flagstaff festival in late September.

Sedona Arts Festival (www.sedonaartsfestival.org) This arts fest in early October has been rated one of the country's top art festivals, showcasing fine arts and crafts, cuisine and entertainment.

Celebraciónes de la Gente Held at the same time of year as Día de los Muertos (Day of the Dead) at the Museum of Northern Arizona in Flagstaff, this late October festival celebrates the town's Latino heritage.

Sedona Plein Air Festival (www.sedonaartscenter.com) Open-air painters from all over the country and the world come to Sedona's spectacular natural setting in late October to paint and show off their works.

Festival of Lights Thousands of luminaria light up Tlaquepaque in Sedona in early December, accompanied by hot cider, live entertainment and holiday festivities.

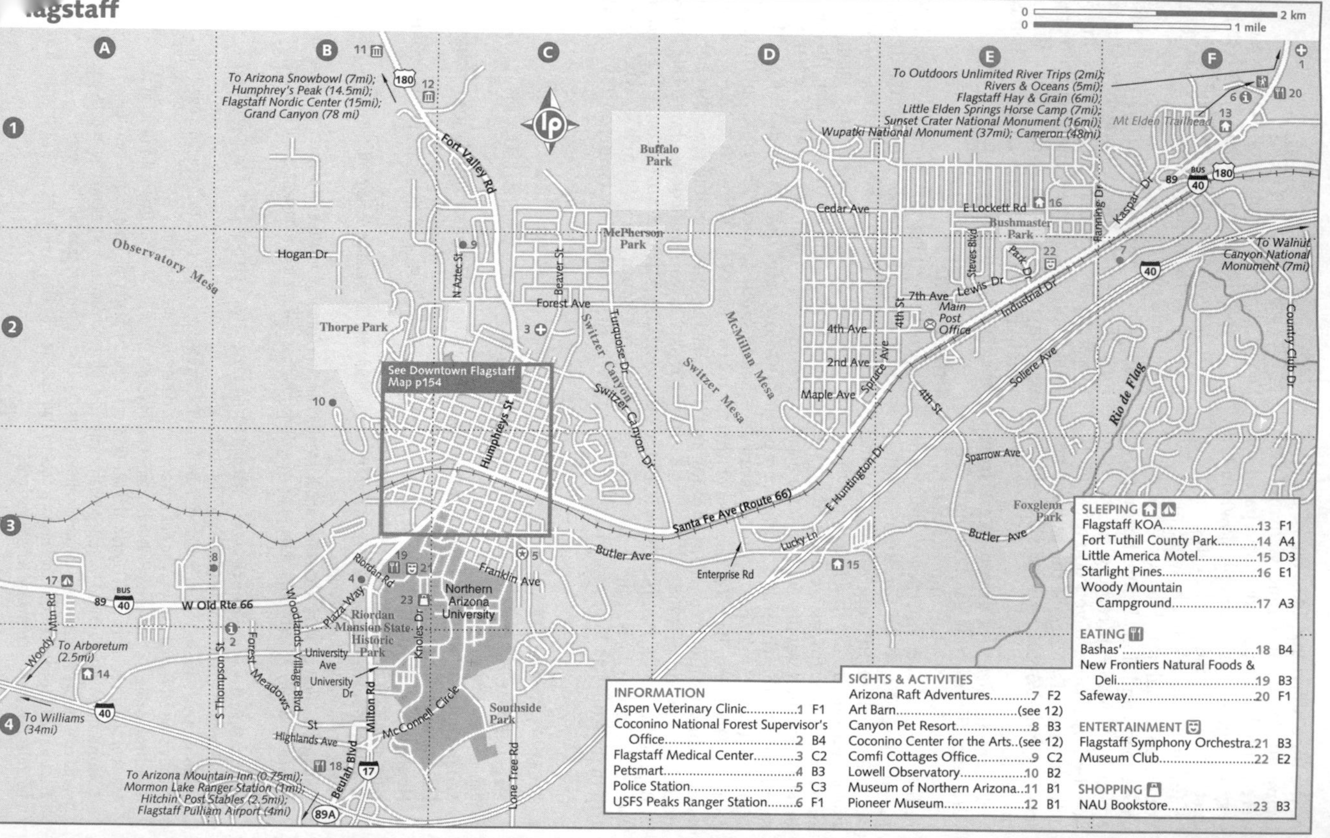
Flagstaff
0 2 km
0 1 mile
To Arizona Snowbowl (7mi); Humphrey's Peak (14.5mi); Flagstaff Nordic Center (15mi); Grand Canyon (78 mi)
To Outdoors Unlimited River Trips (2mi); Rivers & Oceans (5mi); Flagstaff Hay & Grain (6mi); Little Elden Springs Horse Camp (7mi); Sunset Crater National Monument (16mi); Wupatki National Monument (37mi); Cameron (48mi)
Mt Elden Trailhead
To Walnut Canyon National Monument (7mi)
Buffalo Park
McPherson Park
Bushmaster Park
Thorpe Park
Observatory Mesa
McMillan Mesa
Switzer Mesa
Switzer Canyon
Foxglenn Park
Southside Park
Rio de Flag
See Downtown Flagstaff Map p154
Northern Arizona University
Riordan Mansion State Historic Park
Main Post Office
Fort Valley Rd
Hogan Dr
N Aztec St
Beaver St
Forest Ave
Turquoise Dr
Switzer Canyon Dr
Humphreys St
Cedar Ave
E Lockett Rd
Steves Blvd
Park Dr
Lewis Dr
7th Ave
4th St
4th Ave
2nd Ave
Maple Ave
Spruce Ave
Industrial Dr
Kaspar Dr
Fanning Dr
Soliere Ave
Country Club Dr
Sparrow Ave
E Huntington Dr
Santa Fe Ave (Route 66)
Butler Ave
Lucky Ln
Enterprise Rd
Franklin Ave
Riordan Rd
Plaza Way
Knoles Dr
University Ave
University Dr
Milton Rd
McConnell Circle
Lone Tree Rd
Beulah Blvd
Highlands Ave
Woodlands Village Blvd
Forest Meadows St
S Thompson St
W Old Rte 66
Woody Mtn Rd
To Arboretum (2.5mi)
To Williams (34mi)
To Arizona Mountain Inn (0.75mi); Mormon Lake Ranger Station (1mi); Hitchin' Post Stables (2.5mi); Flagstaff Pulliam Airport (4mi)
SLEEPING
Flagstaff KOA.........13 F1
Fort Tuthill County Park.........14 A4
Little America Motel.........15 D3
Starlight Pines.........16 E1
Woody Mountain Campground.........17 A3
EATING
Bashas'.........18 B4
New Frontiers Natural Foods & Deli.........19 B3
Safeway.........20 F1
ENTERTAINMENT
Flagstaff Symphony Orchestra.21 B3
Museum Club.........22 E2
SHOPPING
NAU Bookstore.........23 B3
INFORMATION
Aspen Veterinary Clinic.........1 F1
Coconino National Forest Supervisor's Office.........2 B4
Flagstaff Medical Center.........3 C2
Petsmart.........4 B3
Police Station.........5 C3
USFS Peaks Ranger Station.........6 F1
SIGHTS & ACTIVITIES
Arizona Raft Adventures.........7 F2
Art Barn.........(see 12)
Canyon Pet Resort.........8 B3
Coconino Center for the Arts..(see 12)
Comfi Cottages Office.........9 C2
Lowell Observatory.........10 B2
Museum of Northern Arizona..11 B1
Pioneer Museum.........12 B1

where it meets Hwy 64 heading west to the canyon's East Entrance. Those headed to the North Rim (193 miles) stay on Hwy 89 past Cameron, link up with Alt 89 to Jacob Lake, then take Hwy 67 to the rim.

Information

Coconino National Forest Supervisor's Office (Map p152; ☎ 928-527-3600; 1824 S Thompson St; 7:30am-4:30pm Mon-Fri) For information on hiking, biking and camping in the surrounding national forest.
Flagstaff Medical Center (Map p152; ☎ 928-779-3366; 1200 N Beaver St; emergency 24hr)
Flagstaff Public Library (Map p154; ☎ 928-774-4000; 300 W Aspen Ave; 10am-8pm Mon & Wed, 10am-6pm Tue & Thu, 10am-5pm Fri & Sat, noon-5pm Sun)
Mormon Lake Ranger Station (off Map p152; ☎ 928-774-1147; 4373 Lake Mary Rd; 7:30am-4:30pm Mon-Fri) Focuses on the area south of town.
Police station (Map p152; ☎ 928-556-2316; 911 E Sawmill Rd; emergency 24hr)
Post office (Map p154; ☎ 928-714-9302; 104 N Agassiz St; 9am-5pm Mon-Fri, to 1pm Sat)
USFS Peaks Ranger Station (Map p152; ☎ 928-526-0866; 5075 N Hwy 89; 7:30am-4:30pm Mon-Fri) Provides information on the Mt Elden, Humphreys Peak and O'Leary Peak areas north of Flagstaff.
Visitors center (Map p154; ☎ 928-774-9541, 800-842-7293; www.flagstaff.az.us; 1 E Route 66; 8am-5pm) Inside the Amtrak station, the visitors center has a great Flagstaff Discovery map.

Sights

Flagstaff's laid-back appeal is hard to pin down – it could be the wonderful mix of cultural sites, its historic downtown, the access to outdoorsy pursuits – better you should investigate yourself.

MUSEUM OF NORTHERN ARIZONA

If you have time for only one sight in Flagstaff, this is it. In an attractive Craftsman-style stone building amid a pine grove, this small but excellent **museum** (Map p152; ☎ 928-774-5213; www.musnaz.org; 3101 N Fort Valley Rd; adult/child $7/4; 9am-5pm) features exhibits on local Native American archeology, history and culture, as well as geology, biology and the arts. Don't miss the extensive collection of Hopi katsina (the museum's spelling for 'kachina') dolls and a wonderful variety of Native American basketry and ceramics. The bookstore specializes in regional subjects. Check the website for information on changing exhibits, weekend craft demonstrations and one- to three-day workshops for children and adults. The museum also offers customized trips to the Grand Canyon (see p232).

RIORDAN MANSION STATE HISTORIC PARK

Centered on a beautiful 13,000-sq-ft mansion, this **park** (Map p152; ☎ 928-779-4395; www.pr.state.az.us; 409 W Riordan Rd; adult/child $6/2.50; 8:30am-5pm May-Oct, 10:30am-5pm Nov-Apr) is a must for anyone interested the Arts and Crafts movement. Having made a fortune from their Arizona Lumber Company, brothers Michael and Timothy Riordan had the house built in 1904. The Craftsman-style design was the brainchild of Atchison, Topeka & Santa Fe Railway architect Charles Whittlesey, who also designed El Tovar, on the South Rim. The exterior features hand-split wooden shingles, log-slab siding and rustic stone. Filled with Edison, Stickley, Tiffany and Steinway furniture, the interior is a shrine to Arts and Crafts and looks much as it did when the Riordans lived here. Visitors are welcome to walk the grounds and picnic, but entrance to the house is by guided tour only. Tours leave daily and on the hour; advance reservations are accepted. The visitors center offers a good selection of books on the Arts and Crafts movement, as well as exhibits on Flagstaff's history and architecture.

LOWELL OBSERVATORY

Atop the aptly named Mars Hill a mile west of downtown, this **national historic landmark** (Map p152; ☎ 928-774-3358; www.lowell.edu; 1400 W Mars Hill Rd; adult/child $6/3; 9am-5pm Mar-Oct, noon-5pm Nov-Feb;) was built in 1894 by Percival Lowell. In 1896 Lowell bought a 24in Clark refractor telescope for $20,000 ($6 million in today's dollars) and spent the next 20 years looking for life on Mars. Though he never did spot a Martian, the observatory has witnessed many important discoveries, the most famous of which was the first sighting of Pluto, in 1930. In the '60s NASA used the Clark telescope to map the moon. Weather permitting, visitors can stargaze through the telescope; check the website for the evening schedule. The short, paved Pluto Walk climbs through a scale model of our solar system, providing descriptions of each planet. You can stroll the grounds

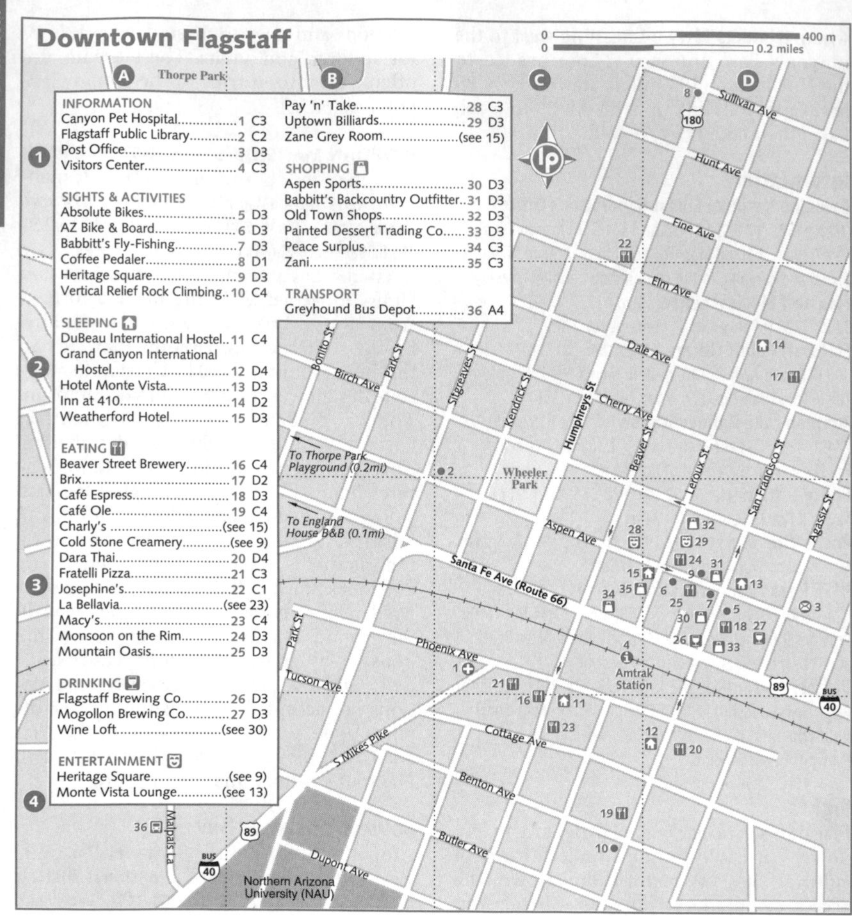

and museum on your own, but the only way to see the telescopes and lovely observatories is on a tour (on the hour from 10am to 4pm in summer; on the hour from 1pm and 4pm in winter). Even those with a passing interest in astronomy will enjoy the tours, as guides do a great job of explaining things in everyday terms.

THE ARBORETUM

More than just an attraction for gardeners and plant-lovers, this 200-acre **arboretum** (Map p152; ☎ 928-774-1442; 4001 S Woody Mountain Rd; www.thearb.org; adult/child $5/2; ⏰ 9am-5pm Apr-Oct, closed Nov 1-Mar 31;) is a lovely spot to take a break and rejuvenate your spirit. Two short wood-chip trails hug a meadow and wind beneath ponderosa pines, passing an herb garden, native plants, vegetables and wildflowers, among other growing things. Plan a picnic at one of the tables scattered throughout the gardens. The arboretum offers tours (11am and 1pm), as well as a summer adventure program for children aged four to 12.

PIONEER MUSEUM & COCONINO CENTER FOR THE ARTS

Housed in the old 1908 county hospital, the **Pioneer Museum** (Map p152; ☎ 928-774-6272; 2340 N Fort Valley Rd; adult/child $3/free; ⏰ 9am-5pm Mon-Sat) preserves Flagstaff's early history in photographs and an eclectic mix of memorabilia – for example, a 1920s-era permanent-wave machine (for curling hair) that looks more like a science-fiction torture device.

Behind the museum, the **Coconino Center for the Arts** (Map p152; ☎ 928-779-2300; www.culturalpartners.org; 2300 N Fort Valley Rd; ⏰ vary) exhibits work by local artists and hosts various performances and programs. Check its website for current exhibitions, performances and events. The adjacent **Art Barn** (Map p152; ☎ 928-774-0822; 2320 N Fort Valley Rd; ⏰ vary) has been displaying and selling local artisans' work for three decades. Here you'll find a good selection of jewelry, photography, painting, pottery and kachina dolls, among other objects.

SUNSET CRATER VOLCANO NATIONAL MONUMENT & WUPATKI NATIONAL MONUMENT

In AD 1064 a volcano erupted on this spot, spewing ash across 800 sq miles, spawning the Kana-A lava flow and leaving behind 8029ft **Sunset Crater** (Map p136). The eruption forced farmers to vacate lands they had cultivated for 400 years. Subsequent eruptions continued for more than 200 years. The **visitor center** (☎ 928-526-0502; www.nps.gov/sucr; park entrance fee $5; ⏰ visitor center 8am-5pm May-Oct, 9am-5pm Nov-Apr, monument sunrise-sunset) houses a seismograph and other exhibits pertaining to volcanology, while viewpoints and a 1-mile interpretive trail through the **Bonito lava flow** (formed c 1180) grant visitors a firsthand look at volcanic features; a shorter 0.3-mile loop is wheelchair accessible. You can also climb **Lenox Crater** (7024ft), a 1-mile round-trip that climbs 300ft. More ambitious hikers and mountain bikers can ascend **O'Leary Peak** (8965ft; 8 miles round-trip), the only way to peer down into Sunset Crater (aside from scenic flights).

The first eruptions enriched the surrounding soil, and ancestors of today's Hopi, Zuni and Navajo people returned to farm the land in the early 1100s. By 1180 thousands were living here in advanced multistory buildings, but by 1250 their pueblos stood abandoned. About 2700 of these structures lie within **Wupatki National Monument** (Map p136; ☎ 928-679-2365; www.nps.gov/wupa; ⏰ 9am-5pm), though only a few are open to the public. A short self-guided tour of the largest dwelling, **Wupatki Pueblo**, begins behind the visitors center. **Lamaki**, **Citadel** and **Nalakihu Pueblos** sit within a half-mile of the loop road just north of the visitors center, and a 2.5-mile road veers west from the center to **Wukoki Pueblo**, the best preserved of the buildings. In April and October rangers lead visitors on a 16-mile round-trip weekend backpacking tour ($50; supply your own food and gear) of **Crack-in-Rock Pueblo** and nearby petroglyphs. Chosen by lottery, only 13 people may join each tour; apply two months in advance via the website or in writing.

Covered by a single $5 entrance fee, both monuments lie along Park Loop Rd 545, a well-marked 36-mile loop that heads east off Hwy 89 about 12 miles north of Flagstaff then rejoins the highway 26 miles north of Flagstaff. Visitors can choose from among several picnic grounds. Rangers offer interpretive programs in summer.

WALNUT CANYON NATIONAL MONUMENT

The Sinagua cliff dwellings at **Walnut Canyon** (Map p136; ☎ 928-526-3367; www.nps.gov/waca; admission $5, valid for 7 days; ⏰ 8am-5pm May-Oct, 9am-5pm Nov-Apr) are set in the nearly vertical walls of a small limestone butte amid this forested canyon. The mile-long **Island Trail** steeply descends 185ft (more than 200 stairs), passing 25 rooms built under the natural overhangs of the curvaceous butte. A shorter, wheelchair-accessible **Rim Trail** affords several views of the cliff dwelling from across the canyon. Even if you're not all that interested in the mysterious Sinagua people, whose origins are unknown and whose site abandonments are still not understood today, Walnut Canyon itself is a beautiful place to visit, not so far from Flagstaff.

METEOR CRATER

A huge meteor crashed into our planet almost 50,000 years ago and produced this **crater** (Map p136; ☎ 928-289-5898, 800-289-5898; www.meteorcrater.com; adult/child $15/7; ⏰ 7am-7pm Jun–mid-Sep, 8am-5pm mid-Sep–May) about 43 miles east of Flagstaff. It is 570ft deep and almost a mile across. It was used as a training ground for some of the *Apollo* astronauts; the on-site museum has exhibits about meteors and space missions. Descending into the crater is not allowed, but you can walk the 3.5-mile Rim Trail. However, apart from a big hole in the ground, there's not much to see, and some readers suggest that it is an overpriced attraction.

The crater is privately owned and operated, and national-park passes are not accepted.

Meteor Crater RV Park (☎ 800-478-4002; RV sites $) has 71 RV sites with hookups. The RV Park has showers, a coin laundry, a playground, a small grocery store and a Subway sandwich shop.

Activities

HIKING & BIKING

Ask at the USFS ranger stations for maps and information about the scores of hiking and mountain-biking trails in and around Flagstaff. Another useful resource is *Flagstaff Hikes: 97 Day Hikes Around Flagstaff*, by Richard and Sherry Mangum (Hexagon Press, 2007), available at the visitors center, La Bellavia restaurant (p159) and Babbitt's Backcountry Outfitter (p162), among other places. For an inside track on the local mountain-biking scene served with a double macchiato, stop by **Coffee Pedaler** (Map p154; ☎ 928-779-5393; www.coffeepedaler.com; 719 W Humphreys St; 6am-4pm;), Flagstaff's awesome full-service bike shop and espresso bar.

Consider tackling the steep, 3-mile one-way hike up 9299ft **Mt Elden** (Map p152) to the ranger station at the top of the peak's tower, which has stairs you can climb to the ranger's lookout. Arizona Snowbowl offers several trails, including the strenuous 4.5-mile one-way hike up 12,633ft **Humphreys Peak** (off Map p152), the highest point in Arizona; wear decent boots, as sections of the trail cross crumbly volcanic rock. In summer, ride the scenic **chairlift** (adult/child $10/6; 10am-4pm Memorial Day-Labor Day) at Arizona Snowbowl (opposite) to 11,500ft, where you can hike, eat lunch on the Agassiz Deck and take in the desert and mountain views. Children under seven ride for free.

There's also a beautiful stretch of the Arizona Trail (see p45) running through the area. If you head toward Walnut Canyon (p155), you'll see a turnoff on the right, leading to the **Walnut Canyon Trailhead**. Drive 1.7 miles down the graded dirt road and you'll come to the trailhead. There are no restrooms, no water, no nothin' – come prepared with a map and supplies if you want to do the Fisher Point Trail (6.7 miles one way) or hike up to Marshall Lake (13.4 miles one way).

Another original, fabulous series of local mountain-biking and hiking guides is penned by local character Cosmic Ray. Pick up a copy of *Fat Tire Tales and Trails* (Cosmic Ray, 2006), with hand-drawn, to-scale maps and colorful, entertaining summaries of each trail – 'epic-didlyicious!' – accompanied with elevation gain, distance, difficulty level and detailed route descriptions. Cosmic Ray also self-publishes the guide *50 Favorite Hikes: Flagstaff and Sedona* (2007), as well as laminated,

FLAGSTAFF FUN STUFF FOR KIDS

- Call on Cold Stone Creamery (p159) for a creative cone
- Boogie to the band and catch a movie outdoors at Heritage Square (Map p154)
- Feed the fawns at Grand Canyon Deer Farm (p140)
- Ride a horse-drawn carriage (opposite) around Flagstaff
- Picnic and play at Thorpe Park playground (opposite)
- Browse books in the children's book section of the library (p153)
- Ride the scenic chairlift at Arizona Snowbowl (opposite)
- Hike through lava flows at Sunset Crater Volcano National Monument (p155)
- Board the Grand Canyon Railway (p244) to the South Rim
- Learn about native flora in the Flagstaff Arboretum (p154) summer adventure program
- Groove to the tunes of the Summer Concert Series at the Arboretum (p154) on the first Saturdays of June, July and August
- Pull up a chair in Heritage Sq (p161) and catch a family-friendly flick on a warm summer weekend

shove-in-your-pocket trail maps for both Flagstaff and Sedona. Look for his books and maps at Macy's (p159), the Coffee Pedaler and regional branches of REI (Recreational Equipment, Inc) – and then hit the trail.

To rent a mountain bike, hit up **Absolute Bikes** (Map p154; ☎ 928-779-5969; www.absolutebikes.net; 18 N San Francisco St; bike rentals per day from $40; ⏰ 9am-7pm Mon-Fri, 10am-6pm Sat, 10am-4pm Sun), or **AZ Bike & Board** (Map p154; ☎ 928-772-9881; 5 E Aspen Ave; bike rentals per day from $30; ⏰ 9am-5pm). Rentals typically include a helmet, patch kit, inner tube, water-bottle cage and pump.

OTHER ACTIVITIES

If you can't guess by glancing around at the townsfolk, Flagstaff is full of active citizens. So there's no shortage of outdoors stores and places to rent camping, biking and skiing equipment. For ski rentals, swing by Peace Surplus (p162) and Babbitt's Backcountry.

About 7 miles north of downtown, **Arizona Snowbowl** (off Map p152; ☎ 928-779-1951; www.arizonasnowbowl.com; Hwy 180 & Snowbowl Rd; adult/child $48/25; ⏰ 9am-4pm) is small but lofty, with four lifts that service 30 ski runs between 9200ft and 11,500ft. You can cross-country ski along 30 groomed trails at the **Flagstaff Nordic Center** (off Map p152; ☎ 928-220-0550; www.flagstaffnordiccenter.com; $10; Hwy 180), 15 miles north of Flagstaff, which offers lessons, rentals and food. Past the Nordic Center off Hwy 180, you'll find plenty of USFS cross-country skiing pullouts, where you can park and ski for free.

Vertical Relief Rock Climbing (Map p154; ☎ 928-556-9909; www.verticalrelief.com; 205 S San Francisco St; rock gym day pass $15; ⏰ 10am-11pm Mon-Fri, noon-8pm Sat & Sun) provides 6000 sq ft of artificial indoor climbing walls. Routes range from beginner to the most difficult grades. The center also offers indoor and outdoor classes as well as information on local climbing routes.

MacDonalds Ranch (☎ 928-774-4481; www.macdonaldsranch.com) offers one- or two-hour guided trail rides and hay rides through Coconino National Forest at Arizona Snowbowl. **Hitchin' Post Stables** (off Map p152; ☎ 928-774-1719; www.hitchinpoststables.com; 4848 Lake Mary Rd; 🚸) offers trail rides to Walnut Canyon and other destinations upon request. **Horse-drawn carriage** rides depart from Heritage Sq (Map p154) on summer weekend evenings.

Fly-fishing opportunities abound in Oak Creek and the lakes surrounding Flagstaff and Williams. **Babbitt's Fly-Fishing** (Map p154; ☎ 928-779-3253; 15 E Aspen Ave; ⏰ 10am-6pm Mon-Fri, 10am-4pm Sun) and Peace Surplus can provide information and equipment, and Babbitt's offers guided trips.

Thorpe Park (off Map p154; ☎ 928-779-7690; 245 N Thorpe Rd) is a great playground for letting the little ones run loose.

Sleeping

One flaw that mars Flagstaff's abundant charm is the frequency of trains traveling through the middle of town (once every 15 minutes, on average). The trains themselves wouldn't be so bothersome if they didn't blare their horns incessantly when chugging through, late at night. Unfortunately, most of Flagstaff's budget accommodations, as well as many others, are near the tracks. If you're a light sleeper, you'll want to bring earplugs – or an anvil to drop on your own head – to facilitate a good night's sleep.

BUDGET

Dozens of nondescript, independent motels, with rates ranging from $30 to $50, line Old Route 66 and the railroad tracks east of downtown (exit 198 off I-40). Check the room before you pay – some are worse than others, and many are loud. You're better off at one of the hostels or historic hotels downtown.

Grand Canyon International Hostel (Map p154; ☎ 928-779-9421, 888-442-2696; www.grandcanyonhostel.com; 19½ S San Francisco St; dm & r $, both incl breakfast; 💻) Housed in a historic building with hardwood floors and Southwestern decor, the bright, homey Grand Canyon Hostel offers budget travelers private rooms or dorms with a four-person maximum. It has a slightly more mellow feel and is just slightly further from the tracks than the DuBeau, which is owned by the same proprietors. The kitchens are spotless, and there's a TV room with a VCR.

DuBeau International Hostel (Map p154; ☎ 928-774-6731, 800-398-7112; www.grandcanyonhostel.com; 19 W Phoenix Ave; dm & r $, both incl breakfast; 💻) Sharing the same owner as the Grand Canyon International Hostel, this independent hostel offers the same friendly service and clean, well-run accommodations. There are also laundry facilities and bright, clean kitchens. Convivial common areas include a nonsmoking lounge with a fireplace, as well as a jukebox, foosball and a pool table – it's a bit livelier over here.

Free dispersed camping is permitted in the national forest surrounding Flagstaff. Also check out p166 for information about USFS campgrounds in Oak Creek Canyon, 15 to 30 miles south of town.

Woody Mountain Campground (Map p152; ☎ 928-774-7727; www.woodymountaincampground.com; 2727 W Route 66; tent & RV sites $; Mar-Oct;) Has 146 sites, a pool, playground and coin laundry; off I-40 at exit 191.

Fort Tuthill County Park (Map p152; ☎ 928-774-3464; tent & RV sites $; May-Sep) Fort Tuthill sits 5 miles south of downtown at exit 337 off I-17; has 100 family sites with water and sewer only, and 150 group sites without utilities.

Flagstaff KOA (Map p152; ☎ 928-526-9926, 800-562-3524; www.flagstaffkoa.com; 5803 N Hwy 89; tent & RV sites $; year-round) One of the biggest campgrounds lies a mile north of I-40 off exit 201, 5 miles northeast of downtown.

Bonito Campground (☎ 928-526-0866; tent & RV sites $; May–mid-Oct) Across from the Sunset Crater Volcano National Monument visitors center (p155), the USFS-run Bonito provides running water and restrooms but no showers or hookups.

MIDRANGE

Chain motels line Milton Rd and Beulah Blvd, clustering around exit 198 off I-40. These are furthest from the train tracks and thus the quietest in Flagstaff.

Weatherford Hotel (Map p154; ☎ 928-779-1919; www.weatherfordhotel.com; 23 N Leroux St; r $$) This historic three-story brick hotel offers eight small, pleasant rooms, five with private bathrooms and all with a turn-of-the-20th-century feel. Since it has two bars, live music (see Charly's, p161) and is within rumble distance of the train station, it can get loud here – if you need silence for sleeping, consider staying elsewhere. If you do stay here, note that there's a 2am curfew. The 3rd-floor Zane Grey Room welcomes hotel guests and visitors with an 1882 bar, a fireplace and an original Thomas Moran painting. Perch along the adjoining wraparound verandah with a drink, admire the distant San Francisco Peaks, and watch passersby on the busy streets below.

our pick **Hotel Monte Vista** (Map p154; ☎ 928-779-6971, 800-545-3068; www.hotelmontevista.com; 100 N San Francisco St; d & ste $$;) A huge, old-fashioned neon sign towers over the roof of this classic 1926 hotel, hinting at what's inside: feather lampshades, antique furniture, bold colors (just try to find a plain white wall) and eclectic decor. Many of the rooms are named for movie stars who slept in them. The Humphrey Bogart room features black-satin bedding, black walls and a yellow ceiling, while the Jane Russell room flaunts a red rug, red walls and a chair in the shape of a high-heeled shoe. In the late '70s a woman died in the rocking chair of the Jon Bon Jovi (!) room and is said to haunt that room. Creepier still is the Gary Cooper room, supposedly haunted by two prostitutes who were stabbed and thrown out its window in the 1930s. The hotel houses a basement bar (deep enough to keep noise to a minimum), a restaurant and an adjoining Aveda spa. Rates rise on weekends and fall in slower seasons.

Arizona Mountain Inn (off Map p152; ☎ 928-774-8959, 800-239-5236; www.arizonamountaininn.com; 4200 Lake Mary Rd; cabins $$;) A-frame and wood cabins outfitted with kitchenettes, some with mountain views and lofts, are scattered around this ponderosa-forested property about 10 minutes' drive south of downtown. Far from the railroad tracks (and pretty much everything else), this is a great getaway for those craving some quiet. Dogs are allowed in most cabins for an extra fee.

Comfi Cottages (Map p152; ☎ 928-774-0731, 888-774-0731; www.comficottages.com; cottages $$-$$$;) If you're tired of hotels and motels, consider these bungalows, which are spread out in residential areas around town and all less than a mile from the historic district. Most were built in the 1920s and '30s and have a homey old feel to them, with wood floors, Craftsman-style kitchens and little lawns. Cabinets are filled with breakfast foods, and each cottage includes a TV, VCR, telephone, bicycles, tennis rackets, a BBQ grill, a picnic table and picnic baskets. The smallest cottage has one bedroom and one bathroom, while the largest has four bedrooms and four bathrooms.

TOP END

Flagstaff has several wonderful B&Bs, most of which are listed on the website www.flagstaff-bed-breakfast.com.

Starlight Pines (Map p152; ☎ 928-527-1912, 800-752-1912; www.starlightpinesbb.com; 3380 E Lockett Rd; r $$-$$$; 💻) On the east side of town, Starlight Pines has four spacious rooms in a Victorian-style house, each decorated meticulously with Tiffany-style lamps, antique clawfoot tubs, Stickley chairs and other lovely touches. Each room is differently themed and individually decorated, with extras like a private balcony overlooking Mt Elden or a fireplace. Your hosts, Michael and Richard, are as welcoming and warm as the house itself and are happy to give travel advice on the Grand Canyon and other local attractions.

England House (Map p154; ☎ 928-214-7350, 877-214-7350; www.englandhousebandb.com; 614 W Santa Fe Ave; r $$-$$$) This exquisitely restored Flagstaff B&B has a distinctive stone exterior made of local Moenkopi and Coconino sandstones. The elegant design of the interior shines from every surface, from the stamped-tin ceilings to the antique French furniture and sumptuous fabrics. Breakfast is served in a sunroom off of the kitchen, or out back if the sun is shining, and guests are encouraged to raid the refrigerator for modern treats like bottled beers and ice-cream bars.

Inn at 410 (Map p154; ☎ 928-774-0088, 800-774-2008; www.inn410.com; 410 N Leroux St; r $$$; 💻) This elegant and fully renovated 1894 house offers nine spacious, beautifully decorated bedrooms, each with a refrigerator and private bathroom. Most rooms also have a fireplace or whirlpool bath and many have four-poster beds and views of the garden or the San Francisco Peaks. It has a shady garden with fruit trees and a cozy dining room, where the full gourmet breakfast and afternoon snack are served and where you can mix yourself a cocktail on a lazy afternoon.

Little America Motel (Map p152; ☎ 928-779-7900, 800-865-1401; www.littleamerica.com; 2515 E Butler Ave; d & ste $$$; 💻 🚭 ♿ 👶) When you reach the adjacent truck stop, don't drive away thinking you have the wrong place. Behind an unassuming exterior is a sprawling hotel with an elegant lobby and spacious rooms, which are beautifully appointed with faux antique furniture, goose-down pillows and rich bedding, refrigerators and large bathrooms. Small patios in each room open on 500 acres of grass and woods, through which a flat 2-mile trail winds. You'll find a playground and a pool with a small bar, and the hotel's many amenities include room service, a coffee shop and an upscale restaurant. This oasis in the most unexpected of places, minutes from downtown, is great for families.

Eating

Flagstaff has the best food scene in the region, not only in terms of variety but for quality and bang for bucks.

BUDGET

Cold Stone Creamery (Map p154; ☎ 928-214-8440; 6 E Aspen Ave; ice cream $; 🕑 1-9pm Mon-Thu, noon-10pm Fri & Sat, noon-9pm Sun; 👶) If you're not familiar with Cold Stone, this ice-cream shop offers all kinds of treats, from gummy bears and brownies to fruit, which are folded into your ice cream on a chilled countertop. Don't be surprised if the staff burst into song.

New Frontiers Natural Foods & Deli (Map p152; ☎ 928-774-5747; 1000 S Milton Rd; mains $; 🕑 8am-8pm) Our favorite place to stock up on groceries for camping or picnics is this deli, which offers a great selection of premade salads, mains and made-to-order sandwiches. To get there, take Route 66 west from downtown and continue south on S Milton Rd; New Frontiers will be on your left about half a mile down.

La Bellavia (Map p154; ☎ 928-774-8301; 18 S Beaver St; mains $; 🕑 6:30am-2pm; ♿ 👶) Be prepared to wait in line at this popular breakfast spot. The seven-grain French toast with bananas, apples or blueberries is excellent, or try one of their egg dishes like Eggs Sardo – with sautéed spinach and artichoke hearts. If you opt for the yummy oat cakes, just one is – how do you say – *substantial*. Lunch includes a grilled portobello-mushroom sandwich and a grilled salmon salad, as well as standard options like grilled cheese, burgers and a tuna melt. If you're lucky, one of the few tables outside will be free. Credit cards are not accepted.

Macy's (Map p154; ☎ 928-774-2243; www.macyscoffee.net; 14 S Beaver St; mains $; 🕑 6am-8pm Mon-Wed, to 10pm Thu-Sun; 💻 Ⓥ ♿) Two doors down from La Bellavia, this vegetarian café is a Flagstaff institution, where students rub shoulders with superior court judges. A co laundry lies between the two restaurants, you can pop in a load and relax with you latte and book. There's an impressive arra of vegan choices on the menu, but if you're more interested in traditional café grub it also whips up the usual pastries, scrambled eggs, yogurt and granola. On late afternoons and evenings, the café presents live music, but at almost any time of day you'll be sipping your joe (or soy chai) alongside a healthy variety of Flagstaffians. Macy's is cash only.

Café Espress (Map p154; 928-774-0541; 16 N San Francisco St; mains $; 7am-9pm;) A sunny, bright café offering coffee and tea drinks, pastries, smoothies and fresh-squeezed juices, this is a great choice for breakfast, lunch or dinner. There's something here for everyone, from the spinach pesto tofu scramble and Italian vegetable frittata to corned beef hash and biscuits and gravy. One order of blueberry whole-grain pancakes is big enough to satisfy two hungry adults. The lunch and dinner menus are equally eclectic, including mahi-mahi tacos, salmon BLTs, turkey burgers and black bean–chicken salad.

Martans Burrito Palace (Map p154; 928-773-4701; 10 N San Francisco St; mains $; 8am-2pm Mon-Fri, 8:30am-1pm Sun;) This local-favorite hole-in-the-wall specializes in chilaquiles (scrambled eggs, red enchilada sauce, cheese and onions on a tortilla). Just about everyone in town recommends it for quick, tasty, low-key Mexican.

Good supermarkets include the local chain **Bashas'** (Map p152; 928-774-3882; www.bashas.com; 2700 S Woodlands Village Blvd; 5am-1am) and of course **Safeway** (Map p152; 928-526-6116; 4910 N Hwy 89; 5am-midnight).

MIDRANGE

Dara Thai (Map p154; 928-774-0047; 14 S San Francisco St; mains $-$$; 11am-10pm Mon-Sat;) Plants and wooden booths give this low-key Thai spot a comfortable feel. To suit every taste, food is available in spice levels, from one to five. The service is friendly, and the food consistently good, with clean flavors and large portions. Consider ordering a selection of appetizers – deep-fried banana slices dipped in tempura batter; lime, ginger, peanut and toasted coconut wrapped in spinach leaves with brown-sugar dip; or chicken satay with peanut sauce and cucumber dip.

Mountain Oasis (Map p154; 928-214-9270; 11 E Aspen; mains $-$$; 11am-9pm;) Vegetarians and vegans will find a bunch of options on this internationally spiced menu. Tasty specialties include the TBLT (tempeh bacon, lettuce and tomato), Thai veggies and tofu with peanut sauce and brown rice, and stuffed grape leaves. Steak and chicken are also featured on the menu, so meat-eaters need not shy away from this relaxed, plant-filled oasis. The fresh-fruit lemonades are just the thing to revive your spirit on a hot afternoon.

Café Olé (Map p154; 928-774-8272; 119 S San Francisco St; mains $-$$; 11am-3pm & 5-8pm Tue-Sat;) For some of the best Mexican food in the region, stop by this brightly colored joint (complete with chili-pepper strings and interior murals). It's a friendly, family-run place – the Aguinaga family has been perfecting their recipes for more than a decade. The food veers towards New Mexican–style, featuring green and red chili sauce, and everything is fresh and healthy (there's no lard in the beans, and they keep frying to a minimum). For spice-lovers, this is Mexican food with a real kick.

Monsoon on the Rim (Map p154; 928-226-8844; 6 E Aspen Ave; mains $-$$; 11:30am-9pm;) Offering good food, patio dining and a large, modern interior just off Heritage Sq, Monsoon is busy with tourists and locals alike. The limited menu features American-style Chinese standards like kung pao chicken and ginger beef, but you can also get a teriyaki burger or decent sushi. Look for interesting daily specials.

Beaver Street Brewery (Map p154; 928-779-0079; www.beaverstreetbrewery.com; 11 S Beaver St; mains $-$$; 11am-midnight;) Beaver Street Brewery, located on the block south of the tracks that's also home to popular Flagstaff haunts like Macy's and La Bellavia, is a bustling place to go for a bite to eat with a pint of local microbrew. It usually has five handmade beers on tap, like its Railhead Red Ale or R&R Oatmeal Stout, and some seasonal brews. The menu is typical brewpub fare, with delicious pizzas, burgers and salads. This place packs them all in – families, river guides, ski bums and businesspeople.

Fratelli Pizza (Map p154; 928-774-9200; 119 W Phoenix; mains $-$$; 11am-10pm Sun-Thu, to 2am Fri & Sat;) Consistently voted Flagstaff's best pizza joint, Fratelli still pulls them in with its handmade, stone oven–baked pizza. Sauce choices include red, BBQ, pesto and white (olive oil with garlic, basil and oregano), and toppings range from standard pepperoni to grilled chicken, walnuts, artichoke hearts and cucumber. It's located just south of the Amtrak station, and offers free parking. But if you'd rather just pop in and out, it also does simple slices for about $2.50.

TOP END

Josephine's (Map p154; ☎ 928-779-3400; www.josephinesrestaurant.com; 503 N Humphreys St; mains $$$; 11am-2:30pm & 5-9pm Mon-Sat, 5-9pm Sun) Josephine's feels more like someone's home than a restaurant, occupying a 1911 Arts & Crafts bungalow. There's pleasant patio dining, although Humphreys St is a bit loud; inside, you'll encounter a great old stone bar, a fireplace, Craftsman light fixtures and dining tables in each room. Dinner features such dishes as seared ahi tuna with ginger mango salsa and cilantro rice, tortilla-encrusted halibut, and lemon-tarragon roasted chicken. Though a bit pricey, it's a reliable option for an upscale meal. Consider stopping for lunch – crab cakes, pecan-encrusted fish tacos and a turkey-and-Brie sandwich are welcome changes from typical lunch fare. Josephine's also has an extensive wine list.

Brix (Map p154; ☎ 928-213-1021; www.brixflagstaff.com; 413 N San Francisco St; mains $$$; 11am-2pm & 5-9pm Mon-Fri, 5-9pm Sat) Situated in a renovated brick carriage house, Brix brings a breath of fresh, unpretentious sophistication to Flagstaff's dining scene. The menu varies seasonally, using to delicious advantage what is fresh and ripe, sometimes organic, for classics like salade Niçoise and roasted rack of lamb. Artisanal cheeses and the well-balanced wine list feature selections whose provenance is as near as Snowflake, Arizona and as far as South Australia. Though the dining room feels a bit too cramped, it does speak of this restaurant's popularity, and there's also a leafy patio out back if weather permits alfresco dining. Reservations are highly recommended.

Drinking

Pay 'n' Take (Map p154; ☎ 928-226-8595; 12 W Aspen Ave; 7am-10pm Mon-Wed, 7am-1am Thu-Sat, 9am-10pm Sun;) The name is self-explanatory, but it's more like pay 'n' hang. This kick-back spot has a great bar where you can enjoy a beer or a coffee. Help yourself to whatever you'd like from the wall refrigerators, and take it to one of the small tables inside or out on the back patio. You can even have pizza delivered or bring your own takeout if you like. Folks here are always happy to shoot the breeze, *and* there's free wi-fi.

Wine Loft (Map p154; ☎ 928-773-9463; thewineloft@yahoo.com; 17 N San Francisco St; 3pm-midnight Sun-Thu, 2pm-1am Fri & Sat) Oenophiles will want to roam this place to try a new-to-you glass of albariño or browse the wares. It hosts tastings ($12) on the first Saturday of the month, each featuring six wines.

Popular with students and outdoors types, the **Flagstaff Brewing Co** (Map p154; ☎ 928-773-1442; www.flagbrew.com; 16 E Route 66; 11am-1am) and **Mogollon Brewing Co** (Map p154; ☎ 928-773-8950; www.mogbrew.com; 15 N Agassiz St; 3pm-12:30am Mon-Fri, noon-12:30am Sat & Sun) serve up handcrafted beer and a variety of live music.

Entertainment

Flagstaff hosts all sorts of festivals and music programs; call the visitors center or log on to its website for details. On summer weekends, people gather on blankets for fun evenings at Heritage Sq (Map p154). Live music (folk, Celtic, children's etc) starts at 6:30pm, followed at 9pm by a kid-friendly movie projected on an adjacent building. Various activities keep (sometimes PJ-clad) kids entertained until the film starts.

Flagstaff Symphony Orchestra (Map p152; ☎ 928-774-5107; www.flagstaffsymphony.org; Suite A 113 E Aspen Ave; 10am-3pm) This holds eight annual performances in the Ardrey Auditorium, on the NAU campus.

Charly's (Map p154; ☎ 928-779-1919; www.weatherfordhotel.com; Weatherford Hotel, 23 N Leroux St; 11am-10pm) This restaurant at the Weatherford Hotel (p158) has more regular live music. Its fireplace and brick walls provide a cozy setting for the blues, jazz and folk played here. Head upstairs to stroll the verandah outside the popular Zane Grey Room, which overlooks the historic district.

Monte Vista Lounge (Map p154; ☎ 928-779-6971, 800-545-3068; www.hotelmontevista.com; Hotel Monte Vista, 100 N San Francisco St; from 4pm) In the Hotel Monte Vista (p158), this hopping lounge hosts DJs most nights, and on weekends welcomes diverse bands, from country to hip-hop to rock.

Museum Club (Map p152; ☎ 928-526-9434; www.museumclub.com; 3404 E Route 66; 11am-2am)

Housed in a 1931 taxidermy museum (hence its nickname, 'The Zoo'), this log cabin–style club has been a roadhouse since 1936. Today, its Route 66 vibe, country music and spacious wooden dance floor attract a lively crowd. The Zoo also provides free taxi service home.

If you're just after a game of pool and a beer, head to the smoke-free **Uptown Billiards** (Map p154; ☎ 928-773-0551; www.uptownbilliards.net; 114 N Leroux St; 🕑 1pm-1am Mon-Sat, 3-11pm Sun).

Shopping

Since it's probably the biggest, baddest metropolis you hit before your Grand Canyon backpacking adventure, Flagstaff is a good place to get last-minute advice and gear up with the best deals on outdoor equipment.

Painted Desert Trading Co (Map p154; ☎ 928-226-8313; www.painteddeserttrading.com; 2 N San Francisco St; 🕑 10am-6pm Mon-Sat, noon-5pm Sun) This shop carries quality Native American crafts and an excellent selection of books on regional topics.

Zani (Map p154; ☎ 928-774-9409, 800-294-9409; 9 N Leroux St; 🕑 10am-6pm Mon-Sat) It's the place to go if you're in the market for a quality futon, but Zani also carries some beautiful Grand Canyon note cards, locally made jewelry of silver or fused glass, leather wallets stamped with natural leaf impressions and Asian-inspired gifts and homewares.

Old Town Shops (Map p154; ☎ 928-774-3100; www.oldtownshops.net; 120 N Leroux St) A cluster of several independent stores, including a novelty shop, a wine merchant and a few indie boutiques, occupies this two-floor space.

NAU Bookstore (Map p152; ☎ 800-426-7674; www.bookstore@nau.edu; cnr S San Francisco St & Mountain View Dr; 🕑 8am-6pm Mon-Thu, 8am-5pm Fri, 10am-4pm Sat) The university bookstore offers one of the best selections of books about Native Americans and the region, as well as field guides and children's books. From downtown Flagstaff, take San Francisco St south past Butler Ave onto the NAU campus. Park in one of the lots at the intersection of S San Francisco and Mountain View and follow the signs to the bookstore.

For books on regional hiking, biking, skiing and camping, as well as gear, clothing, rentals and USGS maps, stop by **Babbitt's Backcountry Outfitter** (Map p154; ☎ 928-774-4775; 12 E Aspen Ave; 🕑 10am-6pm Mon-Sat, noon-5pm Sun) or **Peace Surplus** (Map p154; ☎ 928-779-4521; www.peacesurplus.com; 14 W Route 66; 🕑 8am-9pm Mon-Fri, to 8pm Sat, to 6pm Sun). For gear that's more climbing- and backpacking-oriented, head to **Aspen Sports** (Map p154; ☎ 928-779-1935; 15 N San Francisco St; 🕑 10am-6pm).

Getting There & Away

Flagstaff Pulliam Airport is 4 miles south of town off I-17. **America West Express** (☎ 800-235-9292; www.americawest.com) offers several daily flights from Phoenix Sky Harbor International Airport. **Greyhound** (Map p154; ☎ 928-774-4573, 800-229-9424; www.greyhound.com; 399 S Malpais Ln) stops in Flagstaff en route to/from Albuquerque, Las Vegas, Los Angeles and Phoenix. **Open Road Tours** (☎ 928-226-8060, 800-766-7117; www.openroadtours.com) offers shuttles to the Grand Canyon ($27 one way, with a stop at Williams) and Phoenix Sky Harbor International Airport (one way/round-trip $42/76).

Operated by **Amtrak** (Map p154; ☎ 928-774-8679, 800-872-7245; www.amtrak.com; 1 E Route 66; 🕑 4:15am-12:30pm & 4:15am-11:30pm), the *Southwest Chief* stops at Flagstaff on its daily run between Chicago and Los Angeles.

Getting Around

Mountain Line Transit (☎ 928-779-6624; adult/child $1/0.50) services four local bus routes Monday through Saturday; pick up a user-friendly map at the visitors center. Those with disabilities can use the company's on-call VanGo service.

If you need a taxi, call **Friendly Cab** (☎ 928-774-4444) or **Sun Taxi** (☎ 928-774-7400, 800-483-4488). Several major car-rental agencies operate from the airport and downtown; see p243.

SEDONA

☎ 928 / pop 11,300 / elev 4500ft

Sedona's a stunner, but it's intensely spiritual as well – and some say sacred. If you're driving to or from Flagstaff, it's a challenge to keep your eyes on the road. Winding your way through the ponderosas that give way to oaks growing in the riparian lushness of Oak Creek Canyon, you'll dip through shady curves in the canyon and rise alongside beautiful red-rock walls. The closer you get to Sedona, the more magical the landscape seems to become.

Nestled amid alien-looking red sandstone formations at the south end of the 16-mile gorge that is Oak Creek Canyon, Sedona attracts spiritual seekers, artists and healers, and day-trippers from Phoenix trying to escape the oppressive heat. Many New Age types believe that this area is the center of vortexes that radiate the Earth's power, and Sedona's combination of scenic beauty and mysticism draws throngs of tourists year-round. You'll find all sorts of alternative medicines and practices, from psychic channeling, past-life regression, crystal healing, shamanism and drumming workshops to more traditional massages, yoga, tai chi and acupressure. The surrounding canyons offer excellent hiking and mountain biking, and the town itself bustles with art galleries and expensive gourmet restaurants. Unlike nearby Flagstaff, Sedona's economy is almost entirely driven by tourism, and in summer the traffic and the crowds in town and on the trails can make you feel the antithesis of peace. Remember to breathe, channel those good vibrations and see if you can't feel some of Sedona's essential magic.

Orientation

The town's main drag is Hwy Alt 89, which leads southwest to Prescott (57 miles) and north to Flagstaff (28 miles) through Oak Creek Canyon (Map p136). Uptown Sedona, the pedestrian center where you'll find most of Sedona's hotels, boutiques and restaurants, is northeast of the 'Y,' as the intersection of Hwys Alt 89 and 179 is known. Turning south at the Y will take you down to Tlaquepaque Village (p170); from here you can cross over Oak Creek and continue down to the area known as The Village at Oak Creek, where you'll find more shopping, restaurants and hotels.

A Red Rock Pass ($5/15/20 daily/weekly/annual) is required to park anywhere in the surrounding national forest. You can buy one at the visitors centers, Circle Ks and at some trailheads.

Information

Police station (Map pp164-5; ☎ 928-282-3100; www.sedonaaz.gov; 100 Roadrunner Dr)

Post office (Map pp164-5; ☎ 928-282-3511; 190 W Hwy Alt 89; 8:45am-5pm Mon-Fri)

Sedona Chamber of Commerce Visitor Center (Map pp164-5; ☎ 928-282-7722, 800-288-7336; www.visitsedona.com; Sinagua Plaza, 320 N Hwy Alt 89; 8:30am-5pm Mon-Sat, 9am-3pm Sun) Located in Uptown Sedona, pick up free maps, brochures and get last-minute hotel bookings.

Sedona Public Library (Map pp164-5; ☎ 928-282-7714; 3250 White Bear Rd; 10am-8pm Mon-Sat, noon-5pm Sun;) Free internet access and wi-fi.

USFS South Gateway Visitor Center (off Map pp164-5; ☎ 928-284-5324; www.redrockcountry.org; Tequa Shopping Plaza, 7000 Hwy 179; 8am-5pm) Get a Red Rock Pass here, as well as hiking guides, maps and local national forest information. It's around 7 miles south of town.

Verde Valley Medical Center (Map pp164-5; ☎ 928-204-3000; 3700 W Hwy Alt 89; 24hr)

Sights

CHAPEL OF THE HOLY CROSS

Situated between spectacular, statuesque red-rock columns 3 miles south of town, this modern, nondenominational **chapel** (off Map pp164-5; ☎ 928-282-4069; 780 Chapel Rd; 9am-5pm) was built in 1956 by Marguerite Brunwig Staude in the tradition of Frank Lloyd Wright. There are no services, but even if you're not affiliated with any religion, the soaring chapel and the perch it occupies may move you as it did its architect. There are no restrooms on the site.

SLIDE ROCK STATE PARK

Popular for picnicking and swimming, this **state park** (Map p136; ☎ 928-282-3034; www.azstateparks.com/Parks/parkhtml/sliderock.html; 6871 N Hwy Alt 89; per car Memorial Day-Labor Day $10, Sep-May $8; 8am-7pm Memorial Day-Labor Day, 8am-5pm Sep-May) features a natural rock chute that whisks swimmers through Oak Creek. Bring a blanket and a cooler, or buy drinks and snacks at the small park store. To avoid the long lines and entrance fee, you can park your car on the shoulder just north of the entrance and hike down

JUST ANOTHER SEDONA SUNSET...

In this town, you can't really go wrong at sundown if you have its red rocks in sight. But for a more sublime Sedona sunset, many suggest seeing it from the **airport** (with about 600 other people; Map pp164–5). If you seek solitude, hike up to **Eagle's Nest** at the top of the Eagle's Nest Loop in Red Rock State Park (Map p136) and you may have the 360-degree view all to yourself. If you've procured a Red Rock Pass, drive up **Dry Creek Road** or **Schnebly Hill Road**, find a deserted trailhead, and mosey off into the sunset.

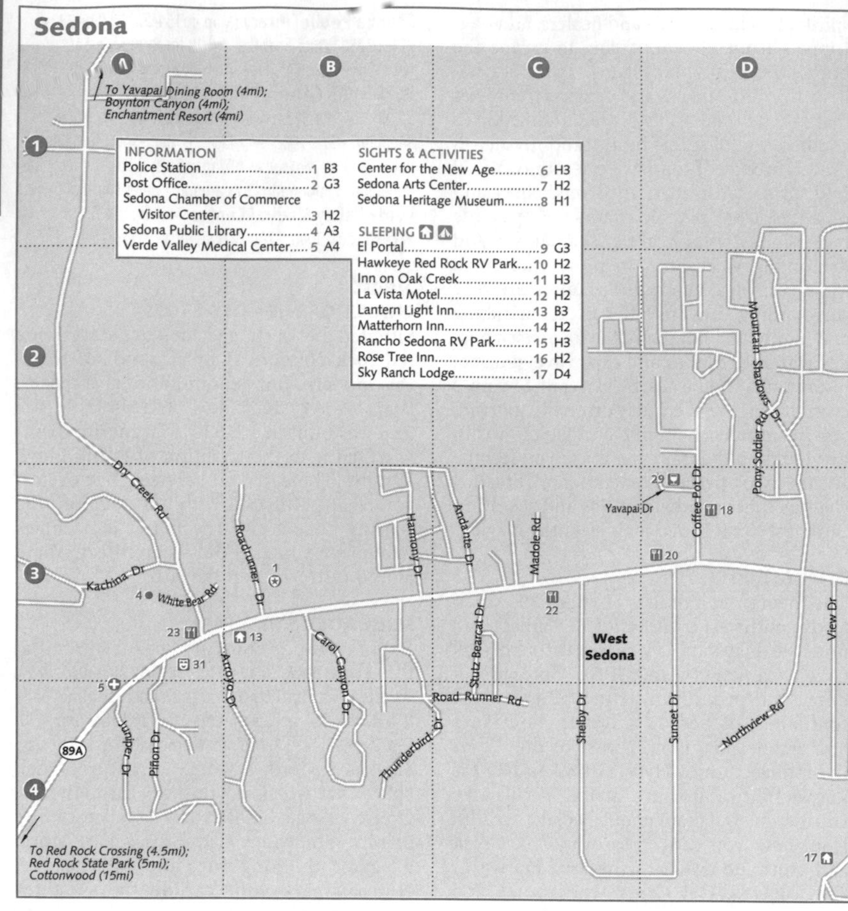

to the rock slide – just follow the crowds. Drive carefully, as lots of pedestrians will be picking their way along and across the highway.

RED ROCK STATE PARK

Sans natural waterslide, this **park** (Map p136; ☎ 928-282-6907; www.pr.state.az.us/Parks/parkhtml/redrock.html; 4050 Red Rock Loop Rd; per car/bicycle or pedestrian $6/2; 8am-8pm) includes an environmental education center, a visitors center, picnic areas and 5 miles of well-marked trails in a riparian habitat amid gorgeous scenery. Ranger-led activities include nature walks, bird walks and full-moon hikes during the warmer months. While popular, it doesn't pack quite as exciting a punch as Slide Rock, meaning it's not so packed, and pleasant because of it. Hours listed here are for summer; it closes earlier in other seasons.

SEDONA ARTS CENTER

The **arts center** (Map pp164-5; ☎ 928-282-3809, 888-954-4442; www.sedonaartscenter.com; 15 Art Barn Rd; 10am-5pm) features changing exhibits of local and regional artists, a gift shop, classes in performing and visual arts, and a variety of cultural events like the Sedona Plein Air Festival (p151).

SEDONA HERITAGE MUSEUM

At this small **heritage museum** (Map pp164-5; ☎ 928-282-7038; www.sedonamuseum.org; 735 N Jordan

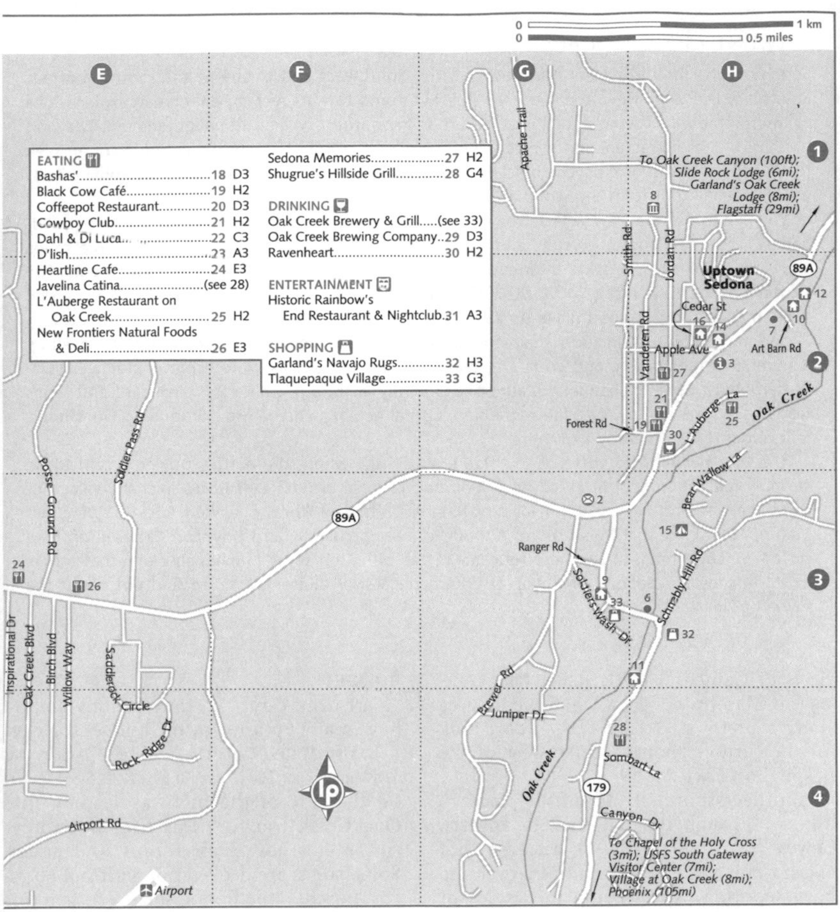

Rd; adult/child $3/free; 11am-3pm), you'll find out who the founding families of Sedona were, and get to know them through quotidian artifacts. Set on the historic farmstead of the Jordan family, the museum displays photos, domestic tools and historical information inside the main house. Outside, the property is home to native flora. Be sure to poke around in the tractor shed out back, where the vintage fire engine and apple-sorting machine reside.

Activities

Hiking and **mountain-biking** trails crisscross the surrounding red-rock country and the woods and meadows of green Oak Creek Canyon (Map p136). Available at the visitors centers and ranger stations, *The Recreation Guide to Red Rock Country* describes hiking and biking trails for all skill levels and includes a map of **scenic drives**. One popular hiking trail in Oak Creek Canyon is the **West Fork Trail**, which follows the creek for 7 miles – the canyon walls rise more than 200ft in places. Wander up as far as you want, splash around and turn back when you've had enough. The trailhead lies about 3 miles north of Slide Rock, in Call of the Canyon Recreation Area.

Oak Creek holds several good **swimming** holes. If Slide Rock (Map p136) is too crowded, check out **Grasshopper Point** ($8 per car), a few miles south. Southwest of town you can splash around and enjoy splendid

IN SEARCH OF THE NEW AGE

Sedona is the foremost New Age center in the Southwest and is one of the most important anywhere. The term 'New Age' loosely refers to a trend toward seeking alternative explanations or interpretations of what constitutes health, religion, the psyche and enlightenment. Drawing upon new and old factual and mystical traditions from around the world, New Agers often seek to transform themselves psychologically and spiritually in the hope that such personal efforts will eventually transform the world at large.

You can't miss the New Age stores in town – many of them have the word 'crystal' in their names. They sell books, crystals and various New Age paraphernalia; distribute free maps showing vortex sites; provide information; and arrange various spiritual or healing events. The **Center for the New Age** (☎ 928-282-2085; www.sedonanewagecenter.com; 341 Hwy 179; 10am-6pm) is open daily and is a good place to start.

Sedona's offerings include mainstream services such as massage, nutrition counseling, acupressure, meditation, and yoga and tai chi classes, as well as more esoteric practices such as herbology, psychic channeling, aura photography, astrology, palmistry, tarot-card and runes readings, aromatherapy, past-life regression, crystal healing, shamanism, drumming workshops, reflexology, hypnotherapy and more.

The four best-known vortexes, or high-energy sites where the earth's power is said to be strongly felt, are in Sedona's Red Rock Mountains. These include **Bell Rock**, near the village of Oak Creek (east of Hwy 179; off Map pp164–5), **Cathedral Rock**, near Red Rock Crossing (off Map pp164–5), **Airport Mesa**, along Airport Rd (Map pp164–5), and **Boynton Canyon** (off Map pp164–5). Local maps show these four main sites, although some individuals claim that others exist. Stop by the Sedona Chamber of Commerce Visitor Center (p163) to find out about the myriad of local vortex tours.

views of Cathedral Rock at **Red Rock Crossing** (off Map pp164–5), a USFS picnic area along a pretty stretch of Oak Creek; look for the turnoff about 2 miles west of the hospital on Hwy Alt 89.

Another stunningly beautiful place to hike is through the red rock of **Boynton Canyon** (off Map pp164–5), an area that exudes spiritual energy and where some have reported experiencing the antics of such energetic spirits (who may not necessarily want them trekking through)! Look for the rock formation known as **Kachina Woman** and try not to be moved. Boynton Canyon is about 5 miles north of Hwy Alt 89 up Dry Creek Rd; get an early start to avoid crowds.

Sleeping

As you might expect from such a scenic town, Sedona is rich with beautiful B&Bs, creekside cabins and full-service resorts, for which you should also expect to pay accordingly. Rates at chain motels range from $75 to $130, reasonable by Sedona standards. Contact the **Sedona Bed & Breakfast Guild** (www.bbsedona.net) for lodging information and suggestions.

BUDGET

Apart from camping, tony Sedona doesn't have many options for the budget traveler.

La Vista Motel (Map pp164-5; ☎ 928-282-7301; www.lavistamotel.com; 500 N Hwy Alt 89; r & ste $-$$) Right on the side of the highway leading into Oak Creek Canyon, this friendly family-run motel has clean rooms and suites. Some suites are decked out with full kitchens, porches, tile floors, sofas, refrigerators and bathtubs. Rooms on the lower level, off the highway, tend to be quieter but more expensive.

Dispersed camping is not permitted in Red Rock Canyon. The **USFS** (☎ 928-282-4119) runs the following campgrounds along Hwy Alt 89 in Oak Creek Canyon (none with hookups). All are nestled in the woods just off the road. It costs $15 to camp, but you don't need a Red Rock Pass. Reservations are accepted for Pine Flat West and Cave Springs; call ☎ 877-444-6777.

Manzanita 18 sites; open year-round; 6 miles north of town.

Bootlegger 10 sites; no water; 8.5 miles north.

Cave Springs 82 sites; showers; 11.5 miles north.

Pine Flat East and Pine Flat West 57 sites; 12.5 miles north.

Rancho Sedona RV Park (Map pp164-5; ☎ 928-282-7255, 888-641-4261; 135 Bear Wallow Lane; RV sites $) includes a laundry, showers and 30 RV sites, most with full hookups. Another option is **Hawkeye Red Rock RV Park** (Map pp164-5; ☎ 928-282-2222; 40 Art Barn Rd; tent & RV sites $).

MIDRANGE

Lantern Light Inn (Map pp164-5; ☎ 928-282-3419, 877-275-4973; www.lanternlightinn.com; 3085 W Hwy Alt 89; r & ste $-$$; 💻) The lovely couple running this small inn in West Sedona put you right at ease in their comfortable antique-filled rooms. Rooms range from small and cozy, overlooking the back deck and garden, to the huge guesthouse in back, but all feel comfortably overstuffed. There's a common room, more of a family library with musical instruments, that can be used for meetings. Higher rates apply on weekends (Friday to Sunday), when guests are treated to a gourmet breakfast.

Sky Ranch Lodge (Map pp164-5; ☎ 928-282-6400, 888-708-6400; www.skyranchlodge.com; Airport Rd; $$; 🚭 ♿) At the top of Airport Rd, with spectacular views of the town and surrounding country, this lodge offers spacious motel rooms, six landscaped acres, and a pool and hot tub. Rates vary according to type of bed and your view. Some include balconies, fireplaces, kitchenettes and/or refrigerators; also available are cottages with vaulted ceilings, exposed beams, kitchenettes and private decks. Away from the Strip and its tourist hordes, this family-run lodge is an excellent deal.

Matterhorn Inn (Map pp164-5; ☎ 928-282-7176, 800-372-8207; www.matterhorninn.com; 230 Apple Ave; r $$; 🚭 ♿) All rooms at this friendly, central motel include refrigerators and have balconies or patios overlooking Uptown Sedona and Oak Creek. Its terraced location is right in the middle of town, right above the highway, and is within walking distance of the shops and restaurants.

Rose Tree Inn (Map pp164-5; ☎ 928-282-2065, 888-282-2065; www.rosetreeinn.com; 376 Cedar St; r $$; 💻 👪) The five homey rooms nestled around this inn's peaceful courtyard garden immediately make you feel as though you're settling in at a friend's place. Some rooms have fireplaces, and all have kitchenettes. It's much cozier and more personable than a hotel and feels a world away from busy Hwy Alt 89 just a block south.

Slide Rock Lodge (off Map pp164-5; ☎ 928-282-3531; www.sliderocklodge.com; 6401 N Hwy Alt 89; r $$; 👪) If you want to stay in Oak Creek Canyon, this is an affordable way to do it. This log-cabin longhouse has rooms along the canyon wall that tend toward the simple and rustic. Some rooms are mustier than others, but all are clean and there's a large grassy area outside to take in the fresh air. The atmosphere is friendly and family-oriented and conducive to a laid-back stay.

Junipine Resort (off Map pp164-5; ☎ 928-282-3375, 800-742-7436; www.junipine.com; 8351 N Hwy Alt 89; r & cottages $$-$$$; 💻 ♿ 👪) In the Oak Creek Canyon woodland, 8 miles north of Sedona, this resort offers spacious, lovely one- and two-bedroom 'creekhouses,' all with kitchens, living/dining rooms, wood-burning stoves and decks – and some with lofts. Some units have creekside views, others have hot tubs, and a few offer both. Two-bedroom units sleep up to four, a great option for families ($25 for each additional person, children under 12 free). The on-site restaurant serves great food as well as microbrews and wine, so you needn't trek all the way into town if you're too relaxed to leave.

TOP END

our pick **Garland's Oak Creek Lodge** (off Map pp164-5; ☎ 928-282-3343; www.garlandslodge.com; Hwy Alt 89; s & d $$; 🕐 closed Sun & mid-Nov–Apr 1; ♿) Set back from Oak Creek on eight secluded acres with broad lawns, an apple orchard and woods, this lodge offers nicely appointed Western log cabins, many with fireplaces. Rates include a full hot breakfast, 4pm tea and a superb gourmet dinner. There's a yoga gazebo overlooking the creek, and you can arrange for massages or spa treatments in its tiny spa cabin. Or just enjoy cocktails at 6pm and the absence of ringing phones. Catering to adults who crave quiet and service, Garland's isn't particularly kid-friendly, charging $60 for each additional guest over the age of two. It's 8 miles north of Sedona and is often booked up a year in advance. If you can't stay overnight, booking dinner is a delicious alternative.

Briar Patch Inn (off Map pp164-5; ☎ 928-282-2342, 888-809-3030; www.briarpatchinn.com; 3190 N Hwy Alt 89; cottages $$$; 💻 ♿ 👪) Nestled in nine wooded acres along Oak Creek, this lovely inn offers 17 log cottages with Southwestern decor and Native American art. All cottages include patios, many have fireplaces, and several lie beside the burbling creek. In summer, a hearty buffet breakfast – including homemade granola, fresh fruit, home-baked breads and pastries, and a quiche of the day – is served on a stone patio that overlooks the creek and is accompanied by live chamber music (Wednesday to Monday). This relaxed, unpretentious spot is a welcome change from the attitude found at some upscale places in town. There's a two-night minimum on weekends and it's best to book at least a few months ahead.

Inn on Oak Creek (Map pp164-5; ☎ 928-282-7896, 800-499-7896; www.innonoakcreek.com; 556 Hwy 179; r $$$; 💻 ♿) Just around the corner from Tlaquepaque, this bright and welcoming country-style B&B boasts an enviable location directly above Oak Creek. Each immaculate, eminently cozy room is decorated according to some individual theme, ranging from old Hollywood to roosters, and all have whirlpool baths and gas fireplaces. Breakfast is a decadent treat here, consisting of several courses that feature freshly squeezed juices, house-baked pastries and gourmet mains, served in the sunny dining room or on the deck above the creek. Nonguests can call the friendly hosts to inquire a day ahead about breakfast reservations.

El Portal (Map pp164-5; ☎ 928-203-9405, 800-313-0017; www.elportalsedona.com; 95 Portal Ln; r $$$$; 💻 ♿) This discreet little inn is a jewel box of Craftsman style, a pocket of relaxed luxury tucked away in a corner near Tlaquepaque. The look is rustic but sophisticated, incorporating reclaimed wood, river rock and thick adobe walls. Each room is meticulously designed and decorated with authentic Stickley and Wright furnishings, exposed beams and antique doorknobs and fixtures. Rooms at the back have incredible red-rock views, and the inn surrounds a peaceful courtyard perfect for sipping a glass of wine. It's one of the few Sedona inns that welcomes dogs, and guests have free pool and spa privileges at the large Los Abrigados resort next door.

Enchantment Resort (off Map pp164-5; ☎ 928-282-2900, 800-826-4180; www.enchantmentresort.com; 525 Boynton Canyon Rd; r $$$$) Based in beautiful Boynton Canyon 5 miles off Hwy Alt 89, this over-the-top-end resort is so exclusive you can't even enter the driveway unless you're staying here or have reservations at one of the three restaurants. Sprawled throughout the grounds, all rooms include patios and expansive views, but the exorbitant rates don't entitle you to extra perks beyond accommodation. Along with the top-notch cuisine the restaurants serve, they also feature gape-worthy views of the surrounding canyon.

Miiamo (☎ 888-749-2137; www.miiamo.com; 3-day packages from $1785) You could also opt to stay here, Enchantment Resort's on-site spa. It offers spa treatments, Ayurvedic programs and tailored journeys addressing your personal health and spiritual goals. Be prepared to pay for the *namaste*.

Eating

Sedona's dining scene caters to sophisticates and to spiritual seekers alike, with an admirable range of vegetarian and health-conscious victuals to choose from. Most Sedona restaurants are as laid-back as elsewhere in the Southwest, but you'll certainly find places to splurge should you feel the urge.

BUDGET

Black Cow Café (Map pp164-5; ☎ 928-203-9868; 229 N Hwy Alt 89; ice creams $; 🕑 8am-9pm) Many claim the Black Cow has the best ice cream in town, and it certainly hits the spot on a hot, dusty day. If you don't want dessert, it also does sandwiches and soup.

New Frontiers Natural Foods & Deli (Map pp164-5; ☎ 928-282-6311; 1420 W Hwy Alt 89; mains $; 🕑 8am-9pm Mon-Sat, to 8pm Sun; ♿) This natural-foods grocery store is a great place to stop for picnic supplies or to grab a smoothie, some vegetarian salads or panini from the deli.

Coffeepot Restaurant (Map pp164-5; ☎ 928-282-6626; 2050 W Hwy Alt 89; mains $; 🕑 6am-2:15pm; ♿ 👶) This has been the go-to breakfast and lunch joint for decades. It's always busy, and service can be slow, but it's friendly, the meals are reasonably priced and the selection is huge – 101 types of omelets (who knew there were that many?) to start with.

D'lish (Map pp164-5; ☎ 928-203-9393; www.dlishvegetarian.com; 3190 W Hwy Alt 89; mains $; 🕑 11am-8pm; Ⓥ ♿) Lots of organic options, all-vegan (!!) menu.

Sedona Memories (Map pp164-5; ☎ 928-282-0032; 321 Jordan Rd; mains $; 🕑 8am-4pm) This low-key sandwich spot a block off Hwy Alt 89 features several vegetarian options, homemade bread and a quiet outdoor patio.

Get groceries at New Frontiers Natural Foods or **Bashas'** (Map pp164-5; ☎ 928-282-5351; 160 Coffee Pot Dr; 🕒 6am-11pm; ♿).

MIDRANGE

Heartline Café (Map pp164-5; ☎ 928-282-0785; www.heartlinecafe.com; 1600-1610 W Hwy Alt 89; mains $$; 🕒 11am-3pm & 5-9pm) This restaurant's name refers to a Zuni Indian symbol for good health and long life, and indeed the imaginative menu offers the kind of fresh, clean and tasty food you might expect. Lunch options include Thai-style vegetables, barbecued pork with apple-onion chutney, pecan-encrusted trout, a hot Cajun turkey sandwich and tea-smoked duck salad. Enclosed in a blue wall covered with flowering vines, the pleasant outdoor patio holds eight tables around a small clay fireplace.

Cowboy Club (Map pp164-5; ☎ 928-282-4200; www.cowboyclub.com; 241 N Hwy Alt 89; mains $$; 🕒 11am-4pm & 5-10pm; ♿) From the outside, it looks like a saloon; inside, the large and determinedly Southwestern Grille Room offers primarily steaks, though you'll also find chicken, fish and vegetarian options. Feeling venturesome? Consider trying rattlesnake. Pricier fine dining is offered in the Silver Saddle Room.

Javelina Cantina (Map pp164-5; ☎ 928-203-9514; www.javelinacantina.com; Hillside Plaza, 671 Hwy 179; mains $$; 🕒 11:30am-9:30pm; ♿) Locals love this place, and while it may not be the best or most authentic Mexican food you'll find in town, you can't beat the view on the patio. The mood is fun, and the food is more than adequate.

Oak Creek Brewery & Grill (Map pp164-5; ☎ 928-282-3300; www.oakcreekpub.com; 336 Hwy 179; mains $$; 🕒 11am-9pm; ♿) At Tlaquepaque Village, this spacious branch of the brewery (right) serves a full menu that includes upmarket pub-style dishes like crab cakes and 'fire-kissed pizzas.' All of the menu offerings are best washed down with a house brew, of course – we're partial to the Oak Creek Amber.

For a memorable brunch on Oak Creek, make a reservation at the **Briar Patch Inn** (off Map pp164-5; ☎ 928-282-2342, 888-809-3030; www.briarpatchinn.com; 3190 N Hwy Alt 89; breakfast $$; 🕒 8:15-9:45am) or, closer to town, at the **Inn on Oak Creek** (Map pp164-5; ☎ 928-282-7896, 800-499-7896; www.innonoakcreek.com; 556 Hwy 179; breakfast $$; 🕒 8-9:30am).

TOP END

Shugrue's Hillside Grill (Map pp164-5; ☎ 928-282-5300; www.shugrues.com; Hillside Plaza, 671 Hwy 179; mains $$$; 🕒 11:30am-3pm & 5-9pm) Promising panoramic views, an outdoor deck from which to enjoy them and consistently excellent food, this restaurant is a great choice for an upscale meal. If it's too chilly to sit outside, don't fret – the walls are mostly glass, so you can still enjoy the scenery. The menu offers everything from steak to ravioli, but it is best known for its wide variety of well-prepared seafood. A jazz ensemble plays on the weekends.

Yavapai Dining Room (Map pp164-5; ☎ 928-282-2900; Enchantment Resort, 525 Boynton Canyon Rd; mains $$$; 🕒 breakfast, lunch & dinner Mon-Sat, 10:30am-2:30pm Sun; ♿) Come here for the delicious and expansive Sunday champagne brunch amid peaceful red-rock surroundings. Dinners are good, if overpriced. You won't be allowed on the premises without advance reservations, and the dress code doesn't allow jeans or athletic shoes.

Dahl & DiLuca Ristorante (Map pp164-5; ☎ 928-282-5219; www.dahlanddiluca.com; 2321 Hwy Alt 89; mains $$$; 🕒 5-10pm; ♿) Though this lovely Italian place fits perfectly into the groove and color scheme of Sedona, at the same time it feels like the kind of place you'd find in a small Italian seaside town. It's a bustling, welcoming spot serving excellent Italian food.

L'Auberge Restaurant on Oak Creek (Map pp164-5; ☎ 928-282-1667; www.lauberge.com; 301 L'Auberge Lane; 🕒 breakfast, lunch & dinner Mon-Sat, 9am-2pm & 5:30-9pm Sun; ♿) Featuring American cuisine with a French accent, the menu at L'Auberge changes seasonally. This creekside spot is a local favorite for celebrating special occasions in elegant environs, with a select wine list to round it off.

Drinking

Ravenheart (Map pp164-5; ☎ 928-282-1070; 206 N Hwy Alt 89; 🕒 6am-9pm; 💻 ♿) Offering a pleasant outdoor patio with good views, this coffee shop is the best spot for a jolt of caffeine and a pastry while you check your email ($2.75 for 15 minutes, $10 for 50 minutes). Despite being on the main drag, it's an oasis of tranquility.

Oak Creek Brewing Company (Map pp164-5; ☎ 928-204-1300; www.oakcreekpub.com; 2050 Yavapai Dr; 🕒 4-9pm Mon-Thu, 11am-midnight Fri-Sun) On a dirt road off Hwy Alt 89, this laid-back place serves handcrafted beers on an outdoor patio and is a laid-back spot to meet locals kicking back with their pals.

Entertainment

Read the monthly *Red Rock Review* for local events. For information about symphony concerts, film festivals, Shakespearean plays and other events, contact the **Sedona Cultural Park** (☎ 928-282-0747, 800-780-2787).

If you're looking for a place to practice your two-step, head to the **Historic Rainbow's End Restaurant & Nightclub** (Map pp164-5; ☎ 928-282-1593; 3235 W Hwy Alt 89; 🕑 11am-1am).

Shopping

Shopping is a big draw in Sedona, and visitors will find everything from expensive boutiques to T-shirt shops. Uptown along Hwy Alt 89 is the place to go souvenir hunting.

Tlaquepaque Village (Map pp164-5; ☎ 928-282-4838; www.tlaq.com; 🕑 vary) Just south of Alt 89 on Hwy 179, this is a series of Mexican-style interconnected plazas that is home to dozens of high-end art galleries, shops and restaurants.

Garland's Navajo Rugs (Map pp164-5; ☎ 928-282-4070; www.garlandsrugs.com; 411 Hwy 179; 🕑 10am-5pm Mon-Sat, 11am-5pm Sun) If you miss the entrance to Tlaquepaque (which is easy enough to do), you'll quickly come upon this place on the other side of the highway. It offers the area's best selection of rugs and also sells other Native American crafts. It's an interesting shop to visit even if you don't plan on buying anything – it displays naturally dyed yarns with their botanical sources of color, as well as bios of the weavers and descriptions of how many hours it takes to create a handwoven rug.

Getting There & Away

Sedona-Phoenix Shuttle (☎ 928-282-2066, 800-448-7988; www.sedona-phoenix-shuttle.com; one way/round-trip $45/85) runs between Phoenix Sky Harbor and Sedona eight times daily; call to make reservations. For door-to-door shuttle service, call **Ace Express** (☎ 928-649-2720, 800-336-2239; one way/round-trip $50/97). **Sedona Taxi Airporter & Tours** (☎ 928-282-5545) offers cab service to Flagstaff. While scenic flights depart from Sedona, the closest commercial airport is Phoenix (two hours) or Flagstaff (30 minutes).

Greyhound (☎ 800-229-9424; www.greyhound.com) stops in Camp Verde, about 30 minutes south of Sedona, and in Flagstaff, about 40 minutes north. **Amtrak** (☎ 800-872-7245; www.amtrak.com) stops in Flagstaff.

Getting Around

Bob's Taxi (☎ 928-282-1234) offers local cab service. Rental cars are available through **Enterprise** (☎ 928-282-2052; www.enterprise.com) and **Sedona Jeep & Car Rentals** (☎ 928-282-2227, 800-879-5337; www.sedonajeeprentals.com).

CAMERON

A tiny, windswept community 32 miles east of the park's East Entrance and 54 miles north of Flagstaff, Cameron sits on the western edge of the Navajo Indian Reservation. There's not much to it; in fact, the town basically comprises just the **Cameron Trading Post & Motel** (☎ 928-679-2231, 800-338-7385; www.camerontradingpost.com; RV sites $, r/ste $/$$; ♿). In the early 1900s Hopis and Navajos came to the trading post to barter wool, blankets and livestock for flour, sugar and other goods. Today visitors can browse a large selection of quality Native American crafts, including Navajo rugs, basketry, jewelry and pottery. Of course, you'll also find the ubiquitous T-shirts, roadrunner knickknacks and other canyon kitsch.

The spacious rooms, many with balconies, feature hand-carved furniture and a Southwestern motif. They are spread out in three two-story adobe-style buildings: the Navajo (doubles with two double beds), the Hopi (two-room suites and doubles with one or two queen beds) and the Apache (doubles with two queen beds). The nicest is the Hopi, set around a lovely, lush garden with fountains and benches – a peaceful spot to sit and relax. Ask for a room with a garden view or a view of the **Little Colorado River Gorge**, which winds around the back of the hotel. RV sites offer hookups, and you can take your meals at **Cameron Trading Post Dining Room** (☎ 928-679-2231, 800-338-7385; mains $-$$; 🕑 6am-10pm), a good place to try the Navajo taco (fried dough with whole beans, ground beef, chili and cheese). If you're driving to the North Rim and need a place to stay en route, or if rooms in the park are booked, this is a great option.

Cameron is also a good spot to break up a long drive: relax at the restaurant for lunch poke around the **art gallery**, and sip a cold drink in the shade of the garden before getting back into the car. Even if the gallery itself is closed, look for the dinosaur footprints left in the flagstone of the gallery's entrance.

LAKE MEAD & HOOVER DAM

Even those who challenge, or at least question, America's commitment to damming the American West have to marvel at the engineering and architecture of the Hoover Dam. Set amid the almost unbearably dry Mohave Desert, the dam towers over Black Canyon and provides electricity for the entire region. Lake Mead is a popular boating, swimming and weekend-camping destination for Las Vegas residents.

Orientation

Hoover Dam created Lake Mead, which boasts 700 miles of shoreline, while Davis Dam created the much smaller Lake Mohave. Black Canyon, the stretch of the Colorado just below Hoover Dam, links the two lakes. All three bodies of water are included in the recreation area, created in 1964. The Colorado feeds into Lake Mead from Grand Canyon National Park, and rafting trips through the canyon finish on the east end of the lake.

Heading north from I-40 at Kingman, Hwy 93 crosses Hoover Dam about 30 minutes southeast of Las Vegas. Traffic across the dam can be terrible; expect delays of at least 30 minutes. The main cities on the south tip of Lake Mead Recreation Area are Bullhead City and Laughlin (see Lonely Planet's *Southwest*). Visitors to the lake will find most services in Boulder City, a small town with a pleasant historic downtown about 7 miles west of the dam and 7 miles south of the visitors center.

Information

The daily fee for the Lake Mead National Recreation Area is $5, payable at the NRA entrances. For emergency help, call ☎ 911, or the park dispatcher at ☎ 702-293-8932 (Nevada) or ☎ 800-680-5851 (Arizona).

Alan Bible Visitor Center (☎ 702-293-8990; www.nps.gov/lame; US 93; 🕒 8:30am-4:30pm) Five miles west of Hoover Dam, and 4 miles east of Boulder City, this is the NPS's main visitors center for the area. Here you'll find information on accommodations, boating and other recreational activities, as well as a small interactive display on desert life.

Boulder City Chamber of Commerce (☎ 702-293-2034; www.boulder-city-chamber.com; 465 Nevada Way, Boulder City, NV; 🕒 9am-5pm Mon-Sat)

Boulder City Hospital (☎ 702-293-4111; www.bouldercityhospital.org; 901 Adams Blvd, Boulder City, NV; 🕒 24hr) Emergency care in the heart of Boulder City.

Katherine Landing Visitor Center (☎ 928-754-3272; 🕒 8:30am-4:30pm) This smaller visitors center is on Lake Mohave at the south tip of the recreation area. Admission is $5 per vehicle and is valid for five days.

Nevada Welcome Center (☎ 702-294-1252; US 93, Boulder City, NV; 🕒 8am-4:30pm)

Sights & Activities

MARINAS

Nine marinas line these lakeshores, offering various recreational opportunities from fishing to houseboating to dinner cruises. Due to droughts, **Las Vegas Bay** is no longer a bay and services at **Overton Beach** are drying up; you'll still find dry storage and campgrounds, but marina services are no longer needed here.

Callville Bay Resort (☎ 702-565-8958; www.callvillebay.com) A well-appointed resort also on the west end of Lake Mead.

Cottonwood Cove (☎ 702-297-1464; www.cottonwoodcoveresort.com) Further south, Cottonwood Cove is one of the two marinas on the shores of Lake Mohave.

Echo Bay (☎ 702-394-4066, 800-752-9669; www.sevencrown.com) You can rent small boats and houseboats at this marina on the west shore of Lake Mead.

Katherine Landing (☎ 928-754-3245; www.sevencrown.com) Katherine Landing is south of Cottonwood Cove.

Temple Bar (☎ 928-767-3211; www.sevencrown.com) On the Arizona shore, Temple Bar is one of the more remote spots on Lake Mead.

Willow Beach (☎ 928-767-4747; www.foreverresorts.com/willowbeach) Willow Beach, on the east side of Black Canyon in Arizona, is a lovely little marina.

HOOVER DAM

A statue of bronze-winged figures stands atop Hoover Dam, memorializing those who built the massive concrete structure. An inscription reads, 'Inspired by a vision of lonely lands made fruitful' – a sentiment that epitomizes America's dam-building frenzy in the 20th century. At 726ft, Hoover Dam remains an engineering and architectural marvel and is one of the world's tallest dams.

Originally named Boulder Dam, Hoover was built between 1931 and 1936 and was the first major dam on the Colorado.

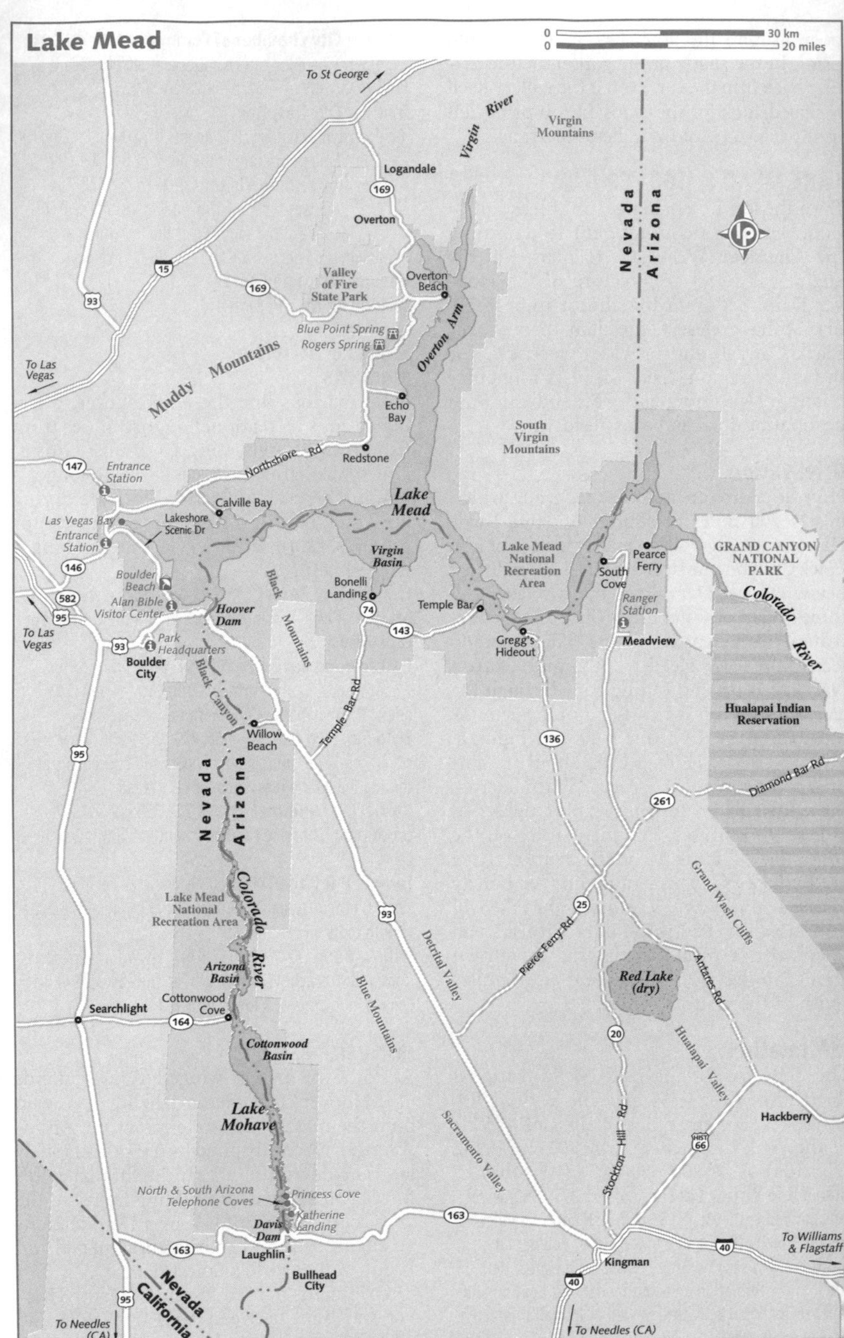
Lake Mead
0 30 km
0 20 miles
To St George
Virgin River
Virgin Mountains
Logandale
169
Overton
15
93
169
Valley of Fire State Park
Overton Beach
Overton Arm
Blue Point Spring
Rogers Spring
Nevada
Arizona
To Las Vegas
Muddy Mountains
Echo Bay
South Virgin Mountains
Northshore Rd
Redstone
147
Entrance Station
Calville Bay
Lake Mead
Las Vegas Bay
Lakeshore Scenic Dr
Entrance Station
Lake Mead National Recreation Area
Virgin Basin
Pearce Ferry
GRAND CANYON NATIONAL PARK
146
Boulder Beach
Black Mountains
Bonelli Landing
South Cove
Colorado River
582
Alan Bible Visitor Center
Hoover Dam
74
Temple Bar
Ranger Station
95
To Las Vegas
143
Gregg's Hideout
Meadview
93
Park Headquarters
Boulder City
Black Canyon
Temple Bar Rd
Hualapai Indian Reservation
Willow Beach
136
95
Diamond Bar Rd
261
Nevada
Arizona
Grand Wash Cliffs
Colorado River
Lake Mead National Recreation Area
25
93
Detrital Valley
Pierce Ferry Rd
Arizona Basin
Antares Rd
Red Lake (dry)
Blue Mountains
Cottonwood Cove
Searchlight
164
20
Hualapai Valley
Cottonwood Basin
Lake Mohave
Hackberry
Sacramento Valley
Stockton Hill Rd
66
North & South Arizona Telephone Coves
Princess Cove
Katherine Landing
163
Davis Dam
To Williams & Flagstaff
163
40
Laughlin
Kingman
Nevada
California
40
Bullhead City
95
To Needles (CA)
To Needles (CA)

Thousands of men and their families, eager for work in the height of the Depression, came to Black Canyon and worked in excruciating conditions – dangling hundreds of feet above the canyon in 120°F desert heat. Hundreds lost their lives. A 25-minute film at the visitors center features original footage of the construction and is an interesting look at the history of not just Hoover Dam, but the sentiments and values that motivated American dam building.

Hoover Dam Visitor Center (☎ 702-293-8321; www.usbr.gov; US 93, NV; tours adult/child $11/6; 🕑 9am-5:30pm), east of Boulder City, offers regular Guided Discovery Tours, which remain fascinating despite tightened restrictions on where in the dam visitors are allowed. Parking costs $5.

BOULDER CITY/HOOVER DAM MUSEUM

In Boulder Dam Hotel in Boulder City, the **Boulder City/Hoover Dam Museum** (☎ 702-294-1988; 1305 Arizona St, Boulder City, NV; adult/child $2/1; 🕑 10am-5pm Mon-Sat, noon-5pm Sun) is worth a visit. It focuses primarily on construction of the dam, with exhibits on Depression-era America and the living conditions of the men and women who came to build the dam. Shot by the Bureau of Reclamation, a 20-minute film features historic footage of the project.

BOATING

Rental boats include personal watercraft, 18ft runabouts for waterskiing and exploring, 24ft patio (pontoon) boats and houseboats (see p174). Call the individual marinas for more information.

You can rent a kayak from **Desert River Outfitters** (☎ 928-763-3033, 888-529-2533; www.desertriveroutfitters.com; 2649 Hwy 95, Bullhead City, AZ). Kayak trips down the Black Canyon start at the base of Hoover Dam, and can be done as a day trip or overnight. Call for details on permits and prices.

FISHING

Fishing for striped largemouth bass is a popular sport on Lake Mead. While fly-fishing is possible, it's difficult and is only recommended at certain times of year. For current conditions, contact Michael Swartz of **Fish Vegas** (☎ 702-293-6294; www.fishvegas.com); he is an expert on Lake Mead fishing. He also offers guided trips for $250 for one or two people and can direct you to other guides.

You must carry a state fishing license, available from the marinas. If your license is from Nevada and you plan on fishing from a boat on Lake Mead or Lake Mohave, or from the Arizona shores, you must also have a use stamp from Arizona (and vice versa). A trout stamp is required if you intend to catch and keep trout. Licenses are not required for children under 14.

CRUISES

If you want to see the lake but don't want to rent a boat, consider a sightseeing tour with **Lake Mead Cruises** (☎ 702-293-6180; www.lakemeadcruises.com). Its boats are triple-decker, air-conditioned Mississippi-style paddlewheelers. Daily tours (adult/child $22/10) leave at noon and 2pm from Hemenway, a couple miles north of the Alan Bible Visitor Center. The company offers a Sunday breakfast cruise (adult/child $36.50/18, departs 10am), dinner cruises ($46/25, departs 6:30pm Sunday to Thursday) and a Saturday dinner and dance cruise ($58, departs 6:30pm). Meal-inclusive cruises are only offered from April through October.

HIKING

Though boating is the primary activity here, you'll find hiking trails throughout the recreation area. Stop by the Alan Bible Visitor Center or one of the ranger stations for information on trails and ranger-led hikes. Hiking in summer is discouraged, as temperatures can reach 120°F in the shade.

SWIMMING

Given the dry heat of the surrounding desert, swimming in Lake Mead is understandably popular. Because water levels vary, what was a beach one year may be a desert the next. Call or stop by the visitors center for a list of recommended beaches, and consider renting a boat to reach suitable water. Two miles north of the Alan Bible Visitor Center, the aptly named Boulder Beach (comprising pebbles and stone, not sand) is one good wading spot. Be sure to ask about pollution levels before swimming – houseboat owners sometimes dump raw sewage into the water rather than usi[ng] pump-out stations.

Sleeping

In addition to the following options, Laughlin and Bullhead City, on the south tip of the recreation area, host several hotel-casinos (RVs can park overnight for free in casino parking lots), independent motels and chain hotels.

CAMPING

The NPS maintains eight campgrounds for tents and RVs (no hookups) in the recreation area (tent & RV sites $; first-come, first-served). All are in or near marinas and offer fire-grills and toilets. The nicest of the west-side campgrounds is **Boulder Beach** (☎ 702-293-2340), overlooking the water and planted with cottonwoods and flowering trees. Set apart from the marina, it's quieter than other campgrounds. The other west-side campgrounds are at **Las Vegas Bay** (☎ 702-565-9111), **Callville Bay** (☎ 702-565-8958) and **Echo Bay** (☎ 702-394-4066). Few sites at Echo Bay (beside the busy marina and hotel) and Las Vegas Bay (a quiet marina, thanks to low water levels) overlook the water.

If you're headed east to the Grand Canyon, your only option is Temple Bar Campground, beside Temple Bar Resort. On Lake Mohave you'll find two campgrounds at Cottonwood Cove and one at Katherine Landing.

Lake Mead RV Village (☎ 702-293-2540; 268 Lakeshore Rd, Boulder City, NV 89005; RV sites $), **Callville Bay Resort** (☎ 702-565-8958; RV sites $), **Echo Bay Resort** (☎ 702-394-4000; RV sites $), **Overton Beach Resort** (☎ 720-394-4040; RV sites $) and **Temple Bar Resort** (☎ 928-767-3211; RV sites $) all offer full RV hookups. On Lake Mohave, RV hookups are available at **Cottonwood Cove Resort** (☎ 702-297-1464; RV sites $) and **Lake Mohave Resort** (☎ 928-754-3245; RV sites $) at Katherine Landing.

HOUSEBOATING

One of the most popular ways to explore Lake Mead is to rent a houseboat, available through **Forever Resorts Houseboats** (☎ 800-255-5561; www.foreverresorts.com) and **Seven Crown Houseboats** (☎ 800-752-9669; www.sevencrown.com). Rates vary widely depending on the season and size of boat. January 1 to June 15 and September 2 to December 31 are 'value seasons,' when rates are about $300 less than the rest of the year. Seven Crown rents the Grand Sierra (six nights for $2450), which has two bathrooms and sleeps 13 if you're packed like sardines; the smaller, more basic Summit (six nights for $2200) sleeps 10. Check the websites for complete information.

HOTELS & MOTELS

Temple Bar Resort (☎ 928-767-3211; www.templebarlakemead.com; cabins $) The only lodging on the Arizona side of the lake is the pleasant and remote Temple Bar Resort, 47 miles east of Hoover Dam. These simple 'fishing' cabins have shared bathrooms and showers, but do include kitchenettes. Some have lake views. If lake levels are high enough, a beach materializes. To get here, head 20 miles south of Hoover Dam on Hwy 93 and look for a marked, paved northbound road.

Best Western North Shore Inn at Lake Mead (☎ 702-397-6000; 520 N Moapa Valley Blvd, Overton, NV; d/ste $/$$) This is one of the best of several chain motels on the north side of the lake in Overton.

Lake Mead Lodge (☎ 702-293-2074; d & ste $-$$;) On the west side of the lake, with a pool overlooking the water, is the one-story Lake Mead Lodge. The place is looking a little worse for wear, but despite its proximity to the marina, beach and campground, it's a quiet spot surrounded by grass and trees and is a five-minute drive from restaurants in Boulder City. Wake early to watch the sun rise over the lake, perhaps in the company of one of the resident roadrunners.

Echo Bay Resort (☎ 702-394-4000; d $$) Also on the west side, this place is about an hour's drive from Boulder City. It's several stories high, has no pool and is rather loud and busy, as it sits amid a large marina. All rooms, even those with lake views, overlook a large parking lot.

Boulder Dam Hotel (☎ 702-293-3510; www.boulderdamhotel.com; 1305 Arizona St, Boulder City, NV; d/ste incl breakfast $$/$$$;) In 1933 this historic hotel opened in Boulder City to accommodate tourists flocking to witness construction of the massive structure. John Wayne, Shirley Temple and President Roosevelt all stayed here. The simple rooms were remodeled in 2001 without regard to historic charm, but the colonial-revival architecture and hint of old-world ambience in the public spaces make this a nice alternative to a standard motel.

Aside from campgrounds and houseboats, the only lodgings on Lake Mead are properties owned by **Seven Crown Resorts** (☎ 800-752-9669;

www.sevencrown.com) and **Forever Resorts** (www.foreverresorts.com). You must call Seven Crown Resorts, rather than the motels themselves, to make reservations. Don't expect a resort in the classic sense of the word – these are more like motels.

There are two motels on Lake Mohave. On the south side, at Katherine Landing, Seven Crown Resorts runs **Lake Mohave Resort** (☎ 928-754-3245; d $$), offering basic motel rooms. **Cottonwood Cove Motel** (☎ 702-297-1464; www.cottonwoodcoveresort.com; d $$) features a swimming beach and rooms with sliding-glass doors that overlook the water.

Several basic motels line Hwy 93 west of Boulder City, the nicest of which are **El Rancho Boulder Motel** (☎ 702-293-1085; 725 Nevada Hwy; s/d $/$$;) and the friendly **Sands Motel** (☎ 702-293-2589; www.sandsmotelbouldercity.com; 809 Nevada Hwy; r $$).

Eating & Drinking

You'll find basic restaurants at the Temple Bar, Boulder Beach and Echo Bay marinas on Lake Mead, and at Cottonwood Cove and Katherine Landing on Lake Mohave. The other marinas provide small convenience stores with snacks and drinks. Otherwise, the best places to eat in the area are in Boulder City.

Carlos Mexican Cafe (☎ 702-294-6640; 651 Hotel Plaza, Boulder City, NV; mains $; lunch & dinner) A cozy little neighborhood spot, this café serves good Mexican food and makes a mean salsa.

Milo's Best Cellars (☎ 702-293-9540; 538 Nevada Hwy; mains $-$$; 11am-10pm Mon-Thu, 11am-midnight Fri & Sat) Milo's feels like a California wine bar, with an extensive wine list and sidewalk seating. It serves sandwiches like the Grecian vegetarian (avocado, sprouts, roasted red pepper, baby greens and garlic mayonnaise served with Terra chips), cheese plates (Spanish Manchego, Italian Asiago, smoked Gouda and olives), baked Brie and fresh salads.

Boulder Dam Brewing (☎ 702-243-2739; 453 Nevada Hwy, NV; mains $-$$; noon-9pm Mon-Thu, to midnight Fri & Sat;) The beer here uses no additives or preservatives, which you can feel good about as you savor a pint with your ploughman's lunch or bratwurst. There's also a patio outfitted with mist sprayers providing welcome humidity on those hot summer evenings.

Getting There & Around

There are no shuttles to or around the recreation area. The only way to travel is by car. You'll find major car-rental agencies in nearby Las Vegas (see p183) and Henderson, Nevada.

LAS VEGAS

☎ 702 / pop 591, 537 / elev 2030ft

This isn't your parents' Vegas, but a blazing oasis of glitz and fantasy aiming to please its nearly 40 million visitors per year. You can still lose your sense of time and lose a bundle among cigarette-huffing oldsters at the nickel slots or with the high rollers at backroom baccarat. Take in a concert, a rollercoaster ride in New York or a gondola ride in Venice, then dance the night away in an after-hours club. The grown-up dining is world-class, the more titillating entertainment can be crass, and though exotic creatures like tigers and dolphins are some of the attractions, this city's human zoo is really where it's at.

But Grand Canyon visitors using Las Vegas as a jumping-off point will also be interested in what many locals quietly enjoy: its proximity to the outdoors. West of town, for example, Red Rock Canyon National Conservation Area (p179) is just a fat-tire hop away.

Orientation

Two interstate highways – I-15 and US Hwy 95 – bisect the city. Most short-term visitors will confine their carousing to S Las Vegas Blvd, the glittering north–south artery also known as the Strip. The upper end begins at the Stratosphere, continuing south into the lower end around the Venetian. Mandalay Bay marks the south end of the Strip, which runs to the airport.

North of the Strip lies Downtown, once the center of the action. Reviving the neighborhood is the Fremont Street Experience, a pedestrian mall that's breathed a little life into old Downtown. The wasteland along Las Vegas Blvd linking Downtown with the Upper Strip has little to offer, and Fremont St east of Downtown is decidedly seedy.

Information

INTERNET ACCESS

Most hotels in Vegas have business cente[rs] that will charge you an arm and a leg for 2[4-hour] internet access; some give it away for f[ree]

LAS VEGAS
0 1 km
0 0.5 miles
A
B
C
D
1
2
3
4
5
6
Washington Ave
E Washington Ave
McWilliams Ave
Bonanza Rd
Owen K Gragson Hwy
Tonopah Hwy
Avalon Ave
Fortune Ave
Twin Lakes Dr
Langtry Dr
Granite Ave
Collins Ave
Wimbledon Dr
Driftwood Dr
Sunland Ave
Rancho Circle
Center St
Alta Dr
Meadows La
Springs Preserve
Canyon Dr
Campbell Dr
Rosemary La
Shadow St
S Martin Luther King Blvd
Grand Central Parkway
Ogden Ave
Post Office
Neon Museum
Stewart Ave
Mesquite Ave
Bonanza Rd
Bell Dr
Carson Ave
Fremont St
Bridger Ave
Lewis Ave
Maryland Parkway
Clark Ave
Bonneville St
Garces Ave
Hoover Ave
Cass St
Main St
Casino Center Blvd
S Las Vegas Blvd
North Las Vegas
Pinto La
Desert La
Goldring Ave
Palomino La
Shetland Rd
Kenny Way
Lacy La
Bedford Rd
To Red Rock Resort (9mi); Red Rock Canyon (20mi)
Rancho La
Charleston Blvd
Huntridge Circle Park
Little White Wedding Chapel
Norman Ave
Chapman Dr
Franklin Ave
Sweeney Ave
Bracken Ave
Wengert Ave
Bruce Ave
Oakey Blvd
Hassett Ave
Canosa Ave
Bonita Ave
St Louis Ave
Phillips Ave
Exley Ave
Tree La
Utah Ave
Commerce St
Rexford Pl
Ellis St
Edgewood Ave
Ashby Ave
Mason Ave
Waldman Ave
Bannie Ave
Bryant Ave
Strong Dr
Silver Ave
Gilmary Ave
Westleigh Ave
Wyoming Ave
La Solana Way
Rancho Dr
Kyrland Ave
Lomond Ave
Highland Ave
Western St
Oakey Blvd
Parque Ave
Plaza de Monte
Valley Vw Blvd
Vista Dr
Hinson St
Melville Dr
Barnard Dr
Douglas Dr
Darmak Dr
Cashman Dr
Calle de Espana
Cahlan Dr
Pine St
Fairfield Ave
Stratosphere Tower
Baltimore Ave
Cleveland Ave
Cincinnati Ave
Santa Clara Dr
Santa Rita Dr
Rexford Dr
Patten Dr
Beverly Way
Van Patten St
Kendale St
State St
Maryland Pkwy
Spencer St
17th St
El Camino Ave
Sahara Ave
San Bernardino Ave
El Conlon Ave
Richfield Blvd
Alcoa Ave
Merritt Ave
Wilmington Way
Sahara Monorail Station
Industrial Rd
Highland Dr
Karen Ave
Laguna St
Del Mar Ave
Vegas Valley Dr
Joe W Brown Dr
Las Vegas Country Club
Bel Air Dr
Tara Ave
Silver Dollar Ave
Penwood Ave
Milo Way
Circus Circus Dr
Riviera Blvd
Las Vegas Hilton Monorail Station
Meade Ave
Rigel Ave
Westwood Dr
Post Office
Palora Ave
Golden Arrow Dr
Silver Mesa Way
Sombrero Dr
Sirius Ave
Wing St
Procyon Ave
Convention Center Dr
Stardust Rd
S Las Vegas Blvd (The Strip)
Pinehurst Dr
Desert Inn Rd
Las Vegas Convention Center Monorail Station
Desert Inn Rd
Brussels St
Rome St
Aztec Way
Pawnee Dr
Pioneer Ave
Western Ave
Fashion Show Dr
Fashion Show Mall
Wynn Golf Course & Country Club
Sierra Vista Dr
Commanche Ave
Spring Mountain Rd
Renate Dr
Vanessa Dr
Schiff Dr
Vegas Plaza Dr
Treasure Island
Sands Ave
Burbank Ave
Edison Cir
Dumont Blvd
Cherokee La
Elm Dr
Country Club La
E Twain Ave
Ottawa Dr
Twain Ave
Wynn Rd
Cinder La
Harrah's Imperial Palace Monorail Station
Cassella Dr
Katie Ave
Swenson St
Cambridge St
Viking Rd
Siegfried & Roy's Secret Garden & Dolphin Habitat
Flamingo
Flamingo/ Caesars Palace Monorail Station
Howard Hughes Parkway
Viking Rd
To McGhies (6.1mi)
Fredrika Dr
Flamingo Wash
Flamingo Rd
Flamingo Rd
Nevso Dr
Tropicana Wash
Bally's & Paris Monorail Station
Charlotte Dr
Rochelle Ave
Valley Vw Blvd
Polaris Ave
Aldebaran Ave
Industrial Rd
The Strip
Audrie St
Koval La
Lana Ave
University of Nevada, Las Vegas
Escondido St
Rochelle Ave
University Ave
Spencer St
Harmon Ave
Naples Dr
Paradise Rd
Mirage Golf Club
Hialeah Dr
Gabriel Dr
Lorilyn Ave
Gym Dr
University Rd
Tompkins Ave
MGM Grand Monorail Station
Deckow La
Henderson
To Siena Deli (0.4mi)
To Orleans (100ft)
Tropicana Ave
Tropicana Ave
Liberace Museum
Arden
Reno Ave
Palo Verde Rd
Lulu Ave
Wilbur St
Escondido St
Tamarus St
Caliente St
Procyon Ave
Ali Baba La
Giles St
McCarran International Airport
Rent A Car Rd
Hacienda Ave
Hacienda Ave
Westminster Ave
1
2
3
4
5
6
7
8
9
10
11
12
13
14
15
16
17
18
19
20
21
22
23
24
25
26
27
28
29
30
31
32
33
34

INFORMATION
American Express....................(see 16)
Cyber Stop....................1 B6
FedEx Kinko's....................2 C5
FedEx Kinko's....................3 C2
Las Vegas Convention & Visitors Authority Visitor Information Center....................4 C4
Sunrise Hospital & Medical Center....................5 D4
University Medical Center of Southern Nevada....................6 B2

SIGHTS & ACTIVITIES
Bellagio....................7 B5
Bellagio Gallery of Fine Art....................(see 7)
Bill's Gamblin' Hall & Saloon....................8 B5
Caesar's Palace....................9 B5
Circus Circus....................10 B4
Circus Circus Adventuredome....................(see 10)
Circus Circus Midway....................(see 10)
Eiffel Tower....................(see 19)
Excalibur....................11 B6
Golden Nugget....................12 C1
Gondola Ride....................(see 22)
Guggenheim Hermitage Museum....................(see 22)
King Tut Museum....................(see 14)
Las Vegas Natural History Museum....................13 D1
Luxor....................14 B6
Mandalay Bay....................15 B6
Manhattan Express Rollercoaster....................(see 18)
MGM Grand....................16 B6
MGM Grand Lion Habitat....................(see 16)
Mirage....................17 B5
New York New York....................18 B6
Paris Las Vegas....................19 B5
Shark Reef....................(see 15)
Stripper 101 Classes....................20 B5
Tropicana....................21 B6
Venetian....................22 B5
Wynn Las Vegas....................23 B4

SLEEPING
USA Hostels Las Vegas....................24 D2

EATING
808....................(see 9)
Aureole....................(see 15)
Buffet at Bellagio....................(see 7)
Café Bellagio....................(see 7)
Carnival World Buffet....................25 A5
Harrie's Bagelmania....................26 C4
House of Blues....................(see 15)
Le Cirque....................(see 7)
Little Buddha....................(see 33)
Nobhill....................(see 16)
Nobu....................(see 28)
Paymon's Mediterranean Café & Lounge....................27 D5
Rainforest Café....................(see 16)

ENTERTAINMENT
Blue Man Group....................(see 14)
Body English....................28 C5
Folies Bergère....................(see 21)
Forty Deuce....................(see 15)
FreeZone....................29 C5
Get Booked....................(see 29)
Ghost Bar....................(see 33)
Gipsy....................30 C5
Hard Rock Hotel & Casino....................(see 28)
Krave....................31 B5
KÀ....................(see 16)
Legends in Concert....................32 B5
Mix....................(see 15)
O....................(see 7)
Palms Casino Resort....................33 A5
Pure....................(see 9)
Tickets2Nite....................(see 16)

TRANSPORT
Greyhound Bus Station....................34 C1

The cafés listed here are your best options if you don't have your own computer.

Cyber Stop (☎ 702-736-4782; Hawaiian Marketplace, Polo Towers Plaza, 3743 S Las Vegas Blvd; per hr $12; 9am-8pm) The only internet café on the Strip.

FedEx Kinko's Downtown (☎ 702-383-7022; 830 S 4th St; per min $0.20; 7am-10pm Mon-Fri, to 5pm Sat); the Strip (☎ 702-951-2400; 395 Hughes Center Dr; per min $0.20; 24hr)

MEDICAL SERVICES

Both these hospitals have 24-hour emergency facilities.

Sunrise Hospital & Medical Center (☎ 702-731-8000, emergency 702-731-8080; 3186 Maryland Parkway)

University Medical Center of Southern Nevada (☎ 702-383-2000, emergency 02-383-2661; 1800 W Charleston Blvd)

MONEY

Every hotel-casino, bank and most convenience stores have ATMs. Fees imposed by casinos to exchange foreign currency tend to be higher than banks but a bit lower than exchange bureaus.

American Express (☎ 702-739-8474; Fashion Show Mall, 3200 S Las Vegas Blvd; 10am-9pm Mon-Fri, 10am-8pm Sat, noon-6pm Sun) Changes currency at competitive rates.

TOURIST INFORMATION

Shops advertising 'tourist information' along the Strip tend not to be official tourist offices but outlets selling helicopter tours and such.

Las Vegas Convention & Visitors Authority hotline (LVCVA; ☎ 702-892-0711; 6am-9pm) Has helpful operators, and recorded entertainment and convention schedules.

Las Vegas Convention & Visitors Authority Visitor Information Center (☎ 702-892-7575, 877-847-4858; www.visitlasvegas.com; 3150 Paradise Rd; 8am-5pm) The city's official tourist office.

Casinos

The casinos might be campy, but just because they bring the bling doesn't mean the draws of Las Vegas have changed all that much. You'll find surprisingly decent room deals in casinos on the Strip, since most make their money in the 24/7 gaming areas.

THE STRIP

Casinos here are listed from south to north.

Mandalay Bay (☎ 702-632-7777, 877-632-7800; www.mandalaybay.com; 3950 S Las Vegas Blvd; r $$;) Tropical-fantasy M-Bay's pool complex is the best on the Strip, a massive affair with a wave po lazy river and clothing-optional beach. Check out the walk-through tunnel going underneath the saltwater aquarium of Shark Reef (702-632-4555; adult/child $15.95/10.95; open 10am to 11pm).

Luxor (702-362-4000, 888-777-0188; www.luxor.com; 3900 S Las Vegas Blvd; r $$;) The Pharaoh-tastic Luxor flaunts a surprisingly elegant Egyptian theme that doesn't stop at the Sphinx in front. Housing the King Tut Museum (702-262-4000; admission $5; open 9am to midnight), this is one of the best midrange accommodation options on the Strip.

Excalibur (702-597-7777, 877-750-5464; www.excalibur.com; 3850 S Las Vegas Blvd; r $;) Fans of Arthurian kitsch will adore the Excalibur's faux-rock castle walls, its Fantasy Faire games, the animatronic fire-breathing dragon battling Merlin, and the 'Tournament of Kings' dinner show featuring live horses and audience participation. Kids under 18 stay for free.

Tropicana (702-739-2222, 888-826-8767; 3801 S Las Vegas Blvd; rooms $$;) The half-century-old Tropicana has had upgrades along the way but still exudes old Vegas. Its pan-cultural tropical theme includes a Wildlife Walk with exotic birds on display, and the palm-fringed pool area has a waterfall and swim-up blackjack tables. The Paradise Tower rooms are still your best bet.

MGM Grand (702-891-7777, 877-880-0880; www.mgmgrand.com; 3799 S Las Vegas Blvd; r $$;) The massive MGM Grand has a lazy river and pool area, the city's most gigantic casino and live lions (see p180), descendants of the MGM studio lion. Rooms echo the look of classic Hollywood bungalows. Don't stay at this sprawling property if you don't like walking.

New York New York (702-740-6969, 866-815-4365; www.nynyhotelcasino.com; 3790 S Las Vegas Blvd; r $$;) This crazy model of the metropolis can feel as crowded as the real NYC, with replicas of the Statue of Liberty, Empire State Building and Brooklyn Bridge all crammed into this minicity of a casino. Yellow cab–styled cars of the Manhattan Express (admission $12.50, re-ride $6; open 11am to 11pm Sunday to Thursday, 10:30am to midnight Friday and Saturday) roar away until late, so avoid lower-level rooms facing the rollercoaster if you want to sleep here.

Paris Las Vegas (702-946-7000, 888-266-5687; www.parislv.com; 3655 S Las Vegas Blvd; rooms $$;) Ah, so romantic…in the brash, Vegas casino manner. Re-creations of the Arc de Triomphe and Champs-Élysées are complemented by accordion players strolling fake cobblestone streets. The centerpiece is the half-scale replica of the Eiffel Tower (adult/child $9/7; open 10am to 1am), with an observation deck overlooking the lights of the Strip.

Bellagio (702-693-7111, 888-987-3456; www.bell[illegible].com; 3600 S Las Vegas Blvd; r $$$;) Out [illegible] the fountain puts on a spectacular show with music, lights and plumes of water. Contributing to the opulent atmosphere are the Mediterranean pool area and artificial lake, Tuscan architecture, European-style casino, gourmet restaurants and Bellagio Gallery of Fine Art (702-693-7871; admission $15; open 9am to 9pm). The under-18 set, while not unwelcome, are subject to restrictions listed on the website.

Caesar's Palace (702-731-7110, 877-427-7243; www.caesarspalace.com; 3570 S Las Vegas Blvd; r $$) Caesar's was one of first luxury mega-resorts and continues to impress with its Greco-Roman fantasyland theme. Marble statuary and bar girls in tiny togas carry on the tradition in swanky style.

Bill's Gamblin' Hall & Saloon (702-737-2100, 866-245-5745; www.billslasvegas.com; 3595 Las Vegas Blvd; r $;) Stained glass and dark polished woods in this casino evoke the exuberant spirit of a turn-of-the-20th-century Barbary Coast brothel. With its corner location and comfortable rooms at civilized prices, this is one of the Strip's sweetest accommodation deals.

Mirage (702-791-7111, 800-374-9000; www.mirage.com; 3400 S Las Vegas Blvd; r $$;) In front of the tropical-themed Mirage lies a 3-acre lagoon, where every night a volcano erupts hourly with a bang. Inside the casino's atrium, palms, bromeliads and cascading water bring some living green and cool relief into this showy casino. Don't miss the teeming 20,000-gallon saltwater aquarium in the registration area.

Venetian (702-414-1000; www.venetian.com; 3355 S Las Vegas Blvd; r $$$;) A gorgeous tribute to the romantic waterways and artistry of Venice – highlights include being serenaded by talented gondoliers on an indoor or outdoor gondola ride (702-414-4500; adult/child/private from $12.50/7.50/50; open 10am to 11pm Sunday to Thursday, to midnight Friday and Saturday) and the Guggenheim Hermitage Museum (702-414-2440; www.guggenheimlasvegas.org; adult/child $15/7; open 9:30am to 7:30pm), whose exhibits hail from the venerable collections of the Hermitage in St Petersburg, Russia, and the Guggenheim in New York. Rooms at the Venetian are unapologetically sumptuous and spacious.

Wynn Las Vegas (702-770-7100; www.wynnlasvegas.com; 3131 Las Vegas Blvd; rooms $$$;) The Strip's latest, greatest splash, the curved bronze-glass Wynn sparkles with luxurious excess and exclusivity. The entrance is discreetly obscured by a fake 7-story mountain. Inside, a profusion of greenery and natural light reflect the landscapes outside, the views of which can be savored through floor-to-ceiling windows from spacious guest rooms. Uniquely, the property includes a country club with a championship golf course.

Circus Circus (702-734-0410, 877-224-7287; www.circuscircus.com; 2880 S Las Vegas Blvd; rooms $;) It's a circus here, literally, with acrobats flying overhead and clowns working the floor – which makes it the most child-friendly casino hotel on the Strip. Free shows on the midway (open 11am to midnight) take place every half-hour, and the arcade's video and carnival games beckon enticingly. Tower rooms are the best choice, and there's an RV park in back. Children under 18 stay for free.

OFF-STRIP

Palms Resort Casino (702-942-7777, 866-942-7770; www.palms.com; 4321 W Flamingo Rd; r $$;) Just off-Strip, the Palms caters to a younger, flashier crowd and is popular for its themed party-floor suites (each sporting accoutrements such as bowling lanes, stripper poles or pool tables) and playpen suites geared toward bachelor and bachelorette parties. For those just here to play and not stay, its lounges and clubs are some of the hottest in town.

Golden Nugget (☎ 702-385-7111; www.goldennugget.com; 129 E Fremont; r $$;) Renovations in the mid-aughts modernized the Golden Nugget while retaining its old-school Vegas appeal. The lavish spa, shark-filled aquarium adjacent to the swimming pool, and understated elegance keep the shine on the Nugget. Standard rooms here are good value; two-level suites are a decadent Downtown splurge.

Orleans (☎ 800-675-3267; www.orleanscasino.com; 4500 W Tropicana Ave; r $;) Several blocks off the Strip, the huge Orleans is decked out in festive Mardi Gras colors and motif. Though the full-service casino also boasts a 70-lane bowling alley, heated pool, and movie theater, shuttles to the Strip depart regularly throughout the day should you need a change of scenery. There's a childcare center on-site.

Red Rock Resort (☎ 702-797-7777, 866-767-7773; www.redrocklasvegas.com; 11011 W Charleston Blvd; r $$$;) If hiking Red Rock Canyon (right) takes priority over strolling the Strip, consider staying at this beautiful resort. With all the amenities of a Vegas casino, it also offers easy access to climbing routes, hiking trails and mountain-biking adventures. It's only 10 miles northwest of the Strip, to which the resort provides a free shuttle.

Other Sights & Activities

Apart from the casino crawl, Las Vegas has myriad other attractions on and around the Strip.

FREMONT STREET EXPERIENCE

A decade ago, Vegas' downtrodden Downtown had lost nearly all of its tourists to the rapidly developing Strip. Always ready for a gamble, city and business boosters came up with a plan, which was realized in December 1995: a $70 million, four-block **pedestrian mall** (☎ 702-373-5200; www.vegasexperience.com; Fremont St, btwn Main St & Las Vegas Blvd). An arched steel canopy lights up with a surround-sound and synchronized light show five times nightly, and it also provides cool relief with its misting system. The gamble paid off, and this self-proclaimed 'vintage Vegas' experience does draw visitors Downtown.

HIKING & MOUNTAIN BIKING

Opened in June 2007, **Springs Preserve** (☎ 702-822-7700; www.springspreserve.org; 333 S Valley View Dr; adult/child $18.95/10.95; 10am-10pm summer, to 6pm winter, trails close at dusk), an oasis in the middle of the city, is sited on a natural spring and is now a 180-acre preserve and educational center. The 1.8 miles of trails meander through botanic gardens to a *ciénega* (wetland area). The trails and gardens are free, but the admission fees grant access to cool interactive exhibits about the secret life of garbage and the Desert Living Center's award-winning green buildings.

Located about 17 miles west of the Strip, **Red Rock Canyon** (☎ 702-515-5350; www.redrockcanyonlv.org, www.nv.blm.gov/redrockcanyon; bicyclists & pedestrians/cars free/$5; visitors center 8am-5pm) is a national conservation area run in conjunction with the Bureau of Land Management (BLM). A 13-mile scenic loop takes drivers through the conservation area, while the short Willow Springs hike leads to a wall of petroglyphs. More strenuous trails lead to riparian areas and good lookouts for expansive valley views. At the park entrance, you'll receive a brochure that contains a map with basic trail information. To get there, take Charleston Blvd, which turns into State Rte 159 and leads to the park entrance.

Check out the following outfits for more information on mountain-biking and hiking trails:

McGhie's (☎ 702-252-8077; www.mcghiesbikes.com; 4035 S Fort Apache Rd; 10am-7pm Mon-Fri, to 6pm Sat, to 5pm Sun) These friendly folks offer excellent service, repairs, bike rentals and guided bike tours.

Hike This (☎ 702-393-4453; www.hikethislasvegas.com) Private and group hiking and scrambling tours in Red Rock Canyon with a fun, eng aging guide; call or email 48 hours in advance for your best chance at a reservation.

Las Vegas for Children

Hotel concierges can refer parents to re[p]table local babysitting agencies, whose [sit]ters are screened and fingerprinted b[y] local sheriff and background-check

STRIP IT GOOD

Fitting as comfortably into Sin City culture as a $10 note tucked into a sequined thong, the striptease dance workout thrives here. Women-only **Stripper 101 classes** (☎ 702-492-3960; Miracle Mile Shops at Planet Hollywood; classes from $40; vary, call for times) take place at least twice daily, offering the chance to learn some actual moves and pole-dancing skills while getting a fun cardio workout in a safe and sexy environment. Meow.

the FBI. One such long-standing agency is **Around the Clock Childcare** (☎ 702-365-1040, 800-798-6768), charging $75 per child (or two siblings) for a four-hour minimum, plus $15 for each additional hour.

Cheap thrills include the following:

Circus Circus Adventuredome (☎ 866-456-8894, 702-794-3939; www.circuscircus.com; Circus Circus; single rides $4-7, day passes $14.95-22.95; 10am-midnight;) Sure, the exuberant acrobats and magicians on the Circus Circus midway are free, but you can also find higher-adrenaline thrills on family-friendly rides at the Adventuredome, the country's largest indoor theme park.

Las Vegas Natural History Museum (☎ 702-384-3466; www.lvnhm.org; 900 N Las Vegas Blvd; adult/child $6/3; 9am-4pm;) If the aquariums, taxidermied wildlife and animatronic T-Rex don't do it for them, the hands-on gallery will pique the little scientists' interest.

MGM Grand Lion Habitat (☎ 702-891-1111; www.mgmgrand.com; MGM Grand; admission free; 11am-10pm;) The MGM Grand showcases several of its 20-odd lions daily in a multilevel enclosure. Visitors can walk down the plexiglass tunnel to get a close-up look at these magnificent creatures (only a few of whom are on duty at a time).

Tours

Las Vegas is a popular gateway for visitors to the Grand Canyon. The following outfits can arrange air tours via small plane and helicopter to the Grand Canyon.

Air Las Vegas (☎ 800-940-2550; www.airvegas.com) Offers tours via helicopter to the West Rim and Colorado River, as well as half-day to full-day rafting trips and bus tours to the West or South Rims.

rand Canyon Helicopters (☎ 702-835-8477; www andcanyonhelicoptersaz.com; tours per person $330- Luxury Grand Canyon flyovers – think champagne at ottom of the western canyon.

Canyon West (☎ 877-716-9378; tours per 240-540) Take a basic trip to the Hualapai Reservation, or fly in style in a helicopter with hors d'oeuvres and champagne before walking the Skywalk (p150) and riding a pontoon boat on the Colorado River.

Maverick Helicopters (☎ 702-261-0007; www.airstar.com; tours $360-520) Offering higher-end tours of the same stripe as Grand Canyon Helicopters.

Papillon (www.papillon.com) This top-flight outfit, offering both small-plane and helicopter tours, also has a base in Tusayan (see p128), just south of the park's South Entrance.

Scenic Airlines (☎ 800-634-6801; www.scenic.com) Offers air tours and day trips to Grand Canyon, as well as bus tours and float trips on motorized rafts on the Colorado.

Sleeping

Las Vegas room rates fluctuate wildly with demand. Prices midweek are often 50% less than weekend rates, but then will triple during big conventions and even quadruple for major holidays like Valentine's Day and New Year's Eve. Remember, Strip properties can offer rooms for the same price as dumpy Downtown joints since they make their money in the gaming areas.

For discounted room rates, check casino websites (see p177) and hotel consolidators like www.travelocity.com, www.hotels.com and www.priceline.com. Consolidators buy up blocks of rooms, and if demand is low they'll sell them off at steep discounts. If you arrive without a reservation, ring the **Las Vegas Convention & Visitors Authority** (LVCVA; ☎ 800-332-5333), who have current rates and availability and can assist you in getting a room.

The most child-friendly casinos, like Circus Circus (p178) and Excalibur (p178), tend to be the least expensive. While there are also decent room deals Downtown, you'll save on time and cab fare if you stay on or near the Strip. **USA Hostels Las Vegas** (☎ 702-385-1150; 1322 Fremont St; dm & r $;) is another excellent budget spot. On the not-so-nice outskirts of Downtown, its top-notch facilities (including a pool, Jacuzzi and bar) and incredibly accommodating staff redeem the location. Call for free pickup from the Greyhound station.

Eating

Because time is irrelevant in this town, meals are timed accordingly – meaning that you could have breakfast at noon or midnight in any casino café. But if you want to do the thing properly, splurge on a weekend champagne brunch buffet. With a glut of excellent restaurants in Las Vegas, we've listed a small variety of favorites here as a starting point.

BUDGET

Siena Deli (☎ 702-736-8424; 2250 E Tropicana Ave; mains $; 8am-6:30pm Mon-Sat) Mama mia, Siena is the best deli in town, hands down. Make a meal out of Sicilian-style flat pizzas, Illy espresso and house-made tiramisu. Or grab a mouthwatering hot or cold deli sandwich.

Harrie's Bagelmania (☎ 702-369-3322; 855 E Twain Ave; mains $; 7am-4pm Mon-Sat) This kosher deli and NYC-style bagelry is the real deal, right down to the chicken in a pot and matzo-ball soup. Harrie's is a great breakfast spot pulling in half the ex-Manhattanites in town.

Paymon's Mediterranean Café & Lounge (☎ 702-731-6030; 4147 S Maryland Parkway; mains $; 11am-1am Mon-Thu, to 3am Fri & Sat) One of the city's few vegetarian spots, Paymon's serves items such as baked eggplant with fresh garlic, baba ghanoush, tabbouleh and hummus. Carnivores should try the kebab sandwich, gyros or rotisserie lamb. The adjacent Hookah Lounge is a tranquil spot to chill with a water pipe and fig-flavored cocktail.

Café Bellagio (Bellagio, 3600 S Las Vegas Blvd; mains $; 24hr) Bellagio's all-hours eatery is among the best in town. The menu features exciting twists on traditional American favorites. Big draws are the delicious coffee drinks, flowery setting and its gorgeous views of the swimming pool and garden areas.

MIDRANGE

House of Blues (☎ 702-632-7600; Mandalay Bay, 3950 S Las Vegas Blvd; mains $$; breakfast, lunch & dinner) This homey roadhouse – serving burgers, salads and BBQ – is a great spot to have a pre-show dinner, since a pre-show dinner receipt whisks you past the show door line for live shows. The swampy bayou atmosphere and down-home Southern cuisine is enhanced by eccentric outsider folk art. For something more appropriate to Sin City than church, let the unlimited champagne flow at the uplifting Sunday Gospel Brunch.

808 (☎ 877-346-4642; Caesar's Palace, 3570 S Las Vegas Blvd; mains $$; 5:30-10:30pm Sun-Thu, to 11pm Fri & Sat) Chef Jean-Marie Joseline dials Hawaii ('eight-oh-eight') daily on the coconut wireless to procure the raw goods that fuel this tropical-island-themed delight. The result is a creative mingling of French, Mediterranean, Indian and Pacific Rim elements. Many locals regard this as their city's top seafood shop.

Little Buddha (☎ 702-942-7778; Palms Resort Casino, 4321 W Flamingo Rd; mains $$; 5:30-11pm Sun-Thu, to 12:30am Fri & Sat) An offshoot of Paris' terribly popular Buddha Bar, it dishes superfresh sushi and French-Chinese fusion at reasonable prices (well, for Las Vegas, that is). Recommended mains include the duck confit, tempura pizza and spicy tuna tartare. The music and interior will sweep you away.

Carnival World Buffet (☎ 702-252-7767; Rio, 3700 W Flamingo Rd; mains $$; 24hr) Food from China, Brazil, Mexico, Italy and the US is showcased at this lavish buffet, one of the town's best. Go for dinner.

Rainforest Café (☎ 702-891-8580; MGM Grand, 3799 S Las Vegas Blvd; mains $$) This jungle-themed restaurant is a perfect place to bring the kids. The food is secondary to the lush faux-forest setting, a host of mechanized exotic animals and simulated tropical downpours. The elephant bellows loud enough to drown out any crying children.

TOP END

Aureole (☎ 702-632-7401; Mandalay Bay, 3950 S Las Vegas Blvd; mains $$$; 6-10:30pm) Chef Charlie Palmer's inspired seasonal American dishes (such as spice-crusted tuna with foie gras) soar to new heights here. The prix-fixe tasting menus ($95) are pure art and it's worth ordering wine just to watch the stewards ascend the four-story tower where the wine is 'cellared'. There's an extensive wine list and formal dress is required. Reservations are essential but difficult.

Le Cirque (☎ 702-693-8100; Bellagio, 3600 S Las Vegas Blvd; mains $$$; dinner) Top toque Marc Poidevin pairs artful haute cuisine with world-class wines in a joyous, intimate setting. The signature dish at this modern French restaurant is rabbit fricassee with Riesling, chanterelles and fava beans. A three-ring tasting menu costs $85, five acts $115. Jacket and tie required.

Nobhill (☎ 702-891-7337; MGM Grand, 3799 S Las Vegas Blvd; mains $$$; 5:30-10:30pm) James B[illegible] Award–winning chef Michael Mina [illegible] out the best of Northern California' [illegible] met cornucopia, including hou[illegible] sourdough breads, farmstead ch[illegible] Monterey Bay abalone. True [illegible] form, the ambience is laid-back yet elegant. Nobhill also offers five-course tasting menus and bar seating.

Nobu (☎ 702-693-5090; Hard Rock Hotel & Casino, 4455 Paradise Rd; mains $$$; 🕓 6-11pm) Iron chef Matsuhisa's sequel to his NYC namesake is every bite as good as the original. The beats are down tempo…the setting pure Zen. Andean influences surface in spicy offerings like *anticucho* chicken skewers. The Kobe beef is suave, the cocktails creative and dessert downright decadent. Feeling flush: try the *omakase* dinner (or 'chef's special,' which means the freshest and most creative of what's available that night). Reservations suggested.

Entertainment

Major sports events, big-ticket performances and over-the-top production shows come through Vegas and sometimes stick around for longer stints. Check current listings at www.whats-on.com. You can also get bargain last-minute show tickets by stopping by **Tickets2Nite** (☎ 702-939-2222; 🕓 10:30am-6pm), located next to the giant Coke bottle next to MGM Grand. Or try **Tix4Tonight** (☎ 877-849-4868; www.tix4tonight.com; 🕓 10:30am-8pm), with four locations (check the website for the location nearest you). At both vendors, available shows are posted at 10:30am daily and go on sale from 11am; you must stop by in person to purchase tickets.

NIGHTCLUBS

It's not as if you'll have a hard time finding a drink in this town – just roam through the front door of any casino. And if you're looking to earn those drinks after a spin on the dance floor, or gawk at pretty people over your top-shelf cocktail, it's merely a matter of knowing where to go.

Body English (☎ 702-693-4000; Hard Rock Hotel & Casino; 4455 Paradise Rd; cover $; 🕓 10:30pm-4am Fri-Sun) This elegant Euro-style club pampers the rich and famous, who mostly hang out in the VIP rooms. Booth reservations require one bottle ($300 minimum) per foursome, but there's a big bar upstairs for smaller spenders. Meanwhile, body English is spoken on the dance floor downstairs, to mainstream house, hip-hop and rock tunes.

Forty Deuce (☎ 702-632-9442; www.fortydeuce.com; Mandalay Bay, 3930 S Las Vegas Blvd; cover $-$$; 🕓 10:30pm-late Thu-Mon) A speakeasy vibe pervades this small but sexy little club. Feast your eyes on the smoking-hot traditional burlesque acts, backed up by a three-piece jazz band, that appear every 90 minutes starting before midnight.

Ghost Bar (☎ 702-942-7777; ghostbar-las-vegas.n9negroup.com; Palms Resort Casino, 4321 W Flamingo Rd; cover $-$$; 🕓 8pm-late) Dress to kill if you want to club with celebrities and wannabes on the 55th floor of the Palms. DJs spin groovy tunes while patrons sip overpriced cocktails amid the sky-high 360-degree panoramas and smart sci-fi decor.

Mix (☎ 702-632-9500; www.chinagrillmgt.com/mixlv; 64th fl, THEhotel at Mandalay Bay, 3950 S Las Vegas Blvd; cover after 10pm $$; 🕓 5pm-2am Sun-Tue, 5pm-4am Wed, Fri & Sat) Arrive before sunset and take a free glass-elevator ride up to this dizzying restaurant lounge with one of the most breathtaking views in Vegas. Take it all in with the glitterati on the vertiginous open-air patio.

Pure (☎ 702-731-7873; www.purethenightclub.com; Caesar's Palace, 3570 S Las Vegas Blvd; admission $-$$$; 🕓 10pm-late Fri-Tue) Dress to code if you want

---

GAY & LESBIAN VENUES

East of the Strip, alongside the UNLV campus, the Fruit Loop triangle is where it's at – or out. Pick up a free copy of *QVegas* (www.qvegas.com) magazine at LGBT retailer **Get Booked** (☎ 702-737-7780; 4640 S Paradise Rd; 🕓 10am-midnight Sun-Thu, to 2am Fri & Sat). Also check out www.outlasvegas.com.

FreeZone (☎ 702-794-2300; 610 E Naples Dr; cover free; 🕓 24hr) What's not to love, with a cool mixed crowd, pool tables and thumping dance floor – all free and all-hours.

[illegible]ipsy (☎ 702-731-1919; www.gipsylv.net; 4605 S Paradise Rd; cover $; 🕓 9pm-late) Always a mixed crowd at [illegible] giant nightclub; drag cabaret shows on Sunday and Latin grooves on Monday.

[illegible]ve (☎ 702-836-0830; www.kravelasvegas.com; 3663 S Las Vegas Blvd; cover $-$$; 🕓 10pm-3am Sun-Thu, [illegible]3am Fri & Sat) Get a table for six for a bottle (minimum $200) and live it up at this classy joint with excellent [illegible]he titillating Fashionistas show happening Monday through Saturday at 8pm. The entrance is off Harmon [illegible]e Desert Passage.

into this chic modern space, done up in electric blue, white and silver. Crowds of fine young thangs lounge inside a labyrinth of rooms that feel a lot like LA (making patrons feel at home, no doubt), all leading up to a gorgeous Strip-view patio.

SHOWS

Popular production shows include these current classics.

Blue Man Group (☎ 702-362-4400, 800-557-7428; Luxor, 3900 S Las Vegas Blvd; admission from $82; shows 7pm & 10pm Mon & Wed-Sat, 7pm Tue & Sun; inquire about additional matinees) A trio of nonspeaking comedic percussionists mix mind-bending audiovisual displays with oddball behavior in a uniquely amusing show. If you're sitting near the front, you may not want to step out in your Sunday best.

Folies Bergère (☎ 800-829-9034; Tropicana, 3801 S Las Vegas Blvd; admission to covered & topless shows $49 & $59; shows covered 7:30pm & topless 10:30pm Mon, Wed, Thu & Sat, topless 8:30pm Tue & Fri) Vegas' longest-running production is a tribute to the Parisian Music Hall and features some of the most beautiful showgirls in town.

Legends in Concert (☎ 877-777-7664; www.imperialpalace.com; Imperial Palace, 3535 S Las Vegas Blvd; admission incl 1 drink $35-60; shows 7:30pm & 10pm Mon-Sat) Around since the early '80s, Vegas' top pop-star impersonator show features real talent – no lip-synching allowed. Video screens beside the stage show real-life concert clips while live back-up dancers spice up the stage.

KÀ (☎ 702-531-2000; MGM Grand, 3799 S Las Vegas Blvd; admission $69-150; shows 7pm & 9:30pm Tue-Sat) Another elegant Cirque du Soleil production, this one an allegorical tale following a set of twins and incorporating elements of martial artistry.

O (Map p176; ☎ 796-9999, 800-963-9634; www.cirquedusoleil.com; Bellagio, 3600 S Las Vegas Blvd; admission $94-150; shows 7:30pm & 10:30pm Wed-Sun) 'Eau' (French for water) is Cirque du Soleil's original epic venture into aquatic theater. A talented international cast – performing in, on and above the precious liquid – create this feast for the eyes and feat of imagination.

Getting There & Away

Las Vegas is served mainly by **McCarran International Airport** (☎ 702-261-5211; www.mccarran.com; 5757 Wayne Newton Blvd), just south of the Strip. Though it's one of the world's 10 busiest airports, it's easy to navigate. Domestic flights use Terminal 1, while international and charter flights depart from Terminal 2.

Long-distance **Greyhound** (☎ 800-231-2222; www.greyhound.com) buses arrive at the Downtown **bus station** (☎ 702-384-9561; 200 S Main St). At the time of writing, Amtrak service did not extend to Las Vegas; closest stations are in Needles, California (106 miles away); Kingman, Arizona (116 miles); and Barstow, California (123 miles). However, Greyhound provides daily connecting buses between Las Vegas and these three cities (fares around $30).

From Las Vegas, it's a 5½-hour drive through the desert to the South Rim.

Getting Around

The McCarran airport Rent-a-Car Center should be your first stop for car rentals; the following companies and others are all based at the airport.

Advantage Rent-a-Car (☎ 702-798-6100; www.advantage.com)
Budget (☎ 800-922-2899; www.budget.com)
Dollar Rent a Car (☎ 800-800-4000; www.dollar.com)
Hertz (☎ 800-654-2210; www.hertz.com)
Thrifty Car Rental (☎ 800-367-2277; www.thrifty.com)

Several convenient public-transportation options exist in the touristed areas, including the Deuce, a 24-hour public bus traveling up and down the Strip (per ride/day $2/5).

The **Las Vegas Strip Trolley** (☎ 702-382-1404; per ride/day or night $2.50/4.25) runs about every 20 minutes from 8:30am to midnight from Mandalay Bay to the Stratosphere, and most resorts not located on the Strip run free shuttles to and from there. Taxis and limousines are readily available, and if you're too drunk to drive, you can even call **Designated Drivers, Inc** (☎ 702-456-7433; depending on mileage $50-60; 24hr) to pick you up and drive your car back to your hotel.

North Rim

On the Grand Canyon's North Rim, solitude reigns supreme. There are no shuttles to overlooks, no museums, no shopping centers, schools or garages, no bus tours or float trips. In fact, there isn't much of anything here beyond a campground, a classic national-park lodge perched directly on the canyon rim, and miles of trails through meadows thick with wildflowers, willowy aspen and towering ponderosa pines. Canyon views peep from behind the trees, and every trail ends with an expansive panorama to enjoy in peace and quiet.

From the lodge, floor-to-ceiling windows offer 180-degree views of the canyon. The small verandah, with a stone fireplace and rough-hewn rocking chairs, fills with dusty, weary hikers, doffing baseball caps, Camelbaks and backpacks at the end of every day. They grab a beer from the saloon and mingle on the porch, comparing notes and sharing experiences. After the sun sets, when most of the children have gone to sleep and darkness has subdued the canyon's ferocity, folks bundle in their fleece and sit quietly, studying the stars, breathing in the canyon's emptiness, listening to the silence.

Everyone here, from families with young children to retirees to wilderness backpackers, seems to settle into the intimate, camplike routine of the North Rim. This is the kinder, gentler Grand Canyon, and once you've been here you'll never want to see the canyon from anywhere else.

HIGHLIGHTS

- Sitting in a rocking chair on the verandah of the **Grand Canyon Lodge** (p197), sipping a North Rim sunset and watching the canyon transform with every shifting nuance of light
- Listening to the silence of the sunrise from the Coconino Overlook on the **North Kaibab** (p194)
- Hiking through aspen, ponderosa and meadows to **Widforss Point** (p192)
- Picnicking and throwing the Frisbee among Indian paintbrush at **Marble View** (p201)
- Belly crawling to the sheer-drop view at **Toroweap** (p189)

ELEVATION: 7865FT TO 8824FT	AVERAGE HIGH/LOW TEMPERATURE IN JULY: 77/46°F

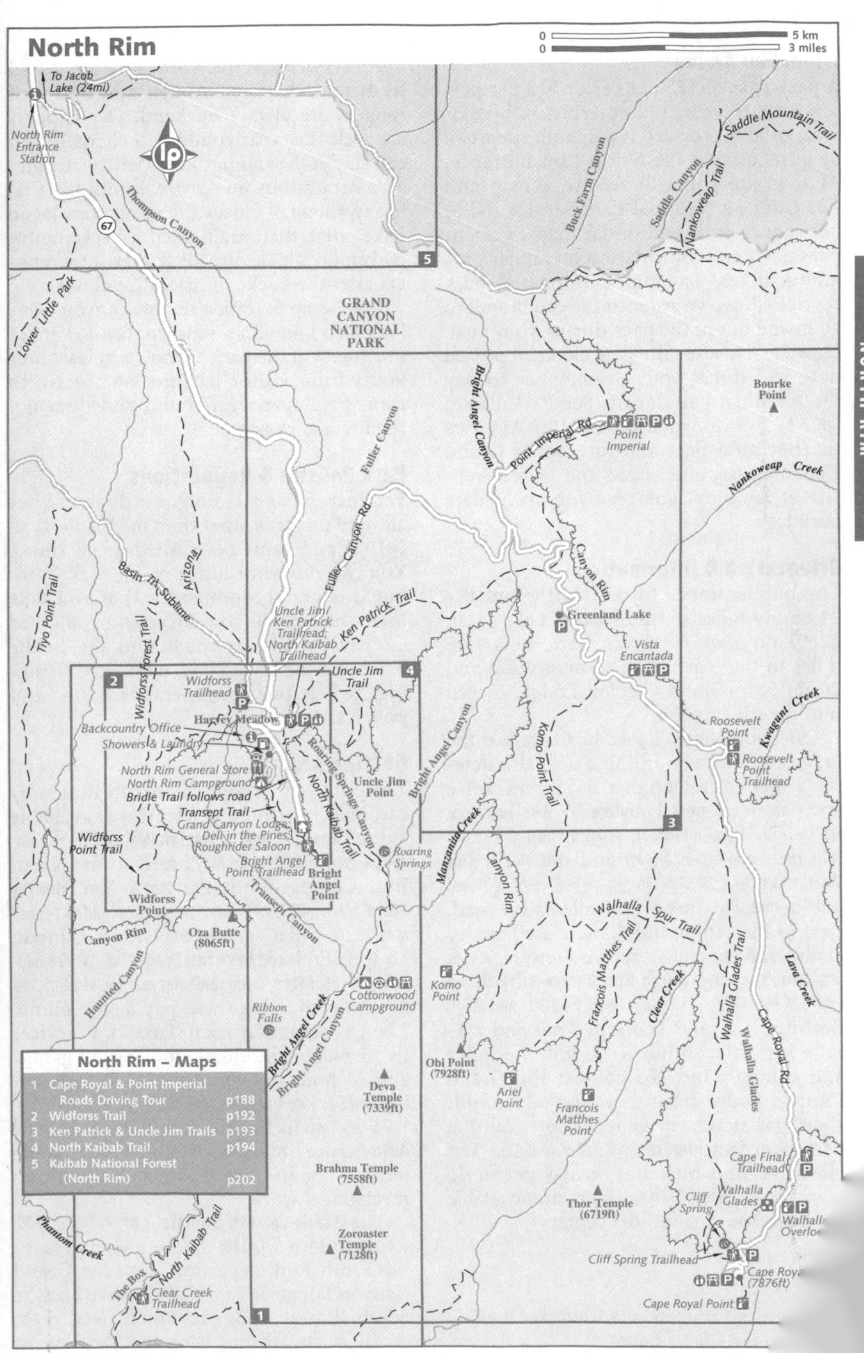

North Rim – Maps

1	Cape Royal & Point Imperial Roads Driving Tour	p188
2	Widforss Trail	p192
3	Ken Patrick & Uncle Jim Trails	p193
4	North Kaibab Trail	p194
5	Kaibab National Forest (North Rim)	p202

When You Arrive

A park pass of $25 per car or $12 per person over 15 years old entering on bike or foot, good for seven days on both rims, can be purchased at the North Rim Entrance. At the gate you will receive a map and *The Guide,* a National Park Service (NPS) newspaper with additional maps, current park news and information on ranger programs, hikes, accommodations and park services. Keep your receipt if you intend to go in and out of the park during your visit. If you arrive after the gate closes, a posted note will direct you – remember to pay the fee when you depart. See Park Passes (p233) for information on the America the Beautiful pass and an annual Grand Canyon pass, and access the park's website at www.nps.gov/grca for up-to-date park fees.

Orientation & Information

The only entrance to the North Rim lies 24 empty miles south of Jacob Lake (Map p200) on Hwy 67. From here, it is 18.5 miles to the North Rim Campground and 20 miles to Grand Canyon Lodge, carved into the canyon rim.

On a horseshoe-shaped boardwalk at the lodge entrance you will find a small cafeteria, a Western saloon that also serves coffee and pastries, a **postal window** (🕑 8am-5pm Mon-Fri, closed mid-Oct–mid-May), a **gift shop** (🕑 8am-9pm, closed mid-Oct–mid-May) and the **North Rim Visitor Center** (☎ 928-638-7864; 🕑 8am-6pm, closed mid-Oct–mid-May). Just over a mile up the road, next to the campground, there are laundry facilities, a general store, fee showers, a gas station and the **North Rim Backcountry Office** (☎ 928-638-7875; 🕑 1-5pm, closed mid-Oct–mid-May). Both the 1.2-mile Transept Trail and a 1-mile leg of the Bridle Trail link the lodge and campground. To contact the Grand Canyon Lodge front desk, the saloon, gift shop, gas station or general store, call the **North Rim Switchboard** (☎ 928-638-2612). The closest ATM, which may or may not work, is in Jacob Lake. Wheelchairs are available for loan from the visitors center.

All services on the North Rim are closed from mid-October through mid-May, but rangers are always on hand. Day-trippers are welcome year-round (no charge). You can stay at the campground (with water and a bathroom but no services) until the first heavy snowfall closes the road from Jacob Lake; after that you'll need a backcountry permit (available directly from winter rangers after the backcountry office closes).

Toroweap (p189), a remote canyon overlook also known as Tuweep, lies 151 miles northwest of the park entrance, at least four hours from visitor facilities on the North Rim. It is open year-round and does not require a park pass.

Park Policies & Regulations

Pets, except signal and guide dogs, are not allowed on trails other than the Bridle Trail (p192) and must be leashed at all times. You can ride your horse on all park trails, but it is not recommended that you take them into the canyon. Bicycles are allowed on paved and dirt roads and the Bridle Trail. See the boxed text, p236, and Bringing the Pets, p62, for general park rules and policies.

Getting Around

The only way to tour the North Rim is by car, bicycle or motorcycle. Gas is available at the **Chevron Service Station** (Map p185; 🕑 7am-7pm, closed mid-Oct–mid-May), next to the North Rim Campground; the **North Rim Country Store** (Map p202; 🕑 7am-7pm, closed mid-Oct–mid-May), 26 miles north of Grand Canyon Lodge; and **Jacob Lake Inn** (Map p200; ☎ 928-643-7232, 🕑 8am-8pm, credit card sales year-round 24hr), 44 miles north, where you pay at the pump. The gas station at Jacob Lake Inn services flat tires, but the closest full-service garage and 24-hour towing service is **Ramsey Towing and Service Garage** (Map p209; ☎ 435-644-2468; 115 S 100 East) in Kanab, 80 miles north. **Judd Auto Service** (☎ 928-643-7107) in Fredonia offers towing and tire repair, but doesn't do mechanical work.

The **Trans-Canyon Shuttle** (☎ 928-638-2820; 1 way/round-trip $70/130) takes passengers to the South Rim, departing from the Grand Canyon Lodge at 7am daily to arrive at the South Rim at 11:30am. You'll need cash; credit cards are not accepted. Reserve at least two weeks in advance (see p245). An

...e is a bathroom and ice-maker (free) ...d the visitors center.

GETTING AWAY FROM IT ALL

It's easy to get away from it all on the North Rim. In fact, coming to the North Rim in the first place is getting away from it all. There are, however, several options for those folk intent on seeing the canyon alone.

Toroweap (p189) requires a two-hour drive from the park entrance, and then a minimum of 2¼ hours on a renowned tire-puncturing dirt road. Within the park's border, Point Sublime (p189) attracts visitors with 4WDs, and overlooks in the Kaibab National Forest just outside the park (see p199) promise solitude. The risk with all these, however, is that you'll take the time and risk the health of your car bumping hours along dirt roads, only to find that others have bumped along to the point as well. To avoid this, head out to Marble View (p201). It's an easy 30-minute drive, and while it doesn't offer a classic canyon overlook, the view from the meadow here is our favorite.

And if you find a handful of other folk out there, you haven't lost much in the effort to escape them. For hikers, several old fire roads off Cape Royal Rd (p188) lead to rarely visited Komo, Ariel and Francois Matthes Points (Map p185).

Come to the park in early October, just before it closes, and you'll have many of the trails, brilliant with fall color and hinting of future frosts, to yourself. Better yet, come to camp after the facilities close in mid-October and before the first snow. Finally, when the snow is deep, park your car at Jacob Lake, snowmobile 44 miles to the rim, and winter camp. Now that's getting away from it all.

informal hikers' shuttle (first/additional passengers $11/7) takes folk from the Grand Canyon Lodge 2 miles to the North Kaibab Trailhead twice daily at roughly 5:30am and 6:30am. You must sign up for it at the front desk; if no one signs up the night before, it will not run.

The nearest bike rental is in Page at Lakeside Bikes (p219), Absolute Bikes in Flagstaff (p157) or **Red Rock Bicycle Company** (☎ 435-674-3185) in St George, Utah.

OVERLOOKS

Every drive, walk and hike on the North Rim includes a canyon overlook. You can drive paved roads to Point Imperial (p189) and Cape Royal (p188) or dirt roads to Point Sublime (p189), Toroweap (p189) and overlooks in the Kaibab National Forest (see p199), including the spectacular Marble View (p201). Widforss Point (p192) and Cape Final (p191) make excellent day-hike destinations, and Bright Angel Point (p190) is an easy stroll.

Steps off the verandah of the Grand Canyon Lodge lead to two rocky overlooks (they don't have a name, but you can't miss them), and the Rainbow Rim Trail (p201) in the Kaibab National Forest connects five overlooks.

DRIVING

Driving on the North Rim involves miles of slow, twisty roads through dense stands of evergreens and aspen to the region's most spectacular overlooks. To reach Cape Royal and Point Imperial Rds, head 3 miles north from Grand Canyon Lodge to the signed right turn. From here, it is 5 miles to the Y-turn for Point Imperial and Cape Royal Rds. The dirt roads to Point Sublime and Toroweap are rough, require high-clearance vehicles and are not recommended for 2WDs.

While the latter two certainly offer amazing views, and promise an escape from crowds, they require at least four hours navigating treacherous roads, and if your goal is absolute solitude, you might be disappointed. You can hike to Point Imperial (see Ken Patrick Trail, p193), but no trails connect the viewpoints.

TIP

Children especially enjoy watching mule deer graze in the meadows along Hwy 67. You can count on seeing them every evening; be careful driving after 5pm, as they regularly leap into the road.

CAPE ROYAL ROAD

Duration 40 minutes one way
Distance 15 miles one way
Start 8 miles north of Grand Canyon Lodge, off Hwy 67
Finish Cape Royal
Nearest Area Grand Canyon Lodge
Summary Quintessential North Rim drive passes several overlooks and an ancient Puebloan site on its way to a 0.6-mile paved path to the magnificent Cape Royal Point.

Descending gradually from 8200ft at Grand Canyon Lodge to 7865ft at Cape Royal, this easy, paved road is a must for any North Rim visitor. From Grand Canyon Lodge it takes about 40 minutes to drive straight to Cape Royal, but once there it's a 20-minute walk to the viewpoint. This road may be closed in the late fall and early spring, and during heavy wind. The only bathrooms are at Cape Royal.

About 2.5 miles after the Y-turn for Point Imperial and Cape Royal Rds, a small parking lot on the right marks **Greenland Lake**. A two-minute walk leads to a meadow and, a few minutes further, an old, empty salt cabin. This is the only stop on the drive without rim views, and it makes an excellent spot for a picnic.

Cape Royal & Point Imperial Roads Driving Tours

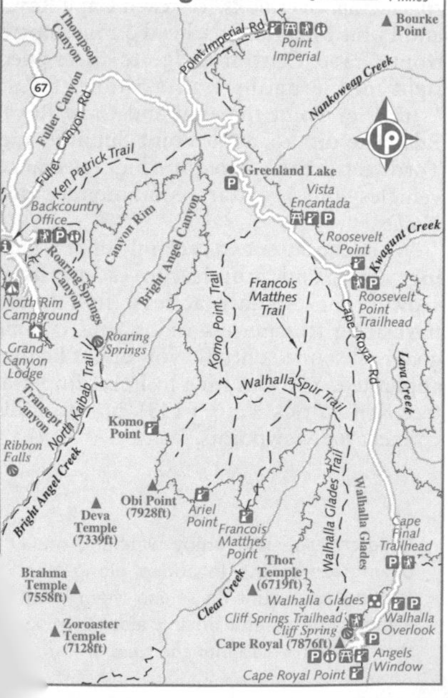

Cape Royal Rd continues 2 miles to **Vista Encantada**. Views from this overlook extend from Nankoweap Creek within the canyon to the Vermilion Cliffs and Painted Desert in the distance. You'll find a few picnic tables, but because the tables are right next to the road and parking lot it's not a particularly nice spot to eat. After taking in the view, continue 1.6 miles to **Roosevelt Point**. From here, you can see the confluence of the Little Colorado and Colorado Rivers, the Navajo Reservation, the Painted Desert and the Hopi Reservation. The easy 0.2-mile round-trip **Roosevelt Point Trail** loops through burnt-out forest to a small bench at the canyon edge.

The next stop is **Walhalla Overlook**, 6.5 miles past Roosevelt Point. Just below the rim lies Unkar Delta, a plateau composed of sand and rocks deposited by Unkar Creek. This was the winter home of ancestral Puebloans from AD 850–1200. On the north side of the parking lot, a path crosses the street and leads to **Walhalla Glades**, the ancient Puebloans' summer home. Because this area sits below most of the North Rim, snow here melted earlier and enabled villagers to grow beans, corn and squash. A short self-guided walk leads past six small ruins; pick up a walking-tour brochure from a small box at the trailhead just off the road.

The road ends 1.5 miles past Walhalla Overlook at the Cape Royal parking lot. From here, a 0.6-mile paved path, lined with piñon, cliffrose and interpretive signs, leads to **Angels Window**, a natural arch, and **Cape Royal Point**, arguably the best view from this side of the canyon. The path splits at the view of Angels Window, a few minutes from the trailhead. To the left, a short path leads to a precipice overlook that juts into the canyon and drops dramatically on three sides – here, you are literally standing atop Angels Window. To the right, the path continues to the rocky outcrop of Cape Royal Point. The Colorado River, 70 miles downstream of Lees Ferry, 18 miles upstream of Phantom Ranch, and 207 miles upstream of Lake Mead, can be seen directly below the point.

While the path is plenty wide for strollers and wheelchairs, they can't access Angels Window and the path from the fork to the end is a bit rough. Several shaded picnic tables sit at the far end of the parking lot. To the left, the **Wedding Site picnic bench** features great canyon views – an ideal spot for a sunrise picnic breakfast.

POINT IMPERIAL ROAD

Duration 10 minutes one way
Distance 3 miles one way
Start 8 miles north of Grand Canyon Lodge, off Hwy 67
Finish Point Imperial
Nearest Area Grand Canyon Lodge
Summary Easy drive through ponderosa and aspen to one of the North Rim's most spectacular overlooks.

At 8803ft, Point Imperial is the highest overlook on either of the rims. Expansive views of the canyon's eastern half and the desert beyond include Nankoweap Creek, the Vermilion Cliffs, the Painted Desert and the Little Colorado River. An interpretive sign identifies the sights and geologic formations, and several shaded picnic tables are set back from the rim. There are no stops along the road to Point Imperial.

POINT SUBLIME

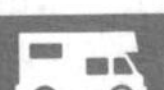

Duration 2 hours one way
Distance 17 miles one way
Start 0.9 miles west of Hwy 67, 2.7 miles north of Grand Canyon Lodge (at sign for Widforss Trail)
Finish Point Sublime
Nearest Area Grand Canyon Lodge
Summary Rough 4WD road to sublime 270-degree overlook.

Touted as one of the more spectacular and remote viewpoints within the park, Point Sublime lives up to its reputation for those with the time and inclination to tackle the grueling four-hour round-trip drive over road that is, in places, almost impassable. The road bumps and winds and bumps some more through ponderosa and aspen, and past several lovely side-canyon views before reaching the piñon and desert shrubs of Point Sublime.

Check road conditions before taking off, and absolutely do not attempt this drive in a 2WD.

Just over 4 miles west of Hwy 67, an old fire-access road heads south for about 4.5 miles to **Tiyo Point**, a quiet overlook and a good backcountry campsite (no facilities). You can't drive, but it's a moderate hike, and you'll more than likely have the point to yourself. Further down the road, about 70 minutes from Hwy 67, a lovely backcountry campsite nestled in a clearing among the trees offers side-canyon views, and there are picnic tables and campsites on the point.

TOROWEAP (OR TUWEEP)

Duration 2¼ hours one way
Distance 61 miles one way
Start BLM Rd 109 (Sunshine Route), off Hwy 389, 9 miles west of Fredonia
Finish Toroweap Overlook
Nearest Town Fredonia (p207)
Summary Washboard road through barren desert to a dramatic, sheer-drop view of Colorado River 3000ft below.

One of the park's most impressive overlooks, Toroweap offers a landscape and views unlike anywhere else on the North Rim. Its 4552ft elevation, lower than either rim, supports piñon, junipers, cacti and small flowering desert plants, and sheer cliffs drop directly into the canyon and the Colorado River below. Toroweap is not for everyone. It's a long way, there are no facilities and it's incredibly hot and dry during the summer. For those who venture out here, however, Toroweap promises a Grand Canyon experience like nothing else. You literally have to crawl on your belly to see the river below, and there are no guardrails. Lava Falls, perhaps the roughest water in the canyon, is visible 1.5 miles downstream, and Vulcans Throne, basalt remnants of a cinder cone eruption 74,000 years ago, rises from the Esplanade

Platform (for more details about this igneous rock, see p68). Across the canyon is the Hualapai Reservation and 25 miles east sits the mouth of Havasu Canyon (p144), home to the Havasupai.

To get here, drive 9 miles west of Fredonia on Hwy 389 and look for a dirt road and the sign 'Toroweap.' Take this road 55 miles south to the **Tuweep Ranger Station** (☎ 928-638-7888), staffed year-round. A free, primitive campground lies 5.4 miles beyond the ranger station and a mile before the rim; a couple of exposed sites sit at the canyon edge.

The road to Toroweap, notorious for flattening tires, keeps garages in Kanab in business. Expect at least one, maybe more, drive under 25mph to minimize your chances, have at least one spare tire, and bring plenty of water. There is none at Toroweap.

About two hours (46 miles) after the turn onto BLM 109 from Hwy 389, just past the park's border, is a sign for Mt Trumbull Rd. Follow this road about 3 miles to **Nampaweap Petroglyphs**; a small parking lot with an interpretive sign marks the short walk to the petroglyphs.

A few moderate hikes offer chances to stretch your legs. The 2.9-mile **Esplanade Loop Trail** begins at the campground. For a shorter hike, try the easy **Saddle Horse Canyon Trail**, a 1.6-mile round-trip to the canyon rim. The easy-to-miss trailhead is 5.7 miles south of the ranger station.

HIKING

Do not underestimate the effect of altitude. If you can, spend a few days acclimating with scenic drives, short walks and lazy days before conquering longer trails. The only maintained rim-to-river trail from the North Rim is the North Kaibab, a steep and difficult 14-mile haul to the river; day hikers will find multiple turnaround spots. Under no circumstances should anyone attempt to hike to the Colorado River and back in one day – as a ranger told us, the Grand Canyon wants to kill you.

See Activities (p41) for general details on walking and hiking in the Grand Canyon; see the Kaibab National Forest (p199) for hikes just outside the park border; and see the boxed text on p196 for info on rigorous unmaintained trails into the canyon.

EASY HIKES

These walks a suitable for those with a modest fitness level.

BRIGHT ANGEL POINT

Duration 30 minutes round-trip
Distance 1 mile round-trip
Difficulty Easy
Start/Finish Log shelter behind visitors center at Grand Canyon Lodge
Nearest Area Grand Canyon Lodge
Transportation Private
Summary Narrow path along rocky outcrop to popular canyon overlook.

More a walk than a hike, this paved trail wraps up, down and out along a narrow finger of an overlook that dangles between The Transept (Transept Canyon) and Roaring Springs Canyon. This is one of the few trails on the North Rim where you feel like you're walking along a precipice, with the canyon dropping off from either side of the trail. Anyone with fear of heights should think twice before strapping on their walking shoes.

There are few guardrails, and the edges are crumbling rock and sand – hold onto your children's hands and do not veer from the established trail. We were there on a windy day, and several folk turned back for fear that a particularly strong gust would simply blow them over the edge. While it is officially paved and easy, the few steep inclines, rocky spots and narrow path make this dangerous for strollers and prohibitive to wheelchairs. A few benches and boulders offer pleasant spots to rest along the way.

The overlook offers unfettered views of the mesas, buttes, spires and temples of Bright Angel Canyon, as well as a straight shot of the South Rim, 11 miles away, and the distant San Francisco Peaks near Flagstaff. If you have a good flashlight or headlamp, visit the point after dusk for unequaled stargazing. For a shorter walk, start at the steps on the east end of the Grand Canyon Lodge verandah and turn left.

TRANSEPT TRAIL

Duration 1½ hours round-trip
Distance 3 miles round-trip
Difficulty Easy
Start/Finish West end of Grand Canyon Lodge verandah
Nearest Area Grand Canyon Lodge
Transportation Private
Summary Wooded walk with sporadic views of Transept Canyon.

Conveniently connecting Grand Canyon Lodge to the campground, this rocky dirt path with moderate inclines meanders through aspens, and is an excellent option for a morning trail run.

From the bottom of the steps off the Grand Canyon Lodge verandah, follow the trail along the rim to the right. In about 15 minutes, you'll come to a log bench with a quiet, lovely view of the canyon. With plenty of room to run, this is a particularly nice spot for a picnic with children. From here, the trail veers from the edge and the path becomes relatively level, more a walk through the woods than a hike. The trail passes a small **ancient Puebloan site** and several viewpoints before reaching the rim-view tent sites of the campground, and the general store beyond.

Snack at the general store and then retrace your steps. Alternatively, return to the lodge on Bridle Trail (p192). You can also walk the trail in reverse; from the campground, the trail begins behind the general store.

CLIFF SPRINGS TRAIL

Duration 45 minutes round-trip
Distance 1 mile round-trip
Difficulty Easy–moderate
Start/Finish Cape Royal Rd 14.5 miles south of Y-junction of Point Imperial Rd and Cape Royal Roads
Nearest Area Grand Canyon Lodge
Transportation Private
Summary Scramble over rocks and under cliffs to hidden side canyon.

While this sweet little trail leads to a lovely hidden dell, stretches can be tricky to negotiate and it's not a particularly pleasant hike. Fortunately, it's short.

The trail immediately heads sharply downhill, over loose rock and through the woods. In about five minutes, you'll come to a stone **ancestral Puebloan granary**, used by the ancestral Puebloans to store corn, beans and squash. The path then makes its way through dry, barren pines and along a short, rocky descent into a ravine. It hugs the wall of a narrow side canyon, passing under the shade of a boulder overhang, for about 10 minutes to its end.

At **Cliff Spring**, a tiny trickle emerges from the ground, forming a large puddle fringed with ferns and verdant thistle, and a huge, flat rock, cooled by steady breezes, offers a shaded spot to sit. The view here is strikingly different from other North Rim trails. You are actually hidden in the canyon, as opposed to sitting on the canyon's edge, and you don't get a sense of the massive vista that so many overlooks boast.

CAPE FINAL

Duration 3 hours round-trip
Distance 4 miles round-trip
Difficulty Easy
Start/Finish Cape Royal Rd 11.8 miles south of Y-junction of Point Imperial Rd and Cape Royal Rd
Nearest Area Grand Canyon Lodge
Transportation Private
Summary Flat hike to one of the most stunning overlooks on the North Rim.

Hike this trail for the destination, not the hike. It's so dry, with nothing but brown ponderosa and brittle needles for most of the hike, that it feels like you're walking through a box of kindling, and what you see at the trailhead is what you'll see for just about the entire hike.

But it's almost completely flat, quite easy, and you're rewarded for tolerating the monochromatic hike with an amazing canyon overlook.

After the initial, moderate 10-minute incline, the trail levels off. In about a half hour, a short side trail veers left to a beautiful view – take a few minutes to rehydrate, and return to the main trail. There is one more view before the trail narrows, turns rocky and head a couple minutes downhill. The ponderosa give way to piñon, sagebrush and cliffrose and a flat, rocky triangle roughly 25ft by 25ft extends into the canyon with incredible views. Hike five more minutes through cactus and scramble up some boulders to **Cape Final**. Here, a small, rocky overlook sits at the edge of the canyon, offering a 270-degree view of lower Marble Canyon, Eastern Grand Canyon and one of the canyon's most famous formations, Vishnu Temple. The ease of this hike makes it great for children, but it's a frighteningly dangerous overlook and there are no guardrails.

POINT IMPERIAL

Duration 2 hours round-trip
Distance 4 miles round-trip
Difficulty Easy
Start/Finish Point Imperial
Nearest Area Grand Canyon Lodge
Transportation Private
Summary Rim trail through burned forest.

From the Point Imperial parking lot this trail heads northeast along the rim through areas burned by the 2000 fire. The trail ends at the park's northern border, where it connects with the Nankoweap Trail (p196) and US Forest Service (USFS) roads. Though this trail rolls gently along the rim, offering views of the eastern canyon, the high elevation (8800ft) can make it seem more difficult.

BRIDLE TRAIL

Duration 80 minute round-trip
Distance 2.4 miles round-trip
Difficulty Easy
Start/Finish Grand Canyon Lodge
Nearest Area Grand Canyon Lodge
Transportation Private
Summary Utilitarian path along the road and through the woods.

This uninspiring trail serves the sole purpose of offering visitors a means of walking from the lodge to the campground, and on to the North Kaibab Trailhead (p194). It hugs the road for 1 mile before climbing through the woods to the Kaibab Trailhead parking lot, just behind the Dennys.

DAY HIKES

The following day hikes allow you to penetrate a little deeper into the canyon.

WIDFORSS TRAIL

Duration 4–6 hours round-trip
Distance 10 miles round-trip
Difficulty Moderate
Start/Finish 1 mile west of Hwy 67, 2.7 miles north of Grand Canyon Lodge
Finish Widforss Point
Nearest Area Grand Canyon Lodge
Transportation Private
Summary Winding trail with views of canyon, meadows and woods, ending at a tranquil overlook.

Named after Gunnar Widforss, an early-20th-century artist who lived, worked, died and was buried at the Grand Canyon, the Widforss Trail meanders through stands of spruce, white fir, ponderosa pine and aspen to **Widforss Point**. Tall trees offer shade, fallen limbs provide pleasant spots to relax, and you likely won't see more than a few people along the trail.

After an initial 15-minute climb, the canyon comes into view. For the next 2 miles, the trail offers wide views of the canyon to one side and meadows and woods to the other. Soon after, about halfway into the hike, the trail jags away from the rim and dips into gullies of lupines and ferns; the

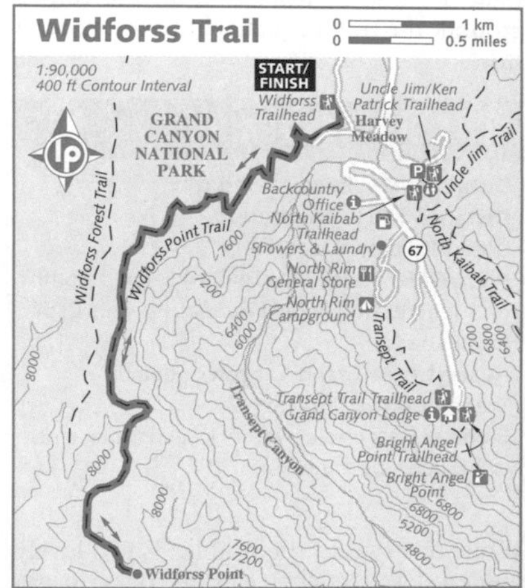

canyon doesn't come into view again until the end. From Widforss Point (elevation 7811ft), take the small path to the left of the picnic table to a flat rock, where you can sit and enjoy your sandwich, the classic view and the silence. Though the total elevation change is only 440ft, rolling terrain makes the first couple of miles a moderate challenge. The park service offers a self-guided trail brochure, available at the trailhead and the visitors center, for the first half of this hike. Follow the trail to the end of the guide and then turn around, and you'll have hiked the best part of the trail. This is a particularly pretty hike in late September or early October when the leaves are golden, and the point makes an excellent backcountry campsite.

KEN PATRICK TRAIL

Duration 6–7 hours one way
Distance 10 miles one way
Difficulty Moderate–difficult
Start North Kaibab trailhead parking lot, Hwy 67 1.5 miles north of Grand Canyon Lodge
Finish Point Imperial
Nearest Area Grand Canyon Lodge
Transportation Private
Summary Deceptively long hike through forest and meadow.

Offering rim and forest views, this challenging trail ascends and descends numerous ravines as it winds through an old, deep forest, crosses **Cape Royal Road** after 7 miles and continues for another 3 miles to **Point Imperial**.

The trail starts with a gentle climb into the woods and winds through gambel oak, ponderosa pine, white fir and aspen woodland. Views are intermittent, offering quick glimpses of Roaring Springs Canyon. The trail sees a lot of mule traffic, and it shows – particularly on the first mile, where the soft dirt path, worn into sandy grooves by hooves and softened by mule urine, can be smelly and hard on the feet. After a mile the mules head off on the Uncle Jim (see right), while the Ken Patrick veers to the left. Beyond this junction the trail grows increasingly serene, at times faint but discernible, and involves several difficult uphill stretches.

For excellent views and a shorter, easier, mule-free walk, start at Point Imperial and hike 3 miles to Cape Royal Rd, and turn

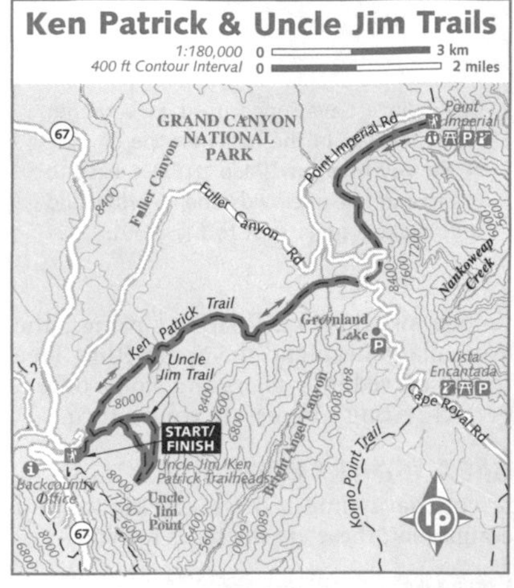

around. This stretch is the steepest but also the prettiest and the quietest. The trail alternates between shady conifer forests and panoramic views of Nankoweap Canyon, the Little Colorado River gorge, Marble Platform and the Painted Desert, and the San Francisco Peaks far to the south. Allow four hours for the round-trip journey.

UNCLE JIM TRAIL

Duration 3 hours round-trip
Distance 5 miles round-trip
Difficulty Moderate
Start/Finish North Kaibab trailhead parking lot, Hwy 67 1.5 miles north of Grand Canyon Lodge
Nearest Area Grand Canyon Lodge
Transportation Private
Summary Wooded trail to picnic spot on canyon overlook.

This spur trail, named for a hunting advocate and forest-service warden who shot hundreds of mountain lions on the Nort
Rim to protect resident deer, shares the K
Patrick Trailhead. The two trails are
same for the first mile (see Ken Pa
left), then Uncle Jim then heads righ
a bit of down and up, the trail soor
the 2-mile loop out to the point
little difference if you go left or
the tie-up area for mules at **U**
you'll have a terrific view

> **TIP**
>
> Uncle Jim's Cave, once used as a ranger residence, lies in the rocks on the far side of **Harvey Meadow** (Map p185) – easy to get to and free of crowds, the meadow and cave make a great spot to hang out.

Kaibab switchbacks, Roaring Springs, the Walhalla Plateau and the South Rim. Tree trunks carved into chairs and stools offer a perfect resting spot before your return.

BACKCOUNTRY HIKES

If you have time, fitness, experience and equipment, these are the hikes for you.

NORTH KAIBAB

Duration 20 hours round-trip
Distance 28.2 miles round-trip
Difficulty Difficult
Start/Finish North Kaibab parking lot, Hwy 67 1.5 miles north of Grand Canyon Lodge
Nearest Area Grand Canyon Lodge
Transportation Private, hikers' shuttle from Grand Canyon Lodge
Summary Dusty trail into the canyon follows Bright Angel Creek for the lower half and offers some of the park's loveliest scenery.

Even the most able-bodied hikers emerge from the pines after a day hike on the North Kaibab and collapse, exhausted and hot, on the stone wall by the trailhead. The 3 miles just below the rim are steep switchback after steep switchback of grinding haul, with no shade and no relief from the heat, made all the more draining by the pools of mule urine blocking the trail. It's not so bad going down, but coming back up is tough – time your hike so you're not tackling this section 'uring the heat of the day. The following de-ription includes an overnight about half- down the trail. With a dawn departure, ould hike down to the river in one day. hike out in one day, however, get on by 3am to avoid midday sun. Note rail drops 4170ft over 7.4 miles n to Cottonwood Campground, ttonwood it levels off to a pleas- line over 7.4 miles.

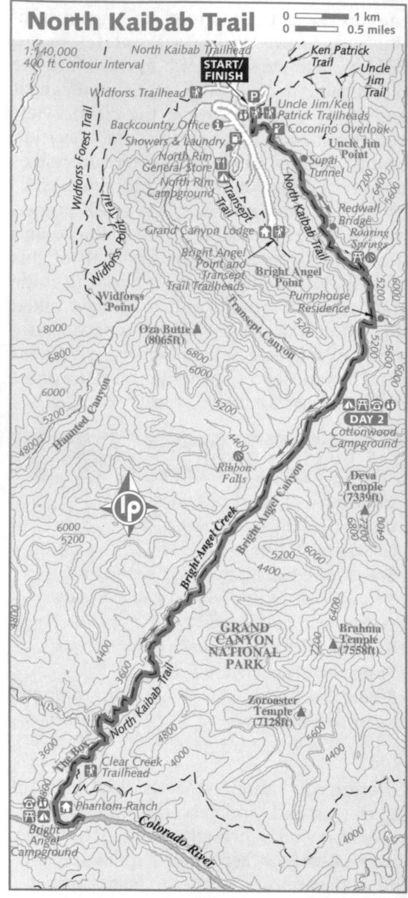

The trailhead lies 2 miles north of Grand Canyon Lodge. The modest parking lot often fills soon after dawn; you can also walk from the lodge or campground on the Bridle Trail (p192) or reserve a spot on the hikers' shuttle (see p187). Potable water is available May through September at Supai Tunnel, Roaring Springs and Cottonwood Campground. The trail remains open year-round, even though the North Rim closes. Snowshoes may be necessary for the upper elevations, and the trail can be dangerous due to ice and snow.

Popular day hikes on the North Kaibab:
Coconino Overlook 1.5 miles/one hour round-trip.
Supai Tunnel 4 miles/three–four hours round-trip.
Redwall Bridge 5.2 miles/four–five hours round-trip.
Roaring Springs 9.4 miles/seven–eight hours round-trip.

DAY 1: NORTH KAIBAB TRAILHEAD TO COTTONWOOD CAMPGROUND

4½ hours; 6.8 miles

The sandy trail begins at 8250ft, under the shade of aspens and pines. Within 10 minutes, the trail emerges from the trees and opens up to canyon views. At **Coconino Overlook** (7450ft), about 25 minutes from the trailhead, a flat ledge offers clear views of Roaring Springs and Bright Angel Canyons.

Forty minutes or so later, the trail comes to a tree-shaded glen with a seasonal water tap and pit toilets, the turn-around for half-day mule trips. Just around a bend is **Supai Tunnel** (6800ft), a short red corridor blasted through the rock when the trail was built in the 1930s. On the other side of the tunnel, views open to an intimidating set of switchbacks beside a knuckle-biting drop-off. It's a tough descent along the switchbacks to **Redwall Bridge** (6100ft). The bridge, built in 1966 when more than 14in of rain fell over 36 hours and washed away huge sections of the North Kaibab Trail, crosses Roaring Springs Canyon. From here, the thin trail hugs the canyon wall to the right and hovers above dramatic sheer drops to the left.

A little over a mile after the bridge, you'll reach the cascading waterfall of **Roaring Springs** (5200ft) itself; take the short detour to the left, where you'll find picnic tables and a pool to cool your feet. Seasonal water is available at the restrooms or 10 minutes down the trail at the **Pumphouse Residence**. New York City–born Grand Canyon artist **Bruce Aiken** (www.bruceaiken.com/index.htm) lived and worked here as the pump operator from 1972 until his retirement in 2006. Park rangers now live here during the summer only.

From Roaring Springs, the trail follows the small and inviting **Bright Angel Creek** 2.1 miles to **Cottonwood Campground** (4080ft). Here, tall cottonwoods offer a shaded spot to relax along the creek. It's a beautiful spot and a welcome oasis after the scorching canyon descent, but the campsites themselves are not shaded. The campground provides drinking water (May 15 to October 15), pit toilets, a phone, a ranger station and an emergency medical facility.

> **TIP**
>
> Bright Angel Creek follows the North Kaibab (opposite) from about 5 miles below the rim all the way to the Colorado – bring a bandana to soak in the water and tie to your head.

DAY 2: COTTONWOOD CAMPGROUND TO COLORADO RIVER

4 hours; 7.3 miles

From the campground, the trail levels off considerably. The steepest grind is over, and it's a gentle downhill walk along Bright Angel Creek to the Colorado River.

After about 30 minutes, you'll see a turnoff on the right for **Ribbon Falls** (3720ft). Take this 0.3-mile spur across the bridge and up to the falls. Here, water mists 100ft over moss-covered stone to a 2in pool surrounded by fern, columbine, and monkeyflower, creating a hidden fairyland. Standing underneath feels like a cold shower, and it's an ideal spot to rest. Retrace your steps to the main trail, and continue to the **Box**, a narrow passage between 2000ft walls that tower over the trail. For about 4 miles, the trail, shaded by canyon walls but with no breeze, follows the stream along almost flat ground. It passes over several bridges before opening up about 20 minutes before Phantom Ranch (p132), Bright Angel Campground (p130) and, a few minutes later, the **Colorado River** (2400ft).

CLEAR CREEK TRAIL

Duration 10 hours round-trip
Distance 17.4 miles round-trip
Difficulty Difficult
Start/Finish North Kaibab Trail, 0.3 miles north of Phantom Ranch
Nearest Area Phantom Ranch
Transportation Private, mule from South Rim to Phantom Ranch
Summary Inner gorge hike to small creek and shaded backcountry camping.

In excellent condition and easy to follow, the enjoyable Clear Creek Trail is one of fe inner-canyon trails on the north side of t Colorado and easily the most popular inr canyon hike. The views into the gorge across the canyon are magnificent. T no drinking water at the creek, so plenty with you and get an early sta

WILDERNESS EXPEDITIONS

Experienced hikers with extensive wilderness experience and GPS navigational systems will find several unmaintained North Rim trails to tackle. These are intense, interior-canyon death traps that should not be attempted by the average canyon visitor.

The **Nankoweap Trail** descends from Marble Canyon 5240ft to the Colorado River. Considered by many to be the toughest hike in the canyon, the grueling 14-mile trail can be tricky to follow in spots and requires a fair amount of maneuvering along steep ledges. Nankoweap Creek, 10.6 mile below the rim, provides a resplendent green oasis for backcountry camping.

From Toroweap (p189), the **Lava Falls Trail** drops 2540ft over a distance of 1.5 miles to the Colorado River. Do not try this treacherous hike in the summer, when temperatures can reach upwards of 115°F.

Other trails include the **Tuckup Trail**, **Bill Hall Trail**, **Thunder River Trail** and **North Bass Trail**. Good day-hike options include Bill Hall 1 mile down to Muav Cabin, or North Bass 1.3 miles to Monument Point. Contact the backcountry office (p186) for maps, guides and current conditions.

Pick up the trail 0.3 mile north of Phantom Ranch. Heading east off the North Kaibab, the trail switchbacks up to the base of Sumner Butte, levels for a bit, then ascends to the Tonto Platform. It then meanders along the contours and canyon folds, passing beneath both Zoroaster and Brahma Temples on the left. Nine miles later it drops down to the streambed, with nice cottonwood-fringed camping spots near the creek. You can spend the night with a backcountry permit, or retrace your steps to Phantom Ranch. Even the first few miles provide gorgeous views, making it equally worthwhile for those desiring a shorter day hike from Phantom Ranch or Bright Angel Campground.

Lots of trails follow the creek's tributaries. The northeast fork of Clear Creek leads up to **Cheyava Falls**, the canyon's tallest (best viewed in spring), but it's a long haul – 10 miles round-trip from Clear Creek.

BIKING

Because bikes are allowed on blacktop roads only, options for biking on the North Rim are limited to Hwy 67 into the park, Point Imperial Rd (p189) and Cape Royal Rd (p188). The two exceptions are the 17-mile rt road to Point Sublime (p189) and the litarian Bridle Trail (p192) that follows road from the campground to the lodge. e surrounding Kaibab National Forest), bikes are allowed on all trails and a gly endless network of forest roads.

OTHER ACTIVITIES

Like everything on the North Rim, activities here are friendly, low-key affairs. If you're here for a few days, park rangers will know you by name.

MULE RIDES

Family-run **Canyon Trail Rides** (☎ 435-679-8665; www.canyonrides.com; ⏲ mid-May–mid-Oct) offer one-hour mule trips through the woods to an overlook, and half- or full-day trips into the canyon on the North Kaibab (p194). The full-day, seven-hour trip ($125) departs at 7:25am daily and descends about 4000ft to **Roaring Springs**. Half-day trips ($65) to **Supai Tunnel** (2000ft below the rim) leave at 7:25am and 12:30pm. Riders spend about 75 minutes on the mule each way. Riders must weigh less than 200lbs and be at least 10/12 years old for the half-/full-day trip. Children seven or older enjoy the one-hour rim ride ($30) to Uncle Jim Point (p193).

To book a mule trip up to 10 days in advance, duck inside the lodge to the **Mule**

TIP

If you think you might take an impromptu mule ride, be sure you have enough cash before entering the park. They don't take credit cards, and the closest ATM to the park is 44 miles away in Jacob Lake (Map p200).

Desk (☎ 928-638-9875; 7am-5pm). Unlike mule trips on the South Rim, you can usually book a trip upon your arrival at the park. To make advance reservations, call Canyon Trail Rides or visit its website. Credit cards are not accepted.

RANGER PROGRAMS

Small, informal gatherings, ranger programs reflect the summer-camp mood of the North Rim. Several afternoon and evening programs are held around the fireplace on the back verandah of Grand Canyon Lodge – a highlight of any visit. When skies are clear, guests gather to gaze through telescopes while a ranger describes the night sky. Other programs are conducted at the campground amphitheater, the Grand Canyon Lodge Auditorium, or the Walhalla Overlook parking lot. *The Guide* publishes a seasonal schedule, and daily events are posted at the visitors center and at the campground.

Children love the Discovery Pack Program and Junior Ranger Program (p60), and many ranger talks are geared toward children.

CROSS-COUNTRY SKIING

Once the first heavy snowfall closes Hwy 67 into the park (as early as late October or as late as January), you can cross-country ski the 44 miles to the rim and camp at the campground (no water, pit toilets). Camping is permitted elsewhere with a backcountry permit, available from rangers year-round. You can ski any of the rim trails, though none are groomed. See Flagstaff (p162) for ski rental.

SLEEPING

The closest lodging outside the park is Kaibab Lodge (p204), 26 miles from the rim, or Jacob Lake Inn (p204), 44 miles from the rim. Beyond that, you'll have to drive 83 miles north to Kanab, Utah (see p211), or 84 miles northeast to Marble Canyon (see p206). As a last resort, try the couple of roadside motels in tiny Fredonia (p207), 7 miles south of Kanab. Contact the backcountry office (p186) or Pipe Spring National Monument (p209) for permits to camp at overlooks and rim trails within the park; you can camp for free without a permit anywhere in the bucolic Kaibab National Forest (p199). A backcountry permit is not required for primitive camping at Toroweap (p189).

TOP FIVE COOL CAMPING SPOTS

- Jumpup Point (Map p202)
- Marble View (Map p202)
- Point Sublime (p189)
- Tiyo Point (p189)
- Toroweap (p189)

North Rim Campground (Map p185; ☎ 928-638-9389, 877-444-6777; www.reserveamerica.com; sites $; ♿) Set back from the road beneath ponderosa, 1.5 miles north of Grand Canyon Lodge, North Rim Campground offers pleasant sites on level ground blanketed in pine needles. Sites 11, 14, 15, 16, 18 and 19 overlook the Transept (a side canyon) and cost a little more. Their proximity to the edge makes these sites unsuitable for children, and while they are beautiful they are particularly windy. Site number 10, backed by woods, and site number eight, nestled in a little aspen grove, are the nicest of the standard sites. The least desirable, with views of the bathrooms, are sites 20, 22, 50 and 51. Reservations are accepted up to six months in advance; hiker/biker sites are usually available without reservation. There are no hookups. The campground remains open once snow closes the road from Jacob Lake, but there are no services (pit toilets only), no water and you must have a backcountry permit (available from on-site rangers after the backcountry office closes).

our pick **Grand Canyon Lodge** (Map p185; ☎ for reservations within 48hr 928-638-2611, for reservations up to 13 months in advance 888-297-2757; www.xanterra.com; r & cabins $$; closed mid-Oct–mid-May; ♿) Made of wood, stone and glass, with a 50 high sunroom, a spacious rimside di room and panoramic canyon views is the canyon as it was meant to b original lodge, designed by Gilbert Underwood and built in 1928 by t Pacific Railroad in anticipation train link to the North Rim, b in 1932. It was rebuilt in 1937

NORTH RIM

TIP

The stone **Moon Room** at Grand Canyon Lodge offers a cool, quiet, safe spot, perfect for parents of young children, to enjoy the canyon. Take the steps on the left side of the lodge's verandah, walk less than a minute, and climb the small unmarked stairs on the left.

and masses of tourists never did come. The lodge, listed on the National Register of Historic Places, remains today much as it did then. Two small stone verandahs, each with rough-hewn rocking chairs and one with a massive fireplace, sit directly on the canyon edge. We've hiked all the trails, seen all the viewpoints and driven all the drives on the North Rim, and these rocking chairs remain our favorite spot. Sitting here with a cold beer after a long, dusty hike, watching the sun set over the canyon – it just doesn't get any better. There are no rooms in the lodge itself. Rustic Frontier cabins (sleeping up to three people) and Pioneer cabins (sleeping up to five people) cluster together, separated by patches of dirt and dirt paths, on the west side of the road just before the lodge. Frontier cabins, which actually occupy half a cabin, include a double and a twin bed and a tiny bathroom (shower only). Someone else occupies the other half, and the walls are thin, so you can hear every word, cough or alarm clock. Pioneer cabins offer two small rooms connected by a bathroom (shower only). Thirteen Pioneer cabins sit on the edge of the woods and offer partial rim views (no extra charge). On the other side of the road, the bright, spacious and recommended Western cabins (sleeping up to five people), made of logs and buffered by trees and grass, provide two queen beds, full bathrooms, gas fireplaces, refrigerators and porches with wicker rocking chairs. Four im-view Western cabins boast spectacular ews of the Grand Canyon. They cost only tle more than a standard Western cabin, ou'll need to reserve them at least a year ance. About 0.5 miles up the road are le motel rooms, each with a queen use access from the parking lot is steps, they're not advisable for hysically impaired. No rooms itioning.

EATING & DRINKING

Part of the North Rim's charm lies in the striking contrast between the the intimacy of its facilities and the wildness of the canyon. With only one restaurant, one cafeteria and one saloon, you'll find yourself bumping into the same folks, sharing stories over a glass of wine. Visitors can contact the following establishments through the **North Rim Switchboard** (☎ 928-638-2612).

North Rim General Store (Map p185; 7am-8pm, closed mid-Oct–mid-May; ♿) Adjacent to the campground and just over a mile from the lodge, the general store primarily services the needs of campers. You'll find canned soup, instant oatmeal, pasta, beer, wine and frozen hamburgers and steak, as well as picnic supplies like bread, cheese, peanut butter and, if you're lucky, a few fresh fruits and vegetables.

Deli in the Pines (Map p185; mains $; 7am-9pm, closed mid-Oct–mid-May) This small cafeteria beside the lodge serves surprisingly good food. The limited menu includes sandwiches, pizza, a chicken-and-rice bowl, beans and rice, a buffalo hot dog and ice cream. There are a few indoor tables, but you're better off taking your plate outside to enjoy the high mountain air.

our pick **Grand Canyon Lodge Dining Room** (Map p185; mains $$-$$$; closed mid-Oct–mid-May; ♿) Some people get downright belligerent if they can't get a window seat, but the canyon-view windows are so huge, it really doesn't matter where you sit. While the solid menu includes buffalo steak and several vegetarian options, don't expect culinary memories. Make reservations in advance of your arrival to guarantee a spot

TOP FIVE SPOTS TO PICK UP A PICNIC LUNCH

- Bean's Coffee (Page, p219)
- Grand Canyon Lodge (North Rim, above)
- Kaibab Lodge (Kaibab National Forest, p204)
- Laid Back Larry's (Kanab, p212)
- North Rim General Store (North Rim, above)

> **TIP**
>
> The life-sized bronze of Brighty the mule in the sunroom of the Grand Canyon Lodge amuses toddlers long enough for adults to enjoy canyon views with a morning coffee or an evening cocktail from the Roughrider Saloon.

for dinner (reservations are not accepted for breakfast or lunch). It will prepare boxed lunches with an hour or two's notice.

Roughrider Saloon (Map p185; snacks $; 5:30-10:30am & 11:30am-11pm, closed mid-Oct–mid-May;) If you're up to catch the sunrise or enjoy an early-morning hike, stop at this small saloon on the boardwalk beside the lodge for an espresso, a fresh-made cinnamon roll and a banana. Starting at 11:30am the saloon serves beer, wine and mixed drinks. Teddy Roosevelt memorabilia lines the walls, honoring his role in the history of the park; ask the bartender for the book about Teddy to browse while you drink. This is the only bar in the lodge, so if you want to enjoy a cocktail on the back verandah or in your room, pick it up here.

BEYOND THE NORTH RIM

The North Rim sits on the southern edge of the spectacular 1010-sq-mile North Kaibab Plateau, refreshingly cool and green at 8000ft and surrounded below by red-rock scenery, miles of hardscrabble trails and vast expanses of desert wilderness. You can easily spend a week exploring the dramatic diversity of the region, boating on Lake Powell (see p217) one day, hiking a slot canyon the next (see p206) and biking through the aspen and meadows of the Kaibab another. Many people combine a visit to the North Rim with Zion and Bryce National Parks (see Lonely Planet's *Zion & Bryce Canyon*), both within a few hours of the park.

KAIBAB NATIONAL FOREST (NORTH RIM)

928 / elev 7900ft–9000ft

Alt 89 winds 5000ft up from the red-rock canyons of the Paria Canyon-Vermilion Cliffs Wilderness, past the Kaibab National Forest boundary and through the eerie black-timbered remains of a 2001 forest fire, to the outpost of Jacob Lake. Nearly everyone heading up to the canyon stops here, piling out of dusty vehicles to breathe in the mountain air, shop for canyon souvenirs and grab a cookie or ice cream before continuing through the meadows, rolling hills, aspen and ponderosa pine of the Kaibab National Forest on their way to the North Rim. On the 24 miles between Jacob Lake and the park entrance, dirt forest-service roads on either side lure curious travelers, offering yellow canopies in the fall, wildflowers in the summer and miles of opportunities for hiking, biking, snowmobiling and cross-country skiing. While most folk simply pass through on their way to the rim, the Kaibab is an idyllic setting in its own right and well worth a couple days to enjoy.

Orientation & Information

Alt 89 to Kanab (38 miles northwest) and Page (80 miles northeast) meets Hwy 67 to the North Rim (44 miles south) at Jacob Lake, which isn't a lake at all but simply a motel with a restaurant and gas station, and a visitors center. The 68,340-acre Kanab Creek Wilderness, comprised of classic canyonland formations cut by Kanab Creek, lies in the southwestern corner of the Kaibab and abuts the western edge of the Kaibab Plateau. Here you'll find many desert trails for experienced hikers; the 21.5-mile Snake Gulch rewards hikers with loads of incredible petroglyphs. On the southeast corner, abutting the eastern edge of the Kaibab Plateau, is the Saddle Mountain Wilderness.

Adjacent to Jacob Lake Inn, the helpful USFS **Kaibab Plateau Visitor Center** (Map p200; 928-643-7298; 8am-5pm, closed Oct-May) features a small museum and bookstore. The Kaibab Lodge, North Rim Country Store and DeMotte campground, the only facilities between Jacob Lake and the park, cluster together 18 miles south of Jacob Lake.

Overlooks

Dirt roads veer off Hwy 67 in both directions to overlooks on the edge of the pl teau. The drives are lovely, particularly in fall when the aspen turn or in late sum when wildflowers and tall grass burst the meadows, but they are long and b Be prepared to drive, even in a 4W snail's pace in some spots. Consider

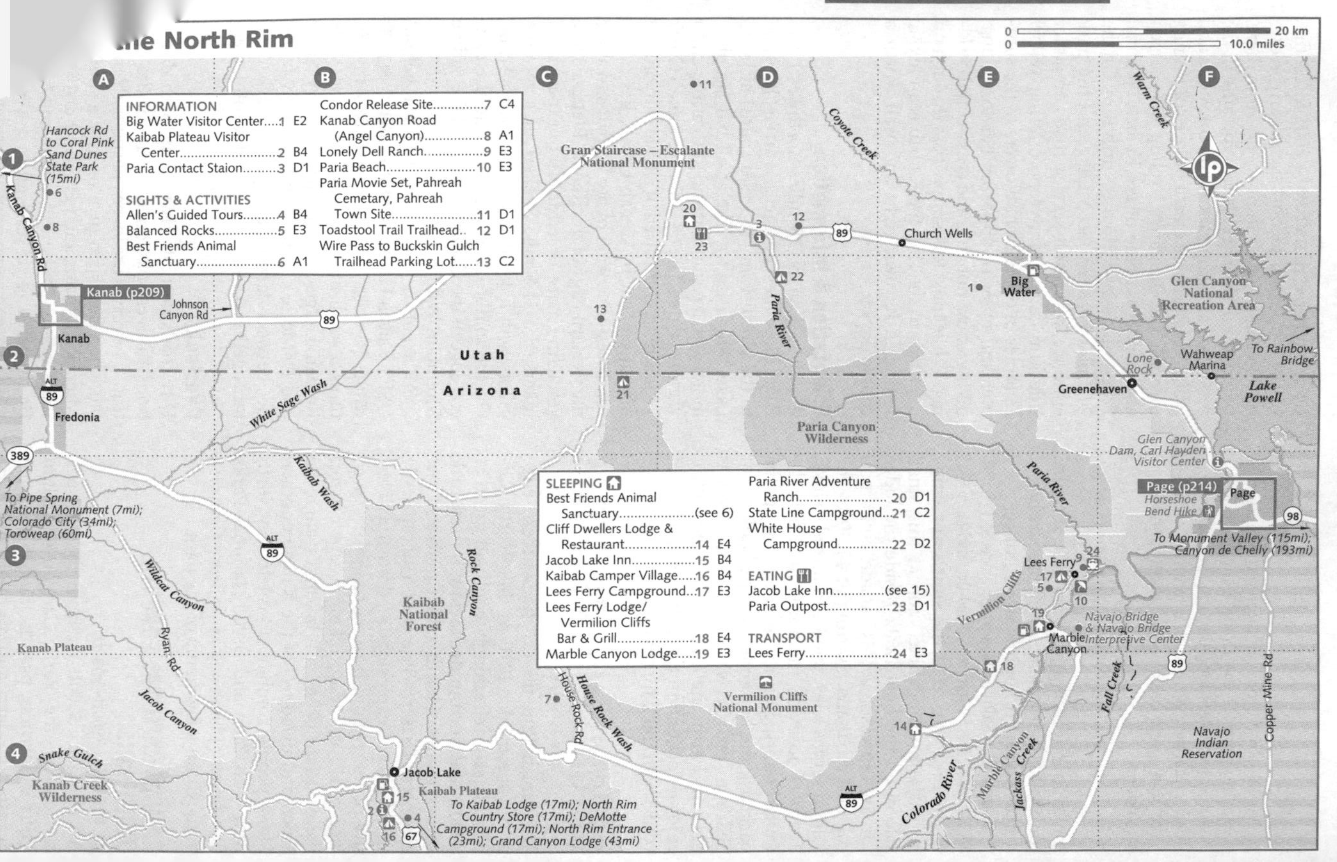

North Rim
INFORMATION
Big Water Visitor Center....1 E2
Kaibab Plateau Visitor Center....2 B4
Paria Contact Staion....3 D1
SIGHTS & ACTIVITIES
Allen's Guided Tours....4 B4
Balanced Rocks....5 E3
Best Friends Animal Sanctuary....6 A1
Condor Release Site....7 C4
Kanab Canyon Road (Angel Canyon)....8 A1
Lonely Dell Ranch....9 E3
Paria Beach....10 E3
Paria Movie Set, Pahreah Cemetary, Pahreah Town Site....11 D1
Toadstool Trail Trailhead....12 D1
Wire Pass to Buckskin Gulch Trailhead Parking Lot....13 C2
SLEEPING
Best Friends Animal Sanctuary....(see 6)
Cliff Dwellers Lodge & Restaurant....14 E4
Jacob Lake Inn....15 B4
Kaibab Camper Village....16 B4
Lees Ferry Campground....17 E3
Lees Ferry Lodge/ Vermilion Cliffs Bar & Grill....18 E4
Marble Canyon Lodge....19 E3
Paria River Adventure Ranch....20 D1
State Line Campground....21 C2
White House Campground....22 D2
EATING
Jacob Lake Inn....(see 15)
Paria Outpost....23 D1
TRANSPORT
Lees Ferry....24 E3
20 km
10.0 miles
Kanab (p209)
Page (p214)
Kanab
Fredonia
Kanab Canyon Rd
Hancock Rd to Coral Pink Sand Dunes State Park (15mi)
Johnson Canyon Rd
To Pipe Spring National Monument (7mi); Colorado City (34mi); Toroweap (60mi)
Kanab Plateau
Kanab Creek Wilderness
Snake Gulch
Jacob Canyon
Ryan Rd
Wildcat Canyon
White Sage Wash
Kaibab Wash
Gran Staircase – Escalante National Monument
Utah
Arizona
Kaibab National Forest
Rock Canyon
Jacob Lake
Kaibab Plateau
To Kaibab Lodge (17mi); North Rim Country Store (17mi); DeMotte Campground (17mi); North Rim Entrance (23mi); Grand Canyon Lodge (43mi)
House Rock Rd
House Rock Wash
Vermilion Cliffs National Monument
Paria Canyon Wilderness
Paria River
Coyote Creek
Church Wells
Big Water
Greenehaven
Lone Rock
Wahweap Marina
Glen Canyon National Recreation Area
Lake Powell
To Rainbow Bridge
Warm Creek
Glen Canyon Dam, Carl Hayden Visitor Center
Horseshoe Bend Hike
Page
To Monument Valley (115mi); Canyon de Chelly (193mi)
Lees Ferry
Vermilion Cliffs
Marble Canyon
Navajo Bridge & Navajo Bridge Interpretive Center
Fall Creek
Jackass Creek
Marble Canyon
Colorado River
Navajo Indian Reservation
Copper Mine Rd

the roads to **Fire Point**, **Crazy Jug**, **Indian Hollow** and the recommended **Jumpup** overlooks (Map p202). The five overlooks connected by Rainbow Rim Trail (right) may see a few more people, but they have the advantage of excellent hiking from each point.

While certainly beautiful, don't expect classic canyon vistas at any of the Kaibab's overlooks; for that, head to the park itself.

MARBLE VIEW

Duration 1 hour round-trip
Distance 22.8 miles round-trip
Start/Finish Hwy 67, 8 miles south of Kaibab Lodge
Nearest Area Kaibab Lodge
Summary A drive from Hwy 67 to an overlook at Marble View: wide dirt road to lovely meadow perched on the plateau's edge.

Our favorite of the many Kaibab Forest overlooks, this viewpoint makes a spectacular picnic or camping spot. From the 1-acre meadow, covered with Indian paintbrush and hiding Coconino sandstone fossils, views extend over the eastern edge of the canyon to the paper-flat expanse beyond. This is not a quintessential Grand Canyon overlook that you see in ubiquitous postcards and Grand Canyon books. Instead, you're looking down where the Colorado first cuts into the rocks from Lees Ferry, at the point where it only hints at the rapids and canyon beyond. The road seems to end at an overlook; be sure to take the narrow road through the woods to the right about 0.25 miles to Marble View.

EAST RIM VIEW

Duration 25 minutes round-trip
Distance 8 miles round-trip
Start/Finish Hwy 67, 8 miles south of Kaibab Lodge
Nearest Area Kaibab Lodge
Summary Easy drive on dirt road and then a short paved walk to overlook.

With views east into the Saddle Mountain Wilderness, Marble Canyon and the Vermilion Cliffs, this easily accessible overlook (elevation 8810ft) is suitable for strollers and wheelchairs. In fact, it's so easy to reach, it's amazing there aren't more people out here. East Rim doesn't offer the inviting picnic and camping opportunities of Marble View, and the views don't inspire comparable awe, but it's a beautiful spot. From the overlook you can hike the **East Rim Trail** 1.5 miles down into the Saddle Mountain Wilderness. The Arizona Trail (p45) runs past the overlook; turn right to take this trail about 6.5 miles to the Park Boundary Trailhead (see p203).

Sights

Three steel towers, all on the National Register of Historic Places, are still used as fire lookouts: built in 1934, **Big Springs** (Map p202) and **Jacob Lake** (p199) stand 100ft tall, while **Dry Park** (Map p202), built in 1944, is 120ft tall. You can drive out to any of them and climb up for great views of the national forest. Though the lookout rooms at the top are locked, if someone is manning the tower, they'll usually let you in.

Biking & Hiking

Stop by the Kaibab Plateau Visitor Center for maps and information on the forest's ubiquitous trails.

RAINBOW RIM TRAIL

Duration 8 hours one way
Distance 18 miles one way
Difficulty Moderate–difficult
Start Timp Point
Finish Parissawampitts
Nearest Area Kaibab Lodge
Transportation Private
Summary Single track trail through woods and meadow connects five canyon overlooks.

The Rainbow Rim Trail (Map p202) connects **Parissawampitts**, **Fence**, **Locust**, **North Timp** and **Timp Points**, each a finger of the Kaibab Plateau that sticks out over the Grand Canyon. While the ride is beautiful, meandering throug meadows, winding up and down with an evation change of no more than 250ft anc lowing the canyon edge for stretches a overlook, none of the viewpoints st from one another and each point stretch drops into a steep side ca a bumpy downhill and a bumpy experienced bikers will find the ing their bikes for long stretch

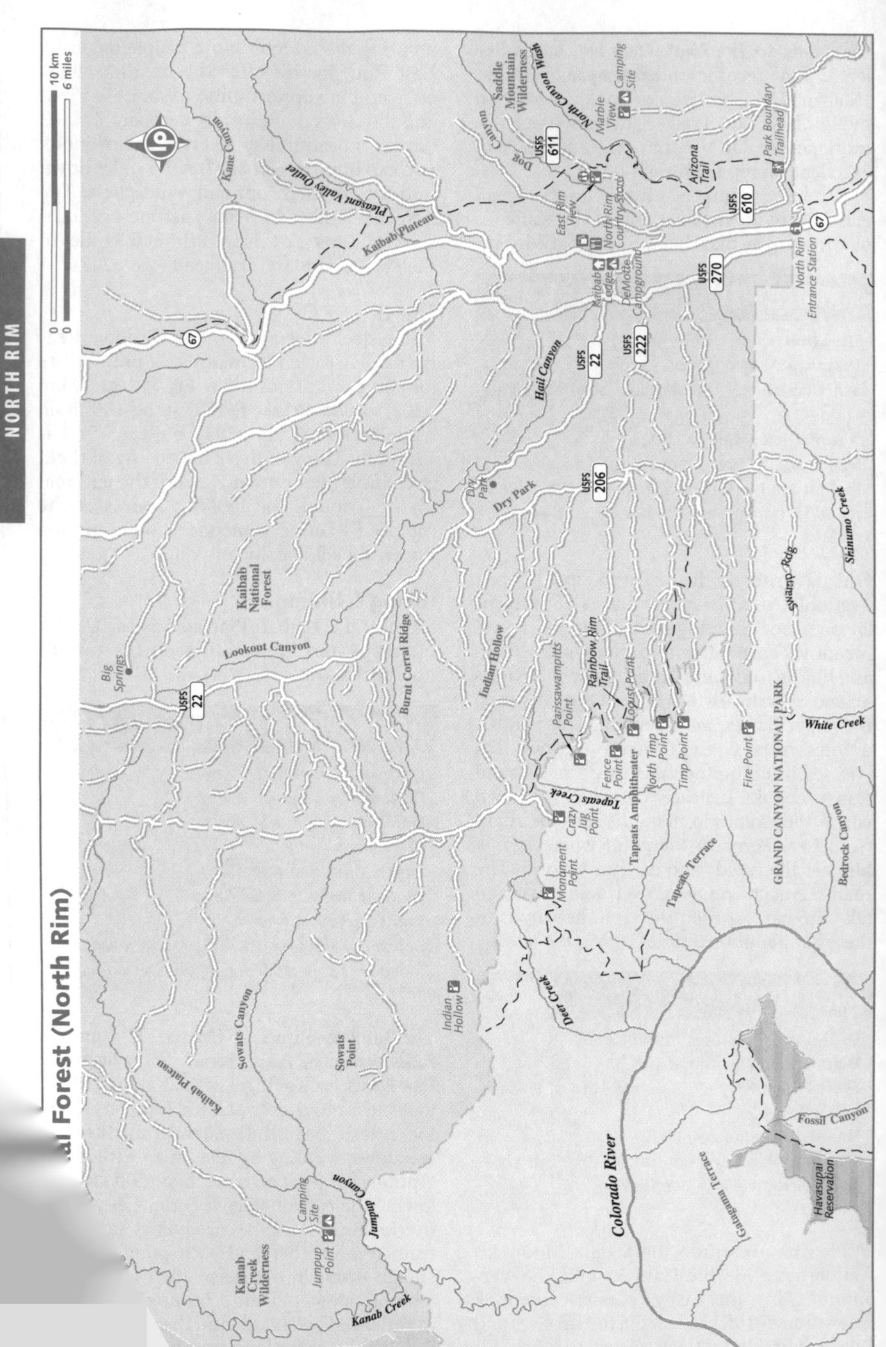

...al Forest (North Rim)
0 10 km
0 6 miles
Kane Canyon
Pleasant Valley Outlet
Kaibab Plateau
Dog Canyon
Saddle Mountain Wilderness
North Canyon Wash
Marble View
Camping Site
USFS 611
East Rim View
North Rim Country Store
Arizona Trail
Park Boundary Trailhead
USFS 610
67
North Rim Entrance Station
Kaibab Lodge
DeMotte Campground
USFS 270
USFS 22
USFS 222
Hail Canyon
Dry Park
USFS 206
Kaibab National Forest
Big Springs
Lookout Canyon
Burnt Corral Ridge
Indian Hollow
Parissawampitts Point
Rainbow Rim Trail
Locust Point
Fence Point
North Timp Point
Timp Point
Fire Point
Swamp Rdg
Skinumo Creek
White Creek
GRAND CANYON NATIONAL PARK
Tapeats Creek
Tapeats Amphitheater
Crazy Jug Point
Monument Point
Tapeats Terrace
Bedrock Canyon
Deer Creek
Sowats Canyon
Sowats Point
Colorado River
Fossil Canyon
Havasupai Reservation
Gatagama Terrace
Jumpup Canyon
Jumpup Point
Kanab Creek Wilderness
Kanab Creek

> **TIP**
>
> For a pleasant, kid-friendly ride to an overlook in the Kaibab, park at FR 206, ride continuously downhill on a forest road to one of the points of the Rainbow Rim Trail (p201) and arrange a ride back.

Shorten the ride by biking between any of the five overlooks, each accessed by a forest service road, and then retracing your steps or arranging for a shuttle to return you to your car. This is also an excellent hiking trail.

To get to Timp Point, turn right onto FR 22 0.7 miles south of Kaibab Lodge. Drive 2 miles to FR 270, turn left, and drive 1 mile to FR 222. Turn right and drive 5 miles to FR 206; turn right and go less than 0.25 miles to FR 271. Follow FR 271 for about 8 miles to the end of the road at Timp Point. Forest-service roads to each of the four other overlooks veer off FR 206 (Map p202). To drive to each view you must backtrack 45 minutes to FR 206, drive up or down a few miles to a different forest road, and then drive about 45 minutes back out to the rim. The rough FR 250 connects the overlooks, but it is only for high-clearance vehicles.

Distances from point to point:

Timp Point to North Timp 3 miles.
North Timp to Locust 6.5 miles.
Locust to Fence 3 miles.
Fence to Parissawampitts 5.5 miles.

ARIZONA TRAIL: PARK BOUNDARY TRAILHEAD TO CRYSTAL SPRING (KAIBAB PLATEAU TRAIL 101)

Duration 4½ hours round-trip
Distance 9.8 miles round-trip
Difficulty Easy–moderate
Start/finish Park Boundary Trailhead: FR 610, 5.8 miles from Hwy 67
Nearest Area Kaibab Lodge
Transportation Private
Summary Peaceful hike through lovely meadows.

This narrow meander through wide meadows bordered by aspen and ponderosa is a hidden gem of the North Kaibab (Map p202). There are no big views or cliffs, but plenty of room to run and scramble. Keep your eye out for fossils in the rocks along the trail. Perfect for families, this hike can be shortened considerably by hiking 2.3 miles to Sourdough Wells and turning around, or lengthen it by hiking an added 1.5 miles to East Rim View (p201). With no grand vista awaiting you at the end, and no one section of the trail more lovely than another, this is the perfect path for strolling as far as you'd like, and then simply turning around, and it makes a great bike ride.

To get to the trailhead, turn east just south of the Kaibab Lodge onto the well-marked FR 611 toward East Rim View. Head 1.2 miles to FR610. Turn right and go 4.6 miles to the Arizona Trail Park Boundary Trailhead, a small, unmarked pullout on the right. There is a restroom but no water. From here, you can either head 0.2 miles east down the road and catch the trail on the left, after it crosses FR611, or you can head a couple of minutes down the path from the bathroom to a big meadow. The trail heads left toward Sourdough Wells and Crystal Spring, or right about 0.25 miles to the national park border.

NORTH RIM

Other Activities

Allen's Guided Tours (Map p200; ☎ 435-644-8150) offers one-hour ($35), two-hour ($60), half-/full-day ($80/125) and custom-designed overnight or multiday horseback rides. Children must be at least five years old. Reservations are not required for short rides – just stop by the corrals.

In the winter, you can **cross-country ski** or **snowmobile** throughout the Kaibab. The Jacob Lake Inn (p204) is open year-round, but the road from Jacob Lake to the North Rim Lodge is not plowed.

Sleeping

You can camp for free anywhere in the national forest, including canyon overlooks.

Kaibab Camper Village (Map p200; ☎ 928-643-7804; www.kaibabcampervillage.com; cabins & sites $; closed mid-Oct–mid-May) Forty-three miles north of North Rim, set back a half-mi from Hwy 67 on a forest-service road j south of Jacob Lake Inn, this privately campground offers the only RV hoo on the North Kaibab Plateau. It's fr and perfectly fine if you need a h but with so many idyllic spots surrounding national forest, where you can pitch a tent for free, there's no reason to camp here except the shower and laundry facilities. The tent sites are crowded and next to an ugly aluminum-sided barn and bathroom.

DeMotte Campground (Map p202; Hwy 67; sites $; 🕑 closed mid-Oct–mid-May) This quiet campground nestled in the forest 18 miles north of the North Rim sits on a slight hill with views of the adjacent meadow. Across the street is a small general store with basic supplies, and the restaurant and bar at Kaibab Lodge are within walking distance. The campground is first come, first served – choose a site before heading for the canyon. All have concrete pads and the best sites, on the eastern side of the first loop, sit under aspen and overlook the meadow. The weather dictates when the campground opens and closes for the year; call the Kaibab Plateau Visitor Center (☎ 928-638-2389).

Jacob Lake Inn (Map p200; ☎ 928-643-7232; www.jacoblake.com; Hwy 67, 44 miles north of North Rim; s, d, f & cabins $$; ♿ 👪) Accommodations here consist of basic cabins with tiny bathrooms (no bathtubs, TVs or phone) tightly packed amid the ponderosa forest, run-down motel rooms, or spacious doubles in the modern hotel-style building. Cabins 18, 19, 20, 21, 28 and 29 overlook the forest. The inn also operates a restaurant (right) with a great bakery, and has a gift shop and a small, bedraggled playground.

Kaibab Lodge (Map p202; ☎ 928-638-2389; www.kaibablodge.com; Hwy 67, 18 miles north of North Rim; r & cabins $$; 🕑 closed mid-Oct–mid-May; ♿ 👪) There's something comforting about this lodge, hugged on two sides by a lovely meadow and on a third by ponderosa and aspen forest. It's a simple, quiet, low-key place, where the biggest excitement comes from counting deer that wander from the woods to graze. The four accommodation options vary considerably, and while they're pleasant, don't expect down comforters, feather pillows and luxurious bath supplies. The oldest, cabins one to six, fer simple, worn-out decor with wood ors and walls, plain beds and a porch looking the meadow. Newer cabins (26) resemble one-room RVs more than , cost a bit more, are quite tiny and have porches with meadow views. the feeling that you're staying in a room c 1952, or perhaps because of it, the older cabins are a better choice. Eight recommended and modern Eastview units, bright earthy orange rooms painted with petroglyphs and furnished with rough-hewn wood beds and nightstands, sit in two two-story log buildings. Each unit has small porch overlooking the woods and field. Three large cabins accommodate four to eight people.

Eating & Drinking

North Rim Country Store (Map p202; ☎ 928-638-2383; Hwy 67; 🕑 7am-7pm, closed mid-Oct–mid-May) Just across Hwy 67 from Kaibab Lodge and DeMotte Campground, 18 miles north of North Rim, this small store and gas station sells a small selection of groceries, including canned goods, cereal, cheese, wine and beer. In July and August, it may stay open until 8pm or 9pm.

Jacob Lake Inn (Map p200; ☎ 928-643-7232; Hwy 67; mains $; 🕑 6:30am-9pm; 👪) This busy, almost festive café is filled with visitors who are either coming from or heading to the North Rim, 44 miles south. The inn does not accept reservations, and the last sitting is at 8pm. An adjacent ice-cream counter offers delicious cookies and desserts. Treat yourself.

Kaibab Lodge (Map p202; ☎ 928-638-2389; Hwy 67; mains $$; 🕑 closed mid-Oct–mid-May; 👪) Eighteen miles north of the North Rim, in a bright, casual room flanked by windows, this restaurant serves basic, tasty fish, burgers and pasta and offers a full bar. Breakfast features whole-wheat pancakes and yogurt with granola, and it'll prepare a picnic lunch with one night's notice.

Getting There & Around

There is no public transportation to Jacob Lake. See p186 for information on gas stations and towing services.

ALONG HIGHWAYS 89 & ALT 89

☎ 435 / elev 3100ft to 6500ft

The interior of the oval formed by these two highways, and the surrounding area, is comprised of the Paria Canyon-Vermilion Cliffs Wilderness (including Vermilion Cliffs National Monument), the southern section of the 1.9-million-acre Grand Staircase-Escalante National Monument, the southeast corner of Glen Canyon

National Recreation Area (p213), the Navajo Indian Reservation (see p216) and the northern tip of the Kaibab National Forest (p199).

For the traveler, however, these are arbitrary distinctions. Whenever you peer out your car window, it's all simply desert. Dry, windy, seemingly endless desert. This is a lonely, desperate kind of wilderness that lures photographers and hikers with its brilliant red and chalky-white buttes, slot canyons and multihued rock formations – the spectacular Vermilion Cliffs tower over a 30-mile stretch of Hwy 89. While dirt roads may tempt drivers into exploring, the roads are sandy and unpredictable; with a little bit of rain, these roads can become impassable within minutes and slot canyons can fill with torrents of water that wash away or kill anything or anyone in their path (see Health & Safety, p251).

Orientation & Information

Kanab and Fredonia to the west, and Page and Lees Ferry to the east, are situated on the ends of the oval formed by Highway 89 and Alt 89. Alt 89, the southern strip of the oval, winds up several thousand feet to Jacob Lake, 41 miles west of Lees Ferry. The stretch of Alt 89 just south and west of Lees Ferry is known as Marble Canyon (confusing, as it is also the name for the northeast leg of the Grand Canyon). Take note of the gas stations, as the only ones outside the towns of Kanab, Fredonia, Jacob Lake and Page are in Big Water (19 miles northwest of Page) and Marble Canyon (38 miles southwest of Page). A post office, Laundromat and pay-showers are adjacent to the gas station in Marble Canyon.

Big Water Visitor Center (Map p200; ☎ 435-675-3200; 🕒 9am-6pm) Small museum, 19 miles northwest of Page, providing information on Grand Staircase-Escalante National Monument and the extensive paleontology research in the area.

Navajo Bridge Interpretive Center (Map p200; ☎ 928-355-2320; Hwy Alt 89; 🕒 9am-5pm, closed Nov-Apr) Forty-five miles southwest of Page, the windswept Glen Canyon National Recreation Area Visitors Center offers historic exhibits in beautiful stone building next to Navajo Bridge (p215).

Paria Contact Station (Map p200; Hwy 89; 🕒 8:30am-4:15pm, closed mid-Nov–mid-Mar) Forty-four miles east of Kanab. Has backcountry permits, maps and daily road and trail information for the Paria Canyon-Vermilion Cliffs Wilderness.

Sights

Thirty-five miles east of Kanab on Hwy 89 is a 5.5-mile dirt road (passable with a 2WD when dry) to the **Paria Movie Set**, **Pahreah Cemetery** and **Pahreah Town Site** (Map p200). Originally settled in 1865, Indian raids forced the town of Pahreah (rhymes with Maria) to move upstream in 1870, and in 1893 floods forced settlers to leave the area altogether. In 1963 Hollywood chose the site to build a Western movie set, and it was used for films and TV shows until 1991. Flooding in 2003 forced local volunteers and the Bureau of Land Management (BLM) to dismantle and move the set to drier ground, only to see it set alight by vandals a couple of years later. A small plaque and fence posts remain, and it is a lovely, quiet spot to poke around. Approximately a mile beyond the set is the town site and the **Paria River**, where you can splash about in the muddy water.

Hiking & Driving

This area boasts picturesque hiking and driving options.

HOUSE ROCK ROAD

Duration 1 hour one way
Distance 29 miles one way
Start Hwy 89 40 miles east of Kanab
Finish Alt 89 14 miles east of Hwy 67 to Jacob Lake
Nearest Town Kanab (p207)
Summary Scenic drive through red dirt and juniper connects Hwy 89 to Alt 89.

While there isn't much in particular to see along the way, this beautiful drive (Map p200) passes through piñon and junipe
hugs the brilliant red sandstone cliffs of t
Vermilion Cliffs National Monument
offers an excellent opportunity to get o
main drag. Ten miles south of Hwy 8
Utah–Arizona state line, the road
from Utah County Rd 700 to BL
Here you will find State Line C
(p206) and a bathroom. The
condor release site (see boxe
miles before reaching Alt 8

TOADSTOOL TRAIL

Duration 1½ hours round-trip
Distance 3 miles round-trip
Difficulty Easy
Start/Finish Hwy 89, 29 miles northwest of Page
Nearest Town Page (p213)
Transportation Private
Summary Easy desert hike to cool rock formations.

This wander gives passersby a taste of the harsh Utah desert. The thin sand trail (p200) meanders through the scrub-brush, massive rocks and boulders about 1 mile to the first toadstool, a sandstone rock in the form of, you guessed it, a toadstool. The unmarked trailhead sits at a small parking area 1.4 miles east of the Paria Contact Station.

WIRE PASS TO BUCKSKIN GULCH

Duration 2 hours round-trip
Distance 3.4 miles round-trip
Difficulty Moderate
Start/Finish House Rock Rd, 8.5 miles south of Hwy 89
Nearest Town Kanab (opposite)
Transportation Private
Summary Squeeze through this slot canyon to the confluence of Buckskin Gulch.

A perfect jaunt for anyone looking to experience Utah's slot canyons without a tour or a commitment to a wilderness expedition, this easily accessible hike (Map p200) requires a bit of scrambling and includes several stretches where the slot canyon is only about 30ft wide and walls tower more than 50ft high. After 1.7 miles the trail reaches uckskin Gulch (see opposite). You can ke this a longer hike by turning right exploring Buckskin Gulch a bit before ing your steps.

& Eating

ter, things around here are pretty urants may or may not be open. Marble Canyon generally tag ning hours, with one open wo are closed.

State Line Campground (Map p200; sites free) There are bathrooms, but no water at this lovely desert spot. Ten miles south of Hwy 89 on House Rock Rd.

White House Campground (Map p200; primitive sites $) Beautiful and quiet, White House offers five sheltered sites, set well apart from one another, each under the shade of a piñon. There are bathrooms, and water is available 3 miles up the dirt road at the Paria Contact Station. The campground is 44 miles east of Kanab on Hwy 89.

Paria River Adventure Ranch (Map p200; ☎ 928-660-2674; www.pariacampground.com; Hwy 89; dm, cabins & campsites $;) Offering horseback rides along the Paria River, all-terrain vehicle rides, and a game house with a pool table and a stereo system with an iPod hookup, this low-key ranch caters to folks looking for some action with their desert silence. It has a two-room cabin and a bunkhouse that sleeps 16, and you can pitch your tent or drive your RV (no hookups) anywhere on its 30 acres. Breakfast and steak dinners are served in a sheltered courtyard decked out with Chinese lanterns. The ranch, 30 miles east of Page, regularly hosts large groups, but can be eerily quiet otherwise.

our pick Lees Ferry Lodge/Vermilion Cliffs Bar & Grill (Map p200; ☎ 928-355-2231; www.leesferrylodge.com; Marble Canyon; d & cabins $$; 6:30am-9pm;) Set under the shadow of the Vermilion Cliffs, this stone building with a stone-walled courtyard is perfect if you want something beyond a roadside motel. The cozy rooms are decorated in different themes. The cowboy room, for example, boasts a Western motif, with animal skins and horseshoes on the wall, horse-print bed covers and a wood-burning stove. Occupying a long room with a rough-hewn beamed ceiling and a pool table, the restaurant-bar serves hearty food and 135 types of beer.

Paria Outpost (Map p200; ☎ 928-691-104; www.paria.com; Hwy 89, 30 miles east of Page) Next door to the Paria River Adventure Ranch, the Paria Outpost has one B&B room. On summer weekends from 5pm to 9pm it serves a tasty barbecue dinner buffet with open-mike Fridays. Throughout the year the outpost hosts Paria River Natural History Association lectures on local geology, paleontology and natural history.

Three windswept motels with restaurants, including **Marble Canyon Lodge** (Map p200;

BACKCOUNTRY HIKES IN THE PARIA CANYON-VERMILION CLIFFS WILDERNESS

Three classic canyon hikes attract photographers and outdoor enthusiasts from around the world. Serious canyoneers can tackle the five-day trek along unforgettable 38-mile **Paria Canyon** from White House Campground (opposite) to Lees Ferry (p215). With numerous stretches of knee-deep muddy water, this hike winds in and out of a slot canyon, past sandstone cliffs, petroglyphs and a handful of campsites. The world-famous 20.3-mile **Buckskin Gulch** (accessed from Wire Pass to Buckskin Gulch trailhead and White House Campground) is the longest and deepest slot canyon in the United States. Be prepared to wade, possibly swim, through sections and to squeeze through 15 miles of canyon with nothing more than glimpses of the sky above. Sandstone walls soar upwards of 200ft, and there are long stretches not much wider than your shoulders. Finally, only 20 people per day are allowed to hike 3.5 miles to **North Coyote Butte** (the Wave) a trailless expanse of slickrock that ends at a smooth, orange-and-white striped rock, shaped into a perfect wave and big enough to climb over. To hike the Wave, reserve online up to seven months ahead. Ten walk-in next-day permits are given out by lottery at the Paria Contact Station (p205). Overnight permits ($5) are required for Paria Canyon and Buckskin Gulch. Only 20 hikers are allowed between the two per day; the Paria Contact Station sells next-day permits when available. Absolutely do not attempt any of these hikes without checking trail conditions and the weather forecast at the Paria Contact Station. Call ☎ 435-688-3246 for details and access www.az.blm.gov/paria for permits.

(☎ 928-355-2225, 800-726-1789; www.marblecanyontrading.com; d & ste $; restaurant 6am-9:30pm; ♿) and **Cliff Dwellers Lodge & Restaurant** (Map p200; ☎ restaurant 928-355-237, lodge 928-355-2261, 800-962-9755; www.cliffdwellerslodge.com; d & ste $; restaurant 6am-9pm; ♿), dot Alt 89 10 miles west of Navajo Bridge Interpretive Center. Also see Lees Ferry Campground (p218).

FREDONIA

☎ 435 / pop 4492 / elev 4925

Tiny blink-and-you-miss-it Fredonia lies 74 miles north of the rim. Here, along Alt 89, you'll find the **Kaibab National Forest District Headquarters** (☎ 928-643-7395; 430 S Main; 8am-5pm Mon-Fri), a **post office** (☎ 928-643-7122; 85 N Main; 8am-4:30pm Mon-Fri) and a **police station** (☎ 928-643-7108; 130 N Main). The welcoming grassy and shaded courtyard at **Grand Canyon Motel** (☎ 928-643-7646; 175 S Main; cabins $) holds a barbecue grill and a few picnic tables, but the interiors of the cute stone cabins that surround it are old and drab. Also try the **Juniper Lodge** (☎ 928-643-7752; 465 S Main; s & d $), with newer rooms and the town's only restaurant. A tiny public swimming pool and park lies a few blocks off Alt 89 – look for the sign.

KANAB

☎ 435 / pop 4492 / elev 4925ft

In 1874 Mormons settled remote Kanab, Utah. Hollywood, drawn by the desert backdrop and stunning red-rock formations, descended on the town in the 1920s. It has since served as a location for hundreds of movies and TV shows, including numerous Westerns and episodes of *The Lone Ranger* and *Gunsmoke*. Though the filmmaking craze here faded, the town still flaunts its silver-screen past. Small-town Kanab offers a tidy, pedestrian-friendly downtown, peaceful surroundings and great food. While not a destination in itself, it offers a quirky taste of the American West and makes a good base for exploring the area.

Orientation & Information

Hwy 89, lined with the town's restaurants and hotels, becomes Main St through town. At the town's only stoplight, Hwy 89 turns east 75 miles to Page; Alt 89 continues south toward Jacob Lake (41 miles); and Hwy 67 heads to the North Rim (85 miles).

Bureau of Land Management (BLM; Map p209; ☎ 435-644-4600; 318 N 100 East; 7:45am-4pm Mon-Fri)

Grand Staircase-Escalante National Monument Visitor Center (Map p209; ☎ 435-644-4680; 745 E Hw 89; 7:30am-5:30pm) For information specific to the national monument.

Kane County Hospital (Map p209; ☎ 435-644-5 355 N Main St; emergency room 24hr) Best op medical services close to the North Rim.

Kane County Travel Council (Map p209; ☎ 5033, 800-733-5263; www.kaneutah.com; 7 9am-7pm Mon-Fri, to 5pm Sat)

Library (Map p209; 435-644-2394; 374 N Main St; 10am-2pm Tue-Thu & Sat, 10am-5pm Mon & Fri)
Police station (Map p209; 435-644-5854; 140 E South)
Post office (Map p209; 435-644-2760; 39 S Main St; 9am-4pm Mon-Fri, to 2pm Sat)
Zion Pharmacy (Map p209; 435-644-2693; 14 E Center St; 9am-6pm Mon-Fri, to noon Sat)

Sights

BEST FRIENDS ANIMAL SANCTUARY

Encompassing 3000 acres of spectacular red-rock desert 5 miles north of Kanab, **Best Friends Animal Sanctuary** (Map p200; 435-644-2001; http://bestfriends.org; Hwy 89; visitors center 9:30am-5:30pm, grounds by tour only;) is the largest no-kill animal rescue center in the country. The staff of 400 full-time employees and 4200 volunteers rescue and take care of abused and abandoned animals from all over the country and the world. Over the course of 249 days, they rescued over 6000 animals from Katrina, mostly dogs and cats, but also an emu that was running down the streets being chased by

ONE MAN, 72 WIVES: POLYGAMY IN THE DESERT

The Fundamentalist Church of Jesus Christ of Latter Day Saints (FLDS), whose founders were excommunicated by the Church of Latter Day Saints (Mormons) and whose members are not welcomed by the Mormon church, cling tenaciously to the doctrine of polygamy. They believe that the only way a man can reach heaven is by having at least three wives, and as many children as possible, and that a woman can reach heaven only through the invitation of a satisfied husband. In the late 19th century, when Mormons abandoned polygamy to satisfy federal requisites for the inclusion of Utah as a state, the sect's early members sought refuge in the remote isolation of the Arizona–Utah border. In the 1920s they settled in the town of what was then called Short Creek, 36 miles west of Fredonia, and were left alone to practice their religion.

On July 26, 1953, Arizona Governor Howard Pyle called upon the Arizona National Guard and state police officers to raid the town and stamp out polygamy. They arrested 122 polygamous men and women, and took 263 children into foster care. National news stories and brutal images of children being torn from their parents caused public outrage against the state's religious intolerance, and authorities were reluctant to enforce polygamy laws again. The town changed its name to Colorado City and the radical sect continued to grow.

Rulon T Jeffs, who led the church from 1986 until his death in 2002, proclaimed himself to be the sole leader, and controlled the city's schools, police and local government. Upon his death, his son Warren Jeffs became the sect's new prophet and leader. Within a week, he had married nearly all of his father's 72 widows and became stepfather to his nearly 65 children. Unlike his father, Warren Jeffs ruled with a power-hungry iron fist. He arranged all the marriages, and he punished disobedient men and women by reassigning wives to different husbands. Told that their salvation depended upon their compliance, girls as young as 12 years old married much older men. If they refused, they were kicked out of their home and the town. Church members were forbidden to watch TV or movies, read newspapers, listen to music, dance or have contact with anyone outside the church, and any infraction could result in banishment from the community. In an effort to ensure that the older members of the church had enough young brides, Jeffs banished more than 400 young boys from the town. The children, known as Lost Boys, taunted as 'plygs' (polygamist kids), and completely unprepared for life outside of the strict confines of Colorado City, were torn from their homes and forbidden to contact their families. Their stories, featured on national TV shows, horrified the American public.

In 2005 authorities cracked down on the isolated enclaves of Colorado City and nearby Hildale, Utah. Placed on the FBI's Ten Most Wanted List, Jeffs was arrested near Las Vegas, Nevada, in August 2006 on a routine traffic violation. He was found with $54,000 in cash, 15 cell phones and hree wigs. At the time of his arrest, Jeffs was estimated to have had 10,000 followers. Polygamist milies in America continue to practice their religion.

everal documentaries, including *Banking on Heaven* and the BBC's *The Man With 80 Wives,* and akauer's highly recommended book *Under the Banner of Heaven,* examine the history, culture igion of Colorado City and FLDS. HBO's TV series *Big Love,* starring Chloe Sevigny, offers ent fictional account, both funny and disturbing, of modern polygamist culture.

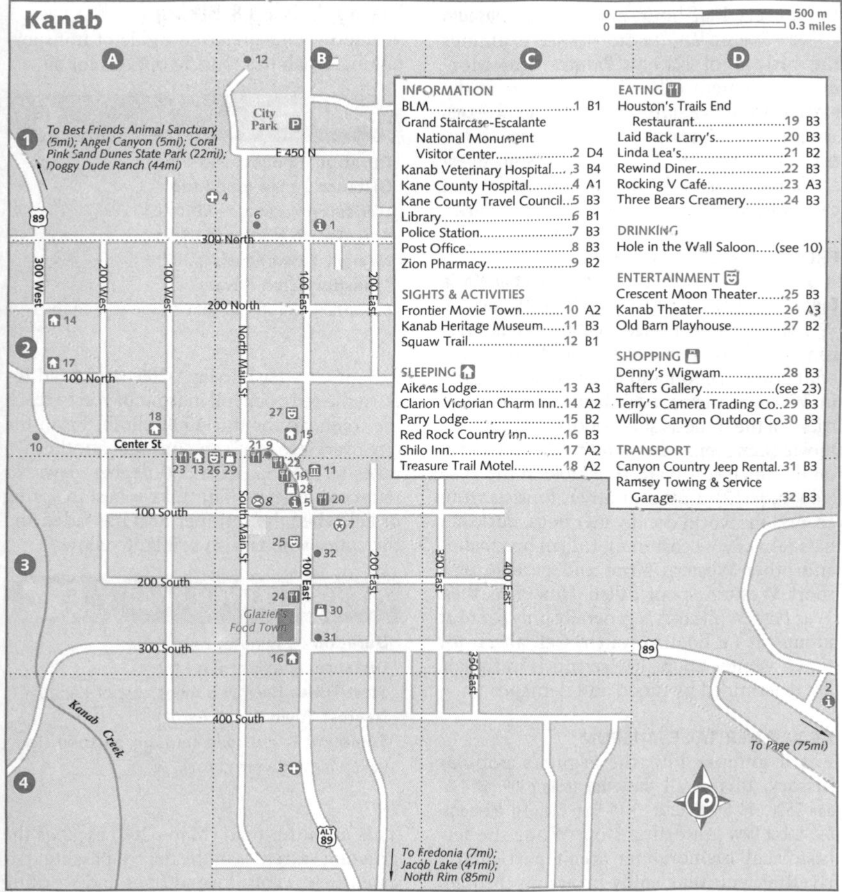

a pack of dogs. In 2006 Best Friends evacuated 300 homeless pets from war-ravaged Beirut and set up 'Little Lebanon' on the grounds. The shelter conducts workshops, offers daily tours of the grounds and hosts open houses of the bunny house and other sections. Every animal is up for adoption, and cabins are available – ask about a sleepover with a borrowed dog, cat or potbelly pig (see Sleeping, p211).

CORAL PINK SAND DUNES STATE PARK

Kids and adults alike can climb, slide and roll through coral-colored sand dunes dotted with junipers and piñon pines at this 3700-acre **state park** (off Map p200; ☎ 435-648-2800; www.utah.com/stateparks/coral_pink.htm; admission $5;). Bring spare clothes, as the dusty sand clings to everything. Don't come during the heat of a summer day when the sand burns feet! The park's 1200-acre off-highway vehicle area is popular with locals.

PIPE SPRING NATIONAL MONUMENT

Used by pioneers as a resting spot and catt[…] ranch, this small and quiet oasis in the des[…] is both lovely and interesting. Visitors […] experience the Old West amid cabi[…] corrals, an orchard, a pond and a […] In summer, rangers and costume[…] teers reenact various pioneer t[…] by Mormons in 1869 for church[…] refuge from Indians, the ston[…] (tours 9am-4pm Sep-May, 8am-4:3[…]

tours every half-hour, and a small **museum** (8am-5pm Sep-May, 7am-5pm May-Aug) examines the history of Kaibab Paiutes and Mormon settlement. The visitors center at the **monument** (off Map p200; 928-643-7105; www.nps.gov/pisp; Hwy 389; admission $5; 7am-5pm Jun-Aug, 8am-5pm Sep-May;), 21 miles southwest of Kanab, sells backcountry permits for rim camping in Grand Canyon National Park.

FRONTIER MOVIE TOWN

A kitschy roadside attraction, **Frontier Movie Town** (Map p209; 435-644-5337; 297 W Center St; 7:30am-11pm;) is classic Americana tourism at its best. You can wander through the bunkhouse, saloon and other buildings used in Western movie sets, brush up on such tricks of the trade as short doorways (to make movie stars seem taller) and relax with a beer on the small courtyard (see Hole in the Wall Saloon, p212). In the summer, tourists from around the world don feather boas, buckskin hats (aka coyote costume), Indian headbands and other Western attire and partake in a short Western spoof called *How The West Was Lost*. While this is generally only for tour groups, it's a hoot to watch. Call ahead for times. Winter hours, like so much in Kanab, are determined by mood and demand.

KANAB HERITAGE MUSEUM

For a glimpse into the region's popular history, this small **museum** (Map p209; 435-644-3506; 13 S 100 East; 9-5pm Mon-Fri Memorial Day-Labor Day) is worth a stop. While the few historical memorabilia aren't particularly riveting, you may enjoy browsing through the 30-plus spiral-bound notebooks filled with movie newspapers, magazine articles, written histories and photographs.

FESTIVALS & EVENTS

Held in late August, the annual **Western Legends Roundup** (www.westernlegendsroundup.com) celebrates Kanab's pioneer and Hollywood past, kicking off with a wagon train, llowed by a film festival, a fiddle compe- on, cowboy poetry, Indian dances and n rides. In Page, the hot-air balloons very November at the **Balloon Re- ahweap Parade of Lights** is a boat lights on Lake Powell on the first ecember.

Hiking, Driving & Biking

Whatever your preferred mode of transportation, Kanab has touring options for all.

SQUAW TRAIL

Duration 1 hour round-trip
Distance 2 mile round-trip
Difficulty Moderate–difficult
Start/Finish North of 100 East
Nearest Town Kanab (p207)
Transportation Private
Summary Climb hill that shadows Kanab.

Park at City Park (Map p209) and head toward the red-rock hill in front of you to reach the trailhead for this 400ft climb. From the city overview, you can continue another 0.5 miles to the top, with 360-degree views, or retrace your steps. This hike is best in spring or fall, when the summer heat has faded and the cottonwoods turn brilliant yellow.

JOHNSON CANYON ROAD

Duration 50 minutes round-trip
Distance 32 miles round-trip
Start/Finish Hwy 89 9 miles east of Kanab
Nearest Town Kanab (p207)
Summary Paved road through pastoral river valley framed by red rock.

This beautiful road (Map p200) escapes the grueling extremes of the desert, passing irrigated fields, cottonwood trees and working ranches. After 16 miles the road turns to dirt – turn around and return to Hwy 89, or continue through Grand Staircase-Escalante National Monument to Cannonville.

KANAB CANYON ROAD (ANGEL CANYON)

Duration 15 minutes one way
Distance 4.5 miles one way
Start Hwy 89, 6 miles northwest of Kanab
Finish Hwy 89, 9.5 miles northwest of Kanab
Nearest Town Kanab (p207)
Summary Loop off Hwy 89 through canyon.

Angel Canyon became the site of scores of movies and TV shows during Kanab's

Hollywood heyday. The public road (Map p200) winds up and down through Best Friends Animal Sanctuary, offering quintessential red-rock scenery and desert views. Just across from the Best Friends Animal Sanctuary Welcome Center, a dirt path veers east about 0.5 miles down to the **Kanab Creek**, a shallow, clear creek that's excellent for dogs and kids. A mile further, just beyond the horse corral on the left, is **Angel's Landing**. This small natural amphitheater borders a grassy field and makes a perfect picnic spot. Angel Canyon also makes a lovely drive.

Tours

Terry at Terry's Camera (p213) has spent years roaming the back roads of the Southwest, photographing landscapes, wildlife, petroglyphs and whatever else he finds, and offers customized **photo tours** of the region. Susan and Steve Dodson at **Paria Outpost** (☎ 928-691-104; www.paria.com) specialize in customized 4WD tours and guided hikes through the rocks and sand of the Grand Staircase-Escalante National Monument and the Paria Canyon-Vermilion Cliffs Wilderness. Rates start at $30 per person, per hour and continue up to $125/175 per person for half-/full-day expeditions. Children's rates are considerably less. These guides can take folks to much more interesting and less busy slot canyons than Antelope Canyon.

Sleeping

Red Rock Country Inn (Map p209; 435-644-8774; www.redrockcountryinn.com; 330 South 100 E; r & f $; closed Dec & Jan;) Little touches give this motel a pleasantly quirky twist. Some rooms have log ceilings, white-brick walls and 1960s Southwest-style furnishings, and most have a refrigerator and microwave. Run by a hiking enthusiast and his brother, the Red Rock caters to desert rats. It has a 'relaxation center' for aching bodies, where you can lie on an aqua-jet massage table (imagine a pulsating waterbed) or soak your feet in a massage bath. Three chairs at the oxygen bar offer 15-minute oxygen treatments, complete with video glasses showing calming nature scenes. The tiny pool sits just off a busy intersection.

ourpick **Best Friends Animal Sanctuary** (Map p200; ☎ 435-644-2001, ext 102; www.bestfriends.org; Hwy 89; sites/cabins $/$$;) With peaceful surrounds and the spectacular red-rock country of Angel Canyon out your door, these bright, modern one-bedroom cottages and two studio cabins overlook the horse pasture at the animal sanctuary (p208). And best of all, you can borrow a dog, cat or potbelly pig for a sleepover! Two RV sites offer the perfect solution for those who want the conveniences of a hookup without the crowds of an RV park, but no tent camping is allowed. Five miles north of Kanab

Kanab Garden Cottages (☎ 435-644-2020, ext 102; www.kanabcottages.com; cottages $$) Beautifully appointed, with handsome furniture and hardwood floors, Kanab Garden rents three cottages spread throughout residential Kanab.

Parry Lodge (Map p209; ☎ 435-644-2601, 888-289-1722; www.parrylodge.com; 89 E Center St; s, d, tw & ste $$;) Rooms at this one-story 1929 motel are set back from the road amid a large, tree-covered parking lot. Some bear the names of movie stars who stayed here while filming in southern Utah, and while it's hard to believe they were ever elegant enough for Gregory Peck or Lana Turner, it's fun to imagine how it must have once been. With a rough-at-the-edges charm, this motel is like walking into the tattered ghost of a more glamorous era. The small, deep pool is a favorite, but avoid the buffet breakfast and rooms in the newer, two-story annex. In the summer, it shows free Western movies in a barn (p212) in the parking lot.

Clarion Victorian Charm Inn (Map p209; ☎ 435-644-8660, 800-738-9643; www.victoriancharminn.com; 190 N 300 West; s & d incl hot breakfast $$;) Hardwood floors, a grand staircase, quilts and four-poster beds lend this hotel an old-time feel, but the building is modern and the antiques are new. There's no escaping the haughty attitude here, and while it is the spiffiest motel in town, that's not saying much. Some rooms have Jacuzzis (in the room itself, to give it that honeymoon-suite feel) and gas fireplaces.

Shilo Inn (Map p209; ☎ 800-222-2244; www.shiloinns.com/utah/kanab/html; 296 W 100 North; s & d $$;) A bowl of dog biscuits welcomes four-legged companions at this bright and tidy chain motel. Unlike most of the places in town, the doors have interior entrance and the feels less like a roadside motel. rooms have a microwave and a refrigerator, and three rooms open directly onto small, fenced-in pool.

In addition to the preceding entries, the friendly **Treasure Trail Motel** (Map p209; ☎ 435-644-2687, 800-603-2687; www.treasuretrailmotel.net; 150 W Center St; s, d & ste $;) and **Aikens Lodge** (Map p209; ☎ 435-644-2625, 800-790-0380; www.aikenslodge.com; 79 W Center St; s, d & ste $;) offer clean, basic rooms, and you can camp at Coral Pink Sand Dunes State Park.

Eating & Drinking

During the winter, most restaurants reduce their hours according to need, mood and available help. As the Rocking V puts it, after Halloween they 'hold a summit to determine the schedule through New Year's.'

Three Bears Creamery (Map p209; ☎ 435-644-3300; 210 S 100 East; mains $; 11am-9pm Mon-Fri, to 8pm Sat, closed Jan;) Serving up fairy-tale themed sundaes like the Goldilocks (caramel sauce over vanilla ice cream – get it?) and the Big Bad Wolf (six scoops with four toppings), Three Bears is the best place for ice cream. It also serves breakfast, sandwiches and soup.

Laid Back Larry's (Map p209; ☎ 435-644-3636; 98 S 100 East; mains $; 7am-4pm Mon-Fri, 8am-4pm Sat & Sun;) The only spot in town for coffee with a kick, this tiny, low-key place has a handful of outdoor tables and a drive-through window. It offers croissant and bagel sandwiches for breakfast, fantastic smoothies, and teriyaki rice bowls (chicken, frozen stir-fry veggies or tofu) and sandwiches for lunch. Try the artichoke hummus and baklava. Parents take note: a sign by the register reads 'Unattended children will be given espresso and a free puppy.'

Linda Lea's (Map p209; ☎ 435-644-8191; 4 E Center St; mains $; 7am-4pm;) Come here for a tasty oatmeal cranberry cookie and a coffee on the pleasant patio. It serves quiche or a breakfast sandwich in the morning and a limited sandwich menu at lunch.

Houston's Trails End Restaurant (Map p209; ☎ 435-644-2488; 132 E Center St; mains $$; 6am-10pm;) Playing on the city's Western heritage, servers at this dependable family-style restaurant dress in cowboy/cowgirl regalia (complete with a gun in the holster), nd the radio plays country music. Expect ner breakfast fare and carnivore classics chicken-fried steak, burgers and ribs.

ewind Diner (Map p209; ☎ 435-644-3200; 18 E St; mains $$; 11am-9pm Tue-Sat;) Betty draped in a red boa, holds the menu outside this retro diner. You can sit at the black-and-white-tiled soda fountain (try the excellent malt) or settle into a red vinyl booth. Vintage movie posters, a Coke-in-the-bottle vending machine and a chrome rotary public phone complete the 1940s ambiance. The menu extends beyond the classic hamburger and sandwich options to include fajitas, wild mushroom pasta and salmon salad. Ask about the falafel sandwich, not on the menu.

our pick **Rocking V Café** (Map p209; ☎ 435-644-8001; 97 W Center St; mains $$-$$$; 11:30am-9pm) Housed in an 1892 storefront and owned by Dallas transplants, this brightly painted café offers a welcome change from basic, uninspired roadside fare. The food is fresh and delicious, and the eclectic menu includes buffalo steak, deep-dish vegetarian enchiladas, Asian chicken salad and a grilled Portobello sandwich. This is the only place in town that serves alcohol beyond beer and wine (with food only), and there are a few sidewalk tables. Dinner reservations are recommended in the summer.

Mormon-influenced Utah laws complicate drinking options. The only place in town where you can enjoy a drink (beer and wine only) without having to order a meal is at the **Hole in the Wall Saloon** (4-10pm) at Frontier Movie Town (p210).

Entertainment

Crescent Moon Theater (Map p209; ☎ 435-644-2350; 150 S 100 East; adult/child $13/6.50) Features Western music and comedy shows. For American West tourism at its kitschiest, catch tour groups putting on a Western show at Frontier Movie Town (p210).

During the summer, the Parry Lodge (p211) shows free classic Western films every night at 7pm in the Old Barn Playhouse behind the lodge. The films are introduced by a true ol' cowboy, the seating ranges from overstuffed to folding wood, and the popcorn and ice cream are cheap. The tiny **Kanab Theater** (Map p209; ☎ 435-644-2334; 29 West Center St; Wed-Sun) screens first-run movies.

Shopping

Willow Canyon Outdoor Co (Map p209; ☎ 435-644-8884; 263 S 100 East; 7:30am-8pm) This tiny place offers an excellent selection of hiking and field guides, camping gear, United

States Geological Survey (USGS) maps, and clothes, as well as an eclectic mix of books, CDs and children's books. It's easy to spend hours just relaxing with a coffee and perusing the books at this markedly urban enclave.

Rafters Gallery (Map p209; ☎ 435-644-8001; ⏰ 11:30am-9pm) Above the Rocking V Café, this decidedly hip gallery shows local artists, with everything from pottery to watercolors, clothes to basketry.

Denny's Wigwam (Map p209; ☎ 435-644-2452; 78 E Center St; ⏰ 8:30am-9:30pm Mon-Sat, 9am-9:30pm Sun) For all kinds of cowboy gear, as well as Native American pottery, jewelry and rugs.

Terry's Camera Trading Co (Map p209; ☎ 435-644-5981; 19 W Center St; ⏰ 8am-6pm Mon-Sat) Terry specializes in camera gear and repair.

Getting There & Around

There's no bus or train service to Kanab, nor are there any taxis. Paria Outpost (p206) offers a shuttle service for the area. The closest car-rental companies are in Page (see p219), but you can rent 4WD jeeps at **Canyon Country Jeep Rental** (Map p209; ☎ 435-644-8250; 285 S 100 East). Las Vegas International Airport (four hours southwest) and Salt Lake City International Airport (five hours north) are the closet airline hubs.

PAGE & GLEN CANYON NATIONAL RECREATION AREA

In 1972 Glen Canyon Dam, Lake Powell, Lees Ferry and more than a million acres of surrounding desert were established as Glen Canyon National Recreation Area (GCNRA). The main attraction here is the 186-mile-long Lake Powell, with 1960 miles of empty shoreline set amid striking red-rock formations, sharply cut canyons and dramatic desert scenery. The windy outpost of Lees Ferry, best known as the jumping-off point for Grand Canyon raft trips, lies 15 miles below the dam.

Orientation & Information

The region's central town is Page, on the southern tip of GCNRA, 142 miles north of Flagstaff and 124 miles northeast of the North Rim. N Lake Powell Blvd in town loops off Hwy 89 and forms the main strip. Twenty-five miles south of Page, Alt 89 spurs west off Hwy 89 toward Jacob Lake and the North Rim. Fourteen miles after the split, Alt 89 crosses the Colorado on the new Navajo Bridge. Just after the bridge, a paved road heads north about 5 miles to Lees Ferry, with historic buildings, a visitors center, a beach on the Colorado River, a campground and some hikes (45 minutes from Page).

The Recreation Area entrance fee, good for up to seven days, is $15 per vehicle or $7 per individual entering on foot or bicycle.

EMERGENCY

Police station (Map p214; ☎ 928-645-2463; 808 Coppermine Rd)

INTERNET ACCESS

Digital Lands (Map p214; ☎ 928-645-2241; 40 S Lake Powell Blvd; per hr $6; ⏰ 10am-10pm)

INTERNET RESOURCES

Aramark (www.lakepowell.com) For marina lodging, boat rentals and boat tours.

Fishing Information (www.wayneswords.com)

Glen Canyon National Recreation Area (www.nps.gov/glca)

Page/Lake Powell Tourism Bureau (www.pagelakepowelltourism.com)

LIBRARIES

Page Public Library (Map p214; ☎ 928-645-4270; 479 S Lake Powell Blvd; ⏰ 10am-8pm Mon-Thu, 10am-5pm Fri & Sat)

MARINAS

Marinas (except for Dangling Rope and Hite) rent boats, host rangers and small supply stores, and sell fuel. **Aramark** (☎ 800-528-6154; www.lakepowell.com) runs all the marinas except for Antelope Point, which is on Navajo Land.

Antelope Point (off Map p214; ☎ 928-645-5900) Peaceful marina 8 miles northeast of Page that opened in 2007.

Bullfrog (☎ 435-684-3000) On Lake Powell's west shore, 290 miles from Page. Connects to Halls Crossing marina by 30-minute ferry.

Dangling Rope Forty lake-miles from Page. Smalles marina, accessible only by boat.

Halls Crossing (☎ 435-684-7000) On Lake Pow shore, 238 miles from Page. Connects to Bullfrog 30-minute ferry.

Hite At Lake Powell's north end, 148 lake-m Page. May be closed due to low water leve

Wahweap (off Map p200; ☎ 928-645 northwest of Page. Frenetic place popu

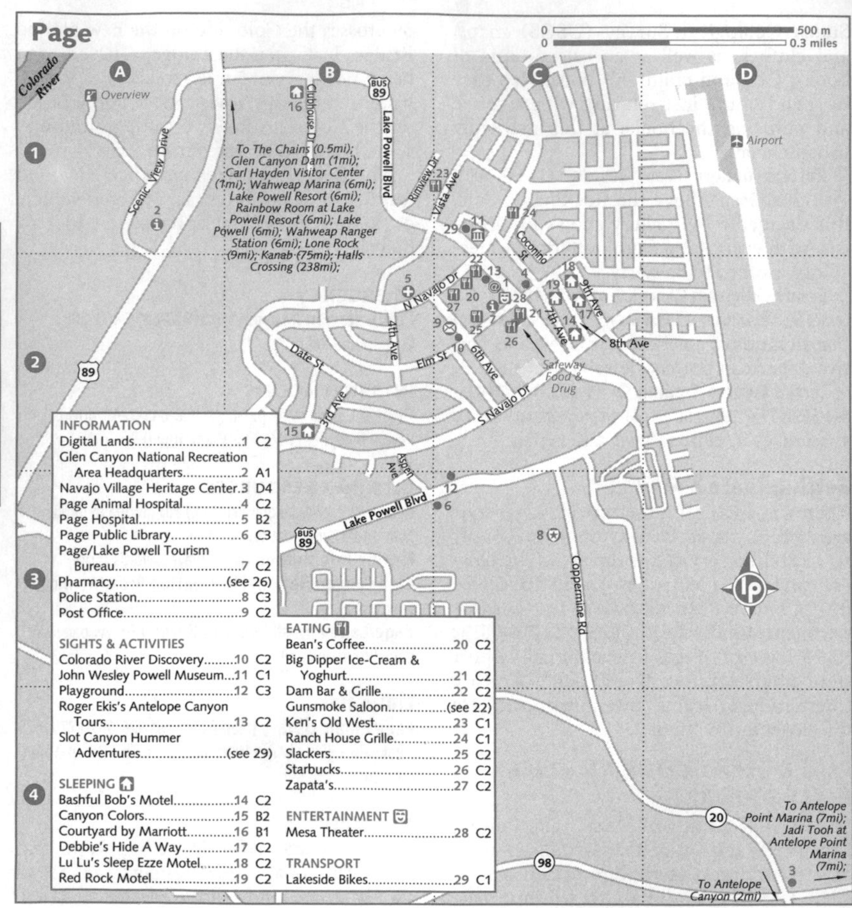

MEDICAL SERVICES

Page Hospital (Map p214; ☎ 928-645-2424; Vista Ave at N Navajo Dr)

Pharmacy (Map p214; ☎ 928-645-8155; 650 Elm St; 9am-8pm Mon-Fri, 9am-6pm Sat, 10am-4pm Sun) Inside the Safeway Food & Drug.

…OST

… office (Map p214; ☎ 928-645-2571; 44 6th Ave; …0am-5pm Mon-Fri)

… STATIONS

…wing GCNRA ranger stations keep …ours.

…er Station (☎ 435-684-7400)

…er Station (☎ 435-826-5651)

…nger Station (☎ 435-684-7460)

Hite Ranger Station (☎ 435-684-2457)

Lees Ferry Ranger Station (☎ 928-355-2234; Lees Ferry)

Wahweap Ranger Station (off Map p214; ☎ 928-608-6531)

TOURIST INFORMATION

In addition to Bullfrog Visitor Center and Carl Hayden Visitor Center, there is a third GCNRA visitors center 39 miles southwest of Page at Navajo Bridge (opposite). Visitors centers for Grand Staircase-Escalante National Monument and the Paria Canyon-Vermilion Cliffs Wilderness lie northwest of Page on Hwy 89 (see p205).

Bullfrog Visitor Center (☎ 435-684-7423; 9am-5pm Wed-Sun, closed Apr-Oct) On the lake's north shore, this is a drive of more than 200 miles from Page.

Carl Hayden Visitor Center (Map p200; ☎ 928-608-6404; 🕑 8am-7pm Memorial Day-Labor Day, to 4pm rest of the year) A well-stocked bookstore and the best source of regional information in Page. It's located at Glen Canyon Dam on Hwy 89, 2 miles north of Page.

Glen Canyon National Recreation Area Headquarters (Map p214; ☎ 928-608-6200; www.nps.gov/glca; 🕑 7am-4pm Mon-Fri, closed noon-1pm)

Glen Canyon Natural History Association (☎ 928-608-6072; www.glencanyonnha.com) Sells maps and guides to Glen Canyon Dam, Grand Staircase-Escalante National Monument, Lake Powell and Vermilion Cliffs National Monument.

Page/Lake Powell Tourism Bureau (Map p214; ☎ 928-645-6870; www.pagelakepowelltourism.com; 647-A Elm St; 🕑 8am-5pm)

Sights

PAGE & LAKE POWELL

Antelope Canyon

Everywhere you look in Page, there seems to be another photo of Antelope Canyon (off Map p214), a scenic slot canyon on the Navajo Indian Reservation, a few miles east of Page and open to tourists by tour only. Year-round, but particularly in the summer, crowds of people pile into shuttles and schlep their tripods and cameras into the narrow canyon. Several tour companies offer trips into upper Antelope Canyon; try **Roger Ekis's Antelope Canyon Tours** (Map p214; ☎ 928-645-9102; www.antelopecanyon.com; 22 S Lake Powell Blvd).

For other slot canyons in the area, see Backcountry Hikes in the Paria Canyon-Vermilion Cliffs Wilderness (p207), the Wire Pass to Buckskin Gulch hike (p206), and Tours in Kanab (p211) and Page (p218).

John Wesley Powell Museum

In 1869 the one-armed John Wesley Powell led the first expedition through the Grand Canyon on the Colorado River (see p92). This recommended **museum** (Map p214; ☎ 928-645-9496, 888-597-6873; www.powellmuseum.org; 64 N Lake Powell Blvd; admission $5; 🕑 9am-5pm, closed mid-Dec–mid-Feb) displays memorabilia of early river runners, including a model of Powell's boat, and photos and illustrations of Powell and his excursions.

Glen Canyon Dam

At 710ft tall, Glen Canyon Dam (Map p200) is the nation's second-highest concrete arch dam – Hoover Dam (p171) is 16ft taller. Construction lasted from 1956 through 1964. From April through October, free 45-minute guided tours depart from the **Carl Hayden Visitor Center** (Map p200; ☎ 928-608-6404; 🕑 8am-7pm Memorial Day-Labor Day, to 4pm rest of the year) and descend deep inside the dam in elevators. A display in the visitors center and three videos tells the story of the dam's construction, complete with technical facts.

The best view of the Colorado River snaking its way through the canyon to Glen Canyon Dam is from an overview (Map p214) just behind the Dennys. A 940ft round-trip walk down stairs and over sandstone leads to a sheltered overlook.

Rainbow Bridge National Monument

On the south shore of Lake Powell, Rainbow Bridge (50 miles by water from Wahweap Marina, Map p200) is the largest natural bridge in the world, measuring 290ft high by 275ft wide. Most visitors arrive by boat and then hike a short trail, though recent droughts have suspended guided tours to the monument. Serious backpackers can drive along dirt roads to access two unmaintained trails to the monument (each 28 miles round-trip). Both trailheads lie on the Navajo Indian Reservation; obtain a tribal permit from the **Navajo Parks & Recreation Department** (☎ 928-871-6647; PO Box 90000, Window Rock, AZ 86515).

LEES FERRY

The town of Lees Ferry (Map p200) was named after John D Lee, who started the Lonely Dell Ranch and a primitive ferry service here in 1872 (see boxed text, p96). The ferry ran until 1929, when the Navajo Bridge opened to a crowd of 5000 people.

Navajo Bridge

Pedestrians are free to walk across the Colorado on the original 834ft-wide, 467ft-hig Navajo Bridge (Map p200), which off great views south down Marble Canyo the northeast lip of the Grand Canyo

Historic Buildings

Walking tour guides, one of (along the river beyond the b and one of **Lonely Dell Ranch** from the river) are availab at the Rainbow Bridge In

HOPI & NAVAJO RESERVATIONS

Many folk zoom past the Hopi and Navajo Reservations, registering them as nothing more than vast desert expanses and a few lonely souvenir huts standing windblown along the road between the North and South Rims. But for those with the time and a willingness to explore the unpolished reality of the American West, a side tour to this desolate area east of the Grand Canyon can be a highlight.

The surreal red-rock formations of **Monument Valley**, featured in hundreds of movies, advertisements, calendars and magazines, emerge magically from the flat and drab landscape 154 miles from Desert View and 246 miles from the North Rim.

Lying 208 miles east of Desert View on the New Mexico border, **Canyon de Chelly**, a many-figured canyon dotted with ancestral Puebloan ruins and etched with pictographs, strikes even the most jaded traveler as hauntingly memorable. Navajo families winter on the rims and move to traditional hogans (one-room structures traditionally built of earth, logs, stone and other materials, with the entrance facing east) on farms on the canyon floor in spring and summer.

Scenic rim drives offer breathtaking beauty, and you can explore the interior on guided hikes or horseback rides.

The private and isolated Hopi communities of **First**, **Second** and **Third Mesas**, about two hours from Desert View (see Entrances, p102), consist of 12 traditional villages perched atop 7200ft mesas. At the end of First Mesa is the tiny village of **Walpi**, the most dramatic of the Hopi enclaves; Hopi guides offer 45-minute walking tours. The **Hopi Cultural Center**, on Second Mesa, has a small museum, and artisans sell woven baskets, kachina dolls and other crafts from roadside booths. On Third Mesa, **Old Oraibi** rivals Taos, New Mexico, and Acoma, New Mexico, as the oldest continuously inhabited village on the continent. Kachina dances are often open to the public, and tribe members sometimes personally invite visitors to other ceremonies. An invitation is an honor; be sure to respect local customs.

The Hopi strictly prohibit alcohol, as well as any form of recording, including sketching. Each of these spots has one or two motels, and there are several chain motels in Kayenta, 24 miles south of Monument Valley. See Lonely Planet's *Southwest USA* for details.

or the Carl Hayden Visitor Center, in Page. Lees Ferry, the site of a ferry-crossing from 1872 to 1978 (see Ferryman of the Colorado, p96) and of Charles Spencer's 1910 effort to extract gold from the surrounding hills, includes a couple of stone buildings and a sunken paddlewheel steamboat, among other things. Lonely Dell Ranch provided for families who worked at the crossing in the 1880s and 1890s. The log cabins, a stone ranch house and a pioneer cemetery remain. Though the main ranch uildings lie only about 700ft up a dirt d from the parking area, a walking tour e entire ranch is a 1-mile round-trip. find picnic tables and an idyllic ap- chard, a sheltered oasis that makes ful picnic spot.

lt 89 take the paved road north Ferry for 5.1 miles, then turn e 0.2 miles to Lonely Dell s Ferry, continue 0.7 miles for Lonely Dell Ranch.

Activities

SWIMMING

The best place to enjoy Lake Powell's cold, clear water (short of jumping off your boat) is at the **Chains** (off Map p214). From the unmarked parking lot just east of the dam, a short walk leads to flat, smooth sandstone that juts directly into the water. Another excellent, if windy, spot to splash around is **Paria Beach** (Map p200), about 45 minutes from Page in Lees Ferry. Here, soft, white sand lines the Colorado River for several hundred feet and the water is calm and shallow halfway across. Stick to wading in the shallows – the deep water of the Colorado is dangerous for swimming.

Nine miles northwest of Page, **Lone Rock** (Map p200) is basically a huge parking lot of sand and gravel set on a thin, mucky finger of Lake Powell. Tents and campers line the shore, there's no shade, and it can get crazy with partygoers during the weekend. A more peaceful option, particularly good for kids, is the boat launch at **Antelope Point Marina** (off Map p214), where you can wade into the water from the small, rocky areas.

FISHING

The calm waters of the Colorado River, deep in a canyon between the dam and Lees Ferry, offer excellent fly-fishing. To fish the Arizona portion of Lake Powell and the Colorado River, you must have an Arizona fishing license ($12.50/26 for one/five days). Fishing the Utah portion of the lake requires a Utah fishing license ($12/32 for one/seven days). Children under 14 years old do not need a license. All marinas sell licenses.

Fly-fishing guides to Lees Ferry and Lake Powell:

Ambassador Guides and Outfitters (☎ 800-256-7596; www.lakepowellanglers.com)
Lees Ferry Anglers (☎ 928-355-2228)
Marble Canyon Guide Service (☎ 800-533-7339, 928-355-2245)

BOATING & CRUISES

The marinas rent kayaks, 18ft runabouts and 14ft fishing boats, as well as water skis and other 'toys.' Distances on Lake Powell are long. To take a powerboat from Page to Rainbow Bridge takes about three hours and at least 10 gallons of gas – that's $120 to $160 for fuel alone – and it's about five hours from the lake's northern to southern tips. Houseboating (below) is hugely popular.

With its many coves and beaches to explore, Lake Powell is perfect for kayaking. To kayak the smooth waters of the Colorado River 15.2 miles from the dam to Lees Ferry, contact Colorado River Discovery (see following). They'll meet you at Lees Ferry at the end of their raft trips and backhaul you upriver to an island just below the dam ($29/$20 person/boat). You can camp at any of the six primitive campsites along the river, or make it a day trip. Call by 7pm the day before you'd like to kayak.

From Wahweap Marina, **Aramark** (☎ 800-528-6154; www.lakepowell.com; ♿) has full-day boat tours to Rainbow Bridge (adult/child $119/79), half-day trips to Navajo Tapestry (adult/child $59/39), and 1½ hour rides to Antelope Canyon (adult/child $31/21), as well as summer dinner cruises to the dam ($61). The largest of the marina's seven boats holds 162 people, and the smallest holds 68, so don't expect an intimate ride.

Colorado River Discovery (Map p214; ☎ 888-522-6644; www.raftthecanyon.com; 130 6th Ave; 🕑 Mar-Nov; ♿) offers a half-day smooth water float trip down the Colorado from Glen Canyon Dam through Marble Canyon to Lees Ferry. Boats stop at petroglyphs, and guides explain the natural and human history along the way. This is a beautiful trip, suitable for children four years old and up. Despite the fact that several boats, each holding 22 people, depart at the same time, the ride is peaceful.

HIKING

Take advantage of the area's excellent short hikes.

HORSESHOE BEND

Duration 25 minutes round-trip
Distance 1.5 miles round-trip
Difficulty Easy–moderate
Start/Finish Hwy 89, 2.5 miles south of Page, just across from mile marker 541
Nearest Town Page (p213)
Transportation Private
Summary Sandy trail to one of the most photographed views of the Colorado River.

This popular hike (Map p200) is short, but the soft sand, shadeless trail and moderate incline makes it a bit trying. Below the overlook, the river bends around a dramatic stone outcrop to form a perfect horseshoe.

HOUSEBOATING ON LAKE POWELL

Lake Powell is famous for its houseboating, and it's a huge attraction for families and college students alike. Though the lake hosts hundreds of houseboats daily, you can explore Lake Powell's secluded inlets, bays, coves and beaches for several days without seeing many folk at all. Contact the recommended **Antelope Point Marina** (off Map p214; ☎ 800-255-5561; www.antelopepointlakepowel .com), which generally has more elegant boats, or **Aramark** (☎ 800-528-6154; www.lakepowell.co for details and reservations.

Toddlers should be secured safely in a backpack, as there are no guardrails at the viewpoint.

RIVER TRAIL

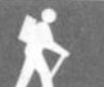

Duration 40 minutes round-trip
Distance 2 miles round-trip
Difficulty Easy
Start/Finish Lees Ferry launch ramp
Nearest Area Navajo Bridge Interpretive Center
Transportation Private
Summary Pleasant desert stroll along the Colorado River.

An excellent choice for families, this easy walk passes the historic buildings of Lees Ferry walking tour (p215) and offers several spots to cool your feet in the icy water of the Colorado.

SPENCER TRAIL

Duration 3 hours round-trip
Distance 4.4 miles round-trip
Difficulty Difficult
Start/Finish Lees Ferry launch ramp
Nearest Area Navajo Bridge Interpretive Center
Transportation Private
Summary Rocky switchbacks climb 1700ft to the rim of the canyon.

A dry, tough climb from the river up the sandstone walls of the canyon, this rocky trail offers spectacular views. The trail begins as part of the River Trail; just past the steel boiler (part of Lees Ferry historic walking tour, p215), it cuts left and winds steadily up to the rim. Bring plenty of water.

Tours

Slot Canyon Hummer Adventures (Map p214; ☎ 928-645-2266; 12 N Lake Powell Blvd) Takes 4WD tours to several slot canyons on Navajo land. With only ix people to a car, and no crowds vying for the perfect gle to shoot a photo, this is an excellent alternative to elope Canyon's mayhem. Tours cost $70/140 per person hree-/five-hour rides.

wind Aviation (☎ 800-245-8668; www.west iation.com) Offers aerial tours from Page Municipal

Sleeping

You can camp anywhere along the Lake Powell shoreline for free as long as you have a portable toilet or toilet facilities on your boat. Six designated primitive campsites, accessible by boat only, sit on the Colorado River between the dam and Lees Ferry. Bullfrog and Hite marinas offer primitive camping, and there are developed campgrounds at Wahweap, Bullfrog and Halls Crossing marinas (call ☎ 800-528-6154 for reservations).

Lees Ferry Campground (Map p200; sites $) This GCNRA campground is a lovely, quiet spot, set up on a small hill with a few shade trees and views of the river, but it's windy, dry and barren. There are toilets and potable water, but no hookups or facilities.

Lone Rock Beach (Map p200; sites $; ♿) Everyone here just pulls up next to the water and sets up house. It's a popular spot with college revelers, and can be busy and loud late into the night during the weekends. Escape to the dunes or the far edges of the lot if you're looking for quiet. There are bathrooms and outdoor cold showers.

Lu Lu's Sleep Ezze Motel (Map p214; ☎ 928-608-0273, 800-553-6211; 105 8th Ave; r $; 💻) Four bright and tidy rooms share a small patio with two large tables, rattan umbrellas, two barbecues, and pebble landscaping.

Debbie's Hide A Way (Map p214; ☎ 928-645-1224; www.debbieshideaway.com; 117 8th Ave; ste $-$$; 💻 👪) The owners encourage you to feel right at home – throw a steak on the grill, leaf through one of several hundred books that line bookshelves, or just hang out with other guests among the rose and fruit trees. In 2007 the rooms received a much-needed face-lift, with new tiles, paint and carpet, and all have kitchens. There are free laundry facilities.

Canyon Colors (Map p214; ☎ 928-645-5979; www.canyoncolors.com; 225 S Navajo; d & f $$; 🚭 👪) Head to this friendly, quiet place in a residential neighborhood to escape the chaos of the main strip, but don't expect elegance. Two rooms, one with a king bed and the other with a queen bed, a futon and a couch, have frills and stuffed animals. In the back yard there is a small grassy area, a patio with a barbecue for guest use, and a raised pool.

Lake Powell Resort (off Map p214; ☎ 928-645-2433, 800-528-6154; www.lakepowell.com; 100 Lake Shore Dr; s, d & ste $$-$$$; 💻 🚭 ♿) This bustling resort on the shores of Lake Powell offers beautiful views and a lovely pool, but it is impersonal and frenetic. Several buildings spread out around the parking lot house basic hotel rooms; rates for lake-view rooms with tiny patios are well worth the extra money. In the lobby you can book boat tours and arrange boat rental.

our pick **Courtyard by Marriott** (Map p214; ☎ 928-645-5000, 800-321-2211; 600 Clubhouse Dr; s & d $$-$$$;) Surrounded by a golf course away from the strip's noise and traffic, with attractive, spacious rooms and a quiet garden courtyard with a large pool, this hotel is a peaceful alternative to other chain hotels. It has a bar and a restaurant, but you'd be better off going elsewhere for a meal.

In addition to these listings, **Bashful Bob's Motel** (Map p214; ☎ 928-645-3919; www.bashfulbobsmotel.com; 750 S Navajo Dr; ste $;) and **Red Rock Motel** (Map p214; ☎ 928-645-0062; www.redrockmotel.com; 114 8th Ave; s, d & ste $) offer friendly, low-key accommodation and outdoor barbecues, and Bullfrog and Halls Crossing marinas have family units and hotels. You'll find standard chain motels along the strip.

Eating & Drinking

Big Dipper Ice-Cream & Yogurt (Map p214; ☎ 928-645-1956; 660 Elm St; ice creams $; 11am-10pm) The only ice-cream store in town; expect a line on summer nights.

Bean's Coffee (Map p214; ☎ 928-645-6858; 644F N Navajo Dr; mains $; 6:30am-6pm Mon-Fri, 7am-6pm Sat, 8am-2pm Sun) While the coffee runs weak, this tiny café serves good breakfast burritos and sandwiches – try the tasty cashew chicken as a picnic lunch to go!

Ranch House Grille (Map p214; ☎ 928-645-1420; 819 N Navajo Dr; mains $; 5am-3pm) The big, white room offers little in terms of ambiance, but the food is good, the portions huge and the service fast. This is your best bet for breakfast.

Slackers (Map p214; 928-645-5267; 662 Elm St; mains $; 11am-9pm Mon-Fri) A chalkboard menu includes excellent burgers (though no kick to the green chili) and hot or cold sub sandwiches. Count on long lunch lines. Picnic tables offer shaded outdoor strip-mall seating.

Zapata's (Map p214; ☎ 928-645-9006; 615 N Navajo Dr; mains $; 4-10pm) Head to this colorful café for standard Mexican fare.

Dam Bar & Grille (Map p214; ☎ 928-645-2161; 644 N Navajo Dr; mains $$; 11:30am-10pm) Raft guides recommend the dependable pub fare, including steak, pasta and ribs. There's a microbrewery feel here, and the patio is pleasant on summer evenings, despite the strip-mall view.

Gunsmoke Saloon (Map p214; ☎ 928-645-2161; 644 N Navajo Dr; mains $$; 5-9pm) This cavernous spot serves barbecue dinners, from sandwiches to racks of ribs with all the fixins'. After dinner it's a popular bar featuring alternative rock and plenty of drunken revelers.

Ken's Old West (Map p214; ☎ 928-645-5160; 718 Vista Ave; mains $$; 4-10pm) Steakhouse aficionados head to Ken's, and from Thursday through Saturday the place is hoppin' with country music and line dancing.

Jadi Tooh (Map p214; ☎ 928-645-5900; Antelope Marina; mains $$-$$$; 10am-4pm & 5pm-10pm) Opened in 2007, this floating restaurant with solid food at the Navajo-owned marina provides a peaceful respite from the bustle of Page, which is 8 miles southwest.

Rainbow Room (Map p200; ☎ 928-645-2433; Lake Powell Resort, 100 Lake Shore Dr; mains $$$; 6-10am, 11am-2pm & 4-11pm) Though the food ranges from nothing special to downright bad, there's something to be said for a meal with a view. Picture windows frame dramatic red-rock formations against blue water. Your best bet is to eat elsewhere and come to the bar here for a sunset drink.

Starbucks (Map p214; ☎ 928-645-8155; 650 Elm St; $; 5am-9pm) Located inside the Safeway, this international coffee chain is the only option for big-city java with a punch.

Entertainment

Navajo Village Heritage Center (Map p214; ☎ 928-660-0304; www.navajo-village.com) On summer evenings this center presents traditional Navajo dancing, song, crafts and food (one/two hours $40/55). Children cost less (under five free). From 9am to 3pm, it's open for self-guided tours of traditional homesites ($5).

Mesa Theater (Map p214; ☎ 928-645-9565; 42 S Lake Powell Blvd) This tiny theater screens first-run movies.

Getting There & Around

Great Lakes Airline (☎ 928-645-1355, 800-554-[illegible] www.greatlakesav.com) offers flights bet[illegible] Page Municipal Airport and Phoenix[illegible] and Avis rent cars from the airport[illegible] services, geared toward hikers, [illegible] able through Paria Outpost (p21[illegible] **Bikes** (Map p214; ☎ 928-645-2266; 1[illegible] Blvd) rents mountain bikes fo[illegible] Ask about negotiable long-t[illegible]

NORTH RIM

Colorado River

A century-and-a-half ago when the Colorado River was but a vast blank space on maps of the West, its mystique was irresistible to truly brave souls like John Wesley Powell. But even now that every river mile has been detailed and its riffles and holes are familiar to skillful guides, its pull has kept thousands of contemporary explorers waiting on lists for 10 years or more to raft it themselves (though – rafters rejoice! – the newly implemented lottery system has slashed wait times). Visitors to the canyon rim can admire the river's glinting bends from up above, marveling at the waterway that has carved the massive natural monument that is the Grand Canyon. Day hikers often find themselves inexplicably drawn by a desire to reach the river, sometimes to their detriment, but who can blame them for the cool, seductive attraction that seems just beyond that next switchback?

Ask any outdoor enthusiast, and chances are good that rafting the Colorado is on his or her Top 10 adventure wish list. It is, as many say, the trip of a lifetime. Not only is it the most exhilarating way to experience the inner gorge, but descending through the layers of rock is to see the geological record move past you, and is nothing short of time travel. Hiking the trails that have been used for centuries, or coming within breathing distance of pictographs painted by ancient inhabitants, connects modern-day visitors with the canyon's human history. On the river, it's possible to see small herds of bighorn sheep and hear the trill of canyon wrens that dwell in this rich ecosystem. More than just the thrill of running its 160-plus rapids, time on the river offers the gift of seeing the canyon's grandeur and scope from the perspective of the water itself as it continues its slow sculptural journey.

HIGHLIGHTS

- Waking on the beach of a river camp as early-morning light reveals reflections of canyon walls in the river below
- Hiking up the steep trail, creeping through a slot canyon and passing pictographs along the way to Deer Creek Falls on one of the most beautiful **hikes** (p227) in the inner gorge
- ouncing down the warm, aquamarine mini-rapids of the **Little Colorado** (p226)
- uting and then slamming through formidable **Lava Falls Rapid** (p226)
- g in the view of an iconic bend in the river from ancient **Puebloan granaries** (p225)

RANCH ELEVATION:	AVERAGE HIGH/LOW TEMPERATURE IN JULY: 106/78°F

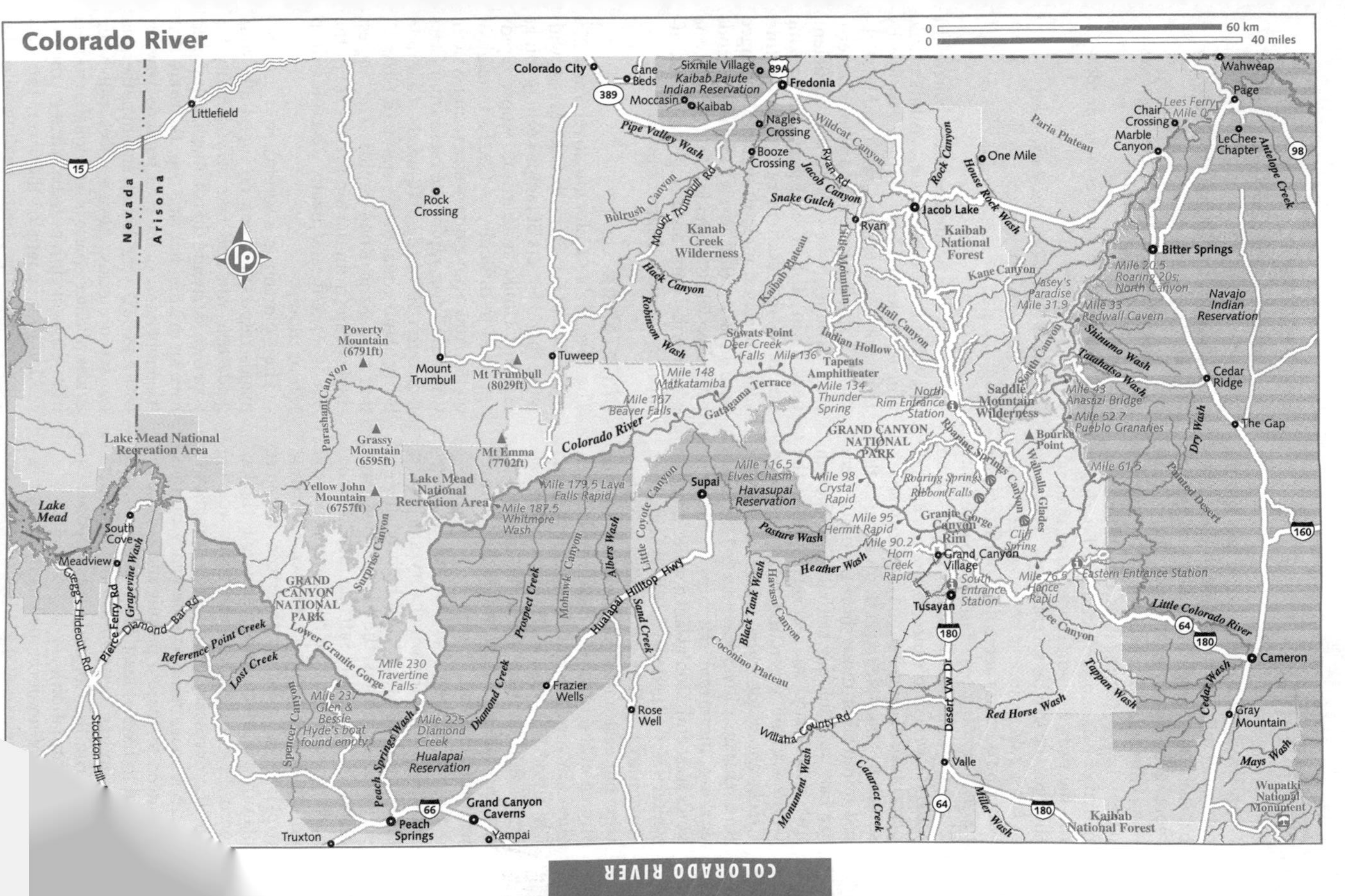
Colorado River
0 60 km
0 40 miles
Nevada
Arizona
Littlefield
Rock Crossing
Colorado City
Cane Beds
Sixmile Village
Kaibab Paiute Indian Reservation
Moccasin
Kaibab
Fredonia
Nagles Crossing
Booze Crossing
Wildcat Canyon
Ryan Rd
Jacob Canyon
Snake Gulch
Ryan
Jacob Lake
Rock Canyon
House Rock Wash
One Mile
Paria Plateau
Kaibab National Forest
Pipe Valley Wash
Bulrush Canyon
Mount Trumbull Rd
Kanab Creek Wilderness
Kaibab Plateau
Little Mountain
Hack Canyon
Robinson Wash
Kane Canyon
Vasey's Paradise Mile 31.9
Chair Crossing
Lees Ferry Mile 0
Marble Canyon
Wahweap
Page
LeChee Chapter
Antelope Creek
Bitter Springs
Mile 20.5 Roaring 20s; North Canyon
Mile 33 Redwall Cavern
Navajo Indian Reservation
Shinumo Wash
Tanhatso Wash
Cedar Ridge
South Canyon
Mile 43 Anasazi Bridge
Mile 52.7 Pueblo Granaries
The Gap
Dry Wash
Poverty Mountain (6791ft)
Parashant Canyon
Mount Trumbull
Mt Trumbull (8029ft)
Tuweep
Sowats Point
Deer Creek Falls
Mile 136
Indian Hollow
Hall Canyon
Tapeats Amphitheater
Mile 134 Thunder Spring
Mile 148 Matkatamiba
Mile 157 Beaver Falls
Gatagama Terrace
North Rim Entrance Station
Saddle Mountain Wilderness
Bourke Point
GRAND CANYON NATIONAL PARK
Grassy Mountain (6595ft)
Mt Emma (7702ft)
Colorado River
Lake Mead National Recreation Area
Lake Mead National Recreation Area
Yellow John Mountain (6757ft)
Mile 179.5 Lava Falls Rapid
Mile 187.5 Whitmore Wash
Little Coyote Canyon
Supai
Mile 116.5 Elves Chasm
Havasupai Reservation
Mile 98 Crystal Rapid
Roaring Springs Canyon
Roaring Springs
Ribbon Falls
Walhalla Glades
Mile 61.5
Painted Desert
Lake Mead
South Cove
Meadview
Grapevine Wash
Gregg's Hideout Rd
Pierce Ferry Rd
Diamond Bar Rd
Stockton Hill
GRAND CANYON NATIONAL PARK
Surprise Canyon
Mohawk Canyon
Prospect Creek
Albers Wash
Sand Creek
Hualapai Hilltop Hwy
Mile 95 Hermit Rapid
Pasture Wash
Mile 90.2 Horn Creek Rapid
Granite Gorge
Canyon Rim
Grand Canyon Village
Cliff Spring
Heather Wash
South Entrance Station
Tusayan
Mile 76.5 Hance Rapid
Eastern Entrance Station
Lee Canyon
Little Colorado River
Cameron
Black Tank Wash
Havasu Canyon
Coconino Plateau
Reference Point Creek
Lost Creek
Lower Granite Gorge
Mile 230 Travertine Falls
Mile 237 Glen & Bessie Hyde's boat found empty
Spencer Canyon
Peach Springs Wash
Mile 225 Diamond Creek
Diamond Creek
Hualapai Reservation
Frazier Wells
Rose Well
Willaha County Rd
Desert Vw Dr
Red Horse Wash
Tappan Wash
Cedar Wash
Gray Mountain
Mays Wash
Wupatki National Monument
Grand Canyon Caverns
Peach Springs
Truxton
Yampai
Monument Wash
Cataract Creek
Valle
Miller Wash
Kaibab National Forest
15
389
89A
98
160
64
180
66

PLANNING

Given two or three weeks, you can run the entire 279 miles of river through the canyon between Lake Powell and Lake Mead. If that's more vacation than you've got, you can raft one of three shorter sections (each 100 miles or less) in four to nine days, or raft a combination of two shorter sections. Choosing to run the river via motorboat rather than raft shortens the trip by several days.

Most rafters join a commercial outing with one of many accredited outfitters (see p224), who offer trips lasting from three to 21 days. Due to their popularity, tours often sell out a year in advance. However, a small percentage of cancellations do occur, so it's sometimes possible to get in on a trip at the last minute. For those short on time, there are half- and full-day rafting trips, though not necessarily on sections within the Grand Canyon. Operating out of Diamond Creek, about four hours from the South Rim, Hualapai River Runners (p225) offers daylong, motorized raft trips in the canyon's west end. Don't want a white-knuckle white-water experience? Wilderness River Adventures (p225) runs half-day rafting trips out east on the silky-smooth 16-mile stretch of the Colorado that flows between Glen Canyon Dam and Lees Ferry. **Xanterra** (☎ 303-287-2757, 888-297-2757; www.xanterra.com) offers full-day trips from the South Rim that bus rafters to Page, where they connect with the float trip.

As part of the Colorado River Management Plan (CRMP), which serves to protect the river and to preserve a high-quality experience for visitors, the park carefully regulates the number of rafts on the Colorado. Each year, a few hundred noncommercial rafting excursions (also known as private trips) are allowed on the river. If you're planning a private trip, *planning* is the key word. Even before you can begin working ut the necessary details, from supplies to ste management to emergency options, need to score a permit and will be re- d to have at least one member of your who has the technical rafting experi- run the Colorado (see opposite for rmation).

re no developed campsites or fa- where along the Colorado. Because this is a wilderness area, where the Leave No Trace ethic applies, visitors should aim to make the least impact possible by removing any waste generated and by sticking to established trails to minimize erosion. Groups on the river are self-sufficient, packing in all food and gear and packing out all waste. Rafters camp on pristine sandy beaches, most of which are fringed with invasive (but lovely) tamarisk stands providing wisps of shade. Usually, only one group will camp on any given beach, affording everyone heaps of privacy.

TOP FIVE RAPIDS

- **Hance** (p225) A thousand yards long with a 30ft drop
- **Horn Creek** (Map p221) A tricky, sticky challenge
- **Hermit** (Map p221) Five giganto waves on this King Kong rapid
- **Crystal** (p226) Another imposing rock-strewn rapid
- **Lava Falls** (p226) The scary, sweet cherry on top

ORIENTATION

The formidable Colorado River runs 279 miles from Lees Ferry to Lake Mead, with more than 160 sets of rapids keeping things exciting. Unlike most rivers, whose rapids are rated in difficulty as Class I through V on the American white-water rating system, Colorado River rapids are rated from Class 1 through 10 (a Class 10 on the Colorado being about equal to the standard Class V; that is, a King Kong rapid). The biggest single drop (from the top to the base of the rapids) is 37ft, and nearly 20 rapids drop 15ft or more.

The Colorado is a serious river and demands respect – if you do everything your guide tells you and take responsibility for your own safety and that of others, you should have an exciting but safe trip. Be aware that the temperature of the river remains between 48°F and 55°F year-round, and hypothermia can set in quickly. Always check with your guides whether a place is far enough removed from the swift current to be safe for a dip.

Along the length of the river, the side canyons and tributaries feeding into the

Colorado provide a wealth of hidden places to explore. Many of the canyon's waterfalls, slot canyons and inviting pools are difficult to reach unless you start from the river, and sights like the Puebloan granaries high in the cliffs above the river can't be seen from the rim. Visits to these remote spots can be the most rewarding part of a river trek.

Put-in & Takeout Points

Put-in and takeout points on the river are obviously limited by accessibility. The only put-in point is at Lees Ferry (p215), 15 miles below the Glen Canyon Dam near Page, Arizona. The takeout point is nearly 300 miles downstream at South Cove on Lake Mead. Though boats must ply the full course, rafters may join, leave or rejoin a river excursion at several points. Rafters doing only the Upper Canyon take out at Phantom Ranch (p132) at Mile 87.5, where they can hike out (usually to the South Rim on the Bright Angel Trail), while others may hike in to do the Middle Canyon. The next takeout point is at Whitmore Wash (Mile 187.5), where rafters are flown up to the rim via helicopter and then usually transferred to a plane for a flight to Las Vegas. Finally, a day's float from South Cove, there's Diamond Creek (Mile 225.6), where a rough road on the Hualapai Reservation (see p150) leads right to the river.

PERMITS & COSTS

When you join a commercial river trip, the operator will take care of your permit. If you plan a private trip, you must apply for your own permit. Before 2006, you would have had to get in line behind the 7500 or so people who were on a 10- to 20-year waitlist! Though the National Park Service (NPS) had a lottery system for a limited number of permits each year, chances were good that you'd be stuck waiting for a decade or so. However, the NPS began transitioning out of the old system in 2006 when they introduced the new weighted lottery system.

To apply for a permit for your group, contact the **Grand Canyon River Permits Office** (☎ 928-638-7843, 800-959-9164; https://npspermits.us; PO Box 129, Grand Canyon, AZ 86023). There's an application fee of $25, and if you're a lucky winner, you'll need to pay an immediate, nonrefundable $400 deposit in order to reserve your slot (the deposit eventually goes toward the cost of the permit, which is $100 per person). Check www.nps.gov/grca/planyourvisit/whitewater-rafting.htm for information on the lottery system, planning tips and a list of reputable outfitters.

BOAT OPTIONS

Do you want to descend the river via oar, paddle or motor power? Your choice will determine the size of the boat, the number of passengers, the noise level, the navigability and stability on the rapids, and the duration of your trip.

The most commonly used boat on the Colorado is an 18ft neoprene raft seating three to five passengers and a guide who rows a set of long wooden oars. Its high center of gravity provides greater stability while giving the guide more power down the big rapids.

Less common is a 14ft neoprene raft on which as many as six passengers and a guide all use single-blade paddles. This style is better suited to high and fast water.

Dories – 17ft rigid, flat-bottomed boats – comfortably seat up to four passengers and a guide who rows a set of long wooden oars. Trips by dory take one or two days longer than rafting trips.

Motorized rafts typically comprise inflatable pontoons lashed together to create a 33ft craft. They seat from eight to 16 passengers and two or three guides.

Hard-shell kayaks are most often used on private trips, while some commercial operators provide inflatable kayaks on request.

WHEN TO GO

The Grand Canyon stretch of the Colorado sees 22,000 annual visitors and is run year-round, though access to some sections is limited under certain conditions. Most commercial trips operate between April and October, with June, July and August being the peak months. While summer draws the most traffic, it also brings more afternoo thunderstorms and searing, triple-di temperatures. The only way to stay co to engage in water fights with fellow r and take quick dips in the face-nu water – controlled releases from Gl yon Dam keep water temperature 48°F and 55°F year-round. Mor in July and August can also floods and increased sedime the water a murky reddish

MATT FAHEY, RIVER GUIDE

River guide and filmmaker Matt Fahey has been guiding for 16 years from the California Salmon to the Futaleufu and Bío-Bío Rivers in Chile, as well as on the Colorado and numerous rivers in between.

What's your favorite aspect about being a river guide? I really like meeting people; I'm gregarious. And generally the people who go out of their way to come here to experience this are pretty cool. Also, I'm a water person…and I enjoy being outdoors, and learning about the geology, botany, ecology and history of the river. **When's your favorite time to be on the river?** October – the light's really good for photography, the days are shorter and it's not so oppressively hot. You can make campfires at night. **Any particularly memorable stories from your time as a guide?** My stories are sort of off-the-cuff – one leads into the next… I remember this one lady from Chicago who'd come on a trip with her husband. She was large and out of shape and had sort of a ho-hum life. Her husband didn't seem that into the trip. She went on a hike up Deer Creek, this really beautiful hike. There's an amazing 120ft waterfall up there, and to get to the source you have to cross this really narrow part – not everyone crosses it. The guide was helping some other people down a ledge so I came over to help her, and she told me, 'I'm so glad I brought my camera, because my friends will never believe I got here!' We have a pretty cool job, bringing people down here. As one of my friends put it, 'Being in the inner gorge makes you feel incredibly special and completely insignificant at the same time.' **Advice to people considering a rafting trip?** Do it.

Veteran river guides suggest you plan a trip in April or between mid-September and mid-October, when air temperatures are mild and rafters can tackle day hikes not possible in summer. Drawbacks of a spring or fall excursion include occasional storms, headwinds and shorter daylight hours. When the weather's cooler and you get splashed, you'll feel it.

RAFTING COMPANIES

Most people join a commercial trip, on which operators provide the boat, all rafting and camping gear, cooking equipment and food. Your multitalented guides wear yet another hat as chefs and prepare all meals. Oar-powered rafting trips cost $200 to $300 per day, while trips via motorboat cost $225 to $325 per day. Children must be 12 or older. The trips are very popular, so make reservations six to 12 months in advance. If
ou feel a little overwhelmed with options,
ntact the Flagstaff-based booking agency
rs & Oceans (off Map p152; ☎ 928-526-4575, 800-
76; www.rivers-oceans.com; 12620 N Copeland Ln,
AZ 86004); it works with all of the com-
unning trips on the Colorado.
listed here are just a sampling of
company offers. Pre- and post-
odations as well as transport
e trip's start/end point may
in the river-trip price. Many companies offer special-interest trips for those interested in subjects as diverse as geology, botany, classical music, art and wine.

Arizona Raft Adventures (Map p152; ☎ 800-786-7238; www.azraft.com; 4050 E Huntington Dr, Flagstaff, AZ 86004; 7-day Upper Canyon hybrid trips/paddle trips $2050/2150, 10-day Full Canyon motor trips $2700) This multigenerational family-run outfit offers paddle, oar, hybrid (with opportunities for both paddling and floating) and motor trips.

Arizona River Runners (☎ 602-867-4866, 800-477-7238; www.raftarizona.com; PO Box 47788, Phoenix, AZ 85068; 8-day Upper Canyon oar trips $1925, 8-day Full Canyon motor trips $2250) Arizona River Runners have been at their game since 1970, offering oar-powered and motorized trips.

Canyon Explorations/Expeditions (☎ 928-774-4559, 800-654-0723; www.canyonexplorations.com; PO Box 310, Flagstaff, AZ 86002; 7-day Upper Canyon trips $1910, 14-day Full Canyon trips $3245) It's possible to kayak the full canyon on paddle trips for an extra $200 (kayakers are accompanied by a kayak guide; and once in a blue moon it offers trips with a string quartet for evening performances on the beach).

Canyoneers (☎ 928-526-0924, 800-525-0924; www.canyoneers.com; PO Box 2997, Flagstaff, AZ 86003; 6-day Upper Canyon oar trips $1695, 7-day Full Canyon motor trips $1895) Some oar-powered trips travel with an historic, restored 'cataract boat' originally used in the '40s.

Colorado River & Trail Expeditions (☎ 801-261-1789, 800-253-7328; www.crateinc.com; PO Box 57575, Salt Lake City, UT 84157; 5-day Upper Canyon oar, paddle or hybrid trips $1715, 9-day motor trips $2515) Offering a range of motorized and oar-powered trips, this outfit also includes transportation to or from Las Vegas.

Diamond River Adventures (☎ 928-645-8866, 800-343-3121; www.diamondriver.com; PO Box 1300, Page, AZ 86040; 5-day Upper Canyon oar trips $1255, 8-day Full Canyon motor trips $1690) Owned and managed by two generations of women in the Diamond family since 1978, this company runs both oar and motorized trips on the river.

Grand Canyon Expeditions (☎ 435-644-2691, 800-544-2691; www.gcex.com; PO Box 0, Kanab, UT 84741; 8-day Full Canyon motor trips $2200, 14-day Full Canyon dory trips $3285) In addition to oar and motor trips, this company also offers dory trips for traveling down the river the old-fashioned way. Transportation to and from Las Vegas is included in all trips.

Hatch River Expeditions (☎ 800-856-8966; www.hatchriverexpeditions.com; HC 67 Box 35, Marble Canyon, AZ 86036; 4-day Upper Canyon motor trips $1085, 7-day Full Canyon motor trips $2075) Hatch has been around since 1929, though of course the motorized rafts are a more recent introduction, and is a reliable company for those seeking a faster trip down the river.

Hualapai River Runners (☎ 928-769-2219, 888-255-9550; www.destinationgrandcanyon.com/runners.html; PO Box 246, Peach Springs, AZ 86434; 1-day motorized trips $330) The only company to do one-day trips on the Colorado. You'll put in at Diamond Creek and upon takeout, will be helicoptered to the rim at Grand Canyon West. Package deals are also offered through Hualapai Lodge (p150) in Peach Springs. Note that Peach Springs is a four-hour drive from the South Rim.

Moki Mac River Expeditions (☎ 801-268-6667, 800-284-7280; www.mokimac.com; PO Box 71242, Salt Lake City, UT 84171; 6-day Upper Canyon oar trips $2130, 8-day Full Canyon motor trips $2650) Trips originate in Las Vegas, and prices include transportation to Vegas and back. Moki Mac is another company that offers dories on some trips.

OARS (☎ 209-736-4677, 800-346-6277; www.oars.com; PO Box 67, Angels Camp, CA 95222; 6-day Upper Canyon oar trips $2255, 15-day Full Canyon dory trips $4720) One of the best outfitters out there, OARS offers oar, paddle and dory trips and offers the option of carbon-offsetting your trip.

Outdoors Unlimited River Trips (off Map p152; ☎ 928-526-4511, 800-637-7238; www.outdoorsunlimited.com; 6900 Townsend Winona Rd, Flagstaff, AZ 86004; 5-day Upper Canyon oar trips $1395, 13-day Full Canyon oar trips $2895) Outdoors Unlimited also offers paddle expeditions but not motorized trips. As with most outfitters, some spring and fall trips stretch one or two days longer to allow more hikes and exploration along the way.

Tour West (☎ 801-225-0755, 800-453-9107; www.twriver.com; PO Box 333, Orem, UT 84059; 9-day Full Canyon motor trips $2230, 13-day Upper & Middle Canyon oar trips $3180) Trips include transportation to Las Vegas at the end of the trip as well as accommodations on the first night. Oar trips take out at Whitmore Wash, where you will be picked up by a helicopter bound for Vegas.

Western River Expeditions (☎ 801-942-6669, 866-904-1160; www.westernriver.com; 7258 Racquet Club Dr, Salt Lake City, UT 84121; 7-day Upper & Middle Canyon motor trips $2430) Taking out at Whitmore Wash, these river trips can last for six or seven days; it also offers half-day to 2-day paddle or inflatable kayak trips starting and ending in Moab, Utah.

Wilderness River Adventures (☎ 928-645-3296, 800-992-8022; www.riveradventures.com; PO Box 717, Page, AZ 86040; 6-day Full Canyon motor trips $2015, 12-day Full Canyon oar trips $3280) Wilderness River Adventures also offers hybrid trips that offer rafters the chance to paddle or float as on an oar-powered trip.

UPPER SECTION: LEES FERRY TO PHANTOM RANCH

(Mile 0 to Mile 87.5)

Beginning at Lees Ferry, where it cuts through the top sedimentary layer of the Moenkopi shale, the upper section of the Colorado River then passes through Marble Canyon and Granite Gorge. The walls of **Marble Canyon** rise higher and higher, quickly exposing layers of rock beneath. Once you hit Mile 20.5, you've entered the **Roaring 20s**, a series of rapids (rated up to 8) that begin with North Canyon Rapid.

At Mile 31.9 you'll see **Vasey's Paradise** springing forth from the wall on your right, a lush green garden nourished from the water escaping the Redwall limestone. Shortly thereafter, the wide, low mouth of the enormous **Redwall Cavern** (Mile 33) appears ahead.

Around Mile 50, the beautiful dark green, burgundy and purple layers of Bright Angel shale appear, as do the doorways of ancient **Pueblo granaries** (Mile 52.7) dating to AD 1100, sitting high above the water. The canyon extends to the confluence with the **Little Colorado River** at Mile 61.5.

This stretch features 28 rapids, 17 c which are rated 5 or higher. Nine rapi drop 15ft or more, including **Hance R** (Mile 76.5), which boasts one of the ri largest single drops, a whopping 30ft Mile 77 the appearance of pink Zo granite intrusions into black Vishr marks the start of **Granite Gorge**.

RUNNING THE LITTLE COLORADO

In drier seasons, the Little Colorado flows down from a mineral spring, which gives the water its tropical warmth and turquoise hue. If the water is clear, the confluence with the big Colorado is a lovely juxtaposition of colors. But hiking about a half-mile up the side canyon will reward you with the chance to hop in and run the tiny mini-rapids of the Little Colorado. It's easy – strap that Personal Flotation Device around your bum (for flotation and protection) and bump on down the fun run.

Side Hike

Boating the Colorado River isn't all about boating. You can stretch your legs too.

NORTH CANYON

Duration 1½ hours round-trip
Distance 2 miles round-trip
Difficulty Moderate
Start/Finish Mile 20.5
Summary Hike up North Canyon to a sculptural pool carved by water.

There isn't much elevation gain involved, but this short hike entails a scramble up a wash to reach the pool. The erosion pattern above the pool has carved its sinuous curves with a design not unlike a three-dimensional topographic map or Georgia O'Keeffe painting.

MIDDLE SECTION: PHANTOM RANCH TO WHITMORE WASH

(Mile 87.5 to Mile 187.5)

Rafters hike from the South Rim to the boat beach near Phantom Ranch to raft **Middle Granite Gorge**, where Tapeats sandstone meets the Vishnu schist.

This section claims the Colorado's biggest white water. It also offers the most technically challenging rapids: **Crystal Rapid** (Mile 98) and the granddaddy **Lava Falls Rapid** (Mile 179.5) with its gut-in-throat drop of 37ft. From Lava [illegible]alls Rapid the next 80 miles downstream are [illegible]eologic marvel. Columnar basalt lines the [illegible]yon walls for thousands of vertical feet.

[illegible] leave Whitmore Wash, rafters take a [illegible]pter from the Hualapai Indian Res[illegible]n (the only place in the canyon [illegible]ers are allowed to land) to the Bar 10 [illegible] miles north of the canyon rim.

The middle section boasts 38 rapids, 23 of which are rated 5 or higher (Crystal and Lava Falls Rapids both rate 10s). Eight rapids drop between 15ft and 18ft. Operators run this stretch between May and July. Between July and September trips continue to **Diamond Creek** (Mile 225). Oar-powered rafts take seven to nine days; motorboats four to five.

Side Hikes

On the Middle Section you can bomb a mossy pool or hike the world's shortest river.

ELVES CHASM

Duration 5 minutes one way
Distance 0.5 miles one way
Difficulty Easy
Start/Finish Mile 116.5
Summary Quick scramble to a pretty grotto.

Ferns, orchids and scarlet monkeyflowers drape the walls of this grotto, where a waterfall tumbles over intricate travertine formations. It takes five minutes to scramble up Royal Arch Creek from the river. Dive into the grotto's pool and swim to the base of the waterfall. Clamber up through the cave to an opening above a moss-draped rocky chute, then jump back into the pool below.

TAPEATS CREEK TO THUNDER SPRING

Duration 4½ hours round-trip
Distance 5 miles round-trip
Difficulty Moderate–difficult
Start/Finish Mile 133.7
Summary Hike to a short river then connect with the Deer Creek Trail.

Thunder Spring, the roaring 100ft waterfall that gushes out of the Muav limestone at Thunder Cave, is the source of Thunder

River, one of the world's shortest rivers. Over its half-mile course it plunges more than 1200ft to the confluence with Tapeats Creek.

Just before Mile 134, follow the **Thunder River Trail** upstream along cottonwood-shaded **Tapeats Creek**, crossing it twice. You'll reach the first crossing, a thigh-deep ford of rushing water, in about 45 minutes. The second crossing, an hour later, is via a fallen log.

Leaving Tapeats Creek, you'll slowly zig-zag up an open slope for 30 minutes to expanding views of **Tapeats Amphitheater** and **Thunder Spring** (3400ft) – you'll hear the roar before seeing the waterfall. Enjoy a picnic in the shade at the base of the fall before retracing your steps (1400ft elevation change).

You can make this a seven-hour near-loop hike by continuing on the Thunder River Trail beyond the waterfall, traversing Surprise Valley and descending the Deer Creek Trail (below) to the Colorado.

DEER CREEK

Duration 2½ hours one way
Distance 3 miles one way
Difficulty Moderate–difficult
Start/Finish Mile 136
Summary One of the inner gorge's finest hikes, with pictographs in a curvy slot canyon, and lush waterfalls.

Downstream from Granite Narrows below Mile 136, **Deer Creek Falls** tumbles into the Colorado. From this welcoming trailhead you head 500ft up a steep, bushy slope to a stunning overlook. From here the trail leads into **Deer Creek Narrows**, an impressive slot canyon whose walls bear remarkable pictographs. The narrows end in an inviting cascade. Above, lush vegetation lines the trail as it meanders along the cottonwood-shaded creek.

The trail crosses the creek and ascends open, rocky slopes to **Deer Creek Spring**, the trail's second waterfall. From here retrace your steps back to the river. Despite having to scramble up and down steep slopes over loose rocks and follow narrow, exposed trails, this hike is one of the inner canyon's best.

MATKATAMIBA

Duration 20 minutes round-trip
Distance 0.8 mile round-trip
Difficulty Moderate
Start/Finish Mile 148
Summary Pull yourself on through the narrows to get to the amphitheater at Matkatamiba.

Matkatamiba, named for a Havasupai family and nicknamed Matkat, is a very narrow Redwall limestone slot canyon that meets the Colorado at Mile 148. So, wet or dry? You must quickly decide how to spend the next 10 minutes heading up to Matkat's acoustically perfect natural **amphitheater**, lined by ferns and wildflowers. On the tricky wet route, you head upstream through the creek – wading when possible, and crawling on all fours and using handholds to pull yourself over slippery boulders.

But hang on, you get wet on the dry route too, since the first 25ft of both routes start by wading through a chest-deep pool, clambering over a boulder as wide as the creek, then wading through yet another pool. Here the dry route leaves the creek and ascends 100ft of steep rock to an exposed trail that overlooks the narrow chasm. At a sculpted curve where the amphitheater emerges, the two routes merge. The wet route is too dangerous to descend, so return via the dry route.

BEAVER FALLS

Duration 4 hours round-trip
Distance 8 miles round-trip
Difficulty Easy–moderate
Start/Finish Mile 157
Summary Explore the blue-green waters of Havasu Canyon from the back side.

The blue-green spring-fed waters of Havasu Creek plunge over a series of five breathtaking waterfalls to the Colorado. Beaver Falls, which tumbles over travertine formations with one prominent fall, is the cascade nearest to the river. Most backpackers hike in only as far as Mooney Falls (p145), s Beaver Falls – 2 miles further – is almc the exclusive domain of rafters.

The slot canyon near Mile 157 doesn't at what lies further up **Havasu Canyon**. A minutes from the Colorado, the rock walls part to reveal wild grapevines, lush ground cover and tall cottonwoods along the level creekside trail. On this gentle hike, you'll spend about 20 minutes in water as you ford Havasu Creek, cross deep pools and wade upstream through knee-deep water. Once through the first and biggest water obstacle – the lovely, chest-deep **Big Kids Pool** – you'll emerge and climb a log staircase through a Muav limestone tunnel. The trail continues upstream to the base of a cliff near the confluence with Beaver Creek. Scramble up the cliff to reach an **overlook** of Beaver Falls. Retrace your steps, relaxing and swimming in the several pools.

LOWER SECTION: WHITMORE WASH TO SOUTH COVE

(Mile 187.5 to beyond Mile 279)

Rafters join the river at Whitmore Wash via helicopter from Bar 10 Ranch. **Lower Granite Gorge**, the third and last of the canyon's sister granite gorges, starts at Mile 215, marked by the appearance of metamorphic and igneous rock. Though it features more flat water than other stretches, this section still boasts great white water, including 11 rapids, seven of which are rated 5 or higher. The two biggest drops are 16ft and 25ft. Oar-powered rafts take four to five days, motorboats three to four days.

In July and August the trip wraps up at **Diamond Creek** (Mile 225). Trips in May and June, however, continue downstream and can catch a glimpse of the water shimmering over the limestone deposits that make **Travertine Falls** (Mile 230) a petrified waterfall.

You might also muse over the unsolved mystery of Glen and Bessie Hyde's disappearance at **Mile 237**, where their flat-bottomed boat was found peacefully floating with everything in it but the Hydes. Eventually, the trip continues beyond the canyon's terminus at **Grand Wash Cliffs** to end at South Cove on Lake Mead. Oar-powered rafts take passengers as far as Mile 240, where they hop on a motorboat for the one-hour ride to South Cove.

Directory

CONTENTS

Accommodations	229
Activities	230
Business Hours	231
Children	231
Climate Charts	231
Courses	232
Discount Cards	233
Festivals & Events	233
Food & Drink	233
Holidays	234
Insurance	234
International Visitors	234
Internet Access	235
Money	235
Post	235
Showers & Laundry	235
Telephone	235
Time	236
Tourist Information	236
Tours	236
Travelers with Disabilities	237
Volunteering	238
Women Travelers	238
Work	239

ACCOMMODATIONS

Accommodations in the park range from historic lodges, with dark beams and overstuffed chairs, to rustic cabins and standard motel rooms.

The South Rim boasts the majority of accommodations, while the North Rim offers just one lodge and one campground. Those descending into the canyon will find a lodge and several backcountry campgrounds. Be sure to book early, particularly if you have a specific lodging in mind (perhaps a rimside cabin on the North Rim or the wonderful Buckey O'Neill Cabin on the South Rim; see p107). If you haven't booked ahead, you still have a chance of finding a great room – a 48-hour advance cancellation policy means that rooms open up all the time (see boxed text, p230).

Budget accommodations in the region range from campgrounds, hostels and roadside motels, with the upper price limit being $75; they are denoted by a $ symbol throughout this book. Quality runs the gamut, and facilities vary widely, with some campgrounds offering nothing but a site to lay your head, while motels might offer amenities like a complimentary continental breakfast. Midrange accommodations ($75 to $150) are marked with a $$ symbol and occupy a place on the hotel or lodge spectrum. Most midrange places have private bathrooms, air-conditioned rooms, TVs, telephones and parking, but of course some have more character than others. (Note that places listed have air-con unless specified otherwise.) Top-end accommodations ($150 to $250) are designated with the $$$ symbol, and if rates soar over $250, they're designated with $$$$. Top-end accommodations in the region tend to be B&Bs or upscale inns, with a resort or two in the mix.

Some hotels maintain the same rates year-round, as at the South Rim lodges. However in the region, room rates drop drastically i the winter. During holidays, special eve and weekends, rates may be higher. C hotels, as well as more atmospheric and B&Bs, often have great online d it's worth shopping around if you last-minute deals outside the pa www.expedia.com, www.travel www.orbitz.com, www.priceline .hotwire.com and www.hotels.

PRACTICALITIES

- Major local papers include the *Arizona Republic, Salt Lake Tribune, Deseret News, Las Vegas Review Journal* and *Las Vegas Sun.*
- Broadcast out of Northern Arizona University, local NPR stations include KNAD (91.7 in Page), KNAG (90.3 at the Grand Canyon) and KNAU (88.7 in Flagstaff).
- The imperial system is used for weights and measures.
- Voltage is 110/120V, 60 cycles.
- Videos are on the NTSC system, which is incompatible with the PAL system.

B&Bs

In the South Rim region, Williams (p140), Sedona (p166) and Flagstaff (p157) have several excellent B&Bs, all of which have their own unique feel. Your hosts at these B&Bs tend to be knowledgeable about the area and offer great advice on things to see and do in their hometowns and at the canyon.

Camping

Free dispersed camping (independent camping at nonestablished sites) is allowed in Kaibab National Forest, which borders both rims. Don't camp within a quarter-mile of the highway or any surface water, within a half-mile of any developed campground or in meadows. Fires are not permitted, and campers are expected to leave no trace (see p250). See the Camping Chart on p131 for a quick overview of campsites on the South Rim; on the North Rim, see p197. Women who are camping solo should also see p238.

Hostels

Noteworthy hostels in the region include the two bright, clean and friendly ones in Flagstaff (p157) and the European-style Grand Canyon Hotel (p141) in Williams.

Hotels & Motels

This being Route 66 territory, some local roadside motels have historical charm emanating from the walls. Others may emanate less pleasant stuff. But generally, motels round these parts can be anything from the tiny, run-down variety or restored, upscale places that stray out of the budget range. For Route 66 flavor, stop in Seligman (p144).

Chain hotels provide the generic but consistent level of quality you would expect, but there are also some great family-run inns and hotels throughout the area.

Lodges & Resorts

Inside the park, lodges are basically the park's hotels, where the rooms are comfortable enough but don't necessarily have the rough-hewn exposed beams and crackling fireplaces the word 'lodge' connotes. However, some lodges – El Tovar (p133) and Grand Canyon Lodge (p197) leap to mind – do have more rustic charm than others.

Resorts are few and far between here, the glaring exception being Sedona's Enchantment Resort (p168) and the lavish casinos (p177) of Las Vegas. Outside Sedona, in Oak Creek Canyon, lie some lovely local inns (p167) that are the perfect antidote to typical resorts.

ACTIVITIES

Hiking is the activity of choice at the Grand Canyon, but it's just one of many pursuits that are possible at the park and in its sur-

LAST-MINUTE ACCOMMODATIONS

It is possible to get last-minute accommodations at the Grand Canyon, even along the South Rim during summer peak season. Your first step should be to call **Xanterra** (☎ 888-297-2757), the official park concessionaire. Reservations may be canceled up to 48 hours in advance, so you never know when a room may be available. If you're looking for same-day accommodations, call the lodges directly through the **North Rim switchboard** (☎ 928-638-2612) or **South Rim switchboard** (☎ 928-638-2631). There's no waiting list, so keep trying.

If you don't find a room on the South Rim, check motels in Tusayan (p138), only 7 miles from the South Entrance, or the motel in Valle (p139), about 15 miles further south. In the middle of nowhere 32 miles east of the East Entrance is the pleasant Cameron Trading Post & Motel (p170), which often has vacancies. Another option is Williams (p140), 59 miles south of the park. Perhaps the safest bet for accommodations is Flagstaff (p157), 80 miles south, where you'll find a couple of wonderful historic hotels, two terrific hostels, B&Bs and lots of independent and chain motels.

The closest places to stay outside the North Rim are Kaibab Lodge (p204), 5 miles from the k entrance, or Jacob Lake Inn (p204), 30 miles north. DeMotte Campground (p204), across from ab Lodge, is arguably the nicest campground in the region and there's also a campground in Lake. If everything is booked, you'll have to head to Kanab (p211), a pleasant town about s north, where you'll find a hostel and several motels with rates from $55 to $90.

lse fails, you can camp for free just about anywhere in Kaibab National Forest (see above) on either rim.

BOOK ACCOMMODATIONS ONLINE

For more accommodations reviews and recommendations by Lonely Planet authors, check out the online booking service at www.lonelyplanet.com. You'll find the true, insider lowdown on the best places to stay. Reviews are thorough and independent. Best of all, you can book online.

rounding areas. Though the park itself isn't such a great mountain-biking venue, there are miles of trails in Kaibab National Forest, Flagstaff and Sedona. Rafters dream of running the Colorado River, while others just wish to fish in it. Winter brings snow-centric opportunities like cross-country skiing and snowshoeing. More relaxed activities include ranger programs, volunteering and drives along the scenic roadways.

For a full rundown of activities in and around the park, see p41.

BUSINESS HOURS

Generally speaking, business hours are from 9am to 5pm. In the bigger towns, supermarkets are open 24 hours a day. Unless there are variances of more than half an hour in either direction, the following serve as regular opening hours throughout this book.

Banks 10am-5pm Mon-Fri
Bars 5pm-2am
Restaurants breakfast 7am-10:30am, lunch 11am-2:30pm, dinner 5-9pm
Shops 9:30am-5:30pm

CHILDREN

Traveling with children during summer in the Southwest means taking it easy. The hot sun, dry climate and high altitude of the region can quickly turn into sunburn, dehydration and fatigue. Break up long car trips with frequent stops, and try not to jam too much activity into one day. See the Kids & Pets chapter (p57) for detailed information and tips for traveling with kids.

CLIMATE CHARTS

Depending on the season and location, weather at and around the Grand Canyon varies wildly. Scorching South Rim summers look nothing like the winter wonderland of the North Rim. See p24 for guidance on planning your trip.

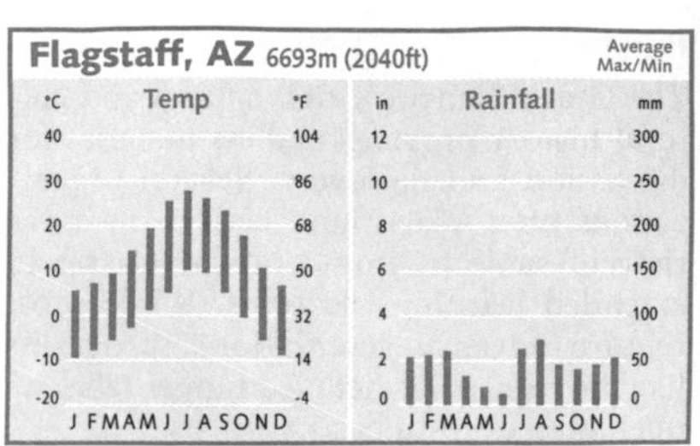

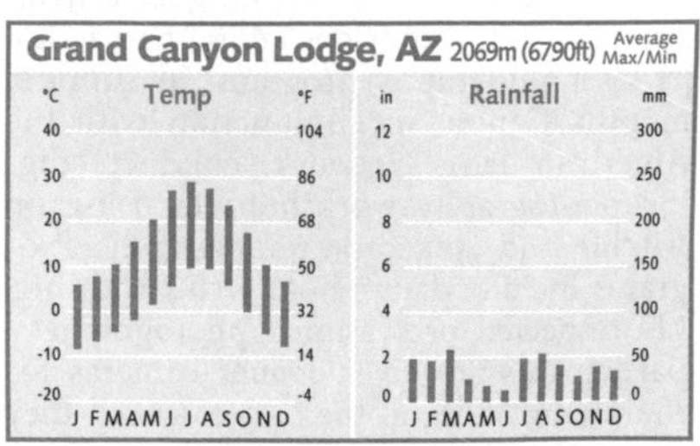

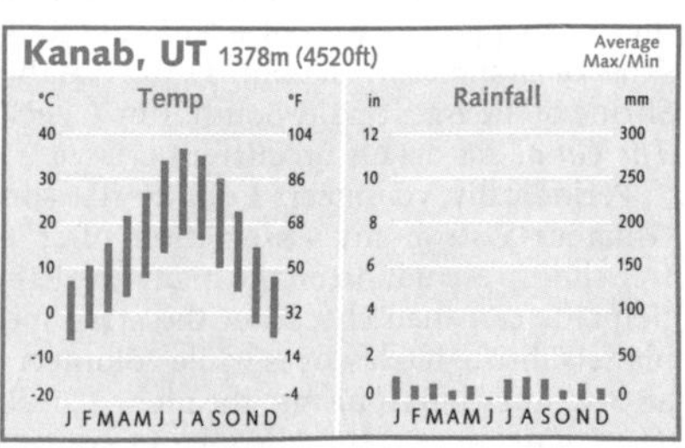

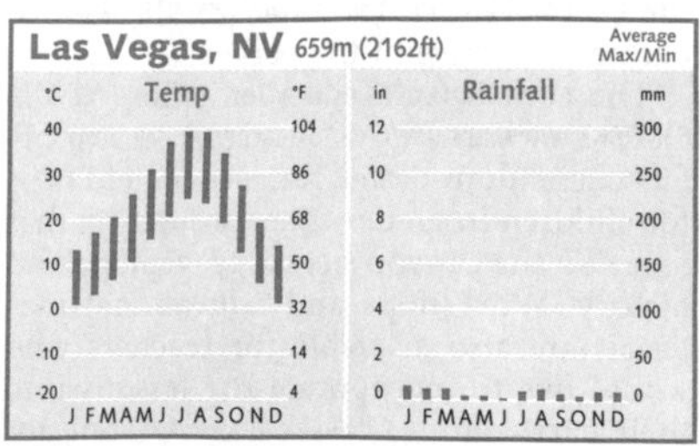

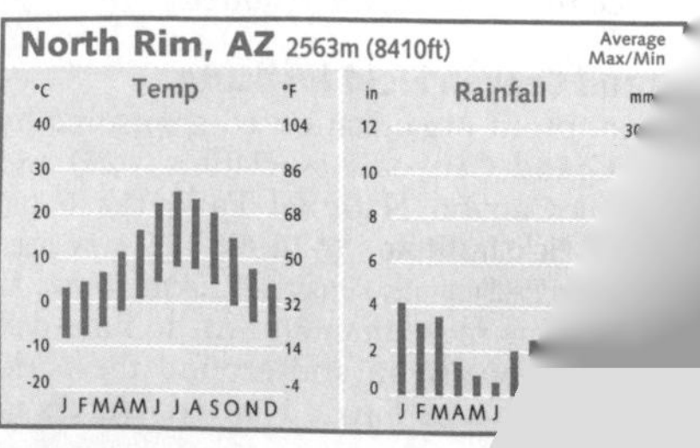

COURSES

The Grand Canyon's rich natural and cultural history provides endless material for discussion and discovery. Several organizations offer year-round classes on a variety of subjects, from one-day classes to extended learning vacations. While most require advance reservations, programs like the regularly scheduled ranger talks are open on a drop-in basis.

If you plan on photographing the canyon (who doesn't?), consider taking part in the park's photography program. In summer months Canon, in conjunction with the American Park Network, conducts digital photography workshops focusing on wildlife and landscape photography. Programs include daily photo walks with hig. hly respected professional photographers; participants are given loaner cameras for the photo walks, at the end of which they receive a CD and prints of the pictures they've snapped. There's also a nightly slide show of Grand Canyon photos shown at the Shrine of the Ages on the South Rim. Check *The Guide* for details on current classes.

Periodically, volunteers from the Tucson Amateur Astronomy Association offer a free slide presentation on the night sky. Participants can then check out the stars and planets through telescopes while volunteers answer questions long into the night. Check *The Guide* for current schedules or contact the **Canyon View Visitor Center** (☎ 928-638-7644) before you arrive in the park.

The **environmental education office** (☎ 928-638-7662; www.nps.gov/grca/forteachers/index.htm) offers curriculum-based, ranger-led field trips for children in grades four through six that focus on the canyon's ecology, geology and history. Workshops and educational materials are also available for teachers who would like to incorporate the lessons into their curriculum. Classes are free, but advance reservations are required.

rand Canyon Field Institute

nonprofit organization co-sponsored by Grand Canyon Association (p29) and d Canyon National Park, the **Grand Field Institute** (☎ 928-638-2485; www.grand /fieldinstitute; PO Box 399, Grand Canyon, AZ rs more than 50 two- to nine-day nually, in and around the park. ctors have advanced degrees in their field of study, have written on their subjects of expertise and have led canyon trips for several years. Courses typically include hikes that range from gentle walks on level terrain to hard-core backpacking excursions.

Subjects on both rims include cultural history, natural history and wilderness studies, women's studies, backcountry medicine and photography expeditions (a fantastic way to explore the backcountry while honing one's skills). The institute also offers service trips, such as Hands-on Archeology, during which participants unearth and catalog artifacts under the guidance of park scientists.

Rates start at $95 for a family (children eight and older) introduction to the canyon, with most courses costing between $300 and $600. Grand Canyon Association Members ($35 annual membership) are eligible for discounts on most institute classes. You can pick up the annual Schedule of Courses from the Canyon View Information Plaza (p104); more detailed course descriptions, as well as information on registration procedures, are available on its website.

Museum of Northern Arizona

The Museum of Northern Arizona organizes an array of customized educational tours led by scientists, writers and artists through its **MNA Ventures program** (☎ 928-774-5213; www.mnaventures.org). Options include hiking, backpacking, river rafting, horseback riding, van tours and hotel-based trips throughout the Southwest.

Northern Arizona University's Grand Canyon Semester

Northern Arizona University offers a three-month interdisciplinary **Grand Canyon Semester** (www.grandcanyonsemester.nau.edu; Northern Arizona University, Grand Canyon Semester, NAU Box 15018, Flagstaff, AZ 86011-5018) that examines the region's geology, history, ecology, geography and politics, among other topics. The 18-credit-hour course, comparable to a semester abroad, spans classroom sessions in Flagstaff, backcountry field trips and rafting excursions down the Colorado. While most participants are college-age students, the course is open to anyone. The semester costs about $4000 for Arizona residents and $9000 for everyone else, including dormitory accommodations and meals.

DISCOUNT CARDS

American Automobile Association (AAA) members can get hotel, rental-car and National Park Pass discounts by showing their cards where such offers are advertised. Backpackers who plan on doing more than one backcountry trek within the space of a year can save on permit fees with a Frequent Hiker Membership (see p45).

Park Passes

If you plan to stay at the park for longer than a week or make a return visit within the year, consider purchasing a $50 Grand Canyon Annual Pass, which allows unlimited visits for 12 months. Better yet, an annual $80 America the Beautiful Annual Pass grants the holder and any accompanying passengers in a private vehicle free admission to any National Park Service (NPS) site in the US, as well as all sites administered by the US Fish & Wildlife Service (USFW), the US Forest Service (USFS) and the Bureau of Land Management (BLM).

If you're 62 or older, purchase the $10 America the Beautiful Senior Pass, which grants access to all NPS, USFW, USFS and BLM sites and is good for the holder's lifetime. An America the Beautiful Access Pass is free to US residents who are permanently disabled, and offers the same benefits as the Senior Pass; you must offer medical proof of your disability to be eligible.

All passes are available at the park entrance stations. The Senior and Access Passes must be purchased in person at a park, but you can get an America the Beautiful Pass in advance with a credit card (☎ 888-275-8747; http://store.usgs.gov/pass/). It takes up to two weeks to receive and there's an additional cost for shipping; priority shipping (five business days) is also available.

Senior Cards

Travelers aged 50 and older can receive rate cuts and benefits in many places. Inquire about discounts at hotels, museums and restaurants before you make reservations or purchase tickets. With an America the Beautiful Senior Pass (above), US citizens aged 62 or over receive free admission to national parks and a 50% discount on camping fees (reserve at www.recreation.gov). Discounts may also be available to over-50s holding membership cards with the **American Association of Retired Persons** (AARP; ☎ 888-687-2277; www.aarp.org; 601 E St NW, Washington, DC 20049; annual membership for individual plus spouse $12.50).

Student & Youth Cards

Museums and theatres often give discounts if you flash a student ID. Some tour operators in the area also give student discounts.

FESTIVALS & EVENTS

Rich with culture, the festivals and special events of the Southwest run from the artistic to the agricultural. Check out p25 for events at the Grand Canyon, and p151 and p210 for events beyond the rims.

FOOD & DRINK

Meals are often an afterthought on a trip to the Grand Canyon, but the park does provide a decent variety of dining options. On either rim you can choose between basic cafeteria eats or upscale continental cuisine. El Tovar and Grand Canyon Lodge offer creative menus with surprisingly good food, although their top-end prices make them ideal for a special occasion rather than every day dining. Prices listed here are for dinner – expect lower prices for breakfast and lunch. Eating listings are detailed in order of ascending price ranges: budget (mains less than $10), midrange (mains from $10 to $20) and top end ($20 or more).

Groceries

Picnicking is a great way to not only save money, but also enjoy some quiet moments. If you're visiting the park for more than a day, buy a small cooler to stow picnic supplies and keep drinks cold; consider a backpack-style cooler so you can easily carry it with you. In-room refrigerators are a rarity in park lodges, but you can get ice at Canyon Village Marketplace (p133), on the South Rim; Desert View Marketplace (p133), at the East Entrance near Desert View Campground; and the North Rim General Store (p198).

Canyon Village Marketplace is the park's only full-size grocery. Desert View Marketplace sells basic grocery items, including canned goods, milk, cereal, beer and cheese. You're best off buying groceries before arriving at the park, as prices are much higher here.

The North Rim General Store offers a small but thorough selection of groceries. You'll find steak, frozen meat, eggs, cheese, diapers, beer, wine and firewood, among other essentials. The closest full grocery store is in Kanab, a 90-minute drive north.

Local Liquor Laws

In Utah, you'll encounter some of the weirdest liquor laws in the country. As everywhere in the US, you must be aged 21 to drink legally. Grocery stores sell near-beer (which doesn't exceed 3.2% alcohol content) seven days a week, but state-run liquor stores sell beer, wine and spirits Monday through Saturday. Lounges and taverns only serve near-beer – stronger drinks are served at restaurants and 'private clubs.' To enter a private club, you must be a member; a temporary membership costs $4 and is valid for three weeks, entitling you to invite seven guests. At restaurants, servers aren't permitted to offer alcoholic drinks or show you a drink menu unless you specifically ask. If you do order a drink, you must also order food, but a snack or appetizer will do. Wherever you're drinking, you can only order one drink for yourself at a time.

Note also that alcohol is prohibited on all Native American reservations and cannot be transported on or through the reservations.

HOLIDAYS

During the winter holiday season (December 24 through January 2), accommodations can get extremely tight at the canyon. Things can also get hectic during the summer high season between Memorial Day and Labor Day. Traffic gets worse around the South Rim on holidays, and people should make reservations for special transportation options like the Grand Canyon Railway trains. Refer to p24 for more seasonal information.

New Year's Day January 1
Martin Luther King, Jr Day 3rd Monday in January
Presidents Day 3rd Monday in February
Easter Late March or early April
Memorial Day Last Monday in May
Independence Day July 4
Labor Day 1st Monday in September
Columbus Day 2nd Monday in October
Veterans Day November 11
Thanksgiving Day 4th Thursday in November
Christmas Day December 25

INSURANCE

The US is an expensive country in which to get sick, crash your car or be robbed, so protect yourself. For car insurance, see p243; for health insurance, see p247. To insure yourself from theft from your car, consult your homeowner's (or renter's) insurance policy before leaving home.

Worldwide travel insurance is available at www.lonelyplanet.com/travel_services. You can buy, extend and claim online any time – even if you're already on the road traveling.

INTERNATIONAL VISITORS

Getting into the US can be a bureaucratic nightmare, depending on your country of origin. For up-to-date information about visas and immigration, check with the **US Department of State** (☎ 202-663-1225; www.travel.state.gov).

Most foreign visitors to the US need a visa, but there's a visa waiver program (VWP) in which citizens of certain countries may enter the US for stays of 90 days or less without first obtaining a visa. At press time, VWP countries include Andorra, Australia, Austria, Belgium, Brunei, Denmark, Finland, France, Germany, Iceland, Ireland, Italy, Japan, Liechtenstein, Luxembourg, Monaco, the Netherlands, New Zealand, Norway, Portugal, San Marino, Singapore, Slovenia, Spain, Sweden, Switzerland and the UK.

As visa waiver status is constantly in flux, contact the Department of State or the **Department of Homeland Security** (www.dhs.gov) for current visa requirements.

Regardless of visa status, your passport should be valid for at least another six months after you leave the US. Visa applications occasionally require proof of financial stability or guarantees from a US resident (particularly for visitors from developing countries), as well as proof of 'binding obligations' that will guarantee that you return to your home country. Because of such requirements, foreign visitors are usually better off applying for US visas before leaving their country of origin.

See p243 for information on international permits and licenses. You cannot obtain an international license once you've arrived in the US.

INTERNET ACCESS

Midrange and top-end hotel rooms usually have high-speed cable, DSL or wireless internet access. Nowadays, many lower-end motels and lodges offer free wi-fi. If you're traveling with a notebook or hand-held computer, be aware that your modem may not work once you leave your home country. The safest option is to buy a reputable 'global' modem before you leave home, or buy a local PC-card modem if you're spending an extended time in any one country. For more information on traveling with a portable computer, see www.teleadapt.com.

If you aren't traveling with your own computer, common places to find internet access are public libraries (where access is usually limited but free) or at local cafés for a small fee. It's usually a good idea not to conduct sensitive business like online banking from public terminals because of security concerns like keystroke-capturing software. You could also consider setting up a trip-specific email address for your travels.

In places where internet access is available, we've used the 🖳 symbol. Look for internet-access points in the Information sections of individual regions. Also see p28 for internet resources.

MONEY

Most hotels, restaurants and shops take cash and credit cards. At restaurants, it's customary to tip waitstaff 15% to 20% of the pretax bill, and tip bartenders $1 per drink as these hardworking folks rely on tips for their livelihoods. Prices in this book are quoted in the local currency, US dollars ($), unless otherwise stated. See p26 for more information on costs.

The only ATM at the park is on the South Rim at the **Chase Bank** (☎ 928-638-2437; 🕑 9am-5pm Mon-Thu, 9am-6pm Fri) in Market Plaza (see p104). During banking hours, you can exchange foreign currency and traveler's checks for US dollars here, but the ATM is open 24 hours a day. There's neither a bank nor an ATM on the North Rim. The nearest ATM is in Jacob Lake, 44 miles north of the lodge.

POST

You'll find a full-service **post office** (☎ 928-638-2512; 🕑 9am-4:30pm Mon-Fri, 11am-3pm Sat) on the South Rim in Market Plaza (see p104). You can buy stamps from machines in the lobby, which is open daily from 5am to 10pm. The concierge at El Tovar also sells stamps.

There's a **postal window** (🕑 11am-4pm Mon-Fri, 8am-1pm Sat) on the covered boardwalk beside the lodge on the North Rim.

SHOWERS & LAUNDRY

The **Camper Services Building** (🕑 6am-11pm) near Mather Campground on the South Rim provides a coin laundry and pay showers. The last laundry load must go in by 9:45pm.

Pay shower and laundry **facilities** (🕑 7am-7pm) on the North Rim are on the access road leading to the campground. Water must be pumped up more than 3000ft from Roaring Springs, so use these services sparingly.

TELEPHONE

Cell-phone reception in the park can be sketchy, depending on your provider network. No one gets reception below the rim, where satellite phones are the only way to call out of the canyon. You can find pay phones in lodge lobbies at the park, as well as at Market Plaza (see p104) and Canyon View Information Plaza (p104) on the South Rim. On the North Rim, find pay phones at the general store and outside the main entrance to the lodge. See the inside back cover for dialing codes and emergency numbers.

LOST & FOUND

If you lose something in or near the lodges or restaurants on the South Rim, call the **main switchboard** (☎ 928-638-2631) and ask to be connected to the place where you last had the item. Otherwise, ask to be connected to lost and found, where all items are eventually returned. If you lose something elsewhere on the South Rim, call the Grand Canyon National Park **Lost and Found Office** (☎ 928-638-7798). The park asks that you turn in found items to Canyon View Information Plaza (p104).

If you lose an item anywhere on the North Rim, contact the **visitors center** (☎ 928-638-7864) or **Grand Canyon Lodge** (☎ 928-638-2612).

PARK POLICIES & REGULATIONS

Bicycles

Bicycles are allowed only on roads open to other vehicles. You cannot take them on any trails in the park, except for the Greenway Trail on the South Rim.

Campfires

This is extremely dry country, and the slightest spark may cause a devastating wildfire. Open fires are only permitted in fire pits at North Rim, and at Desert View and Mather Campgrounds on the South Rim; use camp stoves at other campgrounds and in the backcountry. Throw water on all fires, including those in fire grills, and make sure they're completely out when you leave.

Pets

Dogs are permitted on developed South Rim trails but must be leashed at all times. Pets are not allowed in park lodges or below the rim, unless they are certified service dogs. Pets are allowed in the campgrounds. For more information, see p62.

Weapons

Weapons of any kind, including guns and bows, are prohibited on park grounds.

Wilderness Permits & Regulations

A backcountry permit is required for all overnight camping below the rim and on parkland outside of designated campgrounds. See p44 for details on fees and procedures for obtaining a permit.

Wildlife

It's illegal to feed any wildlife in the park, including jump-in-your-lap squirrels and forward ravens. This is not only for your safety (did you know squirrels can carry bubonic plague?), but also for the safety and well-being of the animals.

TIME

Arizona is on Mountain Standard Time (MST), but the state does not observe Daylight Savings Time (DST). Daylight Savings Time starts on the second Sunday in March and ends on the second Sunday in November. In March, clocks are set ahead one hour; in November, they are set back an hour.

If that isn't confusing enough, the Navajo Reservation *does* observe Mountain Daylight Savings Time during the summer, which means that it is an hour ahead of Arizona during this time and on the same time as Utah and New Mexico.

When it's noon in June in Arizona, it's noon in San Francisco (and Vancouver), 2pm in Chicago, 3pm in New York (and Toronto), 8pm in London and 5am the next day in Melbourne (and Sydney).

TOURIST INFORMATION

Tourist info is easy to come by on either rim and in the surrounding towns. Refer to individual towns and regions for local tourist information.

Canyon View Visitor Center (South Rim) (☎ 928-638-7644)

North Rim Visitor Center (☎ 928-638-7864)

TOURS

Among the best organized tours are those offered via the Grand Canyon Field Institute (p232) and the Museum of Northern Arizona (p232). See also the Activities chapter (p41), which lists the best companies that provide activity-based tours in the region.

The following tours of the South Rim stop at viewpoints and selected sights; most include time for a walk along the rim. Airlines in Tusayan offer scenic canyon tours from Las Vegas (see p128). For details on guided rafting trips, see p224 and the Hualapai Reservation, see p150.

From Flagstaff & Williams

American Dream Tours (☎ 928-527-3369, 888-203-1212; www.americandreamtours.com; day tours adult/child $98/69) Departing from Flagstaff, Williams and Tusayan, each tour takes no more than 14 people per van on all-inclusive one-day trips of the South Rim.

Grand Canyon Railway Does unique train rides to the South Rim, as well as combination train/bus tours. See p244.

Grand Canyon Tours of Splendor (☎ 928-525-2675, 866-525-2675; www.grandcanyonsplendor.com; day tours adult/child $109/79) Has particularly comfortable vans; rates include a ticket for the IMAX movie and a complimentary postcard of you at the Grand Canyon.

Marvelous Marv's (☎ 928-707-0291; www.marvelousmarv.com; per person $85) The best personalized tours around are run by this quirky local. He'll pick you up from your hotel or campground in or around Williams to take you for a full-day tour at the South Rim in his air-conditioned 15-passenger van. Cash, traveler's checks or personal US checks only.

Open Road Tours (☎ 877-226-8060, 800-766-7117; www.openroadtours.com; day tours adult/child $89/45) From Flagstaff, Open Road offers a one-day tour of the park and Navajo Reservation, including a stop at the Cameron Trading Post.

From Las Vegas

Air packages are a popular way to do day tours of the canyon from Las Vegas. For helicopter or plane tours of the canyon, see p180.

Grand Canyon Tour Company (☎ 800-222-6966; www.grandcanyontourcompany.com) Go with a one-day bus trip to the South Rim ($160 for two if booked online), or an air/bus combo tour ($430 for two if booked online); a wide variety of tours are offered on its website.

Sundance Helicopters (☎ 800-653-1881; www.helicoptour.com) Offers trips further west to the Hualapai Reservation, which isn't subject to the same above-the-rim air regulations enforced elsewhere in the canyon; choose from a quick flight down to the river and back (about $89 per person) or a full-day excursion that includes your flight into the canyon and a three-hour rafting trip on the Colorado ($389).

From Kanab

For customized, 4WD photography tours of remote North Rim spots, contact **Terry's Camera Trading Co** (Map p209; ☎ 435-644-5981; 19 W Center St; 8am-6pm Mon-Sat). Terry has been exploring and photographing the canyon and the surrounding desert and plateau country for more than 25 years. Allen's Guided Tours (p203) leads horseback riding tours in Kaibab National Park (North Rim).

TRAVELERS WITH DISABILITIES

Grand Canyon National Park offers many attractions and services for travelers with disabilities. Ask for an updated *Accessibility Guide* when you enter the park, which clearly maps out all the handicapped-accessible bathrooms, showers, campsites, guestrooms and parking lots, describes accessibility at overlooks, and identifies 'windshield view' spots along the South Rim. You can also download a PDF version of the *Accessibility Guide* from the park website (go to www.nps.gov/grca and click through the Plan Your Visit link to Things to Know Before You Come, then Accessibility).

Around the Southwest, public buildings are required to be wheelchair accessible and to have appropriate restroom facilities. Public transportation must be accessible to all, and most chain hotels have rooms or suites for disabled travelers. Telephone companies provide relay operators for the hearing impaired. Many banks provide ATM instructions in braille, curb ramps are common and many busy intersections have audible crossing signals.

Throughout this guide, we've used the ♿ symbol to indicate places with wheelchair access, but which do not necessarily have accessible restrooms.

Useful organizations for disabled travelers include the following:

Mobility International USA (☎ 541-343-1284; www.miusa.org; 132 E Broadway, Suite 343, Eugene, OR 97401) Advises disabled travelers on mobility issues.

Society for Accessible Travel & Hospitality (☎ 212-447-7284; www.sath.org; Suite 605, 347 Fifth Ave, New York, NY 10016) Publishes a quarterly magazine and provides information on travel for the disabled.

Activities

Mule rides are provisionally accessible with advance notice. Contact the **Bright Angel Transportation Desk** (☎ 928-638-2631), and they'll connect you with the barn to discuss your needs with the head wrangler. To secure a bus tour, call at least one week in advance to reserve a seat. The wheelchair-accessible bus has only 30 seats and the standard buses about 56; if a handicapped person books a tour, the concessionaire can limit the number of reservations.

River concessionaires can in many cases accommodate people with disabilities, even on multiday white-water trips. Call **Grand Canyon River Trip Information** (☎ 800-959-9164) for info. If you're not ready for rapids, **Xanterra** (☎ 888-297-2757) offers a bus trip to Page, where rafters can do a half-day float from Glen Canyon to Lees Ferry. Accessible accommodations can be arranged in advance.

Getting Around

Many sites along the South Rim are readily accessible. Free loaner wheelchairs are usually available at the Canyon View Information Plaza (p104). The 2-mile stretch from Mather Point to Bright Angel Lodge is easiest for those who have difficulty walking or use a wheelchair, and a golf cart runs regularly between the information plaza and Mather Point (about 200yd). The Powell, Hopi and Pima Overlooks on Hermit Rd and the Yaki, Grandview, Moran and Desert View Overlooks on Desert View Dr all offer wheelchair access. See p109 for more about these overlooks.

All lodges except Bright Angel offer accessible guestrooms, and Mather, Desert View and Trailer Village Campgrounds include a few accessible campsites. Hopi House is accessible only through a 29in-wide door, while steps and small doors at Kolb and Lookout Studios are more problematic. At the Tusayan Ruins & Museum, a level, paved trail leads into the museum and around the pueblo dwelling.

Descending into the canyon is a different story. The Bright Angel (South Rim) and North Kaibab (North Rim) trails are the least rocky, but even these will pose a challenge. Use extreme caution. Anyone wishing to take a certified service dog below the rim must first check in at the Backcountry Information Center on either rim.

On the North Rim, the best overlook is Cape Royal, where a fairly level, 0.6-mile paved trail leads to several canyon viewpoints. There's a wheelchair-accessible viewing platform at Point Imperial. Public spaces at Grand Canyon Lodge are easily negotiable by people with limited mobility, and four guestrooms have been specially modified. The North Rim Campground provides two accessible sites with picnic tables and one bathroom.

Limited funding has delayed purchase of wheelchair-accessible, alternative-fuel shuttles to replace the current shuttles. At press time, most of the shuttles on the green Village Route and about half those on the red Hermits Rest Route could accommodate wheelchairs. If you want to be assured a wheelchair-accessible shuttle, call ☎ 928-638-0591 a day in advance. Ask at the Canyon View Information Plaza (p104) or any of the transportation desks for a permit to drive a private car into shuttle-only areas. To obtain a permit for designated parking, inquire at an entrance station, Canyon View or the Yavapai Observation Station.

VOLUNTEERING

There are loads of opportunities to volunteer at and around Grand Canyon National Park, for one-day projects or longer-term endeavors. Volunteers can work on trail maintenance, restore grasslands, pull invasive plants from the inner gorge, train to be an interpretive ranger or work with youth organizations.

To find out about volunteer opportunities, see p54.

WOMEN TRAVELERS

Generally speaking, though women travelers should take the same common-sense precautions they would anywhere in the country, Grand Canyon National Park and its surrounding areas are safe places for women traveling solo.

If you feel uncomfortable hiking alone, stick to well-trodden trails where you're likely to meet people at campsites, or try to hook up with a group or companion before hitting the trail; national-park visitor centers and ranger stations often have bulletin boards specifically for this purpose. One place where it's currently inadvisable to travel alone is Havasu Canyon (see boxed text, p148).

If you are assaulted, you do not need to go directly to the police in order to get help. The best course of action is often to call a rape-crisis hotline; contact numbers are usually listed in local telephone directories. Rape-crisis center staff act as a link between medical, legal and social-service systems, advocating on behalf of survivors to ensure their rights are respected and their needs are addressed. Outside urban areas, you can go to the nearest hospital for help first, then decide later whether or not to call the police.

Useful organizations:

National Organization of Women (NOW; ☎ 202-331-0066; www.now.org; 3rd fl, 1100 H St NW, Washington, DC 20005) Good resource for information and can refer you to local chapters.

Planned Parenthood (☎ 212-541-7800; www.plannedparenthood.org; 26 Bleeker St, New York, NY 10012) Can refer you to clinics around the region and advise on medical issues.

WORK

Seasonal work at the park tends to be low-paying service jobs that are mostly filled by young people. For the best shot at seasonal employment, apply well ahead of time through the **NPS website** (www.sep.nps.gov) or **US Federal Government** (www.usajobs.com). Planning ahead is essential, whether you are applying for NPS or park concessionaire jobs – applications for summer jobs are typically due during December and January.

If you are not a US citizen, you must apply for a work visa from the US embassy in your home country before you leave. The type of visa varies, depending on how long you're staying and the kind of work you plan to do. Generally, you need either a J-I visa, which you can obtain by joining a visitor-exchange program (issued mostly to students for work in summer camps), an H-1B visa for skilled professionals or an H-2B visa, when you are sponsored by a US employer. The latter two can be difficult to procure unless you can show that you already have a job offer from an employer who considers your qualifications unique and not readily available in the US.

Transportation

CONTENTS

Getting There & Away	**240**
Air	240
Bus	241
Car & Motorcycle	242
Train	244
Getting Around	**245**
Bicycle	245
Shuttle	245
Car & Motorcycle	245

The adventure of the quintessential road trip defines how most people travel this region. Long hours in the car, driving down the open highways of the Southwest, ultimately brings visitors to Grand Canyon National Park. But many others fly into local air hubs, rent cars and go from there.

However you choose to get here and get around, flights, tours and more can be booked online at www.lonelyplanet.com/travel_services.

GETTING THERE & AWAY

Travelers to the Grand Canyon usually fly or drive to a gateway city, before continuing to the national park via train, car, bus or occasionally on foot or snowshoe.

AIR

Airports

Main air hubs to the park are Las Vegas, Nevada; Phoenix, Arizona; Salt Lake City, Utah; and Albuquerque, New Mexico.

In terms of passenger traffic, **McCarran International Airport** (LAS; Map p176; ☎ 702-261-5211; www.mccarran.com; 5757 Wayne Newton Blvd, Las Vegas, NV 89119) is the sixth busiest airport in the US, but it's also one of the country's more efficient airports. Las Vegas is 290 miles from the South Rim and 277 miles from the North Rim. A 10-minute drive from the Vegas Strip, McCarran is a hub for America West Airlines, Southwest Airlines and US Airways, among others. There are several advantages to flying into Vegas. For one, it's closer to the North Rim, and in order to

CLIMATE CHANGE & TRAVEL

Climate change is a serious threat to the ecosystems that humans rely upon, and air travel is the fastest-growing contributor to the problem. Lonely Planet regards travel, overall, as a global benefit but believes we all have a responsibility to limit our personal impact on global warming.

Flying & Climate Change

Pretty much every form of motorized travel generates CO_2 (the main cause of human-induced climate change) but planes are far and away the worst offenders, not just because of the sheer distances they allow us to travel, but because they release greenhouse gases high into the atmosphere. The statistics are frightening: two people taking a return flight between Europe and the US will contribute as much to climate change as an average household's gas and electricity consumption over a whole year.

Carbon Offset Schemes

Climatecare.org and other websites use 'carbon calculators' that allow travelers to offset the level of greenhouse gases they are responsible for with financial contributions to sustainable travel schemes that reduce global warming – including projects in India, Honduras, Kazakhstan and Uganda.

Lonely Planet, together with Rough Guides and other concerned partners in the travel industry, support the carbon offset scheme run by climatecare.org. Lonely Planet offsets all of its staff and author travel.

For more information check out our website: www.lonelyplanet.com.

> **THINGS CHANGE...**
>
> The information in this chapter is particularly vulnerable to change. Check directly with the airline or a travel agent to make sure you understand how a fare (and ticket you may buy) works and be aware of the security requirements for international travel. Shop carefully. The details given in this chapter should be regarded as pointers and are not a substitute for your own careful, up-to-date research.

attract the gambling set, airlines offer cheap flights and packages to the city year-round. Driving to the park from Vegas is also easy – aside from delays around Hoover Dam, traffic is minimal to either rim.

Phoenix is 220 miles from the South Rim and 335 miles from the North Rim. Three miles southeast of downtown, **Sky Harbor International Airport** (PSH; ☎ 602-273-3300; www.phxskyharbor.com) is another hub for America West and Southwest Airlines. Phoenix offers more connecting airlines and routes, but you risk getting caught in traffic. Once you do escape the city, the drive north on Highways 89 and Alt 89 to Flagstaff is beautiful, passing through several mountain towns and Sedona's celebrated red-rock country. You could easily spend a few leisurely days driving to the park. For a faster option, America West Express offers several flights a day from Phoenix to Flagstaff, 80 miles south of the South Rim.

Along with Las Vegas, **Salt Lake City International Airport** (SLC; ☎ 801-575-2400; www.slcairport.com; 776 N Terminal Dr, Salt Lake City, UT 84116) is a great place to fly into if you're headed for the North Rim. It's served by several airlines, including Delta, Continental, Southwest and United, and has a reputation for being one of the more low-stress airports of its size in the US.

Albuquerque International Sunport Airport (ABQ; ☎ 505-244-7700; www.cabq.gov/airport; 2200 Sunport Blvd SE, Albuquerque, NM 87106) is served by eight major domestic carriers as well as by regional airlines. Of the four airports in the region, this is the least convenient to the Grand Canyon, but it's a good option for those planning on spending time in this part of the Southwest.

Airlines

Discount travel agents in the US are known as consolidators. San Francisco is the ticket consolidator capital of America, although some good deals can be found in Los Angeles, New York and other big cities.

The following agencies are recommended for online bookings:

CheapTickets (www.cheaptickets.com)
Expedia Travel (www.expedia.com)
Lowestfare.com (www.lowestfare.com)
Orbitz (www.orbitz.com)
STA Travel (www.sta.com) For travelers under the age of 26.
Travelocity (www.travelocity.com)

FLIGHTS FROM USA & CANADA

Air Canada (☎ 888-247-2262; www.aircanada.ca)
Alaska Airlines (☎ 800-252-7522; www.alaskaair.com)
America West Airlines (☎ 800-235-9292; www.americawest.com)
American Airlines (☎ 800-223-5436; www.aa.com)
ATA (☎ 800-225-2995; www.ata.com)
Continental Airlines (☎ 800-523-3273; www.continental.com)
Delta (☎ 800-221-1212; www.delta.com)
Frontier (☎ 800-432-1359; www.flyfrontier.com)
JetBlue (☎ 800-538-2583; www.jetblue.com)
Mesa Air (☎ 800-637-2247; www.mesa-air.com)
Northwest Airlines (☎ 800-225-2525; www.nwa.com)
Southwest Airlines (☎ 800-435-9792; www.southwest.com)
United Airlines (☎ 800-241-6522; www.united.com)
US Airways (☎ 800-428-4322; www.usairways.com)

FLIGHTS FROM UK & IRELAND

Aer Lingus (☎ 800-223-6537; www.aerlingus.com)
British Airways (☎ 800-247-9297; www.britishairways.com)
Virgin Atlantic (☎ 800-862-8621; www.virginatlantic.com)

FLIGHTS FROM AUSTRALIA & NEW ZEALAND

Air New Zealand (☎ 800-262-1234; www.airnz.co.nz)
Qantas (☎ 800-227-4500; www.qantas.com.au)

BUS

Greyhound (☎ 928-774-4573, 800-229-9424; www.greyhound.com) stops at Flagstaff to and from Albuquerque ($57, six hours), Las Vegas ($52/61 weekdays/weekends, 4½ hours), Los Angeles ($68, 13 hours) and Phoenix ($28, three hours). From the Flagstaff train depot, a shuttle heads to the park daily.

Open Road Tours (☎ 928-226-8060, 800-766-7117; www.openroadtours.com) offers shuttles from Phoenix's Sky Harbor to Flagstaff that continue on to Williams and the Grand Canyon's South Rim.

CAR & MOTORCYCLE

From Las Vegas, it's an easy drive to either rim. To get to the North Rim, head north on I-15 into Utah. Just past St George, take Hwy 9 east to Hurricane. You can either continue on Hwy 9 through Zion National Park, then connect with Hwy 89 down through Kanab to Fredonia, or take Hwy 59/389 southeast to Fredonia and connect with Alt 89. Alt 89 heads southeast to Jacob Lake, where Hwy 67 leads 30 miles to the park entrance station. The most direct route to the South Rim is Hwy 93 south to I-40, then east to Williams, where you'll turn north on Hwy 64 to Valle, then follow Hwy 180 into the park.

From Phoenix, take I-17 north to Flagstaff and continue on Hwy 180 north to the South Rim. Another option is to take Hwy 60 northwest to Hwy 89 through Prescott, then connect with Alt 89, which winds northeast through forested mountains to Sedona. From there it's a short jaunt north through Oak Creek Canyon to Flagstaff. It is a beautiful drive, but traffic can be brutal in summer, particularly around Sedona. If you're continuing to the North Rim from Flagstaff, take Hwy 89 north. (At Cameron, Hwy 64 leads 32 miles west to the South

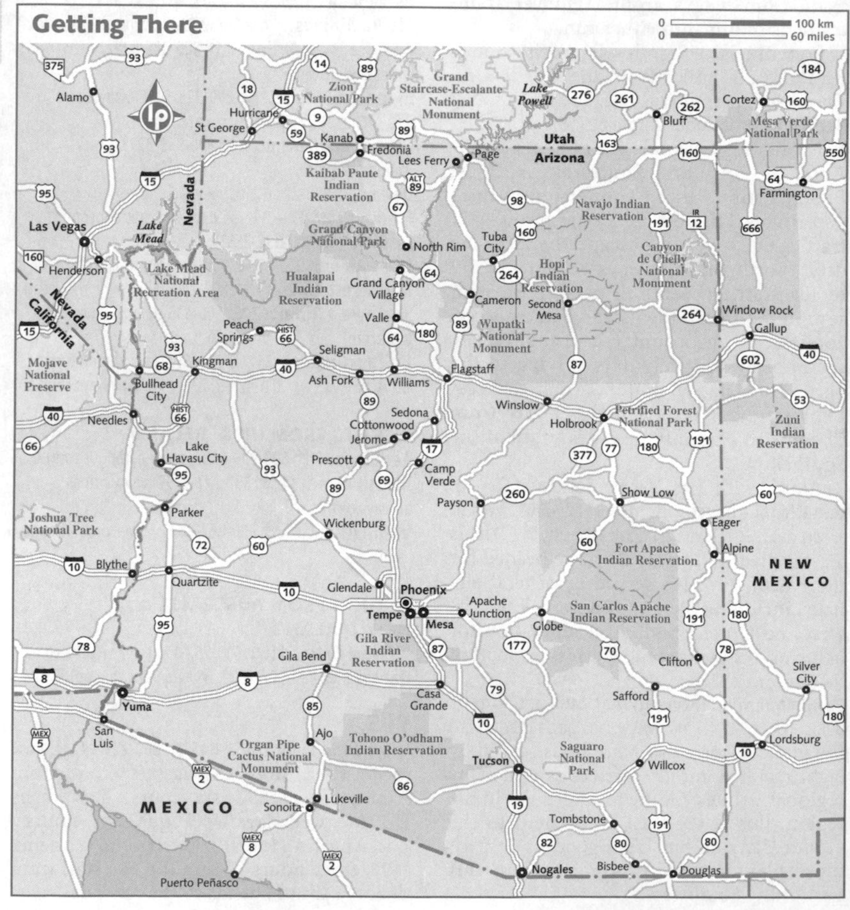

ROAD DISTANCES

From	To	Distance (miles)	Duration (hours)
Albuquerque	South Rim	410	6
Atlanta	Albuquerque	1395	21
Chicago	Denver	1000	14½
Denver	Flagstaff	770	11
Las Vegas	South Rim	280	4½
Las Vegas	South Rim	280	4½
Los Angeles	Las Vegas	270	4
New York	Chicago	790	12½
Salt Lake City	North Rim	390	6½
San Francisco	Salt Lake City	735	10½

Rim's East Entrance.) About 60 miles north of Cameron, Alt 89 turns east through Lees Ferry and Marble Canyon to Jacob Lake.

Automobile Associations

The **American Automobile Association** (AAA; ☎ 800-564-6222; www.aaa.com; basic annual membership $65) provides members with maps and trip-planning information. Members also get discounts on car rentals, air tickets and hotels attractions, as well as emergency roadside service and towing (☎ 800-222-4357). AAA – or 'Triple A' – has reciprocal agreements with automobile associations in other countries, including a long-standing agreement with the **Canadian Automobile Association** (CAA; www.caa.ca). Be sure to bring your membership card from your country of origin.

Driver's License

You will need your vehicle's registration papers, liability insurance and an international driver's permit in addition to your domestic license. Contact your local automobile association for details about all documentation. An international driver's license, obtained in your home country, is only necessary if your country of origin is a non-English-speaking one.

Rental

Most car-rental agencies require renters to be at least 25 years old, and sometimes have an upper age limit as well. When shopping around, always check with the agency itself. It's illegal to drive without automobile insurance, so consult your policy from your home country before leaving. See right for more information on insurance.

The following major car-rental agencies operate out of the airports in Las Vegas and Phoenix. Options include convertibles, minivans and four-wheel-drive vehicles.

Avis (☎ 800-230-4898; www.avis.com)
Budget (☎ 800-527-0700; www.budgetrentacar.com)
Enterprise (☎ 928-526-1377, 800-325-8007; www.pickenterprise.com)
Hertz (☎ 800-654-3131; www.hertz.com)
National (☎ 800-227-7366; www.nationalcar.com)
Thrifty (☎ 800-367-2277; www.thrifty.com)

You can also rent cars in Flagstaff, though rates are higher than in Phoenix or Las Vegas. Enterprise also operates out of Grand Canyon National Park Airport in Tusayan, but rates are higher still and cars may only be available from April through October.

Cruise America (☎ 800-783-3768; www.cruiseamerica.com) rents recreational vehicles nationwide and has offices in Phoenix, Flagstaff and Las Vegas. For one-way rental, call ☎ 800-327-7799. Rates are about $1500 a week. On its website, you'll find the Renters Assistance Guide, which offers RV operating tips. It also rents motorcycles out of the Phoenix office (☎ 480-464-7300).

Insurance

Liability insurance covers people and property that you might hit. For damage to the rental vehicle, a collision damage waiver is available for about $15 per day. If you have collision coverage on your vehicle at home, it might also cover damage to rental cars; check your policy before leaving home. Some credit cards offer reimbursement coverage for collision damage if you rent the car with that credit card, although most do not cover rentals of more than 15 days or exotic models, vans and 4WD vehicles.

Most rental companies stipulate that damage a car sustains while driven on unpaved roads is not covered by the insurance they offer. Check with the agent when you make your reservation.

Road Rules

Throughout the US, cars drive on the right side of the road. Apart from that, road rules differ slightly from state to state, but all require the use of safety belts as well as the proper use of child safety seats for children under the age of five. Speed limits also vary; on rural interstates the speed limit is 75mph, but this drops down to 65mph in urban areas (or 55mph in Arizona).

Pay attention to signs signaling livestock or deer crossings – tangle with a deer, cow or elk and you'll total your car in addition to killing the critter.

The minimum drinking age in the US is 21; you'll need a government-issued photo ID to prove it. Stiff fines, jail time and other penalties can be incurred if you're caught driving under the influence of alcohol. The legal limit for blood alcohol level is 0.08% in Arizona and most other states.

TRAIN

Operated by **Amtrak** (☎ 928-774-8679, 800-872-7245; www.amtrak.com), the *Southwest Chief* makes a daily run between Chicago and Los Angeles, with stops at Flagstaff and Williams. In Williams you can connect with the

RIDING THE RAILS

On September 17, 1901, the Grand Canyon Railway departed Williams to carry its first passengers to the South Rim – and so began the modern era of the canyon as a tourist destination. Absent the hurdle of a long and arduous stagecoach ride, tourists could now travel to the canyon in relative comfort. By 1968 car travel had made the train obsolete – only three passengers were on that year's final trip to the rim. In 1989 Max and Thelma Biegert bought and restored the train and resumed passenger service after a 21-year absence. Today the railway runs a steam locomotive from Memorial Day through September and a diesel locomotive the rest of the year.

Passengers can choose from among five classes of service:

- **coach class** (adult/child $65/30 round-trip) – features a 1923 Harriman-style Pullman car with reversible seats and large wood-framed windows that open to let in the desert breeze; complimentary soft drinks are included
- **club class** ($95/60) – offers a mahogany cash bar and complimentary juice and pastries
- **1st class** ($130/95) – has air-conditioning, the spacious seats recline, and champagne and appetizers are offered during the return trip
- **deluxe observation dome class** (adult/youth $160/135) – features a cash bar and upper-level seating in a glass-enclosed dome; not open to children under 11
- **luxury parlor car** (adult/youth $170/145) – offers incredibly comfortable cushioned window seats and an open-air rear platform; not open to children under 11

A 1952 parlor car doubles as a café, selling coffee, candy, box lunches, sunscreen, water and film.

Even if you're not a train buff, or if you generally shrink from traveling en masse, the train can be a lot of fun if you get into the spirit. A banjo player or another kind of musician wanders the aisles, joking with passengers and strumming such folk classics as 'I've Been Working on the Railroad.' Something about riding the rails, waving your arms out the window or pretending to be FDR stumping on the rear platform brings the kid out in people. A mock horseback chase and train robbery enliven the return trip.

The train departs the 1908 Grand Canyon Railway Depot in Williams at 10am, following a 9:30am Wild West shoot-out by the tracks (a slapstick performance to put you in the mood). You'll arrive at Grand Canyon Depot at 12:15pm. The return train pulls out at 3:30pm, arriving back in Williams at 5:45pm. Most people approach it as a day trip, but you can purchase a one-way ticket or spend a few days in the park and return on a later train. Packages are available through the Fray Marcos Hotel in Williams, and lodgings at the rim. For reservations and details about accommodations, bus tours and meal packages, contact the **Grand Canyon Railway** (☎ 800-843-8724; www.thetrain.com).

historic Grand Canyon Railway (see boxed text, opposite), with original 1923 Pullman cars chugging the scenic 65 miles to the South Rim.

GETTING AROUND

On the South Rim, the most hassle-free way to get around is to drive into the park, park your car and use the convenient shuttles and your own pedestrian power. On the North Rim, unless you're taking the Trans-Canyon Shuttle, you'll have to drive in yourself, as there are few services on this rim (none during the winter).

BICYCLE

Because roads on the South Rim are so heavily trafficked, riding a bike is not the greatest mode of transportation around this rim. However, there is some great mountain biking around Kaibab National Forest (North and South) and Flagstaff. You can ride a bicycle on all roads but not on trails (except the Greenway Trail) on the South Rim. See p254 for more information on bike safety within the park. You can rent mountain bikes in Las Vegas (p179), Flagstaff (p157) and St George (p187) at reasonable daily rates.

CAR & MOTORCYCLE

RV traffic is commonplace in this region, so you won't have any problems finding pull-through campsites and dump stations.

Fuel & Repairs

You'll find a **gas station** (7am-7pm) on the access road to North Rim Campground.

The garage in Grand Canyon Village is open for servicing and repairs weekdays from 8am to 5pm, but parts are limited and you may have to wait a few days for anything but the simplest of repairs. Call ☎ 928-638-2631 for 24-hour emergency towing.

Road Conditions

To check road conditions within the park, call the automated information line at ☎ 928-638-7888. To check conditions in the Kaibab National Forest (South Rim), call the **Tusayan Ranger Station** (☎ 928-638-2443); for conditions in the Kaibab National Forest (North Rim), call the **Kaibab Plateau Visitor Center** (☎ 928-643-7298).

Ranging between 6500ft and 7500ft in elevation, roads in Flagstaff and environs may experience snow and ice from October through April. At elevations approaching 9000ft, roads along the North Rim are even more susceptible to weather. The drive up from deserts north and east of the park climbs about 4000ft, and conditions change rapidly – you may start out in sunny, dry weather in Kanab or Lees Ferry and wind up battling rain, hail or snow in Jacob Lake. The forest service's dirt roads, particularly those in Kaibab National Forest, may be impassable after even a light rain. Always check with a ranger before heading out. You'll need a high-clearance 4WD vehicle to tackle both the 17-mile road to Point Sublime, a minimum two-hour round-trip, and the 60-mile dirt road to Toroweap. Absolutely do not attempt these drives without first telling someone where you're going, and bring plenty of water.

The unpaved road to Grand Canyon West on the Hualapai Reservation is a doozy. If you aren't driving a 4WD vehicle, make sure you know how to change a tire – if you actually get cell-phone reception out there, chances are the towing will cost a few hundred dollars. Regardless of the car you're driving, be sure to start out with a full tank of gas and a good supply of water.

Road Hazards

The main hazard to look out for is wildlife in and around the parks, or livestock in rural areas surrounding the park.

SHUTTLE

Free shuttle buses operate every 10 to 15 minutes along three routes on the South Rim. Hermits Rest Route accesses the 8-mile stretch of rim road west of Grand Canyon Village. This road is closed to private vehicles from March through November; the only way to see the overlooks then is via shuttle or on foot. You can drive to most facilities in the village, but it's easier to park your car and take one of the Village Route shuttles (for details see p105). The Kaibab Trail Route stops at Pipe Creek Vista, South Kaibab Trailhead and Yaki Point, the last of which is closed to private vehicles year-round. Except for an early-morning shuttle to the North Kaibab Trailhead, the only way to explore the North Rim is by car, bicycle or foot.

The **Trans-Canyon Shuttle** (☎ 928-638-2820; adult one way/round-trip $65/110, child 12 & under one way/round-trip $50/90, cash only) offers rim-to-rim shuttle service from mid-May to mid-October (when the North Rim is open). Reservations are required, and infant car seats are not provided. Reserve a seat two weeks in advance to be guaranteed a spot. The shuttle departs Grand Canyon Lodge at 7am, arrives at South Rim's Bright Angel Lodge at 11:30am, then makes the return trip at 1:30pm, arriving at the North Rim at 6pm. The shuttle is a godsend for rim-to-rim hikers, but it's also a good option for those who want to see both rims and don't want to bother with a car.

Call ☎ 928-638-7888 for recorded information on road and weather conditions.

Health & Safety

CONTENTS

Before You Go	**247**
Insurance	247
Medical Checklist	247
Internet Resources	247
Further Reading	248
In the Park	**248**
Medical Assistance	248
Common Ailments	248
Environmental Hazards	249
Safe Hiking	251
Safe Biking	254

Educating yourself on the Grand Canyon's unique environment and hazards will go a long way toward making your visit a safe and healthy one.

BEFORE YOU GO

Even strolling the scenic viewpoints around the Grand Canyon will be easier and more enjoyable if you're somewhat physically fit. If you're not in decent shape and plan on doing any hiking, start getting regular, vigorous physical exercise at least three weeks prior to your trip.

When possible, visitors from lower elevations and cooler climes should allow several days to acclimatize before undertaking any strenuous activity at the Grand Canyon.

INSURANCE

It's definitely a prudent idea to review the terms of your health-insurance policy before going overseas on a trip; some policies don't cover injuries sustained as a result of dangerous activities, which can include such pursuits as rock climbing or mountaineering.

You may also want to double-check that emergency medical care, as well as emergency evacuation to your home country (if you're not from the US), is covered by your policy.

MEDICAL CHECKLIST

Following is a list of items to include in your first-aid kit.

- adhesive tape
- bandages and safety pins
- elasticized support bandage for knees, ankles etc
- gauze swabs
- nonadhesive dressings
- paper stitches
- small pair of scissors
- sterile alcohol wipes
- thermometer (note that mercury thermometers are prohibited by airlines)
- tweezers

Medications & Miscellany

In addition to any regular medications you need, consider including some of these over-the-counter meds in your kit.

- antidiarrhea and antinausea drugs
- antifungal cream or powder
- antihistamines
- antiseptic
- calamine lotion, sting-relief spray or aloe vera
- cold and influenza tablets, throat lozenges and nasal decongestant
- eye drops
- insect repellent
- multivitamins – especially for longer hikes, when dietary vitamin intake may be inadequate
- painkillers (such as aspirin, acetaminophen or ibuprofen)
- rehydration mixture – particularly important when traveling with children
- sunscreen and lip balm
- water-purification tablets or iodine

INTERNET RESOURCES

There's a wealth of travel health advice on the internet. One excellent site that provides cutting-edge wilderness medicine information by using real-life case studies is www.nols.edu/wmi/c urriculum_updates.

Centers for Disease Control & Prevention (www.cdc.gov) Represents US government agencies with a vast amount of relevant information.

International Society for Infectious Diseases (www.isid.org) An international organization representing

numerous agencies and individuals that work in infectious disease research.
Wilderness Medical Society (www.wms.org) A nonprofit organization dedicated to promoting outdoor and emergency knowledge and research.
World Health Organization (www.who.int/en/) Has the latest news on health issues and developments around the world.

FURTHER READING

Backcountry hikers may want to stuff one of these detailed first-aid guides into their packs.

- *Backcountry First Aid and Extended Care* by Buck Tilton (Falcon, 2007) – this pocket-size guide is a compact addition to your kit.
- *Medicine for the Outdoors* by Paul S Auerbach (Lyons Press, 2003) – this layperson's reference gives brief explanations of many medical problems and practical treatment options.
- *Wilderness 911* by Eric A Weiss (Mountaineers Books, 1998) – a step-by-step guide to first aid and advanced care in remote areas when you have limited medical supplies.

IN THE PARK

For the casual visitor to the park, health and safety usually requires little effort apart from keeping sufficiently hydrated and not goofing off near precarious ledges on the rim. However, for those heading below the rim, preparation and taking responsibility for one's own safety are key to a safe adventure. Many emergencies below the rim occur because visitors overestimate their abilities and come underprepared to deal with the consequences.

Always lock your car and put valuables in the trunk, particularly if you park at a trailhead. Physical assault is rare in the park, but use caution when hiking alone.

MEDICAL ASSISTANCE

In an emergency on either rim, dial ☎ 911; from your lodge or cabin, dial ☎ 9-911. Those seeking a higher level of self-reliance might be interested in taking a wilderness medicine course before setting out into the backcountry. Check out the certified Wilderness First Responder (WFR) course offered by the **Wilderness Medicine Institute** (WMI; www.nols.edu/wmi/courses/wildfirstresponder.shtml) or the **Wilderness Medicine Training Center** (WMTC; www.wildmedcenter. com/courses.html).

South Rim

On the South Rim, the **clinic** (Map p103; ☎ 928-638-2551; Grand Canyon Village) offers walk-in medical care from 8am to 6pm and also has a **dentist** (☎ 928-638-2395) available. The clinic's pharmacy can fill prescriptions within 24 hours if you have an original prescription from your doctor; for refills, the nearest pharmacy is 60 miles south at the **Safeway** (Map p141; ☎ 928-635-0500, pharmacy 928-635-5977; 637 W Rte 66; 🕑 5am-10pm) in Williams.

Nearest hospitals to the South Rim are 80 miles south in Flagstaff, including the top-notch **Flagstaff Medical Center** (Map p152; ☎ 928-779-3366; 1200 N Beaver St, Flagstaff, AZ 86001).

North Rim

Rangers provide emergency medical care on the North Rim; the nearest hospital, **Kane County Hospital** (Map p209; ☎ 435-644-5811; 355 North Main St, Kanab, UT 84741), is 80 miles north in Kanab. Also in Kanab is the nearest pharmacy, **Zion Pharmacy** (Map p209; ☎ 435-644-2693; 14 E Center St; 🕑 9am-6pm Mon-Fri, to noon Sat).

Page Hospital (Map p214; ☎ 928-645-2424 501; N Navajo, Page, AZ 86040) is 114 miles from the North Rim in Page, Arizona, where you'll also find a pharmacy at the local **Safeway** (Map p214; ☎ 928-645-8155; 650 Elm St, Page, AZ 86040; 9am-8pm Mon-Fri, 9am-6pm Sat, 10am-4pm Sun).

COMMON AILMENTS

Plaguing hikers in the Grand Canyon and beyond, these common ailments may strike your hike. But come prepared, and they may not pose any problems.

Blisters

To avoid blisters, make sure your walking boots or shoes are well worn in before you hit the trail. Your boots should fit comfortably with enough room to move your toes; boots that are too big or too small will cause blisters. Similarly for socks – be sure they fit properly and are specifically made for walkers; even then, check to make sure that there are no seams across the widest part of your foot. Wet and muddy socks can also cause blisters, so even on a day walk, pack a spare pair of socks. Keep your toenails clipped but not too short. If you do feel a blister coming on, treat it sooner rather then later by applying a bit of moleskin (or duct tape).

Fatigue

A simple statistic: more injuries happen toward the end of the day than earlier, when you're fresher. Although tiredness can simply be a nuisance on an easy walk, it can be life-threatening on narrow exposed ridges or in bad weather. You should never set out on a walk that is beyond your capabilities on the day. If you feel below par, have a day off or hop on a shuttle. To reduce the risk, don't push yourself too hard – take rests every hour or two and build in a good half-hour lunch break. Toward the end of the day, take down the pace and increase your concentration. You should also eat properly throughout the day; nuts, dried fruit and chocolate are all good energy-giving snack foods.

Giardiasis

This parasitic infection of the small intestine occurs throughout North America and the world. Symptoms may include nausea, bloating, cramps and diarrhea, and may last for weeks. To protect yourself from giardia, you should avoid drinking directly from lakes, ponds, streams and rivers, which may be contaminated by animal or human feces. The infection can also be transmitted from person to person if proper hand washing is not performed. Giardiasis is easily diagnosed by a stool test and readily treated with antibiotics.

Knee Strain

Many walkers feel the burn on long, steep descents. Although you can't eliminate strain on the knee joints when dropping steeply, you can reduce it by taking shorter steps that leave your legs slightly bent and ensuring that your heel hits the ground before the rest of your foot. Some walkers find that compression bandages help, and hiking poles are very effective in taking some of the weight off the knees.

Travelers Diarrhea

While a change of water, food or climate may give travelers a case of the runs, serious diarrhea caused by contaminated water is an increasing problem in heavily used backcountry areas. If diarrhea does hit you, fluid replacement is the mainstay of management. Weak black tea with a little sugar; soda water; or soft drinks allowed to go flat and 50% diluted with water are all good. With severe diarrhea, a rehydrating solution is necessary to replace minerals and salts. Commercially available oral rehydration salts (ORS) are very useful. Stick to a bland diet as you recover.

Gut-paralyzing drugs such as diphenoxylate or loperamide can bring relief from symptoms, but they don't actually cure the problem.

ENVIRONMENTAL HAZARDS

Altitude

As the South Rim is more than 7000ft above sea level and the North Rim 8801ft at its highest point, altitude sickness is fairly common. Characterized by shortness of breath, fatigue and headaches, it can be avoided by drinking plenty of water and taking a day or two to acclimatize before attempting any long hikes.

Bites & Stings

Common sense approaches to these concerns are the most effective: wear boots when hiking to protect from snakes, wear long sleeves and pants to prevent tick and mosquito bites.

SCORPIONS

Commonly found in Arizona, the bark scorpion is the only dangerous species of scorpion in the US. If stung, you should immediately apply ice or cold packs, immobilize the affected body part, and go to the nearest emergency room. To prevent scorpion stings, be sure to inspect and shake out clothing, shoes and sleeping bags before use.

SNAKES

Several species of rattlesnake are found in the Grand Canyon. Most snakebites can be prevented by respecting the snake's space – if you encounter one, move away slowly. Those bitten will experience rapid swelling, severe pain and possibly temporary paralysis. Death is rare, but children are at higher risk. Place a light constricting bandage over the bite, keep the wounded part below the level of the heart and move it as little as possible. Attempting to suck out the venom is not generally considered an effective strategy. Stay calm and get to a medical facility for antivenin treatment as soon as possible.

TICKS

Always check your body for ticks after walking through high grass or thickly forested areas. If ticks are found unattached, they can simply be brushed off. If a tick is found attached, press down around the tick's head with tweezers, grab the head and gently pull upwards – do not twist it. (If no tweezers are available, use your fingers, but protect them from contamination with a piece of tissue or paper.) Do not douse the tick with oil, alcohol or petroleum jelly.

Transmitted by ticks, Lyme disease is uncommon in Arizona, but you should consult a doctor if you get sick in the weeks after your trip.

Cold

HYPOTHERMIA

If you hike the canyon in winter, hypothermia is a real danger. This life-threatening condition occurs when prolonged exposure to cold thwarts the body's ability to maintain its core temperature. Hypothermia doesn't just occur in cold weather – dehydration and certain medications can predispose people to hypothermia, especially when they're wet, and even in relatively warm weather.

Symptoms include uncontrolled shivering, poor muscle control and a careless attitude. Remember to dress in layers and wear a windproof outer jacket. If possible, bring a Thermos containing a hot (nonalcoholic) beverage. Treat symptoms by putting on dry clothing, drinking warm fluids and warming the victim through direct body contact with another person.

Heat

DEHYDRATION & HEAT EXHAUSTION

The canyon is a dry, hot place, and even if you're just walking along the rim, lack of water can cause dehydration, which in turn can lead to heat exhaustion. Take time to acclimatize to high temperatures, wear a wide-brimmed hat and make sure to drink enough fluids. Hikers should drink a gallon of water per day. It's also wise to carry jugs of water in your car in case it breaks down. Characterized by fatigue, nausea, headaches, cramps and cool, clammy skin, heat exhaustion should be treated by drinking water, eating high-energy foods, resting in the shade and cooling the skin with a wet cloth.

Heat exhaustion can lead to heatstroke if not addressed promptly.

HEATSTROKE

Long, continuous exposure to high temperatures can lead to heatstroke, a serious, sometimes fatal condition that occurs when

CAMPING RULES

The most important rule to remember when camping in the park or the surrounding Kaibab National Forest is to leave no trace. With so many annual visitors, the park environment is particularly vulnerable to overuse or carelessness.

- Pack out all trash (including food scraps).
- Keep fires in grills (no open campfires); backpackers should use small portable stoves.
- Refrain from gathering wood; instead, purchase wood at **Canyon Village Marketplace** (☎ 928-631-2262; Market Plaza, Grand Canyon Village; 7am-9pm) or the **North Rim General Store** (Map p185; 7am-8pm, closed mid-Oct–mid-May; ♿)
- Never leave fires unattended; extinguish them thoroughly with water.
- Keep all food and fragrant items (soap, deodorant, toothpaste etc) in your car or hang your backpack from a tree overnight to keep coyotes and other critters at bay.
- If pit toilets are unavailable, bury human waste 6in deep and at least 200ft from trails, campsites or water sources.
- Wash dishes at least 200ft from water sources and scatter strained dishwater (waste breaks down slowly in the dry desert climate)

the body's heat-regulating mechanism breaks down and one's body temperature rises to dangerous levels. Other symptoms include flushed, dry skin, a weak and rapid pulse, and poor judgment, inability to focus or delirium. Move the victim to shade, remove clothing, cover them with a wet sheet or towel and fan them continually. Hospitalization is essential for heatstroke.

Some 250 hikers a year on the most popular below-the-rim trails require ranger assistance to get out safely. Several have died. The main problems are too much sun and too little water. Time and again, hikers who have been rescued from the canyon say that their biggest mistake was underestimating just how hot the canyon can be. Even if it turns out you don't need it, carrying extra water into the canyon could save someone else's life.

HYPONATREMIA

While drinking plenty of water is crucial, it's also important to supplement water intake with salty snacks to avoid hyponatremia (a dangerously low sodium level in the blood). In the dry heat of the canyon, sweat can evaporate off of your skin so quickly that you may not notice how much you've perspired. Salt lost through sweating must be replaced in order to keep a balanced sodium level in the blood.

Symptoms of hyponatremia are similar to early signs of heat exhaustion: nausea, vomiting and an altered mental state. Give the victim salty foods and seek immediate help if their mental alertness diminishes.

Sunburn

In the desert and at high altitude you can sunburn in less than an hour, even through cloud cover. Use lots of sunscreen (minimum SPF 15, ideally SPF 45), especially on skin not typically exposed to sun. Be sure to apply sunscreen to young children, particularly babies, and wear wide-brimmed hats.

Weather & Flash Floods

Even if the sky overhead is clear, distant rainstorms can send walls of water, debris and mud roaring through side canyons without warning. Such flash floods have killed people caught in creeks and dry riverbeds. Never camp in dry washes, and be sure to check weather reports for the entire region before venturing into the canyon. This is crucial if you're planning on hiking through any slot canyons. Flash floods are most common during summer storms in July, August and September.

Don't underestimate the summer heat – temperatures routinely soar past 100°F in the canyon.

In winter months, snow and ice can make trails slick and dangerous. Ask a ranger about conditions before heading out.

Wildlife

For their own safety and yours, it's illegal to approach or feed any wildlife – from those chubby South Rim squirrels (who bite!) to seemingly placid elk and reclusive mountain lions. In the canyon, always shake out shoes and sleeping bags to dislodge hiding scorpions. Also keep an ear out for rattlesnakes, who rattle their segmented tails when disturbed.

SAFE HIKING

It's easy to become complacent when hiking in the Grand Canyon, given the thin air, clearly marked trails and relative ease of descent into the canyon. But hiking here can be serious business. On average, there are 400 medical emergencies each year on canyon trails, and more than 250 hikers need to be rescued at their own hefty expense. It's not that hiking itself is an inherently unsafe activity, but the canyon's extreme terrain and climate mean it can quickly turn dangerous.

The best way of ensuring a rewarding hike is proper planning. Learn about the trails, respect your limitations and bring ample supplies. Always tell someone of your plans; cell phones may not work in the park, and they definitely won't get a signal inside the canyon.

In summer, as rim temperatures heat up into the 90s Fahrenheit and the canyon floor often exceeds 110°F, the sun can quickly leave you dehydrated and at risk of heat exhaustion. When undertaking any longer day hike, plan on getting started by 6am and avoiding the sun altogether between 10am and 2pm. Wear a hat with a brim and slather yourself generously in sunscreen.

Before you set out on any trail over a mile, know whether and where water is available. While water is available along Bright Angel and North Kaibab, pipe breakage is common. Elsewhere, such as Hermit Springs, you'll need to treat water before drinking it, either by boiling it for at least five minutes, treating it with iodine tablets or using a filter that screens out giardiasis.

Take note if you haven't had to pee as often as usual or your urine is dark yellow or amber-colored. These are indicators of dehydration, which can rapidly spiral into more dire health concerns. Loss of appetite and thirst may be early symptoms of heat exhaustion, so even if you don't feel thirsty, drink water often and have a salty snack while you're at it. Adding a little electrolyte replacement powder (like Gatorade) to your water is another good way to keep dehydration and hyponatremia at bay. Err on the side of caution and bring more water and food than you think you'll need.

Falls

Just about every year people fall to their death at the Grand Canyon. Stay on the trails, refrain from stepping over guardrails, and absolutely do not allow children to run along the rim. There aren't as many guardrails as you may think, and several stretches have no railing at all. Jokingly posing for 'look, I'm falling over the rim!' photographs are ill-advised, as several unfortunate souls doing so have had vertigo or loose rocks send them over the edge. Parents should consider carrying toddlers in a child-carrier backpack along and below the rim.

When hiking below the rim, wear sturdy shoes or boots with good traction.

Getting Lost

The park comprises 1904 sq miles of desert terrain, and it's easy to lose your way in its labyrinth of side canyons and sheer cliffs.

DON'T HORSE AROUND WITH MULES

Day hikers are bound to encounter mules, who always have the right of way. If you're hiking when a mule train approaches, stand quietly on the inner side of the trail, turn your pack away from the animals (lest one bumps your pack and knocks you off balance) and listen for directions from the guide. Be especially careful if you're hiking with kids.

PREHYDRATION

Since your body can only absorb about a quart of water per hour, it's beneficial to prehydrate before embarking on a long hike. To get a head start on hydration, drink plenty of water the day and evening before your hike, and avoid diuretics like caffeine and alcohol.

It is imperative that you plan any hike carefully and appropriately: for backcountry hikes, bring a topo map, know how to read it and never stray from trails under any circumstances. Leave a detailed itinerary with a friend that includes routes and dates, as well as identifying details of your car, such as the license plate number, make and model.

In the event that you do get lost, search-and-rescue operations may take days to find you. Stay calm and stay put, making your location as visible as possible by spreading out colorful clothing or equipment in an exposed place. Use a signal mirror (an old CD is a good lightweight substitute) and ration food and water. Do not attempt to blaze a shortcut to the river; people have died from falls after stranding themselves on steep, dead-end ledges or ridges.

Whether you're hiking the backcountry or driving one of the region's many dirt roads, always carry an adequate map and bring a gallon of water per person per day.

Lightning

Being below the rim does not protect you from lightning strikes. If a thunderstorm catches you on an exposed ridge or summit, look for a concave rock formation to shelter in, but avoid touching the rock itself. In open areas where there's no shelter, find a depression in the ground and take up a crouched-squatting position with your feet together; do not lie on the ground. Never seek shelter under objects that are isolated or higher than their surroundings. Avoid contact with metallic objects such as pack frames or hiking poles.

Should anyone be struck by lightning, immediately begin first-aid measures such as checking their airway, breathing and pulse, and starting burn treatment. Get the patient to a doctor as quickly as possible.

Rescue & Evacuation

Hikers should take responsibility for their own safety and aim to prevent emergency situations, but even the most safety-conscious hiker may have a serious accident requiring urgent medical attention. In case of accidents, self-rescue should be your first consideration, as search-and-rescue operations into the canyon are very expensive and require emergency personnel to put their own safety at risk.

If a person in your group is injured, leave someone with them while others seek help. If there are only two of you, leave the injured person with as much warm clothing, food and water as it's sensible to spare, plus a whistle and flashlight. Mark their position with something conspicuous – a yellow rain jacket or a large stone cross on the ground.

Rockfall

Always be alert to the danger of rockfall, especially after heavy rains. If you accidentally let loose a rock, loudly warn other hikers below. Bighorn sheep sometimes dislodge rocks, so animal-watchers should be especially vigilant.

Traumatic Injuries

Detailed first-aid instruction is outside the scope of this book, but here are some basic tips and advice. Hikers might consider

SAFETY TIPS FOR HIKING SMART

These are the nuts and bolts for safe hiking in the Grand Canyon:

- **Down = 2x up** – Make this formula your hiking mantra. Generally speaking, it takes twice as long to wheeze back up the canyon as it does to breeze down. So if you'd like to hike for six hours, turn around after two. Most first-time canyon hikers slog uphill at about 1mph.
- **Never leave the trail** – Stay on marked trails, both for safety and erosion control. Nowhere is this more important than in the Grand Canyon, where hazards include stupefying drop-offs. It's also extremely difficult to find a hiker who has wandered off-trail.
- **Don't hike alone** – Most of those who get in trouble in the canyon are solo hikers, for whom the risks are multiplied.
- **Take your time** – Given the altitude and extreme aridity, go slow to avoid overexertion. Ideally, you should be able to speak easily while hiking, regardless of the grade. Be sure to take a five- to 10-minute break every hour to recharge, in the shade if possible.
- **Eat and drink often** – Pay close attention to your intake of food and fluids to guard against dehydration and hyponatremia (low blood sodium level). One good strategy is to check your watch and have a snack and a long drink of water every 20 to 30 minutes. In summer months each hiker should drink about a gallon of water per day; always have at least two pints of water on you. Eat before you're hungry and drink before you're thirsty. Prior to a major hike, eat a healthy breakfast and drink lots of water; afterward, replenish with more water (and perhaps a margarita; see boxed text, p118) and treat yourself to a big dinner.
- **Salty snacks are your friends** – To prevent hyponatremia, eat plenty of carbohydrates and salty snacks before and during your hike.
- **Take care of your feet** – In addition to sturdy, comfortable, broken-in boots and medium-weight socks, bring moleskin for blisters and make sure your toenails are trimmed. On long hikes, soak your feet in streams to reduce inflammation and safeguard against blisters (just be sure to dry them thoroughly before replacing your socks). After hiking, elevate your feet.
- **Don't be overly ambitious** – Particularly for novice hikers, it's a good idea to spend the first day or two gauging your ability and response to the climate and terrain. If you're planning long hikes, test your desert legs on a more level hike or a short round-trip of 2 to 4 miles, then work your way up to more difficult trails.
- **Stay cool** – Hike during the cooler early-morning and late-afternoon hours. Splash water on your face and head at streams and water sources, and soak your shirt or bandana to produce an evaporative cooling effect.

taking a first-aid course before hitting the trail to ensure they know what to do in the event of an injury.

If the victim is unconscious, immediately check if they are breathing. Clear their airway if it's blocked, and check for a pulse – feel the side of the neck rather than the wrist.

Check for wounds and broken bones – ask the person where they have pain if they are conscious, otherwise gently inspect them all over (including their back and the back of the head), moving them as little as possible in case they've sustained a neck or back injury. Control any bleeding by applying firm pressure to the wound. Bleeding from the nose or ear may indicate a fractured skull. Don't give the person anything by mouth.

You'll have to manage the person for shock. Raise their legs above heart level (unless their legs are fractured); dress any wounds and immobilize any fractures; loosen tight clothing; keep the person warm by covering them with a blanket or other dry clothing; insulate them from the ground if possible, but don't heat them.

Some general points to bear in mind:

- Simple fractures take several weeks to heal and don't need fixing straight away, but they should be immobilized to protect them from further injury. Compound fractures need urgent treatment.
- If you do have to splint a broken bone, remember to check regularly that the splint is not cutting off the circulation to the hand or foot.
- Most cases of brief unconsciousness are not associated with any serious internal injury to the brain, but as a general rule of thumb in these circumstances, any person who has been knocked unconscious should be watched for deterioration. If they do deteriorate, seek medical attention immediately.

FRACTURES

Indications of a fracture are pain (tenderness of the affected area), swelling and discoloration, loss of function or deformity of a limb. Unless you know what you're doing, don't try to straighten an obviously displaced broken bone. To protect from further injury, immobilize a nondisplaced fracture (where the broken bones are in alignment) by splinting it, usually in the position found, which will probably be the most comfortable position.

Fractures of the thigh bone require urgent treatment as they involve massive blood loss and pain. Seek help and treat the patient for shock. Compound fractures (associated with open wounds) also require more urgent treatment than simple fractures, as there is a risk of infection. Dislocations, where the bone has come out of the joint, are very painful and should be set as soon as possible.

Broken ribs are painful but usually heal by themselves and do not need splinting. If breathing difficulties occur, or the person coughs up blood, medical attention should be sought urgently, as this may indicate a punctured lung.

INTERNAL INJURIES

These are more difficult to detect and cannot usually be treated in the field. Watch for shock, which is a specific medical condition associated with a failure to maintain circulating blood volume. Signs include a rapid pulse and cold, clammy extremities. A person in shock requires urgent medical attention.

SPRAINS

Ankle and knee sprains are common injuries among hikers, particularly when crossing rugged terrain. To help prevent ankle sprains, wear boots that have adequate ankle support. If you do suffer a sprain, immobilize the joint with a firm bandage, and if possible, immerse the foot in cold water. Distribute the contents of your pack among your companions. Once you reach shelter, relieve pain and swelling by keeping the joint elevated for the first 24 hours and icing the swollen joint. Take over-the-counter painkillers to ease the discomfort. If the sprain is mild, you may be able to continue your hike after a couple of days. For more severe sprains, seek medical attention as an X-ray may be needed to find out if in fact a bone has been broken.

SAFE BIKING

On the South Rim, bicycling is permitted on the Greenway Trail (see boxed text, p105), as well as on all paved and unpaved roads. Other trails are off limits to bikes. Bicyclists must adhere to traffic regulations and should use caution along the heavily trafficked roads, especially during the busy summer season. On Hermit Rd, bicyclists are required to pull off the road to allow vehicles to pass. Always wear a helmet and bright colors to improve your visibility to drivers.

Biking around the North Rim is a whole other animal. Single-track trails and forest roads abound in the Kaibab National Forest for mountain-bikers. Because the area is so remote compared with the developed South Rim, cyclists should wear helmets and come supplied with water, food and first aid. For more information on biking the North Rim, see p51.

Clothing & Equipment

CONTENTS

Clothing	256
Equipment	258
Buying & Renting Locally	261

Arriving outfitted with the proper clothing and equipment will keep you comfortable on a hiking expedition or other adventure. Much of what is appropriate to bring depends on the season you're visiting and what activities you plan to pursue. We've covered most of the basic equipment and attire here, along with buying tips and what to look for.

Many first-time visitors are surprised by the weather, especially the extreme heat of summer and the high-country cold of the North Rim.

Plan carefully for the season, particularly if you're planning to explore the backcountry for the first time. Below the rim, you'll have to be self-sufficient as the only facilities inside the canyon are at riverside Phantom Ranch.

CLOTHING

Modern outdoor garments made from new synthetic fabrics (which are breathable and actively wick moisture away from your skin) are better for hiking than anything made of cotton or wool. The exception to this is if you're hiking out of the canyon in midsummer, when cotton is a godsend. Soak cotton shirts or bandanas with water at every opportunity, and allow the evaporative cooling effect to ease your journey.

Layering

To cope with changing temperatures and exertion, layering your clothing is a good way to regulate your body temperature.

For the upper body, the base layer is typically a light vest or T-shirt made of synthetic thermal fabric (eg Polartec). The second layer is a long-sleeve shirt, and the third layer can be either a synthetic fleece sweater or pile jacket that continues to wick away moisture. The outer shell consists of a weatherproof jacket that also protects against strong cold winds.

For the lower body, shorts will probably be most comfortable in midsummer, although some hikers prefer long pants – light, quick-drying fabric (no more than 30% cotton) is best. As 'longjohn' type underwear can't be easily removed, it is not recommended except when conditions are expected to remain very cold for the whole day (such as from midfall). Waterproof overpants form the outer layer for the lower body.

ROUTE FINDING

While accurate, our maps are not perfect. Inaccuracies in altitudes are commonly caused by air-temperature anomalies. Natural features such as river confluences and mountain peaks are in their true position, but sometimes the location of villages and trails is not always so. This may be because a village is spread over a hillside, or the size of the map does not allow for detail of the trail's twists and turns. However, by using several basic route-finding techniques, you will have few problems following our descriptions:

- Be aware of whether the trail should be climbing or descending.
- Check the north-point arrow on the map and determine the general direction of the trail.
- Time your progress over a known distance and calculate the speed at which you travel in the given terrain. From then on, you can determine with reasonable accuracy how far you have traveled.
- Watch the path – look for boot prints and other signs of previous passage.

EQUIPMENT CHECKLIST

Though it's tempting to simply toss everything into the car at the last minute, taking time to think things through as you pack can save you a lot of headaches down the road. Your list will vary, depending on your travel circumstances.

Clothing

- ☐ broad-brimmed hat (one that ties under the chin is required for all mule trips) in summer
- ☐ hiking boots, or sturdy trail-running shoes, and spare laces
- ☐ river sandals or flip-flops
- ☐ shorts and lightweight trousers or skirt
- ☐ socks and underwear
- ☐ sweater or fleece
- ☐ thermal underwear
- ☐ T-shirt and long-sleeved shirt with collar
- ☐ warm hat, scarf and gloves in winter
- ☐ waterproof jacket
- ☐ waterproof pants

Equipment

- ☐ backpack with waterproof liner
- ☐ first-aid kit
- ☐ high-energy food and snacks and one day's emergency supplies
- ☐ insect repellent
- ☐ map, compass and guidebook
- ☐ map case or clip-seal plastic bags
- ☐ pocket knife
- ☐ sunglasses
- ☐ sunscreen and lip balm
- ☐ survival bag or blanket
- ☐ toilet paper and trowel
- ☐ flashlight or headlamp, spare batteries and bulb
- ☐ watch
- ☐ water container
- ☐ whistle

Overnight Hikes

- ☐ biodegradable soap
- ☐ cooking, eating and drinking utensils
- ☐ matches and lighter
- ☐ sewing/repair kit
- ☐ sleeping bag and/or liner
- ☐ sleeping pad/mat
- ☐ spare cord
- ☐ stove and fuel
- ☐ tent, pegs, poles and guylines
- ☐ toiletries
- ☐ towel
- ☐ water-purification tablets, iodine or filter

Optional Items

- ☐ altimeter
- ☐ backpack cover (waterproof, slip-on)
- ☐ binoculars
- ☐ camera, film and batteries
- ☐ candle
- ☐ emergency distress beacon
- ☐ GPS receiver
- ☐ groundsheet
- ☐ hiking poles
- ☐ mobile phone
- ☐ mosquito net
- ☐ notebook and pen
- ☐ swimsuit

Waterproof Shells

Hikers in the Grand Canyon should always carry a windproof and waterproof rainjacket and pants. It should be properly seam-sealed and have a hood to keep the rain and wind off your head. Gore-Tex or a similar breathable fabric work the best.

Footwear, Socks & Gaiters

It is vital that your boots are properly worn in before you begin any serious hiking. Some hikers prefer the greater agility that lightweight boots allow, while others insist on heavier designs that give firm ankle support and protect feet in rough terrain. Hiking boots should have a flexible (preferably polyurethane) midsole and an insole that supports the arch and heel.

Synthetic socks that draw moisture away from your feet are another must. If you're hiking in wet conditions, like in winter at the North Rim, gaiters will help keep water

NAVIGATION EQUIPMENT

Maps & Compass

You should always carry a good map of the area you are hiking in (see Maps, p28), and know how to read it. Before setting off on your trek, ensure that you understand the contours and the map symbols, plus the main ridge and river systems in the area. Also familiarize yourself with the true north–south directions and the general direction in which you are heading. On the trail, try to identify major landmarks such as mountain ranges and gorges, and locate them on your map. This will give you a better understanding of the region's geography.

Buy a compass and learn how to use it. The attraction of magnetic north varies in different parts of the world, so compasses need to be balanced accordingly.

Compass manufacturers have divided the world into five zones. Make sure your compass is balanced for your destination zone. There are also 'universal' compasses on the market that can be used anywhere in the world.

1 Base plate
2 Direction of travel arrow
3 Dash
4 Bezel
5 Meridian lines
6 Needle
7 Red end
8 N (north point)

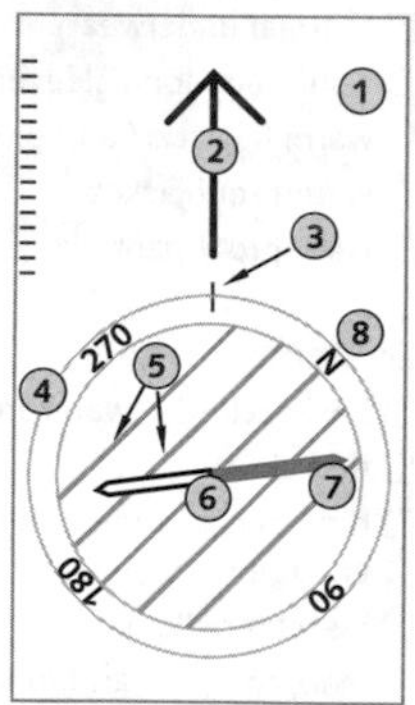

How to Use a Compass

This is a very basic introduction to using a compass and will only be of assistance if you are proficient in map reading. For simplicity, it doesn't take magnetic variation into account. Before using a compass we recommend you obtain further instruction.

Reading a Compass

Hold the compass flat in the palm of your hand. Rotate the bezel so the red end of the needle points to the N on the bezel. The bearing is read from the dash under the bezel.

Orienting the Map

To orient the map so that it aligns with the ground, place the compass flat on the map. Rotate the map until the needle is parallel with the map's north–south grid lines and the red end is pointing to north on the map. You can now identify features around you by aligning them with labeled features on the map.

from running down your waterproof pants into your shoes.

EQUIPMENT

It doesn't have to be fancy or from the highest-end manufacturer's New! Improved! collection, but making sure you have the basic equipment will contribute greatly to a safe and comfortable journey.

Backpacks & Daypacks

A backpack that weighs on your shoulders as you hike is not just uncomfortable, it may be doing permanent injury to your back. The only good backpacks are those with robust, easily adjustable waist-belts that can comfortably support the entire weight carried, effectively transferring the load from your shoulders onto your hips. The shoulder straps should serve only to steady the backpack.

Backpacks with a relatively large capacity (at least 5500 cubic inches) are best for overnight hiking in the backcountry. Internal-frame backpacks fit snugly against your back, keeping the weight close to your center of gravity. Unfortunately, this allows for poor ventilation, so sweat soaks your shirt instead of evaporating to cool your body. Newer, redesigned external-frame packs largely solve this problem, but even the best brands are still slightly cumbersome and about the same price as internal-frame backpacks.

Ultimately, it's about what's most comfortable for you.

For day hikes or side trips from camp, a small daypack should hold all you need. Daypacks that double as hydration systems (like Camelbaks) eliminate the hassle of toting unwieldy water bottles and save space.

Taking a Bearing from the Map

Draw a line on the map between your starting point and your destination. Place the edge of the compass on this line with the direction-of-travel arrow pointing towards your destination. Rotate the bezel until the meridian lines are parallel with the north–south grid lines on the map and the N points to north on the map. Read the bearing from the dash.

Following a Bearing

Rotate the bezel so that the intended bearing is in line with the dash. Place the compass flat in the palm of your hand and rotate the base plate until the red end points to N on the bezel. The direction-of-travel arrow will now point in the direction you need to walk.

Determining Your Bearing

Rotate the bezel so the red end points to the N. Place the compass flat in the palm of your hand and rotate the base plate until the direction of travel arrow points in the direction in which you have been walking/hiking/trekking. Read your bearing from the dash.

GPS

Originally developed by the US Department of Defense, the Global Positioning System (GPS) is a network of more than 20 earth-orbiting satellites that continually beam encoded signals back to earth. Small computer-driven devices (GPS receivers) can decode these signals to give users an extremely accurate reading of their location – to within 30m, anywhere on the planet, at any time of day, in almost any weather.

The cheapest hand-held GPS receivers now cost less than US$100 (although these may not have a built-in averaging system that minimizes signal errors). Other important factors to consider when buying a GPS receiver are its weight and battery life.

Remember that a GPS receiver is of little use to walkers/hikers/trekkers unless used with an accurate topographical map. The receiver simply gives your position, which you must then locate on the local map.

GPS receivers will only work properly in the open. The signals from a crucial satellite may be blocked (or bounce off rock or water) directly below high cliffs, near large bodies of water or in dense tree cover and give inaccurate readings.

GPS receivers are more vulnerable to breakdowns (including dead batteries) than the humble magnetic compass – a low-tech device that has served navigators faithfully for centuries – so don't rely on them entirely.

Tents

A three-season tent will suffice for most backpacking expeditions. If you're planning a backcountry trip during the winter, then you'll need a four-season tent to keep you sheltered from snow and harsh winter conditions.

Sleeping Bag & Mat

As with tents, three-season sleeping bags will serve the needs of most campers. During the summer, the canyon floor is usually sweltering enough to forego a sleeping bag altogether; backcountry campers might consider bringing just a sleeping bag liner or a sheet.

Some even soak a sheet in the river for the evaporative cooling effect for a soothing sleep. Cooler seasons, especially on the North Rim, call for both sleeping bag and a sleeping pad (mat) for insulation from the cold ground.

Stoves & Fuel

The type of fuel you'll use most often will help determine what kind of camp stove is best for you. The following types of fuel can be found in the US, and local outdoors stores can help you choose an appropriate camp stove if you aren't traveling with your own. Canyon Village Marketplace (p133) on the South Rim carries a basic selection of stoves and fuel.

Inexpensive white gas is readily available throughout the country, reliable in all temperatures and clean-burning. It's more volatile than other types of fuel, but overall it's the most efficient and accessible type of fuel used in the US.

Butane, propane and isobutane are clean-burning fuels that come in non-recyclable canisters and tend to be more expensive. These fuels are best for camping in warmer conditions, as their

BUYING TIPS

To help you select outdoor equipment and clothing, here are some things to look for when shopping around.

Backpack

For day hikes, a daypack will usually suffice, but for multiday hikes you'll need a backpack. A good backpack should be made of strong fabric such as canvas or Cordura, have a lightweight internal or external frame and an adjustable, well-padded harness that evenly distributes weight. Even if the manufacturer claims your pack is waterproof, use heavy-duty liners.

Footwear

Trail-running or walking shoes are fine over easy terrain, but for more difficult trails and across rocks and scree, the ankle support offered by boots is invaluable. Nonslip soles (such as Vibram) provide the best grip. Buy boots in warm conditions or go for a walk before trying them on, so that your feet can swell slightly, as they would on a walk.

Most hikers carry a pair of river sandals or flip-flops to wear around camp or at rest stops. River sandals are also useful when fording waterways.

Gaiters

If you will be hiking through snow, deep mud or scratchy vegetation, gaiters will protect your legs and help keep your socks dry. The best are made of strong fabric, with a robust zip protected by a flap, and secure easily around the foot.

Sleeping Bag & Mat

Down fillings are warmer than synthetic for the same weight and bulk but, unlike synthetic fillings, do not retain warmth when wet. Mummy bags are the best shape for weight and warmth. The given figure (-5°C, for instance) is the coldest temperature at which a person should feel comfortable in the bag (although the ratings are notoriously unreliable).

An inner liner helps keep your sleeping bag clean, as well as adding an insulating layer. Silk liners are lightest, but they also come in cotton or polypropylene.

Self-inflating sleeping mats put an air cushion between you and the ground. More importantly they insulate from the cold. Foam mats are a low-cost but less comfortable alternative.

Socks

Hiking socks should be free of ridged seams in the toes and heels; the best types are made from wicking material that draws moisture away from your feet.

Waterproof Jacket & Pants

The ideal specifications for both these items are a breathable, waterproof fabric, a hood that's roomy enough to cover headwear but still allows peripheral vision, a spacious map pocket, and a heavy-gauge zip protected by a storm flap.

When looking for pants, choose a pair with slits for pocket access and long leg zips so that you can pull them on and off over your boots.

Stove

Fuel stoves fall roughly into three categories: multifuel, methylated spirits (ethyl alcohol) and butane gas. Multifuel stoves are small, efficient and ideal for places where a reliable fuel supply is difficult to find. However, they tend to be sooty and require frequent maintenance. Stoves running on methylated spirits are slower and less efficient, but are safe, clean and easy to use. Butane gas stoves are clean and reliable, but can be slow, and the gas canisters can be awkward to carry and a potential litter problem.

Tent

A three-season tent will be sufficient for most backcountry hikers. The floor and the outer shell, or rainfly, should have taped or sealed seams and covered zips to stop leaks. Most hikers find tents of around 5lb or 6lb a comfortable carrying weight. Dome- and tunnel-shaped tents handle windy conditions better than flat-sided tents.

performance markedly decreases in below-freezing temperatures.

The most sustainable alternative is renewable denatured alcohol, which burns slowly but also extremely quietly.

BUYING & RENTING LOCALLY

If you haven't come prepared with all the equipment you need, it can actually be a boon to buy and rent locally, as you can take advantage of local expertise on what works best in the region.

On the South Rim, Canyon Village Marketplace (p133) is the park's only full-sized grocery. But it also sells and rents sleeping bags, tents, backpacks, camping stoves and lanterns, as well as cross-country skis in the winter. It offers the park's largest selection of gear and can even tackle simple repairs. Desert View Marketplace (p133) offers a few camping necessities like flashlights, water-purification tablets and thermal blankets.

The outdoor stores in Flagstaff (p162) sell and rent bikes, cross-country skis and climbing equipment and are great places to get local outdoors advice.

On the North Rim, the North Rim General Store (p198) also sells a limited selection of camping gear, including fuel, insect repellant and lanterns, as well as mats and sleeping bags. Willow Canyon Outdoor Co (p212) in Kanab sells outdoor gear, books and maps.

Glossary

4WD – Four-wheel-drive vehicle

backcountry – anywhere away from roads or other major infrastructure
backpacking – multiday hiking with full camping gear
basalt – hard, dense and very common volcanic rock; solidified lava
BLM – Bureau of Land Management; government agency that controls large areas of public land
butte – prominent hill or mountain standing separate from surrounding ranges

cairn – pile or stack of rocks used to indicate the route or a trail junction
caldera – very large crater that has resulted from a volcanic explosion or the collapse of a volcanic cone
cascade – small waterfall
CR – county road

drainage – course of a creek or streamlet

fire blanket/fire pan – metal sheeting (mandatory in some wilderness areas) to protect the ground from campfires
ford – to cross a river by wading
fork – branch or tributary of a stream or river
FR – forest road

gap – mountain pass or saddle; notch
GPS – Global Positioning System; electronic, satellite-based network that allows for the calculation of position and elevation using a hand-held receiver/decoder
graded – leveled (road or trail)
granite – coarse-grained, often gray, rock formed by the slow cooling of molten rock (magma) deep below the earth
gulch – narrow ravine cut by a river or stream

hogan – one-room Navajo structure traditionally built of earth, logs, stone and other materials, with the entrance facing east
hookup – campground site with electricity

inlet – (principal) stream flowing into a lake

kachina – (or katsina) carved cottonwood dolls that are wooden effigies of spirit beings who guide and protect the Hopi people
karst – a form of limestone
kiva – ceremonial chamber used by ancient and modern Pueblo people
KOA – Kampgrounds of America; a private chain of campgrounds with substantial amenities

limestone – sedimentary rock composed mainly of calcium carbonate

mesa – Spanish word for elevated tableland or plateau
montane – lower forest zone

national forest – area of public land administered by the *USFS*
NPS – National Park Service
NRA – National Recreation Area; similar to wilderness area but with some controlled development; also National Rifle Association

obsidian – black, glassy volcanic rock
old-growth – forest more than 200 years old and never altered by humans
outlet – stream flowing out of a lake

privy – pit toilet at a campsite
public land – any federal or state land, especially that administered by the *BLM*, *NPS* or *USFS*
Pueblo – corn-growing cultures that inhabited the southern Colorado Plateau and the Four Corners Region (Arizona, Utah, Colorado and New Mexico)

quad – 1:24,000 USGS topographic map
quartzite – white or gray sandstone composed primarily of quartz grains

RV – recreational vehicle; motor home

saddle – low place in a ridge
sandstone – sedimentary rock composed of sand grains
scree – weathered rock fragments at the foot of a cliff or on a hillside
sidle – to cut along a slope; contour; see also *traverse*
slickrock – large expanse of exposed rock that has been sculpted and smoothed by erosion
slot canyon – narrow, deep canyon carved by water
snow line – level above which snow remains on the ground throughout the year
spur – small ridge that leads up from a valley to a main ridge; small branch of a main trail
switchback – route that follows a zigzag course on a steep grade

talus – large boulders accumulated on a slope, fanning out at its base
topo – topographic (contoured) map
trail mix – snack-food mixture of nuts, dried fruit, seeds and/or chocolate; also known as gorp
traverse – to cut along a slope (sometimes also along a ridge); see also *sidle*
travertine – calcium carbonate deposits left by water

USFS – United States Forest Service; manages the nation's system of national forests
USGS – United States Geological Survey; national cartographic organization

wilderness – officially designated primitive area
wildland – roadless or primitive area (whether officially designated or not)

Behind the Scenes

THIS BOOK

The 1st edition of *Grand Canyon National Park* was written by Jennifer Denniston, Amy Marr, David Lukas and Kimberley O'Neil. This 2nd edition was researched and written by Wendy Yanagihara, Jennifer Denniston and David Lukas. Thanks also to Sara Benson, who provided some of the Las Vegas text. This guidebook was commissioned in Lonely Planet's Oakland office, and produced by the following:

Series Manager Heather Dickson
Commissioning Editor Suki Gear
Coordinating Editors Charlotte Orr, Simon Williamson
Coordinating Cartographer Anita Banh
Coordinating Layout Designer Pablo Gastar
Senior Editors Helen Christinis, Sasha Baskett
Managing Cartographer Alison Lyall
Managing Layout Designers Adam McCrow, Celia Wood
Assisting Cartographer Andrew Smith
Cover Designer Amy Stephens
Project Manager Eoin Dunlevy

Thanks to Jennifer Garrett, Michelle Glynn, Brice Gosnell, James Hardy, Laura Jane, Lisa Knights, Adriana Mammarella, Raphael Richards, Laura Stansfeld, Glenn van der Knijff

THANKS

WENDY YANAGIHARA

Though the Grand Canyon is mind-blowing enough and the Southwest one of the more stunning landscapes to explore by foot, hoof, wheel and raft, the very many people who befriended and helped me along the way made it even more than 'just' a beautiful research trip. I owe enormous thanks to Estelle Kingston for her kindness, Tim Kingston of course, the generous and delightful Bill and Danna Hendrix, Matt Fahey and the entire Colorado River crew, Al 'Mountain Goat' Astorga, Dr Heather Webb, Cosmic Ray, Thaney da Silva, Rich Hull, John Doskicz, G (my favorite Vietnam vet), the friendly South Rim rangers, Suki Gear for her good humor, Jennifer Denniston for being so wonderful to work with, Becca Blond, Aaron Anderson, Dukey, Dad, Jason, and all those friends and family who helped maintain my sanity as you always do: thank you thank you thank you.

JENNIFER DENNISTON

Thanks to my amazing editor Suki Gear, coauthor Wendy Yanagihara, cartographers Alison Lyall and Anita Banh, and to Charlotte Orr. I can't imagine a better team to work with. To Heather Webb, Mark

THE LONELY PLANET STORY

Fresh from an epic journey across Europe, Asia and Australia in 1972, Tony and Maureen Wheeler sat at their kitchen table stapling together notes. The first Lonely Planet guidebook, *Across Asia on the Cheap,* was born.

Travelers snapped up the guides. Inspired by their success, the Wheelers began publishing books to Southeast Asia, India and beyond. Demand was prodigious, and the Wheelers expanded the business rapidly to keep up. Over the years, Lonely Planet extended its coverage to every country and into the virtual world via lonelyplanet.com and the Thorn Tree message board.

As Lonely Planet became a globally loved brand, Tony and Maureen received several offers for the company. But it wasn't until 2007 that they found a partner whom they trusted to remain true to the company's principles of traveling widely, treading lightly and giving sustainably. In October of that year, BBC Worldwide acquired a 75% share in the company, pledging to uphold Lonely Planet's commitment to independent travel, trustworthy advice and editorial independence.

Today, Lonely Planet has offices in Melbourne, London and Oakland, with over 500 staff members and 300 authors. Tony and Maureen are still actively involved with Lonely Planet. They're traveling more often than ever, and they're devoting their spare time to charitable projects. And the company is still driven by the philosophy of *Across Asia on the Cheap*: 'All you've got to do is decide to go and the hardest part is over. So go!'

Sagarin and their daughters Zoe and Ruby – I wish we could hike together more often. Thanks to Todd Knoop, Kerry Fachan, Christella Sanz Guerrero, the two couples from Kansas City and California whom we met on the North Rim, the Zinkula family, Victor Polyak and Rob Rachowiecki. Thanks to my family – my daughters Anna and Harper, who, despite forays to emergency rooms, sick days in the hotel, cold nights under the stars, and long days in the car, are always happy to hit the road; their adopted grandmother Marj Whitley, who keeps our life in order the many months we're gone; her husband Wes, for sharing her; my parents; and my husband Rhawn, who makes research trips so much fun. I love you.

OUR READERS

Many thanks to the travelers who used the last edition and wrote to us with helpful hints, useful advice and interesting anecdotes:

Rosalyn Jirge, Thomas Kurz, James Schaad, Liz Warnicke

ACKNOWLEDGMENTS

Many thanks to the following for the use of their content:

Internal photographs by Yvette Cardozo/Alamy p15 (#1); Dennis Cox/Alamy p9 (#2); Danita Delimont/Alamy p13 (#4); Keiji Iwai/Alamy p11 (#3); Design Pics Inc./Alamy p6 (#5); Tom Bean/CORBIS p4 (#6), p7 (#3); David Kadlubowski/CORBIS p16. All other photographs by Lonely Planet Images, and by Eddie Brady p4 (#1); Richard Cummins p12, p14; John Elk III p11 (#6); Lee Foster p15 (#5); Holger Leue p3; Andrew Marshall & Leanne Walker p9 (#6); Mark Newman p5 (#4), p8; Andrew Peacock p5 (#5), p7 (#6), p10; Caro Polich p13 (#1); Dallas Stribley p7 (#4).

SEND US YOUR FEEDBACK

We love to hear from travelers – your comments keep us on our toes and help make our books better. Our well-traveled team reads every word on what you loved or loathed about this book. Although we cannot reply individually to postal submissions, we always guarantee that your feedback goes straight to the appropriate authors, in time for the next edition. Each person who sends us information is thanked in the next edition – and the most useful submissions are rewarded with a free book.

To send us your updates – and find out about Lonely Planet events, newsletters and travel news – visit our award-winning website: **www.lonelyplanet.com/feedback**.

Note: we may edit, reproduce and incorporate your comments in Lonely Planet products such as guidebooks, websites and digital products, so let us know if you don't want your comments reproduced or your name acknowledged. For a copy of our privacy policy visit www.lonelyplanet.com/privacy.

Index

See also separate subindex for Hikes (p277).

A

Abyss 109, 111
acacias 79
accommodations 229-30, *see also individual locations*
  children, travel with 59
  costs 26-7
  internet resources 229
  last minute 230
  North Rim 197-8
  South Rim 130-3
activities 41-56, 230-1, *see also individual activities*
acute mountain sickness, *see* altitude sickness
air travel 240-1
airlines 241
airplane tours 53, 180, 218
Airport Mesa 166
airports 240-1
alcohol laws 234
altitude sickness 249
American dippers 75
AmeriCorps 54
amphibians 76
Anasazi, *see* ancestral Puebloans
ancestral Puebloans 85-8, 188, 191, 216, 223
Angel's Landing 62, 211
Angels Window 188
animals 72-7, 251, *see also individual species;* birds; pets, travel with
Antelope Canyon 215
Antelope Point Marina 217
Arboretum, the 154
archeological sites & ruins 113, 125, 155, 191, 216, 223, 225
archeology courses 232
architecture 96, 97, 98, 197
Arizona Trail 45
art galleries
  Cameron 171
  Grand Canyon Village 104
  Kanab 213
  Las Vegas 178
Arthur, President Chester 88
Arts & Crafts movement 153
arts festivals 151
asbestos 94
Ashley, William Henry 90
aspens 77-8
astronomy 232
ATMs 196, 235
automobile associations 243

B

Backcountry Information Center 45
backcountry permits 44-5
backpacking, *see* hiking
backpacks 258, 260
Balanced Rocks 62
Balloon Regatta 210
banana yuccas 79
banded geckos 76
Basketmakers, the 85-7
Bass, William Wallace 94
Beaman, EO 92
Beaver Falls 145, 227
bees 77
Bell Rock 166
Bellagio 178
Berry, Peter 94
Best Friends Animal Sanctuary 208-9
Big Kids Pool 228
big sagebrush 79
Big Springs lookout 201
bighorn sheep 73
biking, *see* cycling, mountain biking
Bill's Gamblin' Hall & Saloon 178
birds 74-6, *see also individual species*
blackbrush 79
black-throated sparrows 74
blisters 248-9
boating, *see also* canoeing & kayaking, rafting
  books 52
  Colorado River 222-8
  Lake Mead 171, 173
  Lake Powell 213, 217
  permits 223
  tours 173, 217, 224
books 27-8
  boating 52
  camping 162
  children's 61
  cycling 52, 162
  dams 27
  environment 47, 72, 78
  first aid 248
  geology 27-8
  Havasupai 88
  hiking 27, 46, 115, 156, 162
  history 27, 88, 92, 98
  rock climbing 56
  skiing 162
Boucher, Louis 'The Hermit' 112
Boulder City/Hoover Dam Museum 173
Box, the 195
Boynton Canyon 166
Bright Angel Canyon 7
Bright Angel Lodge 107
Bright Angel shale 69
Bright Angel Trail 116-17, 122-4, **116, 122**
Buckey O'Neill Cabin 107
Buckskin Gulch 206, 207, 5
bus travel 241-2, 245, *see also* shuttles
bushwalking, *see* hiking
business hours 231

C

cacti 81
Caesar's Palace 178
California condors 75
Cameron 170-1
Cameron, Ralph 94
Cameron Trading Post 62, 170
campfires 236
camping 230, 250, *see also* accommodations, *individual locations*
  books 162
  charts 130-1
  clothing 256-61
  equipment 256-61
  fires 46, 236, 250
  North Rim 197-8
  permits 44-5
  responsible camping 45-7
  South Rim 130-3
  stoves 259-61
canoeing & kayaking, *see also* boating, rafting
  Colorado River 223, 224, 225

000 Map pages
000 Photograph pages

Lake Mead 173
Lake Powell 217
permits 223
Canyon de Chelly 216
canyon wrens 74
Cape Final 192
Cape Royal Point 188
car travel 242-4, 245-6, *see also* driving routes
Cárdenas, García López de 89
carpenter bees 77
casinos
Bellagio 178
Bill's Gamblin' Hall & Saloon 178
Caesar's Palace 178
Circus Circus 178
Excalibur 178
Golden Nugget 179
Luxor 178
Mandalay Bay 177
MGM Grand 178
Mirage 178
New York New York 178
Orleans 179
Palms Resort Casino 179
Paris Las Vegas 178
Red Rock Resort 179
Tropicana 178
Venetian 178
Wynn Las Vegas 178
Cathedral Rock 166
Cathedral Stairs 125
Cedar Mesa 118
Celebraciónes de la Gente 151
cell phones 235
Chapel of the Holy Cross 163
Cheyava Falls 196
chickadees 74
children, travel with 57-64, 156, 231
accommodations 59
attractions 60
books 61
child-friendly hikes 61
food 59
health 59-60
itineraries 38-9, **38-9**
ranger programs 60-1
safety 59-60
chipmunks 73-4
cicadas 77
Circus Circus 178
Citadel Pueblo 155
Cliff Spring 191
climate 231
climate change 240
clothing 256-61
Coconino Center for the Arts 154
Coconino Forest 153
Coconino Overlook 195
Coconino Saddle 119
Coconino sandstone 69, **7**
Colorado River 220-8, **221**, **5**, **10**, **11**
damming 27, 81-2
fishing 217
highlights 220
hiking 226-8
history 93
permits 223
rafting 220-6, 228
Colter, Mary 97, 98
compasses 258-9
condors 75
Confucius Temple 127
copper 94
Coral Pink Sand Dunes State Park 209
Coronado, Francisco Vásquez de 89
costs 26-7, 233, *see also inside back cover*
Cottonwood Campground 195
Cottonwood Cove 171
cottonwoods 78
courses 232
archeology 232
first aid 248
photography 232
coyotes 73
Crack-in-Rock Pueblo 155
Crazy Jug 201
cross-country skiing 55-6, 129, 197, *see also* downhill skiing
Flagstaff 151, 157
Kaibab National Forest (South Rim) 137
cryptobiotic crusts 82
Crystal Rapids 226
cycling 51-2, 126-7, 245, *see also* mountain biking
books 52, 162
Flagstaff 156-7
guided tours 52, 179
Kanab 210-11
North Rim 52, 196
park policies & regulations 236
safety 254-5
South Rim 52, 110, 126-7
Sunset Crater Volcano National Monument 155

D

dams 81-2
Glen Canyon Dam 27, 81-2, 215
Hoover Dam 27, 171-5
Deer Creek Falls 227
Deer Creek Narrows 227
dehydration 250
Dellenbaugh, Frederick Samuel 92
desert trumpet 80
Desert View 109
Desert View Drive 112-14, **113**
Devils Corkscrew 123
Diamond Creek Road 150
diarrhea 249
disabilities, travelers with 237-8
discount cards 233
dogs 63-4
downhill skiing 55-6, *see also* cross-country skiing
drinking 233-4, *see also individual locations*
driver's licenses 243
driving routes, *see also* car travel
Cape Royal Road 188-9, **188**
Desert View Drive 112-14, **113**
East Rim View 201
Hermit Road 110-12, **111**
House Rock Road 205-6
Imperial Point Road 189, **188**
Johnson Canyon Road 210
Marble View 201
Point Sublime 189
Toroweap 189-90
Dry Park lookout 201
Dutton, Clarence Edward 127

E

eagles 75
Eagle's Nest 163
eastern fence lizards 76
Egloffstein, Baron Friedrich W Von 91
El Tovar 106-7, 133
electricity 229
Elves Chasm 226, **11**
emergencies, *see inside back cover*
Engelmann spruce 78
entrance fees 26, 233
environment 65-83, *see also* animals, plants
books 47, 72, 78
environmental issues 81-2
climate change 240
cryptobiotic crusts 82
dams 81-2
light pollution 80

INDEX

environmental issues *continued*
  noise pollution 128
  responsible hiking 251-4
  Skywalk 22
  tamarisk 78
  traffic congestion 105
equipment 256-61
evacuation 247, 253
events, *see* festivals & events
Excalibur 178

F

Fabulous Fourth Festivities 151
falcons 75-6
fatigue 249
fauna, *see* animals
Fence Point 201
fendlerbush 79
Festival of Lights 151
festivals & events 25, 233
  Balloon Regatta 210
  Celebraciónes de la Gente 151
  Fabulous Fourth Festivities 151
  Festival of Lights 151
  Flagstaff Festival of Science 151
  Flagstaff Winterfest 151
  Grand Canyon Music Festival 25
  Heritage Days 25
  Hopi Festival of Arts & Culture 151
  Navajo Festival of Arts & Culture 151
  Sedona Arts Festival 151
  Sedona International Film Festival 151
  Sedona Plein Air Festival 151
  Star Party 25
  Wahweap Parade of Lights 210
  Western Legends Roundup 210
Fire Point 201
firearms 236
first aid 247, 248, 253-4
First Mesa 216
fishing 55, 128-9
  Colorado River 217
  Flagstaff 157
  Lake Mead 173
  Lake Powell 217
  Lees Ferry 217
  licenses & permits 55, 129, 173, 217
  tours 173, 217

000 Map pages
000 Photograph pages

Flagstaff 151-62, **152**, **154**
  accommodations 157-9
  activities 156-7
  attractions 153-6
  drinking 161
  entertainment 161-2
  festivals & events 151
  food 159-61
  shopping 162
  transportation 162
Flagstaff Festival of Science 151
Flagstaff Winterfest 151
flash floods 251
flora, *see* plants
flowers 80-1
food 233-4, *see also individual locations*
  children's meals 59
footwear 257-8, 260
fossils 66, 112, 129
foxes 73
Fredonia 207
Freemont Street Experience 179
Freya Castle 127
frogs 76
Frontier Movie Town 210
frost riving 70
Fundamentalist Church of Jesus Christ of Latter Day Saints 208
fur trade 90

G

Gárces, Francisco Tomás 89
gay travelers 182
geology 65-70
  books 27-8
giardiasis 249
Gila monsters 76
Glen Canyon Dam 27, 81-2, 215
Glen Canyon National Recreation Area 213-19
Global Positioning System 259
gneiss 68
gold 89, 94
golden eagles 75
Golden Nugget 179
GPS 259
Grand Canyon Association 29
Grand Canyon Cemetery 109
Grand Canyon Chamber of Commerce 29
Grand Canyon Deer Farm 140
Grand Canyon Depot 107
Grand Canyon Field Institute 232
Grand Canyon Lodge 197-8, 13

Grand Canyon Music Festival 25
Grand Canyon National Park, *see* North Rim, South Rim
Grand Canyon National Park Foundation 29
Grand Canyon Railway 140
Grand Canyon Skywalk 22, 83, 149-50, 16
Grand Canyon Trust 29, 54
Grand Canyon Village 103-9, **103**
Grand Canyon Volunteers 54
Grand Canyon West 150
Grand Canyon Youth 54
Grand View Hotel 94
Grandview 112
Grandview Lookout 137
Grandview Point 109
granite 65
Granite Rapids 126
Grasshopper Point 165
Greenland Lake 62
Greenway Plan 105
guide dogs 186
guided hikes 47, 53, 128, 211, 216

H

Hance, John 94
Hance Rapids 225
Harvey, Fred 96
Harvey Meadow 62
Havasu Canyon 145-8, 15
Havasu Creek 228
Havasu Falls 145
Havasupai people 146, 148
  books 88
  history 87-90, 116
  reservation 144-9
Havasupai Reservation 144-9
Hayes, President Rutherford 88
health 247-55
  children, travel with 59-60
  environmental hazards 249-51
  insurance 247
  internet resources 247-8
heat exhaustion 250
heatstroke 250-1
helicopter tours 53, 128, 149
Heritage Days 25
Hermit Creek Campground 126
Hermit Rapids 222
Hermit Road 110-12, **111**
Hermit shale 69
Hermits Rest 109, 112, 13
Highway 89 204-7
Highway Alt 89 204-7

hiking 41-7, *see also* Hikes *subindex*
- books 27, 46, 115, 156, 162
- charts 48, 50
- child friendly 61
- clothing 256-61
- Colorado River 226-8
- environmentally friendly 45-7
- equipment 256-61
- Flagstaff 155, 156-7
- guided hikes 47, 53, 128, 211, 216
- Kanab 210
- Lake Mead 173
- Las Vegas 179
- maps 28
- permits 44-5, 207
- safety 42, 46, 251-4
- Sedona 165

Hiller, John 92
history 84-99
- ancestral Puebloans 85-8
- Basketmakers, the 85-8
- books 27, 88, 92, 98
- Colorado River 93
- Native Americans 84-9
- park creation 97
- Spanish exploration 89-90

Hogan, Daniel Lorain 110
holidays 234
Holmes, William Henry 127
Hoover Dam 27, 171-5
Hopi Festival of Arts & Culture 151
Hopi House 108
Hopi people 147
- arts & crafts 147, 151, 216
- history 108, 155
- kachina dolls 147, 153, 216
- reservation 216

Hopi Point 109, 111
Hopi Reservation 216
Hopi Room 114
Horn Creek 222
horseback riding 53
- equestrian facilities 64
- Flagstaff 157
- Havasupai Reservation 149
- Kaibab National Forest (North Rim) 203
- Kaibab National Forest (South Rim) 137
- Paria River 206
- permits 63

Horseshoe Mesa 119
hotels, *see* accommodations
houseboats 174, 217
Hualapai people 146-7
- history 87-9
- reservation 149-51
- Skywalk 22, **16**

hummingbirds 74
Humphreys Peak 156
Hyde, Bessie 93
Hyde, Glen 93
hyponatremia 251, 253
hypothermia 250

I

IMAX Theater 139
Indian Garden 117
Indian Garden Campground 123
Indian Hollow 201
insects 77
insurance 234
- health 247
- vehicle 243-4

international visitors 234
internet access 235
internet resources 28-9, *see also inside front cover*
- accommodations 229
- air tickets 241
- health 247-8

itineraries 19, 30-40
- child friendly 38-9, **38-9**
- North Rim 35-7, 39-40, **35-7, 39-40**
- South Rim 30-4, 38, 40, **30-4, 38, 40**

Ives, Joseph Christmas 91-2

J

Jacob Lake lookout 201
Jacobs, Madelaine 110
Jeffs, Rulon T 208
Jeffs, Warren 208
Jensen, Aldus 95
John Wesley Powell Museum 215
Julien, Denis 90
Jumpup 201
juncos 74
junipers 71, 78

K

Kachina & Thunderbird Lodges 132
kachina dolls 147, 153, 216
Kachina Woman 166
Kaibab limestone 68
Kaibab National Forest (North Rim) 199-204, **202, 9**
- accommodations 203-4
- drinking 204
- driving 201
- food 204
- hiking 201-3
- mountain biking 201-3

Kaibab National Forest (South Rim) 137
Kaibab Uplift 67
Kanab 207-13, **209**
Kanab Heritage Museum 210
katsina dolls, *see* kachina dolls
kayaking, *see* canoeing & kayaking
kennels 63-4
knee pain 249
Kolb, Ellsworth 108-9
Kolb, Emery 108-9
Kolb Studio 108-9
Krishna Shrine 127

L

Lake Mead 171-5, **172**
Lake Powell 213, 215, 216, 217
Lamaki Pueblo 155
landslides 70
Las Vegas 175-83, **176-7**
- accommodations 180
- attractions 177-80
- entertainment 182-3
- food 180-2
- transportation 183

laundry 235
Lava Falls 67
Lava Falls Rapids 189, 226
Leave No Trace ethic 45-7
Lee, John D 96
Lees Ferry 96, 215, 217
Lenox Crater 155
lesbian travelers 182
licenses & permits
- boating 223
- camping 44-5
- fishing 55, 129, 173, 217
- hiking 44-5, 207
- horseback riding 63
- tribal 149

light pollution 80
lightning 252
limestone 68-9
Lipan Point 109, 113
liquor laws 234
literature, *see* books
Little Colorado River Gorge 62, 226
Locust Point 201

Lone Rock 216
Lonely Dell Ranch 62, 215
Lookout Studio 108
lookouts, *see* overlooks
lost & found 235
Lowell Observatory 153
Lower Granite Gorge 228
Luxor 178

M

Mandalay Bay 177
maps 28, 258-9
Maricopa Point 109, 110
Maswik Lodge 132-3
Mather Point 109, 112
Matkatamiba 227
measures 229, *see also inside back cover*
medical services 248, *see also* health
mesquite 79
Meteor Crater 155
metric conversions, *see inside back cover*
Mexican-American War 90
MGM Grand 178
mining 82, 94, 110-11, 112, 119
Mirage 178
missionaries 89-90
mobile phones 235
Mohave Point 109, 111
Mollhausen, Heinrich Baldwin 91
money 26-7, 233, 235, *see also inside back cover*
Monument Valley 216
Mooney Falls 145
Moran Point 109, 113
Moran, Thomas 92, 127
Mormons 95, 96, 208, 209-10
motorcycle travel 242-4, 245-6, *see also* driving routes
Mt Elden 156
mountain biking 51-2, 126-7, 245, *see also* cycling
- books 52
- Coconino Forest 153
- Flagstaff 156-7
- Kaibab National Forest (North Rim) 196, 201, 203
- Kaibab National Forest (South Rim) 137, 196
- Kanab 210-11
- Las Vegas 179
- park policies & regulations 236
- safety 254-5
- Sedona 165
- Sunset Crater National Volcano Monument 155
- Williams 140

mountain lions 72-3, 99, 193
mountaineering, *see* rock climbing
Muav limestone 69
mudstone 68
mule deer 72-3
mule trains 55, 3
- Havasupai Reservation 149
- North Rim 196-7
- safety 252
- South Rim 127-8

Museum of Northern Arizona 153, 232
museums
- Boulder City/Hoover Dam Museum 173
- John Wesley Powell Museum 215
- Kanab Heritage Museum 210
- Museum of Northern Arizona 153, 232
- Pioneer Museum 154-5
- Pipe Spring National Monument Museum 210
- Sedona Heritage Museum 164-5
- Tusayan Ruins & Museum 113

music festivals 25

N

Nalakihu Pueblo 155
Nampaweap Petroglyphs 190
National Park Service 29, 54
Native Americans 146-7, *see also individual peoples*
- Heritage Days 25
- history 84-9, 97
- reservations 144-51, 216

Navajo Bridge 215
Navajo Falls 145
Navajo Festival of Arts & Culture 151
Navajo people 147
- arts & crafts 62, 147, 151, 170, 219, 5
- history 87, 155
- reservation 216

Navajo Point 109, 114
navigation 258-9
Nevills, Norman 93
New York New York 178
newspapers 229
noise pollution 128
North Rim 184-219, **185**
- accommodations 197-8
- cycling 52, 196
- drinking 198-9
- driving routes 187-90
- entrances 186
- fees & passes 26-7, 186, 233
- food 198-9
- highlights 184
- hiking 190-6
- itineraries 35-7, 39-40, **35-7**, **39-40**
- overlooks 187
- park policies & regulations 236
- transportation 186-7
- visitors centers & information stations 186

North Rim Campground 197
North Timp Point 201

O

Oak Creek 165
oaks 78
O'Neill, William Owen 'Buckey' 107, 132
opening hours 231
Orleans 179
Osiris Temple 127
overlooks 7
- Abyss 109, 111
- Cape Final 192
- Cape Royal Point 188
- Coconino Overlook 195
- Crazy Jug 201
- Desert View 109
- Fence Point 201
- Fire Point 201
- Grandview 112
- Grandview Point 109
- Hermits Rest 109, 112
- Hopi Point 109, 111
- Indian Hollow 201
- Jumpup 201
- Lipan Point 109, 113
- Locust Point 201
- Maricopa Point 109, 110
- Mather Point 109, 112
- Mohave Point 109, 111
- Moran Point 109, 113
- Navajo Point 109, 114
- North Timp Point 201
- Parissawampitts Point 201
- Pima Point 109, 111
- Pipe Creek Vista 109, 112
- Plateau Point 117
- Powell Point 109
- Shoshone Point 109

000 Map pages
000 Photograph pages

Timp Point 201
Tiyo Point 189
Trailview Overlook 109, 110
Uncle Jim Point 193
Vista Encantada 188
Yaki Point 109, 112
Owens, Jim 'Uncle Jim' 95
owls 75

P

Page 213-19, **214**
Pahreah Town 205
Paiute people 87-8, 89, 92, 147
Palms Resort Casino 179
Paria Beach 62, 216
Paria River 206
Paris Las Vegas 178
Parissawampitts Point 201
passes 233
passports 234
Peach Springs 144
peregrine falcons 75-6
permits, *see* licenses & permits
petroglyphs 155, 190
pets, travel with 62-4, 236
Phantom Ranch 95, 132
photography 149, 211, 232
picnic spots 134
pictographs 116, 123, 216, 227
Pima Point 109, 111
pines 77-8
piñon pines 78
Pioneer Museum 154-5
Pipe Creek Vista 109, 112
Pipe Spring National Monument 209-10
Pipe Spring National Monument Museum 210
planning 23-9, 233, 256-61, *see also* itineraries
children, travel with 57-64
clothing & equipment 257
discount cards 233
health 247-8
holidays 234
pets, travel with 62-4, 236
plants 71-2, 77-81, *see also individual species*
Plateau Point 117
polygamy 208
postal services 235
Powell, John Wesley 92-3
Powell Memorial 111
Powell Point 109
powwows 149
prehydration 252
Puebloans, *see* ancestral Puebloans
Pumphouse Residence 195

Q

quaking aspen 78

R

radio 229
rafting 50-1, 150, 180, 220-6, 228, *see also* boating, canoeing & kayaking
Rainbow Bridge National Monument 215
ranger programs 53, 60-1, 129, 197
Red Horse 107
Red Rock Canyon 179
Red Rock Crossing 166
Red Rock Resort 179
Red Rock State Park 164
Redwall Bridge 195
Redwall limestone 69, **7**
reptiles 76
rescue 247, 253
Ribbon Falls 195
ringtails 74
Riordan Mansion State Historic Park 153
road rules 244
Roaring Springs 195
rock climbing 56, 157
rockfalls 253
rocks, *see* geology
Roosevelt, President Theodore 'Teddy' 92, 94, 95
Route 66 144, **9**
RVs, *see* car travel

S

safe travel
children, travel with 59-60
cycling 254-5
evacuation 247, 253
first aid 247, 248, 253-4
flash floods 251
GPS 259
hiking 42, 46, 251-4
mules 252
roads 245-6
wildlife 251
women 238
sagebrush 79
sandstone 68
Santa Maria Spring 120
schist 65-6, 68
scorpions 249
seasons 24-5, 72
Second Mesa 216
Sedona 162-70, **164-5**
accommodations 166-8
activities 165-6
attractions 163-5
drinking 169-70
entertainment 170
food 168-9
shopping 170
transportation 170
Sedona Arts Center 164
Sedona Arts Festival 151
Sedona Heritage Museum 164-5
Sedona International Film Festival 151
Sedona Plein Air Festival 151
Seligman 144
senior travelers 233
shale 68
Sherum, Chief 88
shopping, *see individual locations*
Shoshone Point 109
showers 235
shuttles 105-6
Sierra Club, Grand Canyon Chapter 29, 54
silver 94
skiing, *see* cross-country skiing, downhill skiing
Skywalk 22, 83, 149-50, **16**
sleeping bags 259, 260
Slide Rock State Park 163-4, 165
Smith, Harry 94
snakes 76, 249-50
snowmobiling 203
snowshoeing 55-6, 129
South Rim 100-83, **101**
accommodations 130-3
attractions 106-9
cycling 52, 110, 126-7
drinking 135
driving routes 110-14
entrances 102
fees & passes 26-7, 102, 233
food 133-5
highlights 100
hiking 114-26
itineraries 30-4, 38, 40, **30-4**, **38**, **40**
overlooks 109
park policies & regulations 236
tours 106
transportation 105-6
visitors centers & information stations 104-5

INDEX

Spencer, Charles 216
sprains 254
Springs Preserve 179
spruce 77-8
squirrels 73-4
Stanton, Robert Brewster 93
Star Party 25
Stegner, Wallace 92
stoves 259-61
stromatolites 65
Student Conservation Association 54
sunburn 251
Sunset Crater Volcano National Monument 155
Supai 94, 144-5
Supai Group 69
Supai Tunnel 195
Surprise Canyon 70
sustainable travel 82-3
swimming 54
  Elves Chasm 226, **11**
  Grasshopper Point 165
  Havasu Canyon 144, 145
  Havasu Creek 228
  Lake Mead 173
  Lake Powell 216
  Oak Creek 165
  Slide Rock State Park 165

T

tamarisk 78-9
Tapeats Creek 227
Tapeats Narrows 123
Tapeats sandstone 69-70
telephone services 235, *see also inside back cover*
tents 259, 260
Third Mesa 216
Thunder Spring 227
ticks 250
time 236, **278-9**
Timp Point 201
tipping 235
Tiyo Point 189
toads 76
Toroweap Formation 68
tourist information 236
tours 236-7, *see also* driving routes
  airplane 53, 180, 218
  boat 173, 217, 224
  bus 106
  canoeing & kayaking 217, 224
  cycling 52, 179
  driving 144
  fishing 173, 217
  guided hikes 47, 53, 128, 211, 216
  helicopter 53, 128, 149
  horseback riding 137, 157, 203, 237
  photographic 211
  rafting 180, 224-5
  ranger programs 129
Trailview Overlook 109, 110
train travel 244-5
trash 46
transportation **242**, *see also individual locations*
travel to/from Grand Canyon National Park 240-5
travel within Grand Canyon National Park 245-6
traveler's checks 235
Travertine Falls 228
Treaty of Guadalupe Hidalgo 90
trekking, *see* hiking
Tropicana 178
Tusayan 137-9
Tusayan Bike Trail 137
Tusayan Ruins & Museum 113

U

Uncle Jim Point 193
Uncle Jim's Cave 194
Underwood, Gilbert Stanley 96, 197
uranium 82
Utah junipers 78

V

vacations 234
Valle 139
Vasey's Paradise 225
Venetian 178
Verkamp curios 108
veterinarians 63
video systems 229
viewpoints, *see* overlooks
visas 234
Vishnu schist 65-6
Vishnu Temple 7, **6**
Vista Encantada 188
volunteering 54, 238
Vulcans Throne 7, 68

W

Wahweap Parade of Lights 210
Walhalla Glades 188
walking, *see* hiking
Walnut Canyon National Monument 155, **14**
Watchtower 114, **12**
waterfalls
  Beaver Falls 145, 227
  Cheyava Falls 196
  Deer Creek Falls 227
  Havasu Falls 145
  Mooney Falls 145
  Navajo Falls 145
  Ribbon Falls 195
  Roaring Springs 195
  Thunder Spring 227
  Travertine Falls 228
Wauba Yuman, Chief 88
weapons 236
weather 24-5, 231
websites, *see* internet resources, *inside front cover*
weddings 129
weights 229, *see also inside back cover*
Western Legends Roundup 210
white-throated swifts 74
white-water rafting, *see* rafting
wildlife, *see* animals, plants, *individual species*
Williams 140-4, **141**
  accommodations 140-3
  activities 140
  attractions 140
  drinking 143-4
  food 143-4
  transportation 144
Wilson, President Woodrow 97
Winsor Castle 209
women travelers 238
wood rats 74
work 239
Wukoki Pueblo 155
Wupatki National Monument 155
Wupatki Pueblo 155
Wynn Las Vegas 178

X

Xanterra Parks & Resorts 29, 130, 222, 230

Y

Yaki Point 109, 112
Yavapai Lodge 133
Yavapai Observation Station 107
Yavapai Point 109

Z

Zoroaster granite 65

000 Map pages
000 Photograph pages

HIKES

Arizona Trail: Park Boundary Trailhead to Crystal Spring (Kaibab Plateau Trail 101) 203
Beaver Falls 227-8
Bill Hall Trail 196
Bridle Trail 192
Bright Angel Point 190
Bright Angel Trail 122-4, **122**
Bright Angel Trail - Long Day Hike 117, **116**
Bright Angel Trail - Short Day Hike 116, **116**
Buckskin Gulch 207, **5**
Cape Final 191-2
Cedar Ridge Hike 129
Clear Creek Trail 195-6
Cliff Springs 191
Deer Creek 227
Dripping Springs Trail 121
Elves Chasm 226, **11**
Fossil Walk 129
Geology Walk 129
Grand View Trail 119-20
Havasu Canyon to Waterfalls 145-8
Hermit Trail 120, **120**, **4**
Hermit Trail to Bright Angel Trailhead 126, **4**
Hermit Trail to Hermit Creek 125-6, **125**, **4**
Horseshoe Bend 217-18
Hualapai Hilltop to Supai 145
Ken Patrick Trail 193, **193**
Lava Falls Trail 196
Matkatamiba 227
Nankoweap Trail 196
North Bass Trail 196
North Canyon 226
North Coyote Butte 207
North Kaibab 194-5, **194**
Paria Canyon 207
Point Imperial 192
Rainbow Rim Trail 201-2
Rim to Rim 123, **4**
Rim Trail 114
River Trail 218
Shoshone Point 115
South Kaibab 117-19, **118**
South Kaibab to Bright Angel 124-5, **124**
Spencer Trail 218
Squaw Trail 210
Tapeats Creek to Thunder Springs 226-7
Thunder River Trail 196
Toadstool Trail 206
Tonto Trail (South Kaibab to Bright Angel) 121-2
Transept Trail 191
Tuckup Trail 196
Uncle Jim Trail 193-4
Widforss Trail 192-3, **192**
Wire Pass to Buckskin Gulch 206

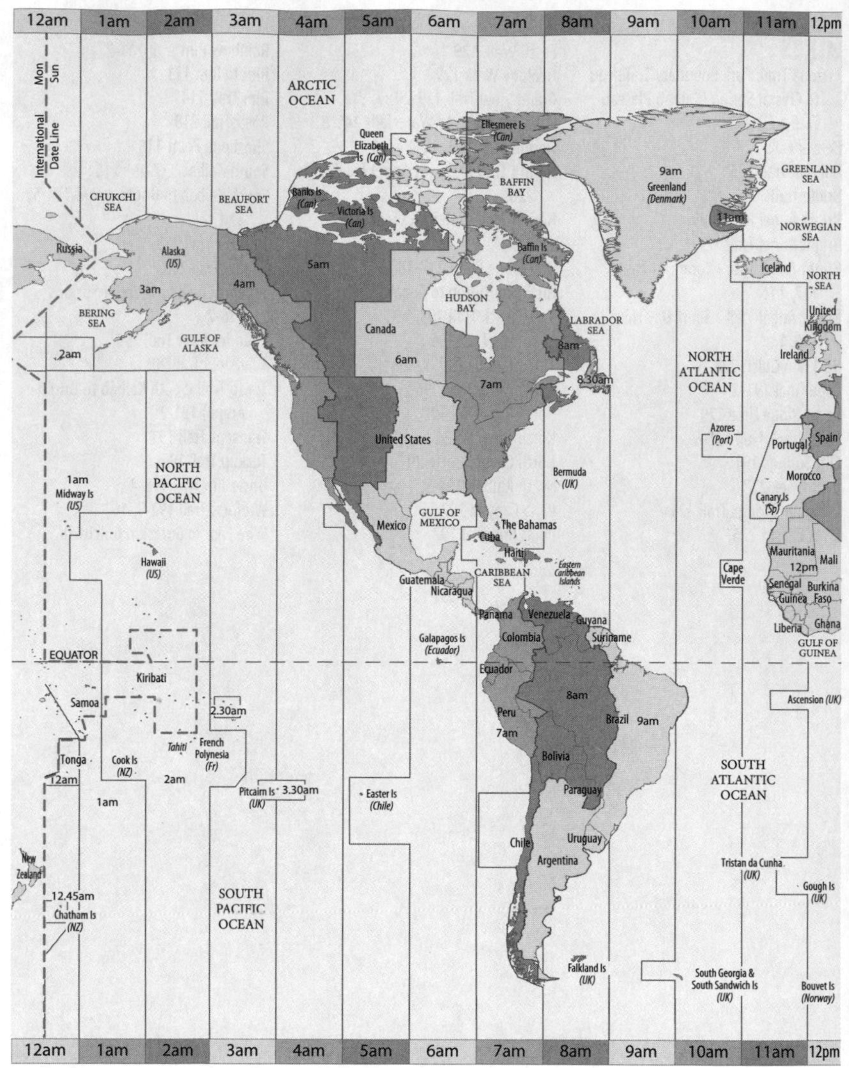
12am
1am
2am
3am
4am
5am
6am
7am
8am
9am
10am
11am
12pm
International Date Line
Mon
Sun
ARCTIC OCEAN
Queen Elizabeth Is (Can)
Ellesmere Is (Can)
Greenland (Denmark)
GREENLAND SEA
NORWEGIAN SEA
CHUKCHI SEA
BEAUFORT SEA
Banks Is (Can)
Victoria Is (Can)
BAFFIN BAY
Baffin Is (Can)
Iceland
NORTH SEA
Russia
Alaska (US)
BERING SEA
GULF OF ALASKA
HUDSON BAY
LABRADOR SEA
United Kingdom
Ireland
Canada
NORTH ATLANTIC OCEAN
United States
Azores (Port)
Portugal
Spain
Morocco
Canary Is (Sp)
NORTH PACIFIC OCEAN
Midway Is (US)
Bermuda (UK)
GULF OF MEXICO
Mexico
The Bahamas
Cuba
Haiti
Eastern Caribbean Islands
Hawaii (US)
CARIBBEAN SEA
Guatemala
Nicaragua
Mauritania
Mali
Cape Verde
Senegal
Guinea
Burkina Faso
Liberia
Ghana
GULF OF GUINEA
Panama
Venezuela
Guyana
Suriname
Colombia
Galapagos Is (Ecuador)
EQUATOR
Ecuador
Kiribati
Samoa
Ascension (UK)
Peru
Brazil
Bolivia
Paraguay
Tahiti
French Polynesia (Fr)
Tonga
Cook Is (NZ)
Pitcairn Is (UK)
Easter Is (Chile)
SOUTH ATLANTIC OCEAN
Chile
Uruguay
Argentina
New Zealand
Chatham Is (NZ)
SOUTH PACIFIC OCEAN
Tristan da Cunha (UK)
Gough Is (UK)
Falkland Is (UK)
South Georgia & South Sandwich Is (UK)
Bouvet Is (Norway)
2.30am
3.30am
8.30am
12.45am

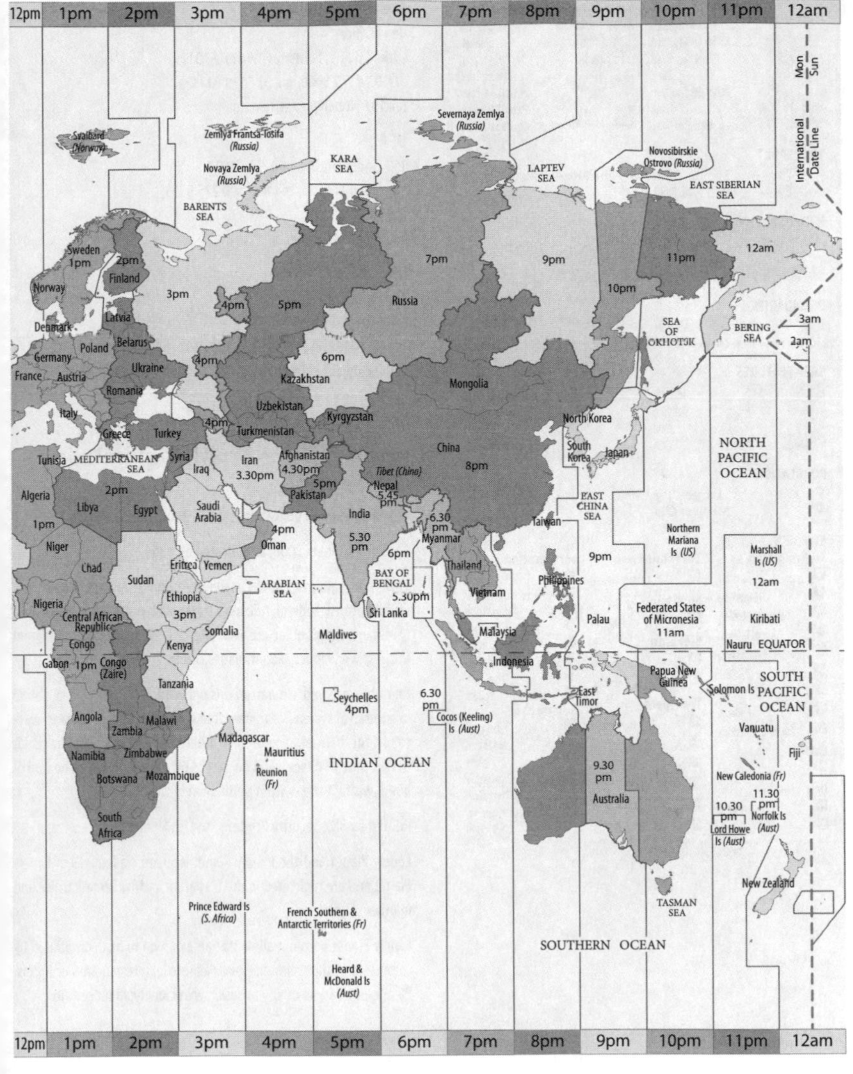
12pm
1pm
2pm
3pm
4pm
5pm
6pm
7pm
8pm
9pm
10pm
11pm
12am
Mon
Sun
International Date Line
Svalbard (Norway)
Zemlya Frantsa-Iosifa (Russia)
Novaya Zemlya (Russia)
Severnaya Zemlya (Russia)
KARA SEA
LAPTEV SEA
Novosibirskie Ostrovo (Russia)
EAST SIBERIAN SEA
BARENTS SEA
Sweden 1pm
2pm
Finland
Norway
3pm
4pm
5pm
7pm
Russia
9pm
10pm
11pm
12am
Denmark
Latvia
Poland
Belarus
Germany
Ukraine
France
Austria
Romania
Italy
Greece
Turkey
Kazakhstan
6pm
Uzbekistan
Turkmenistan
Kyrgyzstan
Mongolia
North Korea
South Korea
Japan
China
8pm
Tibet (China)
SEA OF OKHOTSK
BERING SEA
3am
2am
NORTH PACIFIC OCEAN
Tunisia
MEDITERRANEAN SEA
Syria
Iraq
Iran 3.30pm
Afghanistan 4.30pm
5pm
Nepal 5.45 pm
Pakistan
Algeria
2pm
Libya
Egypt
Saudi Arabia
India 5.30 pm
4pm
Oman
6.30 pm
Myanmar
Taiwan
EAST CHINA SEA
Northern Mariana Is (US)
Marshall Is (US)
1pm
Niger
Chad
Sudan
Eritrea
Yemen
6pm
BAY OF BENGAL
Thailand
9pm
Philippines
12am
ARABIAN SEA
5.30pm
Vietnam
Nigeria
Ethiopia
3pm
Central African Republic
Somalia
Sri Lanka
Palau
Federated States of Micronesia 11am
Kiribati
Congo
Kenya
Maldives
Malaysia
Nauru EQUATOR
Gabon
1pm
Congo (Zaire)
Indonesia
Papua New Guinea
SOUTH PACIFIC OCEAN
Tanzania
Seychelles 4pm
6.30 pm
East Timor
Solomon Is
Angola
Malawi
Zambia
Cocos (Keeling) Is (Aust)
Vanuatu
Madagascar
Namibia
Zimbabwe
Mauritius
INDIAN OCEAN
9.30 pm
Fiji
Botswana
Mozambique
Reunion (Fr)
Australia
New Caledonia (Fr)
11.30 pm
10.30 pm
Norfolk Is (Aust)
South Africa
Lord Howe Is (Aust)
New Zealand
Prince Edward Is (S. Africa)
French Southern & Antarctic Territories (Fr)
TASMAN SEA
SOUTHERN OCEAN
Heard & McDonald Is (Aust)
12pm
1pm
2pm
3pm
4pm
5pm
6pm
7pm
8pm
9pm
10pm
11pm
12am

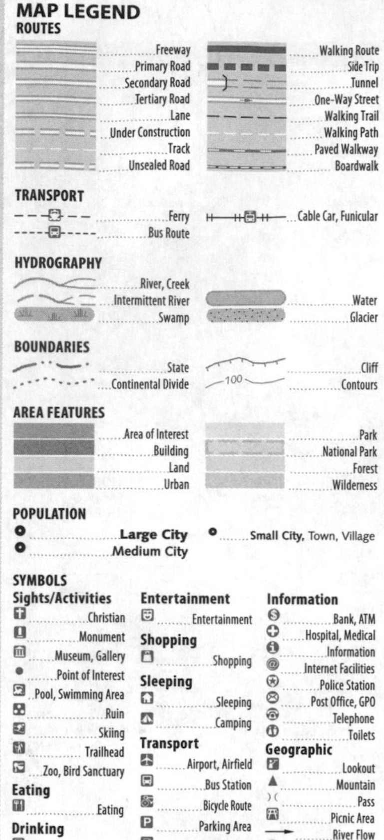

LONELY PLANET OFFICES

Australia
Head Office
Locked Bag 1, Footscray, Victoria 3011
☎ 03 8379 8000, fax 03 8379 8111
talk2us@lonelyplanet.com.au

USA
150 Linden St, Oakland, CA 94607
☎ 510 893 8555, toll free 800 275 8555
fax 510 893 8572
info@lonelyplanet.com

UK
2nd Fl, 186 City Rd
London ECV1 2NT
☎ 020 7106 2100, fax 020 7106 2101
go@lonelyplanet.co.uk

Published by Lonely Planet Publications Pty Ltd
ABN 36 005 607 983

Cover photographs: Grand Canyon from Toroweap Point, Ron Watts/CORBIS (front); Sedona, Arizona, Cheyenne Rouse/LPI (back). Many of the images in this guide are available for licensing from Lonely Planet Images: www.lonelyplanetimages.com.

Printed by SNP Security Printing Pte Ltd, Singapore.